Luigi Daniele • Pierluigi Simone • Roberto Cisotta
Editors

Democracy in the EMU in the Aftermath of the Crisis

G. Giappichelli Editore

Springer

Editors
Luigi Daniele
Department of Public Law
University of Rome "Tor Vergata"
Rome, Italy

Pierluigi Simone
Department of Public Law
University of Rome "Tor Vergata"
Rome, Italy

Roberto Cisotta
Italian Ministry of Foreign Affairs and
International Cooperation
Rome, Italy

ISBN 978-3-319-53894-5 ISBN 978-3-319-53895-2 (eBook)
DOI 10.1007/978-3-319-53895-2

Library of Congress Control Number: 2017939565

Printed on acid-free paper

This Springer imprint is published by Springer Nature
The registered company is Springer International Publishing AG
The registered company address is: Gewerbestrasse 11, 6330 Cham, Switzerland

Preface

1. The aim of this book is to explore the role of the democratic principle in the context of the Economic and Monetary Union (EMU). The time is indeed quite ripe for opening a discussion on such issues.

We all knew that, right from the beginning, the EMU regime had its own features, which distinguished it from any other area of competence of the European Union (EU) and, among others, did not contemplate the conferral of "strong" powers to the European Parliament.

We were also aware that things had not much improved with the Treaty of Lisbon.

However, a certain measure of "democratic deficit" in the area of Economic and Monetary Union policies seemed to be tolerable as long as the economic situation in Europe and particularly for the euro-area Member States remained florid. At that time, the scarce involvement of the European Parliament was regarded as a fair price to pay for a mechanism, which was producing positive results in economic terms for both the Member States and their citizens.

Besides, as far as the Monetary "branch" of EMU was concerned, it was felt that the independence of the European Central Bank (ECB) from the Member States was a sufficient guarantee that the managing of the euro would be correct and impartial and did not require a direct parliamentary interference.

On the other hand, the Treaties only established a rather loose "coordination" of the economic policies of Member States. The procedures laid down to ensure the respect of the Maastricht criteria in terms of ratio between GDP and, respectively, government deficit and debt left a wide margin of manoeuvre for each Member State. Budgetary decisions were still taken at State level, and this allowed National parliaments to play their democratic role.

2. Things changed dramatically as from 2008, with the explosion of the financial and, later, sovereign debt crisis.

Budgetary rules had to be made much tighter than before. Member States, especially those which were having difficulties with their sovereign debt, had to accept a drastic compression of their discretion in economic affairs.

The "golden rule" laid down in the Fiscal Compact now requires States to maintain a balanced budget, by gradually reducing the government debt. The annual budget must now be adopted following a procedure, which is heavily regulated at the European level, and this confers the Commission large possibility of putting pressure on Member States in order to obtain corrections and adaptations.

"Strict conditionality", which is needed for being granted both the financial assistance from the European Stability Mechanism (ESM) and the intervention of the ECB through its unconventional operations like the Outright Monetary Transactions (OMT), means that a Member State is asked to accept specific and targeted measures in the fiscal and economic domain, which must be decided in agreement with the "troika".

The enforcement of the bail-in principle within the Banking Union (BU) will prevent Member States from rescuing a National failing bank, as it was the case in the past.

3. In this new context, far-reaching measures, which may immediately affect the life of individuals, like cutting public salaries or pensions, increasing taxes, privatising public services or putting State assets on the market, preventing Member States from protecting private investors from the risk of losing their money in case of a bank failure, are *de facto* being imposed on a Member State, without neither the European Parliament nor the National parliaments having much to say.

Representative democracy, on which EU should be founded, according to Art. 10.1 of the Treaty on European Union (TEU), would require that decisions are taken by bodies elected by the citizens. However nowadays representative democracy is not anymore regarded as the only possible declination of the principle of democracy.

Article 10.3 and the whole of Art. 11 of the TEU offer several non-representative methods for enhancing democracy. Transparency and publicity of the decisions taken at the European level as well as the right of citizens to make their views known and to be consulted are made compulsory for all institutions, including the ECB.

The right of access to any document of the institutions is now listed among the human rights under Art. 42 of the Charter of Fundamental Rights of the European Union.

Moreover the Court of Justice of the European Union and several courts of Member States, including some Constitutional courts, have asserted their competence to judicially review both the decisions taken by the institutions in the area of EMU and the measures issued by Member States in implementing such decisions.

All in all, the picture is not black or white.

On one side, the lack of a truly effective parliamentary involvement in the running of the EMU indicates that the principle of democracy in terms of representative democracy is not observed. On the other side, the several non-representative instruments of democracy provided might, to a certain extent, make up for such a lack.

As we all know, Economic and Monetary Union policies are a highly technical area, which do not normally afford a wide parliamentary scrutiny even at the level of each State. The very democratic problem with EMU therefore seems to be that decisions are being taken, directly or indirectly, at the European level rather than freely by the individual State. And this brings us back to the core question of the State sovereignty and of the limits that a State may accept in view of the progress of the European integration.

It is this book's aim to help in shedding some more light on this very delicate and intricate situation.

4. The book is made up of five parts.

In **Part I**, it is offered an updated picture of the institutional balance within the scope of EMU that resulted from the recent reforms, including non-EU measures, like the EMS Treaty and the Fiscal Compact.

The core of the analysis is, of course, the role of the European Parliament, as the only institution having a democratic mandate (**Starita**, **Martucci, De la Parra**, **Lionello**, **Simone**).

However, much attention is devoted also to the Commission (**Smits**, **Martines**, **Fasone-Fromage**). Indeed the independent and impartial nature of this institution, coupled with its very wide duty of transparency, participation and dialogue with the European Parliament, the National parliaments and the general public, could somewhat compensate the lack of any real parliamentary involvement.

The rise of the "intergovernmentalism", of which the activism of the European Council is the clearest evidence (**Allemand**), and the tendency towards a more and more centralised system for EMU (**Fabbrini**) are also explored in Part I, as they could both make the democratic control more difficult, whether through the European Parliament or through non-representative methods.

Part II is focused on the ECB.

Nobody ignores that, during the crisis, the EU monetary institution, with its well-timed measures, came to the rescue of both the banking system in need of liquidity and the Member States having difficulties with their sovereign debts. The importance of the ECB's role is self-evident if one only thinks that, at a time when the ECB launched its various programmes, the intergovernmental mechanisms, like the ESM, were not fully operational yet.

However, the fact that the ECB's help came through "unconventional" measures raised several doubts as to whether the ECB was exceeding the limits of its competence under the Treaties. And if this was the case, the democratic principle would be at stake, Indeed, *ultra vires* acts of the institutions, according to the doctrine of the Bundesverfassungsgericht (BVerfG), infringe the Constitutional right of citizens to democracy and to vote. Such doubts were the subject matter of the ruling of the Court of Justice of the European Union (ECJ) in *Gauweiler*. However the distinction between conventional and unconventional measures is still open. Several new programmes have been launched since by the ECB, including the Quantitative Easing

(QE). The ECJ may be called upon to better draw a dividing line between what is "monetary" and merely "economic" (**Cafaro, Bassan**).

Considering that the ECB is independent from the Member States but also from the other EU institutions, including the European Parliament, the fact that some of the ECB unconventional measures like the OMT imposed a "strict conditionality" on Member States also raised a problem of democracy. Indeed a mainly technocratic institution allows itself to dictate harsh conditions upon Member States which might have very negative repercussions on the life of the citizens (**Peroni**).

In **Part III**, an important and much awaited side effect of EMU is under review in terms of democracy: the Banking Union (BU). No doubt, by setting a Single Supervisory Mechanism (SSM) and a Single Resolution Mechanism (SRM), which should be soon completed by the recent European Deposit Insurance Scheme (EDIS), the BU had the effect of transferring most of the monitoring powers on the banking system from the Member State level to the EU one. This new development should help in enhancing a real solidarity between Member States in the financial area (**Viterbo**).

By centralising the banking supervision, the BU should also reduce the mutual influence between the National politicians and the bankers. This should make the banking supervision less exposed to the negative democratic externalities of the past whenever a banking crisis occurs (**Ortino**).

At the same time, full use should be made of the several "tools" of non-representative democratic control inserted in the BU, in terms of transparency and accountability of the activities of the ECB in the area of prudential supervision, as well as the activities of the Single Resolution Board (SRB) and of the Single Resolution Fund (SRF) in the area of banking resolution (**Cisotta**, **Ruccia**).

Part IV deals with the role of the ECJ and that of the Supreme/Constitutional courts of Member States in the area of the reformed EMU law. Indeed democracy is less in danger where a real judicial review of the measures issued by the public powers is ensured.

It is well known that the ECB's OMT programme offered the opportunity for a first "direct" dialogue between the ECJ and the BVerfG. This dialogue took place on the occasion of the already quoted *Gauweiler* case, which was referred by the BVerfG to the ECJ under Art. 267 of the TFEU. Despite a critical approach that one may take of the ECJ's ruling or of some parts of its reasoning, the combined work of the ECJ and of the BVerfG produced the result of drawing some more precise limits of what falls within the power of the ECB and what pertains to the individual competence of Member States under the EMU primary law (**Ruffert**, **Pace**).

A further feature of the role that the ECJ is called upon to play within the EMU area is embedded in Art. 37 of the EMS Treaty, Art. 8 of the Fiscal Compact and Art. 14 of the Agreement on the Transfer and Mutualisation of Contributions to the Single Resolution Fund. All these rules confer to ECJ the task to adjudicate disputes linked to the mentioned Treaties. However the conditions under which the ECJ may perform its adjudicating powers vary from one Treaty to the other and need exploring in the light of other similar cases (**Baratta**).

The book ends in **Part V** with some concluding remarks (**Rossi**).

5. Most of the contributions to this book consist of papers presented at the International Conference held in Rome on 22 January, 2016, at the "Sala della Clemenza", kindly offered by Associazione Bancaria Italiana (ABI).

All papers underwent an accurate updating and extension work in view of the publication. The book also includes some further written contributions prepared by scholars, well distinguished in the area of EMU law, who could not take part in the Rome Conference.

The Rome Conference and this book are part of a research project funded by the Italian Ministry of Public Education, University and Research (MIUR) under the PRIN Programme (Research Projects of National Interest) for 2010–2011 (2010AALBC4_006).

Rome, Italy Luigi Daniele

Peer Review Process

The manuscript has been subjected to the peer review process prior to publication. Peer reviewers' reports are kept by the publishing houses.

Contents

List of Authors

Frédéric Allemand University of Luxembourg, Esch-sur-Alzette, Luxembourg

Roberto Baratta Department of Political Science, University of Macerata, Macerata, Italy

Fabio Bassan International Law, Department of Business Studies, University of Roma Tre, Rome, Italy

Susanna Cafaro Department of Legal Sciences, University of Salento, Lecce, Italy

Roberto Cisotta Italian Ministry of Foreign Affairs and International Cooperation, Rome, Italy

Luigi Daniele Department of Public Law, University of Rome "Tor Vergata", Rome, Italy

Sergio De la Parra Centre Virtuel de la Connaissance sur l'Europe, Sanem, Luxembourg

Federico Fabbrini School of Law & Government, Dublin City University, Dublin, Ireland

Cristina Fasone Department of Political Sciences, LUISS Guido Carli University, Rome, Italy

Diane Fromage Law Faculty, Maastricht University, Maastricht, The Netherlands

Luca Lionello Catholic University of Milan, Milan, Italy

Francesca Martines European Union Law, Law Department, University of Pisa, Pisa, Italy

Francesco Martucci Department of Public Law, University Panthéon-Assas (Paris II), Paris, France

Matteo Ortino Economic Law, University of Verona, Verona, Italy

Lorenzo Federico Pace Department of Economics, University of Molise, Campobasso, Italy

Giulio Peroni Department of Italian and Supranational Pubic Law, University of Milan, Milan, Italy

Lucia Serena Rossi Department of Legal Sciences, University of Bologna, Bologna, Italy

Nicola Ruccia Polytechnic of Bari, Bari, Italy

Matthias Ruffert Department of Public Law and European Law, Humboldt-University, Berlin, Germany

Pierluigi Simone Department of Public Law, University of Rome "Tor Vergata", Rome, Italy

René Smits Law of the Economic and Monetary Union, University of Amsterdam, Amsterdam, The Netherlands

Centre for Commercial Law Studies, Queen Mary University of London, London, UK

Administrative Board of Review, ECB, Frankfurt, Germany

Belgian Competition Authority, Brussels, Belgium

EMU Law and Banking Regulation, RS Law & Society Consulting B.V., Hoofddorp, The Netherlands

Massimo Starita Department of Law, University of Palermo, Palermo, Italy

Annamaria Viterbo International Law, Department of Law, University of Turin, Turin, Italy

Collegio Carlo Alberto Law Affiliate, Turin, Italy

Abbreviations

a.k.a.	Also known as
ABS	Asset-Backed Securities
ABSPP	Asset-Backed Securities Purchase Programme
ADEMU	A Dynamic Economic and Monetary Union
AEUV	Vertrag über die Arbeitsweise der Europäischen Union
AG	Advocate General
AIRF	Autoridad Independiente de Responsabilidad Fiscal
APS	Annual Policy Strategy
AQR	Asset Quality Review
ART	Accountability, Representation and Transparency
BEPGs	Broad Economic Policy Guidelines
BGB	Bürgerliches Gesetzbuch
bn	Billion
BRR	Bank Recovery and Resolution
BRRD	Bank Recovery and Resolution Directive
BU	Banking Union
Bull. EC	Bulletin of the European Communities
BVerfG	Bundesverfassungsgericht
BVerfGE	Entscheidungen des Bundesverfassungsgerichts
BvR	Richter des Bundesverfassungsgerichts
CB	Covered Bonds
CBPP	Covered Bonds Purchase Programme
CEPS	Centre for European Policy Studies
cf.	Confer
cit.	Cited
CO_2	Carbon Dioxide
COSAC	Conference of Parliamentary Committees for Union Affairs of Parliaments of the European Union
CPB	Centraal Planbureau/Netherlands Bureau for Economic Policy Analysis
CRR-CRD	Capital Requirements Regulation and Directive

CSRs	Country-Specific Recommendations
CVCE	Centre Virtuel de la Connaissance sur l'Europe
CWP	Commission's Work Programme
DGS	Deposit Guarantee Scheme
DIF	Deposit Insurance Fund
DOI	Digital Object Identifier
DRI	Direct Recapitalisation Instrument
e.g.	Exempli gratia
EA	Euro Area
EBA	European Banking Authority
EBU	European Banking Union
EC	European Community
ECA	European Court of Auditors
ECB	European Central Bank
ECHR	European Convention on Human Rights
ECI	European Citizens' Initiative
ECJ	European Court of Justice
Ecofin	Economic and Financial Affairs Council
ECtHR	European Court of Human Rights
ECON	European Parliament's Committee on Economic and Monetary Affairs
ECU	European Currency Unit
ed	Editor
ED	Economic Dialogue
EDIS	European Deposit Insurance Scheme
edn.	Edition
EDP	Excessive Deficit Procedure
eds	Editors
EEA	European Economic Area
EEC	European Economic Community
EESC	European Economic and Social Committee
EFB	European Fiscal Bund
EFC	Economic and Financial Committee
EFSF	European Financial Stability Facility
EFSM	European Financial Stabilisation Mechanism
EFTA	European Free Trade Association
EGC	European General Court
EGOV	European Parliament's Economic Governance Support Unit
EIB	European Investment Bank
EIOPA	European Insurance and Occupational Pension Authority
EIP	Economic Imbalances Procedure
ELA	Emergency Liquidity Assistance
EMPL	European Parliament's Employment Committee
EMU	Economic and Monetary Union
EP	European Parliament

EPAP	Enhanced Production Audit Programme
EPP	European People's Party
EPRS	European Parliament Research Services
ESAs	European Supervisory Authorities
ESCB	European System of Central Banks
ESFS	European System of Financial Supervision
ESM	European Stability Mechanism
ESMA	European Securities and Markets Authority
esp.	Especially
ESRB	European Systemic Risk Board
et al.	et alii
et seq.	et sequens
et seqq.	et sequentes
etc.	et cetera
EU	European Union
EUDO	European Union Democracy Observatory
EUI	European University Institute
Eurostat	Statistical Office of the European Union
FIDE	International Federation for European Law
FTT	Financial Transaction Tax
GC	Governing Council
GDP	Gross Domestic Product
GDR	German Democratic Republic
GFCC	German Federal Constitutional Court
GURI	Gazzetta Ufficiale della Repubblica Italiana
HCFP	Haut Conseil des Finances Publiques
HIPC	Harmonised Index of Consumer Prices
HIV	Human Immunodeficiency Virus
HUMANE	Help Us Make a New Europe
i.e.	id est
IAI	Istituto Affari Internazionali
Ibid.	Ibidem
IFIs	Independent Fiscal Institutions
IGA	Intergovernmental Agreement
IIA	Interinstitutional Agreement
IMF	International Monetary Fund
INSEE	Institut National de la Statistique et des Études Économiques
LLR	Lender of Last Resort
LSIs	Less Significant Institutions
LTRO	Long-Term Refinancing Operation
LTROs	Long-Term Refinancing Operations
MEP	Member of the European Parliament
MEPs	Members of the European Parliament
MoU	Memorandum of Understanding

MoUs	Memoranda of Understanding
MP	Member of Parliament
MPs	Members of Parliament
Mr.	Mister
MROs	Main Refinancing Operations
n.	Numéro
NCAs	National Competent Authorities
NCBs	National Central Banks
No.	Number
Nos.	Numbers
NPs	National Parliaments
OECD	Organisation for Economic Co-operation and Development
OJEC	Official Journal of the European Communities
OJEU	Official Journal of the European Union
OL	Organic Law
OMC	Open Method of Coordination
OMT	Outright Monetary Transactions
p.	Page
para.	Paragraph
paras.	Paragraphs
PBO	Parliamentary Budget Office
PIGS	Portugal, Ireland, Italy, Greece, Spain
PM	Prime Minister
pp.	Pages
PS	Post Scriptum
PSOE	Partido Socialista Obrero Español
QE	Quantitative Easing
QVM	Qualified Majority Voting
REFIT	European Commission's Regulatory Fitness and Performance Programme
RSCAS	Robert Schuman Centre for Advanced Studies
SDRM	Sovereign Debt Restructuring Mechanism
sec.	Section
SGP	Stability Growth Pact
SIEPS	Swedish Institute for European Policy Studies
SMP	Securities Markets Programme
SPD	Sozialdemokratische Partei Deutschlands
SRB	Single Resolution Board
SREP	Supervisory Review and Evaluation Process
SRF	Single Resolution Fund
SRM	Single Resolution Mechanism
SSM	Single Supervisory Mechanism
subpara.	Subparagraph
Suppl.	Supplement
TEC	Treaty Establishing the European Community

TESM	Treaty on the European Stability Mechanism
TEU	Treaty on European Union
TFEU	Treaty on the Functioning of the European Union
TLTRO	Targeted Longer-Term Refinancing Operations
TSCG	Treaty on Stability, Coordination and Governance in the Economic and Monetary Union
TTIP	Transatlantic Trade and Investment Partnership
UACES	University Association of Contemporary European Studies
UEFA	Union of European Football Associations
UK	United Kingdom
UPC	Unified Patent Court
URL	Uniform Resource Locator
US	United States
USA	United States of America
v./vs.	Versus
Vol.	Volume
WFD	Water Field Directive
WTO	World Trade Organization

Part I
The New Institutional Balance and Democracy

Democratic Principles and the Economic Branch of the European Monetary Union

Massimo Starita

Abstract After the Treaty of Lisbon a variety of rules referring to democracy were incorporated in Title II of the Treaty establishing the European Union (TEU). The way in which representative and non-representative democratic principles are combined in the European Union legal system is not a unitary one, but it changes depending on the fields of competence of the Union. The paper will focus on the effects that the reforms introduced in the period 2011–2013 had on the combination of representative and non-representative democratic principles in the economic branch of the EMU. To that effect the original design of the role of democratic principles in this field will be briefly described. Then, a brief overview of the different rules included in the new law of Economic and Monetary Union, referring to democratic principles, will be provided. Finally, the contribution will evaluate the overall impact of the reforms carried out on democracy in the EMU. The following issues will be particularly addressed: (A) Are these clauses integrated into a complete strategy concerning channels of democratic legitimacy in the law of the EMU? (B) Is this strategy compatible with the TEU stance on democratic principles? (C) Can non-representative democracy principles be considered a real counterweight to the shrinking of representative democratic legitimacy in the EMU and in the fiscal policy of the Member States?

Contents

M. Starita (✉)
Department of Law, University of Palermo, Palermo, Italy
e-mail: massimo.starita@unipa.it

L. Daniele et al. (eds.), *Democracy in the EMU in the Aftermath of the Crisis*,
DOI 10.1007/978-3-319-53895-2_1

1 Introduction

Much has been written on the implications of the reforms introduced in the architecture of the EMU as a response to the Euro crisis for democratic Government in the EU. This paper addresses this problem from the perspective of the democratic theories or "democratic models." In particular, I will discuss two questions. First, I will try to understand whether or not the reforms of 2011 and 2013 were inspired by a particular conception of democracy or, at least, a particular combination of democratic principles. Second, I will seek to assess the compatibility of this combination with EU primary law concerning democracy.

Taking the perspective of the democratic principles when discussing the problem of democratic legitimacy of the European Union's economic and monetary Union (EMU) is interesting for at least two reasons.

The first reason is that we live in very complex societies and democratic principles cannot but reflect this complexity. As a consequence, a variety of conceptions of democracy compete in the political debate today. Some of them have been conceived as possible answers to some problems that traditional representative democracy is supposed to have. These theories can be considered as non-representative theories of democracy, although, generally speaking, their aim is not to substitute representative democracy. They have been designed to mix with this basic model, instead. In other words, their goal is to introduce in a representative system some non-representative democratic principles and some institutional mechanisms inspired by these principles.[1]

The second reason is that this complexity is reflected in positive law too. As far as EU law is concerned, the Treaty of Lisbon introduced a variety of democratic principles in Title II of the Treaty establishing the European Union (TEU). Indeed, the new Title II of the TEU affirms that the European Union is founded on different democratic underpinnings, both representative and non-representative. While representative democracy is referred to in Article 10, para. 1, as the basic principle on which the functioning of the Union is founded,[2] Articles 10–12 introduce in the EU legal system rules and instruments linkable to non-representative conceptions of democracy.

This article puts forward two main propositions. The first one is that the recent transition to strengthened economic cooperation has been accompanied by a loss of power of both national and European parliaments. This first proposition is rooted in insights from existing literature on "executive dominance" in the reformed EMU governance. The second proposition is that the European legislator, searching to compensate this representative deficit, subverted the basic idea stemming from the TEU that non-representative democratic principles have to be conceived as *complements* to representation, but not as *substitutes* for it.

[1]See, in general on democratic models and conceptions, Held (2006).

[2]"The functioning of the Union shall be founded on representative democracy".

Before going deeper in my presentation, three preliminary observations are needed. The first concerns the subject of my analysis. I will focus only on the "economic branch" of the EMU, leaving aside the monetary one. This is not to deny that the unconventional operations enacted by the European Central Bank (such as the Outright Monetary Transactions and the Quantitative Easing) have had distributional consequences and pose thereby a problem of democratic control, as is showed by the BVerfG judgment of 21 June 2016.[3] The choice not to deal with this subject is due to the fact that, interesting and significant as it could be,[4] it has to be set in the framework of the well established principle of independence of central banks from the executives. This principle, which is enshrined in Article 130 of the Treaty on the Functioning of the European Union (TFEU), as recognised by the Court of Justice in *Gauwelier*,[5] seems to suggest that the legitimacy of the ECB could be based, at least to some extent, on mechanisms of political accountability different from traditional democratic control.[6] The problem of legitimacy of the procedures provided for in the so-called "Six Pack" and "Two Pack" and, outside the EU legal framework, in the European Stability Mechanism (ESM) Treaty and in the so-called Fiscal Compact, is rather *new* instead.

The second preliminary observation concerns the approach that I will follow. Dealing with democratic legitimacy is always a difficult task for lawyers, because *legitimacy* is a political concept. Thus, it is simply impossible to follow a strict or a *pure* legal approach. However, I will try not to be caught in the opposite trap of making purely political considerations. In particular, I will neither deliver opinions on democratic models as such, nor make proposals in order to improve the democratic structure of the EMU.

Thirdly, I will discuss the problem of democratic legitimacy only in relation to the reforms introduced through EU legislation, since those introduced by the conclusion of international agreements (in particular TSCG and ESM) could not be reviewed in light of the principles heralded in the TEU. However, since from a material point of view the reforms are intertwined, the discussion will draw on insights from those international agreements where relevant to the inquiry.

---

[3]Bundesverfassungsgericht, judgment of 21 June 2016, 2 BvR 2728/13, 2 BvR 2729/13, 2 BvR 2730/13, 2 BvR 2731/13, 2 bei 13/13.

[4]See Joerges (2016), who argues that the ECJ "supports the establishment of a technocratic regime with unlimited discretionary powers and without credible autonomy".

[5]See ECJ 16 June 2015, Case C-62/14, *Gauweilier and Others*, para. 40: "Article 130 is, in essence, intended to shield the ESCB from all political pressure in order to enable it effectively to pursue the objectives attributed to its tasks, through the independent exercise of the specific powers conferred on it for that purpose by primary law." On the independence of the ECB see: Zilioli and Selmyar (2000), who regard the ECB as an independent specialised organisation of Community law; Lastra and Louis (2013).

[6]See Zilioli (2003) and Lastra and Louis (2013). Under Article 284, para. 3, TFEU, "The European Central Bank shall address an annual report on the activities of the ESCB and on the monetary policy of both the previous and current year to the European Parliament and the Commission, and also to the European Council. The President of the European Central Bank shall present this report to the Council and to the European Parliament which may hold a general debate on that basis.".

My contribution is made up of five more sections. Section 2 will deal with the original relationship between the EMU and democratic principles. In Sect. 3 I will explain how this relationship was changed by the crisis-led reforms. Then, in the Sect. 4, I will seek to summarise some arguments that have been used to justify the democratic shortfalls of the reforms and the problems with these arguments. The following two sections will be devoted to understanding whether the reforms were inspired by a certain democratic model (or at least a certain idea of combining different democratic conceptions and principles) and whether this conception (or combination) is compatible with the basic idea of democratic governance stemming from Title II of the TEU. This contribution goes a step forward: in its conclusions it suggests, albeit in a short-hand fashion, that the recent EU legislation reforming the economic branch of EMU could be considered, notwithstanding its formal *status*, as instruments of constitutional moment.

2 The Original Relationship Between the EMU and Democratic Principles

Already before the reform, the democratic legitimacy of EU action in the field of economic and monetary union was problematic. As is well known, this question was at the centre of the debate preceding the entry into force of the Maastricht Treaty, although it was focused essentially on the Monetary Union and on the role of the ECB therein, given the huge distance that the Treaty guaranteed to the newly created institution from political pressure.[7] However, Economic Union was problematic too, given the executive-dominated law-making processes that the Treaty outlined in this area of cooperation between Member States.

Indeed, the three basic procedures of the economic coordination policy of the EU were steadily in the hands of the national Governments acting through the Council and the European Council: the procedure for definition of the broad guidelines of the economic policies of the Member States of the Union (from now on, broad guidelines), the multilateral surveillance procedure, and the excessive deficit procedure.

Under the Maastricht Treaty, whose basic provisions regarding economic policy coordination have remained unaltered by the subsequent amending treaties, the broad guidelines are adopted by the Council on the basis of a conclusion discussed by the European Council, acting in turn on the basis of a report from the Council, while the whole process starts with a simple recommendation of the Commission

[7]Leino and Salminen (2013).

(and not with a "proposal" from it, as under the ordinary legislative procedure).[8] The EP has no right to have a say in this quite contorted procedure. All Article 121 TFEU provides in terms of parliamentary control is that

> the Commission shall inform the European Parliament of its recommendation.

The second procedure is the multilateral surveillance procedure organised under Article 121, paras. 3 and 4, TFEU, on the economic policies of the Member States, in order to ensure convergence and consistency with these broad guidelines. This is Council-led too. Here the work is made by the Council, on the basis of reports submitted to it by the Commission,[9] with the EP being simply informed, this time by reports on the results of the multilateral surveillance, formulated by the President of the Council and by the Commission. In addition, the EP may invite the President of the Council to appear before its competent committee if the Council has decided to make public a recommendation addressed to a Member State under the procedure of multilateral surveillance.[10]

Finally, once again a Council-directed surveillance procedure is provided for in Article 126 TFEU for prevention and correction of excessive government deficits by Member States. In this case, the Commission monitors the evolution of the budgetary situation and of the stock of Government debt in Member States (with the participation of the Economic and Financial Committee).[11] However, it is the Council that decides whether an excessive deficit exists (on a proposal of the Commission and having considered any observations the Member State concerned may wish to make) and the consequent recommendations.[12]Furthermore, the Council (acting on a recommendation of the Commission) may address to the Member State concerned decisions concerning corrective measures. Once again, the EP is the recipient of a mere right to be informed.[13]

The Stability and Growth Pact, adopted to ensure stricter budgetary discipline for Member States participating in monetary union, by strengthening the surveillance of the budgetary positions and the coordination of economic policies,

[8]This is a difference of moment, given that "proposals" are the manifestation of the power of legislative initiative accorded to the Commission and, as such, are strongly safeguarded by the Treaties and by the Court of Justice. See Article 293, para. 1, TFEU, providing that, except in the cases referred to in the provisions of the TFEU mentioned by it, where, pursuant to the Treaties, the Council acts on a proposal from the Commission, it may amend that proposal only by acting unanimously, and Article 293, para. 2, TFEU, providing that, as long as the Council has not acted, the Commission may alter its proposal at any time during the procedures leading to the adoption of an EU act. The Court of Justice has been ready to offer even wider—maybe too wide—safeguards to the proposals of the Commission, for example by recognising to it—even if within certain limits—the power of withdrawal. See recently ECJ 14 April 2015, Case C-409/13, *Council of the European Union* v. *European Commission*.

[9]Article 121, para. 4, TFEU.

[10]Article 121, para. 5, TFEU.

[11]Article 126, paras. 2–5, TFEU.

[12]Article 126, paras. 6 and 7, TFEU.

[13]Article 126, para. 11, TFEU.

maintained this scheme, though partly anticipating the alterations that would be introduced by the financial crisis-led reforms.[14]

However, the problem of the marginalisation of the EP in the three procedures summarised above was not considered as serious as today. This can be explained if one considers that the basic constitutional features of the EMU could be seen as respecting or, at least, as not seriously impinging on the *representative* democratic principle, if one understands this principle "holistically", namely in the interrelationship between the EU legal order and the national ones. Member States had of course the legal obligation to avoid excessive government deficits on the basis of the two criteria referred to in Article 126, para. 2, TFEU and specified in the Protocol on the excessive deficit procedure annexed to the Treaties. However, it was largely recognised that national Parliaments "remained in control of their economic policies, including their budgetary and fiscal policy."[15] The EU institutions had a competence of economic co-ordination, but it had to be exercised through the adoption of non-binding acts (i.e. "the broad guidelines"), by means of an intergovernmental and "*consensus*-building" procedure (thanks, in particular, to the participation to the procedure of the European Council),[16] respect for which was guaranteed by a "peer pressure" mechanism.[17] In other words, the almost voluntary character of economic cooperation and the consequent role of national Parliaments in shaping the economic decisions taken at the level of the Member States compensated for the slight influence of the European Parliament over the measures adopted at the EU level.

3 The Relationship Between the EMU and Democratic Principles After the Crisis: A "Strengthened" Representative Democratic Deficit

It is with the adoption of the so-called "Six Pack" and "Two Pack" that the problem of the democratic legitimacy of the EMU has deepened. As Jürgen Habermas observes,

---

[14]The so-called Stability and Growth Pact was originally made up of a European Council Resolution (the resolution adopted by the European Council in Amsterdam in June 1997, OJEC C236, 2 August 1997) and two Council Regulations (Council Regulation (EC) No. 1466/97 of 7 July 1997 on the strengthening of the surveillance of budgetary positions and the coordination of economic policies and Council Regulation (EC) No. 1467/97 of the same day on speeding up and clarifying the implementation of the excessive deficit procedure, both in OJEC L 209, 2 August 1997).

[15]Lenaerts (2014).

[16]Colasanti (1994), Smits (2002) and Bickerton et al. (2015).

[17]Colasanti (1994) and Louis (2009).

> the executive, as always in times of crisis, felt compelled to empower itself. In an alliance with the Commission and the European Central Bank, the national governments assembled in the Eurogroup and of the European Council have extended their scope of action at the cost of their national parliaments, and as a result have greatly exacerbated the existing shortfall in legitimacy.[18]

There are good reasons to share this argument, with the exception of the fact that in the sentence quoted the EP is not mentioned as one of the parties, albeit unenthusiastic, to the "alliance" that Habermas refers to.[19]

There is already a rich literature exploring these developments and analytically discussing the so-called democratic deficit in the new economic governance. This literature has highlighted a number of features that can be considered as the most likely candidates for explaining Habermas' concept of "exacerbation of the existing shortfall in legitimacy." The most important of these features are three.

Firstly, *the reforms have insulated EMU governance from direct parliamentary contestation*. This is the most important feature of the democratic deficit argument in the field of economic co-operation. As has been noted:

> one of the objectives of the reform of the EMU was to free the application of technical rules on fiscal discipline from political interference.[20]

It can be maintained that insulation is the product of two parallel developments. *At the national level*, the disempowerment of Parliaments in the budgetary process is the effect of the obligation of the Eurozone States under the TSCG to recognise in their constitutions the balanced budget or "golden" rule (under which "the budgetary position of the general government of a Contracting Party must be balanced or in surplus").[21] This constitutional guarantee will thereby protect the golden rule, as well as the neo-liberal theory behind it, from democratic political contestation: both the Executive and the Parliament are under the *obligation* to shape the national budgetary laws in order to ensure respect for the golden rule. The legal constraints on the budgetary policies of the Member States seem likely in particular to have weakened national Parliaments. Insofar as they were used to function in the budgetary process as decision-makers or as political overseers, depending on the State's more general institutional framework, their role have become narrower,

[18] Habermas (2014). For consideration of the reforms of the EMU as an example of the general tendency of executives to push aside parliaments in times of crises, see also Curtin (2014) and Polou (2014).

[19] Indeed, the EP was a co-legislator in the adoption of the Six-Pack and the Two-Pack and was allowed to participate in the negotiation of the Fiscal Compact. For a discussion see further Sect. 4.

[20] Lenaerts (2014).

[21] See Article 3 of the Treaty on Stability, Coordination and Governance in the Economic and Monetary Union (TSCG).

technical surveillance, whose aim is limited to making sure that the executive abide by the European legal constraints.[22]

The insulation of the budgetary process from democratic competition came about *at the EU level*, too. Indeed, the reduction of the space of *manoeuvre* of Member States, and in particular of national Parliaments, in shaping their economic policies, has not been compensated for by an empowerment of the EP, which has been left at the borders of the new European economic governance, instead (as we will see in the next sections, the "economic dialogues" provided by the EU legislation do not lead to real involvement in the decision-making process). A different trend may be identified: in short, the reforms empowered those European institutions whose nature (judicial, the first one; quasi-technocratic, the second one) insulates them from direct political contestation.

Under the TSCG an important role of control is given to the Court of Justice of the European Union. Indeed, the supranational judiciary is entrusted with overseeing respect for the obligation of the States to incorporate the "golden rule" in national Constitutional law.[23] Furthermore, there is some force in the argument that the ECJ

> may over time acquire a role in enforcing the obligation of states to respect the golden rule in the budgetary procedure

assuming that

> it is conceivable that the ECJ may be asked to rule on the compatibility of a state budget with the provisions of EU laws

as a matter of interpretation *ex* Article 263 TFEU.[24]

---

[22]It has been argued that the golden rule has depowered national Parliaments only in parliamentary systems where Parliaments function as decision-makers in the budgetary process, while it "may provide instruments for parliamentary opposition to make its voice heard" in "semi-parliamentary systems and in parliamentary systems in which executives have strong and obedient parliamentary majority." Indeed, under this argument, in semi-presidential systems the Executive is already in full control of the budgetary process. Thus, the "golden rule" is likely to give new opportunities for the opposition in Parliament to control the activity of the Executive. See Fabbrini (2013). For a critique to this argument see further Sect. 4.

[23]According to Article 8, para. 1, of the TSCG: "The European Commission is invited to present in due time to the Contracting Parties a report in the provisions adopted by each of them in compliance with Article 3 (2). If the European Commission, after having given the Contracting Party concerned the opportunity to submit its observations, concludes in its report that such Contracting Party has failed to comply with Article 3 (2), the matter will be brought to the Court of Justice of the European Union by one or more Contracting Parties. Where a Contracting Party considers, independently of the Commission's report, that another Contracting Party has failed to comply with Article 3 (2), it may also bring the matter to the Court of Justice. In both cases, the judgment of the Court of Justice shall be binding on the parties to the proceedings, which shall take the necessary measures to comply with the judgment within a period to be decided by the Court." If a Party does not comply with the decision of the Court, a second case can be bought to the Court, which may impose on the State "a lump-sum or a penalty" (Article 8, para. 2, of the TSCG).

[24]Fabbrini (2013).

But concerns about democracy have also been raised relating to the role of the European Commission. Under the "Six Pack", the strengthening of the economic governance at EU level passes through an enhanced role of this institution, both in directing the economic policies of Member States and in controlling their budgetary behavior. A central feature in this turn is the introduction of the rule of "reverse majority voting", under which the Commission's recommendations are adopted unless the Council decides to reject the recommendations within 10 days of their adoption by the Commission. This rule concerns the adoption of decisions of non-compliance as well as decisions providing for sanctions. Decisions of non-compliance can be adopted, on the basis of Regulations that apply to all Member States of the European Union, as part of the strengthened multilateral surveillance of budgetary positions of Member States,[25] as well as being part of the new surveillance procedure for the prevention and the correction of excessive macroeconomic imbalances.[26] The "reverse majority voting" rule also applies to the adoption of sanctions. Decisions imposing interest-bearing deposits, non-interest bearing deposits, or annual fines can be adopted, on the basis of two Regulations whose scope of application is limited to Member States whose currency is the Euro, where the Member State concerned by a decision of non-compliance has not taken the corrective action recommended by the Council in a previous decision of non-compliance.[27]

The second feature seriously challenging democratic legitimacy is that *the reforms have made EMU governance substantially biased*. All the reforms adopted, those introduced by EU acts as well as those introduced by international treaties, are part of an overall, coherent, strategy of response to the crisis agreed among the Member States. Under this strategy, which is reflected in a number of European Council conclusions and whose cornerstone is the concept of budgetary discipline, the scope for welfare expenditure is narrow. Three main mechanisms were introduced, as part of a broader counter-crisis project, whose aim is to enact this concept. I have already mentioned the first two. They are the balanced budget or "golden" rule and stricter surveillance by European institution on Member States' budgetary processes. The third one is the principle of financial assistance conditionality (under which the granting of any financial assistance to Eurozone Countries facing severe financial difficulties is made "subject to strict conditionality", i.e. on the recipient

[25]Here the Council adopts, by the reverse majority rule, on the basis of the Commission's recommendations, decisions of non-compliance by Member States with the medium-term budgetary objectives provided for in the broad guidelines. See Articles 6 and 9 of Regulation (EU) No. 1175/2011 of 16 November 2011.

[26]Here the Council adopts by the reverse majority rule, on the basis of Commission's recommendations, decisions of non-compliance by Member States with recommended corrective action. See Article 10 of Regulation (EU) No. 1176/2011 of 16 November 2011.

[27]See Article 3, para. 3, of Regulation (EU) No. 1174/2011 of 16 November 2011; and Articles 4, para. 2, 5, para. 2, and 6, para. 2, of Regulation (EU) No. 1173/2011 of 16 November 2011.

State's acceptance of a number of detailed economic policy conditions[28] and on respect for the "golden rule").[29]

This second feature of the reforms is also bound to have implications on the question of their democratic legitimacy. Indeed, this turn in economic governance seems to give more weight to the critique that the EU would suffer from a *substantial* democratic deficit because of a neo-liberal bias in its economic constitution. In other words, as Scharpf argues,

> the most important element in a democratic polity is to maintain the balance between market liberalization and social protection.

Yet, under this view, the EU would miss this objective.[30] Before the reforms, this thesis was criticised by a number of scholars, who objected that there was little evidence of a neo-liberal bias of the EU. Furthermore, Moravcsik argued:

> the level of social welfare provision in Europe remains relatively stable.[31]

However, these counter-arguments are less tenable today, as indicated by the broad *consensus* among scholars (and citizenry) that after the reforms the EMU is driving social protection downward.[32]

The third feature of the new EMU governance that the literature has highlighted as likely to enhance the democratic deficit in this field is that *the reforms have narrowed the scope of democratic principles of the TEU as parameters of legitimacy for EMU governance*. This is the consequence of the fact that only some of the reforms have been introduced by EU legislation, while another part of the reforms has been adopted through international treaties formally outside the framework of the EU legal system. This means that the Council can no longer be considered as the only forum to be used by the Member States for their cooperation in this field; accordingly, the EMU can no longer be considered as "a union within the Union", but as an inter-sectional group of rules of economic coordination and direction stemming from both EU law and international law.

The use of parallel paths not only poses a risk to the unity of the system, but also has a consequence on the question of the democratic legitimacy of the reforms. In particular, this choice entails non-applicability of the principles enshrined in Title II of the TEU as parameters of the democratic legitimacy of the international branch of the reforms. Indeed, it is clear that what has been introduced through international agreements formally outside the framework of EU law cannot be challenged for violating EU primary law (unless a compatibility clause is provided for in the agreement).[33]

---

[28]European Council Decision 2011/199/EU amending Article 136 TFEU.

[29]See recital 27 of the TSCG.

[30]Scharpf (1999).

[31]Moravcsik (2002).

[32]Ioannidis (2014) and Polou (2014).

[33]Ruffert (2011) and Leino and Salminen (2013).

4 Views on the EMU Democratic Deficit

While the preceding account can be considered as a representation of a widely perceived democratic deficit of EMU governance, some scholars consider these deficiencies as overstated. In this section I will not review this literature, but I will try briefly to analyze the main arguments under which the democratic deific thesis has been criticised and criticise them in turn.

The first critique of the democratic deficit is based on parliamentary participation in the decision-making processes that led to the adoption of the reforms. Under this argument, either national Parliaments or the EP controlled these processes and finally gave their consent to the entry into force of the reforms. On the one side, those introduced through international agreements were controlled by national Parliaments thanks to their treaty-making powers at the ratification stage.[34] On the other side, most of the reforms introduced through EU legal acts were controlled by the EP insofar as they were adopted through the ordinary legislative procedure.[35]

Yet, as far as the involvement of national Parliaments is concerned it must be borne in mind that, given the general tendency in contemporary democratic states towards executive control over the legislature,

> parliamentary supervision thereafter will usually be interstitial or marginal.[36]

Moreover, the perceived urgency of the measures to be taken and the need to achieve agreements in strict deadlines militated against a thorough deliberation within national parliaments. In almost every state, thereby, "the EFSF, the ESM, and the austerity agreements were passed through parliaments by powerful governments."[37]

This is true even in relation to the EP's role in the decision-making process leading to the adoption of the "Six Pack" and the "Two Pack." The actual capacity of the EP to negotiate in these processes was not only conditioned by pressure under the "urgency" argument, but also by an institutional development, that is the rise of the European Council as a "real" legislative initiator in the EU.[38] Indeed, as is well known, this legislation was adopted on the basis of conclusions of the European Council which instructed the Commission in detail on the proposal to submit to the co-legislators and provided for a strict deadline for the final adoption of the reforms.[39] This evolution is likely to have two consequences on the distributions

---

[34]Von Rompuy (2012), Beukers (2013) and Tosato (2016).

[35]Beukers (2013). See also Poiares Maduro et al. (2012) and Tosato (2016).

[36]Craig (2011).

[37]Hix (2015).

[38]As is well known, with the Lisbon Treaty, the European Council became an institution of the Union. However, its composition seems to make it to some extent immune to the principle of institutional balance, as it is reflected in the Treaties, and able to impinge on this balance. See Starita (2013).

[39]See Starita (2013).

of powers between political institutions in the EU. On the one side, it clearly encroaches upon the Commission's monopoly of legislative initiative.[40] On the other side, it seems to reduce the impact of the EP exercise of its prerogatives on the final outcome of the legislative process, even where legislation has to be adopted under the ordinary legislative process. This interpretation is confirmed by the negotiating history of the Six-Pack, where the EP was able to produce only a "modest"[41] reinforcement of the position originally accorded to it by the European Council.[42]

A second possible critique of the democratic deficit argument, as it is conceived in relation to post-reforms EMU governance, is based on justification of "insulation" in mature democracies. Insulation can be conceived as the practice of delegating powers to organs protected from political contestation. As is well known, prominent scholars have defended the so-called EU democratic deficit, by recalling that insulation is very well known not only to the EU, but also to Member States' constitutional practice. Moreover, insulation at EU level has been justified because of the "regulatory" character of the policies attributed to the European Union, while more politically salient policy areas, with significant "redistributive" consequence, would be left to the Member States.[43]

Yet, even assuming that the opposition, on which this thesis is based, between regulatory and distributive policies is precise and unambiguous,[44] it would be difficult to maintain that this argument can be reasonably used today to justify insulation from direct democratic control of EMU governance measures. Indeed, the deeper economic integration pursued by these measures is likely to have greater redistributive consequences between the creditor and the debtor states as well as within the debtor states.[45]

A third thesis challenging the democratic deficit argument consists of a tentative minimisation of this deficit and is based on the supposed democratic credential of the main institutional rulers in the new EMU architecture. Not only has the enhanced role of the Commission been welcomed by some authors in terms of efficiency.[46] It has also been seen as adequate in terms of democratic legitimacy. Under this view, this role must be evaluated in light of the more general context of the EU system of "checks and balances", together with the principle of political responsibility of the Commission before the EP established therein. This system would give the Commission's new powers in EMU governance a level of democratic accountability adequate to their width and depth.[47] Under this argument, the

[40]Dawson and de Witte (2013), Starita (2013) and Curtin (2014).

[41]Fasone (2012).

[42]See Dawson and de Witte (2013), Keppenne (2014) and Lenaerts (2014).

[43]Majone (1996) and Moravcsik (2002).

[44]See, however, Scharpf (1999) for the thesis that the EU free movements rights have gradually constrained the Member States' capacity to shape their social policy.

[45]Baratta (2013), Dawson and de Witte (2013) and Hix (2015).

[46]See e.g. Smits (2002).

[47]Keppenne (2014).

new investiture procedure of the Commission introduced with the Lisbon Treaty has been highlighted.[48]

However, this view has been criticised by recalling that it is still difficult, even after the Lisbon Treaty, to consider the relationship between the Commission and the EP as one of political responsibility. Hix further contends that

> European Parliament elections are unlikely to provide a sufficiently strong mandate to the European Commission for its role in scrutinizing national economic policies under the emerging new architecture.[49]

In a similar vein, Baratta underlines the semi-technocratic character of this institution, which would not be adequate in terms of democratic legitimacy for such a prominent role and Fabbrini writes that the Commission has proven to be a technocratic structure in support of the European Council's deliberations.[50]

Some have even attempted to minimise the democratic deficit in terms of EP participation in the implementation of European governance by arguing that this institution would have gained influence with the "Six Pack." Under this view, it should be borne in mind that the EP was completely sidelined by the Maastricht Treaty, which considered it as a mere observer in the EMU decision-making process. This situation would have changed with the establishment of "economic dialogue."[51]

The problem with this argument lies in the choice of the EP, as it was considered under the Maastricht Treaty, as a useful basis for comparing the actual prerogatives of this institution. In fact, what is at stake is the democratic quality of the EU decision-making process on coordination of economic policies of Member States as it appears today. Thus, one may wonder if it is more appropriate comparing the powers of the EP today with those of an "historical" EP or with the powers assigned to the other political institutions of the EU under the revised EMU governance.

Some scholars have ventured further in the attempt to trivialise the democratic deficit argument, by arguing that the recent evolution in EMU governance would reinforce the role of *national* Parliaments. This thesis enhances the "democratic" quality of the obligation of the Member States to create national institutions responsible for producing macroeconomic and budgetary forecasts. Indeed, national Parliaments would finally have

> independent bodies at their disposal for helping them to effectively control the economic and fiscal action of the government.[52]

The problem with this thesis is that control of economic data based on transparent information does not necessarily guarantee a "political" control function.

48Von Rompuy (2012).

49Hix (2015).

50Baratta (2013), Fabbrini (2015). On the role of the European Council in the new economic governance see Michéa (2012).

51Keppenne (2014).

52Keppenne (2014).

However performed by Parliaments, this control could have a lighter, apolitical, technical function, where it is not accompanied by the power to decide on basic political choices, such as the distribution of wealth.[53] This is probably what happened to the national Parliaments in the reformed EMU governance, whose prerogatives of control over the executives seem to be conceived as directed essentially at guaranteeing respect for European decisions.

In sum, analysis of the main arguments under which the democratic deficit argument has been criticised allow us to understand that this argument has an important point, if one follows a *representative* democratic approach. Indeed, while significantly reducing the space of *manoeuvre* of Member States *vis à vis* the European Union—and, within Member States, of national Parliaments *vis à vis* the executives—in shaping economic policies, the reforms did not empower the EP, leaving it at the borders of the new European economic governance, instead.

But what happens if one also considers non-representative democratic principles? Will the democratic deficit disappear or, at least, will it appear less serious? This question leads us to the analysis of a constitutional problem on which the last part of our contribution will be focused, that is the problem of assessing the compatibility of the reforms with the "constitutional" democratic principles of the EU, as they are enshrined in Title II of the TEU. Indeed, non-representative democratic principles are expressly mentioned therein.

Two developments in our explanation are needed. First, we need to understand whether a particular model of democracy stems from Title II of the TEU or alternative models are permitted under these provisions, as long as they comply with one or more basic principles (Sect. 5). Once the criteria to assess the compatibility of the reforms with Title II of TEU are supplied, we will try to understand whether the reforms develop a particular model of democracy and then we will finally evaluate the compatibility with EU primary law on democratic governance (Sect. 6).

5 Democratic Principles and Democratic Models Under the Lisbon Treaty

The Lisbon Treaty brought about interesting developments in EU primary law in the field of democracy, expressly introducing the idea that the European Union is founded on the synthesis of at least four conceptions of democracy: representation; deliberation; participation of those affected; transparency.

The development of a more legitimate European law lies thereby both in the idea of representing European citizens in the decision-making processes and in new non-majoritarian strategies. First, there are deliberative conceptions, which focus on the quality of the public debate preceding the adoption of a decision as a

[53] Rosanvallon (2006).

fundamental condition of a legitimate genesis of law.[54] Second, there are participative democratic strategies, which are centred on the principle of the inclusion in the law-making process of stakeholders and those affected by a public decision.[55] Furthermore, market control fashioned democratic strategies, which focus on the transparency principle, according to which a legal system should be

> clear, obvious and understandable without doubt or ambiguity.[56]

In particular, Articles 10–12 introduce in the EU legal system rules and instruments linkable to non-representative conceptions of democracy. First, a very broad right of European citizens to participate in the democratic life of the Union is protected under Article 10, para. 3.[57] Second, under Article 11, para. 1, the European institutions

> shall give citizens and representative associations the opportunity to make known and publicly exchange their views in all areas of Union action.

Third, according to Article 11, para. 2,

> the institutions shall maintain an open, transparent and regular dialogue with representative associations and civil society.

Fourth, a more detailed obligation stems from para. 3 for the European Commission that

> shall carry out broad consultations with parties concerned in order to ensure that the Union's actions are coherent and transparent.

Fifth, Article 11, para. 4, introduces the "European citizens' initiative",[58] a mechanism whose procedures and conditions were determined by Regulation (EU) No. 211/2011.[59] Finally, it must be borne in mind that under Article 12 national Parliaments are now involved in the European inter-institutional machinery ("national parliaments contribute actively to the good functioning of the Union").

---

[54]On democratic deliberation, see Habermas (2008).

[55]On participation in the European Union law, see Mendes (2011).

[56]See the Opinion of Advocate General Ruiz-Jarabo Colomer of 16 December 2004 in Case C-110/03, *Belgium* v. *Commission*, point 44. On transparency in the European Union law, see Driessen (2012). For a crystal-clear analysis of the relationship of the principle of transparency and market surveillance and control of economic data and information, see Rosanvallon (2006).

[57]"Every citizen shall have the right to participate in the democratic life of the Union. Decisions shall be taken as openly and as closely as possible to the citizen.".

[58]"No less than one million citizens who are nationals of a significant number of Member States may take the initiative of inviting the European Commission, within the framework of its powers, to submit any appropriate proposal on matters where citizens consider that a legal act of the Union is required for the purpose of implementing the Treaties.".

[59]Regulation (EU) No. 211/2011 of the European Parliament and of the Council of 16 February 2011 on the citizen's initiative. OJEU L 65, 11 March 2011, pp. 1–22. See Dougan (2011) and Dehousse and Verhoeven (2013).

By the introduction of these rules and principles, the Lisbon Treaty produces a compromise between representative and non-representative conceptions of democracy that can be represented as an "open" one. This openness is twofold.

Firstly, the compromise varies from one field of EU action to another. For example, it is reasonable to suggest that the relative importance of the representative democratic pillar is strictly dependent on the weight of the EP in the institutional balance achieved by the Treaties in each field of EU competence.[60] But the actual relevance of non-democratic principles depends on a variety of unstable factors, i.e. the strength of the role of the European Commission in the legislative process, some of the mechanisms aimed at implementing non-representative principles being more stringent for the European Commission acting as a legislative initiator.

Secondly, the compromise varies with time, not only because it is not immune to Treaty revisions, but also because a number of democratic principles of the TEU have to be implemented by the EU political institutions, both through the adoption of normative acts and their daily behaviour. Thus, the actual capacity of democratic principles to inform the working out of EU decisions largely depends on the political attitudes of men succeeding one another in European offices.

Still, notwithstanding its open nature, the compromise founded in the TEU seems to be characterised by a sort of hierarchy between the representative and the non-representative democratic pillars of legitimacy. Indeed, under Article 10, para. 1, the TEU expressly states that

> the functioning of the Union shall be founded on representative democracy,

thereby relegating participative and deliberative principles to a secondary *status*. This is not to say that the participation of those interested in EU policies and the deliberative quality of EU decisions do not contribute in bolstering the democratic legitimacy of EU law. On the contrary, the "structural" problems that the electoral pillar of EU democracy faces make those concepts of deliberation and participation even more important than they currently are in Member States' political dynamics.[61]

However, as long as Article 10, para. 1, has a "legal" meaning, i.e. a meaning that can be useful to scrutinise the legality of EU legal acts, this is that non-representative democratic concepts can only reinforce representative democracy, without substituting for it. This means that if one wants to "take seriously" Part II of the TEU, any reform introduced through EU secondary acts should comply with this basic criterion.

---

[60]However, respect for representative democracy should be guaranteed, where the EP is not involved in the decision-making process on the same foot as the Council, by the national democratic legitimacy of the Council and the European Council. This is the core concept of the so-called "dual legitimacy" theory, which is enshrined in Article 10, para. 2, TEU.

[61]Rosanvallon (2006).

6 Democratic Principles and Democratic Models Under the "Six Pack" and the "Two Pack" Legislation

The fundamental relationship between representative democracy and non-representative democracy established in Article 10, para. 1, TEU is somehow subverted in the architecture of the post-crisis EMU governance, being founded on the idea that in the budgetary field legitimacy should pass more through non-representative democratic paths than the common channels of representative democracy.

The orientation towards a transformation in this relationship is clear in the express mentioning of some democratic values in the Preambles to the "Six Pack" and the "Two Pack" legislation: public dialogue and debate[62]; accountability and transparency[63]; *consensus*-building and inclusion of stakeholders and social partners.[64] These values evoke non-representative conceptions of democracy: deliberative theories of democracy; participative theories of democracy; and transparency or markets' control fashioned theories.[65]

However, I am not suggesting here that the reforms reflect a unitary, coherent conception of democracy. Arguably, a reading of the relevant legislation could indicate that the European legislator took elements from both participative models and deliberative models of democracy, without assembling them into a unitary shape.

This becomes clear if one moves to the question of mechanisms. In fact, not only does the "Six Pack" and the "Two Pack" legislation mention non-representative democratic values, but it also provides for a set of institutional and procedural rules and mechanisms inspired by these principles. Some of those rules and mechanisms do not pass through any Parliament, but consist of obligations placed both on the Member States' Executives and on the Council and the Commission. Others postulate an active role of the EP and, albeit at a lesser degree, national Parliaments.

Preference for mechanisms and procedures involving national Executives and EU political institutions not directly elected by the European citizens is a trait of the principle of *transparency*. In particular, EU legislation reforming the economic branch of the EMU focuses on transparency of macroeconomic and fiscal data and

---

[62]See recitals 8 and 12 of Regulation (EU) No. 1173/2011; recital 9 of Regulation (EU) No. 1174/2011; recital 11 of Regulation (EU) No. 1175/2011.

[63]See Article 3 of Regulation (EU) No. 1173/2011; Article 6 of Regulation (EU) No. 1174/2011. See also, in Regulation (EU) No. 1175/2011, recital 13 (under which the stability and convergence programmes and the national reform programmes should be made public); recital 20 (under which the Commission should make public the calculation method for the projections it makes on the GDP growth of each Member State); and recital 23.

[64]See Preamble, recital 16 of Regulation (EU) No. 1175/2011; Preamble, recitals 19, 20 and 25 of Regulation (EU) No. 1176/2011; Preamble, recital 11 of Regulation (EU) No. 472/2013.

[65]See *supra*, Section 4.

forecasts and on independent audits in order to control national systems of public accounting and encourage best practices.

A prime example is Directive 2011/85/EU, whose fundamental aim is enhancing the transparency of the budget process by laying down detailed rules concerning the characteristics of the budgetary frameworks of the Member States. It provides that Member States shall abide by a number of transparency-making rules. In particular, they shall have in place public accounting systems subject to internal control and independent audits; shall ensure that fiscal planning is based on realistic macroeconomic and budgetary forecasts; shall have in place numerical fiscal rules which are specific to them; shall establish credible, effective medium-term budgetary frameworks; and shall ensure internal control and auditing of their public accounting systems.[66] However, the European Commission too must take its part in enhancing the transparency of the budget process. The Commission's forecasts have to be taken into account by Member States when preparing their budgetary planning. The Commission shall thereby make public

> the methodologies, assumptions and relevant parameters that underpin its macroeconomic and budgetary forecasts.[67]

The principle of transparency has two dimensions, European and national, also under Regulation (EU) No. 1175/2011. On the one side, obligations are placed on national Executives. First, it is established the principle that the stability and convergence programmes and the national reform programmes shall be made public.[68] Then, in the same vein, the principle of statistical independence is added.[69] On the other side, obligations are placed on the European institutions. First, the Commission is required to pursue an objective of transparency in its surveillance tasks, by making public its findings as well as the calculation method it uses.[70] Then, a principle of transparency through motivation is protected by Regulation (EU) No. 1175/2011, whose Article 4, para. 2, provides that

> the Council is expected, as a rule, to follow the recommendations and proposals of the Commission or explain its position publicly.

A second democratic principle whose implementation is guaranteed under the European legislation though non-parliamentary mechanisms and procedures is *participation*.

---

[66]See Article 3, para. 1, of Directive 2011/85/EU.

[67]See Article 4, para. 2, of Directive 2011/85/EU.

[68]See recital 13 and Article 4, para. 2, of Regulation (EU) No. 1175/2011.

[69]See Article 1, para. 14, of Regulation (EU) No. 1175/2011, under which Member Sates shall ensure the professional independence of national statistical authorities. "As a minimum this shall require (a) transparent recruitment and dismissal processes which must be solely based on professional criteria; (b) budgetary allocations which must be made on an annual or multiannual basis; (c) the date of publication of key statistical information which must be designated in advance."

[70]See recitals 20 and 23, and Article 1, paras. 13 and 15, of Regulation (EU) No. 1175/2011.

Inclusion of public interest groups in the national budget process is protected under both the "Six Pack" and the "Two Pack" legislation. Article 1, para. 3, of Regulation (EU) No. 1175/2011—inserting Sec. 1-A on the European Semester in Regulation (EC) No. 1466/97—provides that:

> relevant stakeholders, in particular the social partners, shall be involved in the European Semester, on the main policy issues where appropriate, in accordance with the provisions of the TEU and national legal and political arrangements.

Article 9, para. 3, of Regulation (EU) No. 1176/2011 provides in the same vein that the Commission, when carrying out enhanced surveillance missions to Member States as part of an excessive imbalance procedure,

> shall, where appropriate, involve social partners and other national stakeholders in a dialogue during those missions.

Similarly, Article 5 requires the Commission to.

> acknowledge the national specificities regarding industrial relations and social dialogue,

when undertaking an in-depth review for each Member State. This trend is buttressed in the "Two Pack." Indeed, Article 8 of Regulation (EU) No. 472/2013 provides that

> the Member State shall seek the views of social partners as well as relevant civil society organizations when preparing its draft macroeconomic adjustment programmes, with a view to contributing to building consensus over its content.

But the most interesting feature of this legislation is that even the national Parliaments and the EP are considered more as instruments to achieve non-representative democratic legitimacy than a true representative democracy. In particular, the role attributed to Parliaments in both legislative "Packs" seems to serve as a means for the implementation of the principle of *deliberation*.

The most important of these mechanisms passes through the EP. Not only is it the recipient of a number of obligations to inform placed on the Council and the Commission. More importantly, all five Regulations adopted as part of the "Six Pack" include provisions on the right to invite other European institutions to economic dialogues between the EP and other institutions.[71] The scope of those dialogues *ratione materiae* is very broad, covering the whole spectrum of acts that can be adopted by the Commission and the Council on economic governance, from mere recommendations to decisions on sanctions and fines. But also wide is the scope of economic dialogues *ratione personae*. The right of the EP extends to dialogues with the President of the Council, the Commission, and, where appropriate, the President of the European Council or the President of the Eurogroup. Arguably, when invited by the EP, all these institutions are under a duty to appear before its competent committee. Moreover, the EP may offer the opportunity to

[71] See Article 3 of Regulation (EU) No. 1173/2011; Article 6 of Regulation (EU) No. 1174/2011; Article 1, para. 4, of Regulation (EU) No. 1175/2011; Article 14 of Regulation (EU) No. 1176/2011; Article 1, para. 3, of Regulation (EU) No. 1177/2011.

participate in an exchange of views to the Member State which is the subject of a Council recommendation or decision, whilst participation in such an exchange of views remains voluntary.

Other procedures allegedly aimed at enhancing the deliberative quality of EMU governance are centred on national Parliaments of the States concerned. In particular, the national Parliament of the Member State which is subject to a macroeconomic adjustment programme has the right to invite the European institutions to appear before them for an "exchange of views" on post-programme surveillance (Article 14, para. 5, of Regulation (EU) No. 472/2013).

The role of the EP in the post-reform EMU, in particular through economic dialogue, has been widely debated in literature. It suffices to underline here that the reforms look at the EP much more as a deliberative forum then as a ruler. In fact, its involvement in the EU governance processes is expressly conceived as serving both the aims of stimulating an open and public debate on EMU governance and accountability of decisions. This approach is clearly stated in Article 1, para. 3, of Regulation (EU) No. 1175/2011 concerning EP involvement in the European Semester:

> the European Parliament shall be duly involved in the European Semester in order to increase the transparency and ownership of, and accountability for the decisions taken, in particular by means of the economic dialogue carried out pursuant to Article 2-ab of this Regulation.

But in all provisions in the "Six-Pack" legislation concerning "economic dialogues" the EP becomes an outspoken feature of deliberation, transparency and accountability. Indeed, under the "Two-Pack" Regulations:

> Rules should be laid down to enhance the dialogue between the Union institutions, in particular the European Parliament, the Council and the Commission, and to ensure greater transparency and accountability.[72]

At first sight, this emphasis on the deliberative and transparency-making virtues of the involvement of the EP more than on its representative democratic legitimacy could be difficult to understand. Yet we see from the foregoing analysis that this is an immediate consequence of the "Government approach" to economic cooperation in Europe on which the reforms are based and on the parallel disempowerment of Parliaments in the budgetary decision-making processes.

I will now rapidly move to the question of the adequacy of these mechanisms. By adequacy I mean their appropriateness to protect deliberative and other non-representative democratic values. I argue that, even if one looks at these procedures from the point of view of deliberative and participatory democracy, they cannot be regarded as an adequate counterweight to the rise of intergovernmental co-operation in this area of law.

---

[72]See Preamble, recital 10 of Regulation (EU) No. 472/2013; Article 15 of Regulation (EU) No. 473/2013.

As far as transparency and participation are concerned, my argument is that provisions in the EMU reform legislation referring to those principles share some of the criticism that can be made of these principles in EU law in general. Some scholars doubt that participation, as it actually functions in the EU law, presents the democratic virtues heralded in the TEU.[73] Thus, for example, Mendes argues that participation

> did not deviate much from the neo-functionalist logic that had grounded participatory mechanisms since the beginning of the integration process [...]. In particular, the deciding bodies have maintained the prerogative of choosing which segments of policy and rule-making and which matters are subject to participation procedures, as well as the relevance attributed to participation.

In a similar vein, Kohler-Koch depicts a number of constraints on participation of civil society, arguing *inter alia* that,

> despite noteworthy efforts to become more open, inclusive and participatory, equal representation has not been achieved.[74]

Arguably, the same critical arguments can be presented against the participatory provisions of the "Six Pack" and the "Two Pack" legislation. First, the wording of these provisions seems to leave room for the Commission concerning both the scope and the relevance of participation. Secondly, all these provisions require the Commission to organise the participation of "stakeholders and social partners" and not of civil society or the interested public at large.[75] After all, it could be naïve to assume that the "Porto Alegre" model of participatory budgeting as such could be transferred from the municipal to the European (as well as to the state) level.

As far as the deliberative democracy principle is concerned, my argument is that the subversion of the relationship between the representative and the non-representative dimensions of the European democracy impinges on the deliberative quality of these mechanisms, in particular on the economic dialogue, whose importance is emphasised in the reforms.

A benevolent reading of these provisions would support the view that economic dialogues were meant to enhance democratic input legitimacy. Indeed, dialogues, by favouring the public giving of reasons as well as the public provision of information, should enable the attribution of accountability. Moreover, as we have seen, the scope *ratione materiae* and *ratione personae* of this mechanism is very broad. It can be applied in the course of all the procedures provided for in the European legislation; it can be applied in order to discuss a great variety of acts and topics; it can be used by the EP to obtain an exchange of views with all the European institutions engaged in the EMU governance. Furthermore, it is

[73] Mendes (2011).

[74] Kohler-Koch (2012).

[75] Only Article 8 of Regulation (EU) No. 472/2013 mentions "civil society organisation". However it is not directed to the Commission, but to Member States, when preparing draft macroeconomic adjustment programmes.

reinforced by the obligation placed on the European Commission to keep the EP constantly and widely informed. Due to these features, economic dialogues could stimulate in principle a more general debate in the public sphere and help in addressing accountability.

Nevertheless, the actual influence of economic dialogues on public opinion has been poor. Economic dialogues that have taken place before the competent Committee of the EP so far have received scarce attention from the mass media and, consequently, from the public at large. Arguably, this could be explained by taking into account their low impact on the law-making process: one could contend that information on economic dialogues is not perceived as relevant by journalists and members of the press since these dialogues have insufficient weight in the decision-making process. In other words, the lack of parliamentary power in the law-making process also reduces the deliberative value of parliamentary economic dialogues. Hence data, reasons and arguments emerging from these dialogues risk not being able to cross their strict institutional boundaries.

7 Conclusions

From the three democratic credentials of the EU identified in the TEU—the principle of "representation"; the principle of "participation"; the principle of "deliberation"—the latter two are at the forefront of the democratic discourse in the EU legislation reforming the EMU. A transformation in the relationship between representative democracy and non-representative democracy has thereby accompanied the process of strengthening of economic cooperation in the EU.

The TEU considers participation and deliberation as *complements* to representation, but not as substitutes for it. By contrast, the new architecture of the EMU pursues a "governance" approach, embedding the national Parliaments of the Member States and reducing the EP to a pale function of promoting "public" debate and control.

This is not simply a theoretical question. Arguably, from a legal point of view, the "Six Pack" and the "Two Pack" legislation pose a problem of compatibility with Article 10, para. 1, TEU and the fundamental principle of relationship between representative and non-representative democratic principles established therein.

However, one could ask whether the "Six Pack" and the "Two Pack" legislation can be considered as "mere" secondary law. It could be argued that those acts reflect an agreement reached between the Member States in the European Council, and accepted, with some minor modifications, by the Commission and the EP under the pressure of urgency. In other words, one could be tempted to consider this case in the context of the more general trend followed by the Member States to use the European Council as a forum to achieve international agreements with an impact on EU primary law, irrespective of the procedures provided for in the TEU. From the viewpoint of a constitutional legal system, this approach could be scarcely justified. In fact, it would be a sign of an internationalist shadow on EU law.[76]

In any case, leaving representative democracy behind in the economic branch of the EMU represented a constitutional turn in EU law. Time will tell if it was also a wise one.

References

Baratta R (2013) Legal issues of the fiscal compact. Searching for a mature democratic governance of the Euro. In: de Witte B, Héritier A, Trechsel A (eds) The Euro crisis and the state of European democracy. European University Institute, Florence

Beukers T (2013) The Eurozone crisis and the legitimacy of differentiated integration. In: de Witte B, Héritier A, Trechsel A (eds) The Euro crisis and the state of European democracy. European University Institute, Florence

Bickerton C, Hodson D, Puetter U (2015) The new intergovernalism: European integration in the post-Maastricht era. J Common Mark Stud 53(4)703–722

Cannizzaro E (2016) Disintegration through Law? Eur Pap 1(1)3–6

Colasanti F (1994) Economic policy co-ordination in stage II of economic and monetary union. ECU Activities 27. Accessible at www.ecu-actvities.be/documents/publications/publication/1994_2/colasanti.html

Craig P (2011) Integration, democracy and legitimacy. In: Craig P, De Burca G (eds) The evolution of EU law. Oxford University Press, Oxford, pp 13–40

Curtin D (2014) Challenging executive dominance in European democracy. Mod Law Rev 77(1) 1–32

Dawson M, de Witte F (2013) Constitutional balance in the EU after the Euro-crisis. Mod Law Rev 76(5)817–844

Dehousse F, Verhoeven D (2013) The European citizen's initiative: next big thing or new false good idea? Egmont Paper 59. Accessible at http://www.egmontinstitute.be/wp-content/uploads/2013/07/Egmont-papers-59.pdf

Dougan M (2011) What are we to make of the citizen's initiative? Common Mark Law Rev 48(6) 1807–1848

Driessen B (2012) Transparency in EU institutional law. Kluwer Law International, Alphen aan den Rjin

Fabbrini F (2013) The fiscal compact, the "golden rule", and the paradox of European federalism. Boston Coll Int Comp Law Rev 36(1)1–38

Fabbrini S (2015) Executive power in the European Union: the implications of the Euro crisis. In: EUSA conference paper. Accessible at https://www.eustudies.org/conference/papers

Fasone C (2012) The struggle of the European Parliament to participate in the new economic governance. EUI Working Papers RSCAS 2012/45. Accessible at http://cadmus.eui.eu/bitstream/handle/1814/23429/RSCAS_2012_45.pdf?sequence=1

Habermas J (2008) Between facts and norms. Contributions to a discourse theory of democracy. Polity Press, Cambridge

Habermas J (2014) Democracy in Europe: why the development of the European Union into a transnational democracy in necessary and how it is possible. Arena Working Papers 13/2014.

[76]For a discussion of "the potentialities offered by international law as an alternative decision-making procedure within the EU legal system", although focused on the EU-Turkey Statement of 18 March 2016, see Cannizzaro (2016).

Accessible at www.sv.uio.no/arena/english/research/publications/arena-working-papers/2014/wp13-14.html
Held D (2006) Models of democracy. Stanford University Press, Stanford
Hix S (2015) Democratizing a macroeconomic union in Europe. In: Cramme O, Hobolt SB (eds) Democratic politics in a European Union under stress. Oxford University Press, Oxford, pp 180–198
Ioannidis M (2014) EU financial assistance conditionality after "two pack". Zeitschrift für Ausländisches Öffentliches und Völkerrecht 74(1)61–104
Joerges C (2016) A disintegration of European studies. Eur Pap 1(1)8–12
Keppenne J-P (2014) Institutional report. In: Neergaard U, Jacqueson C, Danielsen JH (eds) The economic and monetary union: constitutional and institutional aspects of the economic governance within the EU. DIØF Publishing, Copenhagen, pp 179–257
Kohler-Koch B (2012) Post-Maastricht civil society and participatory democracy. J Eur Integr 34 (7):809–824
Lastra R, Louis J-V (2013) European economic and monetary union: history, trends and prospects. Yearb Eur Law 32(1)57–206
Leino P, Salminen J (2013) Should the economic and monetary union be democratic? Ger Law J 14(7)844–868
Lenaerts K (2014) EMU and the European Union's constitutional framework. Eur Law Rev 39(6) 753–769
Louis J-V (2009) L'Union européenne et sa monnaie. Commentaire J. Mégret. Editions de l'Université de Bruxelles, Bruxelles
Majone G (1996) Regulatory legitimacy. In: Majone G (ed) Regulating Europe. Routledge, London, pp 284–301
Mendes J (2011) Participation in EU rule-making. A rights-based approach. Oxford University Press, Oxford
Michéa F (2012) L'appropriation de la gouvernance économique par le Conseil européen. Revue de l'Union européenne, No. 556, pp 169–177
Moravcsik A (2002) In defence of the "democratic deficit": reassessing legitimacy in the European Union. J Common Mark Stud 40(4)603–624
Poiares Maduro M, de Witte B, Kumm M (2012) The Euro crisis and the democratic governance of the Euro: legal and political issues of a fiscal crisis. In: Poiares Maduro M, de Witte B, Kumm M (eds) The democratic governance of the Euro. RSCAS Policy Papers 2012/08, pp 3–11
Polou A (2014) Austerity and European social rights: how can courts protect Europe's lost generation? Ger Law J 15(6)1145–1176
Rosanvallon P (2006) La Contre-démocratie. Editions du Seuil, Paris
Ruffert M (2011) The European debt crisis and European Union law. Common Mark Law Rev 48 (6)1777–1805
Scharpf F (1999) Crisis and choice in European social democracy. Cornell University Press, Ithaca
Smits R (2002) The law of economic and monetary union. Collected Course Hague Acad Int Law 300:309–422
Starita M (2013) Il Consiglio europeo e la crisi del debito sovrano. Rivista di diritto internazionale XCVI(2):385–423
Tosato GL (2016) How to pursue a more efficient and legitimate European economic governance. IAI Working Papers 16/03
Von Rompuy H (2012) Towards a genuine economic and monetary union. Report by the President of the European Council. Accessible at www.consilium.europa.eu/uedocs/cms_data/docs/pressdata/en/ec/134069.pdf
Zilioli C (2003) Accountability and independence: irreconcilable values or complementary instruments for democracy? The specific case of the European Central Bank. In: Vandersanden G (ed) Mélanges en Hommage à Jean-Victor Louis. Editions de l'Université libre de Bruxelles, Bruxelles
Zilioli C, Selmyar M (2000) The European Central Bank: an independent specialized organization of community law. Common Mark Law Rev 37(3)591–644

The Democratic Foundations of the EMU: The European Parliament and the National Parliaments Between Cooperation and Rivalry

Francesco Martucci

Abstract According to Article 10 TEU, the functioning of the Union and of the EMU shall be founded on representative democracy. The democratic principle is all the more necessary since economic governance is characterised by its institutional complexity. It calls for a more empowerment of the European Parliament in the EMU. In the European multilevel democratic system, the national Parliaments shall be involved in the economic governance. However, the involvement of the European Parliament and national Parliaments remains limited. Furthermore, the financial and sovereign debt crises triggered substantial reforms of the EMU that have diminished the role of the Parliaments in the European and national decision-making processes. In contrast, due the so-called "monetary" and "economic" dialogues, there is a promotion of Parliaments in accountability process of the EMU. Finally, an important issue arises with the mutation of parliamentary role: the competition between European Parliament and national Parliaments requires an inter-parliamentary cooperation. Provide legitimacy for the EMU has thus brought changes to the parliamentary role in a multilevel constitutional system.

Contents

F. Martucci (✉)
Department of Public Law, University Panthéon-Assas (Paris II), Paris, France
e-mail: Francesco.Martucci@u-paris2.fr

L. Daniele et al. (eds.), *Democracy in the EMU in the Aftermath of the Crisis*,
DOI 10.1007/978-3-319-53895-2_2

1 Introduction

Is the Lisbon Treaty really "The treaty of the parliaments", as the President of Germany declared when this Treaty entered into force?[1] Several authors doubt that the attempt of the Lisbon Treaty to parliamentary the European Union (EU) has succeeded.[2] And the issue is particularly critical for the Economic and Monetary Union (EMU).

The EU is in essence a multilevel constitutional system whose legitimacy firmly rests on the value of democracy. According to Article 10 TEU,

> the functioning of the Union shall be founded on representative democracy.

The two sources from which the EU derives its democratic legitimacy are thus the citizens, represented, in turn, by both the European Parliament and the national Parliaments. The European Parliament, which derives democratic legitimation from the direct elections by universal suffrage, must be seen as that part of the EU structure which best reflects an effective democracy. Pursuant to Article 12 TEU,

> national Parliaments contribute actively to the good functioning of the Union

in accordance with the provisions of Protocol No. 1. Member States are represented in the European Council by their Heads of State or Government and in the Council by their Governments, themselves democratically accountable either to their national Parliaments, or to their citizens.[3]

As a constitutionally integrated Union, the EU is thus founded on the European Treaties and at the same time on national Constitutions which guarantee the role of the European Parliament and national Parliaments. As evidenced, in particular, in the case-law of the German Constitutional Court,[4] Constitutions of some Member States require that the democracy principle shall be observed in a double dimension: through the involvement of the European Parliament in the EU constitutional system, as well as through the protection of rights and prerogatives of national Parliaments.

The Court of Justice has also recognized the

> fundamental democratic principle that the people should take part in the exercise of power through the intermediary of a representative assembly.[5]

To this end, it is necessary to define the role of Parliament in a democratic system, while also taking into account the specific features of the integrated European Union. What kind of power shall be exercised by a Parliament in a

---

[1]See Lammert (2009).

[2]See Fabbrini et al. (2015).

[3]Article 10, para. 2, TEU.

[4]See for example GFCC, Judgment of the Second Senate of 30 June 2009—2 BvE 2/08.

[5]ECJ 29 October 1980, Case 139/79, *Maizena GmbH* v. *Council of the European Communities*, para. 34.

democracy? As the European Court of Human Rights decided in the *Matthews* case, to ensure an "effective political democracy",[6] the Parliament has a twofold responsibility. To ensure that

> effective political democracy is properly served in the territories to which the Convention applies, and in this context, it must have regard not solely to the strictly legislative powers which a body has, but also to that body's role in the overall legislative process.[7]

The Parliament is an integral part of the legislative process; and it is the main tool of democratic control and political responsibility.

In the multilevel constitutional system of the European Union, the parliamentary role is assumed by both the European Parliament and national Parliaments. To ensure a "truly democratic political regime", in the words of the European Court of Justice,

> the Parliament has a dual responsibility. It is an integral part of the legislative process; and it is the principal instrument of democratic control and political responsibility.[8]

Does the EMU constitute a "truly democratic political regime"? On the one hand, EMU is subject to the democratic principle, given that it is fully integrated in the EU legal system, as recognized by the ECJ in the *Olaf* case.[9] On the other hand, the democratic principle is all the more necessary since economic governance is characterized by tremendous institutional complexity. The democratic principle calls therefore for more empowerment of the European Parliament and national Parliaments in the EMU. Nevertheless, the involvement of both the European and national Parliaments in the economic governance remains limited. Further, the financial and sovereign debt crises have triggered substantial reforms of the EMU which have reduced the role of the Parliaments in the European and national decision-making process. National Parliaments have been deprived of instruments in the new economic governance of the EU, given that the European responses to this crisis are increasingly intergovernmental, with a weak involvement of the European Parliament. This evolution is illustrated by the enhanced role of the Eurogroup and the Euro Summit and the international Treaties concluded by Member States outside the EU framework, as well as by the European Stability Mechanism (ESM) and Treaty on Stability, Coordination and Governance in the EMU (TSCG).

The purpose of my contribution is to assess whether the involvement of the European Parliament and national Parliaments in the EMU contributes to legitimize democratically the economic governance. I will analyse whether the multilevel parliamentary integration constitutes an obstacle to the democratisation of the EMU, insofar as the European Parliament and the national Parliaments compete

---

[6]ECoHR 18 February 1999, No. 24833/94, *Matthews* v. *the United Kingdom*.

[7]*Ibid*., para. 49.

[8]See ECJ 29 October 1980, *Maizena GmbH* v. *Council of the European Communities*, para. 22.

[9]ECJ 10 July 2003, Case C-1/00, *Commission* v. *ECB*.

with each other, rather than cooperate. I will first deal with the participation to the decision-making process and then further elaborate on the democratic control.

2 Parliamentary Relegation in Decision-Making Process

From a parliamentary perspective, the EMU is characterised, and may boil down to one word: relegation. Both the European Parliament and national Parliaments have been relegated in the decision-making process. While the ECB and the national central banks (NCBs) which are independent from the Parliaments, lead the monetary policy, Member States implement their economic and fiscal policy powers within the EU coordination and surveillance framework in which the European Parliament plays an ambiguous role, while the national Parliaments decline.

2.1 The Complete Independence of the Central Banks from the Parliaments

In the Eurozone, the ECB, together with the NCBs, constitute the Eurosystem that leads the monetary policy of the Union. According to Article 127, para. 1, TFEU, the primary objective of the Eurosystem shall be to maintain price stability. Without prejudice to the objective of price stability, it shall support the general economic policies in the Union. The Governing Council of the ECB comprises the members of the Executive Board of the ECB and the Governors of the 19 NCBs of the Eurozone. It shall formulate the monetary policy of the Union including, as appropriate, decisions relating to intermediate monetary objectives, key interest rates and the supply of reserves in the ESCB, and shall establish the necessary guidelines for their implementation.[10] The Executive Board implements monetary policy in accordance with the guidelines and decisions laid down by the Governing Council. The NCBs lead the Eurosystem monetary policy operations.

Pursuant to Articles 130 TFEU and 7 of the Statute,[11] the ECB and the NCBs are both independent when exercising the powers and carrying out the tasks and duties conferred upon them by Article 127 TFEU. As highlighted by the European Monetary Institute in the convergence Report of 1998,[12] independence means that the Eurosystem has the exclusive right and duty to define and to implement monetary policy. The Eurosystem is independent from political authorities insofar as the Governing Council of the ECB define a monetary policy aimed at the statutory

[10]Article 12 of the Statute.

[11]Protocol No. 4 on the Statute of the European System of Central Banks and of the European Central Bank.

[12]Convergence Report, Report required by Article 109, j, TEC.

objective of price stability and the ECB and the NCBs possess the powers necessary to implement monetary policy decisions. Article 130 TFEU and Article 7 of the Statute prohibit the ECB and the NCBs seeking or taking instructions from European institutions or bodies, from any Government of a Member State or from any other body. They also prohibit European institutions and bodies and the Governments of the Member States seeking to influence the members of the decision-making bodies of the ECB or of the NCBs.

There is thus no doubt that European Parliament and national Parliaments shall respect the independence of the ECB and the NCBs guaranteed by Union's primary law. It is not conceivable that Parliaments may participate in monetary policy, if only to define the objectives of this policy. As remarked by an author,

> [t]his omission was understandable. Monetary union was supposed to be a specialized technical subject.[13]

On the contrary, the financial crisis and the sovereign debt crisis have shown the fundamental role of ECB in rescuing the Eurozone. The so-called unconventional measures taken by the Council of Governors—as the purchase of government bonds or the inclusion in the list of collaterals eligible for Eurosystem monetary policy operations—have a technical character. However, these measures make such an impact on the economy that they take on an eminently political character.[14] The OMT Programme decided by the ECB in the wake of the sovereign debt was at the heart of a strong debate in Germany. Parts of the civil society—especially Professors of Law and of Economy—and political parties contested vigorously the unconventional measures of the ECB. The political critics became a judicial case with the *Gauweiler* judgment.[15]

According to Article 14 of the Statute, the Eurosystem is based on the principle of integration. If the statutes of NCBs are rooted in legal system of each Member State, the NCBs act as European bodies when they exercise the powers of the Eurosystem. When carrying out the tasks of monetary policy conferred upon by the Treaty, the NCBs shall be completely independent from the Government or from any other national body, including the national Parliament. Article 130 TFEU applies in the same manner to the ECB and to the NCBs. However, in accordance with the principles of institutional and procedural autonomy, the national laws lay down conditions of the independence. For instance, the first provision of the Statute of *Banque de France* provides that the *Banque de France* is an integral part of the Eurosystem and, in this framework, participates in carrying out the tasks and

[13]Elefteriadis (2014), p. 27.

[14]In a book highlighting the major role of central banks in the resolution of the financial crisis, the author—a journalist fine connoisseur of central banking—has significantly devoted a chapter on the "President of Europe": for him, during the crisis, the real President of the EU was not the President of the European Council, nor the President of the European Commission, but the President of the ECB! See Irwin (2013).

[15]See the special issue of German Law Journal, Vol. 15, No. 2, 2014.

complying with the objectives conferred upon it by the Statute. The provision furthermore adds that

> The Banque de France, represented by its Governor, Deputy Governors or any other member of the Monetary Policy Council, shall neither seek nor accept instructions from the Government or any other body in the performance of the tasks arising from its participation in the European System of Central Banks.[16]

There is no doubt that the French Parliament plays no role in the execution of monetary policy.

2.2 The Ambiguous Role of the European Parliament in the Economic Governance

The economic and fiscal policies remain within national competence which shall be exercised by Member States in the "integrated framework" provided by the Treaty. According to Articles 121 and 126 TFEU, Member States shall coordinate their economic policies within the Council and avoid excessive government deficits. Correlatively, the Council and the Commission exercise power on Member States through procedures provided by European law. In the respect of EU law, the Member States of the Eurozone may grant financial assistance under the ESM, which is subject to strict conditionality. The coordination of economic policies, the budgetary discipline and the financial assistance are the three pillars of the economic governance with variable involvement of Parliaments.

As recognised explicitly by Article 5 TFEU,[17] the EU is competent to coordinate the economic policies. This competence implies two powers. Firstly, on a recommendation of the Commission, the Council may adopt the acts whose purpose is to coordinate European and national economic policies. Most of these acts are adopted under the form of recommendation in sense of Article 288 TFEU. Secondly, the European institutions carry out the multilateral surveillance which is, since the adoption of the Six Pack, materialised by the European Semester. Even if the provisions of the Title I Part One of the TFEU are silent, the Treaty lays out powers of budgetary discipline. Pursuant to Article 126 TFEU, the Council is responsible to ensure that Member States respect the rule of avoiding excessive deficit. The powers of coordination of economic policies and of budgetary discipline are exercised in the "integrated framework" adopted by the European legislator. Before the beginning of the third stage of the EMU, the German Government claimed and obtained to reinforce the budgetary discipline, with the adoption of the Stability and Growth Pact composed by two regulations. Regulation (EC) No. 1466/97 sets up

[16]Article 141-1 of Monetary and Financial Code (code monétaire et financier).

[17]Article 5 TFEU: "The Member States shall coordinate their economic policies within the Union. To this end, the Council shall adopt measures, in particular broad guidelines for these policies. Specific provisions shall apply to those Member States whose currency is the euro".

the preventive arm of the Stability and Growth Pact[18] whereas Regulation (EC) No. 1467/97[19] grounds the corrective and repressive arms of the Pact.

During the crisis, Germans obtained again a reinforcement of the budgetary discipline, as counterpart of the bailing-in in the Eurozone. "Solidarity and responsibility" was the banner of some Member States: solidarity from the European side and responsibility of single States. In fact, due to the strict conditionality required by the financial assistance, the Eurozone is more characterised by discipline rather than by solidarity or even by responsibility. That was clearly the purpose of the Six Pack composed by five regulations and one directive adopted by the European legislator.[20] After the revision of the Treaty in 2011, and the adjunction of Article 136, para. 3, TFEU, the budgetary discipline has been more reinforced in the Eurozone by the Two Pack,[21] which is composed by two regulations adopted in 2013 by the European legislator. The so-called golden rule of the Fiscal Compact—namely the requirement that the budgetary position of the Member States shall be balanced or in *surplus*—set up by Article 3 of TSCG has been integrated into the Union's *acquis* by Regulation (EU) No. 473/2013 of the Two Pack.

The European Parliament has limited involvement in the "integrated framework" of the economic governance. The multilateral surveillance and the excessive deficit procedure are implemented only by the Commission and the Council, whilst the European Council plays its natural role laid down by Article 15 TEU (define the general political directions and priorities of the EU). The President of the Council

---

[18]Council Regulation (EC) No. 1466/97 of 7 July 1997 on the strengthening of the surveillance of budgetary positions and the surveillance and coordination of economic policies, OJEC L 209, 2 August 1997, pp. 1 et seqq., consolidated.

[19]Council Regulation (EC) No 1467/97 of 7 July 1997 on speeding up and clarifying the implementation of the excessive deficit procedure, OJEC L 209, 2 August 1997, pp. 6 et seqq., consolidated.

[20]Regulation (EU) No. 1173/2011 of the European Parliament and of the Council of 16 November 2011 on the effective enforcement of budgetary surveillance in the euro area; Regulation (EU) No. 1174/2011 of the European Parliament and of the Council of 16 November 2011 on enforcement measures to correct excessive macroeconomic imbalances in the euro area; Regulation (EU) No. 1175/2011 of the European Parliament and of the Council of 16 November 2011 amending Council Regulation (EC) No. 1466/97 on the strengthening of the surveillance of budgetary positions and the surveillance and coordination of economic policies; Regulation (EU) No. 1176/2011 of the European Parliament and of the Council of 16 November 2011 on the prevention and correction of macroeconomic imbalances; Council Regulation (EU) No. 1177/2011 of 8 November 2011 amending Regulation (EC) No. 1467/97 on speeding up and clarifying the implementation of the excessive deficit procedure; Council Directive 2011/85/EU of 8 November 2011 on requirements for budgetary frameworks of the Member States. OJEU L 306, 23 November 2011.

[21]Regulation (EU) No. 472/2013 of the European Parliament and of the Council of 21 May 2013 on the strengthening of economic and budgetary surveillance of Member States in the euro area experiencing or threatened with serious difficulties with respect to their financial stability, OJEU L 140, 27 May 2013, pp. 1 et seqq. Regulation (EU) No. 473/2013 of the European Parliament and of the Council of 21 May 2013 on common provisions for monitoring and assessing draft budgetary plans and ensuring the correction of excessive deficit of the Member States in the euro area, OJEU L 140, 27 May 2013, pp. 11 et seqq.

shall inform the European Parliament of the decisions taken in order to sanction a Member State which presents an excessive deficit.[22] The President of the Council and the Commission shall only report the European Parliament the results of multilateral surveillance.[23] The ESM Treaty denies any role of the European Parliament in providing stability support to the Member States of the Eurozone.

Nonetheless, the European Parliament plays a major role as co-legislator in the implementation of the European framework. Article 121, para. 6, TFEU provides for an ordinary legislative procedure to adopt detailed rules for the multilateral surveillance procedure. Article 126, para. 14, TFEU provides for a consultation procedure to enact provisions relating to the implementation of the excessive deficit procedure. Despite the democratic principle, the Lisbon Treaty did not revise the provisions of Article 126, para. 14, TFEU and, therefore, since the Maastricht Treaty, two different procedures have been established by the Treaty in order to legislate in the field of economic governance. Articles 121, para. 6, and 126, para. 14, TFEU are the legal basis for implementing all the legislation relating to economic governance. Although, to adopt the texts, which apply only to the Eurozone, the EU legislator relies also on the special legal basis of Article 136 TFEU. However, Article 136 TFEU shall be used in correlation with Article 121, para. 6, TFEU or Article 126, para. 14, TFEU, so that the procedure remains those lay down in these provisions. For instance, the Two Pack is constituted by two regulations applied only in the Eurozone and adopted on the basis of Articles 121, para. 6, and 136 TFEU and under the ordinary legislative procedure. The European Parliament was fully involved in the decision-making process that led to the "integrated framework".

Such involvement represents undoubtedly a democratic step forward the economic governance. At the same time, it leads to longer delivery times for adopting the regulation, whereas the market requires an immediate response to the crisis. That is why, in 2012, Member States preferred an intergovernmental solution when concluding the TSCG in few months, while it took more than 3 years for the European legislator to adopt the Two Pack. And in the *Pringle* case, the ECJ confirmed that the financial assistance to a Member State of the Eurozone falls within the competence of Member States, so that the ESM is established by a Treaty.[24] Logically, the intergovernmental Treaties almost completely ignore the role of the European Parliament whether to conclude the Treaty or to ratify it.

[22]Article 126, para. 11, TFEU.

[23]Article 121, para. 5, TFEU.

[24]ECJ 27 November 2012, Case C-370/12, *Thomas Pringle* v. *Governement of Ireland, Ireland and The Attorney General.*

2.3 The Decline of National Parliaments

As required by Article 10 TEU and Protocol No. 1, the national Parliaments shall play a role in the "economic governance". They are actually involved to varying degrees.

National Parliaments are necessarily excluded from the legislative procedures laid down by Articles 121 and 126 TFEU. In accordance with Protocol No. 1, they play only a role in monitoring compliance with the principles of proportionality and subsidiarity. Neither the Six Pack nor the Two Pack have been contested on the ground of breaching the principles of proportionality or subsidiarity.[25] By contrast, the ratification process in the Member States of the intergovernmental Treaties (ESM and TSCG) succeeded in the reintegration of the national Parliaments, even if we may only regret the weakness of the public debate in national fora.[26] For instance, in France, while the Fiscal Compact created profound popular revulsion, the French Parliament voted the ratification act without any resistance.

The enhanced "integrated framework" of economic and budgetary policies leads to a weakening of the role of Parliaments in the conduct of economic policies at national level. In the tradition of Member States, the vote on the budget is at the heart of part of the prerogatives of the Parliament, although the European "economic governance" aims clearly at strengthening the capacity of the national Government in the conduct of budgetary and economic policies. By virtue of Article 3 of Protocol No. 12,

> in order to ensure the effectiveness of the excessive deficit procedure, the governments of the Member States shall be responsible under this procedure for the deficits of general government.

Since the beginning of the third stage of the EMU, the budgetary discipline provides a centralisation of power within national Governments, which are the most important interlocutors of the Commission in the implementation of the economic policies and deficit procedures. With the enhanced budgetary discipline required by the Six Pack, the powers of national executives in the conduct of budgetary policy have been strengthened to the detriment of national Parliaments. With the Two Pack, the role of national Parliaments is virtually even more limited, especially for States benefitting from the ESM's financial assistance. Such a role is thus significantly degraded because of the conditionality imposed by the Troika, before being inserted in decisions taken on the basis of Regulation (EU) No. 472/2013. In other words, the involvement of the European Parliament in the legislative procedure establishing the "economic governance" has not gone to the national Parliaments' advantage. To the contrary, the European Parliament has contributed to a striking

---

[25]See report from the Commission on subsidiarity and proportionality, 19th report on Better Lawmaking covering the year 2011, COM/2012/373. Report from the Commission, Annual report 2013 on subsidiarity and proportionality, COM/2014/506.

[26]See Closa Montero and Maatsch (2014) and Piedrafita (2014).

weakening of the national Parliaments' budgetary and economic policies powers. The marginalisation of the Parliaments has led to two constitutional reactions.

Firstly, in the integrated constitutional multi-level system of the EU, the main support to national Parliaments comes from Constitutional Courts of Member States. The position of the BVerfG in Germany provides the most significant illustration since the *Lisbon* decision in which the German judges drew conclusions from the democracy principle enshrined, through the fundamental right of vote, by Article 38.1 of the German Fundamental Law.[27] To ensure citizens' right to vote,

> Article 38.1 first sentence of the Basic Law excludes the possibility, in the area of application of Article 23 of the Basic Law, of depleting the content of the legitimation of state authority, and the influence on the exercise of that authority provided by the election, by transferring the responsibilities and competences of the Bundestag to the European level to such an extent that the principle of democracy is violated.[28]

If the German Court never found a breach of democracy principle and a violation of right to vote, it expressed a reservation on constitutionality of EU acts, requiring a strong involvement of the *Bundestag* in German procedures.[29] Therefore, the German Court decided that the TSCG did

> not entail an impairment of the budgetary sovereignty of the German Bundestag.[30]

And the *Gauweiler* case illustrates the role played by fundamental rights in protecting Member States from *ultra vires* European legislation, whereas the European Court of Justice remains the only one judge competent to declare the invalidity of European law.[31] However, the German Court considered that ECB's OMT Programme,[32] interpreted in accordance with European Court of Justice's judgment, does not present a constitutionally relevant threat to the *Bundestag*'s right to decide on the budget. The jurisdictional protection of Parliament could remain only theoretical.

Secondly, the Greece crisis highlighted how the Government of a Member State may exercise the option of a *referendum* so as to strengthen democratic legitimacy while disputing alleged austerity policies required in the execution of financial assistance. During the Summer 2015, after months of negotiation with creditors (EU, Member States and IMF) represented by the Troika, the Greek Government finally refused to implement the new version of ESM adjustment programme, blocking the disbursement of the last financial assistance tranche. The consequences for Greece were dramatic: the IMF stated on 30 June 2015, that a repayment due by Greece had not been received, which meant Greek default. The Greek

[27]See Berner (2013).

[28]GFCC, Judgment of the Second Senate of 30 June 2009—2 BvE 2/08, para. 175.

[29]GFCC, Judgment of the Second Senate of 30 June 2009—2 BvE 2/08. See also GFCC, Judgment of the Second Senate of 18 March 2014—2 BvR 1390/12.

[30]GFCC, Judgment of the Second Senate of 12 September 2012—2 BvR 1390/12, para. 208.

[31]GFCC, Judgment of the Second Senate of 21 June 2016—2 BvR 2728/13.

[32]ECJ, 16 June 2015, Case C-62/14, *Gauweiler*.

Government played his last card in the "game": the appeal to the people. He called a *referendum* on 5 July 2015, which result was a clear refuse of conditionality programme proposed by the Troika. Finally, a so-called "Agreekment" had already been reached by the European Council on 12 July 2015, opening the way to the third Assistance Programme.[33] The new adjustment programme started on 19 August 2015 and is scheduled to run until 20 August 2018. A financial assistance of up to €86 billion under this programme is provided by the ESM. The Greek Parliament passed a legislation—the so-called "Omnibus law"—that contained the prior measures required by the third assistance programme which compliance with the conditionality had been assessed by the Commission.[34] After elections held in September, the new Parliament has passed all the measures scheduled by the Memorandum of Understanding concluded between the ESM, acting through the Commission, and Greece. It confirms the fact, that the Greek has ever accepted the measures of economic policies provided in the assistance programmes since the beginning of assistance in 2010. The Greek Parliament considered itself bound by these programmes, so that it was not able to impose its own will. From a constitutional point of view, all the measures stem from a discretionary power of the national Parliament; from a factual point of view, there is no choice for the Greek Parliament because, as we saw during the Syriza experience, an opposition of measures required by the Troika would mean the stop or the end of the assistance. Already in 2011, Prime Minister George Papandreou decided therefore to call a *referendum*, before cancelling it under pressure from Troika. The Greek crisis is (not only) characterised not so much by a relegation of Parliament, but more by a defeat of democracy facing market discipline. Finally, in a constitutionally integrated Union, the will of the people of a single Member State cannot go against the democratic process of other Member States, especially given that national Parliaments hold the power to approve the financial conditions of new financial assistance. One must keep in mind that the bail-out assistance is financed through the ESM from the Member States of the Eurozone. So each Parliament of the Eurozone shall approve the budgetary consequences of the assistance granted by the ESM.

3 The Promotion of Parliament in Accountability

In European political system, the Parliament remains the most important instrument of democratic control and political responsibility. However, provide legitimacy for the EMU has brought radical changes to the parliamentary role in a multilevel constitutional system. Facing the independence of central banks, the Parliaments

[33] Remarks by President Donald Tusk after the Euro Summit of 12 July 2015 on Greece, 13 July 2015, Statements and remarks, 579/15.

[34] European Commission, Report on Greece's compliance with the draft MoU commitments and the commitments in the Euro Summit statement of 12 July 2015, 14 August 2015.

have come up with a new form of accountability. Furthermore, the crises have triggered changes that make difficult to identify the policy-makers in the new "economic governance", especially in the Eurozone. The EMU must be described as a "polyarchy" system, in sense of Robert Dahl's theory.[35] "Who governs" in the EMU? The answer would be the ECB, the European Council, the European Commission, the Council of EU, the Eurogroup, the Summit of Eurozone, the Member States ... The governors of NCBs are part of the ECB's Council of Governors, the President of European Commission also sits on the European Council, whereas the Eurogroup brings together the Finance Ministers of Eurozone and the Commissioner responsible for Economic and Financial Affairs, etc. The time for opposing intergovernmentalism to supranationalism is over. This assertion is especially true with the Eurozone, whose governance mixes a denationalised institution (ECB) and a supranational institution (European Commission) with an institution and bodies who represent Member States, even international organisation (IMF through the Troika). Facing such *bric-a-brac*, political actors have built a new form of accountability, whose expression sums up in stakeholders' dialogue. Therefore, the Monetary Union has been a laboratory for a "deliberative accountability". An important issue arises with the mutation of parliamentary role: the competition between European Parliament and national Parliaments and requires an inter-parliamentary cooperation.

3.1 The Monetary Dialogue as Laboratory for Accountability

Unlike the members of the European Commission, the members of the Governing Council of the ECB don't possess a true democratic mandate, insofar as their appointment is not approved by the Parliament and the MEPs may not censure the Governing Council, or compel it to resign through a motion of no confidence. The European Parliament shall thus not affect the principle of independence laid down by Article 130 TFEU. Since the beginning of third stage, the ECB is, however, aware that monetary policy requires a democratic legitimation. Therefore, an implicit *modus vivendi* has been concluded between the ECB and the European Parliament in order to establish the so-called "monetary dialogue" which seems the best way to conciliate independence and accountability, so far as it relies on a "deliberative democracy" model.

To replace the "Westminster model" of accountability, it is necessary to find out a new form of democratic legitimation. In my opinion, the deliberative democracy model developed by Joshua Cohen or Jürgen Habermas provides a conceptual basis on how the ECB's monetary policy could be democratically legitimated without prejudice to independence. In his discursive and argumentative theory of legal theory, Habermas argues that a democratic decision-making process supposes a reasoned discussion based on exchange of arguments in which stakeholders are

[35] See Martucci (2016).

motivated by the democratic ideal of political justification. In Cohen's view, a political power can be legitimately exercised under the condition that the discussion is held publicly between equal actors. Deirdre Curtin highlighted the role of Parliaments—European and national—in the democratic accountability of Executive Power in the EU.

> Accountability is conceptualized as an institutional relation in which an actor can be held to account by a forum.[36]

Accountability is

> relationship between an actor and a forum, in which the actor has an obligation to explain and to justify his or her conduct, the forum can pose questions and pass judgment, and the actor may face consequences.[37]

To be efficient, the accountability requires two elements: firstly, the actor informs the forum about his conduct; secondly, the actor and the forum discuss among themselves.

When applying the deliberative democracy model to the monetary policy, some adaptations are required in order to respect the independence of ECB. The monetary dialogue, especially the hearings of the President of the ECB, has emerged as a result of the need to satisfy the requirement for both independence and accountability. In order to respect the principle of independence, the discussion should be held *ex post*, that means after the adoption of the decisions, to ensure that the ECB's decision remains immunised against political pressure. In a way that respects the independence of the ECB, the European Parliament watches on the monetary policy by two means laid down by Article 284, para. 3, TFEU.

The first sentence of Article 284, para. 3, TFEU provides that the ECB sends its annual report on the monetary policy to the European Parliament, which holds a general debate on that basis. Although this report is also addressed to the Council, the Commission and the European Council, the Members of the European Parliament has come to the fore as a democratic legitimacy provider for the Monetary Union. According to Article 126 of the Rules of Procedure of the European Parliament, the President of the ECB shall present to Parliament the Bank's Annual Report on the activities of the Eurosystem and on the monetary policy of both the previous and the current year. This presentation shall be followed by a general debate, so that the structure of such meetings doesn't allow a genuine debate. After the general debate in which MEPs express their point of view, the Presidents wound up the debate with concluding remarks. In fact, the Economic and Monetary Committee prepares a report on the ECB's annual report, which is subject of a resolution voted by the plenary session. However, the European Parliament has never rejected an annual report. At most, some critics have been expressed by the MEPs on the monetary policy, on the lack of transparency or on other issues.[38]

---

[36]Curtin (2015).

[37]Bovens (2007), p. 450, cited by Curtin (2015).

[38]See for a typical illustration of critics Kiiver (2005).

The second sentence of Article 284, para. 3, TFEU forms the legal basis of this monetary dialogue.[39] It specifies that

> [t]he President of the European Central Bank and the other members of the Executive Board may, at the request of the European Parliament or on their own initiative, be heard by the competent committees of the European Parliament.

Since the beginning of the third stage of EMU, the conditions of this monetary dialogue are set up by a provision of the Rules of Procedure of the European Parliament in order to provide a hearing of members of the Executive Board of the ECB on a quarterly basis. According to Article 126 of the Rules of Procedure, the President of the ECB shall be invited to attend meetings of the Committee responsible, at least four times a year, in order to make a statement and to answer questions. It is added that if the Parliament requests, the President, Vice-President and other Members of the Executive Board of the ECB shall be invited to attend additional meetings. During the hearings, the members of the Executive Board of the ECB explain the decision of monetary policy to the MEPs members of the ECON-Committee. The relationship between the ECB and the European Parliament remains equal, when the hearings are public and *verbatim* report of the proceedings under paras. 3 and 4 shall be drawn up in the official languages.[40]

In the constitutional integrated system, the crisis has led to a nationalisation of monetary dialogue. With respect to national law, the President of the ECB felt the necessity to explain the non-standard monetary policy measures to Parliament of some Member States. He accepted thus the invitation to talk about monetary policy. The most glaring example is given by the visit of M. Draghi to the *Bundestag* on 24 October 2012, few weeks after the adoption of the OMT Programme.[41] The words that M. Draghi stated sum up the debate:

> As President of the European Central Bank (ECB), it is a privilege for me to come to the heart of German democracy to present our policy responses to the challenges facing the euro area economy. I know that central bank actions are often a topic of debate among politicians, the media and the general public in Germany. [...] It is rare for the ECB President to speak in a national parliament. The ECB is accountable to the European Parliament, where we have scheduled hearings every three months and occasional hearings on topical matters. We take these duties of accountability to the citizens of Europe and their elected representatives very seriously.[42]

The national Parliaments also ought to respect the principle of independence, explaining the tensions which have arisen in 2016 between the *Bundestag* and the ECB. In 2016, arguing that the ECB's "ultra easy" monetary policy implemented by very low interest rates was eroding the German financial and banking system, Germany's Social Democrats (SPD) called for Mario Draghi to appear again before

[39]On the topic, see Fasone (2014).

[40]Article 126, para. 5, of the Rules of Procedure.

[41]Opening statement at *Deutscher Bundestag*, Speech by Mario Draghi, President of the ECB, Discussion on ECB policies with Members of Parliament, Berlin, 24 October 2012.

[42]*Ibid.*

the *Bundestag* to discuss the issue. But the President of the ECB acted in a two-faced manner. On the one hand, he responded to the German Tabloid *Bild* that he would accept the invitation of the *Bundestag*.[43] On the other hand, the German Parliament renounced to the invitation after M. Draghi's statement that an excess of critics should affect the efficiency of monetary policy.[44]

In the integrated constitutional system of the Monetary Union, the Eurosystem can also be accountable to national Parliaments. In most Member States, NCBs must thus be accountable to parliamentary bodies. In accordance with the principles of institutional and procedural autonomy, the accountability of the NCB is provided by the national law. For instance, the Governor of the *Banque de France* shall submit to the President of the Republic and Parliament a report at least once a year on the *Banque de France*'s activities, the monetary policy it implements within the framework of the Eurosystem and the outlook for this policy.[45] The French law provides, pursuant to the provisions of Article 130 TFEU, a national monetary dialogue. According to a provision of the Statutes of *Banque de France*,

> the Governor of the Banque de France shall appear before the finance committees of the National Assembly and Senate when so requested, and may ask to appear before them.

Despite to the monetary dialogue between the ECB and the European Parliament, the French Parliament doesn't plan to hold such hearings on a regular basis. At least once a year, the Governor of Banque of France is invited to discuss about the monetary policy of the Eurosystem and, when it is considered necessary by the French members of Parliament, about other relevant issues.[46] The French Parliament may invite for an informal exchange of views members of the Governor Council of the ECB.[47]

---

[43]Mario Draghi: Interview with Bild, Interview with Mario Draghi, President of the ECB, conducted by Kai Diekmann, Nikolaus Blome, Daniel Biskup on 25 April 2016 and published on 28 April 2016.

[44]Kritik an Niedrigzinspolitik: Draghi will Einladung des Bundestags annehmen, brk/dpa/Reuters/AFP, 28 April 2016.

[45]Chapter III: Reporting to the President of the Republic-Parliamentary Oversight Article L. 143-1.

[46]See for example Assemblée nationale, Compte rendu de réunion n. 65, Commission des finances, de l'économie générale et du plan, 17/02/2015, Audition de M. Christian Noyer, gouverneur de la Banque de France, sur la politique monétaire européenne et le soutien financier à la Grèce; Compte rendu de réunion n. 0005 - Commission des affaires européennes, 24/07/2012, Audition, conjointe avec la Commission des finances, de M. Christian Noyer, Gouverneur de la Banque de France, et de M. Ramon Fernandez, Directeur général du Trésor, sur la mise en œuvre de l'accord du 29 juin 2012 relatif au pacte de croissance et à l'union bancaire.

[47]See for example Assemblée nationale, Compte rendu de réunion n. 79, Commission des Finances, de l'économie générale et du contrôle budgétaire, 13/05/2015, Échange de vues informel, conjoint avec la commission des Finances, de l'économie générale et du contrôle budgétaire, avec M. Benoît Coeuré, membre du directoire de la Banque centrale européenne.

3.2 The Uncertain Replication of "Dialogue" Accountability Model to Other Fields

The model of monetary dialogue has been replicated to two other fields of the EU.

In the wake of the crisis, the involvement of Parliaments in the oversight of the economic governance has increased. The "method of dialogue" deployed in the monetary area has been extended to the economic governance by the European legislator in the Six Pack, while taking fully into account the specificities of the economic pillar of the EMU. Outlining that

> the strengthening of economic governance should include a closer and a more timely involvement of the European Parliament and the national parliaments,

Regulation (EU) No. 1175/2011 amends the Stability and Growth Pact to include a chapter entitled "Economic dialogue" in Regulation (EC) No. 1466/97. Regulation (EU) No. 473/2013 of the Two Pack contains also a provision dedicated to the "economic dialogue" which is implemented in the same way. In addition, during the course of the enhanced surveillance process, the European Parliament and the Parliament of the Member State concerned may invite representatives of the Commission, the ECB and, even, the IMF to participate in an economic dialogue. Unlike the "monetary dialogue", the "economic dialogue" is provided by a legislative act which confers it two components. On the one hand, the President of the Council and the Commission, and where appropriate, the President of the Eurogroup, shall report annually to the European Parliament and to the European Council on the results of the multilateral surveillance. On the other hand, in order to

> ensure greater transparency and accountability, the competent committee of the European Parliament may invite the President of the Council, the Commission and, where appropriate, the President of the European Council or the President of the Euro Group to appear before the committee to discuss

several acts adopted in the framework of the economic governance listed in the regulations.[48] While the Six Pack refers especially to the acts adopted within the European Semester,[49] the Two Pack is focused on the acts regarding the

[48] Article 2, ab, 1, of Regulation (EU) No. 1175/2011; Article 15 of Regulation (EU) No. 473/2013.

[49] Broad guidelines of economic policy guidance to Member States issued by the Commission at the beginning of the annual cycle of surveillance; any conclusions drawn by the European Council on orientations for economic policies in the context of the European Semester; the results of multilateral surveillance carried out under this Regulation; any conclusions drawn by the European Council on the orientations for and results of multilateral surveillance; any review of the conduct of multilateral surveillance at the end of the European Semester; Council recommendations addressed to Member States in accordance with Article 121, para. 4, TFEU in the event of significant deviation and the report made by the Council to the European Council as defined in Article 6, para. 2, and Article 10, para. 2, of this Regulation.

national budgetary plans and, in general, the budgetary discipline.[50] As with the Monetary Dialogue, the Committee for Economic and Monetary Affairs of the European Parliament may carry out hearings which are scheduled in the same way as the hearings of the ECB's President. However, so far the economic governance is characterised as a "polyarchy", the "economic dialogue" needs to be adapted. It presents two specific features and has therefore to be distinguished from the monetary dialogue.

Firstly, accountable to the European Parliament are all the institutions and bodies involved in the economic governance. The "economic dialogue" looks like a response to the discourse concerning democracy deficit. From a legal point of view, the Council enacts all the acts of the economic governance (excessive deficit procedure, multilateral surveillance, the excessive imbalance procedure, etc.). It acts on a proposition or a recommendation of the Commission. From a political point of view, the Commission plays a key role in all the mechanisms, in so far as it puts a pressure on the Member States with the purpose of macroeconomic discipline. Although the Eurogroup continues to exist as informal meeting for the exchange of views between Ministers, it makes a major contribution to the fiscal discipline. Concluded in 2012, the TSCG has established the "Euro Summit meeting" which brings together the Heads of State or Government of the Euro area Countries, the Euro Summit President and the President of the European Commission. In charge to provide strategic guidelines on Euro area economic policy, the Euro Summit meeting has become the most important political body of the Eurozone. Though not explicitly mentioned by Regulation (EU) No. 1175/2011 of the Six Pack, it can be presumed that, like the Eurogroup, the Euro Summit is also accountable to the European Parliament.[51]

Secondly, one of the key characteristics of the economic governance is its intergovernmental nature, as a result of the division of competences between EU and Member States. This may explain why the Council, the Commission and the Euro Group report not only to the European Parliament, but also to the European Council, whose democratic legitimacy stems from the national constitutional system. It is necessary to point out that the Member States are represented in the European Council by their Heads of State or Government, themselves democratically accountable either to their national Parliaments, or to their citizen. In addition, the "economic dialogue" may offer an opportunity to participate in an exchange of views with a Member State which is the subject of a procedure that could be an excessive deficit procedure or a macroeconomic balance procedure. The European Parliament becomes thus a *forum* to discuss of the economic policies of Member

[50]The specification of the content of the draft budgetary plan as set out in a harmonised framework established in accordance with Article 6, para. 5; the results of the discussion of the Eurogroup on the Commission opinions adopted in accordance with Article 7, para. 1, to the extent that they have been made public; the overall assessment of the budgetary situation and prospects in the Euro area as a whole made by the Commission in accordance with Article 7, para. 4; Council acts referred to in Article 9, para. 4 and in Article 12, para. 3.

[51]The Eurosummit didn't exist, when the Six Pack was adopted.

States. Beyond the democracy legitimacy, the "economic dialogue" should become an instrument of the economic discipline. In any case, the participation of the Member State in such an exchange of views is essentially voluntary.

The Two Pack has taken a step further in the integration logic because of the involvement of national Parliaments. According to Article 7 of Regulation (EU) No. 473/2013, the Commission's opinion on the draft budgetary plan shall be presented to the Parliament of the Member State concerned at its request. Pursuant to Article 8, para. 11, of Regulation (EU) No. 472/2013, representatives of the Commission may be invited by the Parliament of the Member State concerned to participate in an exchange of views on the progress made in the implementation of its macroeconomic adjustment programme.

With the Banking Union, the question arises whether a "banking dialogue" could be carried out. Although there is no mention of a "dialogue" in Regulation (EU) No. 1024/2013, the ECB shall be accountable to the European Parliament and to the Council for the exercise of the supervisory tasks in the Eurozone in the Single Supervision Mechanism (SSM). The accountability system works in accordance with Article 20 of Regulation (EU) No. 1024/2013. It encompasses ECB's obligations to submit the annual report, to participate in hearings, to reply written and oral questions, etc. Although the European Parliament is the preferred interlocutor of the ECB, the Council, the Commission and the Eurogroup are also involved in the accountability system. The legislator has dedicated a provision to the national Parliaments. According to Article 21 of Regulation (EU) No. 1024/2013, the annual report on the SSM shall be forwarded to the national Parliament concerned which may address to the ECB its reasoned observations on that report. The national Parliament may not only submit written questions to the ECB, but also may invite members of the Supervisory Board of the ECB to participate in an exchange of views. However, the members of the ECB are reluctant to attend a meeting with national MEPs. In 2015, in an answer to a written question asked by Irish MEPs,[52] the ECB refused to take part to an "inquiry committee" regarding the Irish bank guarantee. In 2016, the Vice-President of the ECB declined again the invitation sent by the Portuguese Parliament to participate to a meeting of an inquiry committee regarding the bankrupt of a Portuguese bank.[53] The ECB argued that it is accountable for all its tasks to the European Parliament as a supranational institution and not to individual national delegations. In both cases actually, the questions were not relevant for the supervisory tasks carried out by the ECB within the SSM. According to Article 20 para. 3, of Regulation (EU) No. 1024/2013, the national Parliament

[52]BCE, 23 July 2015 L/MD/15/442, Letter from the MEPs representing Ireland and one MEP representing Northern Ireland.

[53]"Constâncio diz em carta porque não vem à Assembleia da República", 4 May 2016, Observador.pt. See Coelho and Fromage (2016).

> may invite the Chair or a member of the Supervisory Board to participate in an exchange of views in relation to the supervision of credit institutions in that Member State together with a representative of the national competent authority.

There is doubt if the ECB shall accept the invitation made by a national Parliament ("may invite"). In any case, the ECB has to be invited together with a member of the supervisory authority of the Member State.

3.3 The Weaknesses of Interparliamentary Cooperation

The increased role of the national Parliaments in the economic governance implies stronger cooperation with the European Parliament. The Lisbon Treaty has constitutionalised the inter-parliamentary cooperation. Pursuant to Article 12, f, TEU, the European and national Parliaments are invited to strengthen their cooperation. According to Article 9 of Protocol No. 1,

> the European Parliament and national Parliaments shall together determine the organisation and promotion of effective and regular inter-parliamentary cooperation within the Union.

While the cooperation is the task of the Conference of specialised parliamentary committees (COSAC), inter-parliamentary Conferences on specific topics may be organised, in particular to debate matters of common foreign and security policy, including common security and defense policy.[54] Article 13 of the TSCG enables Parliaments to create a special conference for the economic governance composed by representatives of national Parliaments and of the European Parliament which confirms the integrated character of the European constitutional system.

Inter-parliamentary cooperation should not only contribute to reduce the democratic deficit by giving a collective voice to Parliaments. The exchange of information and best practices for individual scrutiny could also lead to stronger parliamentary control of national Governments and European institutions. This would strengthen both elements of the dual integrated legitimacy on which the constitutional system of EU relies. The challenge is to strike a balance between European and national legitimacy. As authors write, two concepts of inter-parliamentary cooperation coexist.[55] "Centralised scrutiny" means that inter-parliamentary cooperation is dominated by the European Parliament. "Joint scrutiny" means a full involvement of national Parliaments.

The European Parliament seems traditionally reluctant to increase the role of national Parliaments in a way that might undermine the European Parliament's prerogatives.[56] In a position on the Report of the Five Presidents, the Committee on

---

[54] Article 10 of Protocol No. 1.

[55] Kreilinger (2015). See also Cooper (2014).

[56] See Kreilinger (2015).

Economic and Monetary Affairs of the European Parliament expressed vehement criticism on the inter-parliamentary cooperation:

> whereas cooperation between Parliament and national parliaments on the basis of Protocol No 1 should be reinforced in order to improve exchange of views and the quality of the parliamentary activity in the field of the EMU governance both at Union and national level; whereas such a cooperation should not be seen as the creation of a new mixed parliamentary body which would be both ineffective and illegitimate on a democratic and constitutional point of view.[57]

The European Commission is also skeptical about the inter-parliamentary cooperation, although its position has been even expressed in more diplomatic terms.[58] If the cooperation between the European Parliament and national Parliaments appears valuable to the Commission, so far

> it builds up mutual understanding and common ownership for EMU as a multilevel governance system.[59]

Nevertheless,

> inter-parliamentary cooperation as such does not, however, ensure democratic legitimacy for EU decisions.[60]

And the Commission concluded explicitly: democratic legitimacy

> requires a parliamentary assembly representatively composed in which votes can be taken. The European Parliament, and only it, is that assembly for the EU and hence for the euro.[61]

Furthermore, the European Council admits that the general objective remains

> to ensure democratic legitimacy and accountability at the level at which decisions are taken and implemented.[62]

So in the multilevel system, two levels of democratic legitimacy coexist. At European level, the legitimacy is provided by the European Parliament. At national level, the democratic principle requires

> that Member States ensure the appropriate involvement of their parliaments.[63]

Inter-parliamentary cooperation is at the heart of the "joint scrutiny" system.[64] In December 2012, the conclusions of the European Council underlined on the

---

[57]European Parliament, Committee on Economic and Monetary Affairs, Report with recommendations to the Commission on the report of the Presidents of the European Council, the European Commission, the European Central Bank and the Eurogroup "*Towards a genuine Economic and Monetary Union*", 24 October 2012, PE 494.867v04-00 A7-0339/2012 (2012/2151(INI)).

[58]Communication from the Commission, *A blueprint for a deep and genuine economic and monetary union Launching a European Debate*, 30 November 2012, COM(2012) 777.

[59]*Ibid.*

[60]*Ibid.*

[61]*Ibid.*

[62]European Council, Conclusions, 13–14 December 2012, point 14.

[63]*Ibid.*

[64]See Kreilinger (2015).

> new mechanisms increasing the level of cooperation between national parliaments and the European Parliament, in line with Article 13 of the TSCG and Protocol (No 1) to the Treaties.

In accordance with Article 12 TFEU and Protocol No. 1, so far the inter-parliamentary cooperation has been limited to the organisation of a conference, which brings together representatives from the European Parliament and the national Parliaments. The aim of such inter-parliamentary cooperation is to permit an involvement of national Parliaments in order to compensate the double transfer of power in the multilevel system of EMU. The integration produces a transfer of power from the national to the European level, while the macro-economic discipline required by the Treaty triggers a transfer of power in economic policies from national Parliaments to their Governments. Furthermore, economic policies, especially in the Eurozone, are conducted by Member States, but in a European framework that strengthen the convergence of these policies. Although there is not yet a European economic policy, the framework is tightening so much that, politically, the parliamentary control should not be exercised by the European Parliament alone. To the contrary, national Parliaments must be involved. Insofar as the new economic governance is based on supranational and intergovernmental mechanisms, only scrutiny cooperation could provide a democratic legitimacy.

The opposition between these two conceptions explains perhaps why 4 years after the entry into force of the TSCG, four sessions of this conference were organised without convincing outputs! It is astonishing that the legal basis of the inter-parliamentary cooperation relies on an international Treaty concluded between 25 Member States. According to Article 9 of Protocol No. 1,

> The European Parliament and national Parliaments shall together determine the organisation and promotion of effective and regular inter-parliamentary cooperation within the Union.

However, this provision does not forbid Member States to use international law, as long as they act in accordance with the principle of loyal cooperation under Article 4, para. 3, TEU. Pursuant to Article 13 of TSCG, it is "as provided for in Title II of Protocol (No 1)" that the European Parliament and the national Parliaments of the Contracting Parties promote their cooperation. They

> will together determine the organisation and promotion of a conference of representatives of the relevant committees of the European Parliament and representatives of the relevant committees of national Parliaments in order to discuss budgetary policies and other issues covered by this Treaty.

Since the first meeting of the Inter-parliamentary Conference on Stability, Economic Coordination and Governance within the EU held in Vilnius in October 2013, the Conference is coming up twice a year.[65] During the meetings, the representatives of Parliaments discuss all issues regarding the EMU. For example, at the Luxembourg Conference, fours panels had been organised, the first one

[65] Slovakia 2016, The Netherlands 2016, Luxembourg 2015, Latvia 2015, Italy 2014, Greece 2014.

focused on parliamentary scrutiny of European economic governance, especially after the crisis, the second one on the Social Dimension of Economic Governance, the third on Fair Tax competition and the fourth on growth and the EMU. Despite the enthusiasm of national parliamentarians, all the sessions show clearly that this conference will be at the most a *forum* of discussion without any decision-making or control powers. It might become a real actor in the EMU, particularly because it is source of proposals, on condition to be institutionalised. However, the meetings did lead to the implementation of rules of procedure only during the fifth Conference in Luxembourg in November 2015.

4 Conclusion

The overarching aim to provide legitimacy for the EMU has brought radical changes to the parliamentary role in such a multilevel constitutional system. Denationalising the budgetary procedures in order to secure the main objective of financial stability has resulted in a relegation of Parliaments to a function of control, whose efficiency depends on an inter-parliamentary cooperation. We are very far from a real parliamentarisation of the economic governance. Perhaps, only a European budget for the Eurozone and the europeanisation of the sovereign issuance would permit the single currency to get a real Parliament of the Eurozone.

References

Berner K (2013) "Sovereignty of parliament" under the Grundgesetz: how the German Constitutional Court discovers parliamentary participation as a means of controlling European integration. Eur Public Law 19(2):249–262

Bovens M (2007) Analising and assessing accountability: a conceptual framework. Eur Law Rev 13(4):447–468

Closa Montero C, Maatsch A (2014) In a spirit of solidarity? Justifying the European Financial Stability Facility (EFSF) in national parliamentary debates. J Common Mark Stud 52(4): 826–842

Coelho N, Fromage D (2016) The ECB in check: a case from Portugal on the new Single Supervisory Mechanism by Nelson Coelho and Diane Fromage, 9 June 2016. https://blogdroiteuropeen.com/2016/06/09/the-ecb-in-check-a-case-from-portugal-on-the-new-single-supervisory-mechanism-by-nelson-coelho-et-diane-fromage

Cooper I (2014) Parliamentary oversight of the EU after the crisis: on the creation of the "Article 13" interparliamentary conference. LUISS Guido Carli School of Government Working Paper No. SOG-WP21/2014

Curtin D (2015) Democratic accountability of EU executive power: a reform agenda for parliaments. In: Fabbrini F, Hirsch Ballin E, Somsen H (eds) What form of government for the European Union and the Eurozone? Hart Publishing, Oxford/Portland, pp 171–194

Eleftheriadis P (2014) Democracy in the Eurozone. In: Ringe WG, Huber PM (eds) Legal challenges in the global financial crisis. Hart Publishing, Oxford, pp 1–35

Fabbrini F, Hirsch Ballin E, Somsen H (eds) (2015) What form of government for the European Union and the Eurozone? Hart Publishing, Oxford/Portland
Fasone C (2014) European economic governance and parliamentary representation: what place for the European Parliament? Eur Law J 20(2):164–185
Irwin N (2013) The Alchemists. The Penguin Press, New York
Kiiver P (2005) The national parliaments in the European Union: a critical view on EU constitution-building. Proefschrift-Universiteit Maastricht, Maastricht
Kreilinger V (2015) Inter-parliamentary cooperation and its challenges: the case of economic and financial governance. In: Fabbrini F, Hirsch Ballin E, Somsen H (eds) What form of government for the European Union and the Eurozone? Hart Publishing, Oxford/Portland, pp 271–288
Lammert N (2009) Festvortrag zum Inkrafttreten des Vertrags von Lissabon am 1. Dezember 2009 in der Humboldt-Universität in Berlin "Europa der Bürger – parlamentarische Perspektiven der Union nach dem Lissabon-Vertrag", 1 December 2009
Martucci F (2016) L'ordre économique et monétaire de l'Union européenne. Bruylant, Bruxelles
Piedrafita S (2014) National parliaments' say on the new EU budgetary constraints: the case of Spain and Ireland. The constitutionalization of European budgetary constraints, pp 319–340

Further Reading

Allemand F, Martucci F (2014) The democratic legitimacy of European economic governance. Change in the role of Parliament. Revue de l'OFCE (134):115–131
Arpio Santacruz M (2012) La démocratie parlementaire dans le Traité de Lisbonne: quel rôle pour les parlements nationaux? A man for all treaties: liber amicorum en l'honneur de Jean-Claude Piris. Bruylant, Bruxelles, pp 1–23
Auel K, Höing O (2014) Parliaments in the euro crisis: can the losers of integration still fight back? J Common Mark Stud 52(6):1184–1193
Benz A (2011) Linking multiple demoi: inter-parliamentary relations in the EU. Europe's constitutional challenges in the light of the recent case law of national constitutional courts, pp 267–277
Clerc O (2012) Les traités SCG et MES et la participation des Parlements nationaux à la gouvernance économique de l'Union: déclin confirmé ou potentiel renouveau? Revue des affaires européennes (4):759–772
Corbett R (2012) The evolving roles of the European Parliament and of national parliaments. In: Biondi A, Eeckhout P, Ripley S (eds) EU law after Lisbon. Oxford University Press, Oxford, pp 248–261
Cooper I (2013) Bicameral or tricameral? National parliaments and representative democracy in the European Union. J Eur Integr 35(5):531–546
Costa O (2001) Le Parlement européen, assemblée délibérante. Université de Bruxelles, Bruxelles
Craig P (2015) The financial crisis, the EU institutional order and constitutional responsibility. In: Fabbrini F, Hirsch Ballin E, Somsen H (eds) What form of government for the European Union and the Eurozone? Hart Publishing, Oxford/Portland, pp 17–36
European Parliament (2012) Report on "Interparliamentary relations between the European Parliament and national parliaments under the Treaty of Lisbon" 2010–2011
Jabko N (2001) Expertise et politique à l'âge de l'euro: la Banque centrale européenne sur le terrain de la démocratie. Revue française de science politique 51(6):903–931
Kornobis Romanowska D (2013) La coopération interparlementaire. In: Auvret-Finck J (dir) Le Parlement européen après l'entrée en vigueur du traité de Lisbonne. Larcier, Bruxelles, pp 227–252
Magnette P (2000) La Banque centrale européenne entre indépendance et responsabilité. Cahiers européens de Sciences Po, No. 1

Martucci F (2003) Le rôle du Parlement européen dans la quête de légitimité démocratique de la BCE, Dialogue monétaire et “accountability délibérative”. Cahiers de droit européen (5–6):549–595

Piattoni S (2015) Is the EU a representative democracy? The normative debate and the impact of the Euro-crisis. In: Fabbrini F, Hirsch Ballin E, Somsen H (eds) What form of government for the European Union and the Eurozone? Hart Publishing, Oxford/Portland, pp 133–150

Rodriguez Iglesias GC, Ortiz Blanco L (eds) (2010) The role of national parliaments in the European Union. In: Proceedings of the FIDE XXIV, Congress Madrid 201, vol 1. Universidad Complutense, Madrid

From Subordinated to Prominent: The Role of the European Commission in EMU. Reflections on Euro Area Democracy

René Smits

Abstract This contribution, based on a Paper for the International Conference on *The Democratic Principle and the Economic and Monetary Union*, held in Rome (Italy) on 22 January 2016, sketches the development of the role of the European Commission in EMU affairs, discusses, in the context of EMU, issues of democracy and legitimacy and puts forward ideas on fostering accountability, representation and transparency, as well as humane outcomes of policies.

Contents

The author gratefully acknowledges research assistance by Oliver Englisch. All errors and omissions are mine.

R. Smits (✉)
Law of the Economic and Monetary Union, University of Amsterdam, Amsterdam, The Netherlands

Centre for Commercial Law Studies, Queen Mary University of London, London, UK

Administrative Board of Review, ECB, Frankfurt, Germany

Belgian Competition Authority, Brussels, Belgium

EMU Law and Banking Regulation, RS Law & Society Consulting B.V., Hoofddorp, The Netherlands
e-mail: rs@renesmits.eu

L. Daniele et al. (eds.), *Democracy in the EMU in the Aftermath of the Crisis*,
DOI 10.1007/978-3-319-53895-2_3

1 In the Beginning: The Commission as a De-legitimised Executive in EMU Affairs

In the late 1980s and early 1990s, when the Maastricht Treaty was negotiated, the free market and deregulation consensus reigned supreme. EMU, although constituting a major transfer of powers from State to Community (Union) level, was based on free markets assisting in the coordination of policies and the disciplining of budgets, and resulting in the appropriate exchange rate for the Euro.[1] This climate is one factor explaining the limited role given to the Commission under EMU law initially. There was no perceived need for strong central guidance, and a naïve belief in the willingness to coordinate among Member States. Another factor was the reluctance of the States to give away more sovereignty than strictly necessary. Thus, economic policy was to remain national.[2] The provisions adopted in Maastricht attribute prominence to the Ecofin Council, and relegate the Commission's role to adopting recommendations and being a "technical secretariat" to the Ecofin Council.[3] Whenever the Commission exerted its limited prerogatives, it was called names: "Brussels statisticians", "unelected bureaucrats".[4] The Court couldn't come to its rescue in full when the two largest Member States flouted their own self-imposed rules under the Stability and Growth Pact (SGP) in 2003.[5]

[1]See the Resolution of the European Council on economic policy co-ordination in Stage 3 of EMU and on Treaty Articles 109 and 109b, 13 December 1997, available at: http://www.europarl.europa.eu/summits/lux1_en.htm#annex1, from which I quote: "in general exchange rates should be seen as the outcome of all other economic policies".

[2]Article 5 TFEU even positions economic policy coordination as a separate category between the exclusive and shared competences. See, also, Article 2(3) TEU which obliges Member States to coordinate their economic and employment policies within Treaty-given arrangements which the Union is competent to provide.

[3]See, again, the statement of the European Council in its conclusions of December 1997: "The defining position of the ECOFIN Council at the centre of the economic coordination and decision-making process affirms the unity and cohesion of the Community"; and: "The Commission should provide analyses to the Council [. . .]".

[4]See, in a different context, the de-legitimisation undertaken by the new Polish Government in respect of the Commission, or by the advocates of the referendum on the EU-Ukraine Association Treaty in the Netherlands.

[5]In its judgment of 13 July 2004 in Case C-27/04 (*Commission* v. *Council*), the Court found that "responsibility for making the Member States observe budgetary discipline lies essentially with the Council". The Court did salvage the Commission's exclusive competence to submit recommendations. It found that "the Council cannot break free from the rules laid down by Article 104 EC [Article 126 TFEU] and those which it set for itself in Regulation No 1467/97. Thus, it cannot have recourse to an alternative procedure, for example in order to adopt a measure which would not be the very decision envisaged at a given stage or which would be adopted in conditions different from those required by the applicable provisions" and that "where the Council has adopted recommendations under Article 104 (7) EC [Article 126, para. 7, TFEU], it cannot subsequently modify them without a fresh recommendation from the Commission since the latter has a right of initiative in the excessive deficit procedure". Since the Council's conclusions on the excessive deficits of France and Germany "were not preceded by

2 Crisis Response: Inter-Governmentalism But, Also, Strengthened Commission Role

The role of the Commission has been particularly strengthened under the Six-Pack[6] (*inter alia*, reverse QMV) and Two-Pack legislation,[7] the European Semester, the ESM Treaty,[8] and the Fiscal Compact Treaty (TSCG).[9] To give just a few examples: the Commission's role under Article 121, para. 4, TFEU, which gives it the *option* to address a warning to a Member States, was fortified in *requiring* it to do so.[10] The Commission's recommendations need to be overturned by qualified majority voting (QMV) in the Council or they stand as adopted.[11] The Member States even agreed beforehand to endorse a finding by the Commission, unless a

Commission recommendations seeking the adoption, on the basis of Article 104(7) EC, of Council recommendations different from those adopted previously", and were adopted in accordance not with the rules applying pursuant to para. 7 (all EU States vote except the State whose deficit is discussed) but under the rules applying pursuant to para. 9 (only Euro Area Member States vote) of Article 104 TEC [Article 126 TFEU], the "decision to adopt those Council recommendations, being contrary to Article 104(7) and (13) EC [Articles 126, paras. 7 and 13, TFEU], is therefore unlawful.".

[6]The "Six-Pack" consists of the following legal acts reproduced in OJEU L 306, 23 November 2011: Council Regulation (EU) No. 1177/2011 of 8 November 2011 amending Regulation (EC) No. 1467/97 on speeding up and clarifying the implementation of the excessive deficit procedure; Regulation (EU) No. 1176/2011 of the European Parliament and of the Council of 16 November 2011 on the prevention and correction of macroeconomic imbalances; Regulation (EU) No. 1175/2011 of the European Parliament and of the Council of 16 November 2011 amending Council Regulation (EC) No. 1466/97 on the strengthening of the surveillance of budgetary positions and the surveillance and coordination of economic policies; Regulation (EU) No. 1174/2011 of the European Parliament and of the Council of 16 November 2011 on enforcement measures to correct excessive macroeconomic imbalances in the Euro area; Regulation (EU) No. 1173/2011 of the European Parliament and of the Council of 16 November 2011 on the effective enforcement of budgetary surveillance in the euro area; and Council Directive 2011/85/EU of 8 November 2011 on requirements for budgetary frameworks of the Member States.

[7]The "Two-Pack" consists of the following legal acts reproduced in OJEU L 140, 27 May 2013: Regulation (EU) No. 473/2013 of the European Parliament and of the Council of 21 May 2013 on common provisions for monitoring and assessing draft budgetary plans and ensuring the correction of excessive deficit of the Member States in the Euro area; and Regulation (EU) No. 472/2013 of the European Parliament and of the Council of 21 May 2013 on the strengthening of economic and budgetary surveillance of Member States in the Euro area experiencing or threatened with serious difficulties with respect to their financial stability.

[8]Treaty establishing the European Stability Mechanism, Brussels, 2 February 2012, as amended, available at: http://www.esm.europa.eu/about/legal-documents/index.htm.

[9]Treaty on Stability, Coordination and Governance in the Economic and Monetary Union (TSCG), Brussels, 2 March 2012, available at: http://europa.eu/rapid/press-release_DOC-12-2_en.htm.

[10]Articles 6, para. 2, ("in" Member States) and 10, para. 2, of Regulation (EC) No. 1466/97 ("out" Member States), as amended by Regulation (EU) No. 1175/2011.

[11]See, notably, Articles 6, para. 2, subpara. 5, and 10, para. 2, subpara. 5, of Regulation (EC) No. 1466/97, as amended [the preventive arm of the SGP]; Articles 4, para. 2, 5, para. 2, and 6, para. 2, of Regulation (EU) No. 1173/2011 [the enforcement of sanctions in relation to budgetary rules in respect of Euro Area Member States]; and Article 3, para. 3, of Regulation (EU) No. 1174/2011 [the enforcement of sanctions in relation to the correction of macro-economic imbalances in respect of Euro Area Member States].

majority among them is against.[12] Beyond economic governance strictly speaking, the Commission has been given a prominent role in banking resolution.[13] Whilst the ESM Treaty and the TSCG are intergovernmental agreements and, thus, would seem not to bolster the prerogatives of the supranational EU executive, this is not the case. The Commission may be considered "The Unexpected Winner of the Crisis", as Bauer and Becker argue.[14] Their thesis has drawn criticism and is not in line with the general impression that the crisis, through its emphasis on intergovernmentalism, has further reduced the role of the EU executive. The latter would be advocated by Puetter whose apt reflections on the coordination mechanisms in European economic governance[15] consider the Council and the European Council core players, the latter "emerg[ing] as the centre of political gravity". According to Puetter, "deliberative processes spread to the highest level of decision-making as ministers and heads of state and government are the only group of actors who can exercise sufficient political leadership to bring domestic policies in line with EU objectives". He discerns "an integration paradox" that explains the focus on inter-governmentalism: Member States don't want to "further compromise their sovereignty" but also do not "want to refrain from advancing European solutions" which are required by the interdependencies so they decide matters at Council and European Council level. I think the Commission's troika role has given the EU executive an even more intrusive role in respect of the economic policy making domain hitherto considered largely a national prerogative,[16] and still so considered, when we hear Governments of "programme States" state they want to exit the programme to "regain sovereignty". Although understandable in view of the uneven distribution of economic policy constraints due to

[12]Article 7 TSCG, which reads as follows: "While fully respecting the procedural requirements of the European Union Treaties, the Contracting Parties whose currency is the euro commit to support the proposals or recommendations submitted by the European Commission where it considers that a Member State of the European Union whose currency is the euro is in breach of the deficit criterion in the framework of an excessive deficit procedure. This obligation shall not apply where it is established among the Contracting Parties whose currency is the euro that a qualified majority of them, calculated by analogy with the relevant provisions of the European Union Treaties without taking into account the position of the Contracting Party concerned, is opposed to the decision proposed or recommended.".

[13]See Regulation (EU) No. 806/2014 of the European Parliament and of the Council of 15 July 2014 establishing uniform rules and a uniform procedure for the resolution of credit institutions and certain investment firms in the framework of a Single Resolution Mechanism and a Single Resolution Fund and amending Regulation (EU) No. 1093/2010, OJEU L 255, 30 July 2014, pp. 1 et seqq. (SRM Regulation), notably Article 18, para. 7.

[14]Bauer and Becker (2014); *contra*: Conceição-Heldt (2015); rebuttal: Bauer and Becker (2016).

[15]Puetter (2012).

[16]Articles 5, 119, para. 1, and 120 TFEU.

intrusive conditionality,[17] such utterances reflect a lack of understanding of the limited scope for "sovereign" action in a monetary union. Economic policy prescriptions for Member States are unavoidable in a monetary union; even as States remain competent to determine *individual budget lines*, the Union is competent to set limits on budget *size*, by primary and secondary law.[18]

3 The Need for a More Inclusive Approach: Three Bold Steps Needed

The debate on which institution came out as "the winner" of the crisis response takes place in the context of the 6 decades-long discussion about the nature, and evolution, of the European Community (Union) and the pros and cons of supranational versus intergovernmental features of the European project. I submit it is time for a broader view than one which is mired in dichotomy and dissension. This is especially so since the crisis has brought a lot of disunity, popular dissatisfaction and loss of confidence by the citizens. The disunity can be identified easily: between "programme States" and creditor States, between "North" and "South", between governments and governed, between those at work or unionised, and those below this threshold, and so on. Begg and others speak of "significant divergences and political conflicts, both among and within Member States, as well as between them and supranational EU institutions".[19]

[17]This term is defined here in the sense given by Bini Smaghi (2015): "Conditionality — which implies setting conditions in order for certain decisions to be implemented, typically by other institutions or countries, in a form of quid pro quo — is a way to coordinate or bind the behavior of institutions which are independent from each other or respond to different layers of government." The author assesses conditionality as a necessity in the current federal make-up of the Union: "Conditionality is needed because the implementation of the 'federal' policy — monetary or financial assistance — requires an assessment about the appropriateness of the actions undertaken by the non-federal level of government (fiscal, structural policies). Given that these policies are still in the hands of national institutions, and likely to remain so long as the Union makes a more decisive move toward political integration, conditionality will remain an important component of the European policy framework.".

[18]The Excessive Deficit Procedure (EDP; Article 126 TFEU) and the Stability and Growth Pact (SGP; Regulations (EC) Nos. 1466/97 and 1467/97, as amended) and the Six-Pack and Two-Pack legal acts mentioned before.

[19]In remarks made in the context of the move towards inter-governmentalism they discern: "The spread of political protests and institutional conflicts, both within and between Member States, highlights the challenges because the economic governance model is one based increasingly on executive rather than representative power." And: "the increased resort to executive decisions in economic governance, leading to significant divergences and political conflicts, both among and within Member States, as well as between them and supranational EU institutions, which have tended to be bypassed by intergovernmental or even bilateral bargaining". See Begg et al. (2015).

To move away from disunity, which the crisis has brought in Europe, we need to take some bold steps:

I. To leave behind standard terms and understandings that are, perhaps, no longer valid, and look afresh at legal concepts. Do we need to think of a "Country"[20] in the terms of the 1933 Montevideo Convention[21] or is a more modern approach called for? In this same vein, let us define terms instead of assuming their meaning. Far too often do we see references to concepts that are considered to be fixed but which are not, except in the mind of the author/speaker: "political union", "federation", "price stability",[22] "financial stability", "democracy". One such (in)famous word is: "political will", a construct that is often invoked but may be a self-reinforcing belief set, undermining imaginative solutions;

II. To broaden the perspective from individual disciplines towards a multi-disciplinary perspective, taking in views from other academic approaches beyond law. Economics, political science, sociology, psychology, cultural anthropology, health studies come to mind—to encapsulate a wider view of the economic policy measures adopted, their effects on society and, in the confines of the law, the issue of Union versus State competences. As Jones and Torres say in a recent article: "The euro area crisis cannot be understood without combining insights from a variety of disciplines"[23];

III. To look at matters in context, beyond the academic approach: what are humane approaches and outcomes?

[20]It may be recalled that mention that the EU, in its public utterances and on its website has adopted this term instead of the word "Member State" again in the wake of the populist nationalist tide.

[21]Montevideo Convention on the Rights and Duties of States, 26 December 1933, available at: http://www.oas.org/juridico/english/treaties/a-40.html. Admittedly, the Convention's definition of a State as possessing the following qualifications (a) a permanent population; (b) a defined territory; (c) Government; and (d) capacity to enter into relations with the other States, may be considered a codification of customary international law. Even so, the evolution of new governance forms, notably the EU, make this definition too narrow a perspective for the twenty-first century and an interconnected world.

[22]Whose definition as below but close to 2% inflation was adopted by the ESCB in the composition of the Eurosystem (Article 282, para. 1, 2nd sentence, TFEU), but is now contested mainly by German critics of the Euro Area's monetary authority. For the Eurosystem's own interpretation of the Treaty term of "price stability" which it is mandated to maintain (Ar 127(6) TFEU), see: the ECB's Monthly Bulletin of January 1999 (p. 46), available at: https://www.ecb.europa.eu/pub/pdf/mobu/mb199901en.pdf.

[23]Jones and Torres (2015).

4 Democracy and Legitimacy

This chapter reflects on the role of the Commission and its effect on democracy from several angles, a legal perspective first and a more comprehensive approach afterwards. Doing so, let me be transparent in what I mean by democracy and legitimacy in a legal context.

Democracy relates to representation (of the popular will through our elected representatives), accountability of the politicians vis-à-vis these same representatives and the public at large (through the media) and transparency (the public, the media, and the representatives of citizens should be able to see what is done and to check this against standards of behaviour and outcome). Together, these elements may be abbreviated as: **ART**. Accountability, Representation and Transparency are, indeed, the art of democracy. Democracy may be considered to feature core elements (like majority rule, protection of minorities, freedom of expression, application of the rule of law) but its precise form may be shaded differently from time to time, and from place to place. In a multi-level governance construct, democracy may be differently understood than at State or sub-State levels, where direct democracy may play a role that may be less appropriate at continental or global levels.[24]

Democracy is often linked to a community of like-minded people: geographically close, linked by language, culture, history. This is, of course, a human construct,[25] and in the case of nation-States, a relatively recent one at that. Without pretending to know this area of academic debate well, I profess to take a European people as appoint of departure: a shared (albeit imperfect) European demos, as Culver and Giudice express it.[26] As these authors argue, the conventional methods of thinking may force one onto the dichotomy of the nation-State versus the European "super-State", which is an unnecessary constraint on creativity.[27]

---

[24]Here, referendums in sub-entities of larger communities come to mind as inherently undemocratic when a majority (if at all, in case of a low turn-out perhaps even a minority) of a minority of citizens decides the future of the whole. Cases in point have been the *referenda* in Ireland on ratification of EU(-related) Treaties, the consultative *referendum* in the Netherlands on the EU-Ukraine Association Agreement and the UK *referendum* on EU membership where issues for a continent are decided by a few citizens only.

[25]For explanations on the role of fictions in shaping human behaviour, see: Yuval Noah Harari, *Sapiens, A Brief History of Humankind*, 2011 (Hebrew), 2014 (English).

[26]Culver and Giudice (2013).

[27]Note the interesting qualification of the European Union as "a constituted 'commonwealth' that marked 'post-sovereign' Europe" by Neil MacCormick in his book *Questioning Sovereignty*, cited by Eleftheriadis (2011), who adds "that the EU did not fit the sovereignty paradigm and was, instead, a mixed entity with a mixed constitution.". McCormick's observations deserve a full quote, again taken from Eleftheriadis: "[T]he idea of a democratic commonwealth [...] is a complex not a simple one. Neither 'rule **by** the people, for the people' nor 'majority rule' nor 'one person, one vote' nor any other simple concept or slogan will capture it. The different aspects of the value of democracy need to be acknowledged, in their parallelism with different elements or aspects of subsidiarity. An enlightened bureaucracy [...] can also be seen to have an essential utility in a well-constituted order.".

In the evolution of "community", I would be inclined towards Habermas'[28] advocacy of a pan-European identity but one which is always open to inclusion of others: other humans elsewhere on this planet, and other sentient beings in the universe. European unity is a tool.

In this contribution I cannot engage further in the discussion of democracy at the European level. Let me confine myself to referring to the interesting concept of demo*i*cracy (not a misspelt word!) by Nicolaïdis[29] and to the many contributions by Weiler.[30]

Legitimacy has two aspects: input (or: process) legitimacy concerns the manner in which decisions are formed, whilst output legitimacy is concerned with whether the decision-making process achieves results that are acceptable when appreciated against a set of standards. As indicated before, these standards should, in my view, be broader than technical or abstract—they should relate to human experiences "on the ground" and be seen in context. European unity is a project that serves "true ends", as Eleftheriadis states.[31] Again, especially in a multi-governance construct like the European Union (Euro Area), re-linking with what actually is perceived and felt at the level of citizens and companies is crucial for the European project to continue and to be of benefit to the people of Europe.

In this context, I recall that, during the oral hearing in the *OMT* case, Gregor Gysi,[32] the advocate of *Die Linke*, the left-wing fraction in the German *Bundestag* which joined the other German claimants in contesting the ECB's competence to engage in Outright Monetary Transactions (OMT), brought the suffering of Greek citizens and residents of other programme States into the Court room.[33] Apart from interfering with Member States' economic policy competences, the ECB's linking of this monetary policy instrument to structural adjustment programmes was alleged to dictate a counterproductive and devastating

---

[28]Habermas (2011).

[29]Nicolaïdis (2013). His definition is worthwhile to be quoted in full: "European demoicracy is a Union of peoples, understood both as states and as citizens, who govern together but not as one. It represents a third way against two alternatives which both equate democracy with a single demos: as a demoicracy-in-the-making, the EU is neither a Union of democratic states as 'sovereigntists' would have it, nor a Union-as-a democratic state *to be* as 'federalists' would have it. A Union-as-demoicracy should remain an open-ended process of transformation which seeks to accommodate the tensions inherent in the pursuit of radical mutual opening between separate peoples".

[30]See Weiler (2012) and further references.

[31]Eleftheriadis (2011).

[32]Quoting Georg Gysi here does not imply support for his political positions. The author is aware of the allegations against the foreman of *Die Linke* concerning alleged collaboration with the secret service of the former German Democratic Republic (GDR) and the concealment of assets of the GDR's ruling Communist Party, allegations that Mr. Gysi denies.

[33]Gysi (2015).

economic policy and, therefore, to violate the Charter of Fundamental Rights.[34] The ECB is bound by this Charter and Gysi, when criticising the conditionality of OMT (which can only be activated for a Member State that has committed to structural reforms under a programme), mentioned figures about the effects on health in Greece: increases in neonatal mortality by 21%, in infant mortality by as much as 43%, the HIV infection rate has risen by 52%, and the suicide rate by 37%. There may be a debate about the causality: did structural reforms actually cause these effects or was it the manner in which the reforms were carried out preserving vested interests?[35] The argument that the ECB has no competence to link its monetary policy instruments to specific economic policy measures is, in my view, flawed. First, the ECB is to support the general economic policies in the Union. Second, as the Court stated in its *Gauweiler* judgment on OMT,[36] linking the activation of this monetary policy instrument to conditionality ensures that the guardian of price stability would not undermine the economic policies pursued by the Member States, acting through the Ecofin Council and the ESM.[37] Finally, the legality of (the effects on economic policy of) the intended monetary policy measures under the Charter may be stronger than advocated by the applicant. But all this is beside the point that Gysi was making. He brought humanity into the Court room. The failure of the AG and the Court to address these issues,[38] understandable though this may have been, is an expression of the lack of connection between decision-making (political, judicial) at EU level and what matters on the ground.

This brief excursion into the effects of the economic policies imposed by way of conditionality on programme States serves to underline two points.

---

[34]The applicant *Die Linke* considered the right of collective bargaining and action (Article 28) to be violated, as well as the right to a fair remuneration (Article 31), the right to engage in work (Article 15), the provision of health care (Article 35), the right to housing and social assistance (Article 34), the right to education (Article 14) and the prohibition of discrimination (Article 21).

[35]See, for a very critical analysis, published just before the Syriza victory in January 2015 parliamentary elections in Greece: Eleftheriadis (2014).

[36]Para. 60 which concludes on the link as follows: "The ESCB thus ensures that the monetary policy measures it has adopted will not work against the effectiveness of the economic policies followed by the Member State". ECJ 16 June 2015, Case C-62/14, *Gauweiler and Others* v. *Deutscher Bundestag*.

[37]The Advocate General quotes *Die Linke* in para. 143 of his Opinion and seems to agree with them that "the ECB, in participating in the assistance programmes concerned, has been actively involved in measures which, in certain circumstances, might be perceived as going beyond 'support' for economic policy.".

[38]Neither addressed the issue of violation of basic rights through the structural adjustment and austerity measures to which the OMT would be linked, with the AG finding that the ECB should refrain from engaging in direct involvement in the monitoring of the financial assistance programme once it would have activated OMT in respect of a Member State—something I called "troixit" in a comment—but not insisting on keeping away from conditionality: his finding "does not prevent the ECB from regularly participating in financial assistance programmes as they are provided for in the ESM Treaty". See paras. 140–151 of the AG's Opinion in Case C-62/14, and Smits (2015).

5 Two Provisional Findings on Economic Policy Decision-Making Thus Far

5.1 Outcome Legitimacy Insufficiently Reflected in Decision-Making Up Till Now

First, the requirement of outcome legitimacy in the European democracy has not been adequately reflected in decision-making during the crisis. The Commission can make a contribution to improving the Union's record by taking a more comprehensive and actual approach to such rights. It is acknowledged that the Commission is, at least on paper, committed to this: apart from references to social justice, fairness, and ability to pay in the August 2015 Memorandum of Understanding with Greece,[39] there has been a Commission Staff Working Document on the estimated social impact of the latest programme.[40] The impact assessment addresses some of the notorious issues of inequality and poverty but fails to address in-depth the kind of figures presented by Gysi before the Court. A stronger commitment to actual effects of conditionality, rather than to gloss over its consequences, would foster democracy. For academic support of "a wider normative approach to the European Stability Mechanism and the preventative agenda of the Stability and Growth Pact's Multilateral Economic Co-ordination and Surveillance, in order to ensure that 'critical social functions' are properly safeguarded", I refer to an upcoming contribution of Professor Singh.[41]

5.2 Policy Prescriptions Sharply Distinguish Between EU Citizens: Dichotomy Leads to Discord

Second, it is clear that the EU's impact on economic policy varies widely across Member States, with the programme States being put under curatorship of the experts in Brussels (Commission), Luxembourg (ESM), Frankfurt (ECB) and Washington (IMF), whereas other States are far more unencumbered in their pursuit of economic policies. This state of affairs must be exceptional and cannot last without putting at serious risk the equality of EU citizens and, therefore, European democracy. The *dichotomy* ("*tweedeling*") between Member States subject to MoUs and others in terms of economic policy coordination, with the former subject to far more substantive rules *and* to larger incentives to comply than the latter, has the ugly potential to leading to *discord* ("*tweespalt*"). Here, I make a call for less

---

[39]Available at: http://ec.europa.eu/economy_finance/assistance_eu_ms/greek_loan_facility/pdf/01_mou_20150811_en.pdf.

[40]European Commission (2015a).

[41]Singh (2016).

divisiveness and more non-duality in European economic policy-making. EU economic governance should become more even-handed, and policy scrutiny should be as involved for larger States as for smaller ones. This plea comes alongside advocacy of profound rethinking of the substance of economic policies, to become more inclusive. More inclusive in terms of effects on citizens and with a keen eye on income distribution but, also, more inclusive in taking on board various policy areas and challenges, combining these to find innovative solutions. Also, I suggest to explore the venue of adopting EU-wide policy measures.

6 Exploring EU-Wide Economic Policy Measures

Progress on EU-wide economic policy measures is needed, beyond the approach envisaged by the Five Presidents' Report, as this is too much focused on more coordination and oversight, precisely the kind of divisive and conflictual methods that we may have to look beyond.[42] Apart from a fiscal stabilisation function for the Euro Area, that the Five Presidents fortunately wish to see explored, we might explore whether EU-wide economic policy measures are in order. This is in line with the Five President's Report insistence that the Euro Area dimension is given more prominence in the European Semester[43] and with the introduction of a Euro Area Stabilisation function.[44] In the past, I have proposed exploring the limits of Article 122, para. 2, TFEU to that effect.[45]

Specifying the substantive issues such measures may address, I offer two examples: population ageing and climate change, both also mentioned by Jones and Torres.[46] The Stability and Growth Pact was adopted partially in view of the ageing of Europe's population: an issue that has not gone away, 18 years later. The greying of Europe's population whose budgetary consequences the SGP sought to address early on has a link to the immigration crisis. There seems to be scope for imaginative measures on a Europe-wide scale that address these twin issues. EU-wide vocational training and acculturation classes help refugees integrate in Europe's society, thus diminishing the effect of the outflow of home-born labour

---

[42]At least partially: such methods do have their proper place but are all we have, and more so in the future if the strengthening of EMU continues along the lines sketched by the Five Presidents. See: Juncker et al. (2015), hereafter: Five President's Report.

[43]Five President's Report, Annex II: A More Integrated European Semester.

[44]Five President's Report, para. 4.2.

[45]By going beyond the areas the provision mentions as examples (supply security, in particular in the area of energy) and adopting "the measures appropriate to the economic situation" that the "spirit of solidarity between Member States" calls for.

[46]Jones and Torres (2015) state: "the key to long-term sustainability requires doing more than just addressing the current crisis; it depends upon policymakers developing institutions and practices that will make it easier to address other future crises as well. The solution to the current problems of the euro area must help us deal with population ageing and climate change.".

from the market. Climate change is another issue that merits Europe-wide policy action. Southern States' solar energy might help address energy shortages, or expensiveness in Germany after the *Energiewende* (the energy transition, away from nuclear power, contemplated since the 1980s but speeded up after the Fukushima nuclear accident in 2011). Thus, CO_2 emissions may be reduced in line with commitments in respect of the climate change challenges. Infrastructure spending on solar energy production in southern nations and on interconnectors between South and North should be explored. By the way, this energy transition is itself hailed as a democratisation process, with decentralised power generation becoming predominant.

7 Another Legal Issue: Transparency (and Enforceability) of Conditionality Through EU Legal Acts

Another issue having to do with transparency, as an element of democracy, is that MoU commitments have not always been translated item by item into EU legal acts, adopted in the context of the programme States' compliance with budgetary rules of the EDP/SGP. A comparison between the MoU of August 2015 with the two secondary law-acts adopted[47] reveals that the practice followed in respect of Greece, Portugal, Ireland and Cyprus before, of detailing conditionality in EU legal acts beside the MoUs, seems to have been abandoned.

This diminishes the transparency of legal acts and negatively affects the enforcement of conditionality. Due to the primacy of EU law, such secondary law provisions take precedence over national (constitutional) law and rulings of national (Constitutional) Courts that may adopt judgments on the validity of their Governments' commitments. It should be recalled that, notably in Portugal and Greece, structural reforms and austerity measures have been challenged before High Administrative Courts, with the Greek *Conseil d'État* invoking the primacy of EU law to fend off some of such claims. The relationship between EU legal acts that reflect commitments undertaken in MoUs, and national law and legal challenges merits in-depth research by legal scholarship. Focusing on the issue of democracy and EMU: the Commission would serve democracy if it ensured that commitments engaged into under an ESM programme are fully reflected in EU legal acts. This makes scrutiny by the European Parliament of the Commission's stance possible, enhances transparency, may permit judicial review and improves enforcement of what are bound to be to some (vested interests) unpopular measures.

[47]Council Decision (EU) 2015/1410 of 19 August 2015 giving notice to Greece to take measures for the deficit reduction judged necessary to remedy the situation of excessive deficit, OJEU L 219, 20 August 2015, pp. 8 et seqq., and Council Implementing Decision (EU) 2015/1411 of 19 August 2015 approving the macroeconomic adjustment programme of Greece, OJEU L 219, 20 August 2015, pp. 12 et seqq.

8 Debate Should Be Held at the European Level, with (Sub) national Input

From a formal point of view, the greater role for the Commission in economic policy making is in line with ideas to strengthen the democratic legitimacy of EMU at Union level.[48] It is, after all, the Commission that is responsible before the European Parliament[49] and, primarily, at the EP level that the policy debate about the appropriate economic policies for Europe, and the Eurozone, should take place. The Economic Dialogue introduced by the Six-Pack and Two-Pack legislation[50] should be used to the full, as should be the option for a national Parliament to request the Commission to present its opinion on a draft State budget before it.[51] Emphasis on the European level of accountability is in line with the option, introduced in the Six-Pack legislative package, that representatives of the Member State affected by executive steps in the application of the reinforced economic governance framework interact with the European Parliament.[52] The normative approach I take here (policy discussions *should* primarily take place at EU level) is based on the experience that the crisis has increased the dissension between States and reinforced the island nature of the debate: Greek, German, Dutch, Italian-centered debates which then translate in inter-State discussions pitting Greeks against Germans, Finns against Portuguese, and so forth. It took the *GroenLinks* (Green Left) leader Klaver[53] to state that a Greek unemployed is as much a matter of concern as a Dutch unemployed but such voices as his are, alas, unusual.

From a wider than legal perspective, the absence of a Europe-wide media space is very much to be deplored. The policy debate at continental level will only reach the households and firms affected if the citizens can follow it in their own (second) language. My preference to focus on the EU level for economic policy debate

---

[48]Five President's Report, Chapter 5.

[49]Article 17, para. 8, TEU; Article 234 TFEU.

[50]Article 2, a-b, of Regulation (EC) No. 1466/97, as amended by Regulation (EU) No. 1175/2011 (preventive arm of the SGP); Article 2 of Regulation (EC) No. 1467/97, as amended by Regulation (EU) No. 1177/2011 (corrective arm of the SGP); Article 3 of Regulation (EU) No. 1173/2011 (enforcement of SGP in EA); Article 6 of Regulation (EU) No. 1174/2011 (enforcement of EIP in EA); Article 14 of Regulation (EU) No. 1176/2011 (EIP); Article 15 of Regulation (EU) No. 473/2013.

[51]Article 7, para. 3, of Regulation (EU) No. 473/2013.

[52]See: Article 2, a-b, notably para. 3, of Regulation (EC) No. 1466/97, as amended [the "preventive arm" of the SGP]; Article 2, a, notably in subpara. 3 of para. 1, of Regulation (EC) No. 1467/97, as amended [the "corrective arm" of the SGP]; Article 14, notably para. 2, of Regulation (EU) No. 1176/2011 establishing the Economic Imbalances Procedure; Article 6, notably subpara. 2, of Regulation (EU) No. 1174/2011 on the enforcement of the Economic Imbalances Procedure in the Euro Area; Article 3, notably subpara. 2, of Regulation (EU) No. 1173/2011 on the effective enforcement of the SGP ("budgetary surveillance") in the Euro Area; Article 15, notably para. 2, of Regulation (EU) No. 473/2013 on monitoring draft budgets and the correction of excessive deficits in the Euro Area.

[53]Klaver (2012).

doesn't imply that national Parliaments or regional Parliaments would not play a role, as well. There is ample scope for looking more at regions, rather than at States. This is not to serve the ends of separatists but to acknowledge that differences in economic performance and cultural preferences may exist between regions which are more prominent than between the nation-States into which economic data and popular preferences are amalgamated. In the run-up to monetary union, there was an expectation that, after the introduction of the single currency, one would no longer focus primarily at how nations fared as the frontiers between them would come down: the relevance of balance of payments figures within the Euro Area, and the importance of competitiveness among nation-States would diminish. With the crisis, we have seen a renewed emphasis on States, quite the opposite of what was expected in the 1990s. A return to "*l'Europe des régions*" is, in my view, called for. For a look across the Atlantic, I note that the Canadian Government consults provincial residents ahead of the adoption of the federal budget in specific calls for Manitobans, Québécois and others to give input.[54] Yet, the crisis instruments' emphasis on national parliamentary involvement runs the risk of exacerbating national divisions. I note Bini Smaghi's reflections regarding the ESM[55]:

> The explicit involvement of national parliaments, especially in Germany, gives the impression that it is ultimately up to the latter to agree on whether another Eurozone country can access the ESM and receive financial assistance. This creates a direct opposition between countries, and their own people and media, which is very detrimental to the process of political integration. The ESM decision-making process should be made more similar to that of the IMF. This does not prevent national parliaments from being involved, but this should be at an early stage, in giving mandate to the respective national representatives in the institution rather as appearing to be the ultimate decision-maker and judge.

It is submitted that any furthering of democratic input in the economic governance of Europe should seek to avoid the divisiveness of the economic governance model adopted. This should also be the case if other fora may play a role in representative democracy, including the Conference of Parliamentary Committees for Union Affairs of Parliaments of the European Union (COSAC).[56] I note that the issue of the legitimacy of the 28-State EP in the 19-State Euro Area merits further reflection.

[54]See, by way of example, these two news releases: http://www.fin.gc.ca/n16/16-005-eng.asp and http://www.fin.gc.ca/n16/16-010-eng.asp, plus many others at: http://www.fin.gc.ca/news-nouvelles/nr-nc-eng.asp.

[55]Bini Smaghi (2015).

[56]See: http://www.cosac.eu/en/.

9 The Commission's Central Role as Accountable to the European Parliament: Four Suggestions

As said, the natural central role of the Commission in economic policy setting and budgetary oversight follows from its democratic accountability vis-à-vis the European Parliament. Its current functioning may be scrutinised more closely, and effectively, by the Parliament, acting in tandem with national Parliaments. Its future role may be strengthened, for which I see a case in four areas.

1. When it comes, as it should, to joint tapping of financial markets, there would seem a natural role for the Commission. Eurobonds should be further explored after the less than enthusiastic report by an expert group.[57] Joint financing of State unemployment insurance mechanisms may also be a prime responsibility for the Commission, thus creating an asymmetric shock absorption mechanism at Euro Area level.[58]
2. A European Treasury belongs with the Commission. An EU Finance Ministry was proposed by Jean-Claude Trichet[59] as "exert[ing] direct responsibilities in three domains" (1) surveillance of fiscal policies and competitiveness policies; (2) typical executive branch responsibilities in respect of the EU "integrated financial sector" and (3) representation of the Union in international financial institutions. The discussion of a European fiscal capacity is on-going. A recent contribution from *Notre Europe* and the *Istituto Affari Internazionali* sketches the long-term choice as between a European monetary fund and the institution of insolvency regimes for Member States, reminiscent of the Sovereign Debt Restructuring Mechanism (SDRM) proposed early this century on a global scale within the IMF[60] The Five Presidents' Report notes that "some decisions will increasingly need to be made collectively while ensuring democratic accountability and legitimacy", concluding that "A future euro area treasury could be the place for such collective decision-making".
3. As Trichet advocated, external representation of the Union in EMU affairs, together with the ECB, seems a natural task for the Commission. A recent proposal on this calls for a few remarks on its contents. The Commission's too modest proposal[61] for external representation not only comes too late (proper arrangements should have been adopted[62] in 1999) but also labours from four

[57]Tumpell-Gugerell (2014).

[58]See: Claeys et al. (2014); and the proposals of the Glienicker Group (2013).

[59]Trichet (2011).

[60]Rubio (2016).

[61]European Commission (2015b).

[62]The Commission's original proposal (European Commission 1998) was withdrawn after 17 years.

faults. It allows too easily a State-centered membership approach because the IMF is based on "countries",[63] a concept that we may have to re-interpret in the light of developments since the 1933 Montevideo Convention and the *status* of EU Member States as less a "country" and more like a constituent element of the European Union.[64] I urge the IMF, and the Commission, to adopt an innovative interpretation of old concepts. Second, the recent Commission proposal envisages representation by the President of the Eurogroup instead of by the Commission. In line with democracy and efficiency, I would argue for the latter as EU's voice on the world stage, alongside the President of the ECB. This is my third issue with the proposal: it seems to neglect ECB independence and the incidence of Article 6 ESCB Statute on the Euro's external representation. Although the latter provision gives precedence to Article 138 TFEU, there is no derogation from the independence of the ECB,[65] which leads me to argue that the proposal is not in line with the ECB's prerogatives.[66] Fourth, as I argued in my thesis,[67] even the payments and capital movements competence of the Union requires single representation at the IMF (which is the global overseer of freedom to effect current transactions[68]). It is not "just" the single monetary policy[69] that argues for single representation at the IMF.

4. Finally, there is a case for mutual representation in decision-making bodies: the ECB President should *ex officio* be invited to Commission meetings, just as the ECB President is invited to Ecofin meetings, and the Commission should be able to table a motion for deliberation at the Governing Council of the ECB.[70] This would imply recognition of the Commission's enhanced role, in line with democracy requirements, and put it at par with the Ecofin President. The latter is invited, together with a member of the Commission, as a non-voting participant to meetings of the ECB's Governing Council but, at present, only the Chairperson of the Ecofin Council may submit a motion[71] and the ECB President is invited to the Ecofin only, not to the Commission's meetings. The necessary policy dialogue, and the umbilical cord to democracy, would both be

[63]Article II of the Articles of Agreement of the International Monetary Fund.

[64]The arguments put forward by Bickerton (2013) may be reflected upon in this context. His book was awarded the Best Book of 2013 prize awarded by the University Association of Contemporary European Studies (UACES).

[65]Article 130 TFEU; Article 7 of the ESCB Statute.

[66]See, again, my line of reasoning back in 1997 on the "tied" competence of the Council to enact provisions on external representation, implying reverence for the inherent own powers of the ECB in the external field: Smits (1997), pp. 412–413, 414.

[67]Smits (1997).

[68]Article VIII, sec. 2(a), of the Articles of Agreement, IMF.

[69]See Smits (1997), p. 433.

[70]Article 284, para. 2, TFEU.

[71]Acknowledging that this formal power has not been used, as far as is known in the public domain.

strengthened by such arrangements (which ultimately require Treaty change but may be adopted on a less formal basis before[72]).

10 The Commission as a Neutral Arbiter or a Political Body?

In the current set-up, the Commission often is called to act as arbiter on pre-established rules. I consider its pivotal role an indispensable element in proper, democratic and legitimate economic policy-making at the European level, subject to improvements and wider perspectives, as emphasised here. The Commission then is not a "neutral" arbiter or a technocratic institution. Rather, it takes a policy stance and needs to get support for this in the European Parliament, and among the European public at large. Of course, alignment with the Member States represented in the Council and predominant in the European Council, is also called for.

One issue in this respect is whether depoliticising the process of economic-policy making, as Singh proposes or, rather, fostering legitimacy and debate, at the appropriate (i.e., EU) level would lead to the best, humane outcomes? By proposing to preserve "critical social functions" in the operation of the ESM, and the establishment of an EU-wide fiscal council to assist in this objective through non-politicised budget assessment, Singh seeks "to depoliticise the process and reposition this part of EU policy within its wider economic and social agenda and values". My inclination would be to consider the impact of technocrats and expert advisors already too big in economic policy-making. Without wishing to underestimate the importance of expert advice, we should avoid a situation in which economic policy decisions and budgetary preferences are solely guided by outside expert advice. This reminds me too much of the situation in the Netherlands where all party programmes and many political ideas are "calculated" and "verified" (for budgetary consequences and effects on income distribution) by the CPB, an independent economic research body which forms part of the public sector. Thus, political preferences are reduced to cold calculations. In the context of EMU, it may be worthwhile to note the discussion about the suitability of the EMU budgetary norm, as calculated by the Commission, by this very CPB. Researchers at the CPB found the structural budget balance indicator to be an imperfect measure of fiscal policy effort of Member States and, because of the major role it plays in the annual cycle of economic policy guidance and surveillance (the European Semester), argued for improvements in the measurement and use of this indicator.[73] Without going into the merits of this discussion, it is noted here for the measure

[72]The announced incorporation of the TSCG into the EU legal framework (Article 16 TSCG) may be an appropriate moment to do so.

[73]Hers and Suyker (2014). CBP stands for: *CPB Netherlands Bureau for Economic Policy Analysis* (CPB), an independent policy research and advice body for the Dutch Government.

of debate possible among experts to whom the role of arbiter in policy choices is too often assigned.

A further point on the issue of expert input and rules determining the policies pursued is the concern whether the necessary rules have not taken up too much room in the debating chambers of Europe. The present-day arrangements for economic policy are often rule-based. To a certain extent, this seems inevitable in a continent-spanning Union with still wide disparities in development, income levels and historical "baggage".[74] Yet, by relying on rules, the Union unconsciously fosters two effects that it may wish to reconsider. First, the adversarial approach lamented throughout this contribution rests on enforcement of rules *against* Member States. Conflict and discord may be necessary elements in a system based on the rule of law but Europe may have neglected the societal effects of its approach, and the disruption that divisions regarding the meaning, or the application, of the rules bring. Of course, free debate may also sow discord but such disunity is the result of freely opposing ideas and inclinations rather than the result of one group enforcing the rules against the other. The uneven distribution of power among the subject of the rules reinforces this divisiveness. Second, by imposing rules, the Union forsakes its policy room, its discretion to reflect on the appropriate course of action given any new challenge. Naturally, such policy discretion requires matureness, of the policy debate, of the politicians and of the electorate. Europe clearly is not yet in such an ideal situation. And, even if it were to evolve into a sufficiently mature construct to develop continental debate, the need for rules remains. What rules should we apply then? Awareness of their origins and functions is needed. Rules emanate from a certain policy *consensus* or, seen somewhat less formally, from the *consensus* reigning in the most powerful States or circles of the Union. They may provide a bar to creative thinking. Reconsidering whether the current rules-dominated policy environment is suitable is what Europeans should be doing, to my mind. I see a link with the ADEMU research agenda. ADEMU stands for: A Dynamic Economic and Monetary Union.[75] This concerns a European Commission-funded research project focusing on the post-crisis policy response maps EMU developments, studies the monetary and fiscal structure of the EU and the Euro Area, and the mechanisms of fiscal policy coordination. Its investigations of risks to the long-run sustainability of EMU should lead to detailed institutional proposals aimed at mitigating these risks.[76]

[74]By way of example, Member States with a collective memory of hyper-inflation, like Germany or Bulgaria, are more likely to insist on price stability and strict budgetary rules than others.

[75]See: http://ademu-project.eu/.

[76]Disclosure: I am a member of the Advisory Committee of this largely macro-economic research project on the theoretical underpinnings of a redesigned institutional structure of EMU. ADEMU brings together eight research groups, headed by the European University Institute (EUI)'s Economics Professor Ramon Marimon; it also touches upon legal issues. The ADEMU project's work is undertaken under the responsibility of a Steering Committee, which has appointed the already mentioned Advisory Committee to provide "an external monitoring role and periodic advice to the ADEMU Consortium". The Advisory Committee also monitors the policy recommendations the Project is required to come forward with.

11 A Wider Perspective

Taking a wider perspective, I would like to end by drawing attention to a forthcoming book that questions whether EU law and policy are sufficiently humane. In his preface to this book,[77] Ferreira reflects:

> [...] the current circumstances, namely financial pressures, budgetary cuts, social instability and the present geographical and policy scope of the EU, require serious introspection and 'soul searching'. What can be done to ensure that the EU does not perish but, hopefully, becomes more a part of the solution than of the problem?.

Isn't is remarkable that a project, a construct that is about unity, is based so much on duality? This tendency to rely on sanctions and adversarial proceedings has only become more acute since the crisis.

As Ferreira rightly states, a dualistic focus, a focus on rights and conflicts, although these "retain an important role in society, as they allow individuals [and their social constructs, including States and regions] their essential space of autonomy, expression and self-esteem", is not conducive to a humane outcome:

> One key question is: where do ordinary human beings, in all their complexity and interconnectedness, feature in these debates?.

And:

> Should law not exist for people, for the sake of people? Can we not think of a more imaginative and just way of 'doing' law and justice, in order to offer a system more inclusive of all voices? Since law is a social, regulatory tool aimed at improving relationships between human beings for the sake of a 'good' society, what values should law promote? And how could these values become rooted in personal ways of life?[78]

The authors brought together in the book Ferreira writes the introduction to wish to engage in "a human-centred analysis", in which "humane-ness"[79] ("*humain*", "*menschlich*") is central. Ferreira defines it as follows: "[h]umaneness is the corrective of humanity when it is not at its best". He cites Rifkin's empathic civilisation vision of a collaborative and caring world, and his characterisation of the European Union as "as a cooperative and networked space, where '[m]ultilevel governance networks are like giant laboratories for the exploration of empathy'.".[80]

Throughout this contribution, the argument has been made that we should take such a wider, more-encompassing perspective. We do so by going beyond the confines of an individual academic perspective (law, economics, political science) and include a multitude of approaches in our research and discussion. We do so by

---

[77] Ferreira (2016).

[78] The personal imperative is clear from this quote by Ferreira (2016), taken from Douzinas (2000): "[...] we have been destined to be near Being and to care for the human as well as the other entities in which Being discloses itself.".

[79] The word humane also forms an acronym: HUMANE: Help Us Make A New Europe, as James Organ, quoted by Ferreira, found.

[80] Rifkin (2004), pp. 280 et seqq.

looking beyond the academic to the world, to include the effects on humans and their habitat of the rules we advocate and the policy choices we prefer. We do so by opening our hearts for, extending compassion to the humans in this land, and those coming to this land, and those beyond this land of ours, and—in line with a Treaty injunction[81]—by extending this compassion to other sentient beings.

References

Bauer MW, Becker S (2014) The unexpected winner of the crisis: the European Commission's strengthened role in economic governance. J Eur Integr 36(3):213–229

Bauer MW, Becker S (2016) Absolute gains are still gains: why the European Commission is a winner of the crisis, and unexpectedly so. A rejoinder to Eugénia da Conceição-Heldt. J Eur Integr 38(1):101–106

Begg I, Bongardt A, Nicolaïdis K, Torres F (2015) EMU and sustainable integration. J Eur Integr 37(7):803–816

Bickerton C (2013) European integration – from nation-states to member states. Oxford University Press, Oxford

Bini Smaghi L (2015) Governance and conditionality: toward a sustainable framework? J Eur Integr 37(7):755–768

Claeys G, Darvas Z, Wolff GB (2014) Benefits and drawbacks of European unemployment insurance. Bruegel Policy Brief 2014/06, September 2014. Available at: http://bruegel.org/wp-content/uploads/imported/publications/pb_2014_06_281114.pdf

Conceição-Heldt E (2015) Why the European Commission is not the "unexpected winner" of the Euro crisis: a comment on Bauer and Becker. J Eur Integr 38(1):1–6

Culver K, Giudice M (2013) Not a system but an order – an inter-institutional view of European Union law. In: Dickson J, Eleftheriadis P (eds) Philosophical foundations of European Union law. Oxford University Press, Oxford

Douzinas C (2000) The end of human rights. Hart, Oxford

Eleftheriadis P (2011) The moral distinctiveness of the European Union. Int J Constit Law 9 (3–4):695–713

Eleftheriadis P (2014) Misrule of the few – how the Oligarchs ruined Greece. Foreign Affairs, pp 139 et seqq

European Commission (1998) Proposal for a council decision on the representation and position taking of the community at international level in the context of economic and monetary union, COM(1998) 0637, 9 November 1998, withdrawn in 2015. OJEU C 392, 25 November 2015, pp 6 et seqq

European Commission (2015a) Assessment of the social impact of the new stability support programme for Greece, SWD(2015) 162 final, 19 August 2015. Available at: http://ec.europa.eu/economy_finance/assistance_eu_ms/greek_loan_facility/pdf/assessment_social_impact_en.pdf

[81]Article 13 TFEU: "In formulating and implementing the Union's agriculture, fisheries, transport, internal market, research and technological development and space policies, *the Union and the Member States shall, since animals are sentient beings, pay full regard to the welfare requirements of animals*, while respecting the legislative or administrative provisions and customs of the Member States relating in particular to religious rites, cultural traditions and regional heritage." (italics added).

European Commission (2015b) Proposal for a council decision laying down measures in view of progressively establishing unified representation of the euro area in the international monetary fund, COM(2015) 603 final, 21 October 2015

Ferreira N (2016) The human face of the European Union: are EU law and policy humane enough? An introduction. In: Ferreira N, Kostakopoulou T (eds) The human face of the European Union. Cambridge University Press, Cambridge (forthcoming). Available since 9 September 2015 at: http://papers.ssrn.com/sol3/papers.cfm?abstract_id=2658106

Glienicker Group (von Bogdandy A, Calliess C, Enderlein H, Fratzscher M, Fuest C, Mayer F, Schwarzer D, Steinbeis M, Stelzenmüller C, von Weizsäcker J, Wolff G) (2013) Towards a Euro Union, 17 October 2013. Available at: http://glienickergruppe.eu/en/towards-a-euro-union/

Gysi G (2015) Wir wollen den Euro retten aber anders ("We want to save the euro, but differently"), presentation before the Court of Justice of the EU during the oral hearing in Case C-62/14 (Gauweiler) concerning the OMT. Available at: http://www.gregorgysi.de/reden/einzelansicht/browse/3/zurueck/dr-gregor-gysi-reden/artikel/wir-wollen-den-euro-auch-retten-aber-anders/

Habermas J (2011) Zur Verfassung Europas. Ein Essay. Suhrkamp-Insel Verlag, Berlin

Hers J, Suyker W (2014) Structural budget balance: a love at first sight turned sour. CPB Policy Briefs, 21 October 2014. Available at: http://www.cpb.nl/en/publication/structural-budget-balance-love-first-sight-turned-sour

Jones E, Torres F (2015) An "economics" window on an interdisciplinary crisis. J Eur Integr 37 (7):713–722

Juncker J-C, Tusk D, Dijsselbloem J, Draghi M, Schulz M (2015) Report completing Europe's economic and monetary union, 22 June 2015. Available at: https://ec.europa.eu/priorities/sites/beta-political/files/5-presidents-report_en.pdf

Klaver J (2012) see: https://groenlinks.nl/mensen/jesse-klaver

Nicolaïdis K (2013) The idea of European demoicracy. In: Dickson J, Eleftheriadis P (eds) Philosophical foundations of European Union law. Oxford University Press, Oxford

Puetter U (2012) Europe's deliberative intergovernmentalism: the role of the Council and European Council in EU economic governance. J Eur Public Policy 19(2):161–178

Rifkin J (2004) The European dream, how europe's vision of the future is quietly eclipsing the American dream. Tarcher/Penguin

Rubio E (2016) Federalising the Eurozone: towards a true European budget? Policy Paper 155, 14 January 2016. Available at: http://www.institutdelors.eu

Singh D (2016) Safeguarding "critical social functions" post the global financial crisis. In: Ferreira N, Kostakopoulou T (eds) The human face of the European Union. Cambridge University Press, Cambridge (forthcoming)

Smits R (1997) The European Central Bank – institutional aspects. Kluwer, The Hague

Smits R (2015) European Central Bank's room for manoeuvre provisionally confirmed, blog on the website of the Amsterdam Center for European Law and Governance. Available at: https://acelg.blogactiv.eu/2015/01/19/european-central-bank%E2%80%99s-room-for-manoeuvre-provisionally-confirmed/

Trichet J-C (2011) Building Europe, building institutions, speech by the President of the ECB on receiving the Karlspreis 2011 in Aachen, 2 June 2011. Available at: https://www.ecb.europa.eu/press/key/date/2011/html/sp110602.en.html

Tumpell-Gugerell G (2014) Expert group on debt redemption fund and Eurobills. Final Report, 31 March 2014. Available at: http://ec.europa.eu/economy_finance/articles/governance/pdf/20140331_report_en.pdf

Weiler JHH (2012) Deciphering the political and legal DNA of European integration – an exploratory essay. In: Dickson J, Eleftheriadis P (eds) Philosophical foundations of European Union law. Oxford University Press, Oxford

More or Less Intergovernmental Cooperation Within the New EMU?

Frédéric Allemand

Abstract This chapter aims to analyse the recent shift in the allocation of powers within the EMU institutional framework. In the words of Angela Merkel, a new Union method is emerging from the Lisbon Treaty. The management of the subprime crisis and sovereign debt crisis gave rise to practical institutional arrangements and the adoption of new secondary law whereby the European Council, as well as the Euro Summit were conferred on new political responsibilities. However, as we argue, this development in intergovernmental cooperation takes place with proper regard for the institutional balance and the complex system for the balancing of powers within the EMU. Following all the crises and reforms, EMU governance is neither more supranational nor more intergovernmental. It is both at once. To our way of thinking, to try to set the two approaches against each other would be a sterile exercise. EMU governance—and, in a broader sense, EU governance—is intergovernmental and supranational. It cannot be otherwise, so long as the EU bears the imprint of a twofold requirement: to achieve unity while respecting diversity.

Contents

1 Introduction

Is European integration on its last legs? If we go along with Charles Kupchan, professor of international relations at Georgetown University and adviser to the National Security Council at the White House, where the risk to Europe lies is not in

F. Allemand (✉)
University of Luxembourg, Esch-sur-Alzette, Luxembourg
e-mail: frederic.allemand@uni.lu

L. Daniele et al. (eds.), *Democracy in the EMU in the Aftermath of the Crisis*,
DOI 10.1007/978-3-319-53895-2_4

the modest prospects of economic growth over the next few years but in the resurgence of State-centric attitudes:

> From London to Berlin to Warsaw, Europe is experiencing a renationalization of political life, with countries clawing back the sovereignty they once willingly sacrificed in pursuit of a collective ideal.[1]

A long time before the sovereign debt crisis started, this feeling had already been expressed at the time of the negotiations over the Lisbon Treaty. The determination to work for "an ever closer union among the peoples of Europe"[2] was still the watchword,[3] though it clashed, when it came to the detail, with a narrow formulation of the idea of shared interest. The expansion in the competences of the European Union (EU) went hand in hand with a reminder of the *Kompetenz-Kompetenz* of the signatory States.[4] The EU was reduced to the condition of being a creature of the Member States: they "confer [on it] competences to attain objectives they have in common,"[5] it being made clear that the principle of conferring competences meant that

> the EU acts *only* within the limits of the competences conferred on it by the Member States in the treaties to attain objectives laid down by those treaties.[6]

Seen in that light, the completion of institutional reform was interpreted as the "fossilising"[7] of a Europe which was at its last gasp. Perhaps these judgements went too far. The ideal of a united Europe is "that small hope" of peace and prosperity of which Charles Péguy wrote that it carries everything along with it. EU law has a transforming capacity[8] capable of running alongside and sustaining the drive for

[1]"*As Nationalism Rises, Will the European Union Fall?*", in Washington Post, 29 August 2010.

[2]Penultimate recital of the Preamble and Article 1, para. 2, TEU.

[3]This expression, which was removed during the discussions in the Convention, was brought back in by chance by the IGC lawyers in the summer of 2007. The new agreement for the United Kingdom in the EU approved by the European Council of 18 and 19 February 2016 made Article 1 TEU entirely devoid of application to the United Kingdom.

[4]Bundesverfassungsgericht, 12 October 1993, 2 BvR 2134/92 and 2 BvR 2159/92, *M. B.* v. *the law of 28 December 1992 on the Treaty on European Union of 7 February 1992* (known as the "Maastricht judgment"); and cited in the judgment on the Lisbon Treaty on 30 June 2009 (joined cases 2 BvE 2/08 and others).

[5]Article 1, subpara. 1, TEU.

[6]Article 5, subpara. 1, TEC lays down that "The Community shall act within the limits of the powers conferred upon it *by this Treaty* and of the objectives assigned to it therein". The replacement of the words "this Treaty" by "the Member States" is telling. Article 2 TFEU, in paras. 1 and 2, says: "When the Treaties confer on the Union [...]". The point of the difference is to emphasise that the EU rests on a double foundation: the wish of the Member States, from which all power derives, and the Treaties.

[7]Hanf (2009).

[8]Simon (2001).

European integration. That forward momentum can be seen at work specifically at times of crisis.

At a time of deadlock, any crisis is redemptive, constituting "the last chance for Europe"[9] to start afresh. In this connection, the subprime crisis in autumn 2008, then the sovereign debt crisis from spring 2010 onwards, were an opportunity for profound soul-searching and resulted in some previously unheard-of reforms in the field of Economic and Monetary Union (EMU). Although the Treaties have remained largely unchanged,[10] secondary law has been radically rewritten and supplemented by a range of instruments which fall within the international legal order or the national orders.[11] Do these developments also mark a change in the method of integration? A great many people have stressed the active involvement of national executive authorities in managing and resolving the subprime crisis and subsequent sovereign debt crisis.[12] There were many initiatives at the bilateral and multilateral levels and through the EU institutions which represent the Member States' interests, in other words the European Council and the Council. With the central position they occupy in terms of attention and discussion, these institutions are said to have contributed, through their involvement in economic governance, to the emergence of a "new intergovernmentalism".[13] A method based on coordination between intergovernmental players is said to be operating, thus safeguarding the fields of sovereignty from invasion by the EU.[14] This ascendancy of the intergovernmental institutions, with the European Council in first place, is indisputable. It does not, however, justify drawing any final conclusion regarding any intergovernmental trend in the EU[15] to the detriment of its supranational dimension. Any development in intergovernmental cooperation takes place with proper regard for the institutional balance (2) and the complex system for the ordering of powers within the EMU (3). In tandem with the affirmation of the political responsibility of the European Council and Euro Summits (4) there is a concomitant tightening up of the powers of the supranational institutions, including the Commission (5). Rather than being a new method for running the EU, this interlinking of intergovernmentalism and supranationalism reflects the subtlety of the integration process, in which there is always a balance between achieving unity and respecting diversity (6).

[9]Boone, Salomon (2009). There would otherwise be a close and present danger, see Tsoukalis (2012).

[10]The only amendment to be mentioned is to Article 136 TFEU, to which a new paragraph was added by decision of the European Council of 25 March 2011. OJEU L 91, 6 April 2011, p. 1.

[11]Allemand (2013) and Allemand and Martucci (2012a, b).

[12]We might also add the migration crisis since summer 2014.

[13]Puetter (2012, 2014).

[14]Majone (2005).

[15]Novak (2014).

2 The Dynamics of Institutional Balance

EU law is not ordinary law: it is supranational. Dressed in the finery of shared sovereign power, it creates rights and duties which directly incorporate the legal heritage of the Member States and their nationals.[16] This is a radical departure from traditional public law, where it is exceptional for a law originating outside the State to be able to pass directly into the national legal order and produce legal effects in it comparable to national law.[17] In the legal order of the EU, this exception becomes the rule. This "denationalisation" of the exercise of sovereign functions by a supranational authority—the European Communities and then the EU—sets a distance between the law and the political power of the masses.[18] Once it has broken loose from "the arrogance of the vassals",[19] the "denationalised" sovereign function recovers its full authority and power. Given the legal effects attaching to supranational law, the question which arises is what checks and balances this new European Leviathan[20] has against its own excesses.

Several safeguard clauses have been put in place. Thus, the EU may exercise only those powers conferred on it by the Treaties, its "constitutional charter" (a material limitation), and must do so in accordance with the objectives defined by its charter (a functional limitation).[21] What is more—and this is a subject to which we will be devoting our full attention—the very exercise of those powers is fragmentary in character. A feature of the institutional system is that there is a sharp distinction between the organ and the function: no organ has the exclusive exercise of a function, and no function is exercised by a single organ.[22] And it goes without saying that each institution acts within the limits of the powers conferred on it by the Treaties.[23] Legislative and budgetary powers are split between the Commission, which has the power of initiative, and the European Parliament and the Council, which share the power to adopt laws.[24] Law-making power may be delegated to the Commission under the supervision of Parliament and the Council. As for executive power, it is shared between the Council and the Commission. This allocation of responsibilities works against any concentration of power and requires continuous cooperation between the various institutions.[25] In so doing, it guarantees that the

---

[16]ECJ 5 February 1963, Case 26/62, *Van Gend en Loos*; 15 July 1964, Case 6/64 *Costa* v. *E.N.E.L.*

[17]Permanent Court of International Justice, 3 March 1928, *Consultative opinion on the powers of the Danzig courts* (Series B, Opinion No. 15, pp. 17–18).

[18]Ortega y Gasset (2010).

[19]Durand (1947).

[20]See, on this point, the serious charge of "despotic bureaucratism" levelled at Europe by Siedentop (2000).

[21]Article 5 TEU.

[22]Simon (2001).

[23]Article 13, para. 2, TEU.

[24]Articles 14, para. 1, and 16, para. 1, TEU.

[25]Article 14, para. 2, TEU.

diversity of legitimacies is expressed in the drafting of the law and, at a more fundamental level, makes it possible

> to ensure that the balance between the institutions provided for in the Treaty is maintained.[26]

The principle of a balance between the institutions is a founding principle,[27] both politically and legally. It shapes the institutional order of the EU. As Walter Ganshof Van der Meersch put it,

> [the] balance between equal and sovereign States is replaced by an institutional balance in which the institutions produce acts and elements which express and pursue the common interest.[28]

The principle of institutional balance indisputably constitutes a general principle of EU law.[29] It also has a meta-constitutional dimension[30] and, in our view, applies to the Member States in the exercise of their constituent power or their reserved legislative powers. It is significant in this connection that the institutionalisation of the European Council reinforces the political responsibility which the Treaties have acknowledged it has borne since the European Single Act—a responsibility which also encompasses its power of appointment. But that acknowledgement has the effect of explicitly ruling out any legislative function.[31] As argued at the time when the draft European Constitution, and then the Lisbon Treaty, were being discussed and adopted, the constitutional revisions helped to strengthen the balance between the institutions.[32]

The revision of Article 136 TFEU and the precautions taken during the negotiations on the Treaty establishing the European Stability Mechanism (ESM) testify to the importance attached to respecting the balance between the institutions. In its opinion on the draft decision amending Article 136 TFEU, the Commission made the requirement to safeguard the competences conferred on the EU and its institutions by the TEU and the TFEU a factor in assessing the validity of the reform, and reached a positive conclusion.[33] Consistency between the ESM and the

---

[26] ECJ 13 March 1992, Case C-282/90, *Industrie- en Handelsonderneming Vreugdenhil BV* v. *Commission*, para. 20.

[27] Schmitter (1993).

[28] Ganshof Van der Meersch (1975).

[29] Simon (1991).

[30] Louis and Ronse (2006).

[31] Article 15, para. 1, TEU.

[32] Valéry Giscard d'Estaing, Presentation of the draft European Constitution to the Thessaloniki European Council, 20 June 2003, quoted by Ponzano (2007); see also European Parliament, Resolution of 7 May 2009 on the impact of the Treaty of Lisbon on the development of the institutional balance of the European Union. OJEU C 212 E, 5 August 2010, p. 82.

[33] Commission, Opinion of 15 February 2011 on the draft European Council Decision amending Article 136 TFEU with regard to a stability mechanism for Member States whose currency is the euro. Brussels, COM(2011) 70 final, recital (12); European Parliament, Resolution of 23 March 2011 on the draft European Council Decision amending Article 136 TFEU, P7_TA(2011)0103, paragraph 19.

competences of the EU and of its institutions is particularly important with the prospect of this financial assistance mechanism being incorporated in the future into the institutional framework of the EU, within the Euro area.[34] The principle of institutional balance also guides the legislative initiatives which the Commission is reportedly taking to strengthen the economic governance of the EU.[35] In the *Pringle* judgment, the Court of Justice confirms that treaties negotiated by the Member States cannot alter the competences which the TEU and TFEU confer on the EU institutions.[36] Where new tasks are assigned to the EU institutions by international treaty, these must *be consistent* with the tasks conferred by the TEU and TFEU.[37] In the case of the Treaty on Stability, Coordination and Governance (TSCG), the planned incorporation of the treaty into EU law requires the principle of its compatibility with the TEU and TFEU to be written into its Preamble.[38] The TSCG may assign new tasks to the EU institutions, on condition that they do not in any way affect the tasks and powers derived by the EU institutions from EU law. Recognition for the meetings of the Heads of State or Government of the Euro area is accepted because the meetings have no legal effect on the institutional balance within the EU and are without prejudice to the powers of the European Council. Such meetings remain informal.

Compliance with the principle of institutional balance does not prohibit the establishment of new institutions, within or outside the framework of the EU Treaties, or amendments to the powers of the existing EU institutions, but such institutional developments must not lead to a revolution in the distribution of powers—unless it is in order to decide to alter the very nature of the EU.[39] If we take the long-term view, this forward momentum in the balance between the institutions offers glimpses of an ongoing process of neutralisation in the emergence of a power, of a legitimacy which is above the others.[40] The strengthening of intergovernmental elements invariably goes hand in hand with a similar pattern of development in the supranational elements and vice versa, according to

[34]Commission, Opinion of 15 February 2011, recital (14), European Parliament, Resolution of 23 March 2011, recital G.

[35]Commission, Opinion of 17 February 2011, recital (14).

[36]ECJ 27 November 2012, Case C-370/12, *Thomas Pringle* v. *Government of Ireland*, para. 158.

[37]*Ibid.*, para. 165.

[38]Article 2, para. 2, TSCG.

[39]In the course of the discussions in the 1970s about the establishment of a European Union, the Commission therefore proposed that there be a reorganisation of powers on the lines advocated by Montesquieu (one body, one function) and that it itself should disappear, to make way for a permanent "European Government" which would hold combined executive and administrative powers. See Commission, Report on European Union. Bull. EC 1975, Suppl. 5/75, p. 31, esp. point 98.

[40]For example: Commission, Report of the Working Party examining the problem of the extension of the powers of the European Parliament [Vedel Report]. Bull. EC, Suppl. 4/72, p. 75; Commission, Communication of 7 October 1981, The institutional system of the Community. Restoring the balance. Brussels, COM(81) 581. Bull. EC, Suppl. 3/82, p. 7.

> a kind of to and fro movement between what comes under the heading of integration and what reminds one of cooperation.[41]

This makes the institutional architecture excessively complicated[42]: the number of bodies and organs, whether institutionalised or not, increases, and their powers grow as time goes by.[43]

3 The Atypical Institutional Character of EMU

Economic and monetary union is not a policy area like others.

> Despite the fact that economic policy and monetary policy are mentioned in the Community part of the Treaty, EMU's institutional mechanisms differ at several points from the traditional 'Community method'

it has been observed.[44] The highly political dimension of monetary unification, the firm hold which the Member States keep on their powers over economic policy, the concern of certain Maastricht Treaty negotiators to make sure that the ECB's interlocutor was an intergovernmental body[45] or indeed the discussions around the question of whether to put EMU into the Community pillar[46] all helped to produce a new kind of outcome in terms of the allocation of economic and monetary responsibilities: a "combination of supranationalism and intergovernmentalism", in the words of Professor Francis Snyder.[47] Some people have interpreted the atypical character of EMU's institutional organisation as the expression of an "independent institutional subsystem which is outside common EU law".[48]

These specific characteristics are widely known. Here is a brief reminder. EMU is based on a "dynamic balance"[49] or a "systematic asymmetry"[50] between two pillars. The nature and distribution of powers within EMU reflect distinct, or indeed opposite, approaches: in response to the supranational integration of monetary policy comes intergovernmental cooperation in the coordination of economic

---

41 Lutton (1985).

42 Monar (2011).

43 Schwarzer (2012).

44 Doutriaux (1992).

45 Balleix-Banerjee and Portelli (1997).

46 See especially Louis (1995).

47 "EMU is a combination of supranationalism and intergovernmentalism". See Snyder (1994), esp. p. 68. As has been widely commented, the balance between these two conflicting approaches is not peculiar to EMU, and it applied to all the fields up for negotiation in 1991. For example: Dehousse (1994).

48 Gautron (2009). The subsystem idea has also been taken up by Pertek (2006).

49 Noël (1990).

50 Louis (2000).

policies, while foreign exchange policy adopts a hybrid approach. These differences can be found in the institutional organisation of EMU.

In the monetary pillar, the Member States which adopted the Euro have transferred their powers over monetary and exchange-rate policy to the EU. The Eurosystem (i.e. the European Central Bank (ECB) and the national central banks of the Member States whose currency is the Euro) is responsible for defining and conducting the EU's monetary policy[51] independently.[52] The exchange-rate policy is run by the Council, working closely with the ECB.[53]

In the economic pillar, the Member States, even if they have adopted the Euro, still retain their competence. However, given the interdependence between national and European economic policies on the one hand, and between those and monetary policy on the other, economic policies have to be conducted in a manner consistent with the general aims of the Treaties and the broad economic policy guidelines (BEPGs) adopted jointly. The EU is competent to coordinate economic policies.[54] Here the intergovernmental institutions have a firm hold. The European Council's power to act as a driving force and give guidelines takes specific form in EMU: the European Council intervenes in the process of drawing up BEPGs by adopting conclusions[55] and in the Euro area enlargement procedure.[56] In the area of employment, which is closely linked to EMU, it examines the employment situation in the EU every year and adopts conclusions and guidelines on the subject.[57] As for the Council, it is the central institution responsible for coordination.[58]

The contrast between the two pillars of EMU diminishes as soon as one takes account of the ways in which legislative or executive functions are exercised within them. Despite the non-standard configuration of the powers conferred on the EU institutions,

> [they] are nevertheless still to be found performing their traditional functions.[59]

A striking feature of the normative power is the abundance of special or *ad hoc* legislative procedures which give the lion's share to the Council, in both the economic and the monetary pillars. The implementing measures for Articles 123 to 125 TFEU are adopted by the Council acting on a proposal from the

[51] Article 127 TFEU.

[52] Article 130 TFEU and Article 7 of the Statutes of the ESCB and the ECB.

[53] Article 219 TFEU.

[54] Article 120 TFEU.

[55] Article 121, para. 2, TFEU.

[56] Article 140, para. 2, TFEU.

[57] Article 148, paras. 1 and 2, TFEU.

[58] Article 16, para. 1, TEU and Article 1 TFEU; conclusions of the Luxembourg European Council, 13 December 1997, DOC C/97/400, para. 44.

[59] Louis (1993).

Commission and after consulting the European Parliament.[60] This procedure replaces the cooperation procedure laid down in *ex* Article 252 TEC and abolished by the Lisbon Treaty. This development is not to the advantage of the European Parliament. It loses its power to block in return for a mere power of consultation. Even so, the ordinary legislative procedure is not completely excluded from EMU. Article 294 TFEU is the legal basis for the adoption of the multilateral surveillance arrangements, the revision of a range of technical provisions in the ESCB and ECB Statutes and, lastly, the adoption of the measures required for the use of the Euro as a single currency.[61] It also applies with regard to the adoption of the surveillance measures specific to the Euro area Member States.[62] Monitoring power is shared between the Council and the Commission. It is the Council's job to adopt the bulk of the legal measures, whether binding or not, regarding the Member States. The Treaties give the Commission autonomous power under the multilateral surveillance procedure. It performs this monitoring task by adopting a "warning" addressed to Member States whose economic policies are not consistent with the BEPGs or which risk jeopardising the functioning of EMU.[63] The Council retains the right to make a back-up recommendation. The difference between what the Commission's action and that of the Council are called makes no difference as regards the legal effects: it emphasises the higher political authority of the Council in the exercise of the power to monitor the Member States' compliance with their obligations in relation to coordinating their economic policies. Nevertheless, the very technical dimension of the economic content means that in practice the Commission's "role as guardian of the Treaties" is strengthened. Its ability to conduct surveillance, perform technical analyses and draw up reports is pivotal to the proper functioning of the economic pillar (see Sect. 5).

In contrast to the economic pillar, the monetary pillar, by its nature, places limits on the development of intergovernmental features. Monetary stability is based on a principle of independence whereby the Eurosystem in general and the ECB in particular have to have the powers needed in order to carry out their missions. An "intrusion" into the monetary pillar by any institution other than the ECB is not prohibited but it is restricted. This applies, in particular, to the adoption by the Council of measures to extend the powers of the monetary institution and to the arrangements governing the specifications of Euro coins or the use of the single currency.[64] Regarding the actual implementation of monetary policy,

---

[60] Article 125, para. 2, TFEU.

[61] Articles 121, para. 6, 129, para. 3, and 133 TEU. However, there are some useful adjustments to the ordinary legislative procedure in the monetary field: consultation of the ECB is allowed for, or the procedure can be initiated by the ECB through the adoption of a recommendation sent to the Council. In the latter case, the Commission is consulted.

[62] Article 136, para. 1, TFEU.

[63] Article 121, para. 4, TFEU.

[64] Articles 127, para. 6, 129, paras. 2 and 3, and 132, para. 3, TFEU.

> the power of appraisal was conferred unreservedly on a Central Bank, with the structure of the European System of Central Banks operating implicitly on a federal basis, but one which was independent of the Community method.[65]

The impermeability of the monetary pillar to the interference of intergovernmental features, in particular, is proving problematic in the area of the legal and political balance which has to be struck between institutions and separate areas of legitimacy within EMU. Since 2012, the ECB has played a major role in the rescue of the Euro area. Maintaining a good balance between the supranational and intergovernmental approaches in EMU involves strengthening the intergovernmental aspects within the economic pillar.[66] That, of course, is what makes the whole subject so complicated. On the one hand, the economic pillar deals with policies essential to the functioning of the welfare State, e.g. budgetary and structural policies. To use a phrase coined by Pierre Werner, they are "the last bastion of sovereignty". This explains why Member States constantly oppose any additional transfer of competences to the EU in this pillar. Only coordination competences are conferred on the EU. At the same time, policy coordination, if it is to be effective, cannot be based on an overly intergovernmental approach.

> [Coordination] is a method which encourages discussion, but it does not lead to decisions,

Jean Monnet considers in his *Mémoires*.

> It is not a way of transforming the relationships between people and between countries in circumstances where unity is required. It is the expression of national power, as it actually is; [...].[67]

The challenge now is to strengthen coordination, in other words to open it up more to the supranational approach, without, however, slipping into integration.[68] In this context, new approaches to the application of the principle of institutional balance need to be adopted; it must be achieved *in another way*.

4 Intergovernmentalism: Special Leadership in Crisis Period

The significant role which the Maastricht Treaty gave to the Heads of State or Government in EMU is well known. Since 2008, this special feature has been heightened by the cross effect of several factors. The Lisbon Treaty institutionalises the European Council: it confirms its role and powers, and formalises and strengthens its internal organisational arrangements. A succession of major

---

[65] Quermonne (2001).

[66] On this question, Jean-Paul Jacqué points out that institutional balance is developing in an uncontrolled way. "It has taken place without prior reflection, simply pulled along by the strongest current." See Jacqué (2004).

[67] Monnet (1976).

[68] Allemand (2009).

financial and economic crises has led the leading European political bodies to show a greater sense of responsibility. The sovereign debt crisis is a forceful reminder of how scant the effectiveness of coordinating economic policies and budgetary discipline is when it is left to the Council. The sense of political responsibilities vested in the Heads of State or Government is supposed to reduce the likelihood of the kinds of unwarranted indulgence we have seen from ministers in the past,[69] while at the same time enabling thoroughgoing, open and direct exchanges to take place between leading figures about the line to be followed when it comes to the sustainability of public finances or macroeconomic imbalance.[70] In addition to this, the crisis period has been a good opportunity for trial-running the concept of "pro-active politics" put forward by Nicolas Sarkozy in the 2007 presidential election campaign and reaffirmed as a solution to the EU's lack of efficiency and legitimacy since he was elected President of the French Republic.[71] There is, too, the straight-forward foreign policy being pursued by Angela Merkel.[72] Lastly, this political affirmation of the European Council and national political leaders is being spurred on by the trend towards pushing the Commission to the back—a development which has been under way since President Santer's Commission resigned in 1999.[73]

Between February 2010 and January 2016, the European Council met 41 times and the Euro area Heads of State or Government 14 times. Never in the history of European integration had there been such a frenetic succession of meetings of Europe's highest political leaders. The European Council staked its claim to be seen as the body directing the integration process. Its conclusions or the press releases eschewed evasive forms of words and set out detailed solutions to be applied by the EU institutions and the Member States. The authority which the European Council's positions must be acknowledged as possessing was stated explicitly with regard to the BEPGs by the Ecofin Council of March 2008:

> Once they [the BEPGs] have been approved by the European Council, the guidelines and recommendations by country will be adopted by the Council *without further debate*.[74]

[69]At the same time, we remember President Nicolas Sarkozy coming to the Ecofin Council of 10 July 2007 to argue the case for the tax shield and defend a postponement of the date for returning to balanced budgets—thus going back on the pledge given by the preceding Government when the Berlin agreement of April 2007 was approved.

[70]On this point, see the firm position in favour of a clear and detailed political dialogue for which Jean-Claude Juncker made a fervent case during the debate on economic governance in the European Parliament on 16 November 2011: "We are not a government if we fail to nurture meaningful debate amongst ourselves [the Heads of State or Government] on the key points of political choices which together we will make but which we will have to apply individually in our different countries." (Jean-Claude Juncker, Speech on the occasion of a priority debate on economic governance at a plenary sitting of the European Parliament, Strasbourg, 16 November 2011).

[71]Allemand (2009).

[72]Fabbrini (2013).

[73]Schwarzer (2012).

[74]Council (Ecofin) press release, 2,857th session, 4 March 2008, 7192/08, p. 7.

This political statement has legal consequences in EMU. The European Council's position in the European Semester and in the budgetary discipline and macroeconomic imbalance procedures has been considerably strengthened. In keeping with its strategic role,[75] the European Council has to keep a close watch on the application of multilateral surveillance by, in particular, examining Council reports on compliance by the Member States with the recommendations adopted pursuant to Article 121, para. 4,[76] or Article 126, para. 8, TFEU.[77] The times at which the Heads of State or Government intervene are not without significance: the Head of State or Government meet and hold discussions just before the financial penalties are adopted by the Council. Some will see this as a last opportunity of persuading the authorities of the Member State concerned to comply with EU requirements before a penalty is applied. This involvement has the effect of including the European Council President among the authorities invited to take part in the economic dialogue with the European Parliament.[78]

These developments do not give a very full picture of the twofold shifting of political authority which was carried out during the crisis. The concentration of difficulties in the Euro area has led to crisis management and the defining of the steps needed to escape from it being dealt with *beforehand* by the Heads of State or Government of the Member States sharing the single currency and then being formalised by the European Council. The idea of regular Euro Summits, promoted by the French authorities,[79] initially met with resistance from the other Member States, including Germany.[80] There were fears that it would lead to the

[75]The link between the European Council's strategic function and the increased part it is called upon to play in implementing the multilateral surveillance procedure is stressed in recital (14) to Regulation (EU) No. 1175/2011 of the European Parliament and of the Council of 16 November 2011 amending Council Regulation (EC) No. 1466/97. OJEU L 306, 23 November 2011, p. 12.

[76]Articles 2, a and b, and 6 of Council Regulation (EC) No. 1466/97, as amended in 2011.

[77]Article 10 of Regulation (EU) No. 1176/2011 of the European Parliament and of the Council cited above, and Article 4, para. 2, of Council Regulation (EC) No. 1467/97, as amended in 2011.

[78]See, in particular, Article 3 of Regulation (EU) No. 1173/2011 of the European Parliament and of the Council of 16 November 2011 on the effective enforcement of budgetary surveillance in the euro area. OJEU L 306, 23 November 2011, p. 1; Article 6 of Regulation (EU) No. 1174/2011 of the European Parliament and of the Council of 16 November 2011 on enforcement measures to correct excessive macroeconomic imbalances in the euro area. OJEU L 306, 23 November 2011, p. 8.

[79]Nicolas Sarkozy, Speech to the European Parliament, Strasbourg, 21 October 2008. [Online] URL: http://www.elysee.fr/president/les-actualites/discours/2008/allocution-devant-le-parlement-europeen.5193.html; and speech by the President of the Republic, Toulon, 11 December 2011. The European Parliament backed the initiative as soon as the first meeting of the Heads of State or Government of the Euro area was held on 12 October 2008. See European Parliament resolution of 22 October 2008 on the European Council of 15 and 16 October 2008, P6_TA(2008)0506, para. 4. For an analysis, see Dyson and Marcussen (2010).

[80]In February 2010 Chancellor Angela Merkel said: "Deshalb ist es für mich auch wichtig, dass wir uns im Sinne einer wirklichen Wirtschaftsregierung als Rat aller 27 europäischen Mitgliedstaaten verstehen" ("To our way of thinking, we see the Council as an economic government of the 27 Member States." Translation taken from a French version produced by the Elysée.) Joint press conference, Paris, 4 February 2010. [Online] URL: http://www.archives.elysee.fr.

independence of the ECB being called into question, and that there would be a risk of the common interest being reduced merely to the interests of the Euro area. It was, of course, pointed out that EMU was a matter that concerned all the members of the EU. All the Member States were expected, eventually, to adopt the single currency.[81] In that respect, being part of the Euro area not only created a responsibility towards the other Member States which had adopted the Euro: it also created a responsibility towards all the Member States and the EU. To twin the European Council with a Euro Summit would have affected the unitary function of the former[82] without guaranteeing that the latter's positions were globally consistent with the common interest. The part played by these select summits in practice between the end of 2008 and the end of 2011 led in the end to their being made official by the TSCG. In the interests of compromise, the TSCG remains vague on the powers of these summits[83,84] and on coordinating the work of this body with the European Council.[85] Article 12, para. 6, TSCG merely requires the President of the Euro Summits to keep the other, non-participating Member States *closely* informed of the preparations for the summits and their conclusions.[86] In addition, there is provision for a special association arrangement for the Heads of State or Government of the States signatory to the TSCG which are not part of the Euro area.[87] The TSCG also lays down that the President of the Euro Summit shall be elected by the Heads of State or Government of the Euro area when they elect the President of the

---

[81]With the notable exceptions of the United Kingdom and Denmark, which have an opt-out clause.

[82]Capotorti (1987).

[83]The ambiguity arises from the difference of approach as between France and Germany with regard to the final aim of these summits, as a comparison of the French and German versions of the joint letter sent by Angela Merkel and Nicolas Sarkozy to the President of the Council on 17 August 2011 suggests. Paris describes the Euro Summits as "*la pierre angulaire du nouveau* gouvernement *économique de la zone euro*". Berlin sees them only "*als Eckpfeiler der verbesserten wirtschaftlichen* Steuerung *des Euro-Währungsgebiet*." (our emphasis). The German concept of *Steuerung* refers to the ability to guide, to stimulate, not to lead or govern (*Regierung*). It is worth pointing out, in particular, that two years of crisis had evidently not narrowed the conceptual gap between the two banks of the Rhine, as that linguistic subtlety was already to be found in the statement by the Heads of State or Government of the Euro area of 25 March 2010.

[84]For a discussion of the responsibilities conferred on the Euro Summit, see below, and also Louis (2012).

[85]The same applies to the debate on the order of precedence as between the Euro Summit and the European Council. The Euro Summit Statement of 26 October 2011 stated that its meetings were held after those of the European Council (see Euro Summit Statement, Annex I, *Ten measures to improve the governance of the Euro area*, para. 1). The TSCG leaves the question open.

[86]A stipulation which is not found in Protocol (No. 14) on the Eurogroup but which still lies behind the Resolution of the European Council on economic policy coordination in stage 3 of EMU and on Treaty Articles 109 and 109b (European Council Presidency Conclusions, Luxembourg, 12 and 13 December 1997, C/97/400, Annex I, para. 6): "Whenever matters of common interest are concerned they will be discussed by Ministers of all Member States."

[87]Article 12, para. 3, TSCG. This keenness to open out to the Member States outside the Euro area led to this provision being the only one to apply to all the contracting States as soon as the TSCG entered into force, including those which had not yet ratified the text (Article 14, para. 4, TSCG).

European Council, for the same term of office. The Treaty does not require these different functions to be performed by the same holder, but it strongly urges that they should be.[88] In fact, on 30 August 2014, the Heads of State or Government of the Euro area elected Donald Tusk to the post of President of the Euro Summit, after he had been appointed President of the European Council.[89]

The second shift in authority is the one which took place to the advantage of the Franco-German tandem. Crisis resolution progressed (or stagnated) in time with the agreements (or disagreements) between the two leading economic powers and main contributors to the Euro area's financial assistance facilities.[90] The adoption of the first rescue plan for Greece, of the Euro Plus Pact and even of the TSCG followed the same pattern: there were joint Franco-German consultations prior to a meeting of representatives of the Euro area Member States which itself took place before a meeting of the European Council. The President of the European Council was kept informed. Thus the crisis management points to there having been competition and a ranking of political responsibilities in order of importance: the European Council was the final stage in a decision-making chain with the Franco-German tandem at the bottom. Even though it did not affect the functioning of the institutions directly, the over-powerful hold which the "Franco-German executive board" had on European affairs fed into a feeling that European governance was being taken hostage by a minority and that there was a breakdown of the balances between "large" and "small" Member States, between the intergovernmental approach and the supranational approach.[91]

The strengthening of the authority of the Heads of State or Government in the governance of the EMU concealed a severe deterioration in the position of the Council.[92] Its negotiating capacity was being hampered by the guidelines—sometimes couched in very precise terms—of the European Council on the political issues of the day. Its negotiating capacity was also faced with competition from—and was being stripped of its content by—the Eurogroup. The Eurogroup asserted itself as the decisive ministerial body, the one where the loose ends of negotiations are tied up. The Eurogroup benefited from official *status* having been conferred on

[88]In its conclusions, the European Council of 23 October 2011 laid down the principles governing the link between the two posts of President; it was also noted that, pending the election of the President of the Euro Summit, the President of the European Council (Herman van Rompuy at the time) would also hold that post in the Euro area.

[89]Decision of the Heads of State or Government of the Contracting Parties to the TSCG whose currency is the euro appointing the President of the Euro Summit. Brussels, 30 August 2014, 11949/14.

[90]de Charentenay (2010), p. 590.

[91]Among the criticisms, there was the firm stand taken by Belgian Commissioner Karel de Gucht in December 2011: "If France and Germany want to concert their positions, that's their right. But Europe cannot function on the basis of an executive board. That has never worked and it never will!" See "*L'Europe ne peut pas fonctionner sur la base d'un directoire franco-allemand!*", in Levif.be, 7 December 2011.

[92]Novak (2014).

the Euro Summits, for which it became the preparatory body. Its structure was reinforced, in particular, by the appointment of a permanent chairman of the Eurogroup Working Group set up within the Economic and Financial Committee (EFC).[93] Against this background, the Ecofin Council was still, formally speaking, the institution responsible for economic policy coordination.[94] But the day-to-day management of the Euro area was set at the level of the Eurogroup, which "will, together with the Commission and the ECB, remain at the core", as the Euro Summit Statement of 26 October 2011 says.[95] A comparison of this text with the European Council Conclusions of December 1997 on the mandate of the Eurogroup and its relations with the Ecofin Council offers a striking contrast: the Ecofin Council's coordinating role is no longer mentioned! The future course seems to have been laid out: the Ecofin Council would, at best, become a place for holding discussions with the Member States not in the Euro area, and, at worst, a mere rubber-stamp. Another cause of the weakening of the Council was inherent in the constitution of the Ecofin Council: the expansion of the fields covered by budgetary discipline and the macroeconomic imbalances procedure mobilised all the configurations of the Council and seemed to set them in competition with the Ecofin configuration when it came to evaluating and monitoring the various macroeconomic policies.[96] Lastly, the introduction of inverse qualified majority voting for the adoption of the surveillance measures or new penalties laid down by the Six Pack was a sign both of a concern for effectiveness and of mistrust of the Council. The weakening of the Council opened up another prospect for the striking of political balance between the institutions: in order to safeguard the balance between intergovernmentalism and supranationalism, the strengthening of one intergovernmental element (European Council, Euro Summit, Eurogroup) was offset by the weakening of another intergovernmental element (Council).

---

[93]Euro Summit Statement, Brussels, 26 October 2011, in Annex I, "Ten measures to improve the governance of the euro area", para. 7. The setting up of this working group was referred to in Article 1 of Protocol (No. 14) on the Eurogroup. The Euro Summit Statement laid down that the President of the Working Group will "In principle [...] be elected at the same time as the chair of the Economic and Financial Committee." It did not define the procedure for appointing its President. Considering the close ties between the Working Group and the EFC, it may be supposed that the rule for appointing the President of the EFC (a majority of its members) would be adopted. The EFC statute revised in 2012 (Council Decision of 26 April 2012. OJEU L 121, 8 May 2012, p. 22) throws light on relations between the Presidents of the EFC and of the Eurogroup Working Group: the President of the latter is among the figures who may be elected to the post of President of the EFC.

[94]Articles 16 TEU and 5 TFEU.

[95]Euro Summit Statement, Brussels, 26 October 2011, para. 32.

[96]Symptomatically, the European Council Conclusions and Euro Summit Statements regularly called for the involvement of all configurations of the Council, without there being any special mention of the Ecofin Council. See, for example, the Euro Plus Pact annexed to the conclusions of the Heads of State or Government of the Euro area, Brussels, 11 March 2011, and Jean-Claude Juncker, Speech on the occasion of a priority debate [...], cited above.

5 Supranationalism: Day-to-Day Leadership by Management

It has looked as if the heavy involvement of the Heads of State or Government in managing and resolving the crises which have hit the EU has stifled the Commission's power of initiative. The reality is more complex and does not warrant the conclusion that the Commission is disappearing from the scene.[97]

Since 2008, the Heads of State or Government and the Commission have undeniably been in competition with each other in the area of political initiatives: the "political impetus" of the former is responded to by the "appropriate initiatives" of the latter. At the European Council of March 2010, the task of giving thought to reforming economic governance was assigned to a special working group directed by the President of the European Council and consisting of representatives of the Member States (i.e. the Finance Ministers), of the rotating Presidency and of the ECB. This group was set up "in cooperation" with the Commission. Before the group had had a chance to submit a preliminary, intermediate report to the European Council of June, the Commission adopted two communications sketching the outlines of a revised EMU.[98] On 29 September, it robbed the working group's final report, scheduled for mid-October,[99] of any effect by publishing a series of six legislative proposals (the Six Pack) which were a radical overhaul of economic governance. Thereafter, the principle of consideration by a working group was dropped in favour of a lighter arrangement centring on the President of the European Council. The President was given responsibility for putting forward proposals, road maps and reports. He was required, however, to act "in *close* consultation",[100] "in *close* cooperation"[101] (our italics) or "in collaboration" with the Presidents of the Commission and the Eurogroup.[102] Although its President was associated in a personal capacity with the discussions led by the President of the

[97]Cisotta (2013) and Bauer and Becker (2014).

[98]Communications from the European Commission, *Reinforcing economic policy coordination*. Brussels, 12 May 2010, COM(2010) 250 final; *Enhancing economic policy coordination for stability, growth and jobs—Tools for stronger EU economic governance*. Brussels, 30 June 2016, COM(2010) 367 final.

[99]Report of the Task Force to the European Council, *Strengthening economic governance in the EU*. Brussels, 21 October 2010. At the same time, the Commission emphasised in the explanatory statement on its legislative proposals that a constructive relationship had been established between the Commission and the working group. It added that the working group had based the bulk of its contributions on the Commission's work.

[100]Statement by the Heads of State or Government of the Euro area and the EU institutions, Brussels, 21 July 2011, para. 16.

[101]Conclusions of the European Council, Brussels, 23 October 2011, para. 7; Euro Summit Statement, Brussels, 26 October 2011 (dated 8 November 2011), para. 35.

[102]Conclusions of the European Council, Brussels, 28 and 29 June 2012, EUCO 76/12, para. 4. Although this had not been provided for in October 2011, the President of the ECB was included in the discussions led by the President of the European Council.

European Council, the Commission retained the right to adopt any appropriate initiative. Once again forestalling the submission of the report by the President of the European Council, the Commission launched the debate concerning a substantial review of EMU by releasing *A blueprint for a deep and genuine economic and monetary union*.[103] A week later, the President of the European Council submitted his report to the European Council.[104] The fact is that since then the only new initiatives have been those adopted by the Commission, whether it be the expert group set up to consider the feasibility of a pooling of public debt or the Task Force set up with the EIB in October 2014 to identify practical steps to stimulate investment. It is worth noting that the Commission's role in providing political impetus was recognised by the Euro Summit of 24 October 2014. The Summit invited the President of the Commission to prepare the next steps for better economic governance in the Euro area, in close cooperation with the Presidents of the Euro Summit, the Eurogroup and the ECB.[105] The next meeting of the European Council, in December, confirmed that invitation. The President of the European Parliament was invited by President Juncker to contribute to the discussions. In the report tabled in June 2015, the President of the Commission announced that his institution intended, in spring 2017, to present a White Paper on the precise arrangements for the transition to a genuine Economic and Monetary Union.[106]

Apart from cases of crisis management, the sharing between the Commission and the European Council of the power to give impetus was formally recognised in the establishment of the European Semester. National reform programmes had to be presented and evaluated in a manner consistent with the general guidelines issued by the Commission and the European Council. This was directed at the Commission's Annual Growth Survey and the conclusions of the March European Council. These guidelines had a structuring effect: they are issued at the beginning of the annual surveillance cycle and serve as points of reference for all the parties involved, from the Member States to the EU institutions, or indeed the social partners. The Euro area Member States' budgetary policies must be consistent with them.[107]

The reforms brought in by the Six Pack extended and deepened the area of practical application of economic policy coordination with a level of detail which verged on integration. This increased the risks of failure to comply with the aims

---

[103]Communication from the Commission, *A blueprint for a deep and genuine economic and monetary union. Launching a European Debate*, Brussels, 30 November 2012, COM(2012) 777 final/2.

[104]Herman van Rompuy, *Towards a genuine Economic and Monetary Union*, Brussels, 5 December 2012.

[105]Euro Summit Statement, Brussels, 24 October 2014.

[106]Juncker et al. (2015), p. 5.

[107]Article 3 of Regulation (EU) No. 473/2013 of the European Parliament and of the Council of 21 May 2013 on common provisions for monitoring and assessing draft budgetary plans and ensuring the correction of excessive deficit of the Member States in the euro area. OJEU L 140, 27 May 2013, p. 11.

and recommendations approved by the Council. The legal and political psychodrama of autumn 2003 over the sanctions against France and Germany showed the limits of economic policy coordination placed under the responsibility of the Council. Political assessment based on extra-legal grounds was damaging not just to the trust between European partners but also to the authority of the rule of law. To put oneself in the hands of political institutions was tantamount to making the principle of equality before the law secondary to economic, financial and geopolitical power relations. The close interdependence between macroeconomic situations required the rules of the game to be the same for all the Member States, as the European Council put it in June 2010. Armed with the experience gained, the legislature did not propose to return to the "mistakes made during the first decade of the economic and monetary union".[108] Greater involvement of the Commission to ensure compliance with EU law was imperative, having regard to its role as the institution which safeguards the overall interests of the EU. Its independence enables it to conduct an assessment which is impartial, objective and equal as regards all the Member States.[109] It ensures that they honour their undertakings on equal terms and that no one can take advantage of breaches or failures to act on the part of its partners in order to fail to comply with its own obligations.[110] During the negotiations on the Six Pack, the European Parliament secured a strengthening of the Commission's powers at each stage in the economic policy surveillance procedure: assessments specific to each Member State, on-site missions, recommendations and warnings. This aspect was mentioned in the recitals to all the regulations, including Regulation (EU) No. 1177/2011 adopted by the Council.[111]

The Commission's most important role is expressed in different forms depending on the areas of economic governance under consideration. The multilateral surveillance procedure for economic policies and budgetary discipline are described in detail in the Treaties, in Articles 121 and 126 TFEU respectively. The Commission's role and powers develop within the limits laid down by these provisions. Thus the new regulations recognise the Commission's power to make a legislative *proposal* for adoption by the Council of measures relating to the provisions in the Treaties which also recognise that power, i.e. Article 121, para. 4, and Article 126, para. 6, TFEU. In other cases (which are the majority), the Commission only has a power of *recommendation*, so that Article 293 TFEU cannot then be invoked. Of a total of 46 measures (decisions or recommendations) to be adopted by

[108]This growing awareness was mentioned in the recitals to the five regulatory texts which comprised the Six Pack. This point was not in the original legislative proposals and was the result of amendments tabled by the European Parliament.

[109]Noël (1962).

[110]*Ibid.*

[111]Recital (10) of Council Regulation (EU) No. 1177/2011; also: recitals (7) of Regulation (EU) No. 1173/2011 of the European Parliament and of the Council and (12) of Regulation (EU) No. 1175/2011 of the European Parliament and of the Council.

the Council, the Commission has a power of proposal in only four cases![112] To minimise this difficulty and re-establish the Commission's authority in the decision-making process, the legislature introduced the principle of inverse qualified majority voting. On the model of the procedures followed in the context of comitology, the principle was a simple one: a Commission recommendation was regarded as having been adopted by the Council unless the Member States (among those qualified to vote) opposed it by qualified majority or simple majority, within a time limit of ten days following its adoption by the Commission. This special voting arrangement applies to sanctions adopted in relation to the preventive and corrective aspects of the SGP and under the procedure for macroeconomic imbalances.

The Commission genuinely gained in terms of responsibility in the new procedures established by the Six Pack and the Two Pack. The Treaty defined the procedures in less detail, leaving more room for manoeuvre for secondary law. This applied to the procedure for preventing and correcting macroeconomic imbalances, the procedure for stronger economic and budgetary surveillance of Member States experiencing or threatened with serious difficulties with respect to their financial stability and the procedure for assessing draft budgetary plans. Without going into detail, let us just observe that the surveillance of budgetary plans removed the Council completely from the system—the Eurogroup is informed and considered the Commission's opinions on national plans. As for the reinforced surveillance system provided for in Regulation (EU) No. 472/2013 of the European Parliament and of the Council, the power of deciding whether it should be applied to a Member State belongs solely to the Commission. Regulation (EU) No. 472/2013, which is based on Article 121 TFEU, exploits its full potential in order to extend and intensify the Commission's surveillance functions. Surveillance is comprehensive, covering the economic, budgetary and financial aspects. The authorities of the Member State under surveillance are bound by obligations to communicate and inform regularly and in detail. Missions in the Member State concerned may be organised. The EFC must be kept regularly informed. The Council intervenes only where surveillance by the Commission and the dialogue set up with the national authorities concerned are not adequate to bring about changes in local economic policies or reduce the risks of instability. The Council, acting on a proposal from the Commission, may recommend appropriate corrective measures to the Member State or that it draw up a macroeconomic adjustment programme.[113]

As many of the parties involved have also pointed out, the Commission's high-level know-how and its experience of assessment have helped to make it one of the key players in implementing the financial assistance arrangements. The Commission is involved in the performance of the tasks of assessing applications for financial assistance, negotiating the memorandum of understanding on the terms

[112]Article 6, para. 6, third indent, Article 10, para. 2, second indent of Council Regulation (EC) No. 1466/97; Article 3, para. 3, of Council Regulation (EC) No. 1467/97; Article 7, para. 2, of Regulation No. 1176/2011 of the European Parliament and of the Council.

[113]Article 3 of Council Regulation (EU) No. 472/2013.

of assistance, monitoring the financial assistance programmes and post-programme surveillance provided for in the Treaty establishing the ESM.[114] The Commission's central responsibility for monitoring the implementation of conditionality, i.e. the macroeconomic adjustment programme, was confirmed at the EU level by Regulation (EU) No. 472/2013 of the European Parliament and of the Council.[115]

The expansion in the Commission's tasks led to the Commissioner for Economic and Monetary Affairs being accorded higher *status* in October 2011. The Commissioner was raised to the rank of Vice-President and was responsible for assisting the President of the Commission in all matters relating to the work of the European Council, the Euro Summits and economic governance and of representing the Commission externally in those fields.[116] A post of Chief Economic Analyst, reporting to him, was created. In addition, the Directorate-General for Eurostat was placed under the responsibility of the Member of the Commission responsible for Taxation and Customs Union, Audit and Anti-Fraud.[117] These developments were hailed by the European Council, which saw in them a means of ensuring that the new economic governance was effectively applied.[118] The renewal of the Commission in November 2014 strengthened its position. One Vice-President whose portfolio includes the Euro and social dialogue is responsible for coordinating the work of several of his peers, including the Commissioner specifically responsible for economic and financial affairs. The post of Chief Economic Analyst was retained, reporting to the Vice-President. As regards staff numbers, the number of officials in the Directorate-General for Economic and Financial Affairs went up by 100 or so between 2009 and 2015.[119]

The expansion of the Commission's evaluation and surveillance tasks is not the expression of any wish on its part to alter the institutional balance in its favour but the consequence of a form of economic governance which is increasingly demanding in terms of the information and technical data which have to be examined. The Council does not have such a capacity for analysis, especially since it would duplicate the capacity of the national authorities. The new economic governance in fact prefers technical dialogue between the analysts at the Commission and in the Member States to political dialogue in the Council. The Council retains its key role in decision-making as it is the institution responsible for coordination. But what it does is confined to ratifying the terms of the negotiations between the two parties or, at the ministerial level, settling a disagreement between a Member State and the

[114]The Court of Justice confirmed that these tasks were lawfully conferred in the judgment of 27 November 2012 in *Pringle*, cited above, paras. 155 et seq.

[115]Article 7, para. 4, of Regulation (EU) No. 472/2013, cited above.

[116]Commission. Press Release. Olli Rehn appointed Vice-President with additional instruments, Algirda Semeta responsible for Eurostat, Brussels, 27 October 2011, IP/11/1284.

[117]*Ibid.*

[118]Conclusions of the European Council, Brussels, 23 October 2011, EUCO 52/11.

[119]DG ECFIN had a staff of 619 in February 2016. See Commission, *Statistical Bulletin on 01/02/2016. Distribution of staff by employment type and directorate-general.* [Online]. Available at: http://ec.europa.eu/civil_service/docs/europa_sp2_bs_dist_staff_en.pdf.

Commission—noting that a debate will already have taken place in the Eurogroup if it concerns a Member State of the Euro area. In their 2011 amended version, Regulations (EC) No. 1466/97 and No. 1467/97 say, on this, that

> The Council is, as a rule, expected to follow the recommendations and proposals of the Commission or explain its position publicly.[120]

Technical options, however, are never free of political considerations, particularly since the implementation of the Stability and Growth Pact (SGP) relies on a series of concepts which have been left undefined, for example the notion of "structural reform". This means there is a high risk of the Commission's interpretation binding the Council and responsibility shifting from the Council to the Commission. There was a case of this happening in 2015, involving the use of the elements of flexibility contained in the SGP. In response to a request from the European Council of June 2014, the Commission presented a communication at the beginning of January 2015 in which it set out its interpretation of a number of elements.[121] The challenge was to reconcile the relaunching of investments or the carrying out of structural reforms, on the one hand, with budgetary discipline, on the other. In an opinion issued on 7 April 2015, the Council's Legal Service pointed out that

> the [Commission]'s interpretation on the SGP enjoys a high likelihood of becoming the final decision of the Council,[122]

having regard to the increased role of the Commission in implementing the new economic governance. In fact the Commission applied its new rules of interpretation for the European Semester of 2015. The Council was taken unawares and there were differences of opinion between the Member States—some of them meant to take advantage of the flexibility of the SGP to secure an extension of the time limit for correcting their public deficits.[123] Building on the changes already made when the SGP was amended in 2005, the Six Pack made it systematic practice to mention the Commission after the Council when the relevant factors to be taken into account in their assessments of the situation of the Member States are described.[124] The

---

[120]Article 2, a and b, of Council Regulation (EC) No. 1466/97 and Article 2, a, 1, of Council Regulation (EC) No. 1467/97.

[121]Communication from the Commission, Making the best use of the flexibility within the existing rules of the Stability and Growth Pact. Brussels, 13 January 2015, COM(2015) 12 final.

[122]Council, Legal Service, Opinion of the Legal Service. Communication from the Commission, Making the best use of the flexibility within the existing rules of SGP—Legal remarks, Brussels, 7 April 2015, 7739/15, para. 14.

[123]"*EU Ministers, Commission to agree on flexibility in budget rules this year*", in Reuters, 12 May 2015. Available at: http://www.reuters.com/article/eu-budget-rules-idUSL5N0Y33MW20150512.

[124]This twofold association of the Council and the Commission applied mainly to Council Regulation (EC) No. 1466/97. The number of occurrences of the words "The Council and the Commission" went up from one to 22! In the case of Regulation (EC) No. 1467/97, this type of amendment had been made in the 2005 reform.

object was to ensure that both institutions should be held to the same principles in applying the rules. In that vein, in spring 2015 the Council's Legal Service defended the introduction of the appropriate clarifications regarding the use of the elements of flexibility in the Code of Conduct for the implementation of the SGP. The document, which is drawn up by the EFC and endorsed by the Council, consists of "Specifications" and "guidelines" and, as such, constitutes *soft law*. The Commission is involved in drawing up the Code, with two representatives as full members of the EFC. This consideration, plus the fact that the Code applied to the States as subjects and objects of economic policy coordination, gave the Council's Legal Service grounds for concluding that the Code applied to the Council, the Member States—and the Commission. In May, the Ecofin Council instructed the EFC to amend the code accordingly. The EFC came to a jointly agreed position at the end of November 2015. According to the Council's Conclusions of 8 December 2015, that position must serve as the basis for an updating of the Code of Conduct. At the beginning of July 2016 the new version of the Code had still not been adopted.

6 Is a New Method of Governance Emerging?

Following all the crises and reforms, EMU governance is neither more supranational nor more intergovernmental. It is both at once. To our way of thinking, to try to set the two approaches against each other would be a sterile exercise. EMU governance—and, in a broader sense, EU governance—is intergovernmental and supranational. It cannot be otherwise, so long as the EU bears the imprint of a twofold requirement: to achieve unity while respecting diversity. This twofold imperative has institutional repercussions in the form of

> the coexistence within the Communities [the EU] of an intergovernmental body [the Council] alongside supranational bodies.[125]

The institutional system of the EU turns out to be based on a compromise between cooperation and integration.[126] It is precisely there, in the competition, reconciliation or cooperation between the intergovernmental and supranational approaches, that the secret of Europe's momentum is forged.

> This undertaking [European integration] has managed to make progress only by alternating and then combining the strategies of integration and cooperation,

noted Rostane Mehdi at the end of a symposium in 2000.

---

[125]Sidjanksi (1961).

[126]Lutton (1985).

> By reconciling apparently contradictory imperatives, this dual approach has proven that it works.[127]

This amalgamation of supranationalism and intergovernmentalism[128] is the defining feature of a non-standard method of governance which some have described as "intergovernmental federalism",[129] "federalism in the European manner"[130] or "special federalism".[131] The characteristics of this open and pragmatic method are said to be a renewal of the Community method through a strengthening of the Council-Commission executive tandem, a consolidation of the European Council Presidency, the institutionalisation of a centre of gravity centred on the Eurogroup and the establishment of a constitutional pact laying down the guiding principles for the exercise of shared powers. In the view of Marc Blanquet, we should not overestimate the alternating character of the new type of governance vis-à-vis the Community method. The main field in which this new form of governance applies and develops consists of areas which fall broadly within the spheres of competence of the Member States: it makes it possible to

> take over areas which had hitherto been addressed applying the intergovernmental approach and for which that approach is not politically acceptable to the Member States.

To a great extent it is said to be a "gateway" to the Community method.[132] Seen in that light, the Open Method of Coordination (OMC) occupies an intermediate position between the intergovernmental cooperation approach and the pure legislative integration approach.[133]

The discussion picked up again on 2 November 2010. In her opening address for the 61st academic year of the College of Europe in Bruges, Angela Merkel detected, behind the developments going on in the EU's institutional framework and the new share-out of powers, the emergence of a new "Union method".[134] To the German Chancellor's mind, this method should be understood as

> [a] coordinated action in a spirit of solidarity – each of us in the area for which we are responsible but all working towards the same goal.[135]

Angela Merkel quoted President van Rompuy's analysis of the functioning of the EU, to the effect that

---

[127]Mehdi (2000).

[128]In a recent contribution, Erik Jones, R. Daniel Kelemen and Sophie Meunier refer to the merging of intergovernmentalism and neofunctionalism. See Jones et al. (2015).

[129]Croisat and Quermonne (1999).

[130]Boyer and Dehove (2001).

[131]Quermonne (2001).

[132]Blanquet (2004).

[133]*Ibid.*

[134]Angela Merkel, Address at the opening ceremony for the 61st academic year at the College of Europe, Bruges, 2 November 2010. Available at: https://archiv.bundesregierung.de/ContentArchiv/EN/Archiv17/Reden/2010/2010-11-02-merkel-bruegge.html.

[135]Angela Merkel, cited above.

> Often the choice is not between the Community method and the intergovernmental method, but between a coordinated European position and nothing at all.[136]

The phrase "Union method" is surprising in the way it seems to imply sweeping aside the Community method. Following her, President Nicolas Sarkozy, high on the political responsibility which the Heads of State or Government shoulder in managing crises, announced that "the intergovernmental approach will be the path to European integration, because Europe is going to have to make strategic choices, political choices."[137]

Should we be concerned at this semantic shift and see it only as the expression of a common-sense observation about the interactions and coordination between the intergovernmental and supranational approaches?[138] Or is it a really new method of governance which is being defended? In a resolution of 7 May 2009, the European Parliament considered that

> the Treaty of Lisbon transforms the former 'Community method', adapting and strengthening it, into a 'Union method'[139]

based on three essential principles: the European Council defines the general political directions and priorities, the Commission promotes the general interest of the Union and takes appropriate initiatives to that end, and the European Parliament and the Council jointly exercise legislative and budgetary functions on the basis of the Commission's proposals. While welcoming this new balance between the institutions, Parliament observed that it demanded that

> each institution play its role in permanent cooperation with the other institutions.[140]

Implicitly, the institutions were reminded that they must respect the principle of conferral of powers and loyal cooperation. Once again, this principle does not set the exercise of powers in stone: it must be capable of adapting to the demands of the moment or it could cause the EU to become obsolete. Changes in the powers or tasks conferred on one institution must not be made at the expense of another institution.

An analysis of the new economic governance tends to show how subtle such an exercise is, where change happens as a follow-on from balances struck previously. As to the substance, it now seems to be a done deal, even if the new system works through increased complexity in the institutional system and less transparency in the governance of EMU. As to what comes after, the challenge for future reforms will be precisely at that point: strengthening the democratic legitimacy of the

---

[136]*Ibid.*

[137]Nicolas Sarkozy. Speech by the President of the Republic. Toulon, 1 December 2011.

[138]Ponzano (2011).

[139]European Parliament Resolution of 7 May 2009 on the impact of the Treaty of Lisbon on the development of the institutional balance of the European Union. P6_TA(2009)038.

[140]*Ibid.*

EMU's decision-making process.[141] The European Parliament and the national Parliaments are still marginalised institutions in EMU, even when the decisions taken in them are of major economic and social importance. The economic dialogue set up by the Six Pack, and the interparliamentary conference provided for by the TSCG,[142] are useful arrangements. They are still poor substitutes for the parliamentarisation of EMU. The European Parliament and the national Parliaments must be given a key part to play.[143]

References

Allemand F (2009) Nicolas Sarkozy's voluntarism in international relations. In: Arvanitopoulos C, Botsiou K (eds) The Constantinos Karamanlis Institute for democracy yearbook. Springer, Berlin

Allemand F (2013) Le développement de la coordination des politiques budgétaires dans l'Union européenne. In: Sorel J-M, Chemain R (eds) Quelle souveraineté budgétaire pour les Etats ? Pédone, Paris

Allemand F, Martucci F (2012a) La nouvelle gouvernance économique européenne. Partie 1. Cahiers de droit européen 48(1):17–99

Allemand F, Martucci F (2012b) La nouvelle gouvernance économique européenne. Partie 2. Cahiers de droit européen 48(2):409–457

Balleix-Banerjee C, Portelli H (eds) (1997) La France et la Banque centrale européenne. Débats politiques et élaboration de la décision (janvier 1988 – septembre 1992). Doctoral thesis in political sciences. Université Panthéon-Assas (Paris II), Paris

Bauer MW, Becker S (2014) La gouvernance économique durant et après la crise: vers la disparition de la Commission européenne? Pouvoirs, No. 149, pp 29–44

Blanquet M (2004) Le système communautaire à l'épreuve de la "gouvernance européenne". Pour une "nouvelle gouvernance" raisonnée. In: Mélanges en hommage à Guy Isaac. 50 ans de droit communautaire. Presses de l'Université des Sciences sociales, Toulouse

Boone L, Salomon R (2009) Crise, l'ultime chance de l'Europe. Le Monde, 2 September 2009

Boyer R, Dehove M (2001) Du "gouvernement économique" au gouvernement tout court. Critique internationale 11(2):179–195

Capotorti F (1987) Le statut juridique du Conseil européen à la lumière de l'Acte unique. In: Capotorti F et al (eds) Du droit international au droit de l'intégration. Liber Amicorum Pierre Pescatore. Nomos, Baden-Baden

Cisotta R (2013) What role for the European Commission in the new governance of the economic and monetary union? Istituto Affari Internazionali Working Papers, No. 13/24

Croisat M, Quermonne J-L (1999) L'Europe et le fédéralisme: contribution à l'émergence d'un fédéralisme intergouvernemental, 2nd edn. Montchrestien, Paris

de Charentenay P (2010) L'Europe empêtrée dans ses nations. Etudes 412(5):583–594

Dehousse R (1994) The legacy of Maastricht: emerging institutional issues. Recueil des cours de l'Académie de droit européen 3(1):181–239

Doutriaux Y (1992) Le traité sur l'Union européenne. Armand Colin, Paris

Durand P (1947) La dissolution de l'État. Droit social, pp 301–341

[141]Repasi (2016).

[142]Article 13 TSCG.

[143]Juncker et al. (2015), p. 17.

Dyson K, Marcussen M (2010) Transverse integration in European economic governance: between unitary and differentiated integration. J Eur Integr 32(1):17–39
Fabbrini S (2013) Intergovernmentalism and its limits: assessing the European Union's answer to the Euro crisis. Comp Pol Stud 46(9):1003–1029
Ganshof Van der Meersch W (1975) L'ordre juridique des Communautés européennes et le droit international. In: Académie de Droit International de La Haye, tome 178. Recueil des cours. Sijthoff & Noordhoff, Alphen aan den Rijn
Gautron J-C (2009) Droit européen. Dalloz, Paris
Hanf D (2009) L'encadrement constitutionnel de l'appartenance de l'Allemagne à l'Union européenne. L'apport de l'arrêt "Lisbonne" de la Cour constitutionnelle fédérale. Cahiers de droit européen 46(5–6):642–710
Jacqué J-P (2004) The principle of institutional balance. Common Mark Law Rev 41(2):383–391
Jones E, Kelemen D, Meunier S (2015) Failing forward? The Euro crisis and the incomplete nature of European integration. Comp Pol Stud 49(7):1010–1034
Juncker J-C, Tusk D, Dijsselbloem J, Draghi M, Schulz M (2015) Completing Europe's economic and monetary union. Brussels, 22 June 2015
Louis J-V (1993) Le lien entre les conférences intergouvernementales sur l'union économique et monétaire et l'union politique. In: Monar J, Ungerer W, Wessels W (eds) The Maastricht Treaty on European Union. European Interuniversity Press, Brussels
Louis J-V (1995) Union économique et monétaire. In: Megret J et al (eds) Droit de la CEE [Commentaire Mégret], 2nd edn. Editions de l'Université libre de Bruxelles, Bruxelles
Louis J-V (2000) EMU and economic governance. The European Union and the EURO: economic, institutional and international aspects. In: Fourth ECSA world conference, Brussels, 17 and 18 September 1998. Publications Office of the European Union, Luxembourg
Louis J-V (2012) Un traité vite fait, bien fait? Le traité du 2 mars 2012 sur la stabilité, la coordination et la gouvernance au sein de l'Union économique et monétaire. Revue trimestrielle de droit européen 48(1):5–22
Louis J-V, Ronse T (2006) L'ordre juridique de l'Union européenne. Helbing & Lichtenhahn, Basel/Bruylant, Bruxelles; Paris
Lutton P (1985) Les équilibres mouvants du système institutionnel de la Communauté économique européenne. Quelques réflexions. Revue française de science politique 35(1):26–45
Majone G (2005) Dilemmas of European integration: the ambiguities and pitfalls of integration by stealth. Oxford University Press, Oxford
Mehdi R (2000) Conclusions générales. In: Hervouët F (ed) Démarche communautaire et intégration européenne. Acts of the CEDECE symposium held in Poitiers on 12, 13 and 14 October 2000, vol 2. La Documentation française, Paris
Monar J (2011) The European Union's institutional balance of power after the Treaty of Lisbon. In: Commission (ed) The European Union after the Treaty of Lisbon. Publications Office of the European Union, Luxembourg
Monnet J (1976) Mémoires. Fayard, Paris
Noël E (1962) How the European economic community's institutions work. Speech to the Conservative Political Centre, Oxford, 7 July 1962. Available at: http://aei.pitt.edu/14827
Noël E (1990) Quelques aspects institutionnels de l'Union économique et monétaire. Recueil des cours de l'Académie de droit européen 1(1):9–26
Novak S (2014) Le grand retour des Etats ? Pouvoirs 149(2):19–27
Ortega y Gasset J (2010) La révolte des masses. Les Belles Lettres, Paris
Pertek J (2006) Droit des institutions de l'Union européenne, 2nd edn. PUF, Paris
Ponzano P (2007) Les institutions de l'Union. Chapter XII. In: Amato G, Bribosia H, de Witte B (eds) Genèse et Destinée de la Constitution européenne. Bruylant, Bruxelles
Ponzano P (2011) Community and intergovernmental method: an irrelevant debate? Notre Europe Policy Brief, No. 23
Puetter U (2012) Europe's deliberative intergovernmentalism: the role of the Council and European Council in EU economic governance. J Eur Public Pol 19(2):161–178

Puetter U (2014) The European Council and the Council: new intergovernmentalism and institutional change. Oxford University Press, Oxford
Quermonne J-L (2001) L'Europe peut-elle inventer un fédéralisme spécifique? Revue internationale et stratégique 42(2):113–123
Repasi R (2016) Implementation of the Lisbon Treaty. Improving functioning of the EU: economic and monetary policy. Study for the AFCO committee [European Parliament], PE 556.952
Schmitter C (1993) Principe d'équilibre institutionnel. In: Barav A, Philip C (eds) Dictionnaire juridique de l'Union européenne. PUF, Paris
Schwarzer D (2012) The Euro area crises, shifting power relations and institutional change in the European Union. Global Pol 3(1):28–41
Sidjanksi D (1961) L'originalité des Communautés européennes et la répartition de leurs pouvoirs. Pédone, Paris
Siedentop L (2000) Democracy in Europe. Penguin Books, London
Simon D (1991) Y a-t-il des principes généraux du droit communautaire? Droits, No. 14, p 73
Simon D (2001) Le système juridique communautaire, 3rd edn. PUF, Paris
Snyder F (1994) EMU – metaphor for European Union? Institutions, rules and types of regulations. In: Dehousse R (ed) Europe after Maastricht. An ever closer union? Beck, Munich
Tsoukalis L (2012) The political economy of the crisis: the end of an era? Global Pol 3(1):42–50

The Economic Dialogue: An Effective Accountability Mechanism?

Sergio De la Parra

Abstract The economic dialogue was created in 2011 in order to increase the European Parliament's scrutiny powers in the framework of the new European economic governance. With this new mechanism, Parliament's Committee on Economic and Monetary Affairs can invite top officials from other EU institutions to take part in an exchange of views, increasing the accountability of the decisions taken and ultimately reinforcing the democratic legitimacy of Economic and Monetary Union (EMU).

A legal analysis suggests that Parliament's limited powers as well as the shortcomings in the economic dialogue provisions are at odds with the ambitions of this mechanism. Practical evidence however shows that the dialogue has proved remarkably adaptable to the new reality of EMU, leading to the development of a forum for regular public exchanges between Parliament and the key players in the new European economic governance. Nevertheless, the superficiality of the debates, demands by MEPs for visibility and Parliament's marginal powers remain major obstacles for a real exercise in accountability.

Contents

A previous version of this paper was presented at the NIAS/EURO-CEFG workshop "EU Decision-Making and Challenges to Economic and Financial Governance" held in Wassenaar (Netherlands) in December 2015. I would like to thank all participants for their useful comments. My thanks also go to the CVCE team for their valuable advice. All remaining errors are mine.

S. De la Parra (✉)
Centre Virtuel de la Connaissance sur l'Europe, Sanem, Luxembourg
e-mail: sergio.delaparra@hotmail.com

L. Daniele et al. (eds.), *Democracy in the EMU in the Aftermath of the Crisis*,
DOI 10.1007/978-3-319-53895-2_5

1 Introduction

The management of the sovereign debt crisis entailed a radical transformation of Economic and Monetary Union (EMU). From an institutional point of view, these developments led to a strengthening of the executive bodies.[1] The European Council, the Council, the Eurogroup and the Commission not only played a leading role in the adoption of anti-crisis measures; their positions within the new EMU governance framework were also considerably reinforced. These changes were not counterbalanced by an equivalent reinforcement of parliamentary bodies, neither at European Union (EU) level nor at national level, further aggravating the parliamentary dimension of EU democratic deficit.

In response to these shortcomings the economic dialogue, introduced by the Six-Pack[2] and the Two-Pack,[3] aimed to enhance the European Parliament's power of scrutiny over other EU institutions. Under this new mechanism, Parliament's Committee on Economic and Monetary Affairs (ECON) can invite the key players in the new European economic governance—the Council, the Eurogroup, the European Council, the Commission, a Member State, the European Central Bank (ECB) and the International Monetary Fund (IMF)—to take part in an exchange of views. These exchanges should contribute

> to ensure greater transparency and accountability[4]

[1]See the contribution by F. Allemand in this volume.

[2]Regulation (EU) No. 1173/2011 on the effective enforcement of budgetary surveillance in the Euro area, OJEU L 306, 23 November 2011, pp. 1 et seqq.; Regulation (EU) No. 1174/2011 on enforcement measures to correct excessive macroeconomic imbalances in the Euro area, OJEU L 306, 23 November 2011, pp. 8 et seqq.; Regulation (EU) No. 1175/2011 amending Council Regulation (EC) No. 1466/97 on the strengthening of the surveillance of budgetary positions and the surveillance and coordination of economic policies, OJEU L 306, 23 November 2011, pp. 12 et seqq.; Regulation (EU) No. 1176/2011 on the prevention and correction of macroeconomic imbalances, OJEU L 306, 23 November 2011, pp. 25 et seqq.; Regulation (EU) No. 1177/2011 amending Regulation (EC) No. 1467/97 on speeding up and clarifying the implementation of the excessive deficit procedure, OJEU L 306, 23 November 2011, pp. 33 et seqq.

[3]Regulation (EU) No. 472/2013 on the strengthening of economic and budgetary surveillance of Member States in the Euro area experiencing or threatened with serious difficulties with respect to their financial stability, OJEU L 140, 27 May 2013, pp. 1 et seqq.; Regulation (EU) No. 473/2013 on common provisions for monitoring and assessing draft budgetary plans and ensuring the correction of excessive deficit of the Member States in the Euro area, OJEU L 140, 27 May 2013, pp. 11 et seqq.

[4]Article 3 of Regulation (EU) No. 1173/2011.

for the decisions taken in the new EMU legal framework.

Four years after it was introduced, there are still no studies on the implementation and effectiveness of this economic dialogue.[5] This paper aims to fill this gap. It compares the legal analysis of the economic dialogue with an assessment of its practical implementation. It ultimately aims to determine to what extent the economic dialogue amounts to an effective accountability mechanism.

The factual assessment is based on a systematic analysis of all the meetings of the European Parliament's ECON Committee between December 2011 and December 2015 at which economic dialogues were held.[6] These observations are supplemented by an interview with two officials from the European Parliament's Economic Governance Support Unit (EGOV), which is involved in the practical organisation of the meetings.[7]

The paper is structured as follows. Section 2 sets out the legal and historical context in which the economic dialogue was created. Section 3 analyses the economic dialogue's legal provisions in order to assess to what extent they create the framework for an effective accountability mechanism. Section 4 describes how the economic dialogue has functioned in practice, providing detailed information on the meetings held, the players involved and the topics discussed. Based on a qualitative analysis of these exchanges, a critical assessment is provided in section 5, highlighting the successes and limitations of this exercise. The conclusion gives some suggestions for improvement.

2 The European Parliament and Economic and Monetary Union

2.1 The European Parliament and EMU After Lisbon

Although the European Parliament gained considerable new powers after the entry into force of the Lisbon Treaty,[8] its role in the area of Economic and Monetary Union (EMU) remains marginal. The monetary policy of the Union is defined and implemented by the European System of Central Banks (ESCB), under the lead of the highly independent European Central Bank (ECB).[9] In the economic pillar, the key player is the Council, which mainly acts on the basis of Commission recommendations.[10]

---

[5]The Commission gives the topic only a brief mention in its review of the new economic governance framework. See European Commission (2014).

[6]For this purpose, the video recordings of the meetings available on Parliament's website have been used.

[7]The interview (hereafter "interview 1") was held in Brussels on 23 September 2015.

[8]de Witte et al. (2010), p. 26.

[9]Article 127 Treaty on the Functioning of the European Union (TFEU).

[10]Articles 121, 122 and 126 TFEU.

Parliament has an *ex post* supervisory role: it is informed of measures taken by the ECB within the monetary pillar[11] and by the Council and the Commission within the economic pillar. On this last point, it is informed of the Broad Economic Policy Guidelines adopted by the Council[12]; of the results of the multilateral surveillance procedure carried out by the Council and the Commission[13]; of the decisions taken by the Council concerning the granting of EU financial assistance to a Member State[14]; and of Council measures taken against non-compliant Member States in the framework of the excessive deficit procedure (EDP).[15]

The Lisbon Treaty also provided Parliament with new legislative powers: it participates as co-legislator in the adoption of rules for the multilateral surveillance procedure,[16] the amendment of some provisions of the Statute of the ESCB and of the ECB[17] and the adoption of specific measures for the use of the euro as the single currency.[18]

Until 2010, this limited involvement was in line with the low impact of EU coordination of national economic policies. The main responsibilities in this area lay at national level, where the involvement of Parliaments guaranteed the legitimacy of the decisions taken. The lack of similar mechanisms at European level and the marginalisation of the European Parliament were not considered to be relevant issues.[19]

2.2 *Crisis, EMU Reforms and the Struggle for a New Role*

This situation ended with the reconfiguration of EMU in response to the sovereign debt crisis. The "constitutional mutation"[20] entailed by these reforms altered the balance on which the old EMU was based,[21] resulting in both a significant transfer of powers from national to EU level and a concentration of these new powers in the hands of executive bodies, at the expense of the European and national Parliaments.

Critics from academia, political circles and civil society pointed out how this situation further eroded the representative democracy principle on which the EU functioning is founded.[22] In particular, the limited involvement of the European

[11]Article 284, para. 3, TFEU.

[12]Article 121, para. 2, TFEU.

[13]Article 121, para. 5, TFEU.

[14]Article 122, para. 2, TFEU.

[15]Article 126, para. 11, TFEU.

[16]Article 121, para. 6, TFEU.

[17]Article 129, para. 3, TFEU.

[18]Article 133 TFEU.

[19]Allemand (2013); Fasone (2014), p. 173; Majone (2014).

[20]Menéndez (2014) and Tuori and Tuori (2014).

[21]Dawson and de Witte (2013).

[22]Article 10 TFEU.

Parliament entailed a segmentation and atomisation of the accountability in EU Member States.[23] Enhancing the European Parliament's prerogatives, especially its power of political control over other EU institutions, was seen as a valid counterweight to these transformations and would strengthen the democratic legitimacy of EMU, according to the principle that

> accountability should occur at the level at which decisions are taken.[24]

The marginalisation of the European Parliament was visible in the very reform process. In May 2010, the European Financial Stabilisation Mechanism was created by a Council Regulation.[25] The following day, the European Financial Stability Facility was set up as a private law company by the Euro area Governments.[26] In September 2010, the first European Semester was launched on the basis of a Commission amendment to the Code of Conduct of the Stability and Growth Pact.[27] In March 2011, the European Council adopted a Decision amending Article 136 TFEU to allow the creation of a European Stability Mechanism, largely ignoring Parliament's recommendations.[28] The same day, the Member States' Heads of Government adopted the Euro-Plus Pact, a soft-law agreement to foster employment and competitiveness, in which Parliament is not even mentioned.

Parliament's demands for greater involvement and the use of EU law[29] were answered to some extent in September 2010, when the Commission published a package of five Regulations and a Directive, the "Six-Pack".[30] This was the first piece of legislation on economic governance in the hands of the European Parliament since the beginning of the crisis: four of the Regulations were enacted with the ordinary legislative procedure provided for in Article 121, para. 6, TFEU. In November 2011 the "Two-Pack" Regulations[31] completed this new governance framework, giving Parliament another opportunity to use its new co-legislative power.

While ideological divisions between MEPs along political lines emerged on matters like the strengthening of the SGP, some transversal issues, like the

---

[23]Maurer (2013), p. 5.

[24]Van Rompuy et al. (2012), p. 16.

[25]Regulation (EU) No. 407/2010 establishing a European financial stabilisation mechanism, OJEU L 118, 12 May 2010, pp. 1 et seqq.

[26]EFSF Framework Agreement, available at http://www.efsf.europa.eu.

[27]Specifications on the implementation of the Stability and Growth Pact and Guidelines on the format and content of Stability and Convergence Programmes, Consolidated version, endorsed by the ECOFIN Council on 7 September 2010, available at http://ec.europa.eu/economy_finance/economic_governance/sgp/pdf/coc/2010-09-07_code_of_conduct_%28consolidated%29_en.pdf.

[28]European Council Decision amending Article 136 of the Treaty on the Functioning of the European Union with regard to a stability mechanism for Member States whose currency is the Euro, OJEU L 91, 6 April 2011, pp. 1–2.

[29]European Parliament (2010a, b, 2011b).

[30]See *supra*, note 2.

[31]See *supra*, note 3.

enhancement of Parliament's role in the new system, resulted in a cross-party *consensus*.[32] The resulting economic dialogue represented a successful use of Parliament's new legislative powers in the field of economic policy.

Indeed, the original aim of the economic dialogue (ED) was to create, within the European Parliament, a forum for exchanges between European institutions and Member States, where the compliance of Member States with EU-level recommendations would be publicly debated. Such debates

> could enable the Member States to take account of the spill-overs of the national decisions and to enable public peer pressure,[33]

strengthening their obligation to

> regard their economic policies as a matter of common concern.[34]

The Council managed to limit the scope of these provisions during the trilogue negotiations. The dialogues would take place only after decisions had been taken, in line with above-mentioned Parliament *ex post* supervisory role, and the exchanges would focus only on situations which were likely to entail negative spillover effects. The final compromise resulted in a limited list of topics open to debate and shifted the emphasis from a dialogue between Parliament and Member States to a dialogue between EU-level institutions.

In this sense, the economic dialogue has largely become a mirror of the already existing "monetary dialogue". This mechanism, created in 1999, consists of a quarterly meeting between the ECON Committee and the ECB President and has been used by MEPs to question the ECB on its conduct of monetary policy.[35]

3 The New Legal Framework

The economic dialogue is based on similar provisions in the Regulations of the Six-Pack and the Two-Pack. They state that

> (i)n order to enhance the dialogue between the institutions of the Union [...] and to ensure greater transparency and accountability, the competent committee of the European Parliament may invite the President of the Council, the Commission and, where appropriate, the President of the European Council or the President of the Eurogroup to appear before the committee to discuss

---

[32] O'Keeffe et al. (2016), p. 226.

[33] European Parliament (2011a), recital 2, h.

[34] Article 121, para. 1, TFEU.

[35] On the monetary dialogue, see Eijffinger and Mujagic (2004), Amtenbrink and van Duin (2009) and Claeys et al. (2014).

particular elements of the Regulation at stake.[36] In most cases, the relevant EP committee

> may offer the opportunity to the Member State concerned [...] to participate in an exchange of views.[37]

In another case, the "troika" is mentioned among the institutions likely to be invited.[38]

The matters open to debate encompass the main documents and procedures involved in the EU's coordination of economic policies: the Broad Economic Policy Guidelines[39]; the Annual Growth Survey[40]; the results of multilateral surveillance[41]; the Stability and Growth Pact and in particular the excessive deficit procedure[42]; the procedure to correct excessive macroeconomic imbalances[43]; the Commission's opinions on national draft budgetary plans[44]; the enhanced surveillance mechanism[45]; and macroeconomic adjustment programmes.[46]

These exchanges are supplemented by a number of reporting requirements. Within the framework of the Stability and Growth Pact, the Council must, as a rule, follow the recommendations of the Commission or explain its position publicly.[47] Moreover, the Commission and the Council are required to inform the European Parliament on a regular basis of the application of these new Regulations.[48]

---

[36] Article 3 of Regulation (EU) No. 1173/2011; Article 6 of Regulation (EU) No. 1174/2011; Article 2, a-b, of Regulation (EC) No. 1466/97 as amended by Regulation (EU) No. 1175/2011; Article 14, para. 1, of Regulation (EU) No. 1176/2011; Article 2, a, of Regulation (EC) No. 1467/97 as amended by Regulation (EU) No. 1177/2011; Article 15 of Regulation (EU) No. 473/2013. See also Articles 3, para. 9, 7, paras. 1, 4 and 10, and 18, of Regulation (EU) No. 472/2013.

[37] *Ibid.*

[38] Article 3, para. 9, of Regulation (EU) No. 472/2013.

[39] Articles 14 of Regulations (EU) Nos. 1175/2011 and 1176/2011.

[40] Articles 14 of Regulations (EU) Nos. 1175/2011 and 1176/2011.

[41] Articles 14 of Regulations (EU) Nos. 1175/2011 and 1176/2011.

[42] Article 3 of Regulation (EU) No. 1173/2011; Regulation (EU) No. 1177/2011.

[43] Article 6 of Regulation (EU) No. 1174/2011.

[44] Articles 7, para. 3, and 15, paras. 1 and 3, of Regulation (EU) No. Reg. 473/2013.

[45] Article 3, para. 9, of Regulation (EU) No. 472/2013.

[46] Article 7, paras. 1, 4 and 10, of Regulation (EU) No. 472/2013.

[47] Article 2, a-b, of Regulation (EC) No. 1466/97 as amended by Regulation (EU) No. 1175/2011; Article 2, a, of Regulation (EC) No. 1467/97 as amended by Article 2, a, of Regulation (EU) No. 1177/2011.

[48] Article 13 of Regulation (EU) No. 1173/2011; Article 7 of Regulation (EU) No. 1174/2011; Article 12 *bis* of Regulation (EC) No. 1466/97 as amended by Regulation (EU) No. 1175/2011; Articles 15 and 16 of Regulation (EU) No. 1176/2011; Article 17 of Regulation (EC) No. 1467/97 as amended by Regulation (EU) No. 1177/2011; Article 18 of Regulation (EU) No. 472/2013; Article 16 of Regulation (EU) No. reg. 473/2013.

Compared with previous forms of exchange with other EU institutions,[49] there are major differences relating to the forum where the economic dialogues take place (the ECON Committee instead of the plenary session), some of the institutions invited (the Eurogroup, the Member States and the troika) and the matters that are discussed (economic matters, specifically those relating to the reformed EMU).

Hereafter, the last two points are examined more closely in order to assess to what extent the economic dialogue can function as an accountability mechanism. We define accountability in a supranational-federalist perspective as the obligation for EU institutions to engage in a dialogue with the European Parliament in order to explain and justify their conduct and face the potential consequences of Parliament's judgement.[50]

3.1 Institutions Invited: Who Can Be Held Accountable?

Does Parliament's "right to invite"[51] create a symmetrical obligation, for the invited institution or the Member State, to accept its invitation and participate in the economic dialogue? In fact the binding character of the mechanism varies widely depending on Parliament's interlocutors.

With regard to the Commission, the provisions for the economic dialogue develop and clarify the Treaty provisions on the function of political control exercised by the European Parliament,[52] and more precisely those relating to the Commission's obligation to reply orally or in writing to its questions.[53] The binding character of the economic dialogue therefore builds upon Parliament's strong "sanctionatory"[54] power of political control over the Commission. The latter is responsible to Parliament,[55] which may vote on a motion of censure of the Commission, entailing its resignation.[56]

In all the other cases, the obligation to accept Parliament's invitations is less clear.

---

[49]These include "structured dialogues" with the Commission, the "monetary dialogue" with the European Central Bank and the regular dialogues with the ECOFIN Council President at the beginning and the end of each six-monthly Council presidency. Cf. Bourgault (2014).

[50]Bovens et al. (2010).

[51]The wording of the provisions is very careful indeed: "the competent committee of the European Parliament *may invite*, where appropriate, etc." (Article 3 of Regulation (EU) No. 1173/2011).

[52]Article 14, para. 1, TEU.

[53]Article 230 TFEU. In the case of multilateral surveillance, this control is also foreseen by Article 121, para. 5, TFEU.

[54]von der Groeben et al. (2015), p. 211.

[55]Article 17, para. 8, TEU.

[56]Article 17, para. 8, TEU and Article 234 TFEU.

Neither the Council nor the European Council is accountable to Parliament, whose power of political control in this case is merely "informative".[57] However, the Treaties provide for the two institutions to be heard by Parliament, in accordance with the conditions laid down in their own Rules of Procedure.[58] The Council has a further obligation to report on the results of multilateral surveillance, in particular when it issues a public recommendation to a Member State.[59] Hence, a refusal to comply with Parliament's invitations in the framework of the economic dialogue could probably be challenged before the Court of Justice for failure to act[60] or breach of the principle of sincere cooperation among institutions.[61]

Whether challenges on such grounds can be raised against the Eurogroup or a Member State—the two main novelties of the economic dialogue—is more questionable. The Treaty provisions on the Eurogroup do not contain any indication about its relationship with Parliament.[62] And it goes without saying that invited representatives of the Member States (in general, the Minister for the Economy) are only accountable to their own Parliament. From a strictly legal point of view, therefore, the Six- and Two-Pack Regulations cannot create new obligations for the Eurogroup or the Member States as long as the Treaties are silent in this regard. If not legally binding, however, the dialogue provisions represent at least a politically binding commitment to submit to Parliament's scrutiny.[63] This fledgling accountability mechanism is all the more relevant in the case of the Eurogroup, an informal[64] institution that has gained considerable new powers in recent years: suffice it to say that its members form the Board of Governors of the European Stability Mechanism.

Lastly, the introduction of "representatives of the Commission, the ECB and the IMF"[65] (the "troika") in the provisions for the economic dialogue is rather curious. The role of the troika in financial assistance programmes has been embedded in EU law through Regulation (EU) No. 472/2013,[66] and the economic dialogue allows Parliament to scrutinise action taken by the Commission and the ECB. However, the IMF, as an international organisation, can hardly be bound by EU law. As will be seen, its willingness to accept these invitations has not been particularly forthcoming.

---

[57] von der Groeben et al. (2015), p. 210.

[58] Article 230, para. 3, TFEU. See also Article 26 of the Council Rules of Procedure and Article 5 of the European Council Rules of Procedure, which define the issue of representation.

[59] Article 121, para. 5, TFEU.

[60] Article 265 TFEU.

[61] Article 13, para. 2, TEU.

[62] Article 137 TFEU; Protocol No. 14 on the Eurogroup.

[63] More precisely, in the case of the Eurogroup the dialogue provisions also formalise an already existing practice of regular exchanges with the ECON Committee.

[64] Article 1 of Protocol No. 14.

[65] Article 3, para. 9, of Regulation (EU) No. 472/2013.

[66] Article 7 of Regulation (EU) No. 472/2013.

3.2 Matters Open to Debate: Accountable for What?

Matters discussed in the framework of the economic dialogue are not restricted to elements from the Six-Pack and the Two-Pack. The topics open to debate range from the multi-annual EU-level objectives set in the Broad Economic Policy Guidelines[67] to the Commission's opinion on a single Member State's draft budgetary plan.[68] Almost all aspects of the EU's coordination of national economic policies are open for discussion.

Two series of limitations apply, however. Firstly, only *certain elements* of each topic are open to debate, in line with Parliament's *ex post* power of political control in the area of EMU. In most cases, discussions can occur only on decisions which have already been taken, leaving no opportunity for Parliament to exert any influence. Secondly, not all topics can be discussed with all institutions.

For example, when it comes to the excessive deficit procedure, the matters open to debate are Council decisions on the existence of an excessive deficit under Article 126, para. 6, TFEU and successive Council acts under Article 126, paras. 7, 9 and 11, TFEU[69]; sanctions granted under the preventive arm of the SGP[70]; and Council opinions on economic partnership programmes adopted by Member States under the EDP.[71] Moreover, should the Council not follow a Commission recommendation, it is required to explain its position.[72] As is well known, a sanction in the framework of the EDP has never been adopted. Much more relevant is the process leading to a decision *not* to give a sanction, and in particular the Commission's recommendations on the basis of which the Council acts. Those issues however are not open to debate.

Another noteworthy element is the debates concerning the granting of financial assistance. In this case, the Commission and the Member State concerned can be invited to discuss the implementation of a Macroeconomic Adjustment Programme.[73] As the negotiation of the third Greek bailout has shown, however, the Commission might not be the key player in these cases. Moreover, the crucial step in the granting of financial assistance is the negotiation of the conditions attached to the assistance. Yet the preparation of the macroeconomic adjustment programme and the monitoring of its implementation are excluded from the economic dialogue: the Commission is merely required to inform the chair and vice-chair of the competent committee in a confidential way.[74]

In sum, the lack of legal basis did not discourage the European Parliament from proactively looking a way to keep other institutions accountable, in the same way as

[67] Article 2, a-b, of Regulation (EC) No. 1466/97 as amended by Regulation (EU) No. 1175/2011.

[68] Article 15, para. 1, of Regulation (EU) No. 473/2013.

[69] Article 1, para. 3, of Regulation (EU) No. 1177/2011.

[70] Article 3 of Regulation (EU) No. 1173/2011.

[71] Article 15, para. 1, d, of Regulation (EU) No. 473/2013.

[72] Article 2, a-b, of Regulation (EC) No. 1466/97 as amended by Regulation (EU) No. 1175/2011.

[73] Article 7, para. 10, of Regulation (EU) No. 472/2013.

[74] Article 7, paras. 1 and 4, of Regulation (EU) No. 472/2013.

it did for the monetary dialogue.[75] Given these legal limitations, it has extended its scrutiny power as much as was possible.[76] Nonetheless, essential elements are lacking in order for the economic dialogue to be considered a proper accountability mechanism.

Firstly, given Parliament's variable power of political control over the other institutions, one of the conditions for the success of the dialogue lies in the willingness of Parliament's interlocutors to participate in this exercise. Secondly, this mechanism is unlikely to entail any consequences for most of the institutions concerned, given the lack of a political relationship between Parliament and its interlocutors. Lastly, while covering a wide range of topics that go beyond the new elements contained in the Six-Pack and the Two-Pack, the list of matters open to debate leaves aside some crucial elements, affecting Parliament's ability to undertake a comprehensive review of the performance of the EU institutions.

4 The Economic Dialogue in Practice

4.1 Calendar, Frequency and Interlocutors

Between December 2011 and December 2015, 48 economic dialogues were held, in other words an average of 12 meetings per year.[77]

Most meetings with institutions take place on a regular basis. Some of these follow the main stages of the European Semester and involve the Commission or the Council. Others follow the 6-month calendar of the rotating Council Presidency, and focus every 6 months on the priorities of the incoming Presidency and an assessment of the outgoing Presidency. Meetings with the Eurogroup do not take place on fixed dates but there are nonetheless two regular meetings each year, one per semester. The calendar of these regular dialogues is reproduced in Table 1.

Other meetings take place on an *ad hoc* basis, depending on relevant economic and political developments in the Euro area and the EU. Examples of such meetings are the dialogues on the crisis in Greece, the adjustment programme in Cyprus, the economic situation in Portugal and the banking crisis in Slovenia. These dialogues mostly involve Member States and the Eurogroup.

As we can see in Table 2, Parliament's main counterparts are the Council and the Commission, the interlocutors in these cases being respectively the ECOFIN President and the Commissioner in charge of Economic Affairs.[78] As mentioned

[75] Amtenbrink and van Duin (2009), p. 569.

[76] Fasone (2014), p. 173.

[77] Some of these meetings, however, lacking a relevant legal basis, should be formally labelled as mere "exchanges of views". They have nonetheless been considered since in practice there is no difference between these and the economic dialogues.

[78] The Commissioner in charge of Employment and Social Affairs is also sometimes invited. See below.

Table 1 Regular economic dialogues

Date	Topic	Institution
1st Semester	Variable	Eurogroup
January	Forthcoming European Semester	Council
April	Macroeconomic imbalances	Commission
June	Draft country-specific recommendations (CSR)	Commission
June	Implementation of the European Semester Adopted CSR	Council
2nd Semester	Variable	Eurogroup
July	Implementation of the European Semester Adopted CSR	Council
September	Draft Annual Growth Survey	Commission[a]
December	Annual Growth Survey Alert Mechanism Report	Commission
December	Opinions on draft budgetary plans	Commission
December	Assessment of completed Semester	Council

[a]First meeting planned for September 2016. See Juncker (2015)

Table 2 Institutions invited during economic dialogues and ECON Committee hearings (2010–2015)

	Commission	Council	Euro-group	Eur. Council	Troika	Member States	Total
2015	5	4	2			1	12
2014	2	2	2			3	9
2013	3	4	3		1[a]	4	15
2012	2	4			1	6	13
2011[b]	4	6	2				12
2010	2	4	2				8

[a]Without the IMF
[b]The dialogue provision entered into force on 23/11/2011

above, meetings with the Eurogroup are more sporadic. Given the lack of binding provisions requiring the Eurogroup President to accept Parliament's invitations, these meetings are mainly dependent on his agenda and good will.

The "troika" took part in two economic dialogues in 2012 and 2013. After the first meeting, however, only representatives from the Commission and the ECB were present. The International Monetary Fund declined all following invitations. IMF experts explained that they are accountable to the IMF Board only and that appearing before the Parliament of a contributor Country could create an unwanted precedent.[79] Yet even after this first and only dialogue with the IMF, confidential meetings were held between some members of the ECON Committee and

[79]Interview 1.

representatives of this institution. Neither the date nor the subject of the discussions was made public.

The President of the European Council never appeared before the ECON Committee but was never invited either. For reasons of prestige, he appears before Parliament at the plenary sessions, where he has made several interventions related to economic matters.

As for the Member States, the following Countries have been invited for an economic dialogue: Hungary, Belgium, Spain (2), Greece, France (2), Germany, Italy, Latvia, Slovenia, Malta, Lithuania and Portugal. The Member State is usually represented by its Minister for Economic Affairs.

Unsurprisingly, the number of dialogues peaked during the most critical moment of the crisis. A fall can be observed in 2014 as a result of reduced parliamentary activity between April and September because of the European elections. In 2015, the number of dialogues rose again but did not reach its pre-election level, probably owing to the more stable economic situation.

Table 2 also reports the number of hearings of the Commission, the Council and the Eurogroup in the 2 years before the creation of the economic dialogue. As can be observed, there were meetings with these institutions before this date. The creation of the dialogue gave a legal basis to some of these meetings (those with the Eurogroup), included new institutions (the European Council and the troika) and Member States, and focused on the new European economic governance mechanisms. The numbers seem to indicate an increase in the frequency of meetings after 2012 compared with pre-dialogue years. This is probably also related to the economic situation in the EU at this time, as mentioned above.

4.2 *The Meetings*

The meetings usually last between 1:30 and 2 h. Most of them take place within the Committee on Economic and Monetary Affairs (ECON), but some dialogues are held before both the ECON and the Employment (EMPL) Committees.

The speaking time is shared between the political groups according to their electoral weight. Each group then provides the ECON Committee Secretariat with a list of the MEPs who will speak.

At the beginning of each meeting, the invited institution or Member State makes a brief introductory statement. Every MEP included in the lists mentioned above then receives a time slot of up to 5 min, to be divided between his or her question (s) and the answer. Given that many MEPs initially tended to use their whole speaking time to word their question, they are now required to ask the question within the first 2 min of their time slot.[80] This should also leave time for the MEP to respond to the answer received.

[80] Interview 1.

Once all the MEPs on the lists have spoken, the remaining time can be used for any additional questions by other MEPs (the "catch-the-eye" procedure).

Before every meeting the ECON Committee Secretariat publishes background notes on the topic of the meeting, which have a significant influence on the questions asked during the debate. Unlike the "monetary dialogue" between Parliament and the European Central Bank, there is no panel of external experts providing background papers before every economic dialogue. In monetary dialogues, the topics of the papers are usually further developed by the ECB President in his introductory speech and serve as a basis for discussion. This system has been introduced since 2014 for economic dialogues with the Eurogroup President.

As with all other European Parliament committee meetings, economic dialogues are broadcasted live on the European Parliament website and remain available there. No detailed minutes or transcriptions of the debates are published.

4.3 Content of the Debates

The issues debated during the meetings largely ignore the limits laid down in the legal provisions for the economic dialogue. In practice the questions cover almost all aspects of economic governance, and more generally any topic related to economic policy. This has never constituted an obstacle to the discussions.

Many questions focused on procedural aspects instead of focusing on content. MEPs are concerned by the very functioning of the reformed Economic and Monetary Union. A large number of questions therefore dealt with legal and institutional issues, such as the many calls for more democratic legitimacy within EMU.

A clear distribution of the topics raised by MEPs emerges, according to their interlocutor.

Most questions on the European Semester[81] were put to the Commission. Commissioners were often asked to justify their positions concerning the application of the Stability and Growth Pact, the content and implementation of the Country-Specific Recommendations and the Commission's opinions on draft budgetary plans, in particular by MEPs from Member States concerned by these decisions. Significantly, great emphasis was put on what MEPs considered an unfair treatment of different Member States. The decision not to take further action against France's excessive deficit and Germany's excessive macroeconomic imbalances during the 2014 and 2015 Semester cycles raised much criticism.[82] This also reveals the extent to which legal provisions on the dialogue were bypassed. In theory, only Council recommendations on these issues would be open to discussion,

---

[81]The European Semester is considered in its "broad format", that is including the 2013 provisions of the Two-Pack.

[82]ECON Committee meetings, 14 April 2015, 15 September 2015 and 1 December 2015.

and not Commission recommendations to the Council. This gap between the legal framework and the content of the debates also appears in the many cases in which MEPs raised questions on draft Country-specific recommendations in order to influence their outcome.[83]

Surprisingly, almost no questions on the Semester were raised during the meetings with the ECOFIN Council, one of the key institutions for the coordination of national economic policies.[84] In practice, as a consequence of the rotating Council Presidency, the ECOFIN President is generally less aware of these issues. Moreover, most decisions concerning the implementation of the Stability and Growth Pact are taken at Commission level and the Council only follows Commission recommendations.[85] Instead, many MEPs take the opportunity to question the ECOFIN President on the priorities of the Presidency, in particular on open legislative procedures relating to economic matters. Many questions were asked, for instance, on the various components of the banking union, in order to obtain information on the negotiations or to try to influence their outcome.[86]

Thanks to his permanent position, the Eurogroup President received many more questions than his ECOFIN colleague on multilateral surveillance in the Euro area. MEPs also consider him to be a privileged interlocutor to debate macroeconomic adjustment programmes[87]—rightly so since the Eurogroup President also chairs the ESM Board of Governors.[88] This represents a twofold departure from the economic dialogue legal framework: not only should these issues be discussed with the Commission, but the only aspect open to debate should be the implementation of the adjustment programmes. In practice, the questions focused on every aspect of the programmes, from the negotiations to the monitoring of their implementation. Many MEPs took this as an opportunity to express their dissatisfaction and ask for justifications for the choices made during the management of the crises in Cyprus and Greece.

Dialogues with Member States were mostly aimed at assessing the reasons for non-compliance with EU guidance.[89] Yet the differing levels of knowledge between MEPs and their interlocutor probably explain why many questions to Member States covered more general economic issues, without any link with those which should form the basis of the economic dialogue.

---

[83]ECON Committee meeting, 23 May 2015.

[84]Articles 120 and 121 TFEU.

[85]Indeed, the "comply or explain" clause of the economic dialogue did not raise much interest: the Council usually submits its explanation in written form, which is largely unobserved.

[86]ECON Committee meetings, 17 December 2013 and 22 January 2014.

[87]ECON Committee meetings, 7 May 2013 and 10 November 2015.

[88]Article 5, para. 2, of the ESM Treaty.

[89]ECON Committee meetings, 28 January 2014, 2 December 2014 and 7 May 2015.

5 Critical Assessment

Overall, the first objective of the economic dialogue has been met. The implementation of this mechanism systematised a pre-existing practice of exchanges with EU institutions, included Member States, and ultimately created a forum for regular public exchanges between Parliament and the key players in the new European economic governance. Within the context of the recent EMU reforms, these debates are a successful application of the principle according to which accountability has to be guaranteed at the level at which decisions are taken.[90]

Practice also revealed the adaptability of this tool to the new reality of Economic and Monetary Union. The Eurogroup and the Member States, even if not legally bound by the Treaties, have more or less willingly agreed to play their part and have become regular interlocutors of the European Parliament. This is all the more relevant in the case of the Eurogroup, for which the economic dialogue represents a (modest) counterweight to the considerable new powers it has gained in recent years. As for the IMF and the European Council, they have other channels through which to meet Parliament's representatives. Finally, with regard to the scope of the exchanges, the dialogues have gone beyond the restricted list laid down in the Six-Pack and the Two-Pack; the topics discussed include all issues related to EU economic affairs.

Yet the mere fact that a certain number of economic dialogues have been held cannot be considered as a success story *per se*. What matters is that many MEPs have been able to use this mechanism successfully: asking relevant questions and obtaining justifications for the decisions taken; expressing relevant and well-argued (usually critical) points of view to EU officials; or even publicly blaming them for their handling of economic matters. In particular, the dialogue has proved very effective in scrutinising each stage of the European Semester, from the Annual Growth Survey to the Commission's opinion on draft budgetary plans.

However, the economic dialogue still underperforms in four main areas.

Firstly, many MEPs do not make optimal use of this new tool. Some use almost their whole speaking time to ask their question, leaving their interlocutor with only a few seconds to answer. Others do not even ask a question but use their entire time slot to raise criticisms. The dialogues certainly provide an opportunity for MEPs to make requests and share their point of view, but the effectiveness of these contributions is questionable.[91] Overall, the impression is that many MEPs consider the economic dialogue merely as an instrument to enhance their own visibility.[92]

Secondly, even when there is an exchange of information between MEPs and EU officials or Member States, the superficiality of the debates is striking. Although the tendency to disregard the restrictive legal framework makes it possible to scrutinise crucial aspects of economic governance, it also contributes to the dispersion of the

[90]European Commission (2012) and European Parliament (2013).

[91]Martin (2011), p. 261.

[92]Martin (2011), p. 267; Sánchez de Dios and Wiberg (2011), pp. 360 and 362.

questions. Many MEPs raise issues for which their interlocutors are not responsible. Moreover, matters such as the effectiveness of austerity, the lack of implementation of country-specific recommendations in the EU and the absence of accountability mechanisms in the new EMU cannot possibly be covered in a satisfactory way within a time slot of a few minutes. The answers provided therefore often remain rather vague. Moreover, follow-up questions are very rare. This is regrettable as it would be the best moment for MEPs to really challenge their interlocutor by deepening, rectifying or contradicting the answer received. Lastly, there is no organisation between the MEPs to explore a single topic more deeply. Instead, the discussion moves from one topic to another every 5 min, adding to this sense of superficiality.

A very detailed and precise discussion, however, may not be entirely satisfactory either. Certain questions focus on highly technical points. While it is certainly very interesting and useful for MEPs to receive first-hand information from top EU officials, there is a difference between the provision of information and accountability.[93] There are many other sources where MEPs could obtain information; accountability, however, involves providing explanations and justifying a political choice.

Thirdly, the debates with the Eurogroup President reveal the limits of Parliament's power. The Eurogroup President attends when it is convenient for him, which means that the dialogues are sometimes held long after the event to which they relate.[94] These meetings often lead to heated exchanges nonetheless. Yet the MEPs are always totally powerless with regard to the Eurogroup President; the only thing they can do is strongly disagree with him. During the exchanges, the Eurogroup President can openly admit that he is not aware of the details of a Memorandum of Understanding,[95] ignore certain questions[96] or even refuse to answer a question,[97] and he will not face any consequences for this.[98] In the best-case scenario, when the MEPs succeed in obtaining explanations or justifications, these dialogues can be considered as an exchange of information—but they are far from representing an exercise in accountability.

Finally, one may wonder whether these exchanges really have an impact on the institutions and Member States invited. A certain number of topics are invariably put forward at each meeting, including objections against the EU austerity drive, calls for more accountable governance mechanisms and their embedding in EU law and protests against the differentiated treatment of small and large Member States

---

[93]Bovens (2007), p. 451; Sánchez de Dios and Wiberg (2011), p. 360.

[94]This was the case with the *ad hoc* dialogue on the third Greek bailout programme, initially scheduled for September 2015 and then postponed to November, some four months after the agreement between the Greek Government and the Eurogroup.

[95]ECON Committee meeting, 24 February 2015.

[96]ECON Committee meeting, 4 September 2014.

[97]As is always the case when asked about Member States' positions within the Eurogroup.

[98]His attitude is actually consistent as he strongly believes that ESM accountability is a matter for national Parliaments, each of them holding its minister to account. See Rittberger (2014), pp. 1178–1179.

when it comes to multilateral surveillance. Yet these recurrent remarks do not seem to have any effect. Paradoxically, more successful requests are also likely to be less visible since the MEPs will not continue to ask them.

6 Conclusion

The economic dialogue was introduced to ensure greater transparency and accountability of the new European economic governance by making the European Parliament the forum where decisions taken are publicly debated with all relevant players.

From the outset, Parliament's limited powers with respect to other EU institutions made the economic dialogue's success dependent on their willingness to participate in this exercise, while excluding any consequence for the institutions involved. Moreover, crucial topics were excluded from the matters open to debate, undermining Parliament's ability to undertake a comprehensive review of its interlocutors' performance.

Evidence reveals that the dialogue has departed from this rigid legal framework and adjusted remarkably to the new reality of Economic and Monetary Union, as regards both the participants and the topics discussed. The resulting regular public exchanges between Parliament and the key players in the new European economic governance are particularly well adapted to scrutiny of the European Semester. Nevertheless, the superficiality of the debates, demands by MEPs for visibility and Parliament's restricted powers, notably with respect to the Eurogroup, limit the dialogue's potential as an effective exercise in accountability.

An assessment of the economic dialogue's added value in terms of accountability has to take into account both its successes and its limitations, bearing in mind that Parliament's instruments are not limited to this mechanism. The other ECON meetings, the meetings of other committees, the role of the plenary sessions and other forums such as the European Parliamentary Week must also be taken into consideration.

As to the way forward, several avenues for improvement can be considered.

In its recent Communication on steps towards completing Economic and Monetary Union, the Commission suggested further aligning the dialogue's meetings with the main stages of the European Semester.[99] More significant progress could undoubtedly be made by amending the list of topics on which the dialogues can focus. A broader selection of topics open to discussion, notably concerning the preparation, implementation and follow-up of financial assistance programmes, should help shed light on one of the most controversial aspects of today's European economic governance.

[99]European Commission (2015).

Yet the main obstacle to a fully effective dialogue comes from the limited competences of Parliament and its very variable power of control over the other institutions. The Five Presidents' Report includes the integration of the ESM into EU law as one of the medium-term targets to be completed as from June 2017.[100] This should allow Parliament to exercise a greater degree of scrutiny over this major pillar of European economic governance and would certainly help overcome many of the current limitations.

In the meantime, the European Parliament should learn how to fully exploit the potential of the tools at its disposal. A number of the dialogue's shortcomings can be addressed by MEPs and political groups. Progressive adaptation and an ongoing learning process should allow them to make better use of this instrument. From this perspective, the current dialogue can be seen as a foretaste of what Parliament's role will be in a more democratic Economic and Monetary Union.

References

Allemand F (2013) Le développement de la coordination des politiques budgétaires dans l'Union Européenne. In: Sorel J-M, Chemain R (eds) Quelle souveraineté budgétaire pour les États? Actes du Colloque du 5 décembre 2012, Palais Brongniart. Pedone, Paris, pp 31–63

Amtenbrink F, van Duin K (2009) The European Central Bank before the European Parliament: theory and practice after 10 years of monetary dialogue. Eur Law Rev 34(4):561–583

Bourgault S (2014) "Dialogues and Accountability Hearings" at a Glance. European Parliament, DG for Internal Policies, Economic Governance Support Unit, Brussels

Bovens M (2007) Analysing and assessing accountability: a conceptual framework. Eur Law J 13 (4):447–468

Bovens M, Curtin D, Hart P (2010) Towards a more accountable EU. Amsterdam Centre for European Law and Governance, Working Paper Series 2010-04, Amsterdam

Claeys G, Hallerberg M, Tschekassin O (2014) European Central Bank accountability: how the monetary dialogue could evolve. Bruegel Policy Contribution, 2014/04 Bruegel, Brussels

Dawson M, de Witte F (2013) Constitutional balance in the EU after the Euro-crisis. Mod Law Rev 76(5):817–844

de Witte B, Trechsel AH, Damjanović D (2010) Legislating after Lisbon. New opportunities for the European Parliament. European University Institute, Robert Schuman Centre for Advanced Studies, Florence

Eijffinger S, Mujagic E (2004) An assessment of the effectiveness of the monetary dialogue on the ECB's accountability and transparency: a qualitative approach. Intereconomics 3(4):190–203

European Commission (2012) Communication from the Commission. A blueprint for a deep and genuine economic and monetary union. Launching a European Debate. COM (2012) 777 final/2

European Commission (2014) Communication from the Commission to the European Parliament, the Council, the European Central Bank, the European Economic and Social Committee and the Committee of the Regions. Economic Governance Review. Report on the Application of Regulations (EU) N° 1173/2011, 1174/2011, 1175/2011, 1176/2011, 1177/2011, 472/2013 and 473/2013. COM (2014) 905 final

[100] Juncker et al. (2015), p. 14.

European Commission (2015) Communication from the Commission on steps towards completing economic and monetary union. COM (2015) 600 final

European Parliament (2010a) Resolution of 16 June 2010 on economic governance. P7_TA(2010) 0224

European Parliament (2010b) Resolution of 20 October 2010 with recommendations to the Commission on improving the economic governance and stability framework of the union, in particular in the Euro area. 2010/2099(INI)

European Parliament (2011a) Amendments adopted on 23 June 2011 to the proposal for a regulation of the European Parliament and of the Council on the effective enforcement of budgetary surveillance in the Euro area. OJEU C 390 E, 18 December 2012, pp 111–120

European Parliament (2011b) European Parliament resolution of 6 July 2011 on the financial, economic and social crisis: recommendations concerning the measures and initiatives to be taken. 2010/2242(INI)

European Parliament (2013) Resolution on constitutional problems of a multitier governance in the European Union. A7-0372/2013

Fasone C (2014) European economic governance and parliamentary representation. What place for the European Parliament? Eur Law J 20(2):164–185

Juncker J-C (2015) Speech before the European Parliament. European Commission, Brussels

Juncker J-C, Tusk D, Dijsselbloem J, Draghi M, Schulz M (2015) Completing Europe's economic and monetary union. European Commission, Brussels

Majone G (2014) From regulatory state to a democratic default. J Common Mark Stud 52 (6):1216–1223

Martin S (2011) Parliamentary questions, the behaviour of legislators, and the function of legislatures: an introduction. J Legis Stud 17(3):259–270

Maurer A (2013) From EMU to DEMU: the democratic legitimacy of the EU and European Parliament. IAI Working Paper 13/11

Menéndez AJ (2014) Editorial: a European Union in constitutional mutation? Eur Law J 20 (2):127–141

O'Keeffe M, Salines M, Wieczorek M (2016) The European Parliament's strategy in EU economic and financial reform. J Eur Public Policy 23(2):217–235

Rittberger B (2014) Integration without representation? The European Parliament and the reform of economic governance in the EU. J Common Mark Stud 52(6):1174–1183

Sánchez de Dios M, Wiberg M (2011) Questioning in European Parliaments. J Legis Stud 17 (3):354–367

Tuori K, Tuori K (2014) The Eurozone crisis: a constitutional analysis. Cambridge University Press, Cambridge

Van Rompuy H, Barroso JM, Juncker J-C, Draghi M (2012) Towards a genuine economic and monetary union. European Council, Brussels

von der Groeben H, Schwarze J, Hatje A (2015) Europäisches Unionsrecht. Nomos Verlagsgesellschaft, Baden-Baden

The Euro-Crisis, EMU and the Perils of Centralisation

Federico Fabbrini

Abstract Since the outburst of the Euro-crisis, legal measures adopted by the Member States and the institutions of the EU have produced a major centralisation of powers in the field of economic governance. Recent proposals to achieve a deeper and more genuine European Economic and Monetary Union—and especially the June 2015 Five Presidents Report on "*Completing Europe's EMU*", and the October 2015 European Commission communication "*On Steps towards Completing EMU*"—have called for further centralisation of powers in the Eurozone. In particular, both documents have proposed the establishment of so-called independent competitiveness councils which would advise State Governments on what structural reforms to undertake nationally as a way to boost growth. The purpose of this contribution is to shed a critical light on these recent proposals discussing the perils that centralisation poses on the balance of power between the EU and the Member States. The chapter, in particular, questions whether the objective of a full centralisation and control of national economic policy can be effective and legitimate. As an alternative, it considers what advantages would be connected to the creation of a genuine EU fiscal capacity: to this end, the chapter explains how an EU fiscal capacity could support the functioning of EMU without bringing about a full centralisation of national economic policies.

Contents

F. Fabbrini (✉)
School of Law & Government, Dublin City University, Dublin, Ireland
e-mail: federico.fabbrini@dcu.ie

L. Daniele et al. (eds.), *Democracy in the EMU in the Aftermath of the Crisis*,
DOI 10.1007/978-3-319-53895-2_6

1 Introduction

Since the outburst of the Euro-crisis, legal measures adopted by the Member States and the institutions of the European Union (EU) have produced a major centralisation of powers in the field of economic governance: from the Fiscal Compact, to the "Two Pack", powers in high-salience areas such as budgetary-making and fiscal policy has been transferred from the Member States to the EU institutions. While this development has been justified as necessary to ensure the survival of the Eurozone, as I have argued elsewhere the centralisation of power emerged in response to the Euro-crisis has been paradoxical when measured by the standard of federal systems.[1]

Recent proposals to achieve a deeper and more genuine European Economic and Monetary Union (EMU)—including the June 2015 Five Presidents Report on "*Completing Europe's EMU*",[2] and the follow-up October 2015 European Commission communication "*On Steps towards Completing EMU*,"[3]—have called for further centralisation of powers in the Eurozone. In particular, the Commission communication proposed the establishment of so-called competitiveness councils, which would advise State Governments on what structural reforms to undertake nationally as a way to boost growth; as well as the creation of an independent fiscal authority, empowered to police even more strictly Member States' compliance with European budgetary rules.

The purpose of this contribution is to shed a critical light on the recent proposals for further legal and institutional reforms in the Eurozone, discussing the perils that centralisation poses on the balance of power between the EU and the Member States.[4] The chapter, in particular, questions whether the objective of a full centralisation and control of national economic policy can be effective and legitimate. As an alternative, it considers what advantages would be connected to the creation of a genuine EU fiscal capacity: to this end, the chapter explains how an EU fiscal capacity could support the functioning of EMU without bringing about a full centralisation of national economic policies as suggested by the latest swath of proposals for EMU reform.

The chapter is structured as follows. Section 2 summarises the main centralising measures adopted in response to the Euro-crisis. Section 3 examines the most recent proposals to reform EMU, explaining the further centralising effects they would produce on the relations of power between the Member States and the EU. Section 4, however, critically discusses the limits associated with this centralisation and suggests that there are plausible arguments why the Member States ought to maintain some autonomy in their budgetary process. Section 5, finally, proposes an alternative to the centralising measures which are currently being proposed and

---

[1]Fabbrini (2016).

[2]President of the European Commission, Report (2015).

[3]European Commission Communication (2015b).

[4]Kollman (2014).

makes the case in favor of a fiscal capacity for the EU: as Sect. 6 claims, giving a modicum of taxing and spending power to the EU would be much less invasive of national autonomy than the current system, where the budgetary policy of the Member States is subject to tight supranational supervision.

2 Responses to the Euro-Crisis

In the efforts to address the Euro-crisis, since 2010 both the EU institutions and the Member States enacted a swath of legal measures aimed at strengthening budgetary constraints at all levels of Government.[5] The objective of ensuring the sustainability of Member State budgets was already enshrined in the Stability and Growth Pact (SGP) originally enacted in two Council Regulations in 1997,[6] and currently attached as Protocol No. 12 to the TFEU,[7] which requires the Member States of the EMU to maintain their public deficit below the yearly *ratio* of 3% of the GDP and the total public debt below 60% of the GDP. The weaknesses of the enforcement mechanisms of the SGP, however, allegedly ensured widespread non-compliance by EMU countries with the SGP.[8] To address this situation, therefore, the EU institutions and the Member States pushed for a tightening of budgetary constraints—at international, supranational and constitutional level.[9]

In November 2011 the EU institutions enacted a package of five EU Regulations and one EU Directive—generally referred to as the "Six Pack"[10]—which profoundly modified the architecture of EU economic governance, enhancing the capacity of EU institutions to prevent and correct Member States deviations from the SGP standards.[11] On the one hand, the "Six Pack" improved the so-called "preventive arm" of the SGP, strengthening the reporting commitments of Member States with respect to their fiscal performance and introducing a new "macroeconomic imbalance procedure" run by the European Commission to alert Member States of the destabilising elements of their economies. On the other hand, the "Six Pack" overhauled the so-called "corrective arm" of the SGP, empowering the Commission to sanction Member States for breaches of the deficit and debt rules and depriving the Council of Minister (the EU body representing the executives of

---

[5]Tuori and Tuori (2014).

[6]Regulation (EC) No. 1466/97; Regulation (EC) No. 1467/97.

[7]Protocol No. 12 on the Excessive Debt Procedure, OJEU C 115, 9 May 2008, pp. 279 et seqq.

[8]Collignon (2004). See also ECJ 13 July 2004, Case C-27/04, *Commission* v. *Council of the EU*, (recognising wide discretion to the Council whether to impose sanctions under the SGP or held in abeyance the excessive deficit procedure against two Member States recommended by the Commission).

[9]Tosato (2014).

[10]Regulation (EU) No. 1173/2011; Regulation (EU) No. 1174/2011; Regulation (EU) No. 1175/2011; Regulation (EU) No. 1176/2011; Regulation (EU) No. 1177/2011; Directive 2011/85/EU.

[11]Craig (2014).

the Member States) of most discretion in the application of fines against States subject to the "excessive deficit procedure." Moreover, the "Six Pack" introduced minimum requirements for the design and operation of State budgetary laws, and gave formal recognition to a new governance framework—the so-called "European Semester", informally set up in 2010[12]—in which Member States submit their draft budgets to the Commission for evaluation and discussion about their compliance with the broader economic forecasts of the EU.

Following on this line of reform, a second set of EU Regulations—generally referred to as the "Two-Pack"[13]—adopted in May 2013, compelled Member States to establish independent national authorities—so-called fiscal councils—entrusted with the task of controlling the quality of the economic forecasts of national Governments.[14] Moreover, it required that Member States submit their draft budget bills to the European Commission for prior assessment of their compliance with the reinforced SGP.[15] Pursuant to this innovation, that integrates the "European Semester," national Governments are required to present to the Commission a draft of their budget bills in September of every year—even before the text is tabled for debate and approval in national Parliaments—and the Commission may demand Member States to introduce changes to their budgetary bills within 3 weeks if these appear to be grossly in deviation of EU standards of budgetary performance.[16]

Besides the reform introduced through EU legislation, another major step toward centralisation in EMU, however, has resulted from measures adopted by the Member States outside the framework of EU law.[17] In particular, 25 out of the (then) 27 EU Member States, agreed to sign in March 2012 a binding international treaty—the Fiscal Compact—which further overhauled the EU architecture of economic governance.[18] The Fiscal Compact, in fact, called for the constitutionalisation of budgetary constraints as the solution for the sovereign debt crisis faced by the Eurozone.[19] First, the Fiscal Compact provides a very detailed and technical "golden rule," which defines in strict mathematical terms the

---

[12]European Council Conclusions (2010), p. 5.

[13]Regulation (EU) No. 473/2013; Regulation (EU) No. 472/2013.

[14]de Streel (2015).

[15]Hinarejos (2015), p. 32.

[16]Art 7, para 2, of Regulation (EU) No. 473/2013 (stating that "where, in exceptional cases, after consulting the Member State concerned within one week of submission of the draft budgetary plan, the Commission identifies particularly serious non-compliance with the budgetary policy obligations laid down in the SGP, the Commission shall adopt its opinion within two weeks of submission of the draft budgetary plan. In its opinion, the Commission shall request that a revised draft budgetary plan be submitted as soon as possible and in any event within three weeks of the date of its opinion.").

[17]Craig (2012).

[18]Treaty on Stability, Coordination and Governance in the Economic and Monetary Union, 2 March 2012, [hereinafter Fiscal Compact], available at http://www.eurozone.europa.eu/media/304649/st00tscg26_en12.pdf (last visited 1 June 2014).

[19]Peers (2012).

yearly structural deficit permitted in every Member State and specifies conditions for disrespecting the rule, as well as automatic mechanisms to ensure compliance.[20] Second, the Fiscal Compact—breaking with the tradition of ordinary international law, which leaves Member States free to choose the domestic means to give effect to the commitments undertaken at the international level—obliges the Contracting Parties to incorporate the "golden rule" in State Constitutions or in other quasi-constitutional sources of law which ought to bind the ordinary budgetary process.[21] Third, the Fiscal Compact sets up an intrusive enforcement mechanism, which authorises contracting parties to bring cases against non-compliant states before the European Court of Justice (ECJ) and empowers the ECJ to sanction disobedient States with substantial financial penalties.[22] Last but not least, the Fiscal Compact, made the introduction of, and compliance with, the "golden rule" a condition to obtain financial assistance under the European Stability Mechanism (ESM).[23]

In conclusion, the reforms adopted in response to the Euro-crisis have produced a remarkable shift of power in the budgetary domain from the Member States to the EU institutions. As Roland Bieber has argued

> [t]he common denominator of those acts is a *reduction* of Member States' competence in matters of general economic policy and a resulting transfer to the Union.[24]

In particular, the "European Semester" requires States to submit every spring to the Commission a draft of their budget laws that takes into account the parameters of the economic situation of the country previously prepared by the Commission. The Commission can request changes when it believes that the draft national budget would run afoul of EU economic and fiscal objectives.[25] Budgets are then presented domestically in Parliaments each fall, after having received the Commission's approval. Moreover, the Fiscal Compact provides another instrument of control for the Commission over the states' budgetary procedures. By relying on the strict and detailed balanced-budget rules mandated by the Fiscal Compact, the Commission is able to exercise a more pervasive *ex ante* scrutiny on the sustainability and appropriateness of the draft budget bills which the Governments submit for approval during the European Semester.[26] At the same time, the Commission has gained more effective powers of *ex post* oversight on the budgetary performances of the states, with the possibility—besides naming the States which have not incorporated the "golden rule," and thus opening the way for a case before the ECJ[27]—of adopting semi-automatic sanctions against States with excessive deficits.[28]

---

[20] Article 3, para. 1, of the Fiscal Compact.

[21] Article 3, para. 2, of the Fiscal Compact.

[22] Article 8 of the Fiscal Compact.

[23] Preamble (recital 27) of the Fiscal Compact.

[24] Bieber (2015), p. 92 (emphasis in original).

[25] Costamagna (2014).

[26] Article 3 of the Fiscal Compact.

[27] Article 8 of the Fiscal Compact.

[28] Article 7 of the Fiscal Compact.

3 New Proposals for EMU Reform

While the reforms adopted in response to the Euro-crisis have sought to limit the weaknesses of EMU, wide-spread *consensus* exists on the need to put the Eurozone on a more stable basis. This has prompted in recent years a flurry of policy proposals—and calls for completing Europe's EMU have not remained a matter of pure academic disquisition but have become a key part of the EU policy-making agenda, at the highest political level.[29] In particular, in December 2012 the President of the European Council produced a report, written in cooperation with the Presidents of the European Commission, the Eurogroup and the European Central Bank (ECB)—the so-called "Four Presidents" Report[30]—in which it outlined a roadmap towards a deeper EMU; and in June 2015, the President of the European Commission published a new report, written in close coordination with the Presidents of the European Council, the Eurogroup, the ECB and also the European Parliament—the so-called "Five Presidents" Report[31]—relaunching steps towards greater integration in EMU, along a time-frame to be accomplished within the next 10 years at maximum. Moreover, calls toward improving EMU have been made by the ECB,[32] the European Commission,[33] the European Parliament,[34] as well as by several national Governments.[35]

Some of the ideas articulated in the current debate on the future of EMU would represent an important improvement of the *status quo*.[36] Nevertheless, a feature running through several of the policy proposals under discussion is the call for endowing the EU institutions with even greater surveillance and police powers over the budgetary policy of the Member States. In other words, while the set of legal and institutional reforms adopted in the aftermath of the Euro-crisis have produced a significant centralising effect, shifting power in the budgetary domains from the Member States to the EU, the trend toward centralisation may not be over yet. In fact, many of the measures under consideration during the recent months in the debates on the reform of the EMU system of governance would promote even greater centralisation, reducing further the ability of Member States to take decisions on their budgets. This development results from two interrelated set of policy proposals: the creation of independent competitiveness councils, and the

---

[29]Mayer (2015).

[30]President of the European Council, Final Report (2012).

[31]President of the European Commission, Report (2015).

[32]Draghi (2015).

[33]European Commission Communication (2012).

[34]E.g. European Parliament Resolution (2012, 2013, 2015b).

[35]In particular, Member States articulated proposals for the future of EMU in response to the questions raised in an Analytical Note prepared by the President of the European Commission, in close cooperation with the Presidents of the European Council, of the Eurogroup and the ECB. See President of the European Commission, Analytical Note (2015).

[36]See *infra*, sec. 5.

institutionalisation of a new European fiscal board, to which in due course the current budgetary surveillance powers of the European Commission could be transferred.

On the one hand, several official documents presented in the last few months have called for the creation of independent competitiveness councils. In particular, the June 2015 Report "*Completing Europe's EMU*" coordinated by the President of the European Commission has recommended the creation

> by each euro area Member State of a national body in charge of tracking performance and policies in the field of competitiveness.[37]

These independent authorities—which would then be placed in a network, to be coordinated by the Commission[38]—ought to provide guidance on structural reforms, removing from the political process, or from labor-management negotiations, the decisions about wage-setting or other regulations affecting economic growth.[39] The idea of a network of competitiveness councils has then been further worked out by the European Commission in its October 2015 communication on the steps toward completing EMU.[40] In this document, the Commission—after stressing the essential role that competitiveness plays in ensuring growth and convergence in the EU[41]—formally advanced a proposal for the establishment of independent competitiveness authorities

> to improve national policymaking by providing independent expertise,[42]

and clarified that determination by these bodies should inform the wage setting processes at national level. Moreover, the idea of competitiveness councils has received a strong backing by President of the Eurogroup Jeroen Dijsselbloem. In a July 2015 letter to the members of the Eurogroup in which he sought re-election by his peers, the President of the Eurogroup clarified his view that

> a framework of national competitiveness councils should be established, to assess the fiscal and macroeconomic implications of planned and implemented reforms, in resemblance of the network of national fiscal councils.[43]

On the other hand, besides the creation of competitiveness councils, calls have been made to create a new independent watchdog—a European fiscal authority—designed to enhance compliance with EU fiscal rules. Building on the Report "*Completing Europe's EMU*",[44] the European Commission has proposed the establishment of a European Fiscal Board, composed of independent fiscal experts, and

---

[37]President of the European Commission, Report (2015), p. 7.

[38]*Ibid.*, p. 8.

[39]*Ibid.*

[40]European Commission Communication (2015b).

[41]*Ibid.*, p. 10.

[42]*Ibid.*

[43]Dijsselbloem (2015), p. 3.

[44]President of the European Commission, Report (2015), p. 7.

tasked to provide recommendations on States' budgetary performance.[45] In the Commission's view, therefore, the Board would work in coordination with the national fiscal councils created pursuant to the "Two Pack", and mostly act as an advisory body.[46] However, the idea of a Fiscal Board has been pushed further in the proposals made by other policy-makers. In Germany, in particular, the creation of an independent EU fiscal body has been hailed as a step toward a strict application of EU fiscal rules.[47] While the German Finance Minister Wolfgang Schäuble has strongly argued in favor of creating a Budget Commissioner empowered to veto national budgets which fail to respect EU deficit and debt rules,[48] the German Central Bank President Jens Weidman has proposed to transfer

> the Commission's current tasks in the field of budgetary surveillance

to such a European fiscal authority.[49] As the President of the German Central Bank complained, the Commission has become too politicised and

> has repeatedly shown that it is prepared to accept compromises at the expenses of fiscal discipline.[50]

To avoid this problem, therefore, he recommended a shift of surveillance powers to a fully-independent fiscal board, which can restore the credibility of EU fiscal rules by applying them blindly, without undue attention toward political realities.

It is clear that if the reform proposals briefly summarised here were to be carried out, they would put in place a new web of restrictions on the budgetary autonomy of the Member States, jeopardising their ability to take meaningful decisions in fiscal and economic matters. The creation of independent competitiveness council, in fact, would remove from the political process decisions on issues like pension reforms, or wage negotiation, delegating to unelected technocrats the power to decide issues of great political significance for the citizenry as a whole. At the same time, the creation of a European fiscal board, in charge of the network of national fiscal councils, would reduce the margin of maneuver of national Parliaments, with the risk of transforming the budgetary decision-making process from a forum in which alternative political movements compete for the allocation of scares resources into a technocratic exercise in which alleged experts decide what is the best economic policy for a country.[51] And of course, if the European fiscal board was to be transformed into a full-fledged EU fiscal watchdog—overtaking the task that the Commission currently performs in the supervision of European budgetary

---

[45]European Commission Communication (2015b), p. 11.

[46]*Ibid.*

[47]Besselink and Reestman (2012).

[48]Schäuble (2014) (speaking in favor of a "European budget commissioner, who would be able to reject national budgets if they don't correspond to the rules we have jointly agreed.").

[49]Weidman (2016).

[50]*Ibid.*

[51]Wyplosz (2005) (emphasising restrictions which fiscal councils would put on parliamentary sovereignty).

rules—the centralising dynamic would reach the zenith: the budgetary policy of the Member States would be subject to strict European policing, with no possibility for the EU countries to negotiate margins of flexibility (as is currently permitted by EU law).[52] While the proposals discussed in this section are all accustomed by a distrust for democracy and elected institutions, it seems apposite to raise the question whether they reflect an effective and legitimate vision for the future of EMU.[53]

4 The Perils of Centralisation

The dynamics of centralisation in the vertical relations of power between the Member States and the EU institutions following the out-burst of the Euro-crisis have been often described as inevitable.[54] The revelations of widespread lack of compliance by the EU Member States with the deficit and debt targets set in the SGP, and the negative externalities that would spill-over from countries in fiscal distress towards other Member States of the Eurozone, have called for greater control at the central level over the budgetary policy of the EU Member States.[55] At the same time, it has been suggested that the constitutionalisation of budgetary constraints into the legal system of the EU Member States, along the model designed in the Fiscal Compact, contributed to the ownership of budgetary rules by the Member States, and strengthened their willingness and ability to abide by them.[56] From a law and economics perspective, therefore, the strengthening of EU budgetary constraints and their domestication in the legal system of the Member States—with the ensuing shift of power from the Member States toward the EU—was a logical step to address collective action problems emerging in the integrated economy of the EMU and to restore Member States commitments towards previously agreed upon fiscal targets.[57]

As Ken Kollman has emphasised, otherwise, federalism-based systems have a tendency to slip towards centralisation.[58] Examining the case of the church, corporations and political unions such as the EU and the United States (US), Ken Kollman has underlined how a common trajectory of centralisation occurs when, in systems of decentralised governance, the emergence of crises creates the need for executive action at the central level and sub-units assent to this development, on the assumption that they can still remain in control of the decision-making process

[52]European Commission Communication (2015a).

[53]Pernice et al. (2012).

[54]Herzog and Hengstermann (2013).

[55]Schelke (2007).

[56]Tuori and Tuori (2014), p. 109.

[57]Antoš (2014) citing Elster (1979).

[58]Kollman (2014), p. 13.

through representative institutions.[59] As he pointed out, the mechanisms of centralisation

> can be summarized by five processes that often happen in rough chronological order: assent, representative centralization, partisanship, executive centralization, and lock-in.[60]

Seen through this prism of analysis, the developments occurring in the EMU appear as largely predictable: after the Member States had assented to the SGP, remaining in control of its enforcement through their action in the Council, the Euro-crisis increasingly created the need for more delegation authority to an independent supranational institution such as the European Commission to effectively enforce these rules.[61] The legislative innovation produced by the "Six-Pack" and the "Two-Pack", coupled with the Fiscal Compact, then, produced an entrenchment of the powers of the Commission, bringing to its extreme the centralisation of budgetary policy in the EU.[62]

Yet, as much as the development recently occurring in the EMU seems to follow a path recurrent in federated system, a crucial question is whether the nature of this centralisation, and its degree, is wholly warranted. Whereas some form of supranational control over state budgetary policies seems inevitable in the EMU, there is a plausible argument that the EU Member States ought to enjoy some degree of autonomy in decisions about taxing and spending. Historically, in Europe the budgetary process has been the battlefield in which national Parliaments have affirmed their role as the institutions representing the popular will, against the wish of the monarchies[63]—and decisions about taxing and spending as reflected through the design of the budgetary act are still today at the core of the ability of democratic States to shape policies.[64] In fact, the literature on fiscal federalism has repeatedly emphasised the advantages which are associated to States' autonomy in the fiscal domain, in terms of experimentation, competition and choice.[65] As Francesco Costamagna emphasised, moreover, in modern welfare States, budgetary decisions profoundly affect the nature of social entitlements that citizens can obtain from the Government, and the existence of budgetary autonomy at the Member States level is a pre-condition for a meaningful political competition on Government policies.[66]

---

[59] *Ibid.*, p. 15.

[60] *Ibid.*, pp. 8–9.

[61] Buti and Carnot (2012).

[62] de Streel (2013).

[63] Delledonne (2014).

[64] Van Malleghem (2014).

[65] Rodriguez-Tejedo and Wallis (2012). See *ceteris paribus* also *New State Ice Co.* v. *Liebmann*, 285 U.S. 262, 311 (1932) (J. Brandeis dissenting, defining as "one of the happy incidents of the federal system [the fact] that a single courageous State may, if its citizens choose, serve as a laboratory; and try novel social and economic experiments without risk to the rest of the country.").

[66] Costamagna (2014).

Acknowledging this point, the Report "*Towards a Genuine Economic and Monetary Union*" delivered in December 2012 by the President of the European Council, underlined that

> [d]ecisions on national budgets are at the heart of Member States' parliamentary democracies.[67]

In other words, relevant constitutional arguments on the role of the EU Member States point in favour of some degree of States' autonomy in the decisions about budget and shed some critical light on the paradox of centralisation produced by the latest legal and institutional responses to the Euro-crisis.[68] The requirement that Member States submit their budget draft to the EU institutions for supranational validation prior to approval in the national Parliaments, coupled with the obligation to enshrine in higher laws fiscal targets policed by supranational institutions, produced a relevant compression on the ability of the Member States to have autonomous deliberations about their budgets. And several of the ongoing proposals for EMU reform would restrict States' budgetary autonomy even further, essentially depoliticising economic policy choices at the national level. Such a development is unlikely to occur without strong national resistances—as evidenced by the skirmishes which have emerged as of late between a plurality of Member States' Government and the EU institutions.[69]

Most crucially, however, it is unconvincing that a significant supranational takeover of the budgetary process of the Member States could not be avoided through other, less restrictive, solutions—which ensured a proper functioning of the EMU and yet secured some autonomy to the Member States. In fact, as I have explained elsewhere, the example of the US points out precisely to such an alternative option.[70] While the US has had to face the challenges of managing an asymmetrical Economic and Monetary Union—much like the EU—is has not found necessary to suspend *tout court* the ability of the Member States to decide autonomously on their budgetary policies.[71] The US States still today remain sovereign in deciding about their domestic taxing and spending, and no federal framework exist to supervise and approve their budgetary laws.[72] Yet, the Federal Government, thanks to a set of constitutional transformations beginning during the Progressiva Era and the New Deal, has acquired other instruments to govern the US economy—notably a fiscal capacity, supported by autonomous revenue sources, to counter-act asymmetric economic shocks occurring in some US States, and prevent contagious effects throughout the US economy.[73] Because such tools have proved valuable to manage

[67] President of the European Council, Final Report (2012), p. 16.

[68] Lindseth (2014).

[69] Dixon (2015).

[70] Fabbrini (2013).

[71] Rodden (2006).

[72] Henning and Kessler (2012).

[73] Super (2015).

the US economy while securing some degree of autonomy to the States, it is worth inquiring whether a similar option may be considered also in the EMU as an alternative to the paradox of centralisation.

5 The Alternative: Fiscal Capacity

As an alternative to the proposals for EMU reform discussed above, an idea which has attracted attention as of late is the creation of a fiscal capacity. The concept of fiscal capacity refers to a Eurozone budget, financed by EU own resources, and designed to perform a fiscal stabilisation function for the EMU.[74] Contrary to the proposals in favor of competitiveness councils and a European fiscal board—which follow the "surveillance model" which has so far inspired responses to the Euro-crisis—the creation of a fiscal capacity would follow the "fiscal federalism model", and complete EMU by endowing the European institutions with a central budget, funded through new own resources, by which to assuage asymmetric shocks and carry out counter-cyclical policies no-longer possible at the national level due to the budgetary constraints.[75] The creation of a fiscal capacity has been hailed by many as a necessary step to transform the EMU from a "rule-based" architecture, into a real system of economic governance, endowed with politics and institutions.[76] From the perspective of this contribution, however, a fiscal capacity would also be a positive step in halting the slide toward centralisation in the budgetary domain. A fiscal capacity, in fact, would endow the EU with the tools to manage the economic challenges emerging in EMU, and yet create space for the States to regain meaningful autonomy in the budgetary domain. With a fiscal capacity, the EU would be able to handle shocks which are created by interdependences and spill-overs, without the need for a full centralisation of controls with regard to budgetary policy.

The idea of a fiscal capacity has received the explicit backing of several prominent institutional players. In particular, the December 2012 Report "*Towards a Genuine EMU*", written by the President of the European Council, clearly linked fiscal capacity to the creation of a "shock-absorption function" to improve the resilience of EMU.[77] As the President's Report clarified, the economic rationale of this instrument lay in the reduction of the impact of country-specific shock and in the prevention of contagious effects across the currency union.[78] Because of its "insurance-type" nature, at the same time, the President's Report suggested alternative macro or micro economic approaches to set-up a fiscal capacity,[79] and

[74]IMF (2013).

[75]Hinarejos (2013).

[76]Enderlein et al. (2005).

[77]President of the European Council, Final Report (2012), p. 5.

[78]*Ibid.*, p. 10.

[79]*Ibid.*, p. 11.

emphasised that its design would still have to avoid "the risk of moral hazard inherent in any insurance system."[80] The idea of a fiscal capacity, moreover, has been strongly supported by the European Parliament, in multiple resolutions,[81] as well as by the European Commission in its November 2012 blueprint "*For a Deep and Genuine EMU*".[82] Finally, the idea of endowing the Eurozone with an autonomous budget has received the individual support of several Member States—with the French President François Hollande,[83] and two Italian Governments openly backing it.[84]

As I have detailed elsewhere, raising a fiscal capacity would trigger important constitutional challenges.[85] But from a strictly legal point of view, there should be no doubt that the current treaty framework already allows for such a development. According to Article 311 TFEU, in fact,

> [t]he Union shall provide itself with the means necessary to attain its objectives and carry through its policies.

And although this clause, which is located in the TFEU's Tile on Financial Provisions, does not mention explicitly EU taxation, it affirms that.

> [w]ithout prejudice to other revenue, the budget shall be financed wholly from own resources.

Moreover, whereas the old text of Article 269 TEC only allowed the Council to lay down provisions relating to the system of own resources of the Community, which it shall recommend to the Member States for adoption in accordance with their respective constitutional requirements, the Lisbon Treaty has now modified Article 311 TFEU, enlarging the power of the Council to shape the own resources of the EU. Pursuant to Article 311, para. 3, TFEU, in fact, the Council, acting unanimously and after consulting the European Parliament shall

> adopt a decision laying down the provisions relating to the system of own resources of the Union. In this context it may establish new categories of own resources or abolish an existing category. That decision shall not enter into force until it is approved by the Member States in accordance with their respective constitutional requirements.

---

[80]*Ibid.*, p. 10.

[81]European Parliament Resolution (2012, 2015b).

[82]European Commission Communication (2012).

[83]Hollande (2013), p. 7 (speaking in favour of "une nouvelle étape d'intégration avec une capacité budgétaire qui serait attribuée à la zone euro") and Hollande (2015) (speaking for "un budget de la zone euro, pour pouvoir agir en termes d'investissements, y compris pour les pays qui sont le plus en retard").

[84]Letta (2013), p. 5 (arguing that "there is room to reflect on a fiscal capacity for the euro area.") and Padoan (2015) (stating that "L'Unione monetaria deve essere affiancata da [...] una autentica unione economica e fiscale, dove al rispetto delle regole si accompagni una altrettanto necessaria condivisione del rischio, necessaria e sostenuta da una adeguata mutualizzazione delle risorse. Il Governo italiano si sta impegnando per portare avanti questa linea").

[85]Fabbrini (2014b).

The exact interpretation of the provisions of the TFEU related to taxes is a matter of debate among tax lawyers.[86] In principle, the Treaties could be construed restrictively, arguing that the own resources clause is intended simply to prohibit the Member States from refusing to contribute to the budget of the Union. The Commission however has interpreted Article 311 TFEU in a more constructive manner and argued that, and, if combined with Article 133 TFEU, it could be read as granting to the EU the power to adopt new taxes for the benefit of the EU budget. In its June 2011 proposal for a Council Decision "*On the system of own resources of the EU*,"[87] in fact, the Commission proposed to the Council to introduce as a new category of own resources under Article 311 TFEU a financial transaction tax (FTT), to be collected by the Member States and transferred to the EU budget in lieu of other contributions currently in place.[88] And in its subsequent proposal for a Council Directive on a FTT,[89] the Commission indicated that its draft legislative text would be based on Article 133 TFEU, thus the harmonisation clause in the TFEU, but that the revenues of the tax would be appropriated by the EU with the aim to feed the EU budget and free the Member States from parts of their current contributions.[90]

As is well known, the requirement that the Council unanimously approves the introduction of new own resources—the tax backbone needed for a fiscal capacity—significantly hampers the ability to establish such a fiscal capacity in the EU. In fact, the proposal to adopt a FTT met with opposition in the Council, and 11 Eurozone Member States—Belgium, Germany, Estonia, Greece, Spain, France, Italy, Austria, Portugal, Slovakia and Slovenia—decided to go ahead on their own and adopt a FTT through enhanced cooperation. The European Parliament consented to the use of enhanced cooperation in December 2012,[91] and the Council authorised it in January 2013.[92] Moreover, in April 2014, the ECJ rejected as inadmissible a challenge by the UK against the Council Decision.[93] Nevertheless, as of the time of writing, the Member States participating to enhanced cooperation have not been able to agree on the substance of FTT legislation. And, in any case, the use of enhanced cooperation for FTT makes it almost impossible to use the revenues of this tax for the purpose of creating a fiscal capacity.[94] Since only a few Member States are collecting the FTT, it would be politically difficult to justify the use of resources gathered within the FTT-zone for the benefit of other Member States too.[95] Be that as it may, however, the example of the FTT shows that—if the

---

[86]Traversa and de la Motte (2015).

[87]Commission Proposal (2011a).

[88]*Ibid.*

[89]Commission Proposal (2011b).

[90]*Ibid.*

[91]European Parliament Legislative Resolution (2012).

[92]Council Decision 2013/52/EU.

[93]ECJ 22 January 2014, Case C-270/12, *United Kingdom* v. *Council.*

[94]Fabbrini (2014a).

[95]European Parliament Legislative Resolution (2013).

political will existed—the EU could be endowed with the financial firepower needed to govern the economic cycle. In other words, a fiscal capacity—that is a new Eurozone budget sustained by real own resources (and to be managed through a reformed political process)[96]—could be a feasible, and legal, alternative to the highly centralising surveillance measures adopted in the aftermath of the crisis, and currently being promoted by some prominent European and national policy-makers.

6 Conclusion

Since the outburst of the Euro-crisis, legal measures adopted by the EU institutions and the Member States have produced a remarkable centralisation of powers at supranational level. Given the perceived weaknesses of the SGP, legal reforms adopted since 2011 have increased the surveillance powers of the EU institutions over the budgetary processes of the Member States. At the same time, proposals currently under considerations have called for further centralising measures in the EMU system of governance: as policy documents drafted by the European Commission, as well as by key national decision-makers have claimed, EMU should be enhanced through the introduction of competitiveness councils and a new Fiscal Board, potentially empowered to enforce the SGP and supervise national budgetary policy in lieu of the Commission.

As this chapter has maintained, however, the calls for further centralisation of power in EMU governance should be resisted. There are in fact strong constitutional arguments why Member States ought to maintain a meaningful autonomy in the decision-making process in the budgetary domain. And the view that economic policy can be removed from the political process and delegated to technocratic institutions clashes with concerns about effectiveness and legitimacy. Moreover, it is highly questionable that the limitation of State budgetary autonomy that is currently under consideration would be necessary: as Alicia Hinarejos has pointed out, the EU is drifting towards a "surveillance model" in which the center has invasive oversight power on the budgetary policies of the Member States because the EU has no fiscal resources of its own.[97]

This chapter has therefore discussed the alternative to such form of centralisation: namely, the creation of a fiscal capacity. As the chapter claimed, if the Eurozone were endowed with a discrete budget, funded by real own resources, it could undertake a counter-cyclical stabilisation function—securing the stability of the EMU without the need to interfere so significantly into the States' budgetary autonomy. In fact, granting a limited taxing and spending power to the EU would be much less invasive of State sovereignty that keeping in place a system where the

[96]Fabbrini (2015).

[97]Hinarejos (2013), p. 1621.

Member States must obtain prior authorisation from the Commission before approving their budget bills, and are subject to strict (and potentially in the future even stricter) oversight by the EU institutions. This is even more the case if—as suggested by the High Level Group of experts on the reform of the EU own resources system chaired by Mario Monti—EU taxes were to be levied on activities which currently fall outside the taxing ability of the Member States.[98]

In conclusion, while the Euro-crisis has promoted a dynamic of centralisation, this development has perils. Moreover, while policy pressures continue to push in the centralisation direction, this dynamic is not inevitable. Fiscal capacity provides a viable, and legal, alternative to complete Europe's EMU, without depriving Member States' of some autonomy in the budgetary domain. A fiscal capacity based on EU taxes levied on activities that currently escape state regulation—including transnational corporations and financial institutions—may even be the instrument to make the EU again popular to its citizens.[99] Contrary to the proposals in favor of creating competitiveness councils and new independent fiscal policemen, the EU should endow itself with the fiscal capacity needed to address the economic emergency of the Eurozone, ensure its future stability and foster its democratic legitimacy.[100]

References

Antoš M (2014) Fiscal stability rules in Central European constitutions. In: Fabbrini F et al (eds) The constitutionalization of European budgetary constraints. Hart Publishing, Oxford, pp 205 et seqq

Besselink L, Reestman JH (2012) Editorial: the fiscal compact and the European constitutions: Europe speaking German. Eur Constit Law Rev 8:1

Bieber R (2015) The allocation of economic policy competences in the European Union. In: Azoulai L (ed) The question of competence in the European Union. Oxford University Press, Oxford

Buti M, Carnot N (2012) The EMU debt crisis: early lessons and reforms. J Common Mark Stud 50:899

Collignon S (2004) The end of the stability and growth pact? Int Econ Econ Policy 1:15

Costamagna F (2014) The impact of stronger economic policy co-ordination on the European social dimension: issues of legitimacy. In: Fabbrini F et al (eds) The constitutionalization of European budgetary constraints. Hart Publishing, Oxford

Craig P (2012) The stability, coordination and governance treaty: principle, politics and pragmatism. Eur Law Rev 37:231

Craig P (2014) Economic governance and the Euro crisis: constitutional architecture and constitutional implications. In: Fabbrini F et al (eds) The constitutionalization of European budgetary constraints. Hart Publishing, Oxford

de Streel A (2013) The evolution of the EU economic governance since the Maastricht Treaty: an unfinished task. Maastricht J Eur Compar Law 20:336

[98]High Level Group on Own Resources (2014).

[99]European Parliament Resolution (2015a).

[100]Maduro (2012), p. 19.

de Streel A (2015) The confusion of tasks in the decision making in the European economic governance. In: Fabbrini F et al (eds) What form of government for the European Union and the Eurozone? Hart Publishing, Oxford
Delledonne G (2014) A legalization of financial constitutions in the EU? Reflections on the German, Spanish, Italian and French experiences. In: Fabbini F et al (eds) The constitutionalization of European budgetary constraints. Hart Publishing, Oxford
Dijsselbloem J (2015) Letter to the members of the Eurogroup, 12 July 2015
Dixon H (2015) In E.U. crises, a decentralized alternative. Reuters Breakingviews, 21 December 2015
Draghi M (2015) Introductory statement in front of the European Parliament, Brussels, 15 June 2015
Elster J (1979) Ulysses and the Sirens. Studies in rationality and irrationality. Cambridge University Press, Cambridge
Enderlein H et al (2005) The EU budget: how much scope for institutional reform? ECB Occasional Paper Series, No. 27/2005
European Commission Communication (2012) A blueprint for a deep and genuine EMU: launching a European debate, 28 November 2012, COM 777 final
European Commission Communication (2015a) Making the best use of the flexibility within the existing rules of the stability and growth pact, 13 January 2015, COM 012 final
European Commission Communication (2015b) On steps toward completing economic and monetary union, 21 October 2015, COM 600 final
European Council Conclusions (2010) EUCO 13/10, 17 June 2010
European Parliament Legislative Resolution (2012) On the proposal for a Council decision authorizing enhanced cooperation in the area of the creation of a FTT, 12 December 2012, P7_TA(2012)0498
European Parliament Legislative Resolution (2013) On the proposal for a Council directive implementing enhanced cooperation in the area of FTT, 3 July 2013, P7_TA(2013)0312
European Parliament Resolution (2012) Towards a genuine EMU, 20 November 2012, P7_TA (2012) 0430
European Parliament Resolution (2013) The constitutional problems of multi-tier governance in the European Union, 12 December 2013, P7_TA(2013)0598
European Parliament Resolution (2015a) Recommendations to the Commission on bringing transparency, coordination and convergence to corporate tax policies in the Union, 16 December 2015, P8_TA(2015)0457
European Parliament Resolution (2015b) The review of economic governance framework: stocktaking and challenges, 24 June 2015, P8_TA (2015) 0238
Fabbrini F (2013) The fiscal compact, the "golden rule" and the paradox of European federalism. Boston Coll Int Compar Law Rev 36:1
Fabbrini F (2014a) Taxing and spending in the Eurozone: legal and political challenges related to the adoption of the financial transaction tax. Eur Law Rev 39:155
Fabbrini F (2014b) From fiscal constraints to fiscal capacity: the future of EMU and its challenges. In: Fabbrini F et al (eds) The constitutionalization of European budgetary constraints. Hart Publishing, Oxford
Fabbrini F (2015) Representation in the European Parliament: of false problems and real challenges. Zeitschrift für ausländisches öffentilches Recht und Völkerrecht 75:823
Fabbrini F (2016) Economic governance in Europe. Oxford University Press, Oxford
Henning R, Kessler M (2012) Fiscal federalism: US history for architects of Europe's fiscal union. Bruegel Essay and Lecture Series, Bruxelles
Herzog B, Hengstermann K (2013) Restoring credible economic governance to the Eurozone. Econ Aff 33:3
High Level Group on Own Resources (2014) First assessment report, 17 December 2014
Hinarejos A (2013) Fiscal federalism in the European Union: evolution and future choices for EMU. Common Mark Law Rev 50:1621

Hinarejos A (2015) The Euro area crisis in constitutional perspective. Oxford University Press, Oxford
Hollande F (2013) Intervention liminaire de lors de la conférence de presse. Paris, 16 May 2013
Hollande F (2015) Entretien à l'occasion du 14 juillet. Paris, 14 July 2015
IMF (2013) Toward a fiscal union for the Euro area. Staff Discussion Note, October 2013
Kollman K (2014) Perils of centralization: lessons from church, state and corporation. Cambridge University Press, Cambridge
Letta E (2013) Keynote speech at annual dinner Brugel, 9 September 2013
Lindseth P (2014) Power & legitimacy in the Eurozone: can integration and democracy be reconciled? In: Fabbrini F et al (eds) The constitutionalization of European budgetary constraints. Hart Publishing, Oxford
Maduro M (2012) A new governance for the European Union and the Euro: democracy and justice. Report commissioned by the European Parliament Constitutional Affairs Committee, September 2012, PE 462.484
Mayer F (2015) Eine Reform der institutionellen Architektur Europas? In: Kadelbach S (ed) Die Europäische Union am Scheideweg: Mehr oder weniger Europa? Nomos, Baden-Baden
Padoan PC (2015) Speech at the Camera dei Deputati, Rome, 29 July 2015
Peers S (2012) The stability treaty: permanent austerity or gesture politics? Eur Constit Law Rev 8:404
Pernice I et al (2012) A democratic solution to the crisis: reform steps towards a democratically based economic and financial constitution for Europe. Nomos, Baden-Baden
President of the European Commission, Analytical Note (2015) Preparing for next steps on better economic governance in the Euro Area, 12 February 2015
President of the European Commission, Report (2015) Completing Europe's EMU, 22 June 2015
President of the European Council, Final Report (2012) Towards a genuine EMU, 5 December 2012
Rodden JA (2006) Hamilton's paradox: the promise and peril of fiscal discipline. Cambridge University Press, Cambridge
Rodriguez-Tejedo I, Wallis JJ (2012) Fiscal institutions and fiscal crises. In: Conti-Brown P, Skeel Jr D (eds) When states go broke: the origins, context and solutions for the American states in fiscal crisis. Cambridge University Press, Cambridge
Schäuble W (2014) Strategy for a European recovery. Keynote speech at the 5th Bruges European business conference, 27 March 2014
Schelke W (2007) EU fiscal governance: hard law in the shadow of soft law? Colum J Eur Law 13:705
Super DA (2015) Rethinking fiscal federalism. Harv Law Rev 118:2544
Tosato GL (2014) La riforma costituzionale sull'equilibrio di bilancio alla luce della normativa dell'Unione: l'interazione fra livello europeo e interno. Rivista di diritto internazionale 5
Traversa E, de la Motte AM (2015) Le fédéralisme économique et la fiscalité dans l'Union européenne. In: De la Rosa S et al (eds) L'Union européene et le fédéralisme économique. Bruylant, Bruxelles
Tuori K, Tuori K (2014) The Eurozone crisis: a constitutional analysis. Cambridge University Press, Cambridge
Van Malleghem PA (2014) (Un)balanced budget rules in Europe and America. In: Fabbrini F et al (eds) The constitutionalization of European budgetary constraints. Hart Publishing, Oxford
Weidman J (2016) Solidity and solidarity in the Euro area. Speech at the German Embassy in Rome, 26 April 2016
Wyplosz C (2005) Fiscal policy: Institutions versus rules. Nat Instit Econ Rev 191:64
Commission Proposal (2011a), for a Council decision "On the system of own resources of the EU", 29 June 2011, COM final
Commission Proposal (2011b), for a Council Directive "On a Common System of FTT", 28 November 2011, COM final
Council Decision 2013/52/EU, OJEU L 22, 25 January 2013, pp 11 et seqq
Directive 2011/85/EU of 8 November 2011 on requirements for budgetary frameworks of the Member States, OJEU L 306, 23 November 2011, pp 41 et seqq

Regulation (EC) No. 1466/97 of the Council of 7 July 1997 on the strengthening of the surveillance of budgetary positions and the surveillance and coordination of economic policies, OJEC L 209, 2 August 1997, pp 1 et seqq
Regulation (EC) No. 1467/97 of the Council of 7 July 1997 on speeding up and clarifying the implementation of the excessive deficit procedure, OJEC L 209, 2 August 1997, pp 6 et seqq
Regulation (EU) No. 472/2013 of 21 May 2013 of the European Parliament and the Council on enhanced surveillance of euro-area Member States experiencing or threatened with serious difficulties with respect to their financial stability, OJEU L 140, 27 May 2013, pp 1 et seqq
Regulation (EU) No. 473/2013 of 21 May 2013 of the European Parliament and the Council on monitoring and assessing draft budgetary plans and ensuring the correction of excessive deficits in euro-area Member States, OJ L 140, 27 May 2013, pp 11 et seqq
Regulation (EU) No. 1173/2011 of the European Parliament and of the Council of 16 November 2011 on the effective enforcement of budgetary surveillance in the Euro area, OJEU L 306, 23 November 2011, pp 1 et seqq
Regulation (EU) No. 1174/2011 of the European Parliament and of the Council of 16 November 2011 on enforcement measures to correct excessive macroeconomic imbalances in the Euro area, OJEU L 306, 23 November 2011, pp 8 et seqq
Regulation (EU) No. 1175/2011 of the European Parliament and of the Council of 16 November 2011 amending Council Regulation (EC) No. 1466/97 on the Strengthening of the surveillance of budgetary positions and the surveillance and coordination of economic policies, OJEU L 306, 23 November 2011, pp 12 et seqq
Regulation (EU) No. 1176/2011 of the European Parliament and of the Council of 16 November 2011 on the prevention and correction of macroeconomic imbalances, OJEU L 306, 23 November 2011, pp 25 et seqq
Regulation (EU) No. 1177/2011 of 8 November 2011 amending Regulation (EC) No. 1467/97 on speeding up and clarifying the implementation of the excessive deficit procedure, OJEU L 306, 23 November 2011, pp 33 et seqq

Institutional Balance, Democracy and Agenda Setting in the European Union

Francesca Martines

Abstract The Commission's exclusive power to initiate legislation is a distinguishing feature of the EU decision-making process. According to some commentators, the Commission's power of proposal is being progressively eroded by the involvement of other actors in the initiative function. This is affecting one of the most significant components of the *Community method*. From a radically different perspective, the Commission's exclusive power of proposal is criticised as a reflection of the EU's democratic deficit, which should be corrected by conferring autonomous power of legislative initiative to the European Parliament. This paper takes a different stand, arguing that the involvement of European Union institutions and of other actors in the first crucial stage of the decision-making process can be appreciated in terms of democracy with reference to standards of transparency, public debate and participation. If these elements of democratic processes were strengthened, it would be possible to maintain the Commission's power to initiate legislation without having to make changes to Treaties that might alter the institutional balance in the European Union and have possible far-reaching consequences.

Contents

F. Martines (✉)
European Union Law, Law Department, University of Pisa, Pisa, Italy
e-mail: francesca.martines@unipi.it

L. Daniele et al. (eds.), *Democracy in the EMU in the Aftermath of the Crisis*,
DOI 10.1007/978-3-319-53895-2_7

1 Introduction

Since the creation of the European Economic Communities, the European Commission, through its initiative power, sets the legislative agenda of the European Union and plays a pivotal role in what is known as the *Community method*.[1]

From one perspective, the Commission's power of proposal has changed and its role has evolved from "autonomous initiator" to "reactive initiator".[2] Its initiative function has been progressively eroded[3] in favour of the European Council, the political driving force of the EU, and of the European Parliament (EP), in particular through the *initiative of the initiative*. More recently, national Parliaments and EU citizens have been involved in the agenda setting process.

From a different perspective, some say that the Commission, which has long been criticised for its (alleged) lack of legitimacy, should share its power of initiative with the European Parliament as an important step towards the establishment of a full European democracy.[4]

This paper argues that a change in the initiative power of the Commission in the direction of conferring the power of proposal to the European Parliament would deeply affect both the institutional balance in the European Union and the legislative procedure without necessarily making the decision-making process more democratic.

One is thus faced with the following dilemma: is it possible to maintain the Commission's exclusive power of initiative and the institutional balance in the ordinary legislative procedure, while improving the decision-making process in terms of democracy?

This work argues that greater involvement of other EU and national institutions in the mechanisms whereby the Commission sets its agenda could strengthen the legitimacy and democracy of the power of initiative and, consequently, of the decision-making process.

---

[1]For a definition, see the contribution from Mr. Barnier and Mr. Vitorino, to the European Convention (2002): "the Commission – the institution representing the general European interest – has a monopoly on initiating legislation, i.e. presents proposals for legislative acts, and the Council – an institution comprising representatives of the Member State governments – and the European Parliament – representing the people of Europe – adopt these acts in co-decision. In particular, the Council votes by qualified majority, with unanimity being required if it wishes to amend the Commission's proposal". The Community Method is not a dogma and can be discussed and modified. See, for example, Angela Merkel's Speech delivered at the opening ceremony of the 61st Academic Year of the College of Europe in Bruges on 2 November 2010, available at https://www.coleurope.eu/events/mrs-angela-merkel-delivered-opening-address-opening-ceremony.

[2]Ponzano et al. (2012), Gianfrancesco (2012).

[3]Höing and Wessels (2013); *contra* Nugent and Rhinard (2015); for a discussion on the role of the Commission in the recent economic crisis, see Bauer and Becker (2014).

[4]Vaubel (1995), Mastroianni (2010), Habermas (2015).

Without dwelling on the much-discussed notion of democratic standards applicable to the EU[5] and to the issue of democratic deficit in the EU decision-making process, this paper analyses the agenda-setting or programming stage from the perspective of participation, public deliberation, debate, accountability and transparency. These can be considered elements of democratic decision-making.

Agenda setting or programming—in the framework of the ordinary legislative procedure and with the exclusion of the European Union's Area of Freedom, Security and Justice[6]—is a component of the power of initiative which, in a broad sense, also covers development of the proposal by the Commission before its formal presentation to legislators (the power of initiative in the narrow sense). The latter will not be addressed in this paper.

The importance of agenda-setting in the policy cycle cannot be overstated. Programming defines the future shape and direction of the EU, helping to determine its identity. The agenda-setting stage is not only important for the issues that will be regulated by the European Union, but also for what will be excluded from future European legislation.

Based on these premises, the paper analyses the contribution of different actors involved in the process of agenda setting and their relations with the programming function of the Commission. The role of the European Council, the Council and Parliament are discussed first. Mention will be made of the contribution of advisory bodies such as the European Economic and Social Committee and the Committee of the Regions. The paper then assesses the role of other actors, in particular of national Parliaments and EU citizens.

2 The Contribution of EU Institutions and Bodies to Agenda Setting

In the European Union, the Commission, the European Council, the Council and the European Parliament, that is the supranational, the intergovernmental, and the democratic components of the Union, help define the agenda.

The Commission is responsible for defining multiannual[7] and annual programming objectives with a view to achieving inter-institutional agreements (Article 17 TEU). Primary EU law thus establishes that the European Parliament and the Council, that is the legislators, shall be involved in shaping the agenda.

---

[5]Majone (1998), Moravcsik (2004), Follesdal and Hix (2006).

[6]In the area of judicial cooperation in criminal matters, police cooperation and on administrative cooperation, the initiative can come from a quarter of EU Member States (Article 76 TFEU). In the area of the Common Foreign Security Policy, Article 30 TEU recognises the power of submitting proposals to the Council and to any Member State, to the High Representative of the Union for Foreign Affairs and Security Policy (who is *ex officio* one of the Commission's Vice-Presidents), either autonomously or with the support of the Commission.

[7]On the relevance of Multiannual programming, see Welle (2015).

The European Council, the supreme political institution in the EU, is entrusted with the definition of policy objectives and priorities (Article 15, para. 1, TEU[8]). This role has been strengthened in the recent economic crisis.[9]

The new and revolutionary method of appointing the President of the Commission after Lisbon, with the European Council voting for the *Spitzenkandidat* of the party having won the European Parliament elections, created a new context in which to set the multiannual agenda but did not modify this model.

The European Union Council has in fact confirmed its political role and its intention to shape the future direction of the Union despite, or possibly due to, the above mentioned development.

It is no coincidence that the European Council's Strategic Agenda was approved in June 2014, that is just after the election of the new European Union Parliament and during the European Council meeting which nominated Jean Claude Juncker, the *Spitzenkandidat* of the EPP, as the new President of the Commission.

The political guidelines of the President-designate ("*A New Start for Europe, My Agenda for Jobs, Growth, Fairness and Democratic Change*") were submitted to the European Parliament on 15 July 2014, before the confirmation vote. They partially reproduced Juncker's programme as *Spitzenkandidat*, but also included the European Council's priorities and some of the issues that the EU Parliament had previously indicated among its priorities[10]. This threefold contribution to the multiannual agenda has been acknowledged by the President-designate himself, who has confirmed that

> Europe's policy agenda must be shaped in close partnership between the European Commission and the European Parliament, and in cooperation with the Member States.[11]

This mechanism reflects the supranational-intergovernmental-democratic representative composition of the EU[12] and gives strong political and democratic legitimacy to the Commission's agenda.

---

[8]Bocquillon and Dobbels (2014).

[9]Carammia et al. (2012), Alexandrova (2015).

[10]See for example the Report Cost of non-Europe, prepared by the Added Value Unit of the EP, which identified the European Union's priorities for the five-year institutional cycle (2014–2019). The Report draws on lists of requests made by the Parliament in its legislative and own-initiative reports and on work undertaken by the Added Value Unit for different Parliamentary Committees. The Report includes references to the Digital Single Market, Transatlantic Trade Agreement, Completion of the Single Market, Integration of energy markets, Reform of the Economic Union. European Added Value Unit, Directorate for Impact Assessment and European Added Value, Directorate-General for Parliamentary Research Services (EPRS), European Parliament, Brussels, 2014. DOI: 10.2861/66747. For a comparative analysis of Juncker's ten priorities and the requests of the European Parliament, see Bassot and Debyser (2014).

[11]See Juncker's Presentation of his agenda to the European Parliament in July 2015. "*A New Start for Europe, My Agenda for Jobs, Growth, Fairness and Democratic Change*".

[12]Although at first sight this looks like the political process in a national parliamentary democracy, where the executive submits its political programme for vote in Parliament. In the case of the European Union, the election of the Commission's President and the Commission requires the absolute majority of the votes of the EP and thus a coalition between the two main groups (EPP and the Socialists).

As for the role of the European Council in programming, the importance of its guidelines lies in the approach it adopts. The guidelines do not contain detailed indications for legislative actions, but provide a clear indication of future lines of action that the executive heads of Member States are willing to pursue.

As the political driving force of the EU, the European Council often calls upon the Commission to present studies, research and proposals. Note that the European Council must often respond to unforeseen events and crises and is primarily concerned with major foreign affairs, as well as economic and financial matters. The European Council agenda is characterised by a certain volatility, whereby some issues are abandoned and replaced by others.[13]

In general, European Council conclusions generally leave the Commission room for manoeuvre in elaborating the content of the draft legislation. This does not mean that the European Council cannot make specific recommendations on the content of the proposal.[14] Nevertheless, legislative acts requested by the European Council often stem from the Commission's preparatory documents and suggestions. The creation of a full-time European Council President strengthened his/her role in directing the work of the European Council and in indicating priorities and issues included in the agenda by the President himself.[15]

It is however misleading to represent the European Council as the material agenda setter and the Commission as the formal agenda setter in the context of a principal-agent relationship. The relationship between the two institutions can be more correctly defined as circular or cooperative.[16] The European Council's requests give political legitimacy to the proposals of the Commission, especially vis-à-vis the Council.[17] The Commission also uses the European Council to strengthen its position.[18] For instance, the Commission felt that agreement with the European Council allowed it to make the detailed proposal forming the climate change package. The European Council's Lisbon Strategy allowed the Commission to better develop the programme's measures.[19]

EU legislators are also involved in the preparation of the Commission's annual Work Programme (CWP).[20] The methods of cooperation with the European Parliament are laid out in the latter's rules of procedure (Rule 37 and Annex XIII

[13]Carammia et al. (2012).

[14]Eggermont (2012), Alexandrova (2015).

[15]Puetter (2014).

[16]Bocquillon and Dobbles (2014).

[17]Craig and de Burca (2011).

[18]Werts (2008).

[19]House of Lords (2008).

[20]It includes soft law initiatives, legislative and non-legislative proposals, repeals, withdrawals and simplification. It contains, if possible, indications on the choice of the type of legal acts, of the legal basis for each proposal, impact assessment, and the indication of timetable. See Interinstitutional Agreement Between the European Parliament, the Council of the European Union and the European Commission on Better Law Making (IIA). OJEU L 123, 12 May 2016, pp. 1 et seqq., para. 8.

reproducing the text of the Framework Agreement between the European Parliament and the Commission).[21]

Bilateral exchanges of views on initiatives for the upcoming year take place before the Commission's President and Vice President submit their "letter of intent" containing details on items of political importance and on the possible withdrawal of the Commission's proposals.

In July, the European Parliament adopts a resolution defining its priorities. In September, the Commission's President delivers[22] the *State of the Union Address*.[23] This provides the basis for dialogue among the Commission, the Council [24] and the European Parliament Committees to define areas of shared priorities.[25]

The Council contributes with the 18-month programme of the Presidency trio and with a joint declaration by the three Presidents (Interinstitutional Agreement 2016, the IIA). The IIA provides for the identification of dossiers of particular relevance that will receive priority in the legislative process (known as Priority Pending Proposals).

After presentation of the Commission's Work Programme,[26] in October a debate takes place in the EP to adopt a resolution[27] on the CWP.

The IIA also establishes that the Commission provides regular updates on its planning throughout the year and gives reason for any delay in the presentation of the proposals included in the Work Programme.[28] The agenda can be modified, for

[21]The Framework Agreement on the relationship between the European Parliament and the Commission is published in OJEU L 304, 20 November 2010, pp. 47 et seqq.

[22]The Commission first prepares the *annual policy strategy* (APS), where it defines its priorities for the year to come. These constitute the basis for its Work Programme.

[23]This is provided for by the 2010 Interinstitutional Agreement between the Commission and the Parliament. See para. 5: "Each year in the first part-session of September, a State of the Union debate will be held in which the President of the Commission shall deliver an address, taking stock of the current year and looking ahead to priorities for the following years. To that end, the President of the Commission will in parallel set out in writing to Parliament the main elements guiding the preparation of the Commission Work Programme for the following year".

[24]See for example the Council's 18-month programme (1 January 2016–30 June 2017), which develops upon the Strategic Agenda. The programme was established by the Netherlands, Slovak and Maltese Presidencies. It covers the period from January 2016 to June 2017. The 18-month programme is explicitly guided by the five priorities of the Strategic Agenda adopted by the European Council in June 2014.

[25]The bilateral dialogue between the Conference of Committee Chairs (it consists of the Chairs of all standing and special committees) and the Vice-President of the Commission continues afterwards in monitoring the implementation of the programme. http://ec.europa.eu/atwork/planning-and-preparing/management-plans/index_en.htm.

[26]See, for example, Commission Communication on the Commission Work Programme 2016: No time for business as usual, COM (2015) 610.

[27]See the European Parliament Resolution on the Commission's Work Programme. 014/2829 (RSP), January 2015.

[28]See the 2010 Interinstitutional Agreement between the EP and the Commission. It establishes that the Commission "shall explain when it cannot deliver individual proposals in its Work Programme for the year in question or when it departs from it" (point 36).

example to respond to unforeseen events, but if the Commission intends to withdraw a proposal, it is required to give reason and consult with the legislators on intended subsequent steps.

The involvement of the Council and the European Parliament in developing the legislative programme is a consequence of the ordinary legislative procedure (former codecision). The Commission benefits from discussion with legislators on shared priorities. The approach is pragmatic and functional to the Commission's interest that the legislators finally adopt the proposed acts.

The sharing of priorities in the agenda by the legislators, public discussion in the European Parliament and the presentation of the programme in advance to the public, all strengthen the legitimacy of the Commission's programme and future proposals in terms of transparency, debate and accountability.

Moreover, this dialogue allows the legislators to have access to information on the activities, priorities and orientation of the Commission at an early stage of the decision-making process, before they are translated into complete draft legislative acts.

Access to information on the objectives and plans of the institutions is important in that this information can influence legislators' decision-making.[29]

While the legislators help develop the agenda they do not have autonomous power of initiative.

The TFEU provides for a pre-initiative power in Articles 225 (for the European Parliament) and 241 (for the Council). European Parliament legislative own-initiative reports contain a detailed draft text of the proposal. They are drawn up by the responsible Committee and adopted in plenary. Although the Commission is not compelled to follow the request, the Interinstitutional Agreement on Better Law-making provides that the institution will give "prompt and detailed consideration to requests for proposals for Union acts". It also establishes that the Commission will respond within three months to the requests of the EP and the Council, stating the follow up it intends to give to the proposals and providing detailed reasons in case it decides not to submit a proposal, including an analysis of possible alternatives. The two legislators thus enjoy an equal position vis-à-vis the Commission as regards their pre-initiative power. This is particularly important for the balance of powers of the two legislators, as explained below.

Note that a European Parliament majority vote is required for approval of a motion for a legislative initiative. This means that the pre-initiative, when approved, has wide support and is difficult for the Commission to ignore. The Commission must present a legislative proposal at latest one year after the request, or must include the proposal in its next CWP.[30]

---

[29] Brandsma (2013).

[30] As mentioned, a European Value Added Assessment supports the legislative own-report initiatives.

The EP is very concerned about its pre-initiative power, as proved by the specific request made to the Commissioners-designate (during the hearing for the formation of the new Commission) in relation to the application of Article 225 TFEU.[31]

The two main advisory bodies also play a role.

The European Economic and Social Committee (EESC), which defined itself as the "privileged intermediary between civil society organisations and the Union institutions",[32] has requested that it be involved from the beginning of the policy cycle. The involvement, although limited, of the EESC is interesting not for its technical contribution but because it is a "vector for the expectations and aspirations of organised civil society".[33] It in fact represents interests that are recognised by the EU legal order.

The EESC adopts own-initiative opinions on issues that could be translated into legal acts.[34] An annual meeting is organised with the President or one of the Vice-Presidents of the Commission to identify priorities requiring cooperation between the bodies.

As for the Committee of the Regions, a framework of inter-institutional cooperation has been established by a Protocol governing arrangements for cooperation with the European Commission.

In particular, as regards its participation in the setting of priorities, administrative-level meetings take place before the adoption of the CWP. The Committee of the Regions provides a link between local and regional authorities and the European Commission by organising Structured Dialogue Meetings.[35] These meetings can convey the priorities of local communities to the Commission. Opinions on pre-legislative documents (Communications, White Papers, Green Papers) offer the Committee the opportunity to influence the content of subsequent initiatives.[36]

---

[31]The question was formulated as follows: "What specific commitments are you prepared to make in terms of enhanced transparency, increased cooperation and effective follow-up to Parliament's positions and requests for legislative initiatives? In relation to planned initiatives or on-going procedures, are you ready to provide Parliament with information and documents on an equal footing with the Council?".

[32]Protocol on Cooperation between the European Commission and the European Economic and Social Committee, 22 February 2012. See also the Opinion of September 2015 on Improving the functioning of the European Union building on the potential of the Lisbon Treaty and on possible evolutions and adjustments of the current institutional set-up of the European Union, available at http://www.eesc.europa.eu/?i=portal.en.institutional-reform-documents-opinions-.36771.

[33]Protocol on Cooperation between the European Commission and the European Economic and Social Committee, 22 February 2012.

[34]In 2007, following a request of the German Presidency in the previous year, the EESC adopted an opinion on the labelling of food. Its position has been mentioned in the recommendation of the Council on Agriculture addressed to the Commission, in which the institution was requested to produce a report leading to a legislative proposal) on the matter.

[35]Communication from the Commission, Dialogue with associations of regional and local authorities on the formulation of European Union policy, COM (2003) 811, Brussels, 19 December 2003.

[36]House of Lords (2008), p. 134.

3 The Contribution of National Parliaments to Agenda Setting

Outside the circle of EU institutions one must consider the role of national Parliaments (NPs)[37].

In Article 12 TEU (Title II, Provisions on Democratic Principles), which describes the different ways in which national Parliaments can contribute to the good functioning of the Union, there is no mention of any specific role in agenda setting or programming.

Subsidiarity control by national Parliaments can result in the withdrawal of a Commission's proposal.[38] However, constructive input is not provided for. To date there is no institutional mechanism assigning NPs an initiative function.

The flow of information from the Commission to the NPs[39] (consultation documents such as Green and White Papers, Communications), in the framework of the Barroso initiative, gives national Parliaments a more active role in shaping policies.[40] They can transmit their opinions on policy issues—often to remark

[37] National Parliaments are considered the main losers in the shift of sovereign powers from national to supranational levels of Government. See O'Brennan (2007).

[38] Article 7, paras. 2 and 3, of the Protocol No. 2 on the Application of the Principles of Subsidiarity and Proportionality. In the hypothesis of the "yellow card" the Commission has to review the draft and then to decide on whether to maintain, amend or withdraw the draft, giving reasons for its decision (Article 7, para. 2, of Protocol No. 2). For the "orange card" (Article 7, para. 3, of the Protocol No. 2), the Commission had similar choices available, but if it decides to maintain the proposal, the Commission has to demonstrate compliance of the act with the subsidiarity principle. National Parliaments, however, cannot block EU legislation (so-called "red card" mechanisms). The European Parliament emphasised that: "the purpose of the early warning mechanism is not to block the European decision-making process, but to improve the quality of EU legislation by ensuring, in particular, that the EU operates within its competences". European Parliament Resolution of 16 April 2014 on Relations between the European Parliament and the National Parliaments, Doc. 2013/2185(INI). The so-called Monti II legislative proposal was withdrawn by the Commission after a yellow card. The Commission claimed that it withdrew the proposal for lack of the necessary political support within the European Parliament and the Council. According to Cooper (2015), however, the yellow card forced the hands of the Commission, proving that national Parliaments can affect the Commission's agenda.

[39] Jančic (2012).

[40] While "reasoned opinions" (provided for in Article 6 of Protocol No. 2) challenge the proposal's compliance with the principle of subsidiarity, each national Parliament can present "opinions" voicing its concerns, objections, comments on the proposal. On the issue of the differentiation between subsidiarity and other arguments which fall outside the scope of the subsidiarity control mechanism, see Jančic (2015). For some examples, see the Report from the Commission, Annual Report 2014 on Relations between the European Commission and National Parliaments, COM (2015) 316 final.

national competence on the issue[41]—and respond to public consultations or comment on policy documents. This involvement is limited but has some potential.[42]

The "green card" initiative[43] proposed in 2014 by the EU Select Committee of the House of Lords is noteworthy. The proposed mechanism would allow a group of national Parliaments to jointly submit proposals to the Commission for future initiatives.

The House of Lords presented a *trial* "green card" initiative on food waste in July 2015 in the form of a letter signed by 16 Chairpersons of National Parliamentary Committees. The aim was to invite the Commission to adopt a strategic approach to food waste in the forthcoming Commission's Circular Economy Package. The proponents considered the "green card" as a form of closer political dialogue with the Commission and an instrument to complement the Commission's right of initiative.

A "green card" initiative could be assessed as a positive contribution to agenda setting, since it conveys the interests of a significant number of national Parliaments, especially if it leaves (as in the case of the trial "green card" initiative mentioned above) the Commission ample autonomy. The proposal on food waste was not detailed: it consisted of five general recommendations, leaving the Commission ample space for manoeuvre in drafting legislation.

The mechanism however, must be considered carefully, particularly in relation to the balance of powers.

The trial green card initiative requested that the Commission "gives due weight" and "responds appropriately" to the proposal "supported by 16 national parliaments and chambers" before the publication of the Circular Economy Package. It also requested that the proposal be "acknowledged and assessed within that package".

It is clear that the green card initiative does not and cannot force the Commission to propose legislation. Neither is the Commission obliged to reply to the initiative.

It would be misleading to draw a parallel with the pre-initiative power of the European Parliament.

Although both national Parliaments and the European Parliament represent EU citizens at different levels, the latter is one of the EU's legislative bodies, the former are not. The role of national Parliaments in the legislative process is to assess the Commission's initiatives, particularly (but not exclusively) with respect to the principle of subsidiarity. National Parliaments also scrutinise their own governments, which are components of the Council (the EU's second legislative chamber).

---

[41]See, for example, the negative comments made on the Commission's Green Paper on pension schemes and the claim of national exclusive competences by several national Parliaments. The Commission decided only to review the EPAP Directive. Report from the Commission, 2010 Annual Report on the Relations between the Commission and National Parliaments, COM (2011) 345 def. 8.

[42]The 2014 Report on the Relation between Commission and National Parliaments, cited above, qualifies this as "untapped potential".

[43]House of Lords (2014), p. 9.

Moreover, there is a difference between a proposal made by one or more national Parliaments in the context of political dialogue and that made by a large number of national Parliaments[44], even following an informal procedure,[45] and requiring that the Commission responds, giving a reason in the case of refusal to take the proposal on board. In other words, once national Parliaments have tabled a proposal, they obviously expect the Commission to explain its position with respect to the request.

In general, the "green card" initiative could have repercussions on institutional balance, particularly as regards the relationship between the Commission and the European Parliament, on the proposal that the latter is required to examine as legislator (overstepped by the other citizens' representatives), and on the position of national Ministers within the Council (consider the position of Ministers whose Parliament backed the proposal) during the adoption of measures.

This explains the position adopted by the Commission: in his response to the "green card" on food waste, Commission Vice-President Timmermans clearly intended to divest the initiative of any legal implications. He insisted on placing the initiative within the context of existing political dialogue with national Parliaments and in qualifying his response to them as "political".[46]

The circular economy package (the withdrawal of the previous proposal and presentation of a new package) mentions food waste in the proposed waste directive but (unsurprisingly) makes no reference to the "green card" initiative.[47] The specific requests of national Parliaments were not taken into consideration.

4 The Contribution of Citizens to Agenda Setting

European citizens take part in the democratic life of the Union through their elected representatives. European democracy is a representative democracy (Article 10 TEU), with participatory democracy[48] playing a complementary role.[49]

---

[44]*Contra* Grinc (2015).

[45]In this case, a letter addressed to the Commission containing details of the proposal.

[46]He also underlined that "The European Commission will not abdicate its exclusive right to introduce legislation. There cannot be any misunderstanding on this issue". He affirmed that the green card could be introduced "in compliance with the Treaties" and at a "political level" and that the European Commission is ready to respond "politically in a positive way if there is widespread support from national parliaments".

[47]Communication from the Commission, Closing the Loop-An EU Action Plan For The Circular Economy, COM (2015) 0614 final.

[48]Bieber and Maiani (2009).

[49]"It would be a mistake to draw too sharp a contrast between participatory democracy, given effect – among other ways – through the ECI, and representative democracy at the EU level. They are mutually reinforcing concepts in the democratic life of the Union. To put this more concretely: the European Parliament, as well as the Commission, has a vital role to play in making a success of the ECI". Decision of the European Ombudsman closing her own-initiative inquiry OI/9/2013/TN concerning the functioning of the European citizens' initiative, 4 March 2015.

Article 11 TEU is the normative basis of EU participatory democracy, which provides for the involvement of representative associations, civil society,[50] parties concerned (stakeholders) and citizens.[51] Such direct participation is ensured through dialogue and public consultations (Article 11, paras. 1, 2 and 3) and through the European Citizens' Initiative (ECI). The latter is discussed below.[52]

The role of the European Citizens' Initiative in strengthening democracy in the EU has been highlighted by the EU General Court, according to which this right

> is intended to reinforce citizenship of the Union and enhance the democratic functioning of the Union through the participation of citizens in the democratic life of the Union.[53]

The Citizens' Initiative is an invitation to the Commission to propose legislation. It must be made by a group of at least one million EU citizens from at least a quarter of the Member States.

> Within the framework of its powers, [the Commission can] submit any appropriate proposal on matters where citizens consider that a legal act of the Union is required for the purpose of implementing the Treaties.

If the request[54] is accepted, the Commission drafts an act to submit to legislators.

Several aspects of the procedure are relevant in terms of the democratic legitimacy of the Commission's power of initiative.

---

[50] On the debate on the definition of civil society, see Kohler-Koch and Quittkat (2009).

[51] Hüller (2010), p. 81. The Commission has a long tradition of consulting interest groups. See the Commission's Communication "*An Open and Structured Dialogue between the Commission and Special Interest Groups*", OJEC C 63, 5 March 1993, pp. 2 et seqq. The White Paper on Governance referred to "civil society's participation in European governance as a chance to get citizens more actively involved in achieving the Union's objectives". Only groups representing economic and social interests were represented at first; consultation has subsequently extended to groups representing more general interests. With the White Paper on EU governance, citizens have been also involved. See Kohler-Koch and Quittkat (2013).

[52] See Regulation (EU) No. 211/2011, which lays out detailed rules and procedures, OJEU L 65, 11 March 2011, pp. 1 et seqq. The Commission refused to register proposals due to the lack of a legal basis in the Treaty. http://ec.europa.eu/citizens-initiative/public/initiatives/non-registered. A Commission's decision not to register the initiative on the State of necessity was challenged before the European General Court, which dismissed the action. EGC 30 September 2015, Case T-450/12, *Anagnostakis* v. *Commission*.

[53] EGC 30 September 2015, Case T-450/12, *Anagnostakis* v. *Commission*. para. 26.

[54] The Fair Transport Europe ECI, for example, invites the Commission to present different proposals. http://ec.europa.eu/citizens-initiative/public/initiatives/open/details/2015/000002.

The Commission is required to give a formal response to organizers (in the form of a Communication (Article 10 of Regulation (EU) No. 211/2011).[55] It can refuse the request but has an obligation to state the reasons for its decision.[56]

In its Communication on the ECI, the Commission must not only give a legal and political response to the Citizens' Initiative but also spell out what action it intends to take, if any, and the reasons for doing or not doing so. In this communication, the Commission gives account of the initiatives that are connected to the citizens' request. The Commission's public and detailed explanation of its political choice cannot but reinforce the transparency of the initiative process.

The procedure generates a public debate before the European Parliament.

Article 11 of Regulation (EU) No. 211/2011 provides that the organisers have the opportunity to present the European Citizens' Initiative at a public hearing at the European Parliament[57] with the participation of the Commission (represented at an appropriate level[58]) and with other institutions and bodies of the Union that wish to participate. The importance of a public hearing has been stressed by the Ombudsman herself in the decision which ended the own-initiative inquiry on the functioning of the European Citizens' Initiative (ECI (OI/9/2013/TN). According to the Ombudsman, the process is in itself valuable as it offers a platform which can generate public debate:

> If public political debate is facilitated properly in the context of the ECI tool, this debate can give the desired effect to this new democratic right for citizens.

Public hearing took place in relation to the Right2Water initiative (accepted by the Commission) and to the One of Us and the Stop Vivisection initiatives (not accepted by the Commission).

Article 218 of the Rules of Procedure of the European Parliament establishes that when a registered initiative cannot be submitted to the Commission because not

[55]According to the EU General Court in Case T-450/12, cit., para. 26, "It is incumbent on the Commission, when it receives a proposal for a citizens' initiative, to appraise it and also to give reasons for any refusal to register it, given the effect of such a refusal on the effective exercise of the right enshrined in the Treaty".

[56]The effectiveness of the procedure could be improved. See the Ombudsman's suggestions to the Commission for increasing the effectiveness of the ECI. Case OI/9/2013/TN, Decision of 4 March 2015. Suggestions focus on the procedural legitimacy of the Commission's decision making. According to the Letter to the European Commission requesting an opinion in the European Ombudsman's own-initiative inquiry OI/9/2013/TN into the functioning of the European citizens' initiative, "The Commission should clearly and unequivocally explain its position on the issue, including the political considerations that it has taken into account. By being clear and frank about the reasons for its choices, the Commission would promote constructive and open debate, thus helping to strengthen the European public sphere and democracy at the EU level".

[57]Article 211 of the EP Rules of Procedure.

[58]Commission Vice-President Katainen represented the Commission at the Stop Vivisection public hearing which took place on 11 May 2015. Commissioners Geoghegan-Quinn and Piebalgs represented the Commission at the EP public hearing on the One of Us initiative held on 10 April 2014. Vice-President Šefčovič represented the Commission at the Right2Water public hearing on 17 February 2014.

all conditions have been complied with, the EP Committee responsible for petitions may nevertheless examine it if follow-up is considered appropriate.

As a follow-up to the Right2Water ECI, the European Parliament adopted an own-initiative Report (2014/2239(INI)[59] in which, besides expressing its views on the ECI, it requested that the Commission

> come forward with legislative proposals, and, if appropriate, a revised WFD directive[60] that would recognise universal access and the human right to water.

The European Parliament considered "regrettable" that this has not been done to date; it believes that if the Commission fails to do so, the ECI "will lose credibility" (para. 10).

If the Commission decides to take action in response to the ECI, the legitimacy of the Commission's proposal is strengthened, even if it is only indirectly connected with the proposal. For example, the amendment of the Drinking Water Directive

> is a response to calls by citizens and the European Parliament to adopt legislation ensuring a better, fair and comprehensive water supply.[61]

As part of the REFIT programme the Commission started an assessment of Drinking Water Directive 98/83/EC, presenting this evaluation as a direct follow-up to the Right2Water ECI. This evaluation was preceded by a public consultation aimed at gaining a better understanding of citizens' views and the possible range of actions which could be taken; the results of the consultation will be used as input to decide if and where the EU Drinking Water Directive 98/83/EC might need improvement.[62] The exclusion of water services from the concession directive was also presented as a follow-up to the Right2Water ECI.[63]

---

[59] Report on the follow-up to the European Citizens' Initiative Right2Water, 15 July 2015 (2014/2239(INI).

[60] Directive 2000/60/EC of the European Parliament and of the Council of 23 October 2000 establishing a framework for Community action in the field of water policy. OJEC L 327, 22 December 2000, pp. 1 et seqq.

[61] EU Commission Press Release, "*EU introduces more efficient monitoring of drinking water for better protection of public health*", 28 October 2015.

[62] http://ec.europa.eu/environment/consultations/water_drink_en.htm.

[63] "The best solution now appears to be to remove water from the scope of the concessions directive. It is our duty to take into account the concerns expressed by so many citizens. I will propose to President Barroso and my fellow commissioners to endorse this decision. The Commission will of course continue to monitor the situation in the water sector closely". Statement of Commissioner Barnier on the exclusion of water from the Concessions Directive, 21 June 2013 (www.ec.europa.eu).

5 Conclusions

This paper has addressed the question of whether it is possible to maintain the (almost) exclusive power of initiative of the Commission as a crucial element of the Community method while improving the EU decision-making process in terms of democracy, understood as participation, public debate, deliberation and transparency.

The focus has been on a limited but important aspect of the Commission's initiative power: agenda setting and programming. This, the first stage of the policy cycle, precedes the drafting of the act and its presentation to EU legislators (under the ordinary legislative procedure). The contribution of different actors to EU agenda setting has been examined in the light of the above-mentioned criteria.

The involvement in programming of political institutions such as the European Union Council, the European Parliament and the Council is not a novelty. However, the entry into force of the Lisbon Treaty changed the dynamics of the legal order, making more complex the relations between the traditional players and involving new actors.

In terms of participation, the involvement of the EU Council, the European Parliament and the Council is established in the Treaty, which states that the three components of the EU legal order shall be represented in agenda setting. The Commission's President-designate sets his agenda taking into account the Commission's programme, European Council Guidelines and the requests of the European Parliament. Such contributions strengthen the political and democratic legitimacy of the Commission's agenda.

Legislators are also involved in drafting the Commission's annual programme. In particular, the involvement of the European Parliament conveys the position of the elected citizens' representatives. The Commission's programme is presented and discussed in the European Parliament, thus enhancing the transparency of the process and the accountability of the Commission.

Moreover, the early transmission and discussion of the Commission's priorities, both in the very first stage of agenda presentation by the President-designate and on the occasion of the State of the Union Address, enable legislators to know the Commission's agenda in advance. The latter's priorities are object of public debate and discussion. The circulation of information is crucial for correct deliberation and thus for democracy.

The representation of institutionally organised interests through consultative bodies is undoubtedly a valuable tool from a democratic perspective, since it allows the participation of different interest groups from a very early stage of the process.

The institutionalised dialogue with National Parliaments (Barroso initiative) was established to strengthen the democratic legitimacy of the European project; however, the contribution of national political actors to the definition of the agenda is at present rather limited and mostly in the form of objections (what not to include in the Agenda). The "green card" option could give more voice to citizens through their elected representatives, but it presents several problematic features.

As for the European Citizens' Initiative, the mechanism provides for the direct participation of citizens. The ECI also has indirect positive effects on transparency and public debate. As discussed earlier, the Commission is required to give reason for its response to the citizens' proposal, which is also assessed in the light of other related Commission's proposals. This compels the Commission to account for its related initiatives openly and clearly. The public hearing before the European Parliament reinforces transparency and the debate.

While the contribution of the above-mentioned players strengthens the Commission's proposals, it remains to be seen whether this involvement deprives the Commission of its power, modifying the institutional balance.

This paper suggests that it is overly simplistic to assert that the present situation is undermining the Commission's agenda-setting prerogative and thus its power of initiative.

It seems that the Commission remains as gatekeeper to the system, especially because it is responsible for preparing the act in details. The Commission is in a win-win situation whereby it strengthens its position with respect to legislators while keeping control of proposal contents.

Although the involvement of other actors in programming can enhance the democratic process in terms of transparency and debate, it raises concerns on the balance of powers in the EU.

The most recent troubling episode is linked to the so-called Brexit and the Commission's declaration that it will modify some EU Directives in accordance with the political deal reached within the European Council.

The European Parliament is clearly striving to acquire the power of initiative and control the agenda. Although its contribution is positive from the standpoint of public debate, transparency and participation, strengthening its role in agenda setting may cause problems with its co-legislator. The question is whether a greater influence of the European Parliament with respect to the Council in the programming stage would affect the decision-making process in the stage of adoption of the proposed act. It is no coincidence that the Better Regulation agreement has tried to improve the balance between the roles of the two legislators in the programming phase.

It is submitted that it would be a mistake to confer the power of initiative upon the European Parliament as a way of correcting the democratic deficit in the European Union decision-making process.

This solution would likely have consequences for the Council, although one could argue that the European Parliament's role in programming is balanced by the European Council's involvement in agenda setting. The latter, however, does not have the power to legislate.

The European Parliament's position may be eroded by the involvement of other actors, for example through a "green card" presented by a significant number of national Parliaments or by an European Citizens' Initiative. The discussion of registered initiatives before the European Parliament, and the fact that the latter can take up the ECI in its own-initiative legislative proposal, clearly indicate that the European Parliament does not wish to be bypassed by citizens.

As for the intervention of national Parliaments, it would be important to find a balance between national democratic representative participation (sensitive to national socio-economic issues, values, history and identity) in policy-making, and the autonomous legislative power of the EU.[64] A development in the direction of greater national Parliaments' involvement in policy-shaping, especially if the "green card" initiative is formalised, should be considered carefully: the involvement of national Parliaments at an early stage of the decision-making process could affect the position of their Government within the Council.

It is also clear that the agenda setting process could become more democratic in terms of participation, dialogue and transparency. For example, the Commission could improve its method of response to the ECI[65] and to suggestions from national Parliaments and provide more exhaustive replies.

In contrast, "parliamentarisation" of the Commission could put its neutrality at risk. The apolitical character of the Commission and its neutrality, a founding principle of the Community Method and of the EU legal order, are important not only for the decision-making process but also for the Commission's other functions, particularly its role as "guardian of the Treaty".

As a final comment, agenda setting is considered the first crucial stage of the Commission's power of initiative. The process of drafting the proposal, in particular impact assessment, and the stage in which the proposal is adopted, particularly the Commission's role in the first reading and the possible withdrawal of the draft proposal, are other issues that may impinge on the democracy of the decision-making process and require further study.

References

Alexandrova P (2015) Analysis of Agenda setting in the European Council 2009–2014. European Parliamentary Research Service, PE 547.543

Bassot E, Debyser A (2014) Setting up Priorities, 2014–2019. The Ten Points of Jean-Claude Juncker's Political Guidelines. European Parliamentary Research Service, Briefing, PE 539.963. https://epthinktank.eu/

Bauer M, Becker S (2014) The unexpected winner of the crisis: the European Commission's strengthened role in economic governance. J Eur Integr 36(3):213–229

Bieber R, Maiani F (2009) Bringing the union closer to its citizens? "Participatory Democracy" and the potential contribution of the Lisbon treaty. Annuaire Suisse de Droit Européen, pp 229–247

Bocquillon P, Dobbels M (2014) An elephant on the 13th floor of the Berlaymont? European Council and Commission Relations in Legislative Agenda Setting. J Eur Public Policy 21 (1):1119–1132

Brandsma GJ (2013) Bending the rules: arrangements for sharing technical and political information between the EU Institutions. In: Ripoll S, Busby A (eds) Agency and influence inside the

[64]Jančic (2015).

[65]Ombudsman own-initiative Report, cit.

EU Institutions. European Integration online Papers, Special Issue 1, Vol. 17, Article 8, pp 1–22. http://eiop.or.at/eiop/texte/2013-008a.htm
Carammia M, Timmermans A, Princen S, Alexandrova P (2012) Analyzing the policy Agenda of the European Council. Perspect Eur 42(2):41–46
Cooper I (2015) A yellow card for the striker: national parliaments and the defeat of EU legislation on the right to strike. J Eur Public Policy 22:1406–1425
Craig P, De Burca G (2011) Text, cases and materials. Oxford University Press, Oxford
Eggermont F (2012) The changing role of the European Council in the Institutional Framework of the European Union. Consequences for the European Integration Process. Interesentia, Cambridge
Follesdal A, Hix S (2006) Why there is a democratic deficit in the EU: a response to Majone and Moravcsik. J Common Mark Stud 44(3):533–562
Gianfrancesco E (2012) Article 17. In: Blanke JH, Mangiameli S (eds) The treaty on European Union. A commentary. Springer, Heildeberg, pp 681–732
Grinc J (2015) Who's Afraid of National Parliaments' "Green Card"? VerfBlog, 17 Feb 2015. http://verfassungsblog.de/whos-afraid-national-parliaments-green-card/
Habermas J (2015) Democracy in Europe: why the development of the EU into a transnational democracy is necessary and how it is possible. Eur Law J 21(4):546–557
Höing O, Wessels W (2013) The European Commission's Position in the post-Lisbon Institutional Balance. Secretariat or Partner to the European Council? In: Chang M, Monar J (eds) The European Commission in the Post-Lisbon Era of crises. College of Europe, Brussels, pp 123–144
House of Lords (2008) Initiation of EU Legislation, European Union Committee, 22nd Report of Session 2007–08. Chapter 4. http://www.publications.parliament.uk/pa/ld200708/ldselect/ldeucom/150/15002.htm
House of Lords (2014) The Role of National Parliaments in the European Union, European Union Committee, 9th Report of Session 2013–2014. http://www.parliament.uk/documents/Role-of-National-Parliaments.pdf
Hüller T (2010) Playground or democratization? New participatory procedures at the European Commission. Swiss Polit Sci Rev 16(1):77–107
Jančic D (2012) The Barroso initiative: window dressing or democracy boost? Utrecht Law Rev 8:78–91
Jančic D (2015) Game of cards: national parliaments in the EU and the future of the early warning mechanism and the political dialogue. Common Mark Law Rev 52:939–976
Kohler-Koch B, Quittkat C (2009) What is civil society and who represents civil society in the EU? Policy Soc 28(1):11–22
Kohler-Koch B, Quittkat C (2013) Involving civil society in EU governance. The consultation regime of the European Commission. In: Kohler-Koch B, Quittkat C (eds) De-Mystification of participatory democracy. OUP, Oxford
Majone G (1998) Europe's "Democratic Deficit": the Question of Standards. Eur Law J 4(1):5–28
Moravcsik A (2004) Is there a "Democratic Deficit" in world politics? a framework for analysis. Gov Opposition 39(2):336–363
Mastroianni R (2010) La procedura legislativa, il Parlamento europeo e i parlamenti nazionali: osservazioni critiche. In: Bassanini F, Tiberi G (eds) Le nuove istituzioni europee. Commento al Trattato di Lisbona. Il Mulino, Bologna
Nugent N, Rhinard M (2015) The European Commission. Palgrave, London
O'Brennan J (2007) Introduction: deparliamentarization through European integration? In: O'Brennan J, Raunio T (eds) National parliaments within the enlarged European Union: from "Victims" of integration to competitive actors? Routledge, Abingdon.
Ponzano P, Hermanin C, Corona D (2012) The power of initiative of the European Commission: a progressive erosion? Study 89, Notre Europe, Paris. http://www.delorsinstitute.eu
Puetter U (2014) The European Council and the Council. New intergovernmentalism and institutional change. Oxford Scholarship Online, Oxford

Vaubel R (1995) The centralization of Western Europe. The common market, political integration and democracy. IEA Hobart Paper, London

Welle K (2015) Democratisation of the European Union. Contribution by Klaus Welle at the 10th European Rendez-vous in Strasbourg. http://www.europarl.europa.eu/the-secretary-general/en/activities.html

Werts J (2008) The European Council. Harper, London

Fiscal Councils: Threat or Opportunity for Democracy in the Post-Crisis Economic and Monetary Union?

Cristina Fasone and Diane Fromage

Abstract After the Eurozone crisis, European Union (EU) Member States have the obligation to establish independent fiscal institutions (IFIs)—also known as fiscal councils—composed of recognised experts responsible for the monitoring of the compliance with fiscal rules in accordance with European norms. Eurozone Countries are the first addressees of this obligation and are bound by stricter legal constraints than States outside the Euro area. The form these IFIs take varies from one Member State to the other and so do their powers. In any event, in requiring their creation, the European norms have potentially led to a reorganisation and a change in the institutional balance at national level. At the same time, they may have participated to the improvement of democracy in ensuring more independent expertise, transparent and public information, and knowledge that Parliaments can use to control and scrutinise their Government's actions, although the fiscal councils themselves remain weak. In this context, this contribution aims to answer the following research question: Do IFIs, according to the new European and national rules of implementation, constitute a threat to democracy or, rather could they, in fact, enhance democracy?

Contents

C. Fasone (✉)
Department of Political Sciences, LUISS Guido Carli University, Rome, Italy
e-mail: cfasone@luiss.it

D. Fromage
Law Faculty, Maastricht University, Maastricht, The Netherlands
e-mail: diane.fromage@maastrichtuniversity.nl

L. Daniele et al. (eds.), *Democracy in the EMU in the Aftermath of the Crisis*,
DOI 10.1007/978-3-319-53895-2_8

1 Introduction

Following the adoption of the complex set of international, EU and national norms that is usually referred to as "Eurocrisis Law", all EU Member States but the United Kingdom have been requested to create (or reform pre-existing) Independent Fiscal Institutions (IFIs). The legal basis for the introduction of IFIs is contained in several EU and non EU documents: Six Pack (Directive 2011/85/EU), TSCG and Two Pack (Regulation (EU) No. 473/2013). Actually, the introduction of IFIs had long been advocated by the OECD, the IMF and the ECB.

The introduction (or the reform) of IFIs has certainly an impact on the form of government and may also positively affect the democratic legitimation of national decision-making. By giving technical and expert inputs, IFIs can entail an increase of the technicality of budgetary procedures but they may also empower national Parliaments. National legislatures and in particular the opposition parties, in having more (independent) information shall be better placed to participate in the Euro-national budgetary procedures and hence be better capable of foreseeing what the consequences of their decisions in this domain might entail. It is, additionally, worth noting that the classification of a national institution as an IFI may differ depending on who the assessing body is: the OECD may for instance consider several institutions as belonging to this category whereas the European Commission may only contemplate one institution, or contemplate different ones.

Against this background, this chapter aims at observing how three Member States—France, Italy and Spain—have adapted to these EU and international obligations and what the consequences have been in terms of democratic legitimation of domestic budgetary procedures. It is argued that the IFIs' potential in this respect has not been fully exploited to date and that the balance between technicality and democracy has not (yet) been struck in a satisfactory manner.

In order to show these effects, the legal framework for the introduction of IFIs shall first be described (Sect. 2) before the three case studies are examined (Sect. 3). Based on this analysis, the final section draws some conclusions on the role of IFIs in Member States' democracies (Sect. 4).

2 Legal Framework for the Creation of IFIs

Directive 2011/85/EU requires all the Member States' fiscal rules excluding the United Kingdom's to be based on

> reliable and independent analysis carried out by independent bodies or bodies endowed with functional autonomy vis-à-vis the fiscal authorities of the Member States (recital 16);

such a need is also anchored in Article 6, para.1, of the Directive. It does not, however, contain any further requirement as to the characteristics or the prerogatives of these institutions.[1] By contrast, Regulation (EU) No. 473/2013—binding on Eurozone Member States only though—does define some of IFIs' features—and, in fact, it sets particular emphasis on IFIs – : already the information contained in the recitals is more detailed than that of Directive 2011/85/EU as it states that

> Unbiased and realistic macroeconomic forecasts can be provided by independent bodies or bodies endowed with functional autonomy vis-à-vis the budgetary authorities of a Member State and *which are underpinned by national legal provisions ensuring a high degree of functional autonomy and accountability* [emphasis added] (recital 10).

Further, some recommendations as to the form IFIs should take are provided:

> Council Directive 2011/85/EU [...] established that monitoring of compliance with country-specific numerical fiscal rules should be supported at national level by independent bodies or bodies endowed with functional autonomy. It is important to note that given the diversity of possible and existing arrangements, while not the preferred option, it should be possible for more than one independent body to be in charge of monitoring compliance with those rules as long as there is a clear allocation of responsibility and as long as there is no overlap of competency over specific aspects of the monitoring. Excessive institutional fragmentation of monitoring tasks should be avoided. (recital 17).

The design of those monitoring bodies should take into account the existing institutional setting and the administrative structure of the Member States concerned. Article 2 further defines the characteristics IFIs should entail in order for their independence to be ensured: they are to be structurally independent or bodies endowed with functional autonomy vis-à-vis the budgetary authorities of the Member State, and which are underpinned by national legal provisions ensuring a high degree of functional autonomy and accountability, including:

> (i) a statutory regime grounded in national laws, regulations or binding administrative provisions;
> (ii) not taking instructions from the budgetary authorities of the Member State concerned or from any other public or private body;
> (iii) the capacity to communicate publicly in a timely manner;
> (iv) procedures for nominating members on the basis of their experience and competence;
> (v) adequate resources and appropriate access to information to carry out their mandate.

Additionally, Article 5 defines the functions IFIs should assume as being in charge of ensuring the compliance with numerical fiscal rules incorporating in the national budgetary processes their medium-term budgetary objective and numerical fiscal rules. They should also

> where appropriate, provide public assessments with respect to national fiscal rules, inter alia relating to: (a) the occurrence of circumstances leading to the activation of the correction mechanism for cases of significant observed deviation from the medium-term objective or the adjustment path towards it [...]; (b) whether the budgetary correction is

[1] More guidance, although the document is not binding, is provided for in European Commission (2012), Annex, point 7.

> proceeding in accordance with national rules and plans; (c) any occurrence or cessation of circumstances referred to in the tenth subparagraph of Article 5(1) of Regulation (EC) No 1466/97 which may allow a temporary deviation from the medium-term budgetary objective or the adjustment path towards it, provided that such a deviation does not endanger fiscal sustainability in the medium term.

The European norms, and in particular Regulation (EU) No. 473/2013, thus define rather general criteria as to the functions and the institutional features of IFIs in EU Member States leaving those to decide how to best fulfil these requirements.[2] As will be illustrated by the cases of France, Italy and Spain, this margin of manoeuvre has led to Member States introducing and having rather different IFIs, both in terms of institutional setting and in terms of prerogatives. However, such flexibility was probably inevitable in the light of the institutional autonomy of the Member States and the respect of their constitutional identity enshrined in the Treaties (Article 4, para. 2, TEU). This was also particularly needed in order to allow Member States to develop the institution(s) that was best suited to their pre-existing institutional framework, although the creation of a new IFI instead of the reform of pre-existing one(s) is not uncontroversial in some Member States such as Italy or Spain.

This situation is further complicated by the fact that an international treaty, the TSCG, also refers to IFIs. Its Article 3, para. 2, addresses their role in the activation of the automatic correction mechanism. Not all provisions of the TSCG apply to all Contracting Parties though[3] and Article 3, para. 2, binds all of them except for Hungary, Poland and Sweden as it is part of Title III (Fiscal Compact). Interestingly, this article is also the only provision of the TSCG eligible for judicial review in accordance with Article 8, para. 1, that reads:

> The European Commission is invited to present in due time to the Contracting Parties a report on the provisions adopted by each of them in compliance with Article 3(2). If the European Commission, after having given the Contracting Party concerned the opportunity to submit its observations, concludes in its report that such Contracting Party has failed to comply with Article 3(2), the matter will be brought to the Court of Justice of the European Union by one or more Contracting Parties (also independently of the Commission's report).

So far, the Commission has not presented this report and it is hence uneasy to predict what the consequences of these provisions will be. On the other hand, whereas Member States had until the end of December 2013 to implement Directive 2011/85/EU, the delay for them to set their national institutions in compliance with Article 5 of Regulation (EU) No. 473/2013 expired on 31 October 2013. This is to say that Member States should have a functioning IFI since over 2 years. Yet, at the end of 2014, seven Member States still had no IFI (Bulgaria, Czech Republic,

[2]More in detail on those requirements, see Fromage (2016a). See also European Commission (2011).

[3]As of May 2016 all EU Members States except for Croatia, the Czech Republic and the United Kingdom have ratified the TSCG.

Greece, Lithuania, Malta, Poland, Slovenia).[4] It seems however that the situation has since evolved positively. It should also be borne in mind that where IFIs already existed, Member States were not necessarily requested to create a new institution: rather they may simply have had to reform these in order to set them in compliance with EU norms. In fact, it will be important to observe how these (sometimes long-existing) national institutions have performed their adaptation from a purely national to new European identity.[5]

3 The French, Italian and Spanish IFIs

3.1 *IFIs' Institutional Settings*

Some Member States have established their IFIs in some form of relationship with the Government or within Parliament but others have opted for more unique settings with Slovakia having established its IFI under the auspices of its central bank for example.[6] As will be illustrated by the three case studies, the choice for one institutional setting or another is nevertheless not void of any consequences for the IFIs' effectiveness as providers of independent information for both governing and opposition parties in order to enhance the democratic legitimacy of budgetary decisions.[7]

3.1.1 France[8]

In France no IFI existed before the European and international obligations were introduced. As a consequence, one single institution, the High Council of Public Finances (*Haut Conseil des Finances Publiques*—HCFP) was created in 2013 following the approval of the Organic Law 2012-1403 on the Programming and the Governance of Public Finances (OL 2012-1403).

This institution is established within the Court of Auditors (Article 11 OL 2012-1403) whose director is also the HCFP's director. The HCFP's tasks are varied: it gives its opinion on the potential GDP and the macroeconomic previsions used as

[4]See the national reports available at eurocrisislaw.eui.eu, EUI Law Project on Constitutional Change Through Eurocrisis Law (2013–2015). See also European Central Bank (2014), p. 97.

[5]This is nevertheless the case for a minority of them as only 10 Member States had an IFI in 2011.

[6]See on this point the report on Slovakia by Dumbrovsky (2014).

[7]See Fasone and Griglio (2013).

[8]Information contained in Gadbled and Fromage (2015) has informed this analysis; so has Fromage (2015).

bases for the proposal of the Programming Act[9] and on the macroeconomic forecasts at the basis of the proposal for yearly Budget Act and Social Security Financing Act; it also provides an opinion on France's Stability programme before it is submitted to the European Commission and it intervenes when the annual Accounting acts are approved. At that point, it shall also evaluate whether France has deviated from its objectives set in the Programming Act and whether the automatic correction mechanism shall be activated. Upon governmental request, it will also determine whether exceptional circumstances—as defined by EU norms—are provided. Note that when the HCFP evaluates the Stability programme it solely assesses the macroeconomic forecasts used by the Government, even if also takes the content of the Programming Act into account.

The HCFP is composed of ten members in addition to its President: four judges of the Court of Auditors, four members nominated respectively by the President of the National Assembly, the President of the Senate, the Presidents of the finance committees of each assembly "because of their competences in the domain of macroeconomic previsions and public finances" (Article 11(2) OL 2012-1403). Before these four last members are nominated, a joint public hearing by the committees of finance and the committee of social affairs of the designating assembly is organised. Actually, the original draft Organic Law foresaw that also the four judges and the member nominated by the President of the Economic, Social and Environmental Council be submitted to a parliamentary hearing. Yet the Constitutional Council struck down this provision to protect the separation of powers in considering that this kind of hearings cannot be contained in an Organic Law and ought to be introduced in the Constitution.[10] Another member is designated by the President of the economic, social and environmental Council because of his or her competences in the domain of macroeconomic forecasts and public finance; it cannot have any elected public function simultaneously either. The General Director of the *Institut national de la statistique et des études économiques* (INSEE—National institute of statistics and economic research) is also a member. Apart from this last person, all members are nominated for a mandate of 5 years. Only the judges among them may be re-elected once. Half of the members are to be designated anew every 30 months and the equality among men and women must be respected (Article 11-4, para. 2, OL 2012-1403).

[9]Programming Acts were introduced by the constitutional reform of 23 July 2008 in Article 34 of the French Constitution. They aim at defining a pluri-annual budgetary framework to reach the objective of budgetary balance. These are ordinary laws that do not constrain neither the Government nor the Parliament at the time of approving annual budgetary acts. But they formalise France's commitment towards its European obligations, in particular since the adoption of OL 2012-1403.

[10]Constitutional Council 13 December 2012, 2012-658 DC and Bourrel (2013), p. 479.

3.1.2 Italy

In Italy, the setting up of an IFI according to the new European legal framework has been preceded by a discussion, at political and institutional level, on whether the existing Court of Auditors could comply with the basic requirements provided for and could fulfil the tasks assigned.[11] Indeed the Italian Court of Auditors is an institution regulated directly in the Constitution (Articles 100 and 103), with a solid reputation in terms of independence and autonomy from political authorities, and with a long standing tradition, as its establishment goes back to 1862.[12]

Constitutional Law No. 1/2012, which among other things introduced into the Italian Constitution the principle of balanced budget, took a clear stance on the form the Italian IFI had to take: a new independent body, established at the two parliamentary chambers "in compliance with their constitutional autonomy, to whom the task to analyse and check the trends in public finance and to assess the respect of budgetary rules are assigned."[13] Hence the new IFI is enabled to accomplish an *ex ante* review.[14]

By contrast, the Court of Auditors is responsible for the *ex post* evaluation of the managements of the budgets of regional and local authorities as well as of non-territorial administrations other than the State, for the coordination of public finance among the level of governments, and the respect of the balanced budget rule by public administrations.[15] For the purpose of the implementation of the reform of the European economic governance, however, the Court of Auditors does not stand as an IFI. The reason lies with its composition and the expertise of its members. In fact they are mostly lawyers, in particular magistrates, who use a legal approach to assess the compliance by public administrations of fiscal rules enshrined in legal provisions. The new IFI, instead, was intended to act according to a more economic-based expertise, in matters of public accounting and financial management.[16]

Soon after the entry into force of Constitutional Law No. 1/2012, a peculiar kind of legal source for the Italian constitutional system was enacted, Law No. 243/2012, which is one of the few examples of legislation passed (and amended) by absolute majority of each house of Parliament rather than simple majority. It is this more rigid source of law compared to ordinary legislation, Law No. 243/2012 (Articles 16 to 19), that regulates in details the "Parliamentary Budget Office", the new IFI.

[11]Fasone (2013).

[12]This is 1 year after the Kingdom of Italy gained independence.

[13]Own translation from the Italian text of Constitutional Law No. 1/2012 (Article 5).

[14]Goretti and Gianniti (2013).

[15]See Article 20 of Law No. 243/2012.

[16]Chiti (2013), Perez (2014).

The Parliamentary Budget Office (PBO) is composed of a Council of three members, one of them acting as the President. Already in the appointment procedure the close link of the IFI with both houses of Parliament is patent. The three members are appointed by agreement between the Presidents of the Senate and of the Chamber of Deputies and are picked and chosen from a list of ten candidates prepared by the standing committees competent on public finance, each one deciding by two-thirds majority.

The appointments, which last for 6 years and are not renewable, must take into account the degree of independence of the candidates, "their renown expertise and experience in the fields of economics and public finance at national and international level (Article 16.2)". Their honorarium shall be equal or comparable to that of the members of other independent authorities.

The headquarter, offices and other instrumental resources for the Parliamentary Budget Office are provided for by the Presidents of the two Chambers; a feature that can trigger some doubts regarding the real independence of the PBO from Parliament as a budgetary authority.[17]

The PBO publishes the macroeconomic and financial forecasts; assesses the macroeconomic impact of the most significant bills, in particular the budget bill and the stability bill ("legge di stabilità"); ascertains the ongoing trends in public finance, also by sub-sector, and the compliance with the budgetary rules; evaluates the sustainability of public finance in the long term and the activation and the use of the correction mechanism and the deviation from the medium term objective under exceptional circumstances (Article 18, a–e).

3.1.3 Spain

Likewise Italy, also Spain had many potential "candidates" to become IFIs when the new European rules entered into force.[18] Indeed, in a report published by the European Commission in 2013, this European institution had identified two IFIs already in place: the Court of Auditors and the National Committee of Local Administration.[19] One more could be added to the list, namely the Oficina Presupuestaria de las Cortes Generales, regulated by Law No. 37/2010 and by the resolution of 19 July 2011 of the Bureaux of the chambers and based at the General-Secretariat of the Congress of Deputies, in the Parliament.[20] However, for different

[17]The same assessment concerns the financial resources for the PBO, as Article 20 of Law No. 243/2012, provides for 3 million euro a year, starting from 2014, for the new IFI. This budget is transfered from the State Budget to the Chambers, which then make these resources available to the Office.

[18]Martínez Lago (2013).

[19]See the list of IFIs available on the website of the European Commission, in particular the fiscal institutions database, at http://ec.europa.eu/economy_finance/db_indicators/fiscal_governance/independent_institutions/index_en.htm.

[20]See Fromage (2016b).

reasons such as the eminently legal expertise of its members (Court of Auditors), the exclusive focus on the state-regional and local relationships on public finance (National Committee of Local Administration), or its late set up (Oficina Presupuestaria de las Cortes Generales),[21] Spain opted for establishing a brand new institution.

In November 2013, to comply with the new European rules, Organic Law No. 6/2013 established "the" Spanish IFI, the Autoridad Independiente de Responsabilidad Fiscal (AIRF), this time at the Ministry of Finance and public administrations, although the main opposition party, the socialist party (PSOE), at that time supported a closer relationship to Parliament and all the opposition parties voted against this Organic Law claiming that the new IFI lacked independence.[22]

The AIRF is to check the compliance of public administrations with the balanced budget principle enshrined in Article 135 of the Spanish Constitution since 2011 (Article 2, Organic Law No. 6/2013). It exercises its functions on the entire Spanish territory, i.e. is entitled to monitor the budgets and prepare the macroeconomic forecasts for the national level of government as well as for the Autonomous Communities (Article 3).

The reports on the macroeconomic forecasts are provided by the AIRF to public administrations to guide them in the preparation of the relevant part of the Budget Bill (ley presupuestaria) and of the Stability Programme (Article 14). Moreover, concerning the Stability Programme as a whole, by 15 April every year the AIRF assesses the suitability of the draft programme to reach the objectives of balanced budget, public debt and spending. By the same token any variation regarding the Stability Programme must be checked by the AIRF (Article 16).[23]

The AIRF also delivers opinions on the follow up of the implementation of the budget by the Ministry of finance and public administrations in relation to the pre-determined objectives, on the sustainability of public finance in the long term and on any other issue provided for by law (Article 23).

The AIRF acts under the direction of its President appointed amongst independent experts in matters of budgetary, economic and financial analysis of the public sector with at least 10 years of professional experience, by the Council of Minister, upon a proposal by the Minister of Finance and public administrations and with the consent of the Congress of Deputies (Article 24, Organic Law No. 6/2013). S/he is heard by the Committee on Finance of the Congress to assess his/her actual ability to fulfill the role and finally has to receive the support of the absolute majority of MPs (simple majority if 15 days after the hearing have elapsed without acceptance of the appointment). Likewise Italy, the term of office of the President is 6 years, non-renewable, and such an appointment is incompatible with any other paid professional activities in the public and private sectors. Her/his cooperation with

---

[21]Bornstein (2013).

[22]Fromage (2016a).

[23]On the many reports that the AIRF is asked to deliver, see, in detail, Martínez Lago (2014), pp. 33–38.

the other bodies in charge of monitoring public finance in Spain is assured by the fact that the President of AIRF participates, without voting rights, in the activities of the Council of Financial and Fiscal Policy, the National Committee of Local Administration and the Financial Committee of Social Security.

In contrast with the involvement of Parliament, in particular the Congress, in the appointment of the President, the other members of AIRF, the Directors of the three Departments (Fiscal, Economic and Legal Departments) are appointed by the Council of Ministers upon a proposal of the President. The link with the executive branch, as the most influential fiscal authority in Spain, is thus very strong, up to the point that the President of AIRF enjoys the *status* of under-secretary at the Ministry of Finance and public administrations.[24] Therefore, pending the publication of the European Commission's report on the implementation of the Fiscal Compact,[25] one can wonder to what extent the Spanish AIRF respects the condition of independence contained in the European provisions, if there is a structural connection with the government, who has even the power to define by decree the statute of the new Authority and provide the funds for its operation (the AIRF is an item in the budget of the Ministry of Finance within the state budget).[26]

3.2 Practice So Far, in Particular with Respect to Relationship with Parliament

Having defined the institutional framework, it is now important to see how these institutions function, especially in their link to parliaments, to assess what their effects are on the democratic "standing" of budgetary procedures.

3.2.1 France

France was particularly prompt in introducing the HCFP after the European obligations were adopted: the decree for its setting up was approved on 18 February 2013, i.e. just over 1 month after the TSCG entered into force. Its members were appointed in March 2013 when it could also be installed. As a consequence, it has been in place for over 4 years now and the first renewal of its members already took place in September 2015. Although it is still a young institution, this functioning period allows to draw some (preliminary) conclusions.

[24]See Fromage (2016b).

[25]The Communication from the European Commission (2006), p. 6, does not contain an assessment in this regard, given the very recent setting up of most IFIs.

[26]According to the fourth final provisions of Organic Law No. 6/2013, "El Consejo de Ministros aprobará, antes del 31 de diciembre de 2013, un Real Decreto por el que se apruebe el Estatuto orgánico de la Autoridad Independiente de Responsabilidad Fiscal.".

First, although the independence of one of the HCFP's members—INSEE's Director—was questioned, it was later deemed sufficient so that the independence of all members is considered to be guaranteed.[27] A balance between opposition and majority is ensured given the fact that the Senate's and the National Assembly's finance committees' Presidents are always members of the opposition.[28]

Its information rights are guaranteed as the Government must provide it with any information it requests. However, whereas preliminary exchanges could take place in preparation for the Budgetary Act and the Social Security Financing Act 2013, these exchanges were not renewed in 2014. Crucially, "A working protocol between the High Council and the Government is being prepared to clarify the content and terms of the exchanges with the administration".[29] In this way, the HCFP would already have the required information when the referral is made and it then has only 7 days to deliver its opinion.[30]

The time the HCFP has to deliver its opinion is indeed particularly limited: since its creation it has had 7 days to do so on average.[31] This is highly challenging when the HCFP has to deliver two opinions at the same time as it was the case in 2014 when it had to examine the Programming Act 2014–2019 and the Budgetary and Social Security Financing Acts for 2015.

Its role appears to be circumscribed as it can only publish an opinion in the cases foreseen by OL 2012-1403. In its own activity report 2013–2015, the HCFP considered, in comparing itself to the other Member States' IFIs introduced following the TSCG's obligation that

> this task is usually less strictly regulated than that of the HCFP, which is centred on the examination of the structural balance and its consistency with the guidelines of a public finance programming law. The mandate of the other IFIs also focuses on the analysis of the actual balance in relation to the 3% rule, on compliance with the MTO and on the structural adjustment (or effort). The debt situation is also often the subject of developments.[32]

However, although its opinions are not binding, they have been used by the Constitutional Council at the time of assessing the sincerity of the draft Budgetary and Social Security Financing Acts. In these cases, the Constitutional Council has nevertheless adopted a very cautious approach in simply stating that

> it [was] not apparent either from the opinion of the High Council of Public Finance or from other elements submitted [to it] that the economic assumptions on which the budget law is based [were] marred by an intention to distort the general outlines of the balance of the referred act.[33]

---

[27]This was due to the fact that the INSEE is associated to the Ministry of Finance. The criterion of independence was later considered to be fulfilled since this independence is recognised by the EU Commission due to the existence of European rules that guarantee it. See Lascombe (2013).

[28]*Ibid.*

[29]High Council of Public Finance (2013–2015), p. 15.

[30]*Ibid.*

[31]*Ibid.*, 3.

[32]*Ibid.*, 10.

[33]*Ibid.*, 11 (translation).

On the other hand, a close relationship could be established with Parliament as eight hearing in the National Assembly and five in the Senate, amounting to a total of thirteen public hearings, broadcast online, could be organised over the first 2, 5 years.[34] Such a possibility is enshrined in Article 10 OL 2012-1403 according to which

> the President of the High Council of Public Finance is heard at any moment at the request of the committees of the National Assembly and the Senate.[35]

Current HCFP's President, Didier Migaud, used to be the President of the National Assembly's Finance Committee which may have contributed to the establishment of this relationship. This is particularly important for the role of Parliament in the budgetary procedure as in the HCFP's own words these debates "give rise to exchanges with parliamentarians who use them during debates on finance bills".[36] Gilles Carrez, the Chairman of the Finance Committee of the National Assembly even stated that "The opinions delivered by the High Council, like the hearings before the Finance Committee which resulted from the opinions, have become a requisite step in budget debates. Their role in the parliamentary procedure is all the more legitimate in that it supports the national representation in its role of monitoring the Government in respects of macroeconomic forecasts".[37] This positive assessment is also shared by Michèle André, the Chairwoman of the Senate Finance Committee.[38] These developments are all the more important as the French parliament had long been left aside during the budgetary procedure and saw its role reinforced as late as 2001 when the Organic Law on the Budgetary Act was approved.[39]

Finally, the creation of the HCFP has not prevented France from falling under the automatic correction mechanism. The Programming Act was since reformed and hence the triggering of the procedure had no effect[40] but as noted by the HCFP "It is not recommended that the LPFP be revised too frequently, in order to ensure the stability of public finance objectives. It would be more appropriate [. . .] to base the objectives set out in the LPFP on adequately prudent assumptions, so that they do not become obsolete too quickly".[41]

---

[34]High Council of Public Finance (2013–2015), p. 5.

[35]*Ibid.*

[36]*Ibid.*

[37]*Ibid.* Testimony included.

[38]*Ibid.*, 12.

[39]Viessant and Philip (2014).

[40]*Ibid.*, 26.

[41]*Ibid.*

3.2.2 Italy

In contrast with France, although the constitutional and legal provisions on the PBO were introduced in 2012, the Italian IFI has been in operation only since September 2014 (the Council was appointed in May 2014, but it started working only in September). The delayed implementation of the national and the European rules on IFIs was partly dependent on the phase of political turbolence that characterised Italy, with the change of two Governments in 1 year following the 2013 parliamentary elections, and partly derived from organisational difficulties.

The symmetric bicameral structure of the Italian Parliament did not help the setting up either. Indeed, both Chambers enjoy exactly the same powers on budgetary matters and both Constitutional Law No. 1/2012 and Law No. 243/2012 repeatedly refer to the rules of procedure of both chambers for the creation of the new IFI. At that time it was no politically feasible to amend the rules of procedure of both Chambers for this purpose—as absolute majority is requested—and, hence, for the first time ever the Senate and Chamber signed a Joint bicameral Protocol with detailed conditions for the establishment and the functioning of the Parliamentary Budget Office.[42] That was the first occasion in which an organisational and procedural decision not dealing with political and parliamentary activities was jointly taken by the two Chambers. Likewise long was the Council appointment procedure as the relevant standing committees had to agree first on ten candidates and then the two Presidents had to choose by common accord the three members.

During the first two years and a half of activity the PBO has further strengthened its relationship with the Parliament.[43] The Office has regularly prepared reports and analyses upon requests of parliamentary committees and the President has been invited to attend committee meetings or to participate in parliamentary hearings almost on a monthly basis, according to a power conferred to the Parliament by Law No. 243/2012 (Article 18.2).

Perhaps one of the most important powers the Italian IFI has, which the Parliament could exploit in the coming years (while it has not done so in 2015 and in 2016), lies in the prerogative to publish independent information that can become a benchmark against governmental information. Should the PBO publish information and data—contained in either Reports, Thematic Focus, or Notes—that are significantly divergent from those of the Government, the executive must appear before one of the committees competent on public finance, upon request by one third of its members (Article 18.3, Law No. 243/2012). Under these circumstances the Government must explain in Parliament why it confirms its own evaluation or, rather, decides to endorse that of the PBO. For example, on the Document of Economics and Finance (DEF) 2015, the main planning document for the medium-term economic and financial strategies of the Country—proposed by the Government

---

[42]See Razza (2013) and Griglio (2014).

[43]It is not by chance that one of the three Council members is a senior parliamentary official and so is the Director General of the Parliamentary Budget Office.

and approved by the Parliament—as subsequently updated in September 2015 the PBO expressed some concerns as for the too optimistic macroeconomic trends depicted by the Government, but that did not trigger the use of the above mentioned procedure.

Although there is potential for expanding the cooperation between the Italian Parliament and the new IFI, the very recent establishment of the latter has allowed the two Chambers to only partially make use of the PBO as a support for an enhanced parliamentary scrutiny and oversight of the executive on public finance.[44] The gradual process of institutionalisation of the PBO is underway.[45] Nevertheless, what is urgently missing is the update of the parliamentary rules of procedure of both Chambers as to detail what is at present simply outlined in the Joint bicameral Protocol and in Law No. 243/2012, namely the ways parliamentary standing committees and the PBO can interact and to create synergies for the Parliament from the role that both the PBO and the Court of Auditors play in the field of public finance.[46]

3.2.3 Spain

Organic Law No. 6/2013 does not establish a close relationship between the Spanish Parliament and the AIRF. Article 24.8 states that the President of AIRF

> appears, at least, once a year before the competent committee [i.e. on Finance and Public Administrations] of the Congress and the Senate.[47]

This is the only explicit obligation of the Spanish IFI vis-à-vis Parliament. The Congress and the Senate can certainly ask for an opinion by the AIRF and they receive the reports prepared by this Authority, which are regularly published on the AIRF's website, but there are no other avenues to foster a more regular exchange with the Parliament as to enhance its oversight on public finance.

Article 24.8 had initially seldom been used by the AIRF to provide information to the Congress and the Senate. Yet, during the first 5 months of 2016, AIRF's President had already appeared twice before Committees of the Congress.[48] Perhaps this indicates a change towards a closer relationship between the Spanish IFI and Parliament, at least as long as Spain is at risk to be fined under the excessive deficit procedure.

---

[44]Such development would be consistent with the explicit acknowledgment of the parliamentary function of control on public finance enshrined in Constitutional Law No. 1/2012.

[45]See Landi (2015). The PBO's Scientific Committee, for instance, has not been established as of May 2016, but its setting up is planned by the end of 2016 according to the PBO Annual Programme (2016), p. 6.

[46]See Lupo (2014), pp. 19–20.

[47]Own translation from the Spanish official version of the Organic Law.

[48]More information on the hearings can be found at: http://www.airef.es/es/contenidos/intervenciones-presidente?page=1.

In 2014 and 2015 the AIRF has published dozens reports and opinions as well as several recommendations addressed to the many public administrations asking to change their course of action in the light of the fiscal and macroeconomic objectives agreed at national and supranational level. However, these recommendations', reports' and opinions' legal effect is unclear as Organic Law No. 6/2013 is rather vague on this point. It only requires that the stability programme shall indicate whether it has received a previous approval by the AIRF (Article 14.1), but it does not detail what happens in the event such an endorsement is lacking.

Just in one case the deviation from the position of the AIRF triggers a specific legal consequence: if the AIRF's report on the macroeconomic forecasts published by the Government points out that they are biased, the Government must take corrective measures and make them public (Article 14.4). This notwithstanding, should the Government disregard the warning launched by the AIRF through its report, the AIRF cannot compel the Government to comply with its recommendations.[49]

It can hence be questioned whether at least the first steps of AIRF have really been contributing to ensure the effectiveness of the macroeconomic and fiscal rules established at European level, which is particularly important in a country, like Spain, subject to an excessive deficit procedure. Additionally, the relatively short activity of the Spanish IFI has also been featured by a direct conflict between the AIRF and the Ministry of Finance. Indeed, in November 2015 the AIRF's President brought an action against the latter before the *Audiencia Nacional* for the alleged violation of the obligation to transmit to the AIRF, according to a ministerial order of June 2015,[50] the relevant information and documents in matter of public finance produced by the public administrations on their behalf (so there is no direct transmission by them in a first moment). This move of the AIRF President had at least two significant effects: to push the Government to negotiate a Protocol with the AIRF on ensuring its good functioning and to show to the public opinion and the Parliament that the AIRF is actually willing to preserve its independence.[51]

4 Concluding Remarks

More than 3 years after the setting up of IFIs has become compulsory the state of the art of the organisation and functioning of IFIs is full of lights and shadows; this and the absence of a report by the Commission render the drawing of conclusions particularly hazardous.

Nevertheless, in particular in France and Italy, the new IFIs may potentially strengthen parliamentary control over the national and European executives. This

[49]See Fromage (2016c).

[50]Orden HAP/1287/2015 of 23 June 2015.

[51]See Fromage (2016a).

would entail positive effects for the improved democratic legitimation of the new Euro-national procedures. Recent developments go precisely along this direction. For example, on 11 September 2015 representatives of the established IFIs came together and established the "Network of EU independent fiscal institutions" aiming to exploit the synergies among these authorities and to coordinate their position vis-à-vis the EU institutions. Indeed, over this short period of time, the Network has already held several meetings with EU officials, workshops, and it has delivered a joint position paper on the initiatives to strengthen the EU fiscal framework.[52] For an initial term of 2 years the Network is presided over by the President of the Spanish AIRF, José Luis Escrivá. With this regard, it appears very interesting that the Spanish provisions on the IFI, contained in Organic Law No. 6/2013, are possibly the only ones in a comparative perspective promoting the AIRF to cooperate with other IFIs as well as with EU institutions and especially the European Commission in the control of public finance along the European Semester (Article 6).

Moreover, following the Five Presidents Report on *Completing Europe's Economic and Monetary Union,*[53] on 21 October 2015 the European Commission adopted the Decision (EU) 2015/1937 establishing an independent advisory European Fiscal Board (EFB), which began working at the end of 2016. Although this new independent body is devoid of implementing powers and is deemed to play mainly a consultative role towards the European Commission i.e. its role differs from that of Member States IFIs, it can potentially strengthen the fiscal coordination within the Euro area and support the institutionalisation and the work of the national IFIs. The EFB is expected to provide the European Commission with an evaluation of the horizontal consistency of the national and European decisions on budgetary surveillance, detecting cases of serious non-compliance, and to advise the Commission on the appropriateness of national fiscal stances for the enforcement of the Stability and Growth Pact, also elaborating on the policy options available (Article 2). The EFB shall "aim at exchanging best practices and facilitating common understanding on matters related to the Union fiscal framework" with national IFIs too (Article 2). The latter task is particularly suitable to the objective of enhancing the institutional capacity of national IFIs, their impact on democratic procedures and credibility at domestic and supranational level, as the first practice after the establishment of the new IFIs has revealed a great variety of approaches among these independent authorities that results from the (necessary) vagueness of the European rules.[54]

[52]See Mijs (2016), pp. 6–7, who is very critical on the current developments and effectiveness of IFIs and their networks. More information on the European Network as well as on the position paper published are available at: http://www.euifis.eu/.

[53]See Five Presidents' Report (2015), pp. 14, 22, annex 3, containing the guiding principles of the advisory European Fiscal Board.

[54]*Ibid.*, p. 2.

The EFB, composed of a Chair and four other members appointed for a 3-year term renewable once, is going to develop a special relationship with the European Commission, in contrast with the national experiences examined where usually democratic legislatures do play a role in the IFIs appointment procedure and/or in the fulfilment of their tasks. In other words, no relationship is foreseen neither with the European Parliament nor with national Parliaments. A more democratic anchoring of the EFB with Parliaments could have probably helped to fill (partially) the democratic legitimacy gap that certainly exists at European level in the management of the economic and fiscal governance. All the processes described—including the recent creation of the EFB—are still underway and time is still needed until the many IFIs of the Economic and Monetary Union become influential in their own domain and reciprocally and can build up an alliance with democratic institutions as to strengthen their scrutiny and oversight powers. Nonetheless, as shown by the three case studies, it is undoubtable that these technical and independent institutions are gradually gaining importance, even when their positions clash with those of the governments, and that they characterise the present and future shape of the Eurozone at domestic and supranational level. Their authority will increase, however, in so far as they will be able to structure solid relationships with the other domestic and supranational institutions, *in primis* legislatures, and to make the result of their work visible and transparent to the people beyond their mere availability on their websites: this still remains a weakness of most IFIs.

References

Bornstein F (2013) Réquiem por un Parlamento inútil: nacimiento y muerte de su Oficina Presupuestaria. http://www.cuartopoder.es/luzdecruce/requiem-por-un-parlamento-inutil-nacimiento-y-muerte-de-su-oficina-presupuestaria/6239

Bourrel R (2013) La validation par le Conseil constitutionnel de la "nouvelle Constitution financière" de la France. L'actualité juridique droit administratif, pp 478 et seq

Chiti MP (2013) L'ufficio parlamentare di bilancio e la nuova governance della finanza pubblica. Rivista italiana di diritto pubblico comunitario, pp 977–990

Dumbrovsky T (2014) Constitutional Change through Euro Crisis Law. http://eurocrisislaw.eui.eu/country/slovakia/topic/six-pack/

European Central Bank (2014) Monthly Bulletin, June 2014

European Commission (2011) Communication containing the Report on the application of Regulations (EU) Nos. 1173/2011, 1174/2011, 1175/2011, 1176/2011, 1177/2011, 472/2013 and 473/2013 – the Economic Governance Review, COM(2014)905 final

European Commission (2012) Communication on Common Principles on national fiscal correction mechanisms, COM(2012) 342 def.

European University Institute, Law Department (2013–2015) Project on Constitutional Change Through Eurocrisis Law. http://eurocrisislaw.eui.eu/

Fasone C (2013) Corte dei Conti v. Ufficio parlamentare di bilancio? In: Witkowski Z (ed) Toruńskie Studia Polsko-Włoskie vol. IX-Studi Polacco-Italiani di Toruń vol. IX. Wydawnictwo UMK, Toruń, pp 171–200

Fasone C, Griglio E (2013) Can fiscal councils enhance the role of national parliaments in the European Union? A comparative analysis. In: de Witte B, Heritier A, Trechsel A (eds) The Euro crisis and the state of European democracy. EUDO, EUI, Florence, pp 264–305

Five Presidents' Report (2015) Jean-Claude Juncker in close cooperation with Donald Tusk, Jeroen Dijsselbloem, Mario Draghi and Martin Schulz, Completing Europe's Economic and Monetary Union, 22 June 2015

French High Council of Public Finance (2013–2015) Activity Report. http://www.hcfp.fr/Avis-et-publication/Actualites/The-2013-2015-Activity-Report-of-the-High-Council-of-Public Finance

Fromage D (2015) Le Haut Conseil des Finances Publiques: quelles consequences deux ans après sa création? Revue du droit public et de la science politique en France et à l'étranger, pp 1107–1125

Fromage D (2016a) Creation and reform of independent fiscal institutions in EU member states: an incomplete and insufficient work in progress?, forthcoming. In: Beukers T, de Witte B, Kilpatrick C (eds) Constitutional change through Euro-crisis law. CUP, Cambridge

Fromage D (2016b) Parlement et Gouvernement espagnols: quelles relations après le Traité de Lisbonne? In: Geslot C, Monjal P-Y, Rossetto J (eds) La responsabilité politique des exécutifs des Etats membres du fait de leur action européenne. Larcier, Bruxelles, pp 77–91

Fromage D (2016c) ¿Una solución al déficit? La Autoridad Independiente de Responsabilidad Fiscal, Agenda Pública. http://agendapublica.es/una-solucion-al-deficit-la-autoridad-independiente-de-responsabilidad-fiscal/

Gadbled R, Fromage D (2015) Constitutional Change through Euro Crisis Law. http://eurocrisislaw.eui.eu/country/france/topic/six-pack/

Goretti C, Gianniti L (2013) Prime note sull'Ufficio parlamentare di bilancio. Rivista giuridica del Mezzogiorno, pp 81–90

Griglio E (2014) Il protocollo sull'Ufficio parlamentare di bilancio: una "fuga" dai regolamenti parlamentari? Quaderni costituzionali, pp 116–118

Italian Parliamentary Budget Office (2016) Annual programme of activities for 2016. http://www.upbilancio.it/wp-content/uploads/2016/03/Programma-annuale-2016.pdf

Landi L (2015) L'ufficio parlamentare di bilancio nell'ordinamento italiano. Rivista trimestrale di diritto dell'economia, pp 177–210

Lascombe M (2013) La nouvelle gouvernance financière. L'actualité juridique droit administratif, pp 228–235

Lupo N (2014) "Codificazione" dei precedenti o valorizzazione del Parlamento? I presupposti dell'ipotesi di reforma del regolamento della Camera e alcune possibili integrazioni. Osservatoriosullefontionline 1:1–20

Martínez Lago MÁ (2013) La autoridad fiscal independiente, III Reunión de Profesores de Derecho Financiero y Tributario, 13-14 2013. Universidad Pompeu Fabra, Barcelona

Martínez Lago MÁ (2014) Reglas fiscales y organismos independientes de supervisión: la autoridad de responsabilidad fiscal española. In: Adame Martínez F, Ramos Prieto J (eds) Estudios sobre el sistema tributario actual y la situación financiera del sector público. Instituto de Estudios Fiscales, Madrid, pp 1–40

Mijs A (2016) The Unsustainability of Independent Fiscal Institutions. Policy Brief – Clingendael Netherland Institute for International Relations, pp 6–7

Perez R (2014) L'ufficio parlamentare di bilancio. Giornale di diritto amministrativo, pp 197–204

Razza A (2013) L'Ufficio parlamentare di bilancio nella nuova governance italiana della finanza pubblica. Rivista giuridica del Mezzogiorno, pp 893–902

Viessant C, Philip L (2014) La loi organique de 2001 relative aux lois de finances. La documentation française, Paris

Does the Eurozone Need Its Own Parliament? Legal Necessity and Feasibility of a Eurozone Parliamentary Scrutiny

Luca Lionello

Abstract The European process of integration is currently suffering an identity crisis. The outbreak of the sovereign debt crisis revealed serious democratic deficits, which have characterised the construction of the Economic and Monetary Union (EMU). The necessary involvement of democratic institutions in the functioning of the new economic governance has to deal with the process of multispeed integration. Pushed by the need to save the single currency from the possibility of collapse, the Member States of the Eurozone have accepted significant limits of their sovereign prerogatives of economic policy and are discussing the establishment of a Fiscal Union. In order to prevent this limitation of national sovereignty from turning into a loss of democracy, it may be opportune to establish a Eurozone parliamentary scrutiny in charge of co-decisions on economic and fiscal matters together with the Eurogroup and the Euro Summit. This proposal has been put forward by a number of European leaders in recent times with increasing pressure. The paper will explore the legal opportunity and feasibility of creating a Eurozone parliamentary scrutiny in the light of the existing political debate on the future of the EMU.

Contents

L. Lionello (✉)
Catholic University of Milan, Milan, Italy
e-mail: luca.lionello@unicatt.it

L. Daniele et al. (eds.), *Democracy in the EMU in the Aftermath of the Crisis*,
DOI 10.1007/978-3-319-53895-2_9

1 Introduction

In the context of the ongoing debate on the reform of the Economic and Monetary Union (EMU), several leaders have proposed the establishment of an *ad hoc* parliamentary scrutiny for the Eurozone or a Eurozone Parliament.[1] The project was specifically put forward in relation to the additional sovereignty transfers that national Governments are considering in order to consolidate the Economic Union. While the recent strengthening of European control over national budgets has already raised serious concerns on the democratic deficits of the new governance, the possible establishment of a Fiscal Union, based on a Eurozone fiscal capacity or budget,[2] would definitely demand stronger guarantees of democratic accountability than the current legal framework is able to provide today.

The article aims to explore the opportunity and feasibility of a Eurozone parliamentary scrutiny from a legal perspective. In the first instance, it will explain the main features that a Eurozone Parliament should reasonably present, as well as its possible tasks. Subsequently, it will explain why the idea of an *ad hoc* assembly has recently come to the fore, despite the consolidating role of the European Parliament over the last decades. The article will then explain why, even considering a number of risks, the creation of a Eurozone Parliament might make sense and should not be a taboo issue. Finally, it will analyse how an *ad hoc* parliamentary scrutiny for the Eurozone may be implemented in concrete in the perspective of a reform of the European Treaties.

2 An *ad hoc* Parliamentary Scrutiny for the Eurozone: Composition and Tasks

The political leaders who have suggested the creation of an *ad hoc* Parliament for the Eurozone have not employed many words to describe the actual features, this assembly should present in concrete. In order to develop a legal analysis on whether the Eurozone needs its own democratic representation, it is necessary nevertheless

---

[1]In a statement of January 2014 the German Minister of Finances Schäuble said that "the European parliament should be involved more effectively in euro zone decisions. It would be relatively easy to achieve this by creating a euro zone parliament consisting of members of parliament from euro zone countries". See *Schäuble advocates separate eurozone parliament,* Euractive, 28 January 2014. Declarations in favour of the establishment of a Eurozone Parliament were also proposed by the French President Francois Hollande in his speech of 14 July 2015 to celebrate the national holiday. See *France's Hollande calls for euro zone parliament,* Reuter, 14 July 2015. Statements in favour of a "Eurozone Parliament" were released by the former French Economy Minister Macron. See *Macron calls for radical reform to save euro,* Financial Time, 24 September 2015.

[2]More precisely, Hollande and Schäuble proposed the establishment of a "Eurozone Parliament" in relation to the creation of a separate budget for the Eurozone.

to add some substance to the general proposal put forward by the politicians and explain what an *ad hoc* parliamentary assembly would realistically look like.

In regard to the composition, it has been said that the establishment of an *ad hoc* parliamentary scrutiny should serve the purpose of providing a genuine democratic representation for the Eurozone. Notably Parliaments have been created in modern history to apply the principle of representative democracy, according to which the members of a political community take part in the decision making process through those people, they trust to speak on their behalf. The exigence of a direct relationship between rulers and ruled makes clear that the elected must be chosen by and among the electors.[3] If the purpose of the Eurozone parliamentary assembly is to represent the people living in the Eurozone and their own interests, such assembly should reasonably consist of citizens from the Member States participating in the Monetary Union. According to the different institutional design that the *ad hoc* parliamentary scrutiny may present in concrete, the right to vote and to stand as a candidate might either apply only to the nationals of Eurozone Countries or be extended to all EU residents in a Member State of the Monetary Union. A different composition of the *ad hoc* parliamentary assembly, for example a committee focused on Eurozone issues, but composed of members of the European Parliament without distinction, wouldn't serve the purpose of providing a democratic representation specifically for the Eurozone.

Coming to the tasks, the Eurozone parliamentary assembly should reasonably take part in the decision making process on those matters concerning the Eurozone as a whole. These are in first instance the decisions on the functioning of the existing economic governance of the Eurozone, including the procedures of the European semester, the common budgetary timeline, the macroeconomic imbalances procedure, the multilateral surveillance and the excessive deficit procedure.[4] A Eurozone Parliament should therefore participate in the adoption of those decisions, which are currently taken by the Commission, the Council and the Eurogroup. At the same time, if the Eurozone was eventually provided with its own fiscal capacity, the *ad hoc* parliamentary assembly should be involved in the management of this instrument for the development of a common economic policy. Its tasks should include the adoption of a possible Eurozone separate budget following a procedure similar to that outlined in Article 314 TFEU for the approval of the EU budget by the European Parliament and the Council.

---

[3] Article 10, para. 1, TEU states that the EU's functioning is based on the principle of representative democracy.

[4] See Verhelst (2014), pp. 4–5. Indeed, even if some of these procedures also apply to EU Members, which are not part of the Monetary Union, they don't foresee sanctions for them.

3 How has the Idea of a Eurozone Parliament Come to the Fore?

When we look at the history of European integration, one of the most important achievements has certainly been the direct election of the European Parliament.[5] Founding its legitimation on the citizens' vote, it has become the home of European democracy and one of the engines of the community method. Over the last decades the European Parliament has progressively strengthened its political role in relation to the Council and the Commission. Considering its progressive involvement in the decision making process, the creation of a separate level of democracy for some Member States would have been simply absurd until a few years ago. Where has the idea of a separate Parliament for the Eurozone then come from? In order to answer this question, we should take into consideration the recent events of the sovereign debt crisis. Something has evidently changed undermining the general trust in the European Parliament to efficiently provide a sufficient level of democracy in the functioning of the Economic and Monetary Union. It is possible to identify in particular two current trends of the integration process, which are helping the idea of an *ad hoc* parliamentary scrutiny for the Eurozone to come to the fore.

First, the measures adopted to deal with the sovereign debt crisis have caused a significant weakening of national democracies in the Member States of the Eurozone. In particular, national Parliaments have limited their margin of action in the exercise of several sovereign prerogatives, notably in the management of fiscal policies.[6] This is the result of the establishment of assisted procedures for the adoption of national budget,[7] the introduction of the golden rule in domestic law[8] and the application of the conditionality policy for those countries requesting the

[5]The first direct election of the European Parliament by universal suffrage took place in 1979.

[6]These limitations of sovereignty are extremely important because they have changed the way Member States conceive their budgetary competence. The Eurozone governance passed from the principle of individual responsibility (*Eigenverantwortlichkeit*) outlined in the Maastricht Treaty to the principle of shared responsibility (*Mitverantwortlichkeit*) of Member States for the management of their budgetary policy. Indeed, due to the strong interdependence within the Eurozone, the decisions of each Government in the field of economic policy must now be confirmed by the other Member States through the intergovernmental supervisory mechanism set up at European level. This is exactly the objective pursued by the strengthening of economic governance over the last years through the reform of the Stability and Growth Pact. The result is a collective management of national budgetary policy under European coordination.

[7]These are the European Semester regulated in Regulation (EU) No. 1175/2011 and the common budgetary timeline regulated in Regulation (EU) No. 473/2013.

[8]In particular, the Treaty on Stability, Coordination and Governance in the Economic and Monetary Union (so called Fiscal Compact) provides that the budgetary position of the general Government of the Contracting Parties must be balanced or in surplus. This provision must be incorporated through provisions of binding force and permanent character, preferably constitutional.

financial assistance of the European Stability Mechanism (ESM).[9] The progressive evaporation of national democracy, however, did not turn into a consolidation of European democracy. Even if the European Parliament has actively participated in the drafting of the Six Pack and the Two Pack and has influenced with its opinions the creation of new intergovernmental instruments, such as the ESM and the Fiscal Compact, its participation in the current management of the economic governance is definitely marginal.[10] The existing accountability mechanisms based on the interinstitutional dialogue[11] are clearly unable to provide the European governance with sufficient democratic legitimation, because citizens cannot influence through their representatives the decisions taken in the framework of economic coordination. The latter has been generally perceived as something intrusive and detached from the mechanism of democratic representation, which characterises the shaping of fiscal policies in modern democracies. At the same time, even if decisions are taken by democratically elected Governments, which often require the authorisation of their national Parliament before acting, the quest for democracy at EU level can only be fully addressed by a European democratic forum, which shall be able to collectively balance the different interests at play in the management of the economic governance. Otherwise there is a serious risk that the limitation of national sovereignty might turn into a loss of democracy, also accelerating the process of detachment between citizens and institutions and definitely undermining people's trust in European integration.

The second fact to take into consideration is that the reforms adopted in response to the Eurozone crisis have caused a significant fracture within the European Union. Pushed by the necessity to save the single currency, the Eurozone Countries have moved forward on the path towards stronger integration, leaving the other EU Member States substantially behind. Despite not having legal personality, the Eurozone has gradually consolidated as one *de facto* entity, which is defined by its own monetary policy and economic governance. The Economic and Monetary Union represents a unique case of multispeed integration because it impinges upon two core elements of national statehood: the shaping of a single monetary policy and the decisions on how Governments can collect and spend public resources. Even if the EMU is characterised by an asymmetry, where monetary policy was transferred at European level, while budgetary policies are only coordinated, the Eurozone has *de facto* gained its own political identity and has been able to determine itself by shaping its own policies and creating its own instruments of

---

[9]Conditions of financial assistance are negotiated by the concerned Member State and the representatives of the Commission, the ECB and the IMF (Troika) in a Memorandum of Understanding (MoU) and then formalised in a financial assistance facility agreement approved by the Board of Governors of the European Stability Mechanism.

[10]See Fasone (2014), pp. 169–174.

[11]The institutions in charge of economic coordination (the Council and the Commission) shall regularly report their decisions to the European Parliament and to the national Parliaments of concerned Member States. At the request of the European Parliament, they shall participate in a hearing, while national Parliaments can also address observations or questions.

crisis management and prevention. The emancipation of the Eurozone from the rest of the EU has also been proven by the progressive consolidation of a separate institutional framework aside from the one, the Treaties foresee for the functioning of the European Union as a whole. The Eurozone can count on its own governance for the economy, which is ruled by the Euro Summit and the Eurogroup,[12] as well as a government of the currency, which is managed by the Executive Board and the Governing Council of the ECB.[13] These are expressions of a variable geometry functioning of European institutions, which *de facto* aims to exclude representatives of non-Euro States from the decision making process according to a principle, we may call "Eurozone representatives decide on the Eurozone matters". The only exception to this principle is clearly represented by the European Commission, which is a supranational institution representing the EU as a whole, but it is strongly involved in the economic governance of the Eurozone by exercising important technical and executive tasks. The emancipation of the Eurozone from the rest of the EU is also proved by the development of its own specific interests, which don't always comply with those of the other Member States. The crisis has been the detector of this fracture of interests, for example in relation to burdening the costs of the rescue mechanisms for those Countries experiencing financial difficulties, the introduction of a single banking supervision or the establishment of a common taxation on financial transactions,[14] all measures in which several non-Euro Member States have categorically refused to participate.[15] In the light of these observations we can notice the existence of a dichotomy between the state of facts and the law. Even if the Treaties literally say that the Euro is the currency of the European Union and the ECB is its central bank, we may wonder whether these statements in reality should apply to the Eurozone alone.

[12]The Eurogroup gathers together the Minister of Finances of the Countries sharing the single currency, representing the Eurozone version of the Ecofin Council. In general, within the Ecofin Council the voting rights of States that did not adopt the Euro are suspended for the adoption of recommendations to those Members whose currency is the Euro. The Euro Summit is instead composed of the Heads of State or Government of the Eurozone, consisting of the Eurozone version of the European Council.

[13]The Governors of Central Banks non participating in the Eurosystem are indeed excluded from these governing bodies.

[14]11 Eurozone Countries (France, Germany, Italy, Spain, Belgium, Portugal, Austria, Estonia, Greece, Slovakia, Slovenia) are negotiating the introduction of a tax on financial transactions by means of an enhanced cooperation. See *Proposal of the European Commission for a Council Directive implementing enhanced cooperation in the area of financial transaction tax*, (COM/2013/71).

[15]The Member States outside of the Eurozone refused to participate in the bailout of Greece and the other Eurozone Countries experiencing financial difficulties. Sweden and the United Kingdom did not participate in the establishment of the Banking Union. The United Kingdom challenged the introduction of a tax on financial transactions before the European Court of Justice, which however dismissed the case on the 30th of April 2014 (see ECJ 30 April 2014, Case C-209/13, *United Kingdom* v. *Council of the European Union*).

4 Can the Eurozone Parliament Serve the Purpose of European Democracy Better Than the European Parliament Itself?

After having identified the reasons why the idea of a Eurozone parliamentary scrutiny has been put forward, we will now analyse the merit of this proposal. The real issue to understand is whether a Eurozone level of democracy could serve the purpose of European democracy better than the European Parliament itself. In order to answer this question, we will adopt a pragmatic approach by considering a number of factors including the relationship between electors and elected, the mandate of parliamentarians, the political role of democratic assemblies in the current process of European integration, as well as the perspectives of further integration and enlargement of the Eurozone.

In the academic debate the project of establishing a Eurozone level of democracy has not been welcomed with enthusiasm.[16] There are in particular four good reasons why the European Parliament should remain the Parliament of the Eurozone. First, the creation of a Eurozone level of democracy would most probably produce a negative political impact on the role of the European Parliament as a whole. The latter would risk being *de facto* obscured by a more compact assembly, which would be involved in the relevant decision making process of the Eurozone economic governance. The political authority of this assembly would reasonably increase, leaving the European Parliament with a role of coordination between the Eurozone and the other Member States.[17] Second, the creation of a separate parliamentary scrutiny for the Eurozone would violate the principle according to which the Members of the European Parliaments (MEPs) represent the European citizens and not their own national people, as provided in Article 14, para 2, TEU. This provision aims to stress the supranational vocation of the European Parliament, which is not a collection of national representations, but it expresses the voice of the European citizens as a whole. By introducing a distinction between MEPs according to their origin, the Parliament would risk being fragmented in many groups and nationalised. Third, considering that the introduction of the single currency is not the only example of multispeed integration in the European Union, the variable geometry composition of parliamentarian representation should also apply to all those cases, where certain Member States have decided to integrate more than others.[18] This would clearly produce the unreasonable result of a Parliament *à la carte*. In other words, we should need as many *ad hoc* parliamentary

---

[16]Concerns were expressed by a number of scholars: Allemand and Martucci (2014), p. 122; Verlhest (2014), pp. 14–19; Fasone (2014), pp. 181–183; Schmidt (2015), p. 50; Fabbrini (2015), pp. 827–834.

[17]This would be similar to the relationship existing within the ECB between the Governing Council and the General Council.

[18]These include for example the adoption of the Schengen Agreements, the Prüm Convention, the Agreement on a Unified Patent Court.

scrutinies, as the existing examples of multispeed integration in the Union. Last, as the EU Treaty foresees that (almost) all Member States are obliged to introduce the Euro,[19] it would make no sense to fragment the European Parliament, because in the future it will almost exclusively be composed of representatives from the Eurozone.

The aforementioned reasons might be sufficient to exclude *a priori* any measure risking to undermine the political role and the legal function of the European Parliament. However, it is important to consider the proposal for an *ad hoc* parliamentary scrutiny in the political context in which it has originated, notably the discussion on the future process of fiscal integration. As we recalled in the introduction, the proposal for a Eurozone level of democracy was put forward specifically in relation to the establishment of a Eurozone fiscal capacity and separate budget.[20] In this regard it is important to stress that the creation of a fiscal power, touching the core state sovereignty, requires a solid source of democratic legitimation. Modern democracies were born to ensure people's control over the government ability to raise new taxes and spend public money. The relationship between the citizens and the fiscal authority in a democratic State has been very well synthesised in one of the mottos of the American revolution, notably the principle of "no taxation without representation". Evidently the creation of a fiscal capacity for the Eurozone would require a stricter compliance with the democratic principle, than the current legal framework is able to offer in regard to other fields of integration. Even the creation of the single currency, which also impinged upon a core element of national sovereignty, did not pose the same challenges in terms of democratic control, because the European Central Bank is an independent institution, whose actions can't be directly influenced by parliamentary bodies.[21] The creation of a Eurozone fiscal capacity instead would require a solid democratic legitimation, meaning that the citizens should be given account of how common resources are spent in the public interest.

---

[19]Notably the United Kingdom and Denmark have an opting-out right on the participation in the Monetary Union.

[20]The establishment of a Fiscal Union in charge of absorbing macroeconomic shocks and supporting structural reforms in the Member States is perceived more and more as a necessary step to stabilise the Eurozone. The European Commission and other European institutions have clearly taken a position in favour of creating a fiscal capacity in the framework of the Monetary Union. See *Towards a Genuine Economic and Monetary Union*, Interim Report by President of the European Council Herman van Rumpoy (in close cooperation with the Presidents of the Commission, the Eurogroup and the European Central Bank), 26 June 2012; Communication from the Commission, *A blueprint for a deep and genuine Economic and Monetary Union. Launching a European Debate*, Brussels, 30 November 2012, COM (2012) 777 final/2; Report *"Completing Europe's Economic and Monetary Union"* by Jean-Claude Juncker in close cooperation with Donald Tusk, Jeroen Dijsselbloem, Mario Draghi and Martin Schulz, 22 June 2015.

[21]The German Constitutional Court itself affirmed that the principle of independence puts a limit on the classic application of democratic principle within parliamentarian systems. See German Federal Constitutional Court, Judgment of 12 October 1993, [BVerfGE 89,155], para. 154.

Once the proposal is contextualised in the process of fiscal integration, it is possible to identify at least three good reasons, why an *ad hoc* parliamentary scrutiny for the Eurozone might serve the purpose of European democracy, better than the European Parliament itself.[22]

First, the creation of an *ad hoc* parliamentary scrutiny for the Eurozone would better comply with the principle of democratic representation, according to which every political power shall be exercised by the representatives of those who are directly subject to its effects.[23] As we have analysed before, the reform of the economic governance has created a number of binding decisions, coordination procedures, legal prohibitions, crisis management tools, which specifically apply to the countries sharing the single currency. These legal instruments and rules are expressions of a new political power, which directly affect only the citizens living in the Eurozone. In order to keep a direct relationship between rulers and ruled, it would then make sense to give the people concerned the power to take part in the decision making process. For this reason, the Eurozone should have its own level of representation not only in intergovernmental bodies, but also in democratic institutions. A strict application of the representative principle is even more important, considering that the impact of the MEPs who don't represent the citizens living in the Eurozone would not be marginal in the results of the voting. Indeed, if the European Parliament as a whole was involved in the management of the Eurozone economic governance (and in perspective of the Fiscal Union), almost one third of MEPs would be elected by citizens, who are not affected by their decisions in these matters.[24]

Second, the existing European Parliament does not ensure the principle of electoral equality of citizens. This is due not only to the fact that MEPs are chosen nationally following different electoral laws, but mostly because the relationship between citizens and their representatives is based on the degressive proportionality rule,[25] according to which MEPs from smaller States represent less citizens than those elected in major States. For example, an Austrian citizen is almost two times more represented than a French citizen, while a Latvian citizen is approximately three times more represented than a Polish citizen. The point has been raised

[22]Positions in favour of a Eurozone level of democracy were expressed by a number of scholars: Meyer (2012); Von Bogdandy et al. (2013); Menéndez (2013), p. 518; Verlhest (2014), pp. 11–13.

[23]Article 10 TEU states that "the functioning of the Union shall be founded on representative democracy. Citizens are directly represented at Union level in the European Parliament".

[24]More precisely, on 504 million EU citizens 167 million come from Countries which are not part of the Eurozone.

[25]In accordance with Article 14 TEU, "representation of citizens shall be degressively proportional, with a minimum threshold of six members per Member State. No Member State shall be allocated more than ninety-six seats". The specific formula for representation is decided by the European Council. The last update in this regard was taken after the accession of Croatia in the EU (European Council Decision No. 2013/312/EU).

already by the German Constitutional Court in the *Lissabon Urteil*:[26] even if the Treaty says that MEPs represent the EU citizens, these are in concrete represented in different ways according to where they come from. Degressive proportionality has been justified on the basis of the legal nature of the EU, which is a Union of States and citizens and for this reason "the representation of citizens must take into account territorial boundaries".[27] Evidently this explanation was quite convincing when the Union had a limited impact on the sovereign prerogatives of State and therefore manipulations in representation were acceptable. However, the ongoing strengthening of the European governance and the perspective of fiscal integration turn things around. The ongoing sovereignty transfers in the framework of the Eurozone require not only the involvement of democratic institutions in the decision making process, but also to make sure that the latter represent citizens in a fair way. As economic and fiscal integration touches the relationship between responsibility and solidarity in a political community, the citizens of Eurozone Member States should all be granted the same voice in the management of the economic governance and fiscal capacity. This can be possible only by making their representation consistent with the principle of electoral equality and direct proportionality.[28] Otherwise, we will incur the awkward situations in which taxpayers of certain Countries may be much more represented than taxpayers of other Countries.

[26]"The degressively proportional composition prescribed for the European Parliament by Article 14.2(1) third sentence Lisbon TEU stands between the principle of equality of states under international law and the state principle of electoral equality. [...]. In federal states, such marked imbalances are, as a general rule, only tolerated for the second chamber existing beside the parliament [...]. They are, however, not accepted in the representative body of the people because otherwise that could not represent the people in a way that does justice to equality based on the principle of personal freedom. The arrangement of the right to vote in the European Union need, however, not be a contradiction to Article 10.1 Lisbon TEU, which provides that the functioning of the Union shall be founded on representative democracy; for the democracies of the Member States with their majorities and decisions on political direction are represented at the level of the European institutions in the Council and also in the Parliament. Thus, this arrangement of representation of the Member States only indirectly represents the distribution of power in the Member States. This is a cogent reason for the fact that it would be perceived as insufficient if for example a small Member State were represented in the European Parliament by only one Member of Parliament if the principle of electoral equality were observed more strictly. The states affected argue that otherwise it would no longer possible to reflect national majority situations in a representative manner at European level. This consideration alone shows that it is not the European people that is represented within the meaning of Article 10.1 Lisbon TEU but the peoples of Europe organised in their states, with their respective distribution of power brought about by democratic elections taking into account the principle of equality and pre-determined by party politics". German Federal Constitutional Court, Judgment of 30 June 2009, [2 BvE 2/08], paras. 284–286.

[27]See Fabbrini (2015), p. 827.

[28]Even if it was impossible to grant full electoral equality in representation, the distortions coming from the principle of degressive proportionality should be significantly reduced.

Such a result would eventually undermine the mutual trust between citizens on which the slow and difficult process of fiscal integration needs to be based on.[29]

Third, the introduction of a Eurozone level of democracy may help the process of European integration to exit the deadlock in which it is currently stuck. Today we are experiencing a difficult situation in which, while Eurozone Countries need to balance the loss of national democracy by strengthening European democracy, other Member States oppose any reform having an impact (even potentially) on their national sovereignty. In this regard, it is important to stress that the involvement of democratic institutions in the decision making process is always responsible for hidden sovereignty transfers to the EU. Indeed, by reducing the intergovernmental functioning of the Union, Member States normally lose a significant part of their grip on the decision making process.[30] This is something that not all Countries are ready to accept. In particular, the Member States not taking part in the Monetary Union may more easily oppose transfers of sovereignty to the European Parliament for at least two reasons: first they don't have the urgency to consolidate European democracy, because their Parliaments are still in charge of most sovereign competences; second some countries might dislike the idea of participating in a reformed European governance, where national Governments have to share their authority with a supranational democratic institution. In the light of this observation, refusing to establish today a Eurozone parliamentary scrutiny with effective powers, hoping that all Member States may accept the authority of EU Parliament on fiscal matters and join in the future the Eurozone is not strategic from the point of view of strengthening European democracy. The Eurozone is experiencing a serious crisis of legitimacy and this is happening now. No other Member State will join the Monetary Union (but on the contrary some may leave)[31] if no effective instruments of democratic control are created at the level where it is required. This level is the Eurozone: the Countries sharing the single currency are obliged by the crisis to take into consideration further transfers

---

[29]The comparative argument according to which other Parliaments also apply the principle of a degressive proportionality is not sufficient to dismiss the criticism regarding the deficits of representation in the European Parliament. By considering the voting power inequality due to skewedness of representation across territorial subdivisions (Voting Gini coefficient), the European Parliament has a coefficient of inequality in representation twenty times higher than the German Parliament and three times higher than the French Parliament. See Véron (2014).

[30]National Governments usually prefer to transfer competences to intergovernmental institutions, they can still participate in and influence. On the contrary, sharing powers with democratic institutions reduces Governments' ability to affect the decision making process at European level on their own. In the light of this consideration, it is unlikely that the process of European democratisation will be accepted by all Member States. Similarly, the Eurogroup and the Euro Summit would probably refuse to share their powers with the entire European Parliament, which may be dominated by majorities not representative of what most of Eurozone citizen's representatives want to do.

[31]For example, the Finnish Parliament has been debating whether the Country should abolish the single currency. See *Finland to discuss leaving eurozone after disgruntled citizens force debate*, The Telegraph, 16 November 2015.

of powers to democratic institutions, especially after they will have decided to create a Fiscal Union.

After having explained, why in the light of the process of fiscal integration a Eurozone level of democracy may serve European democracy better than the European Parliament itself, it is easier to answer two main expressed concerns on the introduction of such an *ad hoc* parliamentary scrutiny.

Regarding the risk of having a European Parliament *à la carte*, we notice that the creation of an *ad hoc* parliamentary scrutiny may make sense for the Eurozone and not for other kinds of multispeed integration. Indeed, the introduction of the single currency has caused a qualitative leap in the process of unification, creating a practical constraint (*Sachzwang*) among the Member States of the Monetary Union towards more integration. The Eurozone has become one entity composed of Countries unified by a solidarity of fact, which means sharing common needs and interests. This was clear during the most acute phase of the sovereign debt crisis when only the Member States of the Monetary Union have been *de facto* obliged to spend billions of Euros to save those Countries risking default. Unfortunately, a similar level of solidarity wasn't achieved by the Schengen Agreements,[32] nor of course by other examples of multispeed integration, such as the Agreement on a Unified Patent Court.[33] Therefore, the creation of *ad hoc* parliamentary scrutiny for the Eurozone should not open the doors to a Parliament *à la carte*, but rather address the current concerns on democratic deficit regarding one of the most important aspects of the integration process, which is the Economic and Monetary Union.

On the possible distinction of MEPs by their origin, the creation of an *ad hoc* parliamentary scrutiny would not necessarily lead to a process of nationalisation, but should on the contrary strengthen the democratic representation of the Eurozone as a whole. A Eurozone parliamentary assembly is meant to be the democratic voice of the Eurozone, not a collection of national representations of the Member States of the Monetary Union. The members of the *ad hoc* parliamentary assembly would slowly emancipate from their national background and put forward the interests of the Eurozone as a whole. Rather than trigger a process of renationalisation of democratic representation, the new assembly should become a core European Parliament.

[32]The current political *momentum* is proving how weak the Schengen *acquis* is compared to other fields of integration, notably the Monetary Union. While the debt crisis has obliged the Eurozone Countries to move forward with integration, national Governments are at the moment struggling to implement a common response to the unprecedented immigration crisis, preferring instead the reintroduction of national borders.

[33]The Agreement on a Unified Patent Court was signed by 26 Member States. It follows the enhanced cooperation in the creation of unitary patent protection adopted in 2011.

5 Different Options for Establishing an *ad hoc* Parliamentary Scrutiny for the Eurozone

If Member States will ever take into consideration the creation of an *ad hoc* democratic representation for the Eurozone, it will be necessary to identify some available solutions to turn this proposal into practice. In this regard the establishment of an *ad hoc* parliamentary scrutiny would most likely require a Treaty change or a new Treaty.[34] Indeed, the current legal framework excludes democratic institutions from the functioning of the economic governance, which is essentially intergovernmental. At the same time, the distinction between the representatives of the EU as a whole and those of the Eurozone is difficult to accomplish without changing the EU Treaties, as the latter exclude for the moment any diversification in the role of parliamentarians according to the constituency, where they were elected.[35]

In the perspective of a Treaty amendment or a new Treaty, it has been possible to identify three alternatives for creating an *ad hoc* parliamentary scrutiny for the Member States participating in the Monetary Union.[36]

First, it may be possible to introduce a democratic representation for the Eurozone within the European Parliament. This may be done by creating an internal committee specifically responsible for the issues regarding the Economic and Monetary Union, composed solely of MEPs elected in the Eurozone Member States. The relationship between the plenary and the committee might have different declinations, but it is important that the latter should be the last resort authority to decide on Eurozone fiscal issues. If the committee remained only a forum of discussion for further decisions to be taken in the plenary, the specific need of democratic representation for the citizens living in the Eurozone would not be

---

[34]Within the limits of the existing legal framework the European Parliament has instead adopted on December 2013 a Resolution to create an informal parliamentary scrutiny for the Economic and Monetary Union on the basis of a political agreement between political groups. "[The European Parliament] stresses that the internal rules of the European Parliament offer a sufficient margin of manoeuvre to organise specific forms of differentiation on the basis of political agreement within and among the political groups in order to provide for appropriate parliamentary scrutiny of the EMU; recalls that Article 3(4) TEU states that 'the Union shall establish an Economic and Monetary Union whose currency is the euro', and that Protocol 14 on the Eurogroup refers to 'the need to lay down special provisions for enhanced dialogue between the Member States whose currency is the euro, pending the euro becoming the currency of all Member States'; points out that, if this supposedly transitory situation is to last, an appropriate accountability mechanism for the current euro area and the Member States committed to joining must be considered within Parliament". European Parliament, "Constitutional problems of a multitier governance in the European Union", Resolution of 12 December 2013, A7-0372/2013, para. 31. Such committee, however, would probably not participate in the economic governance of the Eurozone, but represent only an informal forum of discussion on issues regarding the Economic and Monetary Union.

[35]A Eurozone parliamentary scrutiny provided with effective powers in the economic governance can't be introduced by recurring to enhanced cooperation *ex* Article 20 TEU, which does not allow the reform of the EU institutional framework.

[36]For an overview of the authors in favour of these three options see Verlhest (2014), pp. 17–18.

satisfied. In regard to the possible concretisation of a Eurozone committee within the European Parliament, we notice that the United Kingdom is also considering introducing a variable geometry functioning of the Parliament of Westminster, due to the consequences of asymmetric devolution of competences on representative democracy at state level (so called "West Lothian" question).[37] The creation of a Eurozone committee within the European Parliament would bring a number of advantages and disadvantages. On the one hand the formal integrity of the European Parliament would be safe and it would be easier to coordinate the relationship between the Eurozone representatives and the rest of the MEPs. At the same time, a reform of the EU Treaties in this direction would still require the unanimity of Member States in accordance with the procedures outlined in Article 48 TEU. Also the important passage from degressive proportionality to direct proportionality at least in the election of Eurozone representatives would require the agreement of all Member States. This should not be taken for granted.

A second option for an *ad hoc* parliamentary scrutiny would be creating a lateral Eurozone assembly elected by the citizens of the Eurozone through a separate election, realistically to be taken simultaneously with the vote for the European Parliament. The new Chamber may become a new institution of the EU or an external body like the European Stability Mechanism. While the first formulation would require a Treaty change by unanimity in accordance with Article 48 TEU, the second would need instead an external international agreement between the Eurozone Countries only. The members of the second Chamber should be voted in accordance with a single electoral law by ensuring the direct proportionality in the representation of citizens living in the Eurozone. The clear disadvantages of this proposal are a further complexification of the EU legal framework, as well as the start of a possible competition between the new assembly and the European Parliament. Moreover, the creation of a second Chamber through a separate Treaty may accelerate the fragmentation of the European legal framework confirming the ongoing drift of EU law to international law.[38]

The third possibility would be recurring to inter-parliamentarian cooperation by creating a second level Parliament composed of representatives from the national

[37]The West Lothian Question depends on the not symmetrical devolution process in the United Kingdom that regards Northern Ireland, Scotland and Wales, but not England. The question asks whether it is acceptable that parliamentarians from Northern Ireland, Scotland and Wales shall vote on legislation that mainly affects England alone. In the current situation it is indeed possible that a majority of member of the Parliament from England is overruled by a majority of all United Kingdom parliamentarians on a decision affecting only England. In order to address the West Lothian Question the British Government appointed a Commission chaired by Sir William Robert McKay in 2012. The latter adopted a Report in 2013 making a number of proposals to ensure the principle "English votes for English laws". "Decisions at the United Kingdom level with a separate and distinct effect for England [. . .] should normally be taken only with the consent of a majority of MPs for constituencies in England [. . .]". See *Report of the Commission on the Consequences of Devolution for the House of Commons, (The McKay Commission)*, March 2013, pp. 8–9.

[38]Häde speaks in this regard of "Flucht ins Völkerrecht" (escape to international law). See Häde (2012), pp. 15–16.

Parliaments of Member States participating in the Monetary Union.[39] This option could also be implemented through a Treaty change by unanimity or on the basis of a simple agreement among the Member States of the Eurozone. Quite interestingly, a second level Parliament created along these lines might allow to count not only the majority reached at European level in the new assembly, but also the majorities expressed in each national parliamentarian delegation. This may be necessary in the view of a fiscal integration process, as some national Constitutional Courts might require that also domestic Parliaments agree by majority on those decisions having an impact on the national budget.[40] This condition might be guaranteed as each delegation would present exactly the same proportions between political parties existing within domestic Parliaments. At the same time, the creation of a second level Chamber composed of national parliamentarians would also bring significant disadvantages. Asides from the already mentioned complexification and fragmentation of the EU constitutional system, the main risk is that an inter-parliamentarian assembly would hardly amalgamate national representatives and their interests. As a consequence, this form of parliamentary scrutiny might end up turning into a collection of national democratic representations, rather than being a genuine European forum in charge of European decisions and pursuing the interest of the Eurozone as a whole.

6 Conclusions

The previous analysis has demonstrated how the introduction of an *ad hoc* parliamentary scrutiny for the Eurozone would provide a number of risks, but also some important advantages. While the citizens of the Eurozone Member States definitely need a stronger participation in the management of the economic governance, the fragmentation of parliamentarian representation may achieve the opposite result of weakening European democracy. When then confronted with the choice of whether to support the creation of a separate level of democracy for the Eurozone, it is important to balance the different interests at play in the light of the existing political context. The article suggests that the decisive issue to consider in this debate is that the process of fiscal integration requires not only a significant transfer

[39]The Treaty on the Stability, Coordination and Governance recalled the possibility of inter-parliamentarian cooperation in relation to interinstitutional dialogue. The role for the Conference of National Parliamentary Committees (COSAC), however, is not specified.

[40]In its Judgment on 7 September 2011 the German Constitutional Court stated that the participation of Germany in the rescue mechanisms shall not undermine the full control of the *Bundestag* on the national budget (*Budgethoheit*). For this reason, the *Bundestag* must individually authorise every large-scale aid measure. The Government has to receive in particular the approval of the budgetary Commission of the *Bundestag* before agreeing on financial help within EU institutions. See German Federal Constitutional Court, Judgement of 7 September 2011, [2 BvR 987/10], paras. 121–124.

of sovereignty, but also the creation of a solid and genuine democratic control. The necessary balancing of the asymmetry between the Economic and the Monetary Union represents a challenge in terms of political *consensus* and structural reforms in the functioning of the EU, that only some Countries may be ready to accept. In other words, the introduction of the single currency has created a solidarity of fact between the Eurozone Member States, which may make the difference in the current crisis. Willing or not willing the Countries sharing the single currency have common problems, which require common solutions. For this reason, while some Countries can still have the illusion of having the ability to deal with globalisation on their own, the level of interdependence reached in the Eurozone forces its Governments to continue on the path of an ever-closer union.

In our opinion the most reasonable solution is probably to acknowledge that Europe should proceed at several speeds of integration along two circles. The inner circle is the Eurozone, which will be provided with its own economic Government and democratic representation. The outer circle is the European Union, in which the fundamental factor of cohesion will remain the single market. Its functioning will be more intergovernmental and the democratic legitimation less strong. A reform of the EU treaties should move in this direction.

References

Allemand F, Martucci F (2014) La légitimité démocratique de la gouvernance économique européenne. Revue de l'OFCE/Débats et politiques, pp 115–131

Fabbrini F (2015) Rapresentation in the European Parliament: of False Problems and Real Challenges. Zeitschrift für ausländisches öffentliches Recht und Völkerrecht, pp 823–846

Fasone C (2014) European economic governance and parliamentary representation. What place for the European parliament? Eur Law J 20:164–185

Häde U (2012) Euro-Rettung zwischen Executivprimat und Parlamentsvorbehalt. Nomos, Baden-Baden

Menéndez AJ (2013) The existential crisis of the European Union. German Law J 14:453–526

Meyer H (2012) Why we need a Eurozone Parliament. Soc Eur J, 19 September 2012. Available at https://www.socialeurope.eu/2012/09/why-we-need-a-eurozone-parliament/

Schmidt VA (2015) The Eurozone's Crisis of Democratic Legitimacy: Can the EU Rebuild Public Trust and Support for European Economic Integration? European Commission Directorate-General for Economic and Financial Affairs, Discussion Paper No. 15

Verhelst S (2014) A Eurozone Subcommittee in the European Parliament: High hopes, low results? Egmont European Policy Brief No. 31

Verlhest S (2014) The sense and nonsense of Eurozone level democracy. Egmont Paper No. 70

Véron N (2014) How unequal is the European Parliament's representation? Bruegel Blog Post, 19 May 2014

Von Bogdandy A, Calliess C, Enderlein H, Fratzsche M, Fuest C, Mayer F, Schwarzer D, Steinbeis M, Stelzenmüller C, von Weizsäcker J, Wolff G (2013) Aufbruch in die Euro Union. Zeitschrift für Rechtspolitik, No. 7

Respecting the Democratic Principle in ESM Activities Related to the Context of the Economic and Financial Crisis

Pierluigi Simone

Abstract This chapter is dedicated to the European Stability Mechanism (ESM) and to its compliance with the democratic principle as set out in the European Union (EU) Treaties. Having been established outside the EU legal order, the ESM seems to be inconsistent with the democratic governance and the economic and social rights guaranteed to the EU citizens. The involvement of the EU institutions, the voting rules and the *de facto* absence of transparency are the main critical features of the ESM. The planned full transposition envisaged thereof into EU law might eventually grant the protection of the individuals' rights involved in the Mechanism action and bring this organisation under a democratic control.

Contents

1 Lack of Democratic Legitimacy in the ESM

The European Stability Mechanism (ESM), inaugurated on 8 October 2012, is an intergovernmental organisation under public international law and now a fundamental component of the comprehensive European Union (EU) strategy designed to safeguard the financial stability of the Euro area.[1] Provided with a Board of

[1]Ruffert (2011), p. 1783; Ohler (2012), p. 74 et seqq; Tomkin (2013), p. 66; Schwarz (2014), p. 400; von Bogdandy and Ioannidis (2014), p. 94; Mengozzi (2015), p. 561.

P. Simone (✉)
Department of Public Law, University of Rome "Tor Vergata", Rome, Italy
e-mail: pierluigi.simone@uniroma2.it

L. Daniele et al. (eds.), *Democracy in the EMU in the Aftermath of the Crisis*,
DOI 10.1007/978-3-319-53895-2_10

Governors, a Board of Directors and a Managing Director,[2] the ESM operates as a standing guarantee of financial assistance for its States Parties in difficulty (EU Member States whose currency is the Euro), with a maximum lending capacity of €500 billion (subject to renewal); it has replaced two earlier temporary EU funding programmes: the European Financial Stability Facility (EFSF) and the European Financial Stabilisation Mechanism (EFSM).[3] A Treaty establishing the ESM was originally signed by the Ministers of Finance of the Euro area States on 11 July 2011. A modified, final and definitive version of the Treaty (hereinafter, the "ESM Treaty"), incorporating amendments aimed at improving the effectiveness of the Mechanism, was however signed in Brussels on 2 February 2012 and entered into force on 27 September 2012 following ratification by the Euro area Member States representing no less than 90% of its initial capital requirements.[4]

Although it shows a close connection with the Economic and Monetary Union (EMU), the ESM is at the moment set outside EU law,[5] and is largely unaccountable to EU citizens. As the European Stability Mechanism is not a Union body, it is not subject neither to the EU Treaties, nor to the Charter of Fundamental Rights of the European Union and the general principles of EU law.[6] At the same time, however, the activities of the ESM may weigh heavily upon the economic and social rights protected by the Charter.[7] As it is well known, all financial assistance to Member States is linked to appropriate conditionality. Member States must sign a Memorandum of Understanding (MoU), drafted by the European Commission, in

---

[2]These bodies have a strongly intergovernmental nature and are composed of members with a governmental origin, devoid of individual autonomy. See Ruffert (2011), p. 1783; Rossi (2012), p. 302; Tuori and Tuori (2014), p. 94 et seq; Mengozzi (2015), p. 562; Daniele (2016), p. 265. The ESM also has a Board of Auditors, whose members are appointed by the Board of Governors.

[3]The EFSF was imagined as a temporary crisis resolution mechanism by the Euro area Member States on 7 June 2010. It has provided financial assistance to Ireland, Portugal and Greece, through the issuance of bonds and other debt instruments on capital markets. The final EFSF assistance programme (for Greece) expired on 30 June 2015. The EFSM was instead an emergency funding programme relying upon funds raised on the financial markets and guaranteed by the European Commission, using the budget of the European Union as collateral. It was established under the Council Regulation (EU) No. 407/2010 of 11 May 2010, was managed under the supervision of the European Commission and was aimed at preserving financial stability in Europe by providing financial assistance to Member States of the European Union in economic difficulty. Cf. Ruffert (2011), p. 1779 et seq; Tomkin (2013), p. 66; Tuori and Tuori (2014), p. 90 et seqq; Cucchiara (2015), p. 107 et seq.

[4]See Article 48 of the ESM Treaty (the full text of which is reproduced at www.esm.europa.eu). The current ESM Member States are: Austria, Belgium, Cyprus, Estonia, Finland, France, Germany, Greece, Ireland, Italy, Latvia, Lithuania, Luxembourg, Malta, Netherlands, Portugal, Slovakia, Slovenia and Spain. Latvia and Lithuania were not original signatories of the ESM Treaty but acceded to it later (on 21 February 2014 and 14 January 2015, respectively), after having adopted the Euro.

[5]The Court of Justice, however, affirmed the ESM compatibility with several rules of the EU Treaties in the *Pringle* judgment: see below, Sect. 2.

[6]See Tomkin (2013), p. 80.

[7]See Tomkin (2013), p. 80.

liaison with the European Central Bank (ECB) and, if possible, the International Monetary Fund (IMF), outlining a programme for the needed reforms or fiscal consolidation to be implemented in order to restore the financial stability.[8] The economic terms attached to this financial assistance may therefore potentially impact, in a direct and personal way, on rights such as those concerning the fair and just working conditions, social security and social assistance, and healthcare (all enumerated in Title IV of the Charter).[9] Nevertheless, in performing its functions, the ESM is not subject to review against the provisions of the Charter, and does not operate within the democratic and constitutional limitations of the EU system.[10] Undoubtedly, the creation of a significant permanent institution outside the scope of the EU legal order and beyond the reach of EU citizens and their individual rights, would represent a delicate issue for the European democracy and is inconsistent with the principle of democratic governance.[11]

Based on this background, the Chapter aims to investigate the respect of the democratic principle in relation to the activities that ESM has performed in the recent economic and financial crisis. The issue will be developed with reference to the possibilities and the limits of the EU institutions participation in the decision-making process of ESM and of the judicial review within the organisation (Sect. 2); the voting rules applicable to the ESM bodies (Sect. 3); the manner and the level at which the European Stability Mechanism takes into account the principle of transparency (Sect. 4). Section 5 will draw some conclusions.

2 The Involvement of the EU Institutions

The first element that has to be thoroughly examined to detect a democratic deficiency in the ESM relates to the role played by the EU institutions. The ESM Treaty allocates tasks to the European Commission, the ECB and to the Court of Justice; no functions are provided for the European Parliament, which is not mentioned at all and was kept apart from the negotiations too.[12]

[8]Article 13, paras. 3 and 4, of the ESM Treaty. Cf. Micossi et al. (2011), p. 3 et seqq.

[9]See Tomkin (2013), p. 80.

[10]See Tomkin (2013), p. 80.

[11]Tomkin (2013), pp. 65 and 74.

[12]Ruffert (2011), p. 1790; Fasone (2012), p. 9; Rossi (2012), p. 302; Starita (2013), p. 56; Daniele (2016), p. 271. The European Parliament asked for an involvement in the negotiations with its resolution on "*Conclusions of the European Council meeting (8–9 December 2011) on a draft international agreement on a Fiscal Stability Union*" of 18 January 2012 (point 6), where insisted that "democratic accountability must be respected through a strengthening of Parliamentary participation in all aspects of European economic coordination and governance" (point 4). Cf. furthermore the resolution on "*Draft European Council decision amending Article 136 of the Treaty on the Functioning of the European Union with regard to a stability mechanism for Member States whose currency is the euro*" of 23 March 2011.

As to the European Commission, those tasks consist of assessing requests for stability support; assessing their urgency; negotiating MoUs detailing the conditionality attached to the financial assistances to be granted; monitoring compliance with the conditionality which is to be attached to the financial assistance; and participating in the meetings of the Board of Governors and the Board of Directors as an observer. The tasks entrusted to the ECB consist of assessing the urgency of requests for stability support; participating in the meetings of the Board of Governors and the Board of Directors as an observer; and, in liaison with the European Commission, assessing requests for stability support, negotiating MoUs and monitoring compliance with the conditionality attached to the financial assistance.[13]

These duties were examined by the Court of Justice in the well known *Pringle* judgment of 27 November 2012,[14] and were found compatible with various provisions of the EU Treaties (Articles 4, para. 3, and 13 TEU; Articles 2, para. 3, 3, paras. 1 and 2, 119–123, 125–127 and 282, para. 2, TFEU) as well as with Articles 6.2 and 23 of the Statute of ESCB and of ECB.[15] The reason was that, in areas which do not fall under the exclusive competence of the Union (such as economic policy),

> [...] the Member States are entitled [...] to entrust tasks to the institutions, outside the framework of the Union, such as the task of coordinating a collective action undertaken by the Member States or managing financial assistance [...], provided that those tasks do not alter the essential character of the powers conferred on those institutions by the EU and FEU Treaties [...].[16]

Besides, it should be pointed out that the duties conferred on the European Commission and ECB within the ESM Treaty do not entail any power to make

[13]Articles 4, para. 4, 5, para. 3, 6, para. 2, and 13, paras. 1, 3, 4 and 7, of the ESM Treaty. See Peroni (2012), p. 166; Daniele (2016), pp. 267 and 269.

[14]ECJ 27 November 2012, Case C-370/12, *Pringle*. This judgment has given rise to numerous comments. Cf., among the others, Thym and Wendel (2012), p. 733 et seqq; Craig (2013), p. 3 et seqq; de Witte and Beukers (2013), p. 805 et seqq; Martucci (2013), p. 239 et seqq; Tomkin (2013), p. 68 et seqq; Keppenne (2014), p. 186 et seqq; Mengozzi (2015), p. 565 et seqq.

[15]Protocol No. 4 to the TEU and TFEU, in OJEU C 202, 7 June 2016, pp. 232 and 239 et seq.

[16]ECJ 27 November 2012, *Pringle*, para. 158. See also ECJ 10 April 1992, opinion 1/92, *Draft agreement between the Community and the Countries of the European Free Trade Association relating to the creation of the European Economic Area*, paras. 32 and 41; 30 June 1993, Joined Cases C-181/91 and C-248/91, *Parliament* v. *Council and Commission*, paras. 16, 20 and 22; 2 March 1994, Case C-316/91, *Parliament* v. *Council*, paras. 26, 34 and 41; 18 April 2001, opinion 1/00, *Proposed agreement between the European Community and non-Member States on the establishment of a European Common Aviation Area*, para. 20; 8 March 2011, opinion 1/09, *Agreement creating a Unified Patent Litigation System*, para. 75. Cf. on the matter Rossolillo (2012), p. 14 et seq; de Witte (2013), p. 82 et seqq: he points out, in particular, that the role given to the European Commission and the ECB by Article 13 of the ESM Treaty to negotiate and monitor the MoUs with Countries benefiting from fiscal support is based on the existing model created by Article 3, para. 5, of Council Regulation (EU) No. 407/2010 (already cited above, footnote 3) establishing the EFSM. See furthermore Peers (2013), p. 49 et seqq; Tomkin (2013), p. 73 et seq; Cucchiara (2015), p. 121.

decisions of their own, and that the activities pursued by those institutions within the ESM Treaty solely commit the ESM itself.[17]

The European Commission and the ECB (sometimes together with the IMF) perform their assignments without any involvement of the European Parliament and national Parliaments.[18] Some scholars have described this participation of EU institutions in the intergovernmental cooperation of ESM Member States as giving rise to a "semi-intergovernmental" method or to a form of "hybridity between EU law and the international 'side agreements'".[19] From a more general point of view, it can be observed that Member States, in an attempt to preserve their national sovereignty in budgetary and public finance matters, have preferred to regain a central position; in doing so, they have relegated the EU institutions to an almost instrumental, investigative and monitoring function. In order to deal with the crisis, they have decided to resort to the intergovernmental method, thus escaping the Union legal system and the degree of democratic control ensured by the European Parliament, and weakening at the same time the powers of scrutiny of their national Parliaments.[20] It should also be said that the exclusion of the European Parliament from the procedures of financial assistance to Euro area States in difficulty and the weakening of its role in the economic governance within the EU, expresses a trend in international law in the economic and financial cooperation, being the current historical period marked by an increased incidence of the Summits of Heads of State and Government in the elaboration of programmatic standards in economic and financial matters, and by the failure to provide adequate instruments of democratic control.[21]

As to the role allocated to the Court of Justice, under Article 37 of the ESM Treaty, the Board of Governors is to decide on any dispute arising between an ESM Member and the ESM, or between ESM Members, in connection with the interpretation and application of the ESM Treaty, including any dispute about the compatibility of the decisions adopted by the ESM with that Treaty (para. 2). The dispute is to be submitted to the Court only if an ESM Member contests the decision adopted by the Board of Governors (para. 3). The competence exercised by the Court of Justice, which is different from that provided for in the Treaty on Stability, Coordination and Governance in the Economic and Monetary Union ("TSCG" or "Fiscal Compact"), signed in Brussels on 2 March 2012,[22] is directly based on

[17]Fasone (2012), p. 9 et seqq; Tuori (2012), p. 45; Dawson and de Witte (2013), p. 829; Caruso and Morvillo (2014), p. 699 et seqq; Cucchiara (2015), p. 121 et seq; Mengozzi (2015), p. 571.

[18]Mengozzi (2015), p. 571.

[19]Chiti and Gustavo Teixeira (2013), p. 683 et seqq; Keppenne (2014), p. 203; de Witte (2015), p. 434 et seqq.

[20]Tufano and Pugliese (2014), p. 325 et seqq; Cucchiara (2015), pp. 113 and 128; Mengozzi (2015), pp. 572 et seq. and 575 et seq.

[21]See Starita (2013), p. 58.

[22]See Article 8 of the TSCG. The full text of the TSCG is published in www.consilium.europa.eu; cf. about it, *inter alii*, Baratta (2012), Craig (2012), de Streel and Etienne (2012), Peers (2012), Rossi (2012).

Article 273 TFEU, according to which the Court has jurisdiction in any dispute between Member States related to the subject-matter of the EU Treaties and submitted to it under a special agreement.[23] Therefore the Court (as a second step) may be referred to only by subjects of international law (the ESM Member States, all of which are also EU Members, and the ESM itself), by virtue of a mandatory arbitration clause (Article 37, para. 3).[24]

On the other hand, the ESM Treaty does not provide for any direct control over the legitimacy of the resolutions adopted by the Mechanism bodies,[25] and the democratic principle does not serve as a legal parameter of validity directly applicable to the ESM Treaty rules. The Court of Justice cannot perform such a control neither through an action for annulment as provided for by Article 263 TFEU, nor through an application based on the arbitration clause of Article 37, para. 3, of the ESM Treaty.[26] The democratic principle cannot even be a parameter for assessing the lawfulness of the conduct of Contracting States or international organisations responsible for implementing the ESM Treaty. The jurisdiction of the Court of Justice, in fact, does not arise from the rules contained in the TEU and TFEU and governing its functions in the Union, but rather from the arbitration clause of the ESM Treaty. The legality of the behaviour of a Member State or of the acts adopted by international organisations must be controlled by the Court only with reference to the provisions of the ESM Treaty, while EU law can have at most an interpretative aid.[27]

It is quite clear that the procedure described above escapes the application of the Charter of Fundamental Rights of the European Union,[28] and that, despite what stated by the Court of Justice in the *Pringle* case, the general principle of effective judicial protection is not guaranteed at all.[29] In *Pringle*, the lack of any judicial protection for the economic and social rights of European citizens was among the objections raised by the referring Court (the Supreme Court of Ireland). This Court pointed out that the establishment of the ESM outside the EU legal order could have the consequence that the ESM was removed from the scope of the Charter, and sought therefore to ascertain whether the establishment of the ESM was thereby in breach of Article 47, para. 1, of the Charter itself, which declares that everyone has

---

[23]See recital 16 of the Preamble of the ESM Treaty. Cf. also ECJ 27 November 2012, *Pringle*, para. 171, and Rossi (2012), p. 305; de Witte (2013), p. 83.

[24]ECJ 27 November 2012, *Pringle*, paras. 172 and 175.

[25]Daniele (2016), p. 265. The (indirect) control over the legitimacy of decisions issued by ESM bodies would fall under the jurisdiction of the Court of Justice if such a question should arise in the context of a dispute between an ESM Member and the ESM, or between ESM Members, pursuant to para. 2 of Article 37: cf. Cucchiara (2015), p. 127 et seq.

[26]Cf. Starita (2013), p. 57.

[27]Cf. Starita (2013), p. 57 et seq.

[28]In OJEU C 202, 7 June 2016, p. 389 et seqq.

[29]See Martucci (2013), p. 264 et seq; Schwarz (2014), p. 398 et seqq; Cucchiara (2015), p. 127; Mengozzi (2015), pp. 567 et seq. and 572.

the right to effective judicial protection.[30] Having stressed that the provisions of the Charter are addressed to the Member States only when they are implementing EU law,[31] the Court of Justice observed that

> [...] the Member States are not implementing Union law, within the meaning of Article 51 (1) of the Charter, when they establish a stability mechanism such as the ESM where [...] the EU and FEU Treaties do not confer any specific competence on the Union to establish such a mechanism.[32]

According to the Court of Justice, the general principle of effective judicial protection could preclude neither the conclusion by the Member States whose currency is the Euro of an agreement such as the ESM Treaty nor their ratification of it.[33]

This reasoning deserve being criticised. Advocate General Juliane Kokott has pointed out that EU institutions, even when they act within the framework of the ESM, are as such bound by the full extent of EU law, including the Charter of Fundamental Rights, and that in any event the right of individuals to an effective legal remedy in respect of the activity of the ESM is sufficiently protected because the compatibility with EU law of the acts of Member States within the ESM are subject under the ordinary procedure of Article 267 TFEU to review by the Court of Justice and the national Courts and Tribunals.[34]

In real terms, however, these remedies seem to be still completely insufficient. Firstly, it must be considered that Article 32 of the ESM Treaty sets out some privileges and immunities to enable the ESM to fulfil its purpose. Even if para. 2 of Article 32 states that, in the territory of each ESM Member, the ESM itself has full legal personality and full legal capacity to be a party in legal proceedings (and this would suggest that the ESM does not elude ordinary hearings before national Courts), pursuant to the following para. 3,

> The ESM, its property, funding and assets, wherever located and by whomsoever held, shall enjoy immunity from every form of judicial process except to the extent that the ESM expressly waives its immunity for the purpose of any proceedings or by the terms of any contract, including the documentation of the funding instruments.

The property, funding and assets of the ESM are likewise immune from search, requisition, confiscation, expropriation or any other form of seizure, taking or foreclosure by executive, judicial, administrative or legislative action.[35] Secondly, it must be added to this that, according to Article 35, para. 1, immunities of persons

---

[30] OJEU C 202, 7 June 2016, p. 403. Cf. the Explanations on Article 47 *ibid.*, C 303, 14 December 2007, p. 29 et seq.

[31] See Article 51, para. 1, of the Charter of Fundamental Rights of the European Union.

[32] ECJ 27 November 2012, *Pringle*, para. 180.

[33] ECJ 27 November 2012, *Pringle*, para. 181.

[34] See the View of Advocate General Juliane Kokott about Case C-370/12, *Thomas Pringle* v. *Government of Ireland, Ireland and the Attorney General*, delivered on 26 October 2012, paras. 176, 193 and 194. Cf. also Peers (2013), p. 51 et seqq; Mengozzi (2015), p. 567 et seq.

[35] Article 32, para. 4, of the ESM Treaty.

are also guaranteed: the Chairperson of the Board of Governors, Governors, alternate Governors, Directors, alternate Directors, as well as the Managing Director and other staff members are immune from legal proceedings with respect to acts performed by them in their official capacity.[36] All this involves a contrast between the ESM and the principle of effective judicial protection of the rights and freedoms of individuals; a contrast that is even more serious in the light of the orders, issued by the General Court on 16 October 2014,[37] by which were dismissed, as inadmissible, some individual applications submitted against the European Commission and the ECB for the annulment of the Eurogroup statement of 25 March 2013 concerning the restructuring of the banking sector in Cyprus (implemented through a MoU signed on 26 April 2013 by the European Commission on behalf of the ESM, pursuant to Article 13 of the ESM Treaty). Those applications were considered inadmissible because the contested statement could not be imputed to the defendants. The applicants, however, despite they thought the statement might in any case be attributed to the ESM, brought their actions against the European Commission and the ECB (cited as to the negotiation and signature of the MoUs by Article 13, paras. 3 and 4) since, due to the aforementioned Articles 32 and 35 of the ESM Treaty, it would not have been possible to act directly against the ESM.[38]

3 The Voting Rules Set Out in the ESM Treaty

The voting rules laid down by the ESM Treaty are also a revealing factor of the lowering degree of democracy within the European Stability Mechanism.

The decisions of the Board of Governors and the Board of Directors are taken by mutual agreement, qualified majority or simple majority, and in respect of all decisions must be present a *quorum* of 2/3 of the members representing at least 2/3 of the voting rights.[39] Some important decisions assumed by the Board of Governors require mutual agreement (unanimity of the members participating in the vote, even in presence of abstentions). These include decisions to provide stability support to an ESM Member; the choice of instruments, conditions and terms of such support; calling in authorised unpaid capital (with the exception of emergency capital calls); changing the authorised capital stock and adapting the

---

[36]See Tomkin (2013), p. 80; Schwarz (2014), p. 419 et seqq; Cucchiara (2015), p. 127 et seq; Mengozzi (2015), p. 572.

[37]EGC order 16 October 2014, Case T-327/13, *Mallis and Malli*, paras. 46, 50, 62 and 66; order 16 October 2014, Case T-328/13, *Tameio Pronoias Prosopikou Trapezis Kyprou*, paras. 46, 50, 62 and 66; order 16 October 2014, Case T-329/13, *Chatzithoma and Chatzithoma*, paras. 46, 50, 62 and 66; order 16 October 2014, Case T-330/13, *Chatziioannou*, paras. 46, 50, 62 and 66; order 16 October 2014, Case T-331/13, *Nikolaou*, paras. 46, 50, 62 and 66; order 16 October 2014, Case T-332/13, *Christodoulou and Stavrinou*, paras. 46, 50, 62 and 66.

[38]Cf. on the matter Mengozzi (2015), p. 572.

[39]Article 4, para. 2, of the ESM Treaty. See Mengozzi (2015), p. 562.

maximum lending volume.[40] In most areas, the Board of Governors takes decisions by qualified majority (defined by Article 4, para. 5, of the ESM Treaty as 80% of the votes cast). These areas include setting out the detailed terms of accession of a new Member to the ESM; appointing the Managing Director; establishing the actions for recovering a debt from an ESM Member; approving the annual accounts of the ESM; and waiving the immunity of the Chairperson of the Board of Governors, a Governor, alternate Governor, Director, alternate Director or the Managing Director.[41] As a rule, and unless otherwise stated, the decisions of the Board of Directors are taken by qualified majority.[42]

The ESM Treaty includes also an emergency voting procedure, used where the European Commission and the ECB both conclude that a failure to urgently adopt a decision to grant or implement financial assistance would threaten the economic and financial sustainability of the Euro area. In this case, financial assistance can be granted if supported by a qualified majority of 85% of the votes cast. When this procedure is followed, a transfer from the reserve fund and/or the paid-in-capital to an emergency reserve fund is made in order to cover the risks arising from the financial support granted under the same procedure.[43] The adoption of a decision by simple majority, as specified in the ESM Treaty, requires a majority of the votes cast.[44]

The voting rights of each ESM Member, as exercised by its appointees in the governing bodies of the ESM and briefly described above, are equal to the number of shares allocated to it in the authorised capital stock of the Mechanism as set out in Annex II to the ESM Treaty.[45] It should be born in mind that the ESM has an authorised capital stock of €700 billion, divided into 7 million shares having a nominal value of €100,000 each.[46] This total amount is divided into paid-in shares (€80 billion), provided by the Euro area Member States; and callable shares (€620 billion), that the Board of Governors may require setting an appropriate period for its payment by the ESM Members.[47] ESM Members irrevocably and unconditionally undertake to provide their contribution to the capital stock in accordance with an initial "contribution key" and are bound to meet all capital calls.[48]

---

[40] Articles 4, para. 3, and 5, para. 6, of the ESM Treaty.

[41] Article 5, para. 7, of the ESM Treaty. About the immunity of the members of the Board of Governors, the Board of Directors and the Managing Director pursuant to Article 35, para. 1, of the ESM Treaty, see above, Sect. 2.

[42] Article 6, para. 5, of the ESM Treaty.

[43] Article 4, para. 4, of the ESM Treaty. See Peroni (2012), p. 168; Tuori and Tuori (2014), p. 95.

[44] Article 4, para. 6, of the ESM Treaty.

[45] Article 4, para. 7, of the ESM Treaty.

[46] Article 8, para. 1, of the ESM Treaty. See Peroni (2012), p. 167; Tomkin (2013), p. 66; Tuori and Tuori (2014), p. 95.

[47] Articles 8, paras. 2 and 4, and 9 of the ESM Treaty. See Ruffert (2011), p. 1784; Tuori and Tuori (2014), p. 95; Mengozzi (2015), p. 561.

[48] Article 8, para. 4, of the ESM Treaty. The "contribution key", provided for by Article 11, is calculated for every Member State in Annex I to the same Treaty.

Apart from the fact that each Member State (regardless of its shares) has the power to prevent all deliberations which need mutual consent, Annex II suggests that when a qualified majority is required, the 80% or 85% of votes (shares) can be reached simply if the five biggest contributors (Germany, France, Italy, Spain and the Netherlands) all vote in favour. Germany, France and Italy enjoy a substantial power of veto: Germany and France, each one on its own, are able to prevent the achievement of whichever qualified majority of 80% or 85%, since their respective contributions exceed the 20% threshold of capital; Italy is able to prevent the reaching of 85% required by the emergency voting procedure, as its contribution exceeds the 15% threshold of capital.[49] Moreover, if any ESM Member fails to pay any part of the amounts due in respect of its obligations, that ESM Member shall be unable to exercise any of its voting rights for so long as such failure persists.[50]

The European Stability Mechanism follows therefore the logic of a shareholder-controlled organisation. It has been rightly pointed out, in this regard, that the ESM (unlike the TSCG), due to the composition of its bodies and its voting rules, is inspired, rather than to the intergovernmental method, to an international method similar to the one of the IMF.[51] Indeed, in the IMF legal system the amount of shares paid or subscribed by the Member States is proportional to the economic weight of each of them and determines their voting power, enjoying Member States with an higher number of shares a proportionally higher number of votes.[52] It has been also observed that the power of veto mainly attributed to Germany and France could indicate that the ESM does not really intend to pursue an effective Economic Union, at least in the management of the sovereign debt. Otherwise, instead of a "weighted vote" it would have been preferred the "one man, one vote" formula, according to the natural rule for which, if a body is required to decide, there is no other way than that to perform a count among its members.[53]

---

[49]By Annex II to the ESM Treaty, the number of shares (and the correspondent percentage of contributions in the authorised capital stock) held by Member States, are: Germany, 1,900,248 (27.14%); France, 1,427,013 (20.38%); Italy, 1,253,959 (17.91%); Spain, 833,259 (11.90%); Netherlands, 400,190 (5.71%); Belgium, 243,397 (3.47%); Greece, 197,169 (2.81%); Austria, 194,838 (2.78%); Portugal, 175,644 (2.50%); Finland, 125,818 (1.79%); Ireland, 111,454 (1.59%); Slovakia, 57,680 (0.82%); Slovenia, 29,932 (0.42%); Luxembourg, 17,528 (0.25); Cyprus, 13,734 (0.19%); Estonia, 13,020 (0.18%); Malta, 5,117 (0.07%). Cf. Peroni (2012), p. 168 et seq; Ginter and Narits (2013), p. 65 et seqq; Tuori and Tuori (2014), p. 95; Mengozzi (2015), p. 562.

[50]Article 4, para. 8, of the ESM Treaty.

[51]See Rossi (2012), p. 302, cited by Mengozzi (2015), p. 563. Cf. also Peroni (2012), p. 168.

[52]Cf. Article III of the Articles of Agreement of the International Monetary Fund, adopted in Bretton Woods on 22 July 1944.

[53]For these considerations, see Peroni (2012), p. 169.

4 The Lack of Transparency in ESM Action

Another aspect that needs to be addressed concerns transparency, now regarded not only as a strategic incentive for the democratic rapprochement of citizens towards EU activities and institutions, but even as an empowerment tool for the economic growth in the European legal area. It is in fact necessary to assess whether and to what extent the ESM takes account of this fundamental general principle which, since the early Nineties of the past century, EU has introduced into the action of its institutions.[54]

Measures designed to improve the opportunity for the public to access informations held by the institutions, implemented by Regulation (EC) No. 1049/2001 of the European Parliament and of the Council of 30 May 2001,[55] are widely present in the TEU (Articles 1, 10, para. 3, and 11, paras. 2 and 3), the TFEU (Article 15, paras. 1 and 3) and the Charter of Fundamental Rights of the European Union (Article 42).[56]

Notwithstanding the ESM is at the moment still an international organisation and, as said, is formally placed outside the EU legal order, the matching with the requirements of transparency as a general principle of the institutional action and a fundamental right of the citizen, is not at all unconceivable. Leaving out of consideration that there is an intimate link between transparency and the basic principle of democratic control of public expenditures and budgetary policy (which ESM tasks evidently affect on), it is sufficient here to note that, except IMF, the ESM actors are EU actors as well (Euro area Member States, European Commission, ECB); and that ESM pursues the stability of the Euro, a goal which the EU and its institutions are directly concerned of, being EMU, a relevant sector of EU, in its turn likewise involved.[57]

The ESM Treaty seems to be far from enshrining an acceptable set of standards for transparency. According to Article 32, para. 5, in fact,

> The archives of the ESM and all documents belonging to the ESM or held by it, shall be inviolable.

Article 34 deals with professional secrecy, stating that.

> The Members or former Members of the Board of Governors and of the Board of Directors and any other persons who work or have worked for or in connection with the ESM shall not disclose information that is subject to professional secrecy. They shall be required, even after their duties have ceased, not to disclose information of the kind covered by the obligation of professional secrecy.

---

[54]About the general principle of transparency in the EU legal order, see Driessen (2012).

[55]In OJEC L 145, 31 May 2001, p. 43 et seqq.

[56]Cf. Maubernard (2011), p. 498 et seqq; Starita (2011), p. 15 et seqq; von Bogdandy (2012), p. 315 et seqq.

[57]Cf. Cucchiara (2015), p. 113; De Nes (2015), pp. 131 and 133; Daniele (2016), p. 260 et seq.

Article 35, para. 1, finally, provides that, in the interest of the ESM, the members of the Board of Governors and the Board of Directors, the Managing Director and the other staff members

> [. . .] shall enjoy inviolability in respect of their official papers and documents.

It is therefore evident that the ESM is not obliged to fulfil the same transparency obligations imposed on EU institutions, and that Regulation (EC) No. 1049/2001 is not applicable to it.[58] The ESM Treaty proposes instead what Alicia Hinarejos calls the "closed doors" approach, characteristic of the intergovernmental solutions (also typical of the Fiscal Compact) that Eurozone Member States have given and are giving to the economic and financial crisis.[59]

The lack of transparency in the ESM Treaty and the inevitable need for the introduction of some forms of democratic control in the Mechanism general system have been also highlighted in 2012 by the Constitutional Law Committee (*Perustuslakivaliokunta*) of the Parliament of Finland and the German Federal Constitutional Court (*Bundesverfassungsgericht*). The first, on the one hand, in its opinion of 7 June 2012,[60] noted that

> [. . .] the provision on immunity does not affect the possibility of realising legal ministerial responsibility pursuant to the national constitution.[61]

The second, on the other hand, in its famous judgment of 12 September 2012,[62] while admitting that, on summary review, the ESM Treaty essentially takes account of the requirements of the German Basic Law, asserted that certain interpretations of the provisions on inviolability of documents and professional secrecy of the legal representatives of the ESM might violate the *Bundestag* overall budgetary responsibility. Therefore, such provisions would be compatible with the German Basic Law only if the German Parliament was to receive comprehensive information.[63] Thus,

> Article 32(5), Article 34 and Article 35(1) TESM are [. . .] to be interpreted in such a way that they do not stand in the way of the information of the German *Bundestag*, with the consequence that a violation of the German *Bundestag*'s right [. . .] to be informed comprehensively and at the earliest possible date [. . .] is ruled out from the outset.[64]

---

[58]Poiares Maduro et al. (2012), p. 10; Tuori (2012), p. 47; De Nes (2015), p. 133; Hinarejos (2015), p. 95 et seq.

[59]See Hinarejos (2015), p. 26, and also De Nes (2015), p. 131.

[60]*Perustuslakivaliokunta*, opinion of 7 June 2012 (PeVL 13/2012), available on the Internet at www.eduskunta.fi.

[61]See Tuori and Tuori (2014), p. 219, as reported by De Nes (2015), p. 134. On the opinion of the Finnish Constitutional Law Committee see also Leino Sandberg and Salminen (2014), p. 40.

[62]*Bundesverfassungsgericht*, judgment of 12 September 2012 (2 BvR 1390/12), available on the Internet at www.bundesverfassungsgericht.de. Cf. on it Wendel (2013), p. 37 et seqq; Schwarz (2014), p. 402 et seqq; Mengozzi (2015), p. 563 et seqq.

[63]*Bundesverfassungsgericht*, judgment of 12 September 2012, paras. 135, 136 and 152. Cf. Schneider (2013), p. 54; Majone (2014), p. 146; Rivosecchi (2014), p. 480; Tuori and Tuori (2014), p. 219; Cucchiara (2015), pp. 115 and 129; De Nes (2015), p. 135.

[64]*Bundesverfassungsgericht*, judgment of 12 September 2012, para. 156. See Cucchiara (2015), pp. 115 and 129; De Nes (2015), p. 135; Mengozzi (2015), p. 564; Tosato (2016), p. 226 et seq.

With their statements, anyway, both the *Perustuslakivaliokunta* and *Bundesverfassungsgericht* do not offer a decisive solution to the problem. In talking about "legal ministerial responsibility" (that appears strong only when the ESM Board of Governors decides unanimously, and not when it is necessary to reach the qualified majority of 80%),[65] and about the transmission of elements the German Parliament needs, so to be able to develop an informed opinion (more significant than those of the annual report the Board of Governors has to make accessible to national Parliaments and supreme audit institutions of the ESM Member States),[66] they do not consider the issue of transparency in a direct way that would allow citizens to have a true access to such informations.[67] This could represent an additional damage for the democratic principle, due to the ESM management of a significant amount of financial resources coming from European taxpayers and the relevant impact on redistributive policy that the ESM action has in Member States where aid is provided to tackle financial crises.[68]

The opacity, confidentiality and secrecy that permeate the Mechanism governance in contrast to the clear openings of the EU Treaties, can also be derived from several acts, complementary to the ESM Treaty, issued by the organisation bodies between 2012 and 2016 such as guidelines, principles, lending documentation.[69] Particularly relevant, in this regard, are the By-Laws, adopted on 8 December 2014 by the Board of Governors pursuant to Article 5, para. 9, of the ESM Treaty; and the Code of Conduct binding on the Managing Director, all Directors, alternate Directors and members of the ESM staff, approved in its updated version on 12 May 2016 by the Board of Directors *ex* Article 19 of the aforesaid By-Laws.[70] Although they reveal a veiled attempt of disclosure, the final results are quite modest in substance.

Article 17 of the By-Laws sets forth the conditions under which the ESM communicates documents drawn up or held by the ESM to other persons or entities or otherwise discloses them externally. The rules are very soft, since documents other than minutes and summary records of proceedings of the ESM Boards (generally confidential),[71] "may" be communicated to ESM Members, the

[65]See above, Sect. 3 and footnotes 40 and 41.

[66]Article 30, para. 5, of the ESM Treaty.

[67]De Nes (2015), p. 134 et seq.

[68]See, in this sense, De Nes (2015), p. 135.

[69]See Article 5, para. 2, b, of the Guideline on Precautionary Financial Assistance of 9 October 2012; Article 5, para. 1, of the Guideline on the Secondary Market Support Facility of 9 October 2012; point 3 of the Terms and Conditions on Capital Calls of 9 October 2012; Article 12, para. 1, of the Guideline on Financial Assistance for the Direct Recapitalisation of Institutions of 8 December 2014; clause 6.7, a, ii, of the General Terms for ESM Financial Assistance Facility Agreements of 15 December 2015; clauses 5.1 and 7.2 of the Standard Facility Specific Terms for ESM Financial Assistance Facility Agreements of 15 December 2015; point 5.2 of the High-level Principles for Risk Management of 22 December 2015. All these documents have been adopted by the Board of Directors according to Articles 9, 14, 15, 18 and 21 of the ESM Treaty.

[70]The By-Laws and the Code of Conduct can be found at www.esm.europa.eu.

[71]Article 17, para. 6, of the By-Laws.

European Commission, ECB and IMF subject to appropriate safeguards; and "may" be communicated to other Parties only at the discretion of the Managing Director.[72] No reference is made to informations to be given to national Parliaments, hinting para. 11 only to the fact that the ESM shall refer requests of information or documents by national Parliaments of ESM Member Countries to the Government of the relevant ESM Member.[73] The Board of Governors, acting by qualified majority (80% of the shares), may in any case derogate from all these rules when necessary and appropriate for an overriding public interest or to effect the intent and purpose of the ESM Treaty.[74]

As to the Code of Conduct, its Article 11 confirms the professional secrecy provided for by the ESM Treaty, but without specifying the concrete meaning of it.[75] Para. 1 states in this regard that

> Directors and alternate Directors shall not disclose information that is subject to professional secrecy [. . .]. They are required to ensure the same level of confidentiality when sharing ESM information and documents with their secretariat, national administration or parliament.

Moreover,

> The duty of confidentiality does not prevent Directors and alternate Directors from providing comprehensive information to national parliaments, in case this is foreseen at national level.

Neither this last provision, which evidently refers to the above mentioned judgment of the German Federal Constitutional Court of 2012 (without dictating concrete enforcement procedures on the matter), nor other paragraphs of Article 11 provide for any specific duty to release informations directly to citizens. The Code does not impose the obligation to publish documents on the official website and everything seems to be dependent on the will and evaluation of the Body of Governors, the Body of Directors and the Managing Director.[76]

5 Concluding Remarks

The European Stability Mechanism shows therefore many critical features with respect to the democratic principle. Very low is the range covered by this principle as a yardstick for assessing the overall conduct displayed by the Mechanism and its

[72]See Article 17, paras. 2 and 5, of the By-Laws. Cf. De Nes (2015), p. 136.

[73]De Nes (2015), p. 136. The Board of Governors also publishes an annual report on the main activities of the ESM on its official website (Article 23, para. 3, of the ESM Treaty). Furthermore, according to Article 17, para. 12, of the By-Laws, "The Board of Directors, acting by qualified majority, shall adopt detailed guidelines reflecting the ESM's policy regarding the matters referred to in this Article 17.". Such guidelines do not appear to have been arranged yet.

[74]Article 17, para. 13, of the By-Laws. See De Nes (2015), p. 136.

[75]De Nes (2015), p. 135 et seq.

[76]De Nes (2015), p. 136.

Member States in implementing the relevant norms of the ESM Treaty. The non-involvement of the European Parliament, the existing voting rules and the substantial absence of transparency are all factors to be taken into account. Nevertheless, as it has been rightly observed, although ESM is not part of EU law,

> [...] it is surely part of the economic governance of the Eurozone, and it could threaten the constitutional balance within the Eurozone itself [...].

It could also

> [...] jeopardize social and economic human rights within States that face severe economic conditions [...] and undermine the principle of democratic rule [...].[77]

The ESM has a strong *deficit*, both at the political-democratic level and at the judicial one. The creation of the European Stability Mechanism through an instrument of international law has certainly influenced its relations with EU law and causes that the activities of the ESM are no longer subject to the legislative and democratic safeguards inherent in the Union legal order.[78] The ESM, even if still does not belong to the Union, makes use of various means of forging links with EU institutions, which are considered outside of the legal framework and the decision-making processes that usually belong to them; the use of a purely intergovernmental method clashes in particular with the increased role assigned to the European Parliament by the Lisbon Treaty. The ESM thus emphasises a problem of respecting the institutional balance and democracy, closely related issues already emerging with regard to EMU peculiarities.[79] At the same time, there is a problem of the effectiveness of parliamentary scrutiny over the activities carried out by the representatives of Member States in the context of European economic governance; this effectiveness is significantly affected by the provisions on immunity and the confidentiality clauses of the ESM Treaty.[80]

The judicial review, limited as it is only to disputes between Member States, and the non-compliance with the principle of effective judicial protection laid down by the Charter of Fundamental Rights are even more serious and alarming. The MoUs to be negotiated and then signed, contain some conditionality measures aimed at establishing the financial conditions of the State by imposing austerity policies on important welfare services (such as pensions, healthcare, education and employment), which so well impact upon economic and social rights protected by the

[77]See Ruffert (2011), Dawson and de Witte (2013), Schwarz (2014), Salomon (2015). All these Authors are cited in De Nes (2015), p. 131.

[78]See Tomkin (2013), p. 79.

[79]Cucchiara (2015), pp. 112 and 128 et seqq.

[80]Cucchiara (2015), p. 129.

Charter.[81] Therefore, the rights of citizens to bring a case against the ESM are thus jeopardised in a manner inconsistent with all the international acts on the protection of individual rights currently in force.[82]

The weighted voting system of the Board of Governors and the Board of Directors outlines a further profile of lack of democratic legitimacy. Eurozone Member States have therefore given rise to a (permanent) international financial institution, provided with its own legal personality, which even more looks like to "a European mirror image of the IMF", to a "regional copy of the IMF" or to "the IMF of the EU".[83]

Transparency also does not find an adequate equivalent within the construction of the ESM.[84] It is true that secrecy and confidentiality can be essential since the ESM stirs within the financial market, but it is equally true that the confidentiality clauses in the ESM Treaty and in the documents adopted by its bodies make for an additional obstacle to national parliamentary control and hamper public control by civil society, the media and academia because of the impossibility of accessing to a large number of informations.[85]

A possible solution to try to resolve the disregard of the democratic principle set out in the ESM could come from the full inclusion of the Mechanism in the legal and institutional framework of the Union, also taking into account the already present connection with EU law (higher than that of the TSCG) due to Article 136 TFEU.[86] Most obviously, indeed,

[81]Cf. Tomkin (2013), p. 80; De Nes (2015), p. 132. About the potential of economic conditions attaching to the ESM financial assistance to directly impact on citizen's social rights (despite in these cases the Court of Justice has lacked jurisdiction to hear and determine the requests for a preliminary ruling because of a national legislation not amounting to measures giving effect to EU law), see ECJ order 14 December 2011, Case C-434/11, *Corpul Naţional al Poliţiştilor*, para. 15; order 10 May 2012, Case C-134/12, *Corpul Naţional al Poliţiştilor-Biroul Executiv Central*, para. 12; order 7 March 2013, Case C-128/12, *Sindicato dos Bancários do Norte*, para. 11; order 26 June 2014, Case C-264/12, *Sindicato Nacional dos Profissionais de Seguros e Afins*, para. 20.

[82]Cf. the reference made by Mengozzi (2015), p. 561, footnote 44.

[83]See Ruffert (2011), pp. 1783 and 1789; Schwarz (2014), p. 391, footnote 5; Tuori and Tuori (2014), p. 94; Cucchiara (2015), p. 116. Cf. also Louis (2012), pp. 298 and 319, who warns: "[. . .] It is an embryo of the regional sui generis EMF (European Monetary Fund) that will be born.".

[84]Tuori and Tuori (2014), p. 218; De Nes (2015), p. 131.

[85]See Ruffert (2011), p. 1790; Tuori (2012), p. 47; Schwarz (2014), p. 402; De Nes (2015), p. 133 et seq.

[86]The opening of the negotiations for the ESM Treaty made it necessary to approve an amendment of the EU primary law because it was claimed that ESM itself would not be compatible with the so-called "no bailout clause" referred to in Article 125 TFEU. The new Article 136, para. 3, TFEU, which was adopted by the European Council with Decision 2011/199/EU of 25 March 2011 in the framework of the simplified revision procedure envisaged by Article 48, para. 6, TEU, authorised the establishment of the ESM and entered into force on 1 May 2013. See Ruffert (2011), p. 1782 et seq; de Witte (2011), p. 1 et seq. and (2013), p. 82; Peroni (2012), p. 163 et seqq; Tomkin (2013), p. 67; Tuori and Tuori (2014), p. 94; Cucchiara (2015), p. 109; Mengozzi (2015), p. 563.

> The establishment of a body that is fundamentally and intrinsically concerned with the Union's single currency outside the Union Treaties is not easily reconcilable with the central place of economic and monetary union within the Union legal order.[87]

Such incorporation, to be accomplished by 2025,[88] should be done through the ordinary revision procedure of the Treaties under Article 48 TEU, since new competences would be introduced for the EU institutions.[89] This would give rise to a further hypothesis of enhanced cooperation into the EMU. This cooperation would develop within the Union; the Board of Governors would be perhaps replaced by the Council; the adopted acts would be secondary EU law; these acts would be subject to the procedures and controls already provided for in the Treaties, and would produce for ESM Member States the same effects of EU law; the measures for financial assistance would be guaranteed by the Charter of Fundamental Rights.[90] As to the EU institutions, the new consequential arrangement could be similar to that delineated in Regulation (EU) No. 472/2013 of the European Parliament and of the Council of 21 May 2013.[91] A sort of "reaction" of EU institutions can in fact be seen in the powers entrusted to them by Articles 2, 5 and 7 of this act (one of the measures of the "Two Pack"), which tries to provide a frame, as far as possible, to the functions envisaged in the ESM Treaty.[92]

Nowadays, it is not easy to anticipate the timing within which this hoped integration of the European Stability Mechanism into the EU system may be realised. Moreover, this seems to be the only way to achieve a substantial and judicial protection of the economic and social rights of the people whose lives the ESM is intended to affect, and to bring its actions under the democratic control of the European Parliament and national Parliaments.

References

Baratta R (2012) Legal issues of the Fiscal Compact. Searching for a mature democratic governance of the Euro. Il Diritto dell'Unione Europea 17(4):647–681

Caruso C, Morvillo M (2014) Economic governance and budgetary rules in the European context: a call for a new European constitutionalism. Il Diritto dell'Unione Europea 19(4):699–731

Chiti E, Gustavo Teixeira P (2013) The constitutional implications of the European responses to the financial and public debt crisis. Common Mark Law Rev 50(3):683–708

---

[87]Tomkin (2013), p. 81.

[88]In the medium-term, between 2017 and 2025, it is envisaged that the ESM Treaty should become, from an intergovernmental agreement as it is now, a mechanism fully integrated into the EU law. It should be applying to all Eurozone Member States, so that the ESM could be governed more smoothly by the EU institutions under the competence provided for by the amended Article 136 TFEU. See Juncker et al. (2015), pp. 18 and 21.

[89]See Cucchiara (2015), p. 132 et seq.

[90]Schwarz (2014), p. 418 et seqq; Cucchiara (2015), p. 133; Mengozzi (2015), p. 573.

[91]OJEU L 140, 27 May 2013, p. 1 et seqq.

[92]Cf. Mengozzi (2015), p. 576 et seq.

Craig P (2012) The Stability, Coordination and Governance Treaty: principle, policy and pragmatism. Eur Law Rev 37(2):231–248
Craig P (2013) Pringle: legal reasoning, text, purpose and teleology. Maastricht J Eur Comp Law 20(1):3–11
Cucchiara MF (2015) Fiscal Compact e Meccanismo Europeo di Stabilità: quale impatto sull'equilibrio istituzionale dell'Unione? Il Diritto dell'Unione Europea 20(1):91–135
Daniele L (2016) Misure anti-crisi, riforma della *governance* della zona euro e assetto istituzionale della UEM. In: Tizzano A (ed) Verso i 60 anni dai Trattati di Roma. Stato e prospettive dell'Unione europea. Giappichelli, Torino, pp 253–272
Dawson M, de Witte F (2013) Constitutional balance in the EU after the Euro-crisis. Mod Law Rev 76(5):817–844
De Nes M (2015) The ESM and the principle of transparency. Centro Studi sul Federalismo, Perspect Federalism 7(3):128–141
de Streel A, Etienne J (2012) Le Traité sur la stabilité, la coordination et la gouvernance au sein de l'Union économique et monetaire. Journal de droit européen 6:182–185
de Witte B (2011) The European Treaty amendment for the creation of a financial stability mechanism. Swedish Institute for European Policy Studies (SIEPS), European Policy Analysis, No. 6, pp 1–8
de Witte B (2013) European Stability Mechanism and Treaty on Stability, Coordination and Governance: role of the EU institutions and consistency with the EU legal order. In: European Parliament, Directorate General for Internal Policies-Policy Department C: Citizens' Rights and Constitutional Affairs (ed) Challenges of Multi-tier Governance in the European Union. Effectiveness, efficiency and legitimacy. Compendium of notes. European Parliament, Brussels, pp 78–84
de Witte B (2015) Euro crises responses and the EU legal order: increased institutional variation or constitutional mutation? Eur Const Law Rev 11(3):434–457
de Witte B, Beukers T (2013) The Court of Justice approves the creation of the European Stability Mechanism outside the EU legal order. Common Mark Law Rev 50(3):805–848
Driessen B (2012) Transparency in EU institutional law. Kluwer Law International, Alphen aan den Rijn
Fasone C (2012) The struggle of the European Parliament to participate in the new economic governance. European University Institute-European Union Democracy Observatory (EUDO), EUI Working Paper-Robert Schuman Centre for Advanced Studies (RSCAS) No. 45, pp 1–22
Ginter C, Narits R (2013) The perspective of a small Member State to the democratic deficiency of the ESM. Rev Central East Eur Law 38(1):54–76
Hinarejos A (2015) The Euro area crisis in constitutional perspective. Oxford University Press, Oxford
Juncker J-C, Tusk D, Dijsselbloem J, Draghi M, Schulz M (2015) Completing Europe's Economic and Monetary Union. European Commission, Brussels, pp 1–24
Keppenne JP (2014) Institutional report. In: Neegard U, Jacqueson C, Hartig Danielsen J (eds) The Economic and Monetary Union: constitutional and institutional aspects of the economic governance in the EU. The XXVI FIDE Congress in Copenhagen, 28–31 May 2014, vol 1. DJØF Publishing, Copenhagen, pp 179–257
Leino Sandberg P, Salminen J (2014) Finland. In: European University Institute, Department of Law (ed) Constitutional change through Euro crisis law. A multi-level legal analysis of Economic and Monetary Union. European University Institute, Florence, pp 1–45
Louis J-V (2012) The unexpected revision of the Lisbon Treaty and the establishment of a European Stability Mechanism. In: Ashiagbor D, Countouris N, Lianos I (eds) The European Union after the Treaty of Lisbon. Cambridge University Press, Cambridge, pp 284–320
Majone G (2014) Rethinking the union of Europe post-crisis. Has integration gone too far? Cambridge University Press, Cambridge

Martucci F (2013) La Cour de justice face à la politique économique et monétaire: du droit avant toute chose, du droit pour seule chose. Commentaire de l'arrêt CJUE, 27 novembre 2012, Pringle. Revue trimestrielle de droit européen 49(2):239–266
Maubernard C (2011) Transparence, procès équitable et union de droit. Revue du marché commun et de l'Union européenne 551:498–505
Mengozzi P (2015) La crisi dell'euro e il perseguimento di un equilibrio tra stabilità, democrazia e diritti fondamentali. Studi sull'integrazione europea 10(3):547–598
Micossi S, Carmassi J, Peirce F (2011) On the tasks of the European Stability Mechanism. Centre for European Policy Studies, CEPS Policy Brief, No. 235, pp 1–12
Ohler C (2012) The European Stability Mechanism: the long road to financial stability in the Euro area. German Yearb Int Law 54(1):47–74
Peers S (2012) The Stability Treaty: permanent austerity or gesture politics? Eur Const Law Rev 8(3):404–441
Peers S (2013) Towards a new form of EU law? The use of EU institutions outside the EU legal framework. Eur Const Law Rev 9(1):37–72
Peroni G (2012) La crisi dell'euro: limiti e rimedi dell'Unione economica e monetaria. Giuffrè, Milano
Poiares Maduro M, de Witte B, Kumm M (2012) The Euro crisis and the democratic governance of the Euro: legal and political issues of a fiscal crisis. In: Poiares Maduro M, de Witte B, Kumm M (eds) The democratic governance of the Euro. European University Institute, Robert Schuman Centre for Advanced Studies (RSCAS) Policy Paper No. 8, pp 3–11
Rivosecchi G (2014) Il Trattato sul Mes e il *Fiscal Compact* al vaglio del Tribunale Costituzionale Federale e della Corte di Giustizia. Giornale di diritto amministrativo 16(5):478–487
Rossi LS (2012) "Fiscal Compact" e Trattato sul Meccanismo di Stabilità: aspetti istituzionali e conseguenze dell'integrazione differenziata nell'UE. Il Diritto dell'Unione Europea 17(2): 293–307
Rossolillo G (2012) The Fiscal Compact, the European Stability Mechanism and a two-speed Europe: institutional proposals for a government of the Eurozone. Federalist LIV:10–22
Ruffert M (2011) The European debt crisis and European Union law. Common Mark Law Rev 48(6):1777–1805
Salomon ME (2015) Of austerity, human rights and international institutions. London School of Economics and Political Science Law Department, Law, Society and Economy (LSE) Working Papers, No. 2, pp 1–29
Schneider K (2013) Yes but ... one more thing: Karlsruhe's ruling on the European Stability Mechanism. German Law J 14(1):53–74
Schwarz M (2014) A memorandum of misunderstanding – the doomed road of the European Stability Mechanism and a possible way out: enhanced cooperation. Common Mark Law Rev 51(2):389–423
Starita M (2011) I principi democratici nel diritto dell'Unione europea. Giappichelli, Torino
Starita M (2013) *Governance* economica europea e principi democratici dell'UE. In: Bartoloni ME, Caligiuri A, Ubertazzi B (eds) L'Unione europea e la riforma del governo economico della zona euro. Editoriale Scientifica, Napoli, pp 46–58
Thym D, Wendel M (2012) Préserver le respect du droit dans la crise: la Cour de Justice, le MES et le mythe du déclin de la Communauté de droit (arrêt Pringle). Cahiers de droit européen 48(3):733–757
Tomkin J (2013) Contradiction, circumvention and conceptual gymnastics: the impact of the adoption of the ESM Treaty on the state of European democracy. In: de Witte B, Héritier A, Trechsel AH (eds) The Euro crisis and the state of European democracy. Contributions from the 2012 European Union Democracy Observatory (EUDO) Dissemination Conference. European University Institute, Robert Schuman Centre for Advanced Studies (RSCAS), Florence, pp 64–81
Tosato GL (2016) L'Unione Economica e Monetaria: evoluzione e criticità legali. In: Tizzano A (ed) Verso i 60 anni dai Trattati di Roma. Stato e prospettive dell'Unione europea. Giappichelli, Torino, pp 223–240

Tufano ML, Pugliese S (2014) Il nuovo strumento di convergenza e competitività: verso una governance negoziata per l'UEM? Il Diritto dell'Unione Europea 19(2):317–342

Tuori K (2012) The European financial crisis – constitutional aspects and implications. EUI Working Papers, Law, No. 28, pp 1–57

Tuori K, Tuori K (2014) The Eurozone crisis. A constitutional analysis. Cambridge University Press, Cambridge

von Bogdandy A (2012) The European lesson for international democracy: the significance of Article 9–12 EU Treaty for international organizations. Eur J Int Law 23(2):315–334

von Bogdandy A, Ioannidis M (2014) Systemic deficiency with the rule of law: what it is, what has been done, what can be done. Common Mark Law Rev 51(1):59–96

Wendel M (2013) Judicial restraint and the return to openness: the decision of the German Federal Constitutional Court on the ESM and Fiscal Treaty of 12 September 2012. German Law J 14(1):21–52

Part II
The European Central Bank and Democracy

How the ECB Reinterpreted Its Mandate During the Euro-Crisis (and Why It Was Right in Doing So)

Susanna Cafaro

Abstract During the long years of the Euro-crisis, the European Central Bank (hereinafter ECB) played (and still plays) a really significant role to support states in crisis or banks facing lack of liquidity. As a consequence, it has been accused in the political, but also academic debate to exceed its own powers. First of all, the allegations were related to the scarce respect of its own legal framework (competences and limits established by the EU Treaties); secondly, they regarded her invasion of the field of economic policy while it had to limit its intervention to monetary policy; finally, it was pointed out how it played a too "political" role. This chapter aims to dismantle such criticisms showing how the ECB's intervention—even if unconventional—was required by the critical moment and felt within the scope and the borders of monetary policy. Finally, it will address the peculiar "political" activity of the ECB, which is a technocratic institution inevitably called to exercise a discretion within the range of multiple policy options. Its freedom of judgment has to be grounded and duly motivated on economic reasoning, relating it to price stability. Nonetheless, it remains relevant.

Contents

S. Cafaro (✉)
Department of Legal Sciences, University of Salento, Lecce, Italy
e-mail: susanna.cafaro@unisalento.it

L. Daniele et al. (eds.), *Democracy in the EMU in the Aftermath of the Crisis*,
DOI 10.1007/978-3-319-53895-2_11

1 Introduction

The legitimacy of the role played by the ECB during the Euro-crisis has been much debated by scholars and even challenged by the German Constitutional Court in the famous (and first) referral for preliminary ruling in the *OMT* case.[1] The European Court of Justice (ECJ) has eventually given its blessing to the line of action chosen by the monetary institution, even if equipped with further guarantees. Nonetheless, the topic still remains controversial because behind an apparently legal technical point lay more substantial issues: which is the role of a central bank in a crisis situation? Which level of intervention in the real economy is appropriate or desirable?

The circumstance that the ECB is not the central bank of a State nor of an entity having sovereignty over economic policy makes the even evaluation even more complex.

In the following paragraphs, the competence of the ECB will be examined as it is defined by the Treaty on the Functioning of the European Union (hereinafter TFEU), the Statute and other relevant documents. The Euro-crisis offered a powerful test of compliance for the monetary institution as it had to face the crisis creating new tools, respectful of the spirit and *ratio* of the European Treaties. This operation was not an easy or indisputable one as its competence's limits were stretched to the maximum extent. Nonetheless, the special occurrence required special action, often unconventional.

What made the evaluation of the ECB's choices even more controversial was the clear distinction in the EU Treaties between monetary policy, assigned to the ECB and economic policy, still in the hands of the Member States and subject to coordination at European level. Defining the uncertain border between the two was the exercise carried out by the ECJ. The solution offered—a teleological test for the measures adopted—puts the ECB in its political dimension, although technocratic. It is the natural dimension of a European institution in charge for monetary *policy*.

2 The Tasks and Competences of the European Central Bank

According to Article 127 TFEU, the ECB has a primary and a secondary objective and four basic tasks.

The objectives are spelled out in para. 1:

> The primary objective of the European System of Central Banks [hereinafter referred to as 'the ESCB'] shall be to maintain price stability. Without prejudice to the objective of price

[1] ECJ 16 June 2015, Case C-62/14, *Gauweiler*.

stability, the ESCB shall support the general economic policies in the Union with a view to contributing to the achievement of the objectives of the Union.

The (basic) tasks are listed in para. 2, they are:

— to define and implement the monetary policy of the Union,
— to conduct foreign-exchange operations consistent with the provisions of Article 219,
— to hold and manage the official foreign reserves of the Member States,
— to promote the smooth operation of payment systems.

A fifth task was added recently, but it was already foreseen in para. 6:

The Council, acting by means of regulations in accordance with a special legislative procedure, may unanimously, and after consulting the European Parliament and the European Central Bank, confer specific tasks upon the European Central Bank concerning policies relating to the prudential supervision of credit institutions and other financial institutions with the exception of insurance undertakings.

All of this functions are managed by the ESCB under the guidance of the ECB's decision-making bodies—the Governing Council and the Executive Board—acting in full independence.[2]

This great independence is balanced by the determination of the tasks already observed and especially by the clear objective pursued by the ECB: price stability. Even if the ECB enjoys broad discretion regarding the means by which to achieve price stability, its activity can be defined more technocratic than political.

Moreover, its independence cannot be defined as absolute: it is attributed to the ECB "in exercising the powers and carrying out the tasks and duties"[3] assigned to the system. This independence is therefore far from being unlimited or subtract from the functioning of the general principles of EU law[4] and it is clearly balanced by a rich basket of accountability provisions.

The aim of these accountability tools is monitoring ECB's compliance with the objective of price stability: in all documents and interviews the ECB is required to

[2]On the governance and functioning of the ECB we suggest the following readings: Smits (1997), Zilioli and Selmayr (2001), Malatesta (2003), Louis (2009). On its independence see also Beukers (2013).

[3]So in Article 130 TFEU.

[4]"[...] such independence does not have the consequence of separating it entirely from the European Community and exempting it from every rule of Community law", ECJ 10 July 2003, Case C-11/00 *Commission of the European Communities* v. *the European Central Bank* (*Olaf* Case), para. 135.

justify its activity and it does so by explaining its monetary policy strategy in detail.[5]

It still unclear—and extensively debated in doctrine—the role of the "secondary objective" of the ECB, that "support" to the general economic policies in the Union, which can be pursued without prejudice of price stability. We will come back to it later.

To narrow the already limited discretion intervenes also the prohibition of monetary financing of debt in Article 123 TFEU:

> 1. Overdraft facilities or any other type of credit facility with the European Central Bank or with the central banks of the Member States (hereinafter referred to as 'national central banks') in favor of Union institutions, bodies, offices or agencies, central governments, regional, local or other public authorities, other bodies governed by public law, or public undertakings of Member States shall be prohibited, as shall the purchase directly from them by the European Central Bank or national central banks of debt instruments.

Finally, there is the well–known principle of "no bail out" in Article 125 TFEU. The provision refers to the Union as a whole and the ECB, as an institution of the Union, is also concerned:

> 1. The Union shall not be liable for or assume the commitments of central governments, regional, local or other public authorities, other bodies governed by public law, or public undertakings of any Member State, without prejudice to mutual financial guarantees for the joint execution of a specific project. A Member State shall not be liable for or assume the commitments of central governments, regional, local or other public authorities, other bodies governed by public law, or public undertakings of another Member State, without prejudice to mutual financial guarantees for the joint execution of a specific project.

---

[5]The ECB website so defines accountability: "it is a founding principle of democratic societies that any independent institution bestowed with a public function should be accountable to citizens and their elected representatives for the conduct of its policies. Accountability is therefore an important counterpart of central bank independence." (https://www.ecb.europa.eu). There are several accountability tools provided by the European Treaties and by the ESCB Statute: the ECB President regularly reports on the bank's monetary policy and other duties during his quarterly hearings before the European Parliament's Committee on Economic and Monetary Affairs. In addition, the President of the ECB and the other members of the Executive Board may be heard by the competent Committees of the European Parliament on their own initiative or at the request of these. Besides, MEPs may address written questions to the bank; ECB's compulsory replies are published in the Official Journal of the EU and on the bank's website. As part of the ECB's reporting obligations, the ECB also addresses an Annual Report to the Council and Parliament. This monetary dialogue is grounded on Article 284, para. 3, TFEU—and developed well further than foreseen by the Treaty—as detailed by Article 126 of the EP Rules of Procedure. Other accountability instruments are directly addressed to experts and informed public opinion as communication tools.

As foreseen by Article 15 of the Statute, the ECB has to publish quarterly reports on the activities of the ESCB as well as a consolidated weekly financial statement. There is then the already mentioned Annual Report. Moreover, the ECB also publishes a Monthly Bulletin plus a wide range of other task-related publications. Shortly after each monetary policy meeting of the Governing Council, decisions are explained in a press conference by the President. Since February 2015, the ECB also publishes the summary of the minutes of the governing council, as "account of the monetary policy meeting".

The two provisions have been often recalled to question the legitimacy of the ECB's intervention, particularly with regard to purchase of state bonds.

This is not all. In case of crisis management and need for support to national budgets, we see in the EU Treaties a clear option in favor of the competence of the political institutions (see Articles. 122 and 136—last paragraph added). The same happens about the surveillance of national budgets (Articles. 121 and 126, plus all the Regulations that have followed over time to implement the Stability and Growth Pact, most recently the Six-Pack plus Two-Pack[6]).

All of these norms and Regulations show a clear preference for the intergovernmental approach—as all the macroeconomic chapter of the TFEU: the ultimate responsibility lies with the Council and the European Council while the supervisory powers over national budgets belong to the Commission.

The ECB therefore has a margin of action which is specifically limited and it is required to justify its activities as functional to the objective of price stability. Nonetheless, it enjoys a wide competence in defining price stability.[7] This is made clear by Article 12 of the ESCB Statute attached to the Treaty:

> 1. The Governing Council shall adopt the guidelines and take the decisions necessary to ensure the performance of the tasks entrusted to the ESCB under these Treaties and this Statute. The Governing Council shall formulate the monetary policy of the Union including, as appropriate, decisions relating to *intermediate monetary objectives*, key interest rates and the supply of reserves in the ESCB, and shall establish the necessary guidelines for their implementation. (italic added)

In these "intermediate monetary objectives" we find the ECB's definitions of price stability, which can be found in two important decisions, adopted in 1998 and 2003.[8] By setting a quantitative definition of price stability, the ECB has created a benchmark against which its performance can be assessed. Indeed, the more clearly and precisely the objective is defined, the easier it is to monitor whether the ECB complies with it.

[6]The so-called "Six-Pack" entered into force on 13 December 2011. It is composed of five EU Regulations: four adopted by the Council of the Union and the European Parliament (Nos. 1173/2011, 1174/2011, 1175/2011, 1176/2011) and one by the Council (No. 1177/2011) on 16 November 2011 (in OJEU L 306, 23 November 2011); and of one Directive adopted by the Council (2011/85/EU) on 8 November 2011. All these acts apply to the 28 Member States, with some specific rules for Euro area Member States, especially regarding financial sanctions. A second reform package, the so-called "Two-Pack", entered into force on 30 May 2013 in all Euro area Member States: the Regulations (EU) Nos. 472/2013 and 473/2013 both adopted on 21 May 2013 (in OJEU L 140, 27 May 2013).

[7]See Martucci (2012), p. 96.

[8]These are the monetary policy strategy adopted on 13 October 1998 and its amendment, adopted on 8 May 2003, both atypical acts appeared in the form of press release, see www.ecb.int/press/pr/date/2003/html/pr030508_2.it.html.

In the 2003 Press release we find both the definition of price stability as well as the overall monetary policy strategy.[9] What is interesting, the Governing Council clarifies that in the President's communication on the risks to price stability we find an economic analysis including "an analysis of shocks hitting the Euro area economy and projections of key macroeconomic variables" as well as a monetary analysis, so making clear the interdependence between the two.

3 The Intervention of the ECB in the Euro-Crisis

The financial crisis generated a fragmentation of the financial market, exacerbating the differences between the costs of the bank loans, reducing access to the financial market while the increase of interest rates on government bonds impacted on costs of borrowing from domestic banks. As a consequence, the liquidity crisis made more difficult the transmission of impulses coming from the ECB's monetary policy. Less cash was put into circulation by banks, the economy continued to contract, worsening the position of national budgets and driving up even more interest on government bonds: a vicious circle. So, it is not surprising that the ECB, to correct the situation and ultimately maintain price stability had to intervene in national crises.[10]

---

[9]We read in the Press release: "This strategy, which was announced on 13 October 1998, consists of three main elements: a quantitative definition of price stability, a prominent role for money in the assessment of risks to price stability, and a broadly based assessment of the outlook for price developments". More than 4 years of implementation have worked satisfactorily. Nevertheless, the Governing Council deemed it useful to evaluate the strategy in the light of this experience, taking into account the public debate and a series of studies undertaken by staff of the Eurosystem. "Price stability is defined as a year-on-year increase in the Harmonised Index of Consumer Prices (HICP) for the euro area of below 2%. Price stability is to be maintained over the medium term." Today, the Governing Council confirmed this definition (which it announced in 1998). At the same time, the Governing Council agreed that in the pursuit of price stability it will aim to maintain inflation rates close to 2% over the medium term. This clarification underlines the ECB's commitment to provide a sufficient safety margin to guard against the risks of deflation. It also addresses the issue of the possible presence of a measurement bias in the HICP and the implications of inflation differentials within the Euro area. The Governing Council confirmed that its monetary policy decisions will continue to be based on a comprehensive analysis of the risks to price stability. Over time, analysis under both pillars of the monetary policy strategy has been deepened and extended. This practice will be continued. However, the Governing Council wishes to clarify communication on the cross-checking of information in coming to its unified overall judgement on the risks to price stability. To this end, the introductory statement of the President will henceforth follow a new structure. It will start with the **economic analysis** to identify short to medium-term risks to price stability. As in the past, this will include an analysis of shocks hitting the euro area economy and projections of key macroeconomic variables. The **monetary analysis** will then follow to assess medium to long-term trends in inflation in view of the close relationship between money and prices over extended horizons. As in the past, monetary analysis will take into account developments in a wide range of monetary indicators including M3, its components and counterparts, notably credit, and various measures of excess liquidity.

[10]As it is clearly explained by Mario Draghi in the speech opening the academic year at Università Bocconi (Milan) on 15 November 2012.

In more general terms, it was necessary to analyze potential and current crises and intervene with proper means to guarantee price stability; this is part of the ECB's competence as the ECB itself defines it.[11]

The provisions concerning ECB competences and monetary policy in the EU Treaties worked well during the Euro's first decade of life, their interpretation was undisputed. Unfortunately, they were written for good times. When the Euro-crisis exploded in 2010, new tools had to be invented in the midst of the crisis. This evolution was legitimated by the circumstances, in particular by a sense of urgency that limited the debate and validated "technical" solutions.

One of the consequences of the lack of a European economic government has been the need for the ECB to deploy creative efforts to manage the crisis and to guarantee the survival of the currency itself. Nobody could deny that the European monetary institution stretched its mandate and competences to the limits of possible and with remarkable results.[12]

The ECB, in fact, improved its role—similarly to many powerful central banks around the world[13]—acting as (indirect) lender of last resort, through the adoption of a number of unconventional monetary measures,[14] so contributing significantly to the management of the crisis.[15]

The intervention of the ECB to support States in crisis increased gradually. It started with the long-term refinancing operations in December 2011 and February 2012 (long-term refinancing operation or LTRO). It was followed by a purchasing programme of State bonds on secondary markets: the Securities Market Programme (SMP), which consisted of purchasing government debt on the secondary markets (Greek, Irish and Portuguese bonds in 2010, Italian and Spanish ones in 2011), so increasing the size of the ECB's balance sheet. Other relevant measures were the significant reduction in interest rates and the authorisation to national central banks

[11]As stated by Cœuré (2013) "When we look at the history of central banks, contributing to financial stability was one of their roles in most countries, although to varying degrees. Even when central banks were assigned a relatively narrow mandate, such as that of inflation targeting in recent years, they often played a decisive part as soon as financial instability struck. In particular, their ability to act as lender of last resort in the financial system and to manage liquidity in the interbank market typically made them a key player in crisis management. Even in normal times, the central role of bank deposits in the stock of money makes monetary stability dependent on the soundness of the banking sector. In sum, in the late Tommaso Padoa-Schioppa's words, financial stability has been part of the 'genetic code' of central banks".

[12]Cafaro (2013), pp. 49–68.

[13]In late November 2011, the Federal Reserve, the ECB and Canadian Swiss, Japanese and English central banks announced a coordinated action "to enhance their capacity to provide liquidity support to the global financial system, an intervention of strong symbolic impact showing the will central banks to actively participate in the restoration of financial stability", see the press release by the Federal Reserve's Board of Governors, 30 November 2011, http://www.federalreserve.gov/newsevents/press/monetary/20111130a.htm.

[14]On the topic see Bini Smaghi (2009), Bossone (2013), Bassan (2014).

[15]Cafaro (2013), p. 49 et seq.

interventions a.k.a. emergency liquidity assistance (ELA), due to exceptional circumstances.[16]

The mere announcement of the ECB's willingness to defend the Euro, calmed the markets and led to a significant reduction of interest rates on State bonds. The London speech by Mario Draghi in July 2012 proved to be in itself one of the most powerful unconventional monetary tools.[17] Even bigger miracles operated the announcement of the adoption of the instrument known as *outright monetary transactions* (OMT), on September 2012.[18]

Lately, in January 2015, the ECB adopted—not without inner discussions—a "quantitative easing" (QE) policy, thus mirroring the choices of other important central banks.

All these interventions were only indirectly related to the aim of price stability. The ECB had in fact to guarantee a number of pre-conditions for the correct management of monetary policy in times of crisis, such as to maintain the efficient functioning of the market for sovereign debt bonds, to remedy the liquidity crisis that struck the banking sector, to restore the transmission mechanisms of monetary policy through interest rates and more generally to restore trust. We can assume that the ECB in fact recognised to itself a large role in crisis management, through monetary policy tools, pursuing monetary policy goals.

The two keys which opened the door for this ECB's increased role were; (a) a broad notion of financial stability considered as a precondition for an efficient management of monetary policy[19]; (b) a commitment to guarantee the survival of the currency itself.[20] Such role—even if not different from the one played by other central banks—was in fact even more necessary in Europe because of the lack of a common economic governance framework. By the way, unconventional monetary policy which was considered pretty heretic in economic doctrine only 10 years ago, is nowadays the "new normal".[21]

4 Legitimacy of the Interventions and Conditions Attached to Them

The ECB justified such interventions stretching its own powers and competences but showing due respect for the provisions laid out in the Treaties, which were originally reinterpreted, never dismissed or ignored. The European Court of Justice

[16]Viterbo and Cisotta (2010, 2012).

[17]Draghi (2012b).

[18]See the transcript of the press conference http://www.ecb.europa.eu/press/pressconf/2012/html/is120906.en.html.

[19]Library of the EP (2012).

[20]In its famous London speech on 26 July 2012, Mario Draghi declared that he was prepared to do "whatever it takes to preserve the euro"; Draghi (2012a).

[21]See Roubini (2016).

validated the ECB's course of action in the *Gauweiler* case (a.k.a. *OMT* case), a reference for a preliminary ruling submitted by the German Constitutional Court challenging the legitimacy of the adoption of the OMT programme by the ECB and its compliance with its own competencies.[22] The *OMT* case, deserves here a detailed analysis as it is exemplary in showing both the resistances to the ECB's course of action as well as the reasons and legal grounding for this and other unconventional monetary measures.

Moreover, the reference was the first ever submitted by the German Constitutional Court, and its tone was not exactly friendly: the German Constitutional Court asserted among the lines its own doubts about the illegality of the programme and the compliance of the ECB's activity of crisis management with the European Treaties. As the ECJ maintains clearly a different point, there is, still, potential for conflict between the two Courts.

On the European side, the legitimacy of the outright monetary transactions (OMT) was explained first by the ECB itself in its monthly Bulletin (September 2012), then it has been defended by the Advocate General Cruz Villalón in his conclusions in the *Gauweiler* case, finally it is declared by the EU Court of Justice in its decision on 16 June 2015. The three explanations are not perfectly identical, but are all grounded on the Treaty and—even if only the last one is the final word on the issue—we can see how the Treaty is a powerful benchmark to measure the legitimacy of the ECB's action and a necessary one. For this reason, we suggest to read all these explanations not as alternative ways to justify ECB's interventions, but as a sum, all adding useful elements to the legal reasoning.

4.1 *The Legal Reasoning of the ECB*

In the ECB's monthly bulletin released on September 2012, we find a series of considerations to assert the lawfulness of the OMT programme:

> To comply with the monetary financing prohibition (article 123 of the Treaty on the functioning of the European Union), (i) purchases will be conducted in the secondary market only. (ii) The application of strict conditionality will ensure fiscal discipline in countries eligible for OMTs. In deciding on these transactions, the ECB acts with the aim of countering risks to price stability over the medium term emerging from destructive tail scenarios with potentially severe challenges for price stability in the Euro area. Therefore OMT are fully in line with the primary mandate of the ECB. In addition, (iii) all decisions on OMTs are taken by the governing Council acting in full independence. To further support the effectiveness of OMTs, the Eurosystem will clarify in the relevant legal act that (iv) it accepts the same (*pari passu*) treatment as private or other creditors with respect to bonds issued by Euro area countries and purchased by the Eurosystem through OMTs, in accordance with the terms of such bonds. (v) Furthermore the liquidity created through OMTs will be fully sterilised.[23]

[22]See ECJ 16 June 2015, Case C-62/14, *Gauweiler*.

[23]See the ECB Monthly Bulletin, September 2012, p. 12, on the website www.ecb.int.

The reasons given by the ECB in support of the legality of this intervention may, as well, justify *ex post* all the previous purchasing plans of State bonds on the secondary market, being them supported by the same logic and grounded on the same legal bases.

The ECB highlights how the features of this intervention have been designed in view of compliance with Article 123. It is true that this article prohibits the use of monetary financing of public debt, and it is equally true that the purchase of securities on the secondary market may seem too simple a way to circumvent this prohibition (a point raised by the German Constitutional Court),[24] however the substantial argument used by the Bank is the non-contradiction with the *rationale* of the rule.

The *rationale* of that article is in fact (1) preventing the ECB from moving away from the goal of price stability; (2) avoiding an undue influence of the States on the ECB so impairing its independence; (3) not pushing States to an excessive issuance of bonds, so encouraging the loosening of their budget discipline.

The ECB therefore accepts full responsibility for the choices made: a demonstration of its independence. It must be said that controversies were not lacking, both in doctrine,[25] in politics and within the bank itself, well before the adoption of the OMT programme.[26] Particularly difficult became the relationship between the bank and Germany, which proved to be a far more rigorous guardian of the Treaty's orthodoxy.

If we go fast forward to the *Gauweiler* proceedings we find two more sets of reasons to assert the legitimacy of the *OMT* case. Once again, I want to underline how the *OMT* case is just the latest test-bed to verify the legitimacy of the ECB interventions over the crisis. In other words, if the OMT are lawful, the previous actions—being more limited and less risky—are lawful as well.

This may appear a bit paradoxical as the OMT purchasing programme has just be announced, but never applied. So, it was not a legal act, but an announcement without legal effects, still waiting to be implemented through an ad hoc Regulation. So, the Court of justice could have had easily dismissed the case as inadmissible or just hypothetical. Refusing to second-guess the German Court's assessment of the

---

[24]See para. 278 "For an acquisition of government bonds on the secondary market by the European Central Bank aiming at financing the Members' budgets independently of the capital markets is prohibited as well, as it would circumvent the prohibition of monetary financing (see also recital 7 of Council Regulation (EC) No. 3603/93 of 13 December 1993 (OJEC L 332, 31 December 1993, p. 1)). This is taken account of by the Treaty establishing the European Stability Mechanism, whose recital 4 calls for strict observance of the European Union framework, the integrated macroeconomic surveillance, in particular the Stability and Growth Pact, the macroeconomic imbalances framework and the economic governance rules of the European Union. Article 123 TFEU is one of these rules.".

[25]As reported by Ruffert (2011), p. 1785; Allemand and Martucci (2012), p. 21.

[26]See the resignations presented by Axel Weber on 14 February 2011 and by Jürgen Stark on 30 April 2011.

need for a preliminary ruling, the ECJ reaffirms its role vis-à-vis national courts, accepting the challenge to legitimise the ECB's intervention.

4.2 *The Reasons Offered by the Advocate General Cruz Villalón in the OMT Case*[27]

To the Advocate General, too, the OMTs are lawful. The first reason for this is the wide technique discretion enjoyed by the ECB: its responsibility and exclusive competence in the conduct of monetary policy includes interpretation and definition of the goal of price stability. For this reason the Advocate General chooses not to venture on the technical ground and advises judges to adopt a similar self-restraint (para. 111).

Nonetheless, he enters in this slippery ground to respond to a relevant point raised by the German Constitutional Court: the classification of OMTs as economic policy measures instead of (outright!) monetary ones because of the role that the ECB would play in the management of economic conditionality accompanying the adjustment programme. To make the ECB's intervention more neutral and avoiding any conflict of interests, the AG suggests that the ECB should not negotiate and manage such conditionality itself. In other words, if it the ECB were assisting a State in crisis through the OMT programme, it should make a considerable step back compared to the role that it normally plays as a member of the Troika or under mandate of the ESM in relation to the definition and monitoring of programmes of economic recovery.

Two further conditions are presented as necessary for the legitimacy of the OMT: the respect of EU primary law (and therefore of the prohibitions laid down in the Treaty) and the respect for the principle of proportionality. The first is due to make the ECB's course of action compatible with the *rationale* of Article 123, taking into account the exceptional circumstances pushing for an interpretation even more flexible than it would be otherwise.

Particularly interesting is his argument on the principle of proportionality, which leads straight to a focal point: ECB's accountability. The monetary institution has, in fact, an obligation to justify its choices on a case by case basis, so the need for intervention has to be explained with regard to the specific circumstances, to its opportunity and proportionality and to the expected goal.

If the programme as a whole is already, even if summarily, motivated, it is in the concrete management that the requirement of proportionality will find its final legitimacy test.

---

[27]See the Opinion of Advocate General Cruz Villalón, delivered on 14 January 2015 in the Case C-62/14.

4.3 *The Court's Decision*[28]

The Court points out, first of all, that the open market operations—buying and selling securities—are actually foreseen by the Union's primary law, in Article 18.1 of the Statute of the European System of Central Banks.

In addressing the issue of proportionality, the Court delves deeper into the arguments put forward by the ECB in support of the OMT programme (or, we should say, "proposed actions") and—while recognizing to the Bank a technical discretion on the threshold of which the judge must stop (para. 68) and that does not necessarily have to be spelled out step by step in the motivations of the act (para. 70)—it recognises that the measure was certainly useful and properly pondered by the institution (points 72–80). It is also proportional: the purchasing programme of debt securities, although defined as unlimited, is de facto limited because: (1) it refers to short-term securities (maturity of less than 3 years); (2) it addresses states which are subject to macroeconomic adjustment programmes and (3) only if the situation is not so deteriorated yet by not having access to the market.

On the last point—the compliance with Article 123—the Court openly follows the path opened by the Advocate General Cruz Villalón that is indeed the wake of the reasoning of the ECB itself: the article prohibits the monetary financing of the debt in order to prevent a potential relaxation of public finances or the excessive emission by Member of debt securities. This prohibition appears bypassed by a purchase on the secondary market, but it is not, because of a number of already announced guarantees: (1) the ECB will not announce in advance the purchase; (2) this will take place at market prices and (3) only regarding those Countries whose budgetary discipline is guaranteed by strict conditionality as part of an adjustment programme of the European Stability Mechanism. A second risk, the inflation, would be also sterilised by the ECB through a withdrawal of liquidity of the same size. All the guarantees surrounding such operations, in short, will be sufficient to ensure the respect off the *rationale* of Article 123.

4.4 *More Unconventional Measures: The Quantitative Easing Programme*

On January 2015, the ECB launched its strategy of quantitative easing[29]—an expanded asset purchase programme of public and private sector securities—so continuing its "interventionist" attitude. QE differs deeply form OMT as in the latest the liquidity created through bond purchasing is sterilised while the aim of QE

[28]The already mentioned decision of ECJ in Case C-62/14, adopted on 16 June 2015, for a detailed analysis see Munari (2015).

[29]The first "account of the monetary policy meeting", published on 19 February 2015, reveals how controversial the adoption of the "quantitative easing" policy was http://www.ecb.europa.eu/press/accounts/2015/html/mg150219.en.pdf.

is, conversely, to increase the quantity of money, in the hope that banks will lend more to the private sector (nonetheless, this is outside ECB's control). It is an attempt to stimulate economy in a situation of interest rates nearing zero, a bet over markets to avert deflation.

The programme is not free from risks: risks of inflation, risk of excessive costs, risk of moral hazard. So, even if there was unanimity in the Governing Council that such a QE programme is actually legal, there was disagreement on whether it should be used just yet and some Members maintained it to be considered just as a "last resort" tool. The original guidelines for the (QE) programme evolved since the programme started in January 2015, particularly to expand the universe of purchasable assets and give some flexibility to the ECB.

Thanks to all the legal reasoning above summarised, there isn't any specific reason to re-open the Pandora's vase of legitimacy of ECB's intervention: first of all, there is no doubt on the monetary policy nature of the QE as it is a direct intervention on the liquidity level in the Eurozone; second, it's another open market intervention grounded on Article 18.1 of the ESCB Statute; third, it is a purchasing programme on the secondary market as the OMT, so once again acceptable (or assumed as acceptable, according to Article 123). The only questionable (not irrelevant) point seems to be its appropriateness to guarantee price stability.

Once again, the warning by the advocate general seems appropriate: it is difficult (and risky) for those who are not bankers to venture on such a technical ground. The last word on this unconventional monetary policy tool cannot be a legal one. The markets will tell us if the ECB has won its bet to beat deflation.

5 The Unclear Borders of Monetary Policy

There is no doubt that the ECB interpreted originally its mandate to give itself permission to use unconventional monetary measures to face the financial crisis and the sovereign debt crisis in the Eurozone.

Its interpretation was in line with the rationale of Article 123, and even more with the neglected principle of solidarity (as recalled by the AG in the *Pringle* case), even if the compliance with the letter of Articles 123 and 125 could be challenged in courts. The European Court of Justice, defending the legitimacy of the ECB's intervention (or the simple perspective of intervention) as in the *OMT* case, gave its blessing to the interpretation of the Treaty operated by the monetary institution.

Unfortunately, other, more substantial objections remain to the action of the bank. They do not pertain strictly to the sphere of legal reasoning, they regard respectively the thin border between monetary and economic policy and the even more subtle difference between technocratic and political action.

The artificial division between monetary policy and economic policy was developed in modern times for a practical reason: unfasten monetary policy from the short sight of economic policy as it is managed by governments and political elites, living in the short term of the electoral mandate. Independent monetary institutions—central banks—were entrusted with the task of managing monetary policy in full independence with a strict mandate. Such solution proved empirically to work better but it is far from being an axiom.

We cannot underestimate the fact that monetary policy is ultimately a piece of economic policy, distinct, also, for reasons pertaining the sharing of competences in the European Union both horizontally (between the ECB and the Union's political institutions) and vertically (between the ECB and Member States). Monetary policy is an exclusive Union's competence for the Member States that have adopted the Euro, while economic policy remains largely within the Member States subject to certain principles, prohibitions and procedures and a duty of coordination in the EU institutional frame.

The boundaries of monetary policy are then interpreted by the ECB while choosing its course of action. It's undeniable how in a situation of exceptional circumstances, the tools used by central banks (all of them) are much more invasive of the economic field. Moreover, the two reasons the ECB used to justify its exceptional intervention: financial stability and survival of the Euro, connect deeply economic and monetary policy, as economic policy and politics in more general terms—too—have a say over financial stability and survival of the monetary union.

Finally, under Articles 127, para.1, TFEU and 282, para. 2, TFEU, the primary objective of the Union's monetary policy is to maintain price stability, but—as already observed—the same provisions further stipulate that the European System of Central Banks ('ESCB') is to support the general economic policies in the Union, with a view to contributing to the achievement of its objectives, as laid down in Article 3 TEU.

The Court in the *Pringle* judgment in 2012, as well as the Advocate General and the Court in the *Gauweiler* case made some distinctions between monetary policy and economic policy. Regarding the role to be played by the European Stability Mechanism, it pointed out that:

> the objective pursued by that mechanism, which is to safeguard the stability of the euro area as a whole [. . .] is clearly distinct from the objective of maintaining price stability, which is the primary objective of the Union's monetary policy. Even though the stability of the euro area may have repercussions on the stability of the currency used within that area, an economic policy measure cannot be treated as equivalent to a monetary policy measure for the sole reason that it may have indirect effects on the stability of the euro." (para. 56) and later on that "In the light of the objectives to be attained by the stability mechanism [. . .], the instruments provided in order to achieve those objectives and the close link between that mechanism, the provisions of the TFEU Treaty relating to economic policy and the regulatory framework for strengthened economic governance of the Union, it must be concluded that the establishment of that mechanism falls within the area of economic policy (para. 60).

The objectives, as we know are basically the management of financial crises.

The AG in the *Gauweiler* case suggests a similar approach to distinguish between economic and monetary policy, he maintains that both the objective (as the Court in *Pringle*) *and* the instruments define a policy as either "monetary" or "economic" in Treaty terms, whilst both should adhere to the Treaty general principles and EMU fundamentals.[30]

The Court follows the AG: similarly to what stated in the *Pringle* case, it argues that possible indirect effects of the OMT programme could manifest in economic policy (safeguarding the stability of the Euro area) but this doesn't mean that such measure should be classified as an economic policy tool. Both objectives and instruments of the OMT programme—and thus the programme itself—fall within the scope of monetary policy.

The ECB, by the way, has argued that the aim of the scheme is not to facilitate the financing conditions of certain Member States, or to determine their economic policies, but rather to "unblock" the ECB's monetary policy transmission channels.

So what appears to be in the Treaties as a clear sharing of competence—economic policy to the Member States, coordinated by the Council and the European Council, and monetary policy to the ECB—appears to be more a functional assignment of priorities. Monetary policy decisions may well have an influence over economic policy as economic policy decisions may reflect over monetary policy. It couldn't be otherwise. In this sense, the role of the ECB of support to the general economic policies in the Union with a view to contributing to the achievement of the objectives of the Union—without prejudice of price stability—makes finally sense.

6 Is the Activity of Central Banking "Political"?

Is the ECB playing a political role? Is it central banking a political role? In our opinion the answer is yes to both the questions.

In the Collins English dictionary we read that politics is "the practice or study of the art and science of forming, directing, and administrating states and other political units; the art and science of government".

For his part, the management of the currency (a medium of exchange that is in current use in a particular Country or area), a central bank plays an evident political role managing a little but relevant slice of sovereignty.

It is undeniable that managing monetary policy requires discretion and an evaluation of the public interest, finally it requires an adjustment to external conditions. No doubts that in times of crisis tools and actions change dramatically: the creation of unconventional monetary tools, the brilliant use of communication all show how the ECB was able to navigate the crisis, acting out of necessity.

Nonetheless, the adjective "political" next to "central bank" sounds scary. Why?

Central banks are usually defined as technocratic institutions and, for sure, they are. Technocracy means literally power in the hands of technicians or experts. And experts are selected after the evaluation of knowledge assets and experience. So, if

[30]As underlined by Smits (2015); see also Hinarejos (2015).

an institution is an example of technocracy—the syllogism goes—it is not an example of democracy, that's why the adjective political—side by side with a central bank—sounds scary.

In the case of central banking, there are very good reasons to choose technocracy over democracy and we are not here to challenge them. First of all, decisions in the field of monetary policy are just too difficult for non-experts: stating which is the right amount of money to print or which is the correct interest rate to keep prices stable in the current circumstances is the result of a knowledge-based approach. Only few people are qualified enough to understand the difficult mathematical reasoning behind this kind of decisions.

Second, there is a need of independent, impartial decisions. A central bank under political influence or pressure by public opinion wouldn't manage properly its tasks.

Nonetheless, technocratic institutions are not simply technical, their decisions are the result of evaluation and discretion. And here comes the political side: it's impossible that such decisions are shared or appreciated by everybody, not even by all the "technicians" in the same field. This should not be scary at all. Monetary policy is, in the end, a policy.

The ECB, as all of the technocratic institutions shows two basic features to guarantee that its power will not be abused: a clear mandate and an accountability framework. It doesn't operate in a splendid isolation, but motivates regularly its choices, explains them and justify them on the legal ground of EU primary law, through an open dialogue with political institutions and ad hoc communication tools. For sure it enjoys wide competence to interpret its conferred competences, but the use it has done of them and the validation by the ECJ show that the legal bases together with the exceptional circumstances made them acceptable. At any stage, the monetary institution showed the due respect to the aims and the rationale of the interpreted norms and acted as an institution of the Union.

Specific circumstances—as the lack of real European economic governance i.e. of a common fiscal policy—is the background scenario for this exercise of powers. In our opinion it has played quite a relevant role, but this falls outside the scope of the present chapter.

References

Allemand F, Martucci F (2012) La nouvelle gouvernance économique européenne. Cahiers de droit européen 48(1):21 et seqq

Bassan F (2014) Le operazioni non convenzionali della BCE al vaglio della Corte costituzionale tedesca. Rivista di Diritto internazionale 97:361–393

Beukers T (2013) The new ECB and its relationship with the Eurozone Member States: between Central Bank Independence and Central Bank and Central Bank Intervention. Common Mark Law Rev 50:1579 et seqq

Bini Smaghi L (2009) Conventional and Unconventional Monetary Policy. Keynote lecture at the International Center for Monetary and Banking Studies (ICMB). Geneva, 28 April 2009, on www.ecb.europa.eu
Bossone B (2013) Unconventional Monetary Policies Revisited (Part I), October 4, 2013 and Unconventional Monetary Policies Revisited (Part II), October 5, 2013, http://www.voxeu.org
Cafaro S (2013) L'azione della BCE nella crisi dell'area dell'euro alla luce del diritto dell'Unione europea. In: Adinolfi G, Vellano M (eds) La crisi del debito sovrano degli Stati dell'area dell'euro. Profili giuridici. Giappichelli, Torino, pp 49–68
Cœuré B (2013) Monetary Policy and Banking Supervision, Symposium: "Central Banking: Where Are We Headed?" in honour of Stefan Gerlach's contribution to the Institute for Monetary and Financial Stability. Goethe University, Frankfurt, 7 February 2013, http://www.ecb.europa.eu
Draghi M (2012a) Speech at the Global Investment Conference in London, 26 July 2012, on http://www.ecb.europa.eu
Draghi M (2012b) Speech opening the academic year at Università Bocconi (Milan) on 15 November 2012, on www.ecb.europa.eu/press/key/date/2012/html/sp120726.en.html
Hinarejos A (2015) post "Is the ECB's OMT programme legal? The Advocate-General's Opinion in Gauweiler", on http://eulawanalysis.blogspot.it
Library of the European Parliament (2012) European Central Bank: (Un)Conventional Policy Measures, Library Briefing 02/10/2012, Bruxelles
Louis JV (2009) L'Union européenne et sa monnaie, 3ème edn. Université de Bruxelles, Bruxelles
Malatesta A (2003) La Banca centrale Europea. Giuffrè, Milano
Martucci F (2012) Objectifs et compétences en union économique et monétaire: réflexions sur l'objectif de la stabilité des prix. In: Neframi E (ed) Objectifs et compétences dans l'Union européenne. Bruylant, Bruxelles, pp 96 et seqq
Munari F (2015) Da *Pringle* a *Gauweiler*: i tormentati anni dell'unione monetaria e i loro effetti sull'ordinamento giuridico europeo. Il Diritto dell'Unione europea 4:723–755
Roubini N (2016) The new abnormal for a troubled global economy. Time, January 14, 2016
Ruffert M (2011) The European debt crisis and European Union law. Common Mark Law Rev 48:1777–1806
Smits R (1997) The European Central Bank. Kluwer Law International, The Hague
Smits R (2015) post "European Central Bank's Room for Manoeuvre Provisionally Confirmed", on https://acelg.blogactiv.eu
Viterbo A, Cisotta R (2010) La crisi della Grecia, l'attacco speculativo all'euro e le risposte dell'Unione europea. Il Diritto dell'Unione europea 4:961 et seqq
Viterbo A, Cisotta R (2012) La crisi del debito sovrano e gli interventi dell'UE: dai primi strumenti finanziari al Fiscal Compact. Il Diritto dell'Unione europea 2:323 et seqq
Zilioli C, Selmayr M (2001) The law of the European Central Bank. Hart, Portland

Criteria for Determining the Legality of the ECB's Unconventional Measures

Fabio Bassan

Abstract In the past 7 years, the EU has adopted various measures to react to a banking crisis. In a context where the incompleteness of political union has been one of the major drawbacks to the European reaction to the crisis, the European Central Bank (ECB) has had to play a role as substitute for political institutions. The ECB's interventions have been both conventional and unconventional; the latter often criticised and challenged in European and national Courts. The first part of this study aims to define the ECB's "unconventional" measures, which derive from the economic practice. Then the applicable rules to ECB actions are discussed, together with their interpretation, provided by the Court of Justice of the European Union and the German Federal Constitutional Court, the latter being particularly active on the point. Finally, the study attempts to apply these principles and practices to the unconventional measures adopted by the ECB to verify their effective implementation.

Contents

F. Bassan (✉)
International Law, Department of Business Studies, University of Roma Tre, Rome, Italy
e-mail: fabio.bassan@uniroma3.it

L. Daniele et al. (eds.), *Democracy in the EMU in the Aftermath of the Crisis*,
DOI 10.1007/978-3-319-53895-2_12

1 Introduction

In the past 9 years, the EU has adopted various measures to react to a banking crisis imported from the United States and for which there were not (especially in Europe) suitable antibodies. In a context where the incompleteness of political union has been one of the major drawbacks to the European reaction to the crisis, the European Central Bank (ECB) has had to play a role as substitute for political institutions, by applying an expansionary monetary policy often at odds with the States' restrictive economic policies (under close EU coordination). Hence the reduced effectiveness and the contradictory nature of its interventions.

The ECB's interventions have been both conventional and unconventional; the latter often criticised and challenged in European and national Courts. However, to date, one legally relevant aspect of the phenomenon does not seem to have been highlighted properly, which is the need to identify a measure of the legality of the ECB's actions. On the one hand, the Treaties grant to the ECB wide discretion in its intervention. On the other hand, the ECB often adopts measures on the basis of mere press releases, later accompanied by the implementation of schemes that are very detailed, but only technically. This highlights gaps in the intermediate level and the difficulty of identifying not only the legal basis of the action but also (and especially) the criterion of the legality of the measures, punctually challenged precisely under this aspect.

The first part of this study aims to define the ECB's "unconventional" measures, which derive from the economic practice, without a legal approach. Then the applicable rules to ECB actions will be discussed, together with their interpretation, provided by the Court of Justice of the European Union and the German Federal Constitutional Court, the latter being particularly active on the point. Finally, this study will attempt to apply these principles and practices to the unconventional measures adopted by the ECB to verify their effective implementation.

2 The ECB's Unconventional Measures: A Legal Definition

The distinction between conventional and unconventional measure comes from the economic analysis, not from the legal one. It cannot be compared to the distinction between typical or atypical measures, as there is no provision in the Treaties to this regard. Nor does the Statute of the ECB provide a listing.

All the measures adopted by the ECB were aimed at reaching the primary objective of price stability, measured by many parameters, including inflation rate (less than, but close to 2% per annum). The measure is economically legitimate if functional to this goal. Here we jurists get some challenges: because the goal that the ECB must achieve is different when acting as legislator or as regulator. Because the goal is claimed *ex ante*, but not necessarily achieved *ex post*. Because it introduces a subjective element—according to which purposes become critical—

and a prognostic analysis that is more befitting to UK regulations than to continental ones, the latter being based on objective market criteria investigated retrospectively. Because there may be more than one objective. Because the goal may be achieved with a direct or indirect, primary or secondary tool (i.e. medium to long-term price stability is always the final goal). Because side effects (or secondary objectives) in the actual practice often become, sometimes unintentionally, more important than primary goals. Because the lack of information provided by the ECB in the press releases (not amended by technical details regarding their implementation) authorises conflicting interpretations.

When it comes to a definition, according to the economic perspective it is not necessary to define a measure a priori. A measure is conventional or not depending on whether it was used previously. The interest of the economist is not in the definition but in the classification, functional to the identification of the correct type of unconventional measure according to the case. That of legitimacy, is a purely legal issue. But of course, a classification without a prior definition, is pointless.

The conventional or non-conventional character of the instrument of monetary policy depends, according to the economic analysis, on space and time: the national practices and the period examined. So much so, that "conventional" is often considered synonymous with "standard". So, in many States, the operations of central banks designed to control the nominal interest rate in the short term ("interest rate policy") are now considered conventional, while unconventional measures belong to the set of budgetary policies, through which central banks generally affect prices and financial instruments other than short-term interest rate.

On this basis, we could give the following legal definition of the unconventional measures enacted by the European Central Bank:

> all monetary policy instruments setting targets for the medium/long term that do not directly affect the interest rate.

A measure aimed at ensuring price stability in the medium term is unconventional.

Starting from this assumption, we can try to translate the economic practice into legal terms. Unconventional measures do not constitute an extension of the powers of the ECB. We do not refer to the case law of conferred/implied powers. Independence and exclusivity on the execution of delegated powers—provided for by the Treaties—give the ECB the right to freely choose the most appropriate means to achieve its goal. In the physiological phase, decisions on interest rates are sufficient; in times of crisis, the spectrum of actions is wider. It is the perimeter of the action that expands and retracts according to the needs, not the power. The only limit that cannot be exceeded is represented by the obligations under the Treaty (including the prohibition of direct financing to the States per Article 123, para. 1, TFEU).

In conclusion, the gap in terms of definition and the confusion in terms of classification make the jurist's interpretative job an arduous one. At least in abstract terms. But more concretely, if we examine the activities of the ECB during the crisis in relation to the powers conferred upon it by the Treaties and the Statute.

3 The Rules Applicable in the Treaties and the ECB Statute

According to Article 127 TFEU (para. 1) the main objective of the European System of Central Banks (ESCB) is "price stability". Without prejudice to this objective, the ESCB must support general economic policies in the Union to contribute to the objectives defined in Article 3 TEU. Among these objectives, there is the Economic and Monetary Union based on the Euro. The tasks entrusted by the ESCB are, among others, the definition and implementation of monetary policy and the promotion of the smooth operation of payment systems (Article 127, para. 2, TFEU).

So far, objectives and tasks. As for the instruments, the ECB, as an independent institution (Article 130 TFEU) is free to adopt (or even create) the most suitable ones, in accordance with the general principles of the Union, first and foremost the principle of proportionality. Indeed, the ECB's independence, compared to the national central banks, is "enhanced" by the rigidity of its *status*, that may be changed only with an amendment to the Treaties.

Article 18 of the Statute of the ECB annexed to the Treaties states that the ECB and the national central banks may: (a) operate in the financial markets by buying and selling outright (spot and forward) or under repurchase term lending or borrowing claims and marketable instruments; (b) conduct credit operations with credit institutions and other market participants, with lending being based on adequate collateral.

The second paragraph of Article 18 of the Statute makes it clear that

> The ECB shall establish general principles for open market and credit operations carried out by itself or the national central banks, including for the announcement of conditions under which they stand ready to enter into such transactions.

Again, the independence given to it by the Treaties guarantees to the ECB the power to define the content of the measures to be taken in open markets.

Finally, Article 20 of the Statute permits to the Governing Council of the ECB

> by a majority of two thirds of the voters [the] use of such other operational methods of monetary control as it sees fit.

This last provision, especially in the absence of a comprehensive catalogue, seems to legitimate all the instruments adopted by the ECB, including other than those established under Article 18 of its Statute, provided that they are consistent with and functional to the achievement of price stability.

As for the scope of the powers instead, Articles 123 TFEU and 21, para. 1, of the Statute prohibit the ECB's direct purchase of government securities on the primary market. The purpose of this standard is to prevent the financing of public debt of the Member States. Accordingly, to ensure the practical effect of the provision, also secondary market purchase, under certain conditions, should not be permitted, if directed (even through intermediaries) to circumvent the ban.

4 The Unconventional Measures Taken by the ECB During the Crisis

In the recent years of crisis, the ECB has adopted unconventional measures ranging from long-term auctions (LTRO) for the purchase of government bonds on the secondary market for distressed Countries (SMP), to OMT, targeted long-term auctions (TLTRO), purchase of ABS and covered bonds (ABSPP), and Quantitative Easing (QE).

4.1 LTRO

The Eurosystem's open market operations consist of the provision of liquidity in the short term (1 week: the Main Refinancing Operations, MROs) or in a longer time (3 years: the Longer-Term Refinancing Operations, LTROs). These provide alternative funding to the financial system in cases where the ordinary means are not effective. On 22 December 2011 and 29 February 2012, the ECB launched two LTRO auctions with maturity of 3 years. In these two LTROs, 523 banks participated with a request for €490 billion, and 800 banks with a request for €530 billion, for a total of more than €1000 billion.

4.2 SMP

Starting from 10 May 2010 and until September 2012, the central banks of the Euro purchased securities within the context of the Securities Markets Programme (SMP), with the aim of reducing the tensions that threatened to undermine the chain of transmission of the monetary policy.

4.3 OMT

The OMT, announced by the Governing Council of the ECB on 2 August 2012 and illustrated in a press release on 6 September 2012, constitute the content of the report (known as "speech in London"), held by ECB President Mario Draghi on 26 July 2012 at the Global Investment Conference.[1]

[1]President Draghi said that "the ECB is ready to do whatever it takes to preserve the euro", and added unequivocally, "and believe me, it will be enough". Consequently, prices of sovereign debt of peripheral Eurozone States, like Spain and Italy, suddenly jumped. All in all, such a strong announcement was enough to calm financial market operators' uneasiness.

The OMT consist of the purchase by the ECB of short-term government bonds (with maturity between one and 3 years) issued by Member States in a situation of serious macroeconomic difficulty (requirement of compliance), certified by the start of a programme of financial aid or a precautionary programme with the European Stability Mechanism or the European Framework for Financial Stability. The start, duration and end of the OMT programme are decided by the Governing Council of the ECB. There is no limit to the amount of transactions, which take place only on the secondary market, not on the primary one. With the OMT, the ECB accepts the same treatment as a private lender: it receives equal remuneration and cannot claim any priority in the event of a debt restructuring (*pari passu*). The liquidity injected into the market on purchases of government bonds by the ECB is sterilised (i.e. reabsorbed by selling other securities) to prevent the OMT from interfering with other monetary policy instruments and in particular from increasing the inflation rate. The ECB will publish on a monthly basis both the amount of OMT launched, broken down by Country, and the market value of the assets acquired.

The stated aim of the OMT is to safeguard the transmission channel of the monetary policy for the Euro area and to prevent tensions on the markets of government bonds from causing excessive rises in interest rates. The potentially unlimited amount of the OMT reduces both tensions on the bond markets of the Euro area and premiums, for the risk that the fear of the reversibility of the Euro pushes on Member States in macro-economic difficulties; therefore it supports the efforts of Member States towards recovery and debt consolidation.

This is the information available, as the only official document published by the ECB on the OMT is a press release. The ECB has not adopted nor published any document illustrating in detail the procedures, conditions and limits of the OMT. Not having the OMT yet had any implementation, the absence of information on the application rules has not worried the financial markets.

4.4 ABSPP

In 2009 and 2011, the ECB announced two programmes to purchase, on the primary and secondary markets, covered bonds (CBPP and CBPP2). The two programmes terminated, respectively, on 30 June 2010 (after reaching a nominal amount of €60 billion) and in October 2012 (for a total amount of €40 billion).

In September 2014, the ECB announced the launch of an ABS purchase programme (ABSPP) and a third bond purchase programme (CBPP3). The ABSPP and CBPP3 are part of the joint action of the ECB and the Bank of England "for a better functioning securitisation market in the European Union".

4.5 *TLTRO*

On 5 June 2014, the Board of Governors of the ECB decided to launch eight long-term refinancing operations (TLTRO, Targeted Longer-Term Refinancing Operations) conditioning the use of funding by banks to achieve a particular target. The intention is to overcome the limitations of auctions launched late in 2011 and early in 2012, which have not injected to the markets (in particular, to households and companies) the liquidity provided by the ECB. Based on a decision of 29 July 2014 (Decision ECB/2014/34), the first TLTRO auctions were launched in September 2014 and in December 2014, and starting from March 2015 they were launched on a quarterly basis.

4.6 *Quantitative Easing*

On 22 January 2015, the ECB announced an "expanded asset purchase programme", renamed European Quantitative Easing (QE), directed to overcome the risks of a prolonged period of low inflation. With the QE, the ECB, but also national central banks, purchased on secondary markets, on terms similar to those of private operators (*pari passu*), public debt of member States or bonds issued by private companies, for an amount not exceeding €60 billion/month. Each national central bank buys bonds of its own Country, and assures that only 20% are shared (in so much is the purchase of securities by the ECB).

5 The Court of Justice and the BVerfG

Some of the unconventional measures taken by the ECB have been submitted to the judgment of the Court of Justice of the European Union and of the German Federal Constitutional Court (BVerfG), which have addressed in detail the question of the legality of ECB actions in relation to the powers granted to it under the Treaties. Rulings of the Courts have focused precisely on this issue in the cases *Pringle* (Court of Justice of the European Union)[2] and *OMT* (both the German Federal Constitutional Court and the Court of Justice).[3] A new question on the Quantitative Easing (QE), is currently subject to the BVerfG.

[2]ECJ 27 November 2012, Case C-370/12, *Thomas Pringle* v. *The Government of Ireland, Ireland and the Attorney General.*

[3]BVerfG (German Constitutional Court), Order of 14 January 2014, BvR 2728/13 (*OMT Decision*); ECJ 16 June 2015, Case C-62/14, *Gauweiler and Others* v. *Deutscher Bundestag*; BVerfG, Judgment of 21 June 2016.

A first point about legitimacy evaluated by the Courts concerns the classification of the ECB's unconventional measures as acts of monetary policy or economic policy. Of course, the action could be legitimate only in the former case. A second aspect concerns the limits of ECB action, which indirectly might finance the public debt of the Member States, circumventing the prohibition in Article 123, para. 1, TFEU. The limits of the questions did not allow the Court to address systematically the more general theme, which is to identify the parameters to assess the legality of the ECB's unconventional measures. The answers to the questions raised, however, could lead to identifying a starting point and a possible path for a response.

5.1 Economic and Monetary Policy

As to the first issue, the Treaties confer on the ECB exclusive powers on monetary policy, aimed at maintaining price stability. The separation between monetary policy, which is of exclusive competence of the Union, and the economic policies of the Member States, that the EU can only coordinate, is not simple. An attempt to do so was made recently by the Court of Justice, in the judgment (preliminary rulings) delivered in the *Pringle* case. Here the Court made it clear that the Decision 2011/199/EU, that amended Article 136 TFEU, adding a third paragraph which authorised Member States of the Euro area to create a "stability mechanism", constituted an act of economic and not monetary policy. The evaluation was based on three criteria: the aim of the measure (to safeguard the stability of the Euro area as a whole), the instruments used (financial assistance to the Member State in difficulty) to reach the target, and the connection with other provisions of the Treaty (all related to the strengthening of economic governance in the Union).

The German Federal Constitutional Court (BVerfG) has stepped in to define the parameters of monetary policy, in order to assess whether the unconventional measures of the ECB (the OMT in the case at hand) were part of it, and to what extent. In the absence of definitions in the Treaties, the BVerfG assessed the scope of competence of the ECB in monetary policy on the basis of the three parameters established by the Court in the *Pringle* case: the immediate objective of the action, to be evaluated with objective criteria, the tools used to reach the target and the relationship with other provisions of the Treaties. Following this reasoning, the BVerfG argued that the purchase, even on the secondary market, of bonds of Member States in financial difficulty was aimed at stabilising the Euro area, an objective—as the Court already found in the *Pringle* case—typical of economic policy, and that produces only indirect effects on monetary policy. As for tools, financial assistance to the States is an action that goes beyond monetary policy interventions. Furthermore, the close connection with the assistance programmes of the ESM fund shows, according to the German Court, that OMT are instruments of economic policy, equivalent to a measure of financial assistance but deprived of the democratic legitimacy and the control mechanisms available to the latter. Finally, the selectivity of the OMT programme contrasts in itself with the model of a monetary policy action, which is neutral by definition.

What did the ECJ say on this perspective? Advocate General Cruz Villalón, moving from a functional approach so extreme that borders on tautology ("every measure that is given effect through monetary policy instruments constitutes monetary policy"), suggests giving priority to the teleological aspect (the primary purpose of the measure) and to the formal one (the use of an instrument of monetary policy expressly provided for by the Treaties) to qualify the measure as monetary.

Conversely, the Court of Justice of the European Union has clarified the parameters of the legality of the ECB's unconventional measures addressing both goals, and the tools used to achieve them, the latter examined in relation to their conditionality and selectivity, parameterised on the general criterion of proportionality. The Court holds that the objective of the OMT unconventional measure announced by the ECB is to

> preserve at the same time an adequate transmission of monetary policy and the uniqueness of this policy (para. 47).

Since the deterioration of the transmission mechanism of monetary policy affects the price stability (para. 50) the protection of which is the primary mandate of the ECB, the measure falls within the objectives for which the treaties allow the ECB to act. Except that, on the one hand, on an objective level (paras. 76 and 77) the objective worthy of protection is found also in the stability of the euro: purpose of economic, not monetary policy. On the other hand (para. 80), the (subjective) evaluation of the ESCB when enacting the measure (prognostic) is considered relevant. So, if one considers unstable the frontier between economic and monetary policy, the Court acknowledges a wide discretion to the ECB, that the Court itself does not hesitate to call technical discretionary power (*infra*, para. 5.3).

As regards the means to achieve the goal, the Court points out that Article 18, para. 1, of the Protocol of the ECB and the ESCB, entitles the ECB to operate in the financial markets by buying and selling securities. And indeed, this is an unconventional measure, when instrumental to control short-term interest rates. If the measure is proportional, selectivity and conditionality do not affect its validity.

Proportionality is ensured, according to the Court, by the limits to the potential scope of the OMT programme (para. 85), which is only open to: (a) government bonds of the Member States admitted to a programme of economic adjustment, and (b) having still (or again) access to the bond market and (c) with maturities of less than 3 years, (d) subject to the ESCB reserve to resell securities purchased at any time. These limits allow the ESCB to establish the OMT programme without first setting a quantitative limit, which would make it less effective (para. 88).

Finally, the fact that the implementation of the OMT programme is subject to full compliance with the macroeconomic adjustment programmes of the EFSF or the ESM (conditionality), it cannot be turned into an instrument of economic policy (para. 57 et seqq.). Without prejudice to price stability, the Treaty expressly provides that the ESCB should support the general economic policy of the Union. And indeed, conditionality, by making the implementation of OMT contingent upon the full respect of adjustment programmes, requires the beneficiary States not to deteriorate their situation and is thus an instrument to support the general economic policy of the Union.

5.2 Funding to Member States

Coming to the second set of questions relating to the compliance with the prohibition of direct financing of Member States (Article 123, para. 1, TFEU), and therefore the purchase of public debt bonds of the States only on the secondary market, the ECB argued that it had acted within the limits of its powers and of the mandate conferred on it by the Treaties. The assumption is based on the fact that Article 123 TFEU prohibits the funding of State debt and therefore the purchase of sovereign debt on the primary market, not even on the secondary market, when focused on monetary policy operations. The Court of Justice has already judged (again, reference is made to the *Pringle* case) on the legality of EU interventions under Article 125 TFEU, when necessary to safeguard the stability of the Euro area as a whole and subject to strict conditions. In addition, the purchase of public debt bonds of the States, of limited duration (no more than 3 years) is subject to the occurrence of three main conditions, detailed in the ECB's response brief, which would reveal the purely monetary aim of the measure.

Now, Articles 123 TFEU and 21, para. 1, of the ECB Statute prohibit the ECB's direct purchase of the Member States' government bonds on the primary market. The purpose of the rule, as stated, is to prevent the financing of the public debt of the Member States. It follows that the purchase on the secondary market, if designed to circumvent the ban, must be regarded as not admissible. That this was the purpose of the ECB action is shown, according to the BVerfG, by many elements, ranging from the (implicit) target of reducing the spread of interest rates of the peripheral Countries, to the selectivity of the measure, to the parallel programmes of assistance by the EFSF and ESM funds, and by other elements. Among these, the following are relevant: (a) the unprivileged *status* acquired by the ECB with the OMT programme, which involves a possible participation in the restructuring and the subsequent waiver of the receivables due from the Country in difficulty (*pari passu*). (b) Taking an unconditional risk of the waiver of the credit relative to government bonds purchased in the absence of criteria and limits defined a priori. (c) The option of maintaining securities until maturity (not expressly excluded by the ECB), which entails the removal from the market of the securities purchased and is therefore in essence a direct financing of the public debt of the State. (d) The interference with market price formation, when securities are purchased on the secondary market by the ECB immediately after their issuance in the primary market. (e) The implicit encouragement to operators to buy government bonds on the primary market because of the guarantee of their repurchase on the secondary one.

Many of these critical elements arise, however, from the lack of clarification on the part of the ECB, that in the absence of specific guidelines, merely illustrated the principles of the OMT programme in a press release and then in the defense brief filed for the hearing before the BVerfG.

On this second point (i.e., the funding of Member States), Advocate General Cruz Villalón, in the *OMT* case, after having reclassified the findings of the BVerfG into four categories (conditionality, parallelism, selectivity and circumvention of the prohibition) found it necessary and sufficient that the OMT programme respects an "embargo clause", according to which the purchase of securities of the States on the secondary market is allowed only after a period of time (not pre-determined, in order not to interfere with the markets) sufficient to allow the formation of a price on the secondary market.

The assessment of the Court of Justice on the issue is more complex. Initially (paras. 102 et seqq.), the Court supported the view of the Advocate General, and considered that the purchase of government bonds on the secondary market is subject to guarantees sufficient and appropriate to make them compliant with the prohibition under Article 123, para. 1, so that the effect of the intervention on the secondary market is not equivalent to the direct purchase of securities on the primary market. The guarantees are specifically mentioned by the Court (para. 106):

> The Governing Council [of the ECB] is to be responsible for deciding on the scope, the start, the continuation and the suspension of the intervention on the secondary market envisaged by such a programme. The ECB has also made clear before the Court that the ESCB intends, first, to ensure that a minimum period is observed between the issue of a security on the primary market and its purchase on the secondary market and, secondly, to refrain from making any prior announcement concerning either its decision to carry out such purchases or the volume of purchases envisaged.

Conditionality then, is a further (indirect) guarantee of the compliance with the prohibition of direct financing, since it sterilises the potential elusiveness of the measure, imposing to beneficiary Member States specific commitments in their economic policy that prevent the risk of abuse of a typical loan. Conditionality, in short, has a deterrent effect and allows some form of control in the implementation of other measures.

5.3 *The General Theme: Independence and Discretion of the ECB*

Both the two profiles examined, relevant for assessing the legality of the unconventional measures taken by the ECB, lead to one single point: the independence of the central bank. In fact, to enable it to pursue the objectives set out in Articles 119 and 127, the TFEU gives full independence to the ECB (Article 130). The independence of the central bank is indeed a best practice in all industrialised Countries, and guarantees the autonomy of monetary policy. Now, the question raised by the *OMT* case, but applicable to all ECB unconventional measures, may be simplified as follows: according to the German Constitutional Court, the independence of the ECB should be limited to certain non-conventional instruments; otherwise an absolute freedom of choice would give the ECB a "competence of competence".

This is the point, on the merit, that from a procedural standpoint is due to the standard of judicial review of the ECB measures. The BVerfG challenges the objective of monetary policy of the ECB (the restoration of the transmission chain of the currency) and—in order to apply the *Pringle* pattern—replaces it with another goal of economic policy (the reduction of the interest rate spread of public debt).

Of course, it comes from our assumption that the purpose of a measure is a decisive factor for assessing the legality of the ECB action. In this respect, on a procedural level, the scope of the judicial review of the Court of Justice on ECB actions is defined by a clear case law. Of course, so far the Court has evaluated the independence of the ECB on the monetary policy only in relation to other EU institutions, not to Member States.[4]

In the *OMT* case, the European Court of Justice suggested for the first time a general pattern. The independence granted to the ECB by the Treaties gives it a wide technical discretionary power. The Court should limit itself to judge whether the ECB's unconventional measure manifestly exceeds the competences attributed to the European Central Bank.

The OMT programme is a measure of monetary policy, which is also supporting the general economic policy of the Union (Article 127 TFEU). If this is the scope of the action, the discretionary power of the ECB is unlikely to be challenged without calling into question simultaneously its independence.

6 The General Principles that Flow from the Law: The Criterion for Determining the Legality of the ECB's Non-Standard Measures

Unconventional measures are those that the ECB adopts for purposes other than controlling the nominal rate in the short term. Not the measure itself, but the goal it pursues indicates the classification. There are no typical measures, as the Treaty did

---

[4]See ECJ 10 July 2003, Case C-11/00, *Commission of the European Communities* v. *The European Central Bank* (*Olaf*), Opinion of Advocate General Jacobs (3 October 2002) para. 150: "That provision establishes, according to its wording, a principle of central bank independence. It is, as the ECB itself points out, clear that the independence thus established is not an end in itself; it serves a specific purpose. By shielding the decision-making process of the ECB from short-term political pressures the principle of independence aims to enable the ECB effectively to pursue the aim of price stability and, without prejudice to that aim, support the economic policies of the Community as required by Article 105(1) EC". He also pointed out that "the Treaty and the Statute confer upon the ECB a high level of independence which is equivalent to, or perhaps greater than, the independence of the national central banks [. . .] However, the principle of independence does not imply a total isolation from, or a complete absence of cooperation with, the institutions and bodies of the Community. The Treaty prohibits only influence which is liable to undermine the ability of the ECB to carry out its tasks effectively with a view to price stability, and which must therefore be regarded as undue" (para. 155).

not provide for a list. So, each measure announced or adopted by the ECB is legitimate, in abstract terms. The legitimacy of the intervention, in practice, is measured on the parameter of proportionality, according to the ECB's self-binding principles, not measured in practice *ex post*, but in abstract *ex ante*, on the basis of the prognosis made by the ECB when adopting or implementing the measure. The technical discretion guaranteed to the ECB by its independence as prescribed by the Treaties, requires the Courts (the Court of Justice of the EU in particular) merely to decide on a manifest error or inadequate ruling justification.

So, if their goal is the only requirement that may be used to narrow down the scope of legitimacy of the ECB's unconventional measures, the separation between economic and monetary policy, on which the Court has focused so far, is almost pointless. The goal that the ECB is entitled and indeed obliged to pursue (Article 127, para. 1, TFEU) is the "maintenance of price stability". Notwithstanding this, the ESCB shall support the general economic policies in the Union to contribute to the objectives defined in Article 3 TEU, including the Economic and Monetary Union based on the Euro. Therefore, the unconventional measure is legitimate if the ECB believes that it is necessary to maintain price stability or to support the general economic policies of the Union and not those of one or more Member States. Thus, selectivity should be evaluated not in relation to the application of a measure in a Member State, but to its theoretical applicability to all the States that request it.

7 Application of the Principles to Specific Cases

The limits to the action of the ECB that the BVerfG and the Court of Justice have traced to define the border of the legitimacy of OMT, relate to profiles that can also be applied to other unconventional measures taken by the ECB: the TLTRO, the purchase of ABS, the QE and any other instruments will all respect the constraints identified by BVerG, to the extent that were confirmed or interpreted by the European Court of Justice. Therefore, we can verify whether the measures taken so far by the ECB do respect the constraints of both the Treaties and the Constitutions of the Member States (the German one in particular), as interpreted by the case law so far. In these tests of resistance, the BVerfG constraints are the stronger ones, therefore we will start from these.

The TLTRO do not seem contrary to the Treaties, even when interpreted on the basis of the reasoning of the BVerfG. They are in fact long-term loans granted to banks (individually or in groups) and not to Member States, with constraints on the use of the funds lent. The goal is to ensure the re-entry of the money lent by the ECB through the normal banking channels. The measure also provides for appropriate tools for assessment and verification.

With reference to the types (as defined by the ECB "simple and transparent") of asset-backed securities (ABS) and to programmes for the purchase of covered bonds (CB), the measures are characterised by the fact that not only ABS and CB will be accepted as collateral but they will be purchased by the ECB, when secured and rated adequately. They are "collateralised" by loans to the real economy and not involving public debt securities of the States. Again, the principles and requirements listed by the BVerfG are still met, since it is not the public debt but the private sector being funded.

The story is different for the quantitative easing (QE) which is, at least in abstract, the more challenging unconventional measure already adopted by the ECB. To prevent the violations that the BVerfG highlighted in relation to the OMT, the QE must meet the following criteria:

(a) It should not discriminate between States. The ECB should buy bonds of all Countries, not just those in trouble. The intervention must be pro rata (in relation to ECB shares held by each Member). Non-discrimination between the public debts must still be applied only to bonds exceeding a minimum rating defined a priori;
(b) It should be unlimited, and therefore have a threshold defined *ex ante*;
(c) It shouldn't be bound to compliance with ESM or other procedures;
(d) It shouldn't be restricted to the secondary market, and therefore comply with an "embargo period";
(e) It should not provide for preferential treatment for the ECB (*pari passu* rule).

Clearly, these are conditions that transform the QE in a measure of a general nature, intended to restore the transmission chain of the currency, and not to support the bonds of Countries in difficulty.

The QE adopted by the ECB respects the constraints mentioned above as they emerge from the recent case law. It is not selective, being directed to all Member States, and is not bound to conditionality. It is limited to the secondary market, and respects "embargo periods" which, to date, have proved to be sufficient. It is limited in amount (€60 billion is the monthly threshold) and in duration (18 months, possibly extendable if required). It does not provide for preferential treatment over other creditors. It does not require holding the securities until maturity.

The unconventional measures taken by the ECB during the crisis are not in the Treaties nor in the Statute: both constrain the central bank as to the purpose (of price stability and inflation control) leaving the choice of instruments to achieve it. The legitimacy of the instrument used should be assessed, therefore, in relation both to its instrumentality to the target and to the compliance with the prohibitions by which the Treaties and the ECB Statute surround the border of monetary policy.

If in the Member States the independence of the central bank is a suitable guarantee of the autonomy of monetary policy with respect to economic policy, the current European institutional incompleteness requires instead operators and scholars to develop principles of separation between the two policies. This gives rise to different interpretations, justified by the lack of definition in the Treaties and in the Statute of the ECB. On closer inspection, however, part of this effort is useless.

I have tried to evaluate the unconventional measures adopted so far by the ECB through the lens of conventional case law, which appears to be the unit of measurement used properly by the ECB. However, there is still room for greater accuracy in the drafting of criteria and principles that the unconventional measures should comply with.

The European Central Bank (ECB) and European Democracy: A Technocratic Institution to Rule All European States?

Giulio Peroni

Abstract The crisis has shown how the financial markets move very rapidly and the reaction times of democratic institutions are too slow for preventing the negative effects of financial turmoil. In this framework, the ECB has been very active since the beginning of the crisis and its action helped the Eurozone to avoid its economic and political collapse. Nevertheless, the ECB's action has been strongly criticised because it would appear to contravene EU rules and have probably had the effect to modify its role. The ECB would no longer be a technocratic institution, but the central hub of EU economy policy making, without any democratic effective control. This chapter intends to underline how the supposed democratic deficit can be avoided or limited by strengthening the ECB's transparency and accountability, safeguarding its independence from political influence.

Contents

1 The Crisis and the Reasons of the ECB's Action

The crisis that has hit the global economy since the Summer of 2007, is usually described with the metaphor: "A perfect storm". In fact, no other economic and financial turmoil, after the end of the World War II, has been as deep as the current recession.[1]

[1]Roubini and Uzan (2005), Christodoulakis (2015), Jordà et al. (2016).

G. Peroni (✉)
Department of Italian and Supranational Pubic Law, University of Milan, Milan, Italy
e-mail: giulio.peroni@unimi.it

L. Daniele et al. (eds.), *Democracy in the EMU in the Aftermath of the Crisis*,
DOI 10.1007/978-3-319-53895-2_13

For finding an economic event so serious, we have to call to mind the Great Depression of 1929.[2] During the course of the financial turmoil, Governments and monetary authorities have clearly demonstrated that they are well aware of the need not to repeat the errors of the past. In fact, monetary policy has been more aggressively and Governments have, with their fiscal policy, sought to stimulate as much as possible their respective industries with the aim of protecting their economy. Unlike the 1929 crisis, political and technocratic authorities have not resorted to protectionism, safeguarding, in this way, the free international trade.

The crisis was preceded by a relatively long period of rapid credit growth, large availability of liquidity, development of bubbles, especially in the real estate sector. This interacted with new, complex and opaque financial products with companies that failed to follow their own risk management procedure and with regulators and supervisors that not succeeded in keeping under control excessive risk taking. In this framework, it was very easy for many banks and financial players to veil the underlying risks to their customers.

When the crisis broke in the August of 2007 in the USA, owing to the burst of the real estate bubble which has strictly linked to the phenomenon of subprime loans,[3] uncertainty arose, among economic operators and above all with reference to the capacity of banks to manage the mentioned risks. As a result, the interbank market virtually closed and risks premiums on interbank loans soared. Banks faced a severe liquidity problem. Since the crisis originated in USA, there was the belief that the European Union (EU) economy would have not suffered the financial turmoil had it had a sound financial structure.

In September 2008, the world economic scenario dramatically changed with the default of Lehmann Brothers,[4] a global bank that almost brought down the world's financial institutions. Panic broke in markets, confidence collapse and investors decided massively "to get rid" of their positions. At the same time, the transmission of financial deterioration to the real economy evolved rapidly creating emergency fiscal positions in the so called PIGS States (Portugal, Ireland, Italy, Greece and Spain),[5] owing to their low rate of gross domestic product (GDP).

As a consequence, PIGS were no longer able to respect the strict fiscal constraints established by the Maastricht Treaty, in Articles 121, para. 1, 122, para. 2, and 123, para. 5 (then transposed with the Lisbon Treaty, in Article 140 TFEU) and in the Stability Growth Pact (SGP).[6]

Thus, the idea spread that it would be very difficult for said Countries to repay or refinance their public debt, without the financial assistance of Third

[2]Almunia et al. (2009), Krugman (2009).

[3]Mostacci (2009), Markan (2015).

[4]Markan (2015).

[5]Rosenthal (2012), Weeks (2014).

[6]On the SGP and its functioning see Hahn (1998), and more recently Louis (2007). The SGP was fortified, expanded and supplemented by the so-called "Six Pack" (five Regulations and one Directive entered into force on 13 December 2011). See Laffan and Schlosser (2016).

Parties, especially with the aid of the International Monetary Fund (IMF). Inevitably, the issue of sovereign debt rose,[7] representing the climax of the current economic and financial aftermath.

This last point has clearly shown the fragilities of the Economic and Monetary Union (EMU)[8] in front of the financial and economic downturn of such particular intensity and, above all, the lack of confidence of the financial markets in the economic stability of the Eurozone and in the survival of its single currency: the Euro.[9] Even if the possibility of one of Euro Members leaving the Eurozone is not mentioned by any primary rules of the EU treaties,[10] this solution has not been excluded.[11] But, if it were to happen, the legal, economic and political effects on the Eurozone could probably be very severe.[12] In fact, firstly, an Euro exit by one of its Members would definitively demonstrate the inability to respect the EMU macroeconomic provisions and to repay its debts. Secondly, it would be evident to the EU the impossibility to continue in the path of the economic and political integration between the Member States, as, despite its limits, the EMU remains the unique example of sovereign power completely delegated from Member States to the European Union.

In order to avoid the dissolution of the Eurozone, the EU has, during the last six years, developed a set of new rules, directed to the creation of a crisis management system. It is the case, for example, of the European Stability Mechanism (ESM), that establishes a permanent emergency fund which entered in force in September 2012, and the so called *Fiscal Compact*, agreed in March 2012, that mainly increases budgetary discipline.[13]

At the same time, the Euro Members in financial difficulty, for meeting the strict budgetary constraints imposed by the Maastricht provisions and for recovering the confidence of financial markets, have taken significant fiscal measures according to a political and economic model, inspired by the so called *Washington consensus* paradigm.[14]

---

[7]Gros and Mayer (2010), Cisotta and Viterbo (2012), Napoletano (2012), Starita (2013), Viterbo (2014).

[8]De Grauwe (2011).

[9]De Grauwe (2010), Peel (2010).

[10]Article 50 TEU only provides the possibility for a Member State to withdraw the EU intended as a whole.

[11]On the admissibility of a withdrawal from the Eurozone, see Hofmeister (2011), Dammann (2013), Peroni (2015). For an opposite point of view, see Athanassiou (2009).

[12]Goodhart (2007), Villata (2013), Gross and Gummer (2014).

[13]These new international treaties raise interesting questions with particular reference to their compatibility with the EU law as represent a solution of the crisis that is outside the European institutional system. See De Witte (2011), Baratta (2012), Craig (2012), Rossi (2012), Tosato (2012).

[14]Essentially characterised by a strong reduction of public sectors to finance, particularly, welfare system associated with a significant increase of taxation. See Peroni (2017).

All that has, inevitably, involved a general impoverishment to different layers of the European population, in some cases jeopardising even the access to certain essential public services, particularly in the field of education and health. Besides, the aforementioned measures have had the effect to greatly exacerbate the social tensions within PIGS citizens, also due to the political contexts of the said countries, characterised by a high level of unemployment rates and an increasing demand of economic support by a large number of people.[15]

2 The ECB's Action: A Necessary Intervention to Safeguard the Euro

Within the framework described, a central and decisive role in managing the crisis has been carried out by the European Central Bank (ECB),[16] the monetary authority of the 19 EU Countries which have adopted the Euro, whose main task is to ensure price stability,[17] in order to preserve the purchasing power of the single currency.

The ECB has been very active since the beginning of the crisis, and its action helped the European financial and banking sector to avoid their collapse and to limit the consequences for the real economy. In particular way, the ECB has had to react strongly to unprecedented threats to monetary stability in the Eurozone, owing to the "burst" of sovereignty debt crisis of PIGS Countries. In particular, the ECB's policy answer to the crisis was essentially aimed at ensuring the provision of liquidity and repairing banks lending channel. In order to pursue this aim, the Eurotower, in full consistency of its mandate reduced its key policy interest rate rapidly between October 2008 and May 2009 from 4.25% to 1% and increased the average maturity of its refinancing operations from months to years.

The ECB also took additional non standard measures[18] to ensure that its interest rate decisions were transmitted effectively to the "real economy" despite the volatilities of the financial markets. The main ECB's idea was to give support to banks that could not easily access the money markets or other sources of finance

---

[15] Peroni (2013), Viterbo and Costamagna (2013), De Pasquale (2014), Fabbrini (2014).

[16] On the legal nature, structure, functions and objectives of ECB: Malatesta (2003), de Haan (2005), Zilioli and Selmayr (2007), Harold (2012).

[17] Price stability is mentioned in Articles 3 TEU, and 119, paras. 2 and 3, TFEU; in Article 127, para. 1, TFEU and in Article 2, para. 1, of the Statute of the ESCB and ECB. Price stability is also one of the convergence criteria for the adoption of the Euro (see Article 140, para. 1, TFEU). The mandate of ECB is essentially confined to the maintenance of price stability. Contrary to the US Federal Reserve that is also committed to support growth and employment. According to the liberal theory, see Arndt (1996), price stability can be regarded as a value that stands above democracy.

[18] On ECB unconventional measures see Cafaro (2013), Contaldi (2014), Bassan (2015). From an economic perspective see Eser and Schwaab (2013), Szczerbowicz (2015).

and so have difficulty in providing credit to firms, companies and individuals. Consequently, the ECB for enhancing the provisions of liquidity to the banking system, decided to introduce two very long term refinancing operations (LTRO)[19] with a maturity of three years which were conducted in December 2011 and in February 2012. In addition, the ECB adopted the Securities Market Programme (SMP)[20] and the Covered Bonds Purchase Programme (CBPP)[21] used to buy particular assets like government bonds from PIGS States in order to address the acute tensions in the financial markets and to repair the monetary transmission channel in the Euro area.

Owing to the limited impact and short lived said measures, the ECB launched the Outright Monetary Transaction (OMT)[22] with the aim of purchasing unlimited amounts of government bonds of Member States subject to the ESM financial programme. Indeed, the OMT has not yet been used, but its announcement had a significant impact on government bond yields on the EMU Member States as it demonstrated to financial markets the steady purpose of the European Central Bank to safeguard the stability of the Eurozone.[23]

Nevertheless, the ECB's action has been strongly criticised because it would appear to contravene the EU legislation which clearly prohibits any mone tarizationand bail-out options and any form of financial and economic solidarity between EU and its Member states.[24] Specifically, Article 123 TFEU (repeated in Article 21 of the Statute of the ESCB and the ECB) forbids any form of monetary

[19]Buiter and Rahbari (2012).

[20]The SMP is a measure of monetary policy and consist of an open market operation directed to ensure liquidity in those market segments that are dysfunctional. It found its legal basis in Article 12, para. 1, Article 13, para. 1, and in particular in Article 18, para. 1, of the ESCB Statute. This is a Protocol (No. 4) to the European Treaties and has, according to Article 51 TEU, the same legal value of the EU primary rules. On the implementation of the SMP, during the development of the financial crisis for the purchase of the PIGS bonds, see Pace (2014).

[21]It was adopted by the ECB Governing Council in 2009 to stabilize financial market and help resolve banks' refinancing problems. It is also a programme finalised to improve the transmission of monetary policy by easing the provision of credit, and return inflation rates to levels closer to 2%; the inflation target usually fixed by ECB (see also note 29).

[22]See ECB (2012), p. 7. Thanks to the OMT for the ECB, it is possible to purchase the sovereign bonds of specific Euro area Countries, always, on secondary markets with no set *ex ante* quantitative limits. The ECB Governing Council's aim in implementing this programme is to safeguard an appropriate monetary transmission process and the singleness of monetary policy. For the purchasing of the governments bonds, the OMT programme establishes that the State in question complies with conditions specified in European Stability Mechanism, as we have seen before, that establishes a permanent emergency fund which entered in force in September 2012.

[23]In these terms consider the famous Draghi's phrase "The ECB within its mandate will do whatever it takes to save the euro and believe me it will be enough", uttered during a financial conference in London in July 2012, that signed the beginning of the OMT programme of bond purchase for Eurozone States that were in a situation of financial and economic crisis. The integral Draghi's speech can be consulted in http://www.ecb.europa.eu/press7key/date72012/html/sp120726.en.html. On the influence of Draghi's speech on the evolution of the economic crisis in the Eurozone, see Eichegreen (2013).

[24]Kontochristou and Masha (2014), Closa and Maatsch (2014), Peroni (2016).

financing of deficits or public debt; while Article 124 TFEU rules out privileged access to financial institutions by the public sector and Article 125 TFEU, with the "no-bail-out clause", precludes EU institutions and any one Member State becoming liable for the financial liabilities of another State of the Eurozone, with the one exception concerning "mutual financial guarantees for the joint execution of a specific project".[25]

The mentioned EU primary rules are based on clear and sound economic principles and are an essential part of the EU "budgetary code" that establishes the responsibility of each Member State for its own public finance.[26] So, it is evident the objectives are to avoid: firstly, financial transfers between European institutions to Member States and especially those, that could favour significant "moral hazard effects"[27] in the beneficiary Countries encouraging opportunistic behaviour, undermining the credibility of the EMU within the international and financial community[28]. Secondly, the monetarization of sovereign debt, that could lead to a higher inflation and instability of the prices. Indeed, at the moment, this last risk does not exist as the price level in the Euro area has been falling since late 2011 and has been below 1% since October 2013. So, it is possible to affirm that a slight rise of prices, as a possible effect of ECB purchasing sovereign bonds, not only can be considered acceptable, but decisevely useful in preserving the financial stability of the EMU.[29]

3 The Critics Moved to ECB: A Technocratic Institution Free to Act Without any Democratic Control?

The strong activism that has characterised up until now the ECB's action, since the beginning of the crisis, would have probably had the effect to modify its role.[30] The ECB would be no longer a technocratic institution, devoted to managing the EU,

[25]The above mentioned three prohibitions are linked with the obligation of Member States under Article 126 TFEU to avoid excessive deficits and with correlated SGP.

[26]The States have to finance themselves, if necessary, on the Market and at the conditions set by the Market. The Market is the "Judge" of their financial health. A Member State must borrow on the financial markets in the same way as, and in competition with, other borrowers, including large corporations. See Townsed (2007).

[27]According to Mankiw (2007) moral hazard is "the tendency of a person or entity that is imperfectly monitored to engage in undesirable behaviour.".

[28]This could be the risk if the ECB guarantees that money will always be obtainable to pay out sovereign bond holders, it could lead Governments to issue too much debt. See De Grauwe (2011).

[29]While the Treaty clearly establishes the fundamental objective of the Eurotower, it does not give a quantitative definition of what is meant by price stability. The ECB's Governing Council announced a quantitative definition of price stability in these terms: "Price stability is defined as a year-on-year increase in the Harmonized Index of Consumer Prices (HICP) for the euro area of below 2%.". See ECB (2003).

[30]De Grauwe (2009), Buiter and Rahbari (2012), Peroni (2012), Quadrio Curzio (2012), De Sousa, Papadia (2013).

monetary policy for ensuring price stability and the Euro's purchasing power, but the central hub of the European economic policy,[31] able to impose,[32] its economic recipes to the Eurozone's Countries thanks to the recourse to the conditionality method, without any effective democratic control[33] by either national Parliaments or the European one.

Traditionally, monetary policy includes balancing Parliamentary and the Government control on the one hand and the central monetary authority on the other. On the contrary, in the European Union the ECB does not have equivalent counterpart, and moreover it is not obliged to interact with national Governments. This aspect implies that political pressure is within the European context weaker than the national one.

In support of the thesis for which ECB is fundamentally free to act so to change its role becoming a "policymaker", the critics of the Eurotower's action make reference to two crucial events.[34] The first, occurred at the end of June 2015, when the Eurotower decided not to offer the Greek banking system any emergency liquidity assistance (ELA) until the celebration of *popular referendum*, wanted by Tspiras's Government, to determine whether Greece was to accept the bail out conditions proposed by the "Troika" (International Monetary Fund, EU Commission and ECB). In this case, it has been claimed that the ECB's determination represented a political decision that has nothing to do with its core function, consisting of ensuring the prices stability. On the contrary, it was considered a form of pressure on the Greek electorate in order to influence final results of the *referendum*. In other terms, the ECB has proved to be an institution free to act without reference to any democratic authority able to intervene in a democratic process of a Eurozone State.[35]

Secondly, other event could seem to confirm ECB's political intervention in the internal affairs of EU Members.[36] On this specific point, we have to remember the confidential letters sent to Italian and Spanish Governments on August 2011, were

---

[31]Torres (2013), Wilsher (2014), Braun (2015), Fontan (2014), Giannone (2015), Lombardi and Moschella (2016).

[32]Conditionality makes reference to the commitments contained within loan or grant contract that Countries in financial difficulty must adhere to if they are to receive all or part of the financial aid requested. In the case of Greek crisis, we assist to two different types of macroeconomic conditions: quantitative conditions and structural conditions. The first involved a set of economic targets influencing the level of fiscal deficit or public debt that a Government is allowed to go into. Structural conditions implied institutional and legislative reforms including deregulation, privatisation and liberalisation. See Featherstone (2015).

[33]Democratic control usually consists of monitoring and checking that the people exercise over their representatives and institutions to verify how they get and use the delegated power. In the recent years, the democratic control of the Union governance has received particular attention because it is functional to guarantee the legitimacy of the acts of the EU institutions; in other words, the justification, the acceptance of authorities and of their exercising power. On this topic, see Crum (2013).

[34]Giannone (2015).

[35]Bredt (2011), Majone (2014).

[36]Tremonti (2013).

considered as the *Manifesto* of the monetary and economic policy of ECB, demanding budget cuts and far reaching reforms in return for the purchase of Italian and Spanish bonds. Particularly, for the "Eurotower" the Italian and Spanish Governments needed to take immediate and drastic measures to ensure the sustainability of their public finance, considered the essential condition to guaranting the irreversibility of their participation to the Eurozone and to restore investors' confidence within the international and european capital market. For the ECB, said aims had to be achieved

> mainly via expenditure cuts: reducing the cost of public employees, by strengthening turnover rules and if necessary, by reducing wages and by full liberalization of public services [. . .] though a large scale of privatizations.

To pursue these economic objectives has been considered on the one hand the necessary condition for the Eurotower to purchase in the secondary market[37] sovereign Italian and Spanish bonds and on the other hand, the means for realizing a radical reform of the welfare state, public services goods and labour which is perfectly in line with the *well-known Washington consensus* economic model.[38]

The critics of the ECB's action concerned also the method suggested by the Eurotower to adopt for carrying out said policies:

> in view of the severity of the current financial market situation [. . .] all actions listed [. . .] be taken as soon as possible with decree laws followed by Parliamentary ratification.

This last passage of the letter would prove the clear determination of the ECB to transfrom national Governments into mere executors of its economic political actions without any power to propose, debate and amend laws by their respective Parliaments limiting in this way the democratic debate.

In truth, we believe that the critics moved till now to the ECB's action are in most cases specious and strongly characterised by populist traits. The ECB has succeeded, over the course of the crisis, in inserting itself, at European and national level, in almost of important economic and political decisions, becoming a "policymaker" However, the crisis has required massive sustained intervention by all central banks and the measures taken by the "Eurotower", in the EU "hour of need", have been absolutely necessary to safeguard the single currency receiving a formal investiture at European political, institutional and legal level.

Particularly, we observe how with the Treaty establishing the ESM the EU Members have given a clear mandate to ECB to negotiate the conditionality that characterises ESM's lending activity with regard to the approval of financial aid to

---

[37]Secondary markets are markets where Government securities are traded after they have been issued or sold on primary market. The secondary market is an important source of price signals and is therefore essential for the orderly funding of Government financing requirements, especially in less-developed. On the contrary, the primary market is the market where Government securities are first issued and sold, typically by means of some form of tender or auction process.

[38]See *supra*, note 14.

States in difficulty (in these terms, see Article 4, paras. 4, 5 and 6, g).[39] In the meantime, the EU Court of Justice with some important decisions,[40] considered the monetary measures taken by the ECB in line with the primary provisions established by the EU Treaties as able to restore the proper functioning of the monetary transmission mechanisms severely compromised by the crisis, in order to guarantee the unity of the monetary policy and to save the single currency.

So, we consider that the question of the lack of democracy about ECB's action is misplaced, because the Eurotower's action occurred in the light of exceptional circumstances. An extraordinary moment characterised by the presence of global financial markets players, that have currently the power to overflow and even to ignore the national borders.[41] At the moment, financial markets players are able to force national Governments and other political institutions to follow their respective diktats, even if these are contrary to the political programmes chosen by the sovereign people through democratic elections.

In other words, the ECB has become necessarily the supervisor of the national Governments in driving their political economy only when the latter have shown that they are not being able to manage the effects of the sovereign debt crisis in front of the speculative attacks moved by the financial markets.

Indeed, we think that the critics moved to ECB are essentially used for masking other crucial aspects connected to the current crisis. For example the weakness shown by other European Institutions in the managing the crisis and in trying to establish a new model of economic governance in line with the aim to realize a social market economy (see Article 3, para. 3 TEU).[42] In fact, the crisis has clearly highlighted how the markets have the power to move capitals to countries and places where they can increase their profit, with the effect that each State, for being more attractive than any other, aims at demonstrating its capacity to satisfy the requests of financial players. We are cleary in front of an "external constraint", imposed by the most important economic actors, like hedge funds, sovereignty wealth funds, multinational enterprises and investments banks essentially favoured by the lack of a set of rules at international level able to regulate financial markets effectively.[43]

At the moment, it seems that only complying with market needs States can refinance their public debt on the financial markets. This aspect inevitably raises the

---

[39]With reference to the validity of European Council Decision 2011/199/EU of 25 March 2011 amending Article 136 TFEU with regard to the introduction of ESM, see ECJ 27 November 2012, Case C-370/12, *Thomas Pringle* v. *Government of Ireland*.

[40]See in particular way ECJ 16 June 2015, Case C-62-14, *Peter Gauweiler* v. *Deutscher Bundestag*. In that occasion, the Court of Justice confirmed the legality of the OMT. Consider also that on 7 October 7 2015, the General Court of the EU issued its decision in the case of *Alessandro Accorinti and Others* v. *ECB*, and ruled that the Eurotower was not responsible for the losses of private investors resulting from the restructuring plan of Greece's public debt.

[41]We make reference, in particular way, to hedge funds, sovereign wealth funds, rating agencies. See, respectively, Paredes (2006), Bassan (2011), Gigante and Ligustro (2010).

[42]See *Strengthening Economic Governance in the EU*, Report of the Task Force to the European Council, 21 October 2010; Blanke (2011).

[43]Gari (2014).

crucial question of the temporal dimension of the different interests involved. In fact, in most cases the interest of financial operations is clearly in contrast with those of modern democracy usually founded on the scrutiny of their respective Parliaments. Markets are usually looking for short-term private earnings, and normally operate according to mere selfish logic, while Governments have the duty to define and implement reforms that requires long time to be understood and accepted by their citizens. Nevertheless, not infrequently Governments are induced to adopt immediately, on the basis of conditions of urgency and necessity, as happened during the crisis, specific economic policies, to please the markets even when it is clear that these policies do not match the real and general interests of the Nation.

The approval of fiscal measures that can have a particular impact on the life of people, like occurred, for example, in Italy with the introduction of the reform of pension system (with the so called "Legge Fornero"),[44] require time and involve debates, round tables, conferences, meetings and discussions that in any modern democracy are essential. But, all that increases uncertainty about the final outcome and thus induces markets players to rapidly liquidate their financial investments.

This occurred, particularly, in Greece in the Summer of 2015, during the period of Tsipras *referendum*. We assisted to a strong increase in the budget deficit, public debt and the need for an even larger support package. Probably, the total cost of funding to Greece would have been lower, if the decisions of its Government had been taken more quickly.

This is the context in which the ECB has had to act. In addition, we have to remember that the national Parliaments and Governments of the Members of the Eurozone decided with the signature of Maastricth Treaty to transfer their control over monetary policy without giving any authority in this area to the European Parliament (EP). Inevitably, the ECB is free to operate in a European political *vacuum*, without any European institutions able to balance its powers (with the only exception of the European Court of Justice),[45] and in the absence of an effective mechanism able to prevent the market speculative attacks to sovereign debt of State.[46]

---

[44]See Law 28 June 2012, No. 92 ("Disposizioni in materia di riforma del mercato del lavoro in una prospettiva di crescita"), GURI No. 153, 3 July 2012.

[45]According to Article 263 TFEU "The Court of Justice of the European Union shall review the legality of legislative acts, of acts [. . .] of the European Central Bank intended to produce legal effects vis-à-vis third parties.".

[46]On the legal effects depending on State's default, see Malaguti (2011), Frigo (2012), Tanzi (2012).

4 Improving the ECB's Transparency and Accountability, Defending Its Independence

It is a general principle of democracy that any entity or person with an authoritative power, whose exercise can produce effects on the population, must be considered accountable for its actions in front of its community. But, on the one hand, if the technical and complex issues of monetary policy require that the ECB must be independent[47] from any form of political influence,[48] on the other hand, the ECB can not be considered free of responsibility towards European citizens who can endure, the effects of its monetary decisions.

Particularly, it has been noted that ECB, differently from what happens for other monetary authorities, has a double form of independence with reference to the fundamental target of price stability: goal independence (Governments, usually, fix the politically acceptable level of inflation) and the instrument independence (Governments usually leave free the monetary authority to decide how best to achieve the inflation target). The said double independence would be at the basis of the issue of the lack of democracy concerning the ECB's action. Thus, in order to solve that issue, the Eurotower should "evolve towards a governance model excluding goal independence.".[49]

In the light of the current situation, we believe that the democratic legitimacy of the ECB's action cannot be satisfied by the exclusion of the ECB from the quantitative determination of the rate of inflation, even if a specific inflation target set with the "contribution" of the other EU institutions (especially, the EU Commission and the EU Parliament) could better define the ECB's mandate.

In truth, we consider that a strengthened accountability of the Eurotower which implies a deep reform regarding the transparency of the decision-of its managing board could be the "key" to make the ECB's action more acceptable to EU citizens.[50] In fact, the accumulation of influence and power at ECB level has not been matched by significant improvements in the transparency and accountability of its decisions. In these terms, the Eurotower seems to lack of the good practices implemented by its central banking peers around the World, with particular reference to the publication of meeting minutes and voting records; the external independent membership of boards and a strong parliamentary oversight.[51]

---

[47]On the independence of ECB, see Hayat, Farvaque (2012), Beukers (2013).

[48]It is a common opinion that central banks need to be credible in front the market players to carry out effectively their function. Fort this reason, the said credibility is best achieved trough transparency of its actions and independence from Governments.

[49]In said terms, see Gormley and de Hann (1996), Majone (2010).

[50]On the profile of accountability applied to the ECB, see Kaltenthaler and Miller (2010), Mény (2014), Wandersman (2014).

[51]See the Report "*Transparency International. The global coalition against corruption. Improving the accountability and transparency of the European Central Bank*", available at www.transaprencyinetrnational.eu.

Central banks, in order to carry out their functions effectively, need to be credible in front of market actors and the general public. For this reason, it is a general opinion, that their credibility is best achieved through independence from any form of political influence and the transparency of its operations. Transparency applied to central banks should cover a wide range of issues, concerning above all the econometric targets, models and the effectiveness of monetary instruments used, the way and the reasons by which monetary decisions are taken.[52] The release of minutes and voting records could be a good way to ensure transparency[53]; but, at the EU level, this is a method, at the moment, not considered, according to Article 10, para. 4, of Protocol No. 4 on the Statute of ESCB and ECB.

Transparency at ECB level should also include prompt announcement of policy decisions and indications of likely future policy actions through formal and public records of the decision making process without providing explanations of monetary policy decisions at press conference or in monthly bulletin. In this context particular attention could be paid on ECB rules about public access to documents. Indeed, this is a very sensitive issue, because Article 15 TFEU establishes that the ECB is subject to transparency, but only in the exercise of its administrative duties. These said limitation, clearly acceptable when a publication of a document could damage the financial stability of the EU or a Member State, in the other cases, can ensure the ECB a certain power of discretion on which documents to release.

As regards the accountability, usually considered as the counterpart of independence from political pressure in monetary decision-making recognised to monetary authorities, the ECB should be not considered different from any other public authority. In other terms, if it is fundamental to preserve central bank officials from rushed dismissal or other forms of pressure simply by taking decisions that are not in line with politician determinations; it is also important to strengthen the parliamentary oversight. On this aspect, the ECB is currently accountable to the EP, through the "monetary policy dialogues" with Members of the EP Economic and Monetary Policy Committee.[54]Specifically, the Eurotower must respond to written questions from EP Members and "Strasbourg" has the right to request hearings with ECB's Members Executive Board (see Article 284, para. 3, TFEU and Article 15, para. 3, of Protocol No. 4). It also presents its annual report to Parliament. But, a stronger oversight powers should be granted to the EP foreseeing, for example, that membership should be subject to its approval, favoring as much as possible external membership, in order to strengthen the accountability of its boards. In addition, parliamentary control should imply the possibility to conduct investigations, to scrutinise operational budgets and to dismiss Board Members in cases of malpractices.

All that, without obviously any intention to be exhaustive, can contribute to reduce the distance between the Eurotower and EU citizens and avoid the ECB

[52]See Dai (2016).

[53]For a different perspective, see Bini Smaghi and Gros (2001).

[54]Amtenbrink and van Duin (2009).

being considered a technocratic institution able to rule all EU Member States. Besides, it could be possible to give an effective fulfillment to Article 13 TEU that inserted the European Central Bank in the circuit of EU Institutions. This last provision, introduced with the Lisbon Treaty, has not only solved the issue about the legal nature of ECB, but, above all it has been allowed the Eurotower not to be longer considered an "external body" with respect to the european institutional architecture.

The reforms, briefly suggested, aim at favoring ECB's action in solving the Eurocrisis, without forgetting that the Euroepan Union is still far from having the features of a Federal State. It follows, that any reform concerning, in particular way, fiscal policy, is doomed to affect deeply the States' sovereignty, raising inevitably new crucial legal issues.

References

Almunia M et al (2009) From great depression to great credit crisis: similarities, differences and lessons. National Bureau of Economic Research, Cambridge

Amtenbrink F, van Duin K (2009) The European Central Bank before the European parliament: theory and practice after 10 years of monetary dialogue. Eur Law Rev 34:561–583

Arndt H (1996) Zur Frage der Legitimität der Europäischen Zentralbankautonomie. In: Maure A, Thiele B (eds) Legitimationsprobleme und Demokratisierung der Europäischen union. Schüren Presseverlag, Marburg, pp 208–228

Athanassiou P (2009) Withdrawal and Expulsion from the EU and EMU: Some Reflections. ECB Legal Working Paper Series, 10:1–43

Baratta R (2012) Legal issues of the fiscal compact. Searching for a mature democratic governance of the Euro. Il Diritto dell'Unione Europea 4:647–681

Bassan F (2011) The law of sovereign wealth funds. Edward Elgar, Cheltenham-Northampton

Bassan F (2015) Il parametro di legittimità delle misure non convenzionali della BCE. Banca Impresa Società 2:173–198

Beukers T (2013) The new ECB and its relationship with the Eurozone member states: between central bank independence and central bank intervention. Common Mark Law Rev 50:1579–1620

Bini Smaghi L, Gros D (2001) Is the ECB accountable and transparent? Enepri, Working Paper No. 7

Blanke HJ (2011) The European economic and monetary union. Between vulnerability and reform. Int J Public Law Policy 1(4):402–433

Braun B (2015) Governing the future: the European Central Bank's expectation management during the great moderation. Econ Soc 44:367–391

Bredt S (2011) Prospects and limits of democratic governance in the EU. Eur Law J 17:35–65

Buiter WH, Rahbari E (2012) The ECB as Lender of Last Resort for Sovereigns in the Euro Area. CEPR Discussion Paper Series, No. 8974

Cafaro S (2013) L'azione della BCE nella crisi dell'area dell'euro alla luce del diritto dell'Unione europea. In: Adinolfi G, Vellano M (eds) La crisi del debito sovrano degli Stati dell'area euro. Profili giuridici. Giappichelli, Torino, pp 55–63

Christodoulakis NM (2015) How crises shaped economic ideas and policies: wiser after the events? Springer, Princeton

Cisotta R, Viterbo A (2012) La crisi del debito sovrano e gli interventi dell'UE: dai primi strumenti finanziari al "fiscal compact". Il Diritto dell'Unione Europea 2:323–366

Closa C, Maatsch A (2014) In a Spirit of solidarity? Justifying the European financial stability facility (EFSF) in National Parliamentary Debates. J Common Mark Stud 52:826–842
Contaldi GL (2014) Politica Economica e Monetaria (Diritto dell'Unione europea). Enciclopedia del Diritto (Voce degli Annali VII) 825–827
Craig P (2012) The stability, coordination and governance treaty: principle, policy and pragmatism. Eur Law Rev 37:231–248
Crum B (2013) Saving the Euro at the cost of democracy. J Common Mark Stud 51:614–630
Dai M (2016) Static and dynamic effect of central bank transparency. Bull Econ Res 68:55–78
Dammann JC (2013) The right to leave the Eurozone. Texas Int Law J 48:125–155
De Grauwe P (2009) Economia dell'Unione monetaria? Il Mulino, Bologna
De Grauwe P (2010) Crisis in the Eurozone and how to deal with it. CEPS Policy Brief
De Grauwe P (2011) Only a more active ECB can solve the Euro crisis. CEPS Policy Brief
De Haan J (2005) The European Central Bank: credibility, transparency and centralization. Mit Press, Cambridge
De Pasquale P (2014) L'economia sociale di mercato nell'Unione europea. Studi sull'integrazione europea 2:265–278
De Sousa C, Papadia F (2013) Has the European Central Bank transformed itself into a hedge funds? www.bruegel.org, 8 March 2013
De Witte B (2011) The European treaty amendement for the creation of a financial stability mechanism. Eur Policy An 6:1-8
ECB Montlhy Bulletin, June 2003, pp 85 et seqq
ECB Monthly Bulletin, September 2012, pp 3 et seqq
Eichegreen B (2013) BCE: parole forti come azioni. Il Sole 24 Ore. 14 August 2013
Eser F, Schwaab B (2013) Evaluating the impact of unconventional monetary policy measures: empirical evidence from the ECB's securities markets program. J Financ Econ 119:147–167
Fabbrini F (2014) The Euro crisis and the courts: judicial review and political process. comparative perspective. Berkley J Int Law 32.64–123
Featherstone K (2015) External conditionality and the debt crisis: the "troika" and public administration reform in Greece. J Eur Public Policy 22:295–314
Fontan C (2014) The European Central Bank and the crisis: who decides what? Pouvoirs: Revue d'Etudes constitutionnelles et politiques 149:91–100
Frigo M (2012) Insolvenza delle imprese e insolvenza degli Stati: analogie ed elementi di differenziazione. Rivista di diritto internazionale privato e processuale 4:865–878
Gari G (2014) GATS disciplines on capital transfers and short-term capital inflows: time for change? J Int Econ Law 17:399–435
Giannone D (2015) Suspending democracy? The governance of the EU's political and economic crisis as a process of neoliberal restructuring. In: Kyriakos ND (ed) The European Union in crisis: explorations in representation and democratic legitimacy. Springer, London, pp 105–119
Gigante A, Ligustro A (2010) Il diritto internazionale degli investimenti alla sfida dei fondi sovrani. Diritto pubblico comparato ed europeo 34:1179–1221
Goodhart C (2007) Currency unions: some lessons from the Euro-zone. Atl Econ J 35:1–21
Gormley LW, de Hann J (1996) The democratic deficit of the European Centrak Bank. Eur Law Rev 5:95–111
Gros D, Mayer T (2010) How to deal with sovereign default in Europe: towards a European monetary fund. CEPS Policy Brief
Gross SG, Gummer SC (2014) Ghost of the hasburg empire. Collapsing currency unions and lessons for the Eurozone. East Eur Polit Soc 28:252–265
Hahn HJ (1998) The stability pact for European monetary union: compliance with deficit limits a constant legal duty. Common Mark Law Rev 77–100
Harold J (2012) Making the European monetary union: the role of the committee of central bank governors and the origins of the European Central Bank. Princeton University Press, Priceton

Hayat MA, Farvaque E (2012) Public attitudes towards central bank independence: lessons from the foundation of the ECB. Eur J Polit Econ 35:512–523
Hofmeister H (2011) Goodbye Euro: legal aspects of withdrawal from the Eurozone. Columb J Eur Law 18:111–134
Jordà O et al (2016) Sovereigns versus banks: credit, crises, and consequences. J Eur Econ Assoc 14:45–79
Kaltenthaler K, Miller CJ (2010) Accountability and independent central banks: Europeans and distrust of the European Central Bank. J Common Mark Stud 48:1261–1281
Kontochristou M, Masha E (2014) The Euro crisis and the question of solidarity in the European Union: disclosures and manifestations in the European Press. Rev Eur Stud 6:50–62
Krugman P (2009) The return of depression economics and the crisis of 2008. Norton, New York
Laffan B, Schlosser P (2016) Public finances in Europe: fortifying EU economic governance in the shadow of the crisis. J Eur Integr 38:237–249
Lombardi D, Moschella M (2016) The government bond buying programs of the European Central Bank: an analysis of their policy settings. J Eur Public Policy 23:851–870
Louis JV (2007) The legal foundations of the SGP in primary and secondary EC law. In: Bresuss F (ed) The stability and growth pact: experiences and future aspects. Springer, Berlin
Majone G (2010) Transaction-cost efficiency and the democratic deficit. J Eur Public Policy 150–175
Majone G (2014) From regulatory state to a democratic default. J Common Mark Stud 52:1216–1223
Malaguti MC (2011) Se a fallire sono gli Stati. In: Ligustro A, Sacerdoti G (eds) Problemi e tendenze del diritto internazionale dell'economia. Liber amicorum in onore di Paolo Picone. Editoriale Scientifica, Napoli, pp 213–230
Malatesta A (2003) La Banca Centrale Europea. Gli aspetti istituzionali della banca centrale della Comunità europea. Giuffrè, Milano
Mankiw G (2007) Principles of economics. Thompson South Western, Boston
Markan JW (2015) A financial history of the United States from Eron's scandal to the great recession 2004–2009. Routdlege, New York
Mény Y (2014) Managing the EU crises: another way of integration by stealth? West Eur Polit 37:1336–1353
Mostacci E (2009) Stati finanziari e mercati sovrani: la crisi economica e gli strumenti per fronteggiarla. Diritto pubblico comparato ed europeo, 3:305–324
Napoletano G (2012) La risposta europea alla crisi del debito sovrano: il rafforzamento dell'Unione economica e monetaria. Verso l'Unione bancaria. Banca borsa e titoli di credito 16:747–765
Pace LF (2014) La crisi del sistema euro (2009–2013): cause, fasi, players e soluzioni. Studi in onore di Giuseppe Tesauro, Napoli, pp 2152 et seqq
Paredes TA (2006) On the decision to regulate hedge funds: the SEC's regulatory philosophy style and mission. Washington U. School of Law Working Paper No. 06-03-02
Peel Q (2010) Paris and Berlin at odds over default system. Financial Times, 26 Oct 2010
Peroni G (2012) La crisi dell'Euro: limiti e rimedi dell'Unione economica e monetaria. Giuffrè, Milano
Peroni G (2013) L'azione dell'Unione europea in campo sociale e la crisi economica. In: Daniele L et al (eds) Il Trattato di Lisbona: due anni d'applicazione. Editoriale Scientifica, Napoli, pp 409–424
Peroni G (2015) Il recesso dall'euro: una via percorribile, ma non auspicabile. Studi sull'integrazione europea 85–108
Peroni G (2016) Il difficile equilibrio tra austerità e solidarietà nell'Unione economica e monetaria. In: Mascia M, Velo F (eds) L'Unione economica europea: aspetti economici, sociali e istituzionali. Cacucci, Bari, pp. 73-82

Peroni G (2017) The constitutionalization of the Washington consensus in the European Union: like giving up the social market economy. In: Sciso E (ed) Transparency and democracy in The Bretton Woods Institutions. Springer-Giappichelli, London-Turin
Quadrio Curzio A (2012) Economia oltre la crisi. La Scuola, Brescia
Rosenthal J (2012) Germany and the Euro crisis: is the powerhouse really so pure? Available at www.worldaffairs.journal.org
Rossi LS (2012) Fiscal compact e Trattato sul Meccanismo di Stabilità: aspetti istituzionali e conseguenze dell'integrazione differenziata nell'UE. Il Diritto dell'Unione Europea 2:293–307
Roubini N, Uzan M (2005) International financial crisis and the new international financial architecture. Edward Elgar, Cheltenham-Northampton
Starita M (2013) Il Consiglio europeo e la crisi del debito sovrano. Rivista di diritto internazionale 2:385–423
Szczerbowicz U (2015) The ECB unconventional monetary policies: have they lowered market borrowing costs for banks and governments? Int J Central Bank 8:91–127
Tanzi A (2012) Sull'insolvenza degli Stati nel diritto internazionale. Rivista di diritto internazionale 1:66–88
Torres FS (2013) The EMU's legitimacy and the ECB as a strategic political player in the crisis context. J Eur Int 35:287–300
Tosato GL (2012) L'integrazione europea ai tempi dell'euro. Rivista di diritto internazionale 3:681–703
Townsed M (2007) The Euro and EMU. An historical institutional and economic description. John Harper Publishing, London
Tremonti G (2013) Quella lettera della banca Centrale diktat che violò le regole europee. Corriere della Sera. 25 July 2013
Villata FC (2013) Osservazioni alla ristrutturazione del debito sovrano greco nel 2012: tra accordi di scelta di legge e nuove regole europee sugli strumenti derivati. Rivista di diritto internazionale privato e processuale 2:325–356
Viterbo A, Costamagna F (2013) L'impatto sociale della politica di condizionalità nel contesto della crisi dell'euro. In: Napoletano G, Saccucci A (eds) Gestione internazionale delle emergenze globali. Regole e valori. Editoriale Scientifica, Napoli, pp 163 et seqq
Viterbo A (2014) I meccanismi per la risoluzione delle crisi del debito sovrano: alla ricerca di un difficile bilanciamento tra interessi pubblici e privati. Diritti umani e diritto internazionale 23:351–370
Wandersman A (2014) Moving forward with the science and practice of evaluation capacity building (ECB): the why, how, what, and outcomes of ECB. Am J Eval 35:87-89
Weeks J (2014) Euro crisis and Euro scams: trade non debt and deficits tell the tale. Rev Polit Econ 26:171–189
Wilsher D (2014) Law and the financial crisis: searching for Europe's new gold standard. Eur Law J 20:241–283
Zilioli C, Selmayr M (2007) La Banca centrale europea. Giuffrè, Milano

Part III
The EMU and the Banking System

Financial Challenges to Solidarity: Building the European Banking Union in Times of Crisis

Annamaria Viterbo

Abstract The purpose of this chapter is to single out the features of the European Banking Union that are most problematic to achieve solidarity among Member States. The focus will be on three elements of the European Banking Union where solidarity proves particularly difficult to be achieved: the Single Resolution Fund, the direct recapitalisation instrument of the European Stability Mechanism and the European Deposit Insurance Scheme.

Contents

1 Introduction

The full realisation of the European Banking Union is faltering and, without solidarity, it will remain a half-way system unable to achieve its objectives.

Solidarity has always been a founding value of European integration. In the words of Robert Schuman "*L'Europe ne se fera pas d'un coup ni dans une construction d'ensemble: elle se fera pour des réalisations concrètes, créant d'abord une solidarité de fait*."[1] In the 1980s, Jacques Delors defined his idea of Europe listing the three cornerstones of the Union: "Competition that stimulates,

[1]Schuman (1950) Déclaration Schuman, 9 May 1950.

A. Viterbo (✉)
International Law, Department of Law, University of Turin, Turin, Italy

Collegio Carlo Alberto Law Affiliate, Turin, Italy
e-mail: anna.viterbo@unito.it

L. Daniele et al. (eds.), *Democracy in the EMU in the Aftermath of the Crisis*,
DOI 10.1007/978-3-319-53895-2_14

cooperation that strengthens, and solidarity that unites".[2] The principle acquired even more prominence with the Treaty of Lisbon, with its meaning formally broadened to include also solidarity among generations (see Articles 2 and 3 TEU, as well as Title V of the Charter of Fundamental Rights of the European Union).

Three different dimensions of solidarity can be identified: solidarity among Member States, solidarity between Member States and individuals subject to their jurisdiction, and inter-generational solidarity.[3] This article focuses on solidarity among States, which in the EU Treaties is strictly linked to the reciprocity principle.

In the aftermath of the financial crisis, inter-State solidarity helped avoid the worst, contributing to structure the new European economic governance, although not without tensions. Some Member States and political parties feared that the creation of a Banking Union would ultimately lead to a transfer union, with wealthier Countries like France or Germany forced to provide financial support to economically weaker ones like Greece.

Tension was partially caused by the different scope of the meaning given to the concept of solidarity across Europe.[4] In southern Countries solidarity entails helping people in need regardless of the circumstances, while in northern Countries, to prevent moral hazard, help should only be provided when deserved and under strict conditions.

Germany in particular continues to condition financial burden-sharing to structural reforms and austerity measures. In December 2015, Angela Merkel, commending the Country's Minister of Finance Wolfgang Schaeuble for his role during the Greek negotiations, reminded that the German Government standards were and still are: "No aid without conditionality. Responsibility and solidarity go together and it must remain this way".[5]

George Soros predicted that Germany's fear of becoming the deep pocket of Europe would be fatal for the European Union: "Germany is afraid of becoming the deep pocket of Europe in a transfer union. That attitude has been fatal for the European Union. If you think about normal nation-states, every country is in some sense a 'transfer union'. It is always the more-productive, more-successful parts of a country that have to support the less-developed regions."[6]

A solidarity mechanism which makes assistance to other Countries mandatory certainly interferes with critical national sovereignty aspects. It follows that a clear definition of the criteria for its activation is of the utmost importance. Neither

---

[2]Delors (2003), p. 462.

[3]Domurath (2013), Hilpold (2015), Ross (2010), Sangiovanni (2013). Over the years, forms of transnational solidarity have emerged, as mobile EU citizens seek access to social benefits in a host Member State: see de Witte (2015).

[4]Dammann (2014), p. 1066.

[5]Merkel (2015).

[6]Soros and Schmitz (2014), p. 40.

overly strict criteria nor relaxed standards can contribute to the achievement of solidarity purposes. In fact, while extreme austerity may undermine the effects of solidarity, the opposite may lead some States to threaten the withdrawal of their support fearing that an endless call for support would be triggered.[7]

We can therefore agree with Lorenzo Bini-Smaghi: "The search for the correct balance between providing adequate support to those in need and avoiding moral hazard represents today the most complex point of the European political debate."[8]

Before addressing the features of the European Banking Union standing in the way of an effective achievement of solidarity among Member States, it is worth to briefly describe its structure.

The European Banking Union (EBU) is made up of three pillars.[9]

The first pillar is represented by the Single Supervisory Mechanism (SSM),[10] under which the European Central Bank (ECB) became the central prudential supervisor for the most significant banks, with national supervisors continuing to monitor the remaining banks. Not all EU Member States take part in the SSM, as participation is mandatory only for Euro area Countries. Non-Euro Countries, however, may enter into "close cooperation agreements" with the ECB.[11]

The second pillar is represented by the Single Resolution Mechanism (SRM), which establishes uniform rules and procedures for the resolution of failing credit institutions.

The SRM Regulation[12] concerns banks covered by the SSM and, like the SSM, it includes all banks in the Euro area, with other States eligible to join. Its purpose is

---

[7]On solidarity within the European Monetary Union see Hilpold (2015), p. 15.

[8]Bini-Smaghi (2015).

[9]Baglioni (2016), Baroncelli (2014), Bush and Ferrarini (2015), de Witte (2013, 2015),. Hinojosa-Martinez and Beneyto (2015), Lastra (2013) and Pugliese (2014).

[10]The SSM founding texts consist of a Regulation that confers supervisory tasks on the ECB and an amended Regulation on the European Banking Authority: Council Regulation (EU) No. 1024/2013 conferring specific tasks on the European Central Bank concerning policies relating to the prudential supervision of credit institutions, OJEU L 287, 29 October 2013, pp. 63 et seqq.; Regulation (EU) No. 1022/2013 of the European Parliament and of the Council of 22 October 2013 amending Regulation (EU) No. 1093/2010 establishing a European Supervisory Authority (European Banking Authority) as regards the conferral of specific tasks on the European Central Bank pursuant to Council Regulation (EU) No. 1024/2013, OJEU L 287, 29 October 2013, pp. 5 et seqq.

[11]The main conditions for the establishment of a close cooperation between the ECB and the competent authorities of a Member State whose currency is not the Euro are defined in Article 7 of the SSM Regulation, while the procedural aspects are set out in a decision adopted by the ECB (Decision of the European Central Bank of 31 January 2014 on the close cooperation with the national competent authorities of participating Member States whose currency is not the Euro (Decision ECB/2014/5)).

[12]Regulation (EU) No. 806/2014 of the European Parliament and of the Council of 15 July 2014 establishing uniform rules and a uniform procedure for the resolution of credit institutions and certain investment firms in the framework of a Single Resolution Mechanism and a Single Resolution Fund and amending Regulation (EU) No. 1093/2010, OJEU L 225, 30 July 2014, pp. 1 et seqq.

to ensure a timely and orderly resolution of failing banks, limiting the costs borne by taxpayers, further developing the principles contained in the Bank Recovery and Resolution Directive (BRRD), which applies across the EU.[13] The SRM has been fully operational since 1 January 2016.

When, in spite of stronger EU supervision, a bank is likely to fail, the Single Resolution Board (SRB) decides whether and when to place the bank into resolution *status*, defining the course of action to be followed. These measures are financed by the Single Resolution Fund (SRF) once all other options, including bail-in, have been adopted.

The third pillar is still under construction. The European Commission has recently put forward a proposal for a European Deposit Insurance Scheme (EDIS),[14] aimed at providing greater and uniform protection of depositors throughout the Euro area. The EDIS will consist of a common fund collecting contributions from banks in EBU Countries. Should a bank fail, its depositors across the EU would be protected up to a defined (harmonised) amount by national deposit guarantee schemes.[15]

These three pillars rest on a set of legislative acts (the so-called single rulebook) mandatory for all financial institutions in the EU and are not just limited to banks operating in euro area countries. These acts are intended to create a level-playing field in financial services, harmonising capital requirements standards, national deposit guarantee schemes and bank recovery and resolution procedures.[16]

The next paragraphs focus on the areas in which solidarity proved particularly difficult to be achieved: (1) the functioning of the Single Resolution Fund within the SRM; (2) the functioning of the Direct Recapitalisation Instrument of the European Stability Mechanism (DRI); and (3) the set-up of a pan-European Deposit Insurance Scheme (EDIS).

---

[13]Directive 2014/59/EU of the European Parliament and of the Council of 15 May 2014 establishing a framework for the recovery and resolution of credit institutions and investment firms and amending Council Directive 82/891/EEC, and Directives 2001/24/EC, 2002/47/EC, 2004/25/EC, 2005/56/EC, 2007/36/EC, 2011/35/EU, 2012/30/EU and 2013/36/EU, and Regulations (EU) No. 1093/2010 and (EU) No. 648/2012, of the European Parliament and of the Council, OJEU L 173, 12 June 2014, pp. 190 et seqq.

[14]European Commission, Proposal for a Regulation of the European Parliament and of the Council amending Regulation (EU) No. 806/2014 in order to establish a European Deposit Insurance Scheme (COM/2015/0586 final).

[15]Directive 2014/49/EU of the European Parliament and of the Council of 16 April 2014 on deposit guarantee schemes, OJEU L 173, 12 June 2014, pp. 149 et seqq.

[16]The single rulebook includes the BRRD and the deposit guarantee schemes Directives mentioned above as well as: Regulation (EU) No. 575/2013 of the European Parliament and of the Council of 26 June 2013 on prudential credit requirements for credit institutions and investment firms and amending Regulation (EU) No. 648/2012, OJEU L 176, 27 June 2013, pp. 1 et seqq.; and Directive 2013/36/EU of the European Parliament and of the Council of 26 June 2013 on access to the activity of credit institutions and the prudential supervision of credit institutions and investment firms, amending Directive 2002/87/EC and repealing Directives 2006/48/EC and 2006/49/EC, OJEU L 176, 27 June 2013, pp. 338 et seqq.

2 Solidarity Within the Single Resolution Mechanism: The Functioning of the Single Resolution Fund

The SRM Regulation ensures the orderly restructuring of failing banks operating under the Single Supervisory Mechanism.[17] After all other financing sources—including bail-in[18]—have been exhausted, resolution is financed by the Single Resolution Fund (SRF), with a view to limit resort to taxpayers' money. Decisions on resolution schemes and on the use of SRF's resources are taken by the Single Resolution Board (SRB).

The SRF is not intended to replace private investors in absorbing losses and in providing new capital to a bank, but its backing support is essential since it enables a bank (either in its original form, by means of a bridge bank or through an asset management vehicle) to continue to operate while it is being restructured. In the short to the medium-term, the Fund provides guarantees or loans to a bank being restructured, restoring its full business viability while at same time safeguarding the Euro area financial stability.[19]

As set forth by the SRM Regulation, the SRF is directly financed by *ex ante* contributions from the banking sector: all credit institutions within the scope of the mechanism contribute to the Fund in accordance to their size and risk profile.[20]

One of the key issues during negotiations revolved around the most appropriate way to provide adequate funding to the SRF. Another item of discussion, no less contentious, concerned the achievement of a smooth transition from the existing national resolution funds to the SRF, pooling national contributions while gradually increasing mutualisation of their usage.

The adoption of an intergovernmental agreement was made necessary because some Member States, concerned about their budgetary sovereignty, maintained that the imposition of an obligation to mutualise resolution funds would require amending the EU Treaties.[21]

---

[17]The SRM is fully operational since 1 January 2016.

[18]A bail-in occurs when a bank's investors are forced to bear some of the burden by having a portion of their holdings written off to avoid bankruptcy.

[19]Fabbrini (2014), Zavvos and Kaltsoumi (2015), p. 140; Gortsos (2015), Huhtaniemi et al. (2015), p. 114.

[20]See Council Implementing Regulation (EU) No. 2015/81 of 19 December 2014 specifying uniform conditions of application of Regulation (EU) No. 806/2014 of the European Parliament and of the Council with regard to ex ante contributions to the Single Resolution Fund, OJEU L 15, 22 January 2015, pp. 1 et seqq.

[21]See de Witte (2013); Fabbrini (2014); Kern (2015), p. 176; Moloney (2014), p. 1658. See also the legal opinion delivered by the Council Legal Service: Council, Opinion of the Legal Service, 2013/0253 (COD), 13524/13, LIMITE, JUR 458, ECOFIN 787; and European Parliament Committee on Economic and Monetary Affairs, Letter to the Council Presidency of the EU regarding the intergovernmental agreement negotiated within the framework of the SRM Regulation, 15 January 2014.

The creation of a supranational fund was deemed crucial for the correct functioning of the SRM. If the cost involved in a bank's resolution were to remain national, the link between sovereigns and the banking sector would not be fully severed, and investors' behaviour would continue to be influenced by the fiscal position of the State where the bank is established rather than to its creditworthiness.

The Agreement on the transfer and mutualisation of contributions to the SRF (SRF Agreement)[22] details how bank contributions are collected by national authorities and how they are gradually pooled at Union level during an 8-year transition period.

Only in 2024 the Fund is expected to reach the target level of €55 billion (estimated to be equivalent to 1% of covered deposits of all credit institutions authorised in the Banking Union), a sum which nevertheless appears to be inadequate when considering that the Euro area banking sector is worth €22 trillion.[23] Legitimate concerns were therefore expressed that the SRF would not be able to withstand a major banking crisis.

Capacity constraints are even more likely in the initial years, as the Fund will be structured in separate national compartments. Pursuant to Article 4 of the SRF Agreement, contributions levied on banks at domestic level are kept by the Fund in separate "national compartments". These compartments will only be used for the resolution of institutions established or authorised in the contributing State.

National compartments will be gradually abandoned to shift to a system in which contributions from all compartments may be used, irrespective of their origin or of the Country where the banks in distress is authorised to operate.

When the funds of a compartment are insufficient to finance a particular resolution, Article 7 of the SRF Agreement envisions the possibility of temporary transfers among national compartments.

In spite of the above, solidarity is difficult to be achieved. In fact, the Agreement contains a number of safeguards. For instance, a State may reject lending requests on different grounds: when a transfer request exceeds a given threshold, when a Member State is going to face other resolutions in the near future, or when the receiving Member State cannot provide sufficient guarantees of repayment (Article 7.4 of the SRF Agreement).

Even the most recent developments are showing lack of political will and of a common vision. To avoid funding shortfalls as well as loans among national compartments, in December 2015 Member States agreed to put in place a system

[22]Agreement on the transfer and mutualisation of contributions to the SRF (Council Document 8457/14, ECOFIN 342), available at http://register.consilium.europa.eu/doc/srv?l=EN&fST%208457%202014%20INIT. The Agreement was signed on 21 May 2014 by all EU Member States except Sweden and the United Kingdom, and ratified by all Euro area Member States by December 2015, with Luxembourg joining on 11 January 2016. The obligation to transfer the contributions raised at domestic level to the SRF does not derive from EU law. Besides, the Agreement affirms that all the rights and obligations laid down in its articles are valid provided that the principle of reciprocity is respected (see recital 20 of the Preamble).

[23]See IMF (2015), p. 18, which also advocated for an acceleration in the mutualisation of national compartments from the planned eight-year transition period. See also IMF (2013).

of public bridge financing arrangements for the transitional period, committing to back their national compartments through loans to the SRB.[24]

In practice, by the end of 2016, each participating Member State will enter into harmonised Loan Facility Agreements with the SRB in order to provide a national credit line to the latter. These national credit lines will be used to back national compartments in the SRF in the case of funding shortfalls stemming from the resolution of banks within the Member State concerned. Banks operating in the requesting Member State will be ultimately liable for the repayment of the amounts withdrawn from the credit line.

EBU Member States also acknowledged that the current set-up does not entirely eliminate the risk that public funding may be required for bank resolution operations. For this reason, they agreed to develop a common backstop to temporary mutualise fiscal risk to be used only as a last resort measure.[25] However, to sever the bank-sovereign link, the common backstop to the SRF will have to be fiscally neutral in the medium term: public funds will be reimbursed over time by banks via *ex post* contributions to the SRF. The mechanism is expected to be fully operational at the latest by the end of the transitional period, at the end of 2023.

Nevertheless, heated debate over the new system of bridge financing and the common fiscal backstop makes it clear that Euro area Member States are not ready to share risk, not even on a temporary basis. Consequently, it is reasonable to assume that full and effective solidarity within the SRM pillar of the Banking Union will take far more than the 8 years initially planned.

3 Solidarity Within the European Stability Mechanism: The Direct Recapitalisation Instrument

Another tool through which Euro area Member States may implement solidarity is the Direct Recapitalisation Instrument (DRI) of the European Stability Mechanism (ESM).[26]

[24]Statement of the ECOFIN Ministers on Banking Union and bridge financing arrangements for the Single Resolution Fund of 8 December 2015. In December 2013 Member States had already committed to put in place a bridge financing mechanism to back national compartments in case of funding shortfalls during the transition period (see Statement of the Eurogroup and of the ECOFIN Ministers of 18 December 2013). See also: Five Presidents' Report (2015), p. 11.

[25]Statement of the ECOFIN Ministers on Banking Union and bridge financing arrangements for the Single Resolution Fund of 8 December 2015. See also Statement of Eurogroup and Ecofin Ministers on the SRM backstop, 18 December 2013, http://www.consilium.europa.eu/en/council-eu/eurogroup/pdf/20131218-SRM-backstop-statement_pdf.

[26]The ESM is the permanent crisis resolution mechanism for the Euro area Countries. It provides financial assistance to Member States experiencing, or threatened by, severe financing problems. The Treaty establishing the ESM was originally signed by Finance Ministers of the 17 Euro area Countries on 11 July 2011. However, a modified version of the Treaty, incorporating amendments aimed at improving the effectiveness of the mechanism, was signed in Brussels on 2 February 2012. The ESM Treaty entered into force on 27 September 2012. The current version of the Treaty, amended following the accession of Latvia and Lithuania to the ESM, entered into force on 3 February 2015.

The origins of the DRI stem from the 2008 European financial crisis, when a number of banks in distress had to be recapitalised by the States in which they operated.[27] As a common resolution framework did not exist at the time (and until the entry into force of the 2014 BRRD Directive[28]), the recapitalisation of banks was considered a national problem. Bail-outs were mainly financed with taxpayers' money, increasing the vicious circle between banks and sovereigns.

Moreover, in the cases of Ireland and Spain, the costs of national recapitalisation proved to be particularly burdensome and spurred a sovereign debt crisis that prompted the two States to request a European rescue package.

The ESM financial assistance programme for Spain had, for the first time, as its very objective the recapitalisation and restructuring of that Country's banking sector. ESM financial assistance was provided in the form of debt securities to the Spanish national recapitalisation fund. Therefore, this recapitalisation was indirect since it was carried out through ESM loans granted to the Government, which in turns allocated and transferred the funds to the concerned financial institutions. Such assistance, however, had the effect of increasing the recipient Country's budget deficit and public debt, prompting doubts over its creditworthiness in financial markets, with sovereign ratings plummeting as a consequence.

It was in this broader context that, in June 2012 (a few weeks before Spain made an official request for financial assistance) the Eurosummit started to discuss the introduction of a direct recapitalisation mechanism to allow banks to strengthen their capital position without placing a heavy burden on the Country where they are incorporated.[29]

In December 2012, the European Council recognised the urgent need to sever the link between banks and sovereigns and to proceed towards a Banking Union.[30] It was then agreed that, once the SSM would enter into force, the funding arrangements of the SRM were to include the direct recapitalisation of banks by the ESM (that is: the ESM would have the ability to acquire ordinary shares of troubled financial institutions without first channelling resources through the State).

This meant that the burden of recapitalisation would be partially shifted on all ESM Member States, even if only temporarily.[31] However, not all ESM Members were ready for this new kind of solidarity and, as a result, defining the features of the DRI proved highly contentious.

---

[27]Corti Varela (2015); Merler (2014).

[28]See *supra*.

[29]Euro Area Summit Statement, Brussels, 29 June 2012.

[30]European Council Conclusions on completing EMU, Brussels, 14 December 2012.

[31]The ESM has a total subscribed capital of €704.8 billion, with a paid-in capital of €80.5 billion, and it raises funds by issuing bonds on capital markets. The liability of each ESM Member is limited to its quota in the ESM capital (cf. the ESM shareholder contribution key annexed to the ESM Treaty).

The DRI was finally introduced in December 2014 through a unanimous resolution of the ESM Board of Governors,[32] and once all Euro area Members completed their national approval procedures.[33] The DRI was, however, received with criticism, especially for its overly restrictive eligibility criteria.[34] In fact, the DRI features seem to undermine the very purpose for which it was conceived.

First of all, Member States of the ESM agreed a self-imposed ceiling, capping at €60 billion the amount of resources available under the DRI. The decision was taken by the Board of Governors with a view to preserve the ESM's lending capacity for other instruments, to protect its creditworthiness and minimise the risk of loss. The IMF however considered the ceiling too low to handle stress in the case of large banks.[35] As a comparison, in 2012 the ESM provided €41.3 billion to Spain for the indirect recapitalisation of the banking sector.

Second, the request for DRI funding still has to be made by a Member State, with sovereigns remaining firmly at the center of the mechanism. The requesting State should be unable to provide financial assistance to troubled institutions (through a national recapitalisation process or an indirect recapitalisation via an ESM loan), as this would greatly affect the Country's fiscal sustainability or its continuous market access. The DRI is, therefore, available to a Member State only as a last resort.

This notwithstanding, pursuant to Article 9 of the ESM DRI Guideline, before the ESM becomes a shareholder of the institution, the State has to make a contribution to the recapitalisation operation. This contribution can be waived by the ESM Board of Governors only under exceptional circumstances related to the Country's weak fiscal position or difficult market access. In this case, though, the Country should commit to indemnify the ESM for any further loss incurred and to accept supplementary macroeconomic conditionality. In other words, even a State in distress has to contribute to the recapitalisation of its banks, thus increasing its public debt.

Fourth, to reduce moral hazard, various forms of conditionality are attached to the DRI, including compliance with State-aid rules. Conditions can be institution-specific or addressed to the requesting State; in the latter case, reform may relate to the Country's financial sector or to its general economic policies. A Memorandum

[32]The resolution of the ESM Board of Governors (that is, the Finance Ministers of the Countries of the Euro area, chaired by the Eurogroup President) was taken on the basis of Article 19 of the ESM Treaty. ESM, Board of Governors Resolution No. 4 of 8 December 2014: Establishment of the Instrument for the Direct Recapitalisation of Institutions (SG/BoG/2014/05/04). See also ESM, Guideline on Financial Assistance for the Direct Recapitalisation of Institutions, 8 December 2014 as well as ESM, Guideline on Financial Assistance for the Recapitalisation of Financial Institutions (which applies to the ESM indirect bank recapitalisation instrument under Article 15 of the ESM Treaty).

[33]A political understanding was reached already in June 2014. See Statement by the President of the Eurogroup on the ESM Direct Recapitalisation Instrument, 10 June 2014.

[34]Five Presidents' Report (2015), p. 11.

[35]IMF (2015).

of Understanding will be negotiated by the European Commission, in liaison with the ECB, the ESM Managing Director and, wherever appropriate, by the IMF.

Besides, the DRI is available only for systemically relevant institutions operating under the ECB's supervision, that would pose a serious threat to the financial stability of the Euro area as a whole or of the requesting Member State. The instrument concerns institutions breaching capital requirements which are unable to raise capital from private investors.[36]

Finally, according to Article 8 of the ESM DRI Guideline, a set of preconditions should also be met: the bail-in by private investors, which will have to contribute for not less than 8% of total liabilities; a contribution by the SRF covering up to 5% of total liabilities; and the write-down or conversion in full of all unsecured and non-preferred liabilities other than eligible deposits.

In conclusion, Euro area Members consented to the introduction of the DRI but only under the condition of an appropriate burden sharing structure and of the application of adequate conditionality.[37]

The activation of the DRI in fact requires the bail-in of private stakeholders and the avoidance of public assistance which is limited only to the most extreme circumstances (these also being the characteristics of the European approach to bank resolution set forth in the BRRD). Thus, the primary responsibility for resolution remains at national level, with mutualised financial assistance provided by the ESM only as a last resort. Moreover, even in the unlikely event that a State seeks financial assistance under the DRI, it will have to contribute to the recapitalisation of banks, thus increasing its public debt, impairing market access and reinforcing the vicious circle between sovereigns and banks, rather than severing it.[38]

4 Solidarity and the Protection of Deposits: The Establishment of a European Deposit Insurance Scheme

The third pillar of the Banking Union, a pan-EU deposit insurance scheme, is still under construction, its negotiations proving rather difficult.

[36]See Article 1 of the ESM Guideline on Financial Assistance for the Direct Recapitalisation of Institutions as well as footnote 2, which broadens the concept of systemic relevance.

[37]It is worth mentioning that according to Article 4(1)2 of the German implementation law of the ESM Treaty (ESM *Finanzierungsgesetz* of 13 September 2012, as amended on 29 November 2014), the disbursement of ESM financial assistance for the direct recapitalisation of institutions will require the prior approval of the Bundestag's plenary session.

[38]Hadjiemmanuil (2015), p. 22.

In 2010, the European Commission put forward a proposal to amend the Directive on Deposit Guarantee Schemes (DGSs)[39] to increase confidence and further harmonise existing national schemes.[40]

In its impact assessment, the Commission highlighted the disproportion between the financing level of national DGSs and the worth of covered deposits in the EU, with some DGS not even able to withstand a medium-size bank failure. The situation was made worse by the lack of solidarity among schemes.

Being the establishment of a single European DGS unfeasible at the time, the European Commission proposed the introduction of a "mutual borrowing facility", granting a national scheme the right to borrow from other schemes, should its resources be insufficient.[41]

In 2013, once an agreement on the new Directive[42] was finally reached, the text adopted was watered down compared to the proposal put forward by the Commission. In the version approved, Article 12 of the DGS Directive read:

> Borrowing between DGSs: 1. Members States *may allow* DGSs to lend to other DGSs within the Union *on a voluntary basis* [emphasis added],

provided that a set of conditions was met.

As a result, under the current legal framework, borrowings among DGSs are based on voluntary lending arrangements rather than on a mandatory scheme. Moreover, the lending procedure can only be activated when: a DGS is unable to fulfil its obligations because of lack of means; the DGS has already made recourse to the extraordinary contributions of its members; and the DGS has repaid previous loans.

Besides, the amount of money requested by a DGS cannot exceed 0.5% of its covered deposits and the loan and interests have to be repaid within 5 years.

However, as pointed out by the Five Presidents' Report[43] and also by the IMF,[44] the current national set-up remains vulnerable to sizeable local shocks, in particular when both the sovereign and its national banking sector are perceived as frail.

---

[39]Directive 94/19/EC on deposit guarantee schemes was first amended in 2009 by Directive 2009/14/EC of the European Parliament and of the Council of 11 March 2009, OJEU L 68, 13 March 2009, pp. 3 et seqq., in particular with a view to increase deposits coverage level from €20,000 to €100,000 by the end of 2010.

[40]European Commission, Proposal for a Directive on deposit guarantee schemes, COM(2010)368 final, 12 July 2010.

[41]See Article 10 of the European Commission's proposal: "1. A scheme shall have *the right to borrow* from all other Deposit Guarantee Schemes referred to in Article 1(2) within the Union provided that all of the following conditions are met: [...] [emphasis added]".

[42]Directive 2014/49/EU of the European Parliament and of the Council of 16 April 2014 on deposit guarantee schemes, OJEU L 173, 12 June 2014, pp. 149 et seqq. On the EDIS see Gros (2014, 2015a, 2015b); Kleftouri (2015).

[43]Five Presidents' Report (2015), p. 11.

[44]IMF (2015), p. 18: "To discourage liquidity 'ring-fencing' within national jurisdictions, a pan-European DGS should be established. Since such a pan-European DGS will take time,

Moreover, in case of a large or systemic crisis, it is not possible to exclude recourse to a public backstop if ultimately needed. In such case, Member States will continue to bear the burden of protecting deposits, at least temporarily.

It is in this context that the European Commission has recently put forward a proposal[45] for a European Deposit Insurance Scheme (EDIS) and a Deposit Insurance Fund (DIF) on the basis of Article 114 TFEU.[46]

The Single Resolution Board would administer both the DIF and the SRF, which would coexist. The DIF would complement existing national deposit guarantee funds and it would serve the purpose of reassuring citizens that the safety of their savings does not depend on geographical location. Participation in EDIS would be mandatory for Euro area Members, but it would also cover DGSs of non-Euro States which have established a close cooperation with the ECB on a voluntary basis.

Like in the case of the SRF, the DIF would be privately funded through *ex ante* fees paid by the banks of participating Member States. Riskier banks would be requested to make higher contributions. The DIF would gradually pool the funds: banks' contributions to national schemes would be gradually reduced, in parallel with their increased contributions to the DIF.

Moreover, to reduce moral hazard risk and avoid free riding, the EDIS would only be available to Countries complying with EU rules[47] and to DGSs reaching the harmonised target level of funding in accordance with the prescribed path.

According to the Commission's proposal, the EDIS would be implemented in three phases: i.e. re-insurance, co-insurance and full insurance.

In an initial 3-year phase, the EDIS would function as a joint re-insurance fund, supplemental to existing national DGSs. Access to EDIS funds would be granted only when a DGS depleted its own resources. The reinsurance scheme would cover the liquidity shortfall or excess losses of a participating DGS, up to a certain

---

consideration should be given now to developing a common fiscal backstop to national DGSs, perhaps through the ESM".

[45]European Commission, Proposal for a Regulation of the European Parliament and of the Council amending Regulation (EU) 806/2014 in order to establish a European Deposit Insurance Scheme, 24 November 2015, COM(2015) 586 final. See also Communication from the Commission to the European Parliament, the Council and the European Central Bank, On steps towards completing Economic and Monetary Union, 21 October 2015, COM(2015) 600 final; Communication from the Commission to the European Parliament, the Council, the European Central Bank, the European Economic and Social Committee and the Committee of the Regions, Towards the completion of the Banking Union, 24 November 2015, COM(2015) 587 final.

[46]In its April 2016 legal opinion for the German Banking Industry Committee, prof Matthias Herdegen considers Article 114 TFEU not an adequate legal basis for the EDIS. Transferring fiscal competence to an EU body which would collect financial contributions from banks would require recourse to Article 352 TFEU and unanimity in the Council. See https://die-dk.de/themen/pressemitteilungen/opinion-confirms-inadequate-legal-basis-european-deposit-insurance-scheme-edis/.

[47]In particular, with the DGS Directive, the Bank Recovery and Resolution Directive and the obligations that will arise from the EDIS Regulation.

percentage and with an overall cap on EDIS contributions. At this stage, EDIS coverage would be limited to resolution proceedings conducted by the SRB.

In a 4-year intermediate period, the EDIS would also apply to purely national resolution proceedings, providing funding and covering losses. During this co-insurance phase, the EDIS would contribute from the moment in which depositors are entitled to be reimbursed, even if DGS's resources have not been depleted. Over the years, the EDIS would cover an increasing share of liquidity needs and losses of participating DGSs. There would be no cap on the intervention by EDIS.

Finally, from 2024, the EDIS would fully insure depositor risk across the Banking Union, providing participating DGSs full funding of their liquidity needs, also covering any losses arising from a payout or a request to contribute to resolution.

The establishment of the EDIS as the third pillar of the Banking Union would fill a gap in the current framework: while banks are already subject to common European supervision and resolution rules, responsibility for deposits protection is still at national level. Because of this asymmetry, depositor confidence continues to be negatively influenced by a sovereign's weak fiscal position. This may lead to market fragmentation and competitive distortion and, possibly, to bank runs and financial instability.

However, money can be truly single only if confidence in the safety of bank deposits is the same irrespective of the Member State in which a bank operates.[48] According to the ECB,

> Full monetary union and a single banking system cannot exist without 'single money', which has to be fungible whatever form it takes, independent of its location within the euro area. Therefore, the concept of 'single money' requires deposits to inspire the same degree of confidence, regardless of the Member State of the banking union where they are located. An EDIS would be an effective tool to promote a uniform level of depositor confidence and to help ensure the true 'singleness' of the euro.[49]

For these reasons as well as others, the ECB declared to fully support the establishment of the EDIS.[50] In its opinion on the proposal presented by the Commission, however, the European Central Bank also expressed the view that the EDIS would need to be complemented with a credible common public backstop, intervening in a scenario in which EDIS resources are insufficient to fully reimburse depositors, and *ex post* contributions from the banking sector are not enough. A mechanism similar to the one about to be introduced for the SRF should be adopted also for the EDIS. The ESM could be the institution in charge of providing this kind of last resort funding.

---

[48]Five Presidents' Report (2015), p. 11.

[49]ECB (2016), p. 36, Financial Integration in Europe 2016, Frankfurt am Main.

[50]See European Central Bank (2016), p. 9, Opinion on a proposal for a Regulation of the European Parliament and of the Council amending Regulation (EU) No. 806/2014 in order to establish a European Deposit Insurance Scheme (CON/2016/26), 20 April 2016.

In spite of support by the ECB, some Member States fear that the EDIS would result in a mutualisation of losses. Countries with a strong fiscal position, a sound banking system and a well-capitalised DGS are not willing to pay for the shortcomings of others. Indeed, in the case of a systemic crisis, the EDIS might lead to potentially large transfers among national banking sectors.[51] Furthermore, if recourse to a public backstop is required, this may also lead—at least temporarily[52]—to burden-sharing among participating States.

As advocated by Andrew Duff in his Protocol of Frankfurt: "The Banking union will remain inherently unstable in the absence of a federal European deposit insurance scheme, enjoying the joint and several guarantee of the eurozone members [. . .].".[53]

To win support on the EDIS proposal, it seems however that the European Commission should devise further measures to avoid the risk of moral hazard (like a cap on banks' holdings of domestic government bonds).[54]

Otherwise, the fully mutualised scheme proposed by the European Commission would not win support, with some observers advocating that implementing the re-insurance stage would be enough to achieve the desired objective.[55]

What described above demonstrates that the major obstacle in building a true Banking Union is the absence of solidarity. Without further risk-sharing, the Banking Union would remain incomplete and unable to delink the funding cost of weak sovereigns from that of their banks.

References

Baglioni A (2016) The European banking union: a critical assessment. Palgrave MacMillan, London

Baroncelli S (2014) L'Unione bancaria europea e il meccanismo di risoluzione delle crisi. In: Quaderni costituzionali, pp 447 et seqq

Bini-Smaghi L (2015) What We Mean When We Talk About Solidarity, in Eutopia, 12 October 2015. Available at http://eutopiamagazine.eu/en/lorenzo-bini-smaghi/speakers-corner/what-we-mean-when-we-talk-about-solidarity

[51]In some Member States, banks have large holdings of domestic sovereign bonds and of non-performing loans.

[52]Banks will have to pay back any funds used from a public backstop through ex post contributions.

[53]Duff (2016).

[54]Italy and Spain are strong opponents of a common upper limit on banks' holdings of domestic sovereign debt. Almost 22% of the Italian sovereign debt is owned by its banks. It is worth noting that Germany made the adoption of sovereign debt ceilings a precondition for further discussions on the EDIS.

[55]Daniel Gros of the Centre for European Policy Studies expressed this view on 23 May 2016 during the public hearing of the Committee on Economic and Monetary Affairs of the European Parliament which was held on the EDIS.

Bush D, Ferrarini G (2015) European banking union. Oxford University Press, Oxford
Corti Varela J (2015) Direct recapitalization of banks and sovereign debt: the ESM direct recapitalization instrument and its impact on sovereign debt. In: Hinojosa-Martinez L, Beneyto JM (eds) European banking union: the new regime. Wolters Kluwer, Alphen aan den Rijn, pp 121–135
Dammann J (2014) The Banking union: flawed by design. Georgetown J Int Law 45:1057 et seqq
de Witte B (2013) Using International Law in the Euro Crisis. Arena Working Paper 4/2013
de Witte F (2015) Justice in the EU: the emergence of transnational solidarity. Oxford University Press, Oxford
Delors J (2003) Memoires. Plon, Paris
Domurath I (2013) The three dimensions of solidarity in the EU legal order: limits of the judicial and legal approach. Eur Integr 35:459–475
Duff A (2016) The protocol of Frankfurt: a new treaty for the Eurozone. European Policy Centre. Available at: http://www.epc.eu/documents/uploads/pub_6229_protocol_of_frankfurt.pdf
ECB (2016) Financial Integration in Europe 2016, Frankfurt am Main
Fabbrini F (2014) On banks, courts and international law: the intergovernmental agreement on the Single resolution fund in context. Maastricht J Eur Comp Law 21:444–463
Five Presidents' Report (2015) Completing Europe's Economic and Monetary Union. Available at https://ec.europa.eu/priorities/publications/five-presidents-report-completing-europes-economic-and-monetary-union_en
Gortsos CV (2015) The Single Resolution Mechanism (SRM) and the Single Resolution Fund (SRF): A Comprehensive Review of the Second Main Pillar of the European Banking Union. European Center of Economic and Financial Law. Available at http;//www.ecefil.eu
Gros S (2014) European deposit insurance and resolution in the banking union. J Common Mark Stud 52:529–546
Gros D (2015a) Completing the Banking Union: Deposit Insurance. CEPS Policy Brief No. 335
Gros D (2015b) Deposit insurance: how to deal with the missing pillar of banking union. In: Hinojosa-Martinez L, Beneyto JM (eds) European banking union: the new regime. Wolters Kluwer, Alphen aan den Rijn, pp 139–154
Hadjiemmanuil C (2015) Bank Resolution Financing in the Banking Union. LSE Law, Society and Economy Working Papers 6/2015
Hilpold P (2015) Understanding solidarity within EU law: an analysis of the "Islands of Solidarity" with particular regard to monetary union. Yearb Eur Law 34:257–285
Hinojosa-Martinez L, Beneyto JM (eds) (2015) European banking union: the new regime. Wolters Kluwer, Alphen aan den Rijn
Huhtaniemi H, Nava M, Tornese E (2015) The establishment of a EU-wide framework for the resolution of banks and financial institutions. In: Hinojosa-Martinez L, Beneyto JM (eds) European banking union: the new regime. Wolters Kluwer, Alphen aan den Rijn, pp. 99-119
IMF (2013) A Banking Union for the Euro Area. IMF Staff Discussion Note SDN/13/01
IMF (2015) Euro Area Policies: 2015 Article IV Consultation. IMF Country Report No. 15/204
Kern A (2015) European banking union: a legal and institutional analysis of the single supervisory mechanism and the single resolution mechanism. Eur Law Rev 40(2):154–187
Kleftouri N (2015) Deposit protection and bank resolution. Oxford University Press, Oxford
Lastra RM (2013) Banking union and single market: conflict or companionship? Fordham Int Law J 36:1190 et seqq
Merkel A (2015) Merkel thanks Schaeuble for role in Greek negotiations. Ekathimerini, 14 December 2015. http://www.ekathimerini.com/204320/article/ekathimerini/news/merkel-thanks-schaeuble-for-role-in-greek-negotiations
Merler S (2014) Comfortably Numb: ESM Direct Recapitalization–Too Late to Solve the Current Crisis, Too Little to Deter Future Crises. Bruegel.org. Available at http://www.bruegel.org/nc/blog/detail/article/1369-comfortably-numb-esm-direct-recapitalization
Moloney N (2014) European banking union: assessing its risks and resilience. Common Mark Law Rev 51:1609–1670

Pugliese S (2014) L'unione bancaria europea tra esigenze di coerenza interna e risposte alle sfide globali. Il diritto dell'Unione Europea 19:831 et seqq
Ross M (2010) Promoting solidarity in the European Union. Oxford University Press, Oxford
Sangiovanni A (2013) Solidarity in the European Union. Oxford J Leg Stud. doi:10.1093/ojls/gqs033
Schuman R (1950) Déclaration Schuman du 9 Mai 1950
Soros G, Schmitz GP (2014) The tragedy of the European Union: disintegration or revival? Public Affairs, New York
Zavvos GS, Kaltsoumi S (2015) The Single resolution mechanism in the European banking union: legal foundation, governance structure and financing. In: Haentjens M, Wessels B (eds) Research handbook on crisis management in the banking sector. Edward Elgar, Cheltenham, pp 117–149

The Quest for Financial Stability and Democracy in the Banking Union: Promoting Institutional Transformation and Regulatory Evolution Through Unconventional Means

Roberto Cisotta

Abstract In the context of the new legislation establishing a banking union in the EU, some reporting and democratic accountability duties have been established for the Single Supervisory Mechanism (SSM) and the Single Resolution Board (SRB), essentially to the benefit of the European Parliament and of national Parliaments, as well as of the Council of the EU. These democratic tools reflect in their conception and first applicative praxis those existing for the ECB and can be considered a first attempt to counterweight the marginalisation of the democratically elected bodies in the adoption of responses to the financial and economic crisis. Being it conceived as an esthetic operation or not, and notwithstanding their mild pervasive power, these democratic tools can play a role in strengthening the legitimacy of the SSM and SRB and their actual capacity to make a contribution to preserving financial stability in the EU.

Contents

The opinions expressed are strictly personal and do not engage the Italian Ministry of Foreign Affairs.

R. Cisotta (✉)
Italian Ministry of Foreign Affairs and International Cooperation, Rome, Italy
e-mail: roberto.cisotta@esteri.it

L. Daniele et al. (eds.), *Democracy in the EMU in the Aftermath of the Crisis*,
DOI 10.1007/978-3-319-53895-2_15

1 Introduction

Setting up a banking union in the Eurozone is deemed to be a crucial step to strengthen the soundness of the financial sector of the Union and its capacity to withstand bad financial weather.[1] However, the achievement of these goals has proven to be difficult, due to the reluctance of Member States to confer on the EU new regulatory powers in such a sensitive sector, thus the compromise on which the new legal framework is based has been reached after intense bargaining. Furthermore, a deal has still not been reached as regards some elements which should constitute the banking union, and namely the introduction of a European deposit guarantee scheme (or EDIS, European Deposit Insurance Scheme).[2] There has been much talk about the constituting instruments of the banking union and one may wonder in particular whether the political compromise on which they are based is appropriately fine-tuned for the effectiveness of the new regulation of the sector.[3] In this respect, it has to be considered that a relevant share of competences has shifted from the national to the EU level and therefore rules regarding the division (between the national and European level) and exercise of these new competences are crucial to assess the effectiveness of the system and of the concrete workability of the political equilibrium on which it is built.

The complex legal framework of the baking union will not be wholly evaluated here, however, one element in particular has to be highlighted for the sake of the present analysis: the ECB has been entrusted with new tasks, with a view to ensuring financial stability. This mandate might, in principle, be considered in contrast with its primary objective of maintaining price stability (see Article 127, para. 1, TFEU). Some mechanisms aimed at keeping monetary functions separated from the new tasks have been provided (see in particular Article 25 of Regulation (EU) No. 1024/2013 establishing the Single Supervisory Mechanism—SSM),[4] nevertheless they raise some concerns as to if and to what extent the ECB's institutional profile—and therefore also the way markets may now look at it—has

---

[1]See Communication from the Commission to the European Parliament and the Council "*A Roadmap towards a Banking Union*", COM (2012) 510, 12 September 2012, esp. section 4; Five Presidents' Report of 22 June 2015 on "*Completing Europe's Economic and Monetary Union*" http://ec.europa.eu/priorities/economic-monetary-union/docs/5-presidents-report_en.pdf (hereinafter, Five Presidents' Report), p. 11 et seq.; Communication from the Commission to the European Parliament, the Council and the European Central Bank on steps towards Completing Economic and Monetary Union, COM(2015) 600 final, 21 October 2015, section 5.

[2]See now the Proposal for a Regulation of the European Parliament and of the Council amending Regulation (EU) No. 806/2014 in order to establish a European Deposit Insurance Scheme, COM (2015) 586 final, 24 November 2016; the proposal is based on Article 114 and the legislative procedure [2015/0270(COD)] is still under way at the moment of completion of this chapter.

[3]Alexander (2011), p. 229 et seqq. and (2013), p. 281 et seqq.; Louis (2012), p. 289 et seqq.

[4]Council Regulation (EU) No. 1024/2013 of 15 October 2013 conferring specific tasks on the European Central Bank concerning policies relating to the prudential supervision of credit institutions, OJEU L 287, 29 October 2013, pp. 63–89.

been blunted.[5] The mere hint at this issue—which will not be treated in this chapter—is one of the examples of how the establishment of the banking union can affect delicate aspects of the institutional equilibrium of the EU.

One has to bear in mind the quickly depicted background to analyze the democratic tools[6] introduced in such framework[7] and this will be the object of these pages. The first emerging issue regards the enduring effectiveness of such tools to maintain the overarching objective which, at the end of the day, all the reforms introduced in the course of the crisis tend to attain: the safeguard of financial stability of the Euro area.[8]

A second issue arises with reference to the very reason of the introduction of a democratic foundation for the new banking union, and namely for the new supervisory and resolution functions with which European Institutions and Agencies have been endowed. One may find that banking regulation and supervision is a matter of technical decisions, to be adopted by technical bodies, thus an activity on which only weak democratic and political control is usually exercised. In a purely descriptive perspective, one may say that it is for the sensitivity of the new powers to be exercised at the European level, as well as for their relevance for the solidity of the new machinery aimed at avoiding new financial turmoil, that a series of new democratic tools have been conceived for the new mechanisms.[9]

The two issues, linked, as they are, to the preservation of financial stability, are clearly intertwined.

To see it in a rather skeptical perspective, democratic tools might have been conceived as a purely esthetic operation, with a view to contrast, in a preventive way, possible objections related to the deprivation of the national level of crucial powers in the banking field. Thus, the conferral upon the EU of certain powers can

[5]Di Marco (2013), p. 549 et seqq.; Wolfers, Voland (2014), p. 1463 et seqq.

[6]In this chapter the expressions "mechanisms" or "tools" will be used promiscuously to indicate the components of the democratic machinery presented in Sect. 2.

[7]Ibrido (2016), p. 377 et seqq.

[8]See Cisotta (2015), p. 283 et seqq.

[9]This *prima facie* impression seems confirmed by the somewhat apodictic explanation for the introduction of democratic tools contained in recital (55) of Regulation (EU) No. 1024/2013 (see footnote 14), according to which "[a]ny shift of supervisory powers from the Member State to the Union level should be balanced by appropriate transparency and accountability requirements" (see also recital (D) of Interinstitutional Agreement between the European Parliament and the European Central Bank on the practical modalities of the exercise of democratic accountability and oversight over the exercise of the tasks conferred on the ECB within the framework of the Single Supervisory Mechanism (see footnote 22) and recital (D) of the MoU between the Council and the ECB on the cooperation procedures related to the SSM (see footnote 24)). Regulation (EU) No. 806/2014 (see footnote 16) does not even try to offer a justification (see recital (42)), but see recital (D) of the Agreement between the European Parliament and the Single Resolution Board on the practical modalities of the exercise of democratic accountability and oversight over the exercise of the tasks conferred on the Single Resolution Board within the framework of the Single Resolution Mechanism (see footnote 22), where a wording similar to that used in recital (55) of Regulation (EU) No. 1024/2013 is used.

be more acceptable: the old and newly established European regulators, taking the place of the national ones, will be put under democratic control, in order to reduce the possible *méfiance* towards them. According to this view, democratic legitimacy could deflate grievances related to the appropriateness of a political choice—as giving the EU new powers, although the operation is already envisaged by the Treaties at least in one of the cases which will be considered,[10] is no doubt a political move. If this basis for the introduction of democratic tools may be found poorly convincing, the reason why democratic tools should make the whole machinery more effective—i.e. more apt to pursue the financial stability of the Euro area—may be found even less persuasive and more obscure: indeed, political debates could prove to be inconclusive and endanger the confidentiality—extremely needed on many occasions in the banking field–, as well as the *pure* technicality of decision processes of the competent bodies.

Nonetheless, sane democracy can help new technical bodies to perform well and make them flourish as estimated regulators. Thus, in addition to the intrinsic benefits of a sound democratic structure, one should bear in mind how precious good reputation—i.e. trust and credibility—is on international markets: exposure to questions and debates can reinforce the transparency and soundness of the decision making process, by clarifying to the public the technical and political foundation of choices. At the end, the independence and reputation of technical bodies on the market can take great advantage from democratic mechanisms (also elementary ones, like accountability and reporting) and this is why accountability tools are recommended, for instance, also at the international level.[11] Conceptually, benefits may be considered similar to those experienced in central banking.[12]

Hence, in addition to their primary *raison d'être*, democratic tools should be intended as mechanisms aimed at increasing the credibility and genuine *technical force* of the bodies submitted thereto. In this enquiry, the democratic tools established under the banking union will be analyzed under this light.

2 A Short Presentation of the Democratic Tools of the Banking Union

In the preceding section, the scene has been set to give a first understanding of how democratic tools should be understood—and therefore scrutinised—in the context of the banking union. In this section, the democratic tools will be presented, as they

---

[10]See Article 127, para. 6, laying down the procedure to entrust the ECB with "specific tasks [. . .] concerning policies relating to the prudential supervision of credit institutions and other financial institutions with the exception of insurance undertakings", used as a legal basis for Regulation (EU) No. 1024/2013 (see footnote 14).

[11]Ter Kuile et al. (2015), p. 164 et seqq.

[12]Zilioli (2003), p. 395 et seqq.

have been shaped in the founding texts of the banking union. The avenues through which accountability may be granted can be classified and evaluated in many different ways[13]: here a descriptive approach is adopted to show the mechanisms as they are laid down in normative texts, then a practical evaluation will be carried out with reference to the actual usefulness such mechanisms have demonstrated and are apt to demonstrate.

2.1 The SSM

Starting with the aforementioned Regulation (EU) No. 1024/2013, reference has to be made to Article 20, which lay down a series of rules regarding the duties of the ECB, in its capacity as a supervisor, *vis-à-vis* the European Parliament. Article 21 provides something unprecedented, granting national Parliaments some rights to intervene.

As regards the first aspect, Article 20, paras. 1–6, lays the basic rules:

> 1. The ECB shall be accountable to the European Parliament and to the Council for the implementation of this Regulation, in accordance with this Chapter.
> 2. The ECB shall submit on an annual basis to the European Parliament, to the Council, to the Commission and to the euro Group a report on the execution of the tasks conferred on it by this Regulation, including information on the envisaged evolution of the structure and amount of the supervisory fees mentioned in Article 30.
> 3. The Chair of the Supervisory Board of the ECB shall present that report in public to the European Parliament, and to the euro Group in the presence of representatives from any participating Member State whose currency is not the euro.
> 4. The Chair of the Supervisory Board of the ECB may, at the request of the euro Group, be heard on the execution of its supervisory tasks by the euro Group in the presence of representatives from any participating Member States whose currency is not the euro.
> 5. At the request of the European Parliament, the Chair of the Supervisory Board of the ECB shall participate in a hearing on the execution of its supervisory tasks by the competent committees of the European Parliament.
> 6. The ECB shall reply orally or in writing to questions put to it by the European Parliament, or by the euro Group in accordance with the its own procedures and in the presence of representatives from any participating Member States whose currency is not the euro.

These provisions echo Article 284, para. 3, TFEU and Article 15, para. 3, of Protocol (No. 4) on the Statute of the European System of Central Banks and of the European Central Bank, which provide the accountability tools as regards the exercise of the general functions of the ESCB and of the ECB. Of course, Article 20 of Regulation (EU) No. 1024/2013 provides some more details concerning the specific functions of the ECB as banking supervisor and others stemming from the particular structure of the SSM: first of all, it is the Chair of the Supervisory Board that acts representing the ECB in its capacity as a supervisor, not the president of

[13] Ter Kuile et al. (2015), p. 155 et seqq.

the ECB (like in procedures under Article 284 TFEU). This choice reflects, in the field of democratic tools, the need to separate monetary and supervisory functions.

In the second place, para. 3 specifies that representatives of participating Member States with derogation take part in meetings of the Eurogroup when the Chair of the Supervisory Board of the ECB presents the report on the performance by the SSM of its tasks.

Under Article 284, para. 3, TFEU and Article 15, para. 3, of Protocol (No. 4), it is not the Eurogroup that (in addition to the Council) receives the report. Only the Council in its full composition is involved in that exercise. One may argue that in the context of supervisory functions the degree of integration reached by the Euro area and by participating Member States is more advanced (than in the case of "ordinary" accountability of the ECB); therefore, the technical nature of the activity on which the Chair of the Supervisory Board has to report has led to a specific participation of the Ministries responsible for the economic and financial issues. In the perspective adopted in this chapter, it has to be noted that supervisory functions are indeed relevant for the financial stability of the Euro area and, at the end, of the European Union in its entirety. However, the solution is clearly logical and full accountability is not impaired; it is, on the contrary, enhanced by virtue of the public character of the report.

In the third place, para. 2 imposes the Chair to focus "on the envisaged evolution of the structure and amount of the supervisory fees". Article 30 empowers the ECB to levy such fees on supervised

> credit institutions established in the participating Member States and branches established in a participating Member State by a credit institution established in a non-participating Member State

for the coverage of the expenses incurred in the performance of the tasks conferred by the Regulation and also provides some basic rules on their calculation.

The following paragraphs of Article 20 contain some provisions related to particular situations or inter-institutional relationships. It is worth quoting them, too:

> 7. When the European Court of Auditors examines the operational efficiency of the management of the ECB under Article 27.2 of the Statute of the ESCB and of the ECB, it shall also take into account the supervisory tasks conferred on the ECB by this Regulation.
>
> 8. Upon request the Chair of the Supervisory Board of the ECB shall hold confidential oral discussions behind closed doors with the Chair and Vice-Chairs of the competent committee of the European Parliament concerning its supervisory tasks where such discussions are required for the exercise of the European Parliament's powers under the TFEU. An agreement shall be concluded between the European Parliament and the ECB on the detailed arrangements for organising such discussions, with a view to ensuring full confidentiality in accordance with the confidentiality obligations imposed on the ECB as a competent authority under relevant Union law.
>
> 9. The ECB shall cooperate sincerely with any investigations by the European Parliament, subject to the TFEU. The ECB and the European Parliament shall conclude appropriate arrangements on the practical modalities of the exercise of democratic accountability and oversight over the exercise of the tasks conferred on the ECB by this Regulation. Those

arrangements shall cover, inter alia, access to information, cooperation in investigations and information on the selection procedure of the Chair of the Supervisory Board.

Para. 7 relates to the operational efficiency scrutiny carried out by the Court of Auditors under Article 27, para. 2, of the Statute of the ESCB and of the ECB. This last provision actually limits the scope of the examination of the Court of Auditors, ordinary audit being carried out by external auditors according to Article 27, para. 1, of the Statute. This limitation is due to the protection of the independence of the ECB, as granted, in general, by Article 282, para. 3, TFEU. In this context, the object of the protection is its independence from other EU Institutions, in particular as regards the management of its finances.[14]

Para. 8 envisages the case of confidential oral discussions between the Chair of the Supervisory Board and the Chair and Vice-Chairs of the competent committee of the European Parliament, where needed "for the exercise of the European Parliament's powers under the TFEU". This latter expression appears rather vague and it would be interesting to analyze its future interpretation. The arrangements between the ECB and the Parliament, envisaged also by para. 9 of Article 20, will be the object of separate evaluation.[15]

As to the prerogatives of national Parliaments, they are laid down in Article 21 of Regulation (EU) No. 1024/2013:

1. When submitting the report provided for in Article 20(2), the ECB shall simultaneously forward that report directly to the national parliaments of the participating Member States.

National parliaments may address to the ECB their reasoned observations on that report.

2. National parliaments of the participating Member States, through their own procedures, may request the ECB to reply in writing to any observations or questions submitted by them to the ECB in respect of the tasks of the ECB under this Regulation.

3. The national parliament of a participating Member State may invite the Chair or a member of the Supervisory Board to participate in an exchange of views in relation to the supervision of credit institutions in that Member State together with a representative of the national competent authority.

4. This Regulation is without prejudice to the accountability of national competent authorities to national parliaments in accordance with national law for the performance of tasks not conferred on the ECB by this Regulation and for the performance of activities carried out by them in accordance with Article 6.

As noted above, this is the first time where national Parliaments are empowered to exercise democratic control over a European Institution, although in the mild version consisting in reporting duties and democratic accountability. The following are key expressions in the reported provisions, confirming the soft nature of the control exercised: "reasoned observation" (that can be addressed by national Parliaments to the ECB on its report), (again national Parliaments) "may request

---

[14]As regards the independence of the ECB, see also Articles 130 TFEU and 7 of the Statute of the ESCB and of the ECB. In general, the ECB conceives four "dimensions" of its own independence: institutional, functional, personal, financial: see European Central Bank (1998), p. 23. In the case considered in the main text, institutional, functional and financial independence seem all, in different respects, object of protection.

[15]See *infra*, following section.

the ECB to reply in writing", "exchange of views" (to which the Chair of the Supervisory Board may be invited by the national Parliament of a participating Member State).

Given the particular interaction between national and European regulators established in banking supervision, the last paragraph makes it clear that national mechanisms (between the national competent authority and national Parliaments) are kept out the reach of the new national-European accountability relation established in the preceding paragraphs.

2.2 The SRM

As regards the Single Resolution Mechanism (SRM), Articles 45 and 46 of Regulation (EU) No. 806/2014 (the SRM Regulation)[16] are relevant and the wording echoes that of the aforementioned provisions of Regulation (EU) No. 1024/2013. It seems nevertheless useful to quote the whole texts of those provisions, then offering a brief analysis of the differences with the rules regarding the SSM.

Let us start with Article 45:

> 1. The Board shall be accountable to the European Parliament, the Council and the Commission for the implementation of this Regulation, in accordance with paragraphs 2 to 8.
>
> 2. The Board shall submit an annual report to the European Parliament, the national parliaments of participating Member States in accordance with Article 46, the Council, the Commission and the European Court of Auditors on the performance of the tasks conferred on it by this Regulation. Subject to the requirements of professional secrecy, that report shall be published on the Board's website.
>
> 3. The Chair shall present that report in public to the European Parliament, and to the Council.
>
> 4. At the request of the European Parliament, the Chair shall participate in a hearing by the competent committee of the European Parliament on the performance of the resolution tasks by the Board. A hearing shall take place at least annually.
>
> 5. The Chair may be heard by the Council, at the Council's request, on the performance of the resolution tasks by the Board.
>
> 6. The Board shall reply orally or in writing to questions addressed to it by the European Parliament or by the Council, in accordance with its own procedures and in any event within five weeks of receipt of a question.
>
> 7. Upon request, the Chair shall hold confidential oral discussions behind closed doors with the Chair and Vice-Chairs of the competent committee of the European Parliament where such discussions are required for the exercise of the European Parliament's powers under the TFEU. An agreement shall be concluded between the European Parliament and the Board on the detailed modalities of organising such discussions, with a view to ensuring

[16] Regulation (EU) No. 806/2014 of the European Parliament and of the Council of 15 July 2014 establishing uniform rules and a uniform procedure for the resolution of credit institutions and certain investment firms in the framework of a Single Resolution Mechanism and a Single Resolution Fund and amending Regulation (EU) No. 1093/2010, OJEU L 225, 30 July 2014, pp. 1–90. It is worth noting that the legal basis is provided by Article 114 TFEU.

full confidentiality in accordance with the requirements of professional secrecy imposed on the Board by this Regulation and when the Board is acting as a national resolution authority under the relevant Union law.

8. During any investigations by the European Parliament, the Board shall cooperate with the European Parliament, subject to the TFEU and regulations referred to in Article 226 thereof. Within six months of the appointment of the Chair, the Board and the European Parliament shall conclude appropriate arrangements on the practical modalities of the exercise of democratic accountability and oversight over the exercise of the tasks conferred on the Board by this Regulation. Subject to the power of the European Parliament pursuant to Article 226 TFEU, those arrangements shall cover, inter alia, access to information, including rules on the handling and protection of classified or otherwise confidential information, cooperation in hearings, as referred to in Article 45(4) of this Regulation, confidential oral discussions, reports, responding to questions, investigations and information on the selection procedure of the Chair, the Vice-Chair, and the four members referred to in Article 43(1)(b) of this Regulation.

Essential differences emerges in relation to the different institutional standing held by the SRM, if compared with the SSM. The latter is accountable only to the European Parliament and the Council, while the SRM has to refer also to the Commission (as stated by para. 1). Reports have to be filed (in addition to the addressees envisaged for the report of the SSM also) to national Parliaments of participating Member States and to the European Court of Auditors. Publication of the report on the SRM website is also required, while no such publication is envisaged by Article 20 of Regulation (EU) No. 1024/2013 for the SSM report.[17] In the mechanisms concerning the SSM there is a stronger relation to the bodies governing the Euro area: in particular, requested hearing of the respective Chairs take place before the Eurogroup for the SSM and before the Council for the SRM; the same applies to responses given orally or in written to questions. The duty of cooperation with the European Parliament is laid down in the last paragraph both of Article 20 of Regulation (EU) No. 1024/2013 and of Article 45 of Regulation (EU) No. 806/2014, with the latter stating in some more detail the duties referred to the power of Parliament to establish temporary Committees of Enquiry (Article 226 TFEU).[18]

The SRM is not included in the list of the EU Institutions provided for in Article 13 TEU, while the SSM is attracted, as seen, in the ECB. This inclusion of banking supervision amongst the tasks performed by the ECB is envisaged by the Treaties,[19] while resolution functions have been attracted within EU competences via Article

[17]However, publication of the report on the SSM website is required by Article 1 of the Interinstitutional Agreement between the European Parliament and the European Central Bank on the practical modalities of the exercise of democratic accountability and oversight over the exercise of the tasks conferred on the ECB within the framework of the Single Supervisory Mechanism (see footnote 22).

[18]However, more specific provisions concerning Article 226 TFEU can be found in section 3 of the Interinstitutional Agreement between the European Parliament and the European Central Bank, cit.

[19]As seen above, Article 127, para. 6, TFEU provides such possibility and has offered the legal basis for the adoption of Regulation (EU) No. 1024/2013.

114 TFEU.[20] This is reflected also in the highlighted different dynamics of democratic tools and the difference is especially evident in two of the referred situations. An EU Institution, whose independence is strongly defended by primary law, like the ECB, cannot, in particular, be accountable to the Commission, but to co-legislators only.[21] On the contrary, an agency like the SRM is subjected also to the Commission. Furthermore, the European Court of Auditors has more intrusive powers *vis-à-vis* the SRM, while with the ECB the pre-existing limitations to its action also apply to the performance of its tasks in the context of banking supervision.

The SRM is subjected to some control of national Parliaments, too, as provided by Article 46 of the SRM Regulation:

> 1. Due to the specific tasks that are conferred on the Board by this Regulation, national parliaments of the participating Member States, by means of their own procedures, may request the Board to reply and the Board is obliged to reply in writing to any observations or questions submitted by them to the Board in respect of the functions of the Board under this Regulation.
>
> 2. When submitting the report provided for in Article 45(2), the Board shall simultaneously submit that report directly to the national parliaments of the participating Member States. National parliaments may address to the Board their reasoned observations on that report. The Board shall reply orally or in writing to any observations or questions addressed to it by the national parliaments of the participating Member States, in accordance with its own procedures.
>
> 3. The national parliament of a participating Member State may invite the Chair to participate in an exchange of views in relation to the resolution of entities referred to in Article 2 in that Member State together with a representative of the national resolution authority. The Chair is obliged to follow such invitation.
>
> 4. This Regulation shall be without prejudice to the accountability of national resolution authorities to national parliaments in accordance with national law for the performance of tasks not conferred on the Board, the Council or the Commission by this Regulation and for the performance of activities carried out by them in accordance with Article 7(3).

Two important differences with the rules on the SSM, regarding the existence of two additional statutory duties, emerge. The first is established by the referred para. 1 of Article 46 of the SRM Regulation, and regards the obligation of the SRM Board to reply to any "reasoned observation" addressed by national Parliaments as regards its report. The second is provided for by para. 3, according to which the Chair "is obliged to follow" the invitation to take part in an "exchange of views" (which regards the resolution of Article 2 entities in the Member State in question; a representative of the national resolution authority will also take part in the exercise).

The Agreements with the European Parliament As required by Articles 20, paras. 8 and 9, of Regulation (EU) No. 1024/2013 and 45, paras. 7 and 8, of Regulation (EU) No. 806/2014, two agreements have been concluded with the

[20]See *supra*, footnote 14.

[21]See recital (55) of Regulation (EU) No. 1024/2013.

European Parliament respectively by the ECB and by the SRB.[22] The two instruments are focused essentially on some topics, like confidentiality, and contain the detailed rules for a series of functions to be performed by the two "actors" in cooperation, including in particular provisions on the appointment respectively of the Chair of the SSM Board, and of the Chair, Vice-Chair and Members of the SRM Board. What has to be underlined here is that the first instrument, concluded by the European Parliament with the SSM, is an "Interinstitutional agreement", while the second one is referred to as a simple "Agreement". This confirms the reconstruction proposed above,[23] whereby in the first case two Institutions of the EU find arrangements for certain particular procedures; in the second one, only one of the two parties is an EU Institution, therefore the adjective "interinstitutional" cannot be used.

The MoU Between the Council and the ECB on the Cooperation Procedures Related to the SSM Following the interinstitutional agreement between the European Parliament and the ECB, also a MoU between the latter and the Council has been signed.[24] It should be argued that, short of a provision directly envisaging such instrument in Regulation (EU) No. 1024/2013, it could not be qualified as an interinstitutional agreement, but should be considered as a simple Memorandum of Understanding. The MoU lays down the necessary content of the report, procedural norms on various issues including on hearings, exchange of views, questions asked to the ECB, the selection procedure for the Chair of the SSM and ensures confidentiality, where needed, and protection of classified information.

3 Obtaining Information and Asking Questions

The presented legal framework, given its recent introduction, has been applied for just a short time. The first reports, as well as the available information on hearings and questions asked are however instructive as regards how the newly established machinery is working and what are the most debated issues.[25]

---

[22]Interinstitutional Agreement between the European Parliament and the European Central Bank on the practical modalities of the exercise of democratic accountability and oversight over the exercise of the tasks conferred on the ECB within the framework of the Single Supervisory Mechanism, 2013/694/EU, OJEU L 320, 30 November 2013, pp. 1–6; Agreement between the European Parliament and the Single Resolution Board on the practical modalities of the exercise of democratic accountability and oversight over the exercise of the tasks conferred on the Single Resolution Board within the framework of the Single Resolution Mechanism, OJEU L 339, 24 December 2015, pp. 58–65.

[23]See *supra*, Sect. 2.2.

[24]Memorandum of Understanding between the Council of the European Union and the European Central Bank on the cooperation on procedures related to the Single Supervisory Mechanism (SSM), https://www.ecb.europa.eu/ecb/legal/pdf/mou_between_eucouncil_ecb.pdf.

[25]A comprehensive evaluation of the activities of the SSM and of the SRM cannot be provided here. The relevant documents will be analysed only with reference to the kind of information provided—and without summarising all the details provided therein—and their usefulness for the system of democratic accountability.

3.1 To the SSM

As regards the SSM, two annual report are available to date: the first, regarding 2014 and published in March 2015,[26] and the second, regarding 2015 and published in March 2016. The first report is aimed at offering a picture of the experience of the first pioneering year of European banking supervision. Details are provided as regards the basic legal framework and the first activities carried out by the Board. What appears significant is the will to underline the strength of a European supervisory model, stressing the capacities of the SSM in comparison with national supervisors. In a kind of apologetic endeavour, the chance to assess risks throughout a wider market and the possibility to refine reference instruments for supervision is offered as a surplus of the existing system, gravitating to a European (although not unique) supervisor.[27] In other terms, these strengths should be seen as the advantages of the single market reflected in the field of banking supervision and the referred apologetic endeavour seems aimed at justifying on the basis of the principle of subsidiarity the very existence of the SSM.

The second report of the SSM,[28] in addition to informing on the remaining operational set-up of the machinery, is more focused on presenting the significance of the work of the Mechanism for the preservation of financial stability.[29] The activities are shown in the light of their contribution to the robustness of the banking sector of the EU and of the importance of setting up a common regulatory framework, also with a view to providing consistent information throughout the States participating in this integration experiment.

The evolution of the approach seems also substantially confirmed by the regular hearings of the Chair of the Board before the European Parliament's Economic and Monetary Affairs Committee.[30]

---

[26]European central Bank (2014).

[27]A passage from the foreword by Danièle Nouy, Chair of the Supervisory Board, is particularly clear in this respect: "The most important objective of the SSM is to improve the quality and consistency of banking supervision within the euro area. The SSM will deliver increased opportunities for benchmarking and peer comparison among banks across the euro area. The SSM will allow us to improve the tools of supervisory risk assessment, with due regard to the diversity of banks' business models within Europe—which I believe is a clear strength. The SSM is certainly very well placed to assess, monitor and address the risks in the banking sector on a European scale. Its micro-prudential view is enriched by its macro-prudential responsibilities for monitoring and addressing risks from a system-wide perspective. In addition, the SSM gives us a stronger consolidated perspective, and enhances efficiency in the allocation and transfer of intra-group capital and liquidity.". (p. 5 of the Report, cit.).

[28]European Central Bank (2015).

[29]Chapter 2 of the report is significantly entitled "Supervisory contribution to financial stability".

[30]The texts of the speeches are available on-line: https://www.bankingsupervision.europa.eu/press/speeches/date/2016/html/index.en.html.

Questions asked to the SSM and responses given in particular to MEPs are also instructive.[31] Such questions often concern specific cases, probably related to situations under the attention of the MEP asking the question. In other cases, questions concern rather technical issues and, in particular, the review processes carried out by the SSM, like a question recently filed to the Chair on the Supervisory Review and Evaluation Process (SREP).[32] More in general, MEPs show concern as regards the impact of banking regulation on the stability of credit institutions, sometimes in view of broad reforms of the banking sector[33] (maybe in relation in particular with some of such institutions under their attention for whatever reason). Some issues touched upon by MEPs, although in a minority of the whole number of the questions asked, are especially interesting, as they reveal the consciousness of the delicate application of the traditional criteria of the single market to the new supervisory system. This is shown by a question on proportionality.[34] The respect of the principle was assessed with reference to "Less significant institutions" (LSIs) (a category often under the attention of MEPs) as regards accounting requirements and thematic review of such institutions. As a third branch of the evaluation, proportionality was assessed in the context of, again, the SREP. In the response it was assessed that reporting requirements for LSIs are reduced, but the answer was rather generic as regards thematic reviews.[35] The most interesting part of the response regards the SREP, where an attempt is made to explain how supervisory benchmarks are shaped and refined, also with reference to the tools provided by EBA, as well as to illustrate how discretion is exercised in setting capital requirements to avoid abuses (and namely respecting the principle of proportionality). In an older response,[36] it is remarkable that stress was put on the fact that criteria for

[31]Responses are available on-line under the "Publications" section of the website of the SSM: https://www.bankingsupervision.europa.eu/press/publications/date/2016/html/index.en.html.

[32]See the response by the Chair to Mr. Sven Giegold, MEP, 11 July 2016, https://www.bankingsupervision.europa.eu/ecb/pub/pdf/160711letter_giegold_1.en.pdf.

[33]See the responses by the Chair to Mr. Mario Borghezio, MEP, respectively 6 April 2016, and 2 March 2016, https://www.bankingsupervision.europa.eu/ecb/pub/pdf/160406letter_borghezio.en.pdf and https://www.bankingsupervision.europa.eu/ecb/pub/pdf/160302letter_borghezio.en.pdf.

[34]See the response by the Chair to Mr. Sven Giegold, MEP, 20 November 2015, https://www.bankingsupervision.europa.eu/ecb/pub/pdf/151120letter_giegold.en.pdf. See also the response by the Chair to Mr. Sven Giegold, MEP, 2 October 2015, https://www.bankingsupervision.europa.eu/ecb/pub/pdf/151002letter_giegold_2.en.pdf.

[35]The following sentence of the response seems at the same time reassuring, but quite generic (which is not uncommon feature of responses in the context of accountability mechanism, as responses should anyway be, at the same time, straight-to-the-point and understandable to the public): "I can assure you that both the ECB and the NCAs [National Competent Authorities] are very much aware of the specificities of small LSIs, and we design the thematic reviews in such a way that the burden on small LSIs, for instance in terms of reporting and the resources involved, is kept to a minimum.".

[36]See the response by the Chair to Mr. Markus Ferber, MEP, 18 July 2014, https://www.bankingsupervision.europa.eu/ecb/pub/pdf/20140718ssm-reply_to_mep_ferberen.pdf.

supervision are consistent throughout the participating Countries, both if applied by national authorities and by the SSM. Moreover, as regards a specific exercise (asset quality review—AQR), the Chair underlined the right of the SSM to carry out it also for all less significant banks (even if this was not under consideration at that moment). Leaving aside all specific consideration regarding that kind of exercise and the precise moment in which the response was given, it should be noted how the needed effective supervision may sometimes require discretional moves by regulators which, at first sight, exceed what could in principle be considered as a proportional action (also in line with the principle of subsidiarity).

3.2 And the SRM

The SRB has published only one report to date regarding its activities in 2015.[37] Given the taking up of operations in March 2015, that year "might best be described as the start-up phase of the SRB".[38] Therefore, the report essentially informs about the transitional and capacity building processes carried out in that year, and on the basic structure of the Agency.

Three hearings of the Chair of the SRB have been held before the European Parliament's Economic and Monetary Affairs Committee and they have been dominated by the need to present the toolkit at the disposal of the Agency, as well as its setting up and working plan for the first period. Some insights have been dedicated to the vulnerable banks under the supervision of the SSM.

No document is available at the time of writing regarding questions or responses to the SRB.[39]

4 Final Remarks

This enquiry—despite relying on a limited number of sources, in particular because of the young life of the actors considered—has led to highlight some points. Such results should be read in the light of researches carried out on the similar democratic accountability tools existing for the ECB. In that context, it had been noted that the dialogue between the European Parliament and the ECB had become more mature over time (in particular in the first 10 years of ECB life), shifting from the focus on

[37]Single Resolution Board (2015).

[38]See Report, cit, foreword by the Chair, p. 4.

[39]Some questions have been addressed as regards, in particular, the establishment of the SRM and the starting of activity of the Single Resolution Fund, for instance to the Council: see e.g. the written question submitted by E. Ferreira on 20 November 2015, http://www.europarl.europa.eu/sides/getAllAnswers.do?reference=E-2015-014924&language=EN and the relative response: http://www.europarl.europa.eu/sides/getAllAnswers.do?reference=E-2015-014924&language=EN.

price stability, transparency and mandate of the Bank, to more general topics related to economic policy.[40] This can be considered a quite natural trajectory, reproduced also in the (still short) dialogues between the European Parliament and the SSM and the SRB. The European Parliament just needed to get in touch with the mandate of the new subjects, but then, especially with reference to the SSM, it could build upon the experience obtained with the ECB. Therefore, as seen, at the beginning the interest concerned the structure and mandate of the SSM and SRM; then, it is already evident that it is shifting to the systemic implications of the activity of the new subjects, in particular in terms of preservation of the financial stability (which has anyway become a common concern over the last years).

Again with reference to the ECB experience, the mildly pervasive nature of the democratic tools has led to a certain skepticism in some authors[41] and others have noted that the flaws of such system reflects those of the whole system of the EU legal order.[42] Nevertheless, such tools offer a non-substitutable occasion to put issues on the spotlight, leaving to more refined mechanisms, like legal review or scientific analysis (which could not, on their turn, be substituted by democratic tools), to enter into some detail.

It must be said that the highly technical nature of the issues treated both by the SSM and the SRM makes it difficult to offer food for sane politically profiled debates in the European Parliament. This sometimes may lead MEPs to bring the regulators on unfriendly grounds, trying to carve out of the responses they may provide elements which could offer some kind of satisfaction to their constituencies, or which can be (mis)used for more general criticisms against EU conduct of economic policies.

Nevertheless, some pieces of good practice are also emerging. The accent put by observers and legal doctrine[43] on the relationships between the banking union and internal market law has influenced also debates in the European Parliament on the activities of the SSM and of the SRB. Apart from what has already been seen before on the problematic nature of the relationships between banking union and internal market rules, it clearly stems from the philosophy of the latter that promoting common standards leads to achieve a level playing field and economic advantages in the medium and long run. Therefore, a virtuous circle could slowly be alimented also thanks to democratic tools, leading to appreciate the positive outcomes of pioneering integration projects in areas like banking supervision and resolution.

[40] Amtenbrink and Van Duin (2009), p. 561 et seqq.

[41] Amtenbrink and Van Duin (2009), p. 561 et seqq.

[42] Zilioli and Selmayr (2006), p. 89.

[43] Lastra (2013), p. 1190 et seqq.

References

Alexander K (2011) Reforming European financial supervision: adapting EU institutions to market structures. ERA Forum 12:229–252
Alexander K (2013) Bank resolution and recovery in the EU: enhancing banking union? ERA Forum 14:81–93
Amtenbrink F, Van Duin K (2009) The European Central Bank before the parliament: theory and practice after 10 years of monetary dialogue. Eur Law Rev 34:561–583
Cisotta R (2015) Financial stability and the reconstruction of the EU legal order in the aftermath of the crisis. In: European Central Bank (ed) From monetary union to banking union, on the way to capital markets union–new opportunities for European integration. European Central Bank, Frankfurt am Main, pp 283-304
Di Marco A (2013) Il controllo delle banche nell'UEM: la (problematica) nascita di un sistema integrato di vigilanza prudenziale. Il Diritto dell'Unione europea 18:549–592
European Central Bank (1998) Monthly Bulletin, 10th Anniversary of the ECB
European Central Bank (2014) Annual Report on Banking Supervision, available on-line. https://www.bankingsupervision.europa.eu/ecb/pub/pdf/ssmar2014.en.pdf?c50e4de7ccc030381567868a76b97e1d
European Central Bank (2015) Annual Report on Banking Supervision, available on-line. https://www.bankingsupervision.europa.eu/ecb/pub/pdf/ssmar2015.en.pdf?76bfa705d9eb131ceed673b36b94079a
Ibrido R (2016) Le nuove procedure di accountability democratica nel quadro del secondo pilastro della banking union. Quaderni Costituzionali 36:377–380
Lastra MR (2013) Banking union and single market: conflict or companionship? Fordham Int Law J 36:1190–1224
Louis J-V (2012) Éditorial, Vers l'Union bancaire. Cahiers de droit européen 48:289–304
Single Resolution Board (2015) Annual Report, available on-line. http://srb.europa.eu/sites/srbsite/files/srb_annual_report_2015_en_0.pdf
Ter Kuile G, Wissink L, Bovenschen W (2015) Tailor-made accountability within the single supervisory mechanism. Common Mark Law Rev 52:155–190
Wolfers B, Voland T (2014) Level the playing field: the new supervision of credit institutions by the European Central Bank. Common Mark Law Rev 51:1463–1496
Zilioli C (2003) Accountability and independence: irreconcilable values or complementary instruments for democracy? The specific case of the European Central Bank. In: Van der Sanden G, De Walsche A (eds) Mélanges en hommage à Jean-Victor Louis, vol II. Editions de l'Université de Bruxelles, Institut d'Etudes Européennes, Bruxelles, pp 395–422
Zilioli C, Selmayr M (2006) Recents developments in the law of the European Central Bank. Yearb Eur Law 25:1–89

Negative Democratic Externalities in the European Banking System

Matteo Ortino

Abstract In this contribution, the recent institutional reforms introduced by the EU in the banking sector—in particular, the establishment of the European Banking Authority and the Banking Union—will be analysed and assessed against the democratic requirements of representation, accountability and the pursuit of the people's interests. The analysis will assume that three institutional features are crucial for the fulfilment of these three democratic requirements, and thus for assessing the democratic legitimacy of the new institutional set-up. These determinants are: centralisation, independence and the regime of accountability. As result of the examination, various democratic institutional weaknesses will be highlighted.

Contents

1 Democratic Failures in the Governance of the EU Banking System

In democratic systems, political decisions are sanctioned by the people and are implemented with the goal of satisfying the people's preferences. Democratic political power is thus based on two pillars: the first is the people's *ex ante* and *ex post* input—representation and accountability—, the second is the pursuit of the people's preferences. In Abraham Lincoln's famous words, the Government is carried out "by the people" and "for the people".

M. Ortino (✉)
Economic Law, University of Verona, Verona, Italy
e-mail: matteo.ortino@univr.it

L. Daniele et al. (eds.), *Democracy in the EMU in the Aftermath of the Crisis*,
DOI 10.1007/978-3-319-53895-2_16

The institutional reforms recently adopted in the banking sector in the EU can be seen from the perspective of democratic requirements, and explained as an attempt to correct the democratic failures existing in the relative governance. The expressions "governance of the banking sector" or "banking regulation *lato sensu*" are meant here to refer to the various public powers governing the banking sector. These powers essentially are legislative and administrative rule-making, supervision, enforcement and crisis management. The organisational and institutional arrangements in place (at national/EU level) before and during the banking and the Euro crisis, with regards to such powers, did not fully meet the democratic requirements. They did not provide adequate guarantees in terms of democratic representation, accountability and pursuit of the people's interests.

At least two groups of democratic failures could be highlighted in the governance of the EU banking sector. They both represent different forms of "negative democratic externalities". This concept refers to the situation in which the general community is being burdened with costs resulting from activities carried out by specific subjects for their own purposes, disregarding the community's will and general interest. As regards the banking regulation, these other subjects are in particular national authorities and financial institutions (e.g. banks). The governance of the banking system at the time of the financial and Euro crises was not democratic to the extent that it allowed political and private interests to be pursued without effective democratic control and to the detriment of the public good.

The first democratic externality that was present in the governance of the banking sector concerns the conflict between private and public interests: this can be referred as the "private/public externality". It is the conflict between the interests of a limited number of (legal or physical) persons, acting and organised in a "professional" capacity, on the one hand, and the interests of a much wider group of unorganised and "unprofessional" individuals or of the general public at large, on the other hand. The former group is exemplified by politicians and bankers, while the latter by retail clients, investors and taxpayers. This is a conflict underlying the exercise of all public powers concerning the banking field that form banking regulation *lato sensu*. The private/public negative democratic externality occurs when banking regulation *lato sensu* allows the financial industry to dump its costs on others (e.g. the public at large). For example, a weak crisis-prevention regulation increases the risks of individual and systemic bank failures, to the detriment of third parties who will bear most of the costs of these failures (e.g. real economy firms severely damaged by the credit crunch triggered by a banking systemic crisis). Another example is the political management of a banking crisis that is mainly based on the use of public resources to bail out (mostly private) financial institutions, and more generally to try and correct their mistakes and excessive risk-taking profit-oriented conduct.

The above scenarios constitute not only market failures, but also failures of the democratic process. The political decision-making organisational set-up fails to ensure an adequate degree of *representation*, *accountability* and/or effective *protection of the public good*. The political decision to structure banking regulation *lato sensu* so as to allow the financial industry to externalise most of the costs (e.g. risks) of their activities does not surely represent the will/interest of the community at large, nor the protection of fundamental private rights. Banking regulation *lato sensu* is often being shaped by politicians' (political and personal) objectives and by the interests of the financial industry at the expense of public interests (e.g. financial stability, interests of banks' clients and of taxpayers). In many respects the (formal and informal) links between the political system and the banking system are stronger than the links between the former and its citizens. National political institutions, in charge of laying down banking legislation, find it difficult to deprive themselves of levers to influence banking activities for political reasons. National independent supervisory authorities have not solved the problem. Furthermore at EU level, the governance of the legislative process has a poor record in representing general interests such as those of retail banking clients.

The second group of democratic negative externalities can be referred to as the "national/foreign externality". It originates from the mismatch between the wide integration of European markets and the narrow scope of democratic decision-making processes. Because of the interconnection and overlap among national banking systems within the EU, inadequate national regulation and supervision of banks in one Member State may easily produce negative consequences on another State's citizens, but without the former State having to take into account the interests of these citizens in its decision-making process.[1] Again, costs are imposed on others who do not have the democratic means to have a say in the matter. In Maduro's words, "[t]he scope and level of politics has not mirrored the scope and level of the political problems facing Europe".[2] For this type of externalities both myopic/selfish Member States and inadequate EU decision-making architecture share the blame. Again, the underlying causes are rooted in the design and/or in the functioning of the institutional mechanisms that fail to ensure the right degree of democratic representation, accountability and public interest protection.

In this contribution, the recent institutional reforms introduced by the EU in the banking sector will be analysed and assessed in relation to their ability to address these two types of democratic externalities.

2 Democratic Legitimacy of the Reformed Governance of the EU Banking Sector. Three Determinants: Centralisation, Independence and Accountability

Banking regulation *lato sensu* can be divided in legislative and administrative powers. Banking legislation is where the people's representatives make the fundamental political and policy choices underlying this field, and determine the general regulatory structure thereof. These choices are (or should be) then implemented by

[1]Maduro (2011).

[2]Maduro (2011).

means of administrative activities: technical rule-making, supervision over the compliance with, and enforcement of, the resulting legislative and administrative layers of banking rules.

The most important banking institutional reforms recently enacted in the EU are the establishment of the European Banking Authority (EBA) and the Banking Union (BU). These reforms have left the legislative power unchanged, while introducing some profound institutional changes to the administrative sphere of banking regulation.

Established in 2010, the EBA's tasks are to improve the functioning of the internal market, in particular by ensuring a high, effective and consistent level of banking regulation and supervision taking account of the varying interests of all Member States and the different nature of financial institutions.[3] In order to carry out its tasks, the EBA has been given various powers, which produce different legal effects: binding,[4] quasi-binding[5] and non-binding.[6] These powers concern banking administrative rule-making (e.g. technical standards) and supervisory functions, addressed at competent authorities (which includes the ECB, after the establishment of the Banking Union)[7] and/or at financial institutions[8] and financial markets.[9]

The EBA's central organ is the Board of Supervisors: its voting members are the heads of national banking supervisory authorities (the BU has not altered this national-based voting membership: the EBA Board of Supervisors comprises one representative nominated by the ECB Supervisory Board, but he/she shall be non-voting[10]). Technical standards are approved by qualified majority voting, and by double simple majority of Member States participating and non-participating in the BU.[11]

In 2011 the Euro crisis forced a second wave of institutional banking reforms, which, unlike EBA, are not involving all Member States (but only Member States whose currency is the Euro and some non-Euro Member States). The Euro Area

---

[3]As regards EBA's tasks, see recital 11 and Articles 8 and 9 of the 2010 EBA Regulation.

[4]E.g. measures adopted in case of breach of banking rules, Article 17, para. 6, of the 2010 EBA Regulation.

[5]Quasi-binding powers do not produce *per se* legally binding measures but "form part of a process that leads to legally binding instruments" (Wymeersch 2012). See e.g. the power to draft technical standards, Articles 10 and 11 of the 2010 EBA Regulation.

[6]E.g. issue of guidelines and recommendations, Article 16 of the 2010 EBA Regulation. While not mandatory, they are inspired by the principle of "comply or explain".

[7]Article 4, para. 2, of the 2010 EBA Regulation.

[8]Guidelines and recommendations issued under Article 16 of the 2010 EBA Regulation are addressed at competent authorities or financial institutions.

[9]E.g. task of carrying economic analysis of the market in which financial institutions operate and assessment of the impact of potential market developments on such institutions (Article 32 of the 2010 EBA Regulation).

[10]Article 40, para. 1, d, of the 2010 EBA Regulation.

[11]Article 44 of the 2010 EBA Regulation (as amended with the establishment of the Banking Union).

Summit of June 2012 approved the BU project proposed by the Commission. Currently, two of the three pillars of the BU have been realised: the Single Supervisory Mechanism (SSM)[12] which revolves around the ECB as the new supervisor; and the Single Resolution Mechanism (SRM),[13] managed by a Single Resolution Board (SRB), a newly established EU agency, in charged of taking decision concerning the resolution of banks. The third pillar, i.e. the Common Deposit Insurance, is still being negotiated.

The new EU institutional financial architecture resulting from the introduction of the EBA and from the BU, is to be evaluated against the democratic requirements: representation, accountability and protection of the people's interests. The analysis assumes that three institutional features are of central importance for the fulfilment of these democratic requirements, and therefore for assessing the democratic legitimacy of the new institutional set-up. These determinants are: *centralisation*, *independence* and the regime of *accountability*. This contribution aims at verifying whether, how and to what extent, these three institutional elements are present in the reformed EU governance of the banking sector, and whether they are effectively able to prevent negative democratic externalities.

Before proceeding with the assessment, the general conceptual meaning of the three determinants needs some clarification.

Centralisation refers to the shift of tasks from the national to the EU level and to the creation of tasks at EU level. In order to understand the functional connection between centralisation and democracy, it is important to stress the *raison d'être* of European integration. The allocation of powers to EU institutions and bodies follows the same logic underlying the very creation and functioning of the EU, and particularly the constitutional principle of subsidiarity. The Union's *raison d'être* is to enable the Member States to pursue their common objectives (Article 1 TEU). These objectives are, or may be, out of reach for the Member States alone, which thus need the Union to achieve them. To that end, Member States provide the latter with the necessary powers. Non-exclusive EU powers can be actually exercised only if and to the extent that the pursued objectives cannot be sufficiently achieved by the Member States (Article 5 TEU). Thus, the principle of subsidiarity follows the same logic of necessity underlying the EU as a whole[14]: in order to achieve certain political goals, it may be concluded that the relevant power must be exercised at a higher level of Government. The outcome of this assessment is context-based: for example, what is considered necessary may change in time.

---

[12]Council Regulation (EU) No. 1024/2013 of 15 October 2013 conferring specific tasks on the European Central Bank concerning policies relating to the prudential supervision of credit institutions, OJEU L 287, 29 October 2013, pp. 63 et seqq. [2013 SSM/ECB Regulation].

[13]Regulation (EU) No. 806/2014 of the European Parliament and of the Council of 15 July 2014 establishing uniform rules and a uniform procedure for the resolution of credit institutions and certain investment firms in the framework of a Single Resolution Mechanism and a Single Resolution Fund and amending Regulation (EU) No. 1093/2010, OJEU L 225, 30 July 2014, pp. 1 et seqq.

[14]Ortino (1993).

Democracy is among the fundamental values that must be safeguarded in, and by, the EU (Article 2 TEU). In case of negative democratic externalities, such as those in place in the banking field, the value of democracy is not sufficiently protected by the Member States. Hence, a higher degree of centralisation of power, in the hands of EU institutions or bodies, is required by democratic imperatives.

The second determinant is independence. In EU institutional law, in relation to a public body, independence

> normally means a status which ensures that the body concerned can act completely freely, without taking any instructions or being put under any pressure.[15]

The external influence the *status* of independence is meant to protect from may be of a political nature, coming from national or other EU authorities, or of a private nature, coming from market economic stakeholders. Independence is strictly connected to the need for effectiveness. "[I]ndependent bodies are deemed better able to perform certain functions and to achieve certain goals".[16] In particular, in the EU, independence is generally considered a necessary feature of public authorities that are entrusted with the task of promoting the "interests of the EU as a whole", as opposed to national interests (e.g. Commission, ECB), or with the task of protecting the correct functioning of the EU legal system (e.g. the Court of the EU).

In relation to democratic requirements, independent authorities fall outside the classic parliamentary and administrative mechanism of electoral-political representation and accountability. However non-majoritarian entities are not precluded by the principle of democracy, provided that there are other mechanisms of representation and accountability in place.[17] Not only independent authorities do not *per se* conflict with democracy, but their existence and functions can even be considered as required by democratic imperatives. The functional chain that links an independent judiciary, the rule of law and democracy clearly proves this point. Without an independent Court, the rule of law in the EU legal system would be at risk, and with it the democratic functioning of the political system at EU and national level. A Government not bound by law is not likely to be a Government by the people and for the people. By the same logic, if and to the extent that an independent authority is deemed to be necessary for the effective achievement of a policy goal decided upon by democratically-elected officials (like the case of independent central banks for the goal of monetary stability; of independent financial supervisors for the goal of financial stability), the existence of such authority becomes required by democratic legitimacy. Through independence, the will of the people and/or of the people's representatives, transposed into a regulatory act, may be more faithfully implemented and carried through, to the benefit thus of democratic representation and of the people's perceived public interest.

---

[15] ECJ 9 March 2010, Case C-518/07, *Commission* v. *Germany*, para 18.

[16] Ritleng (2016).

[17] ECJ 9 March 2010, Case C-518/07, *Commission* v. *Germany*, paras. 42–46.

In this regard, it is imperative that independent authorities be also subject to adequate accountability mechanisms. Effectiveness, independence and accountability are strictly intertwined. Like independence, accountability is aimed at increasing the effectiveness of certain public powers, at ensuring that public authorities duly undertake the tasks that they have been assigned. Among the various forms of accountability, judicial accountability promotes effectiveness from a legality perspective: successfully carrying out a task entails, *inter alia*, complying with the relevant legal rules. Performance accountability (e.g. through parliamentary hearings or annual reports), instead, promotes effectiveness from a substantive perspective, ensuring that the body's activities are not only legal but also materially capable of achieving the goal.

3 Democratic Legitimacy of the Reformed EU Institutional Banking Architecture: The Assessment

The assessment as to the democratic legitimacy of the reformed governance of the EU banking system must be carried out in relation to its components: legislative and administrative powers.

3.1 The Making of EU Banking Legislation

The first stage of the banking rule-making process is the adoption of legislative rules. In banking law fields such as prudential regulation, over the last decades it is EU legislators that have been given the task to take the fundamental political and policy choices. National prudential legislations have been harmonised (although not to a sufficient degree, see below).

The EU legislative process of harmonisation is governed by EU Treaties rules, which were left unchanged by the double crisis-induced reforms. The legislative rule-making procedure applicable to the banking sector is usually the "ordinary" one (Article 294 TFEU), based on the Commission's proposal, and on the approval by the Council and the EU Parliament. In general—that is, not just when applied to banking regulation—this legislative process does not fare the democratic legitimacy test well, as least as regards two of the above-said requirements: representation and accountability. J. Weiler's critical assessment of the general EU governance[18] can be applied to the specific exercise of the legislative power under Article 294 TFEU. As regards representation,

> there is simply no moment in the civic calendar of Europe where the citizen can influence directly the outcome of any policy choice facing [. . .] the Union in the way that citizens can

[18]Weiler (2012).

> when choosing between parties which offer sharply distinct programs at the national level. The political colour of the European Parliament only very weakly gets translated into the legislative and administrative output of the Union.

As to the Council—I would add—, its members are—at least for the moment—normally by-products of nationally-focused political competitions, and sometimes not even involving voters.[19] All this makes the voters' input in the EU political process—in terms of the impact of their preferences among various policies options—quite weak. As regards accountability,

> even the basic condition of representative democracy that at election time the citizens can 'throw the scoundrels out' – that is replace the government – does not operate in Europe. [...] Dismissing the Commission by Parliament (or approving the appointment of the Commission President) is not quite the same, not even remotely so.[20]

The weak link between European votes and the activities of the EU co-legislators renders the latter's electoral accountability not effective.

Weak popular representation and accountability makes the EU political system an even more fertile ground than national systems for regulatory capture by the financial industry. This increases the risk and the magnitude of public/private externality. Large financial institutions will likely continue to have a disproportionate influence over the policy and rule-making process. As this process is increasingly taking place at EU level (to regulate banking activities carried out within and outside the Union, e.g. TTIP negotiations between the EU and the USA), lobbying is being targeted at both domestic and European politics. In economic boom times the perception of financial risks and the attention of voters on financial regulation tends to naturally decrease, thus making lobbying regulators for market liberalisation more effective. But also in economic crises, the vital role of the financial system for the whole economy provides financial institutions (already strained by the crisis) with a political lever against restrictive regulation. This is particular true in the current EU financial system, for two reasons: the first is that, due to various factors, the EU banking system is still in precarious financial conditions; the second is that traditionally the European financial system relies excessively on banks, as opposed to financial markets, to finance the real economy and sovereign debt.[21] Not surprisingly, US authorities currently hold the belief that European regulators (in both EU and national sense) are excessively porous to the influence and demands of the financial industry (the watered-down implementation of the Basel III Accord in the EU could confirm this view).[22]

---

[19]For example, the previous Italian Prime Minister, M. Renzi, did not participate in the national general election, and the political programme of his Government, including the policies it was promoting in the Council, was never subject to voters' approval in any democratic election.

[20]Weiler (2012).

[21]"These kinds of relations explain why even without strong pressures by the financial industry, governments feel compelled to consider that the interests of the financial sector are aligned with those of the economy and the country as a whole", see Monnet et al. (2014).

[22]Jones and Macartney (2016).

In sum, for the above reasons, the gap between democratic credentials of legislators at EU level and the ideals of democracy is even wider then at national level (for banking regulatory policies). On the other hand, however, the centralisation of the legislative function in the hands of EU institutions could be an important factor for correcting the undemocratic "national/foreign" externality. Representatives from all Member States participate in the EU legislative process, and thus have at least the opportunity to express their views on the banking regulation that is going to affect all citizens of Europe even if applied by foreign national authorities. In this sense, the centralisation of legislative law-making strengthens political representation and, at the same time, the protection of European citizens' interests. But the fact that in the Council some Member States could be outvoted, allowing the majority to create externalities for the minority, means that the risk of externality is not eliminated by shifting the decision making at EU level. The only difference in this case is that the externality is created by a group of States, and not by an individual State, at the cost of the other States. This variation of the national/foreign externality can be referred to as the "majority/ minority externality". As it will be explained below, this variation can also be found in the EU regulatory stages following the adoption of EU legislation.

The risk of majority/minority externality is in part mitigated by the Commission. Its role in the legislative process and its *status* as independent EU institution are important in addressing the national/foreign externality. The Commission is able to address this externality, not from a "representational" perspective—i.e. not as the Government "by the people"—, but acting as a government "for the people". Having the quasi-exclusive right of legislative initiative, and having the duty to exercise it in the "general interest of the Union" and in complete independence from national and private interferences (Article 17 TEU), the Commission is able to safeguard—at least to a certain extent (under Article 294 TFEU, in the third reading the Council and the Parliament enjoy more freedom to change the legislative text)—the general European interest, as opposed to the interests of individual Member States and of the majority of States, in that sector.

The presence of the majority/minority externality is not the only reason why centralisation of legislative function does not eliminate the risk of national/foreign externality. An insufficient degree of rule harmonisation may also allow this risk to persist: to the extent that national authorities can find room to implement and/or to apply EU rules differently, the risk of negative externalities will continue to exist. This is a democratic deficit not caused by the structure of EU governance *per se*, but by political difficulties of agreeing on common rules during the legislative process. It often has to do with Member States' natural tendency to safeguard their national regulatory autonomy as much as possible, by limiting the extent of EU harmonisation.

An inadequate level of centralisation/harmonisation can be found in the current EU primary prudential legislation. In the wake of the financial crisis, the lack of a consistent set of rules of EU banking regulation was highlighted as one of the urgent problems to solve. In 2009 the de Larosière Report stated that

> The present regulatory framework in Europe lacks cohesiveness. The main cause of this situation stems from the options provided to EU members in the [implementation] of common directives. These options lead to a wide diversity of national transpositions related to local traditions, legislations and practices.[23]

The problem has not yet been solved. "The CRDIV-CRR include 80 options and national discretions left to Member States or competent authorities. The number goes up to 155 if we consider also the options and discretions that are applied by competent authorities on a case by case basis (i.e. individual institutions)."[24] As will be shown below, the sources of regulatory diversity among national banking legal systems can also be found in the other stages of banking regulation *lato sensu*. Options and discretions left by EU legislation to the Member States are a particularly fertile ground for national/foreign externality: they can be used for "protectionist purposes or supervisory forbearance, eventually conducing to distortions of competition and threatening the integrity of the Single Market".[25] The need to address particular aspects and elements of domestic financial markets (e.g. non-mainstream business models and practices) must be managed directly at EU level, and its management must not be left to unilateral measures of Member States.[26] Therefore, if one size does not fit all national financial markets, because, for example, the size of one Member State's financial sector requires higher prudential standards than the rest of the EU,[27] the appropriate derogatory legal regime should be produced at EU level and not left to the discretion of the former Member State.

3.2 The Administrative Powers

3.2.1 The European Banking Authority

The lack of consistent banking regulation *lato sensu* in the EU was one of the main problems that prompted the EU to introduce the EBA as a new actor in the governance of the EU banking sector. The EBA has been created mainly to deal with deficiencies of the banking regulatory process following the legislative phase, consisting of technical/national specification and implementation of legislative rules, and application of the resulting body of (legislative and administrative)

[23]De Larosière Report (2009).

[24]Enria (2015).

[25]Enria (2015).

[26]Enria (2015).

[27]Lastra (2015), who highlights the risk that prudential standards set by EU maximum harmonisation law may not be sufficiently high in relation to specific features of a national financial sector (e.g. the size of the UK financial sector). This, just as the "opposite" scenario of different national banking laws, is a source of financial instability for the whole EU. In my opinion, both risks must be managed at EU level.

law. The fundamental problems were, *inter alia*, "the lack of a consistent set of rules"[28] throughout the EU, and the lack of consistent supervisory practices among national authorities. The two main causes behind the divergent national banking rules stemmed, firstly, from the implementation options left to Member States by EU legislative acts (directives), and secondly, from the diverse interpretations of EU rules, even when national options were not included.

At the root of (almost) all deficiencies is the national-based approach to banking regulation. National-based regulatory and supervisory models have failed in dealing with the integrated and interconnected reality of European financial markets.[29] They have failed in protecting the people's interest, in its European and national dimension (the public power was not exercised "for the people"). National financial markets were not adequately monitored and national authorities failed to address, unilaterally and in cooperation with each other, cross-border issues and risks. The national based models also failed in democratic representation (the public power was not exercised "by the people"). Under this model, national authorities are able "to unduly favour their own national banking system and economy, regardless of outward spill-overs that lie beyond their mandates".[30] "The regulatory approach based on minimum harmonisation coupled with the home-host cooperation allowed national authorities to use the regulatory lever to favour national champions and attract business to national markets, thus weakening the overall regulatory framework"[31] and damaging the realisation of a EU-wide internal financial market by ring-fencing domestic markets and by creating an uneven playing field.

In response to the democratic failings of national-based governance structure, the EU has increased the degree of centralisation of non-legislative rule making, supervision and enforcement. The EU-wide reforms revolve around the work of the EBA and the Commission, but the Council, the EU Parliament, and sometimes national Government's representatives (through comitology committees) are also involved.

The EBA is the engine behind the new EU power of setting binding technical standards aimed at increasing the level of harmonisation.[32] It is the EBA that drafts technical standards, which then have to be endorsed by the Commission. In case of regulatory technical standards, once adopted by the Commission, the Council or the European Parliament may veto their entry into force (Article 290 TFEU and Article 13 of the 2010 EBA Regulation). In case of implementing technical standards, the Commission's exercise of implementing powers can also be subject to the comitology-based control of Member States (Article 291, para. 3 TFEU and Regulation (EU) No. 182/2001).

---

[28] De Larosière Report (2009).

[29] Recital 1 of the 2010 EBA Regulation.

[30] Enoch et al. (2013).

[31] Enria (2015).

[32] Avgouleas (2012) refers to "maximum harmonisation". However, the EBA's President has highlighted the various obstacles that are still obstructing the achievement of such level of harmonistion, see Enria (2015).

The question is whether the new governance is able to prevent the two negative democratic externalities from occurring in the post-legislative phases of banking regulation *lato sensu*. Doubts about its full effectiveness are due to the seemingly insufficient degree of centralisation and independence, in addition to structural fragilities in the accountability mechanism.

As regards the public/private externality, some of its underlying causes still persist. The new governance has not severed the structural features allowing or even favouring the "special" relations between policy/rule-makers and financial institutions. First, with (especially continental) European economic systems still bank-based and the sovereign debt risks still looming, financial industry lobbies continue to have "bargaining power" in the regulatory process. Such power can be used to extract concessions from regulators and supervisors, both at national and at EU level. Second, the governance is still dominated by national authorities (as will be explained below). To the extent that in the past these authorities favoured banks over the public good because of national politics, the new governance will not stop them now. In other words, as national interests are still able to find their way in the regulatory and supervisory process within the reformed EU institutional framework, so will the disproportionate political weight of the financial industries that come with those interests. Third, and strictly connected to the previous point, the performance accountability of national competent authorities (NCAs) to national political institutions is bound to be stronger than to EU political institutions (EU Parliament and Council). Strictly speaking NCAs are accountable to the latter only indirectly: under Article 3 of the 2010 EBA Regulation, it is the EBA—not the NCAs—to be accountable to the European Parliament and to the Council. Furthermore, NCAs are expression of national legal and political decisions (e.g. the heads of such authorities are nominated by national institutions) and mainly work in the national social and economic environment (e.g. subject to the scrutiny of national media). To the extent that the national political institutions, in turn, continue to be more responsive to the demands of the financial industry than to the public good, the public/private externality will persist.

The fact that national authorities are still in control of post-legislative phases of banking regulation gives rise not only to public/private externality, as just mentioned, but also to the "national/foreign" one. Within the new governance framework national authorities still enjoy enough regulatory space to create costs for other Member States without the latter's consent.

As far as centralisation is concerned, the shift of power from national to EU level is incomplete: it is not deep enough to iron out undue differences between national regulations and between national supervisory practices. There are various factors at play. Some have to do with the specific mandates given to the EBA by the co-legislators. In some cases, the EBA is tasked with developing technical standards from minimum harmonisation directives. "Implementing those Directives through immediately applicable Regulations is a source of complexity and it is often used to refrain from full harmonisation".[33] Other factors concern the scope of

[33]Enria (2015).

EBA's powers, as provided for by its foundational legal act. Member States remain in charge of implementing and/or applying the common rules and standards adopted at EU legislative and administrative level. Differentiated national practices can preserve legal fragmentation and thus regulatory competition and cross-border externalities or spill-overs within the EU banking sector. Enforcement of banking regulation against financial institutions is still a national competence. Only the enforcement against Member States is centralised. In this regard, however, the EBA has no enforcement powers. In case of non-compliance, only the Commission can act against a Member State on the basis of general enforcement procedures provided for by Article 258 TFEU.[34] The Commission's intervention, with the possible involvement of the Court, certainly represents the highest form of centralisation; however it is questionable whether that system is able to manage effectively all the cases for non-implementation of EU banking law arising from the activities of national authorities in the 28 Member States.[35]

Insufficient independence is the second weakness of the new EU governance of the banking system. In order for the national/foreign externality to be corrected, shifting power from the national to the EU level is not the only necessary condition. The "national/foreign" logic must also be removed from the exercise of power at EU level. And its place must be taken by the "EU as a whole" logic. The EBA's internal decision making is still dominated by national perspectives and national tendencies: the 28 voting members of the Board of Supervisors are the heads of national supervisory authorities.[36] Standard-making decisions are taken by qualified majority of its members. The Board of Supervisors' composition and voting system are likely to raise the risk that nationally-focused politics steer the Board's decisions. As regards the standards drafted by the EBA, the national/foreign externality may be removed from the action of individual Member States, but not from the collective action of Member States forming the majority. Decisions might be taken to further the common national interests of the majority, instead of the interests of the EU as a whole. The existence of such risk finds confirmation in the 2013 amendment of voting procedures within the EBA Boards of Supervisors: because of fears that the group of national authorities participating in the ECB/SSM might dominate the EBA's rule-making function, the revised Article 44 of the 2010 EBA Regulation provides that a double majority (participating/non participating States) is required.

Besides the relation between the ECB and the EBA, if the latter were to act with a view to furthering the banking interests of the majority of its members, it would be liable for exercising its powers in violation of its duties: the Chairperson and the voting members of the Board of Supervisors are under the obligation to

---

[34]Besides private enforcement against the State or the national competent authority at national level.

[35]Wymeersch (2012).

[36]EBA Chairman, Andrea Enria, has warned that national tendencies in the Supervisory Board may negatively affect the Authority's tasks, in Jenkins and Fleming (2013).

act independently and objectively in the sole interests of the Union as a whole.[37]

The issue here is not so much the illegality of EBA's actions, but the undemocratic structure of its decision making mechanism. The democratic failures are rooted in the very structure of EBA's internal governance. The people's input is not implemented: non-majoritarian authorities, like the EBA, are legitimate if and to the extent that they enact policy decisions taken by the people's representatives. In this case, the latter, i.e. the Parliament and the Council, have imposed the EBA the duty to pursue the "sole interests of the Union as a whole". As its decision making process *de facto* leads the EBA instead to act not in pursuit of that goal, but of other—possibly conflicting—goals (i.e. the interests of the majority of States), the governance of the EBA is not in line with the requirement of democratic representation. The second failure concerns the protection of the people's interest. As the EBA is structurally biased in favour of the majority's interests, possibly in conflict with what has been democratically determined to be the public interest to be pursued, i.e. the interests of EU citizens as a whole, the governance of EBA is in conflict with an exercise of public power "for the people".

It could be argued that the role of the Commission ensures the EU governance of the banking system with adequate independence. The Commission has in fact the last word on most of the EBA's proposed measures. It is the Commission that adopts the technical standards (Articles 290 and 291 TFEU), that forces a Member State to comply with EU banking rules[38] and that adopts emergency measures.[39] The central role of the Commission certainly increases the likelihood that a supranational perspective on the governance of the EU banking system is adopted, without however providing absolute guarantees of that. The technical regulatory standards must meet the (tacit) approval of the Council (national interests) (Article 290 TFEU), and sometimes the implementing technical standards have to go through the comitology process (national interests) (Article 291 TFEU). Furthermore, because of its specific banking expertise and information, it is likely that on the more technical aspects of EU banking regulation *lato sensu*, it is the EBA that will be in the driver's seat.

Will the EBA's accountability regime be able to steer the EBA towards the protection of EU interests from conflicting domestic interests? As far as the effectiveness of performance accountability is concerned, what said above about the private/public externality applies here as well. As regards judicial accountability, it is not likely to have a significant impact on the exercise of most relevant powers of the EBA, that is, the quasi-regulatory powers. Technical standards are formally adopted by the Commission and, besides respecting the legal limits of the EU legislators' delegation, the degree of discretion inherent in their creation will leave them mostly outside the reach of judicial review.

[37]Article 42 of the 2010 EBA Regulation.

[38]Article 17 of the 2010 EBA Regulation.

[39]Article 18 of the 2010 EBA Regulation.

3.2.2 The Banking Union

Within the personal and material scope of the BU, centralisation deficits have been reduced, but not eliminated. And the independence of decision-makers within the BU is still fragile.

The BU project has been conceived exactly to increase the degree of European integration as regards prudential supervision, enforcement and crisis management. The conviction is that in the field of prudential supervision and bank resolution, powers need to be transferred to the EU level in order to be effective, and the exercise of national powers need to be subject to a stronger control and management by EU authorities. Past models of governance based on mere coordination/cooperation have proved to be insufficient for ensuring effective prudential supervision, crisis management and consistent application of EU common rules.[40] For this reason, some of the national decision-making powers have been transferred to the ECB (e.g. authorisation of credit institutions) and to a EU agency, the Single Resolution Board (SRB) (e.g. adoption of resolution plans for banks), within the framework of the Single Supervisory Mechanism (SSM)[41] and the Single Resolution Mechanism (SRM),[42] respectively. Both mechanisms are composed also of national competent authorities (and, in the case of the SRM, the Commission and the Council): the logic behind them is not just an upward shift of powers, but a EU-led stronger multi-level integration and cooperation. For example, the ECB's decision to authorise a bank to take up its business is based on a draft decision proposed by the relevant national competent authority.[43]

The goal of addressing negative democratic externalities underlies the political decision to step up centralisation through the SSM and the SRM. For space constraints, examples from the SSM will be used in the following analysis. The preoccupation with the national/foreign negative externality is particularly clear. As regards the SSM, the EU legislators justify replacing national competences with EU powers by making an explicit reference to the risk of "the impact of failures of credit institutions on other Member States".[44] In the context of a single currency, a EU governance based on mere coordination between national authorities is particularly ineffective, and the risk and consequences of negative externalities of the national/foreign type are particularly serious.[45] Because of "the close links and interactions"[46] between Euro-area Member States, the concerns of negative externalities are not only related to the banking markets, but also to the sovereign debt

[40]Recitals 5 and 87 of the 2013 ECB/SSM Regulation.

[41]Article 6 of the 2013 ECB/SSM Regulation.

[42]Article 1 of the 2014 SRM Regulation.

[43]Article 14 of the 2013 ECB/SSM Regulation.

[44]*Ibid.*, recital 87.

[45]*Ibid.*, recitals 5 and 11.

[46]*Ibid.*, recital 11.

market and the functioning of the single currency and monetary policy. For this reason at least all Euro-area Members State must join the BU.

Centralisation through the BU has reduced without eliminating negative democratic externalities. The SSM leaves open the possibility of negative cross-border externalities between participating and non-participating Member States. Inadequate supervision of banks outside the BU can give rise to instability in the banking markets within the EU, and vice-versa. Again, in theory the member of the SSM are to protect not simply the interests of the Euro-area and those of other participating Member States, but the interests of the whole EU. But in practice priorities may be different.

Furthermore, centralisation does not necessarily equate with independence. The composition of the Supervisory Board is for the most part made of "representatives" of the national competent authorities of each participating Member State.[47] In theory, they are supposed to act in the sole interest of the Union as a whole, disregarding the interests of their home Country.

> The members of the Supervisory Board [. . .] shall act independently and objectively in the interest of the Union as a whole and shall neither seek nor take instructions from the institutions or bodies of the Union, from any government of a Member State or form any other public or private body.[48]

> All member of the Supervisory Board shall act in the interest of the Union as a whole.[49]

Will they comply with this obligation? There seems to be a contradiction: on the one hand, supervisory tasks have been taken away from individual national authorities also because they were carried out with too much focus on national interests; on the other hand, however, the planning and execution of supervision in the SSM is still to be undertaken by a body composed by a majority of national authorities.[50] True supranational decisions are needed to pursue a truly European interest, and cannot be trusted to a body composed of national authorities. It leaves too much room for national-oriented perspectives, and for conflicts both between national interests and between national interests and the interest of the EU as a whole.[51] The ECB might be accused of

[47]*Ibid.*, Article 26.

[48]*Ibid.*, Article 19.

[49]*Ibid.*, Article 26.

[50]It is commonly believed that, because of the *Meroni* case-law, the Supervisory Board may not be delegated to take supervisory decisions. It is tasked with preparatory works and with proposing to the ECB Governing Council complete drafts decisions (Article 26, para. 8, of the 2013 ECB/SSM Regulation). Formally, it is always the ECB Governing Council that adopts such decisions. However, the latter may only approve or object (but not modify) the proposals of the Supervisory Board; in case of objections it has to state its reasons in writing, and it has only a 10 working days (or 48 h in case of emergency) timeframe to present its objections. For these reasons, it is reasonable to assume that, normally, the Governing Council will not have time to review day-to-day supervision and approve the Supervisory Board's proposal by silence, making it "in practice a co-decision-making body", see Hinojosa-Martinez (2015).

[51]See Hinojosa-Martinez (2015), who believes that "the supranational context of this decision-making and its highly technical background provide an environment that favours objectivity.".

carrying out its supervisory tasks without impartiality if, for example, its decisions would favour the banking systems of certain Member States to the detriment of the others. By focusing on credit risk and ignoring market and legal risk, the ECB has already been "suspected" of favouring northern European Member States in which banks focus more on trading and/or are currently involved in costly lawsuits (like Deutsche Bank).[52]

Majority/minority negative dynamics can also arise in the adoption of decisions by the ECB's Governing Council (GC), which is the SSM final decision maker, and in which non-Euro SSM participating Member States are absent. For this reason, the GC is expected to invite representatives from those Member States whenever it is planning to object to a Supervisory Board's draft decisions or whenever the concerned national competent authorities inform the GC of their reasoned disagreement with a draft decision of the Supervisory Board addressed to national authorities concerning banks from non-Euro SSM participating Member States.[53] The GC must promptly decide on any draft decision of the Supervisory Board with which a non-Euro participating Member State disagrees, taking fully into account the latter's reasons and explain in writing its decision to the Member State concerned. The latter may request the ECB to leave the close cooperation with immediate effect and will not be bound by the ensuing decision.[54] These special rules are double-edged sword. On one hand, they increase democratic representation and attenuate the risk of majority/minority externality. On the other hand, by identifying a national supervisor with its Member State, a Member State with "its" banks, and by allowing a Member State to threat leaving the BU for individual decisions concerning its banks, show how the nationally-focused perspective can still permeate EU decision making, thus weakening the pursuit of the interests of the EU as a whole.

A particular obligation aimed at ensuring impartiality in the exercise of supervisory tasks by national authorities, and thus preventing the national/foreign externality, is exemplified by Article 31 of the 2013 ECB/SSM Regulation. The ECB has the power to impose a multi-national composition of supervisory teams of national authorities taking supervisory actions regarding a financial institution. Requiring the involvement of staff from foreign supervisory authorities, thus making possible for national authorities to monitor and keep in check one another on an on-going basis,[55] is meant to ensure that supervision is carried out for the interests of the EU as a whole, as oppose to national interests. The EU wants to avoid conflict of interest situations,[56] in which, in particular, national authorities may be tempted to subordinate EU interests to the protection of national champions.

---

52 Baglioni (2016).

53 Recital 72 of the 2013 SSM Regulation.

54 Article 7, para. 8, of the SSM 2013 Regulation.

55 Recital 79 of the SSM 2013 Regulation.

56 Recital 40 of the 2012 SSM Commission Proposal ("Where necessary to avoid conflicts of interest, particularly in the supervision of large banks").

Overall, ECB's accountability safeguards provided for by EU legislation appear to be of a good standard.[57] The ECB is accountable to both sources of democratic legitimacy in the EU: the totality of EU citizens (EU Parliament) and Member States' democratically organised peoples (Council and national Parliaments).[58] Of particular interest is a national Parliament's possibility of inviting the Chair or a member of the Supervisory Board for

> an exchange of view in relation to the supervision of credit institutions in that Member State[59]:

this is certainly an important means to enhance transparency and thus accountability and a crucial moment to correctly understand and manage in practice the possible duality between national interests and EU interest. To make ECB's accountability (and independence) more effective, the transparency of its activities should be enhanced, for instance, by providing through its website a level of information adequate enough to enable the general public—through the intermediation of market analysts, academic commentators, consumer associations and the media—to evaluate the ECB's conduct, in terms of impartiality, coherence and effectiveness.

One aspect deserving particular attention is the power of the EU Parliament and of the Council to "pressure" the ECB into removing the Chair or the Vice Chair of the Supervisory Board when he no longer fulfils the "conditions required for the performance of his duties".[60] These conditions are not sufficiently clear.

The ECB is also accountable to judicial and administrative review mechanisms, activated by individual persons who are subject to or affected by its supervisory decisions. Legal instruments like the duty of due process, the internal administrative review and the right to bring proceedings before the Court of Justice, are particularly important for keeping the ECB in check as regards the correct implementation of its mandate.

References

Avgouleas E (2012) Governance of global financial markets. Cambridge University Press, Cambridge

Baglioni A (2016) The European banking union. A critical assessment. Palgrave, Basingstoke

De Larosière Report (2009) The High-Level Group on financial supervision in the EU, chaired by J. de Larosière

Enoch C et al (eds) (2013) From fragmentation to financial integration in Europe. IMF

Enria A (2015) The single rulebook in banking: is it "single" enough? In: Lectio Magistralis. University of Padova, Padova

[57] See Masciandaro and Nieto (2013).

[58] Articles 20 and 21 of the 2013 ECB/SMM Regulation.

[59] Recital 26 and Article 21 of the 2013 ECB/SSM Regulation.

[60] *Ibid.*, Article 26, para. 4.

Hinojosa-Martinez LM (2015) The role of the ECB in the supervision of credit institutions. In: Hinojosa-Martinez LM, Beneyto JM (eds) European banking union. The new regime. Wolters Kluwer, The Hague

Jenkins P, Fleming S (2013) Euro bank watchdog attacks unwieldy governance. Financial Times, 17 November 2013

Jones E, Macartney H (2016) TTIP and the "finance exception": venue-shopping and the breakdown of financial regulatory coordination. J Bank Regul 17:4–20

Lastra R (2015) International financial and monetary law, 2nd edn. Oxford University Press, Oxford

Maduro MP (2011) A new governance for the European Union and the Euro: democracy and justice. EUI/RSCAS Policy Papers, No. 11

Masciandaro D, Nieto M (2013) Gouvernance du Mécanisme de Supervision Unique: Quelques Réflexions. Revue d'Economie Financière, No. 4, pp 51 et seqq

Monnet E, Pagliari S, Vallée S (2014) Europe between financial repression and regulatory capture. Bruegel Working Paper, No. 8

Ortino S (1993) Introduzione al diritto costituzionale federativo. Giappichelli, Torino

Ritleng D (2016) Introduction. In: Ritleng D (ed) Independence and legitimacy in the institutional system of the European Union. Oxford University Press, Oxford

Weiler JHH (2012) In the face of crisis: input legitimacy, output legitimacy and the political Messianism of European integration. J Eur Integr 34(7):825–841

Wymeersch E (2012) The European financial supervisory authorities or ESAS. In: Wymeersch E et al (eds) Financial regulation and supervision. Oxford University Press, Oxford

The Single Resolution Mechanism and the Single Resolution Fund: Substantive Issues and the Contradictory Democratic Deficit

Nicola Ruccia

Abstract This paper is aimed to examine the Single Resolution Mechanism (SRM) and the Single Resolution Fund (SRF), with particular reference to the effective level of control on their activity and the potential democratic deficit stemming from them. To this end, it first provides a definition of resolution for banks, followed by the examination of why the efficiency of prudential supervision in the Euro area is significantly linked to a centralised system of resolution. Within this ambit, it illustrates that the SRF is financed by contributions from the banking sector which transfer is based on a separate intergovernmental agreement between the Member States of the Euro area. After, it analyses the relationships between the SRM and the European Banking Authority (EBA) and their several implications. Finally, the paper tries to show whether, and to what extent, it is possible to overcome the democratic deficit in the SRM and the SRF and its contradictions.

Contents

1 Introduction

The financial crisis in the Economic and Monetary Union (EMU), following the entry into force of the Treaty of Lisbon, has highlighted the link between bank risk and sovereign risk. The former is the uncertainty about future cash flows of a bank,

N. Ruccia (✉)
Polytechnic of Bari, Bari, Italy
e-mail: ruccia.nicola@libero.it

L. Daniele et al. (eds.), *Democracy in the EMU in the Aftermath of the Crisis*,
DOI 10.1007/978-3-319-53895-2_17

the probability of loss or revenue shortfall—compared with the planned—of its resources as a result of certain financial transactions. It can lead to the recourse to central bank or Government liquidity.[1] The latter refers to the danger of Government default on a loan made to a Member State or guaranteed by it.

Public intervention on troubled banks has generated an increase of the level of debt for some Member States while the purchase, by banks, of bonds of Member States with large deficits has undermined their financial stability. This spiral, within the EMU, has taken on a cross-border dimension that has often questioned the confidence in the Euro.

The provision of a system limiting one of those risks to reduce the other one had proved unworkable due to the low level of banking integration. Therefore, an action characterised by two parallel aims of financial stability—one concerning the Member States and one regarding their banks—both converging to the overall stability of the system, became necessary.

The EU, with regard to the sovereign risk, intervened with measures provided both by primary[2] and secondary law.[3] Instead, with reference to banking risk, it has issued only secondary legislation. The first step was represented by the European System of Financial Supervision (ESFS) which, however, from the beginning proved to be inadequate to ensure the general stabilisation of the banking sector in the EMU.[4]

---

[1]Altunbas et al. (2011).

[2]The European Stability Mechanism and the Fiscal Compact signed, respectively, on 2 February and on 2 March 2012.

[3]For example: i) Council Regulation (EU) No. 407/2010 of 11 May 2010 establishing a European financial stabilisation mechanism; ii) the so called Six Pack, that includes: Regulation (EU) No. 1173/2011 of the European Parliament and of the Council of 16 November 2011 on the effective enforcement of budgetary surveillance in the Euro area, Regulation (EU) No. 1174/2011 of the European Parliament and of the Council of 16 November 2011 on enforcement measures to correct excessive macroeconomic imbalances in the Euro area, Regulation (EU) No. 1175/2011 of the European Parliament and of the Council of 16 November 2011 amending Council Regulation (EC) No. 1466/97 on the strengthening of the surveillance of budgetary positions and the surveillance and coordination of economic policies, Regulation (EU) No. 1176/2011 of the European Parliament and of the Council of 16 November 2011 on the prevention and correction of macroeconomic imbalances, Council Regulation (EU) No. 1177/2011 of 8 November 2011 amending Regulation (EC) No. 1467/97 on speeding up and clarifying the implementation of the excessive deficit procedure and Council Directive 2011/85/EU of 8 November 2011 on require ments for budgetary frameworks of the Member States; iii) the so called Two Pack, that includes: Regulation (EU) No. 472/2013 of the European Parliament and of the Council of 21 May 2013 on the strengthening of economic and budgetary surveillance of Member States in the Euro area experiencing or threatened with serious difficulties with respect to their financial stability and Regulation (EU) No. 473/2013 of the European Parliament and of the Council of 21 May 2013 on common provisions for monitoring and assessing draft budgetary plans and ensuring the correction of excessive deficit of the Member States in the Euro area.

[4]The ESFS is a system of micro and macro prudential supervision consisting of European and national supervisors. The micro prudential pillar at EU level includes the European Banking Authority (EBA), the European Insurance and Occupational Pension Authority (EIOPA), the European Securities and Markets Authority (ESMA), which work together in the Joint Committee of the European Supervisory Authorities (ESAs). Macro prudential supervision is performed by the European Systemic Risk Board (ESRB). The national supervisory authorities also take part of the EFSF.

As a result, a general reform of the sector was needed. It led to the so called Banking Union, which is based on three complementary pillars:

(i) the Single Supervisory Mechanism (SSM), established by Regulation (EU) No. 1024/2013[5];
(ii) the Single Resolution Mechanism (SRM) and the Single Resolution Fund (SRF), both established by Regulation (EU) No. 806/2014[6];
(iii) the European Deposit Insurance Scheme (EDIS), under construction.[7]

This paper is devoted to analyse the SRM and the SRF, with particular regard to the effective level of control on their activity and the potential democratic deficit stemming from them. Under these profiles it first provides a definition of resolution for banks followed by the examination of why the efficiency of prudential supervision in the Euro area is significantly linked to a centralised system of resolution. Within this ambit, it illustrates that the SRF is financed by contributions from the banking sector which transfer is based on a separate intergovernmental agreement between the Member States of the Euro area. After, the analysis of the relationships between the SRM and the European Banking Authority (EBA) and their several implications will be made and finally, the paper tries to show whether, and to what extent, it is possible to overcome the democratic deficit in the SRM and the SRF and its contradictions.

2 Definition of Resolution for Banks

At EU level, the resolution for banks is defined in secondary law.[8] The legislation aims at ensuring the continuity of the critical functions of a bank under financial stress, to avoid significant adverse effects on the financial system, to protect public

---

[5]Council Regulation (EU) No. 1024/2013 of 15 October 2013 conferring specific tasks on the European Central Bank concerning policies relating to the prudential supervision of credit institutions.

[6]Regulation (EU) No. 806/2014 of the European Parliament and of the Council of 15 July 2014 establishing uniform rules and a uniform procedure for the resolution of credit institutions and certain investment firms in the framework of a Single Resolution Mechanism and a Single Resolution Fund and amending Regulation (EU) No. 1093/2010.

[7]Proposal for a Regulation of the European Parliament and of the Council amending Regulation (EU) No. 806/2014 in order to establish a European Deposit Insurance Scheme, COM (2015) 586 final.

[8]Directive 2014/59/EU of the European Parliament and of the Council of 15 May 2014 establishing a framework for the recovery and resolution of credit institutions and investment firms and amending Council Directive 82/891/EEC, and Directives 2001/24/EC, 2002/47/EC, 2004/25/EC, 2005/56/EC, 2007/36/EC, 2011/35/EU, 2012/30/EU and 2013/36/EU; Regulation (EU) No. 1093/2010 of the European Parliament and of the Council of 24 November 2010 establishing a European Supervisory Authority (European Banking Authority), amending Decision 716/2009/EC and repealing Commission Decision 2009/78/EC. See Babis (2014).

funds by minimising reliance on extraordinary public financial support and, finally, to protect depositors, investors, client funds and client assets.[9]

Resolution actions are taken if a bank is failing or is likely to fail and—having regard to timing and other relevant circumstances—there is no realistic prospect that any alternative private sector measures would prevent its failure within a reasonable timeframe. Finally, they must be necessary in the public interest.[10] These actions must minimise the cost of resolution and avoid destruction of value unless necessary to achieve the resolution aims.

Under the technical profile, there are four types of resolution instruments: the sale of the business, the establishment of a bridge institution, the asset separation and the bail-in.[11]

The first is the transfer to a purchaser, on commercial terms and without requiring the consent of shareholders, of the whole or part of the shares or other instruments of ownership or any assets, rights or liabilities of the bank concerned.[12]

The second is a temporary tool. It consists in a legal person—controlled by public authorities—created for the purpose of receiving and holding some or all of the shares or other instruments of ownership of the bank involved, or its assets, rights and liabilities with a view to maintaining access to critical functions and selling it when market conditions will be appropriate.[13]

The third—that can be admitted only in conjunction with another tool, in order to minimise competitive distortion—allows the transfer of impaired assets to an asset management vehicle, with the aim to permit them to be managed and sold over time.[14]

The fourth is the most contested and controversial.[15] It is conceived to recapitalise a bank to the extent necessary to restore its ability to comply with its authorisation conditions and to continue to carry out its activities.[16] Furthermore, this instrument must contribute to sustain sufficient market confidence in the bank under resolution and to convert to equity or reduce the principal amount of claims or debt instruments that are transferred to a bridge institution with a view to providing capital for that bridge institution or under the sale of business tool or the asset separation tool.[17] In other words, the bail-in clause consents to write down the claims of unsecured creditors and to convert debt into equity. It seeks to use debt capital as means to absorb bank losses in advance of using public funds.[18]

---

[9]Article 31, para. 2, of Directive 2014/59/EU. See Schillig (2013).

[10]Article 33 of Directive 2014/59/EU.

[11]Article 37, para. 3, of Directive 2014/59/EU. See Schillig (2014).

[12]Article 38 of Directive 2014/59/EU. See Schillig (2015).

[13]Article 40, para. 2, of Directive 2014/59/EU. See Schillig (2015).

[14]Article 42 of Directive 2014/59/EU. See Schillig (2015) and Wellerdt (2015).

[15]Moloney (2014).

[16]Boccuzzi (2015), Forestieri (2014), Huertas (2013) and Schillig (2015).

[17]Article 43, para. 2, of Directive 2014/59/EU.

[18]Kokkinis (2015).

3 Connection between Supervision and Resolution

Banking Union is based on awareness that centralisation of prudential supervision at the EU level is not enough to break the perverse link between sovereigns and the banking sector if resolution of credit institutions continues to be provided by national authorities.[19] In the latter hypothesis, costs of resolution would weigh on Member States triggering, one more time, the above mentioned link. Instead, a centralised approach for the evaluation of the balance sheets of banks and for their eventual recapitalisation would lead to the expected results of their business recovery.[20]

Therefore, effective prudential supervision at EU level is strictly related to an European mechanism of bank resolution. The latter must provide private financial assistance instead of the public one and, for cross-border banking groups, the allocation of losses in the Member States involved. The aim is to avoid that capital investments in banks would be less dangerous that the ones operated in other sectors, generating cases of moral hazard.[21]

The SRM and the SSM will help break the aforesaid link between banks and sovereigns in the Member States and reverse the current process of financial market fragmentation.

Without a strong SRM complementing the SSM, the credibility and effectiveness of the European Banking Union would be modest. Leaving resolution tools at national level while supervision is centralised implies considerable risks, such as keeping alive bank-sovereigns links and creating potential conflicts among national authorities in cross border resolution.

Conversely, an European authority, as presumptive receiver of failed banks, can facilitate timely resolution, including cross-border banks. It would provide an instrument to internalise home-host concerns and would reach agreement on burden-sharing when common backstops are needed and would be, therefore, essential to guarantee effectiveness of centralised supervision. It could thus contribute to avoid the expensive and prolonged resolutions that occurred, for example, in the cases of *Dexia* and of *Fortis*.[22] It is also indispensable to line up inducements for least-cost resolution, because a common backstop in a decentralised mechanism would provide incentives to shift residual losses from national taxpayers to those of the Euro area.

Furthermore, centralisation of bank resolution would achieve economies of scale, avoid incoherence and duplication, align incentives and accumulate expertise including for preparation and implementation of recovery and resolution plans for systemic institutions.[23]

---

[19] Huertas (2016).

[20] Véron and Wolff (2013).

[21] Allen and Carletti (2015).

[22] Avgouleas (2012).

[23] Tressel (2014).

Finally, centralisation of resolution decisions—including on the use of funding raised at EU level—is fundamental for the completion of the internal market in financial services since the failure of banks in one Member State may affect its stability.

Indeed, banks in the internal market are highly interconnected and have a large percentage of foreign assets. In the absence of a centralised resolution authority, bank crises in Member States participating in the integrated prudential supervision would have a stronger negative systemic impact also in non-participating Member States. As a result, uniform resolution rules and equal conditions of resolution financing across Member States are in the best interests not only of the Member States in which banks operate but also of all Member States considered as a whole, ensuring a level competitive playing field and improving the functioning of the internal market. In other words, a centralised authority would guarantee a neutral approach in dealing with failing banks. It would increase stability of the banks of the participating Member States and prevent the spill-over of crises into non-participating Member States and will thus facilitate the functioning of the internal market as a whole.[24]

4 The Single Resolution Fund

The SRF is a paramount element for the attainment of the Banking Union's aims. Particularly, it has been established for the purpose of ensuring the efficient implementation of resolution tools and powers, and for the equalisation across Member States of banks' bailout prospects. Without it, investors would persist to establish borrowing conditions according to the place of establishment of the banks rather than to their creditworthiness.[25] In this contest it must be noted that the SRM and the SRF are established under Article 114 TFEU. It is the legal basis enabling the European institutions to adopt measures aimed at the approximation of national provisions, regulations and administrative practices that have as their objective the establishment and the functioning of the internal market.[26]

The SRF is pre-funded with bank contributions, which are raised at the national level but pooled at EU level. These contributions from individual banks must be raised *ex ante*, in order to attain a determined target level of pre-funding, able to guarantee resources available under any circumstances and to avoid destabilising effects of an *ex post* levy on other banks. Its accessible financial means will reach at least 1% of the amount of covered deposits of all credit institutions authorised in all of the participating Member States. This level must be reached gradually over a

[24]See recital 12 of Regulation (EU) No. 806/2014; Gallagher (2014). On the internal market, its establishment and completion, see Daniele (2012).

[25]Recital 19 of Regulation (EU) No. 806/2014.

[26]Maletić (2013).

period of 8 years which could be extended, by up to four more years, if it has made cumulative disbursements of more than 0.5% of covered deposits. Thereafter, if its financial resources fall below the target, they must be refilled through supplementary contributions.[27] The latter can also be imposed on an extraordinary basis and up to a limit *ex post*, if the pre-funded resources are insufficient to cover the cost of resolution actions.[28]

The SRF's resources must be used exclusively for the implementation of resolution tools and resolution powers.[29] They can provide extended short-term funding to a failed bank or a bridge entity, guarantees to potential purchasers of a failed bank or injection of capital in a bridge entity but they cannot be used directly to absorb losses of the failed bank or to recapitalise it.

Finally, any decisions on the use of the resources must be taken by the Single Resolution Board (SRB) of the SRM, which is responsible for its administration.[30] Within this ambit it must be noted that, while the resources are drawn from the private banking sector—not from the taxpayer—any resolution action involving the SRF needs the approval of the European Commission, just as if it were a type of state aid.[31]

While the SRF has been established by secondary law, arrangements regarding the transfer to and the mutualisation of contributions to it have been defined in an international agreement signed by the Member States participating in the SSM.[32] This agreement would enter into force on the first day of the second month following deposit of ratification by Member States that represent 90% of the aggregate of the weighted votes of all Member States participating in the SSM and in the SRM.[33] On 30 November 2015 a sufficient number of Member States has ratified it, allowing full operationalisation of the SRF. As a result, the SRM and SRF entered into force on 1 January 2016.

The adoption of the IGA concerning the SRF implies some legal questions.[34]

The first regards the compliance of the SRF with the principle of autonomy of EU law.

Since the IGA would enter into force under the above mentioned conditions, the eventual failure to ratify it would render inapplicable several provisions of Regulation (EU) No. 806/2014. Even though the IGA has been ratified, one cannot exclude that its potential revision would be in contrast with the same Regulation. This implies a breach of the principle of autonomy of EU law for which its scope,

[27] Article 69, paras. 1, 3 and 4, of Regulation (EU) No. 806/2014.

[28] *Ibid.*, Article 71, para. 1.

[29] *Ibid.*, Article 76.

[30] *Ibid.*, Articles 42–56.

[31] Hadjiemmanuil (2015).

[32] Articles 1 and 77 of Regulation (EU) No. 806/2014.

[33] Article 1, para. 2, of the Agreement on the Transfer and Mutualisation of Contributions to the Single Resolution Fund (SRF IGA), signed on 14 May 2014.

[34] Zavvos and Kaltsouni (2015).

validity, interpretation and application are independent from any other rule or system of law, national as well as international, due to its special nature.[35] As a result, powers of the EU and its institutions cannot be affected by intergovernmental agreements.[36] Nonetheless, in this case it would seem that such powers could be substantially affected by the SRF IGA. As a matter of fact, Regulation (EU) No. 806/2014 cannot be applied without the adoption of a parallel intergovernmental agreement. The effective application of its rules on the use of the SRF is only possible after the ratification of the connected agreement by the majority of contracting Member States. Furthermore, even if ratified, the intergovernmental agreement could be amended in a sense contrary to EU law.

The second important question stemming from the adoption of the SRF IGA concerns the future of decision-making procedures.

SRF IGA is the last international agreement adopting measures in response to the EU financial crisis, after the Fiscal Compact Treaty and the European Stability Mechanism Treaty.[37] One can observe that there is a new trend in the EU decision-making in the economic and monetary field, favouring the intergovernmental method for coordinated action in the spirit of solidarity rather than the community method.[38] However, while the latter empowers the European Commission to analyse national positions before determining the EU general interest, the former, taken outside the EU institutional framework, seeks to delineate the lowest common ground allowing Member States to attain unanimity more easily. The intergovernmental method gives some Countries more weight during the negotiations of the agreements and conducts to the isolation of other Countries not in line with the concessions needed for attaining unanimity.[39]

Moreover, one must notice the absence of the European Parliament from the decision-making with this method. Thus, the democratic legitimacy of the measures concerned is reduced.[40] Differently, if these agreements would be adopted within the EU institutional framework, the European Parliament would have a well-delineated role, either as a co-legislator or by granting its consent throughout the flexibility clause. Consequently, they would obtain an increased democratic legitimacy.[41]

[35]Barents (2004).

[36]van Rossem (2013).

[37]See para. 1.

[38]De Schoutheete (2011).

[39]Ponzano (2011).

[40]Ponzano (2011).

[41]Zavvos and Kaltsouni (2015).

5 The Relationship between the Single Resolution Mechanism and the European Banking Authority

The establishment of the SRM requires the examination of its relationship with EBA,[42] especially with regard to the division of their tasks—and to their potential overlap—and the way in which the former may participate in the decision-making of the latter.

Firstly, it must be noted that Article 8, para. 1, i, of Regulation (EU) No. 1093/2010[43] assigns to EBA an active role in the development and coordination of recovery and resolution plans. It provides a high level of protection to depositors and investors throughout the EU and elaborates methods for the resolution of failing banks as well as an estimation of the need for adequate financing tools. In accordance with Article 27, it also contributes to the evaluation of the need for a robust funding mechanism connected to a set of coordinated national crisis management measures. Indeed, since its establishment, it was also expected the enhancement of its role in a framework of crisis resolution and, if necessary, the creation of an EU resolution fund. As reported in Article 25, the aim is to minimise the systemic impact of any failures, with particular reference to those that may involve a systemic risk, in order to avoid contagion and to permit failing banks to be wound in a timely manner.[44] As a result, EBA can identify best practises for facilitating the resolution of failing banks, particularly cross-border groups, and may develop regulatory and implementing technical standards.

In other words, EBA has the power to enact binding legal acts.[45] This involves a questionable power shift that must be analysed with regard to the balance of powers.[46]

To this end, one must observe that the SRB, pursuant to Article 5, para. 2, of Regulation (EU) No. 806/2014, is subject to the above mentioned binding regulatory and implementing technical standards and to any guidelines and recommendations developed by EBA. It is also subject to any decision of EBA in case of settlement of disagreements between competent authorities in cross-border situations provided for in Article 19 of Regulation (EU) No. 1093/2010. According to the latter, EBA, in order to prevent a Balkanisation of the resolution planning process, acts at the first stage as a mediator. However, if the competent authorities concerned fail to reach an agreement, it may take a decision requiring them to take specific action or to refrain from action in order to settle the matter, with binding effects for them and for the banks involved. The aim is to preserve the coherence of group-wide resolution planning.[47]

---

[42] *Supra*, para. 1.

[43] *Supra*, para. 2.

[44] De Meester (2014).

[45] Magiera and Weiß (2014).

[46] Wellerdt (2015).

[47] Davies (2015).

Moreover, EBA must ensure compliance with EU law. Within this ambit, one must pay attention to recital 18 of Regulation (EU) No. 806/2014, which affirms that in cases where EU law confers discretion on competent authorities, EBA's decisions cannot replace the exercise in compliance with EU law of that discretion. Under this principle it must perform its tasks.

It can be noted, therefore, that the SRM—despite its heading role in resolution for banks in EMU—is placed, in the relationship with EBA, at the same level of national authorities, with two orders of consequences.

First of all, even with regard to the SRM, the acts that EBA may issue in place of the national authorities, if necessary conditions are met, would be adopted.

Furthermore, EBA would be given the role of the regulatory authority for resolution across the EU considered as a whole. It would be the main guarantor of financial stability of the latter, having specific powers to intervene on national authorities and banks of all Member States, including cross-border groups.

Another matter of considerable complexity is represented by the participation of the SRM in the decision-making of EBA.

According to Article 30, para. 5, of Regulation (EU) No. 806/2014, the SRB shall appoint a representative which shall participate in the Resolution Committee of EBA, which is a permanent internal Committee established for the purpose of preparing EBA decisions—including draft regulatory technical standards and draft implementing technical standards—relating to tasks that have been conferred on resolution authorities as provided for in Directive 2014/59/EU. This Committee promotes the development and coordination of resolution plans and develops methods for the resolution of failing banks.[48] Within this ambit, EBA must ensure structural separation between the Resolution Committee and other functions referred to in Regulation (EU) No. 1093/2010. The scope is to avoid conflicts of interest that occurs when the impartial and objective exercise of its powers in resolution for banks is compromised for reasons involving any other of its institutional functions.

With regard to the meeting of the SRB one must note that, according to Article 51, para. 3, of Regulation (EU) No. 806/2014, it may invite observers to participate in its plenary session, including a representative of EBA.

As stated in Article 32, para. 4, of Regulation (EU) No. 806/2014, the SRB may conclude, on behalf of the national resolution authorities of participating Member States, non-binding cooperation arrangements in line with the EBA framework cooperation arrangements, which must be notified to EBA. Article 32 also provides for consultation of—and cooperation with—non-participating Member States. In these cases, the SRB represents the national resolution authorities of the participating Member States for the purposes of consultation and cooperation with non-participating Member States. To this end, it can conclude, in accordance with

[48] Article 127 of Directive 2014/59/EU.

the ECB, a memorandum of understanding describing the general terms of cooperation in line with EBA's policies.

Furthermore, Article 94 of Regulation (EU) No. 806/2014 establishes that by 31 December 2018, and every 3 years thereafter, the Commission must publish a report evaluating, among other things, the functioning of the SRM—assessing whether cooperation between it and EBA, within the ambit of the ESFS,[49] is appropriate—and the level of the interaction between the SRB and EBA.

Finally, with regard to the connection of the SRB with other public financial stability facilities, Article 30, para. 6, of Regulation (EU) No. 806/2014 provides for its close cooperation with the European Financial Stability Facility (EFSF)[50] and the European Stability Mechanism (ESM).[51] This applies, particularly, in the extraordinary circumstances which require further funding that may be sought from alternative financing sources and where such a facility could grant financial assistance to entities established in a participating Member State. To this end, a memorandum of understanding with the ECB and the national resolution authorities, describing in general terms how they will cooperate in the performance of their respective tasks under EU law, can be concluded.[52]

6 Democracy in the Single Resolution Mechanism and in the Single Resolution Fund

From the beginning of the financial crisis onwards debate within the EMU highlighted its democratic deficit, particularly with regard to the repartition of banks' losses. On the one hand, the bailing in of bondholders, affirmed in Article 27 of Regulation (EU) No. 806/2014, has been justified on the basis that, in the internal market, it should be market participants rather than the Member State that price in and carry the risk undertaken by market participants themselves. On the other hand, permitting bondholders to suffer significant losses could cause withdrawal of market support, letting go the banks concerned and pushing the other operators involved also towards distress. Within this ambit, the connection among different necessities must be made with democratic direction of the policies adopted.[53]

Firstly, it should remain for each Member State to debate and define how it wants to allocate the risks posed by its banks. If, through the democratic process, it is

---

[49] *Supra*, para. 1.

[50] It was created as a temporary crisis resolution mechanism in the form of a company incorporated in Luxembourg under Luxembourgish law on 7 June 2010. Its shareholders are EMU Member States with the exception of Latvia and Lithuania.

[51] *Supra*, para 1.

[52] Article 30, para. 7, of Regulation (EU) No. 806/2014.

[53] Dorn (2015).

stated that the principle of creditor bail-in should be or not be applied, it would be difficult to take an opposite decision.

Secondly, resolution plans imply expert judgment-making about decisions that must be taken rapidly escaping, generally, democratic procedures.

Thirdly, if the bail-in clause does not apply, and bonds are paid with public sources, the public actor involved gives profit to the speculator. Finally, citizens in one EMU Member State may find themselves paying not only to bail out another EMU Member State but also to pay private funds, undermining, very much, solidarity.

Therefore, one can affirm that the SRM cannot be simply seen as technocratic harmonisation at EU level of resolution for banks or as a system to apply after the failure of prudential supervision. It is a new policy frontier in the financial market regulation that contributes, enormously, at redefining it.[54]

Within this ambit, one must observe that Regulation (EU) No. 806/2014 establishes some forms of democratic control on the SRB. According to Article 45, the latter must be accountable to the European Parliament, the Council and the Commission for the implementation of the SRM. It must submit an annual report to them as well as to the national Parliaments of participating Member States and to the European Court of Auditors, on the performance of its tasks. Furthermore, its President must present that report to the European Parliament and to the Council.

At the request of the European Parliament, the President participates in a hearing by the competent committee of the European Parliament on the performance of the resolution tasks of the SRB. However, a hearing must take place at least annually. The SRB can reply orally or in writing to questions addressed to it by the European Parliament or by the Council, within 5 weeks of receipt of a question.

Finally, during any investigations by the European Parliament, the SRB must cooperate with it, under Article 226 TFEU. Thus, Regulation (EU) No. 806/2014 expressly requires the involvement of the European Parliament at committee level to conduct inquiries on the activity of the SRB.

Within 6 months of the appointment of the President, the SRB and the European Parliament conclude appropriate arrangements on the practical modalities of the exercise of democratic accountability and oversight over the exercise of the tasks conferred on the SRB.[55] The allocation of powers of the latter should guarantee that an institution with democratic credentials, i.e. the European Parliament, exercises control over the implementation of EU policy, i.e. the resolution plans, for which it can be held accountable to the electorate through the democratic process.[56] The aim

---

[54]Dorn (2015).

[55]Interinstitutional agreement between the European Parliament and the Single Resolution Board on the practical modalities of the exercise of democratic accountability and oversight over the exercise of the tasks conferred on the Single Resolution Board within the framework of the Single Resolution Mechanism, signed on 16 December 2015.

[56]Craig (2015).

of the rule, in accordance with the general concept of democratic accountability, is to contribute to assign political responsibility to the SRB.[57]

Finally, as stated in Article 46, national Parliaments of the participating Member States may request the SRB to reply to any observations or questions submitted by them in respect of the functions of the SRB itself. They may also address to it their reasoned observations on its annual report. Furthermore, the national Parliament of a participating Member State may invite the President of the SRB to participate in an exchange of views in relation to the resolution of banks in that Member State together with a representative of the national resolution authority. The President is obliged to follow such invitation. Thus, this rule confers to national Parliaments certain powers to be exercised within the SRM, representing directly their people in dealing with the SRB. It is aimed to ensure that the democratic control on the latter can be also exercised at the national level of the banks involved. This determines a further form of direct popular representation.[58]

References

Allen F, Carletti E (2015) Systemic risk and macroprudential regulation. In: Micklitz HM, Tridimas T (eds) Risk and EU law. Elgar Publishing, Cheltenham-Northampton

Altunbas Y et al (2011) Bank risk during the financial crisis. Do business models matter? ECB Working Papers, No. 1394

Avgouleas E (2012) Governance of global financial markets. The law, the economics, the politics. Cambridge University Press, Cambridge

Babis VSG (2014) European bank recovery and resolution directive: recovery proceedings for cross-border banking groups. Eur Bus Law Rev (3):459–480

Barents R (2004) The autonomy of community law. Kluwer Law International, The Hague-London-New York

Boccuzzi G (2015) La gestione delle crisi bancarie nel quadro dell'Unione bancaria europea. Bancaria (2):2–11

Craig P (2015) Accountability. In: Arnull A, Chalmers D (eds) The Oxford handbook of European Union law. Oxford University Press, Oxford

Crum B, Curtin D (2015) The challenge of making European Union executive power accountable. In: Piattoni S (ed) The European Union: democratic principles and institutional architectures in times of crisis. Oxford University Press, Oxford

Daniele L (2012) Diritto del mercato unico europeo. II edn. Giuffrè, Milano

Davies P (2015) Resolution of cross-border groups. In: Haentjens M, Wessels B (eds) Researching handbook on crisis management in the banking sector. Elgar Publishing, Cheltenham-Northampton

De Meester B (2014) Liberalization of trade in banking services. An international and European perspective. Cambridge University Press, Cambridge

De Schoutheete P (2011) Decision-making in the Union. Notre Europe Policy Brief, No. 24

Dorn N (2015) Democracy and diversity in financial market regulation. Routledge, New York

---

[57]Crum and Curtin (2015).

[58]Villani (2016).

Forestieri G (2014) L'Unione bancaria europea e l'impatto sulle banche. Banca Impresa Società (3):489–504
Gallagher P (2014) The financial crisis, banking union and the rule of law. In: Bradley K et al (eds) Of courts and constitutions. Liber amicorum in Honour of Nial Fennely. Hart Publishing, Oxford-Portland
Hadjiemmanuil C (2015) Bank resolution financing in the Banking Union. LSE Law, Society and Economy Working Papers, No. 6
Huertas TF (2013) The case for bail-ins. In: Dombret A, Kenadijan PS (eds) The bank recovery and resolution directive: Europe's solution for "Too Big To Fail?". de Gruyter, Berlin-Boston
Huertas TF (2016) Banking Union. The way forward. In: Castañeda JE et al (eds) European Banking Union. Prospects and challenges. Routledge, New York
Kokkinis A (2015) A primer on corporate governance in banks and financial institutions: are banks special? In: Chiu I, McKee M (eds) The law on corporate governance in banks. Elgar Publishing, Cheltenham-Northampton
Magiera S, Weiß W (2014) Alternative dispute resolution mechanisms in the European Union law. In: Dragos D, Neamtu B (eds) Alternative dispute resolution in European administrative law. Springer, Heidelberg-New York-Dordrecht-London
Maletić I (2013) The law and policy of harmonisation in Europe's internal market. Elgar Publishing, Cheltenham-Northampton
Moloney N (2014) EU securities and financial markets regulation, 3rd edn. Oxford University Press, Oxford
Ponzano P (2011) Community and intergovernmental method: an irrelevant debate? Notre Europe Policy Brief, No. 23
Schillig M (2013) Bank resolution regimes in Europe-Part I: recovery and resolution planning, early intervention. Eur Bus Law Rev (6):751–779
Schillig M (2014) Bank resolution regimes in Europe-Part II: resolution tools and powers. Eur Bus Law Rev (6):67–102
Schillig M (2015) The EU resolution toolbox. In: Haentjens M, Wessels B (eds) Researching handbook on crisis management in the banking sector. Elgar Publishing, Cheltenham-Northampton
Tressel T (2014) Banking Union and single market: consistent setup and risk mitigation. In: Enoch C et al (eds) From fragmentation to financial integration in Europe. International Monetary Fund, Washington
van Rossem JW (2013) The autonomy of EU law. In: Wessel RA, Blockmans S (eds) Between autonomy and dependence: the EU legal order under the influence of international organisations. T.M.C. Asser Press, The Hague
Véron N, Wolff GB (2013) From supervision to resolution: next steps on the road to European Banking Union. Bruegel Policy Contribution, No. 4
Villani U (2016) Istituzioni di Diritto dell'Unione europea, IV edn. Cacucci, Bari
Wellerdt A (2015) Organisation of banking regulation. Springer, Heidelberg-New York-Dordrecht-London
Zavvos GS, Kaltsouni S (2015) The single resolution mechanism in the European Banking Union: legal foundation, governance structure and financing. In: Haentjens M, Wessels B (eds) Researching handbook on crisis management in the banking sector. Elgar Publishing, Cheltenham-Northampton

Part IV
EMU as a Field of Dialogue or Conflict Between National and European Courts?

The EMU in the ECJ: A New Dimension of Dispute Resolution in the Process of European Integration

Matthias Ruffert

Abstract Contrary to common expectations, the importance of EU law has grown during the State debt crisis. Law is used as an argument, it may be a tool of power, it can learn and it may reach its limits. EU law scholarship must react upon this greater role of law. Influences by national traditions must be detected and simplifications in transdisciplinary discourse eliminated. There are many untenable assumptions that are taken for granted in the current debate.

Contents

1 EU Law in the Economic and Monetary Union

The importance of EU law has significantly risen following the establishment of the EMU and in particular in the course of its crisis. If EU law does not live up to this importance, it will run the risk of depreciation and might totally lose its influence.

The message of this initial statement is not obvious. What is currently visible are severe troubles in the State debt crisis since 2010, apparent through deep changes in party politics all over Europe or in the deterioration of the relationship between Germany and Greece, which was rather harmonious before.[1] However, a closer look reveals that within the Economic and Monetary Union, European Union law has been attributed a new task: to regulate the relationship between the Union and its Member States and above all between the Member States in a crucial political field—their economic opportunities and their financial performance. This is a completely novel and fundamental task. We know comparable regulatory

[1]Cf. only Seidel (2015); Höpner (2015).

M. Ruffert (✉)
Department of Public Law and European Law, Humboldt-University, Berlin, Germany
e-mail: matthias.ruffert@rewi.hu-berlin.de

L. Daniele et al. (eds.), *Democracy in the EMU in the Aftermath of the Crisis*,
DOI 10.1007/978-3-319-53895-2_18

challenges only from the early phase of European integration or from complicated accessions.[2] Even central questions of EU constitutional law such as the direct effect and primacy of the fundamental freedoms, the relationship between the EU and the EEA and the WTO or the protection of human rights within the EU including its accession to the ECHR are far below the importance of the aforementioned matter.[3] What are the rules on the "purity" of spaghetti or beer, what is price-building in the banana market or the UEFA transfer system, what is even the free-movement of the "Polish plumber" against the limitation of State influence on the potential of development of European national economies?[4]

It is obvious that this core role of EU law must be reflected in the jurisprudence of its Court, the ECJ, which has delivered two important judgments so far: *Pringle* and *Gauweiler*; both at the same time carefully elaborated albeit not without methodological uncertainties. Instead of just commenting on both of them, the following contribution tries to localise the ECJ following the initial assessment in an analysis of four different positions the law may have in providing the structural coupling between politics, economics and itself: law as an argument, law as power, learning law and limits of government through law. The analysis will end up in the formulation of a line of core tasks for European legal scholarship ensuing from the debate around the judgments.

2 EU Law and the ECJ in the State Debt Crisis: Structural Couplings Between Law, Economics and Politics

2.1 Law as an Argument: The Function of the No Bail Out-Clause

The structural coupling of political interest and the functional logic of economics on the one hand with legal argumentation on the other hand became virulent during the State debt crisis in the interpretation of the no bail out-clause (Article 125, para. 1, TFEU). With respect to capital transfers to States in crisis, the political interests at stake are evident: States that entered the EMU with competitive economies do not wish to become continuous payers, and those who lost their ability to boost their domestic economies by devaluating their currency may

[2]Cf. for historical analysis Schulz-Forberg and Stråth (2010); Schorkopf (2015).

[3]ECJ 5 February 1963, Case 26/62, *Van Gend en Loos*; Opinion 15 November 1994, 1/94, *Competence of the Community to conclude international agreements concerning services and the protection of intellectual property*; Order 7 May 2013, Case C-617/10, *Åkerberg Fransson*; Opinion 14 October 2014, 1/13, *Convention on the civil aspects of international child abduction*.

[4]ECJ 12 March 1987, Case 178/84, *Commission* v. *Germany*; 14 July 1988, Case 90/86, *Zoni*; 5 October 1994, Case C-280/93, *Germany* v. *Council*; 15 December 1995, Case C-415/93, *Bosman*.

promote the idea of capital transfers from the stronger Members. True, in the economic theory of the ideal currency area, capital transfers are one of two carrying pillars,[5] but it can reasonably be submitted that the EMU is more likely to be construed around the other pillar which is factor mobility. Considering the ratio and genesis of the EMU in the late 1980s/early 1990s, it is quite obviously a continuation of the achievements of the single market which has factor mobility as its core aim, and transfers are concentrated on common projects in the framework of social and structural funds as well as trans-European networks which is reflected in the Treaty.[6] Further, EMU follows a model underlining Member States' responsibility for their budgetary performance.[7] Expectations formulated with respect to EMU when the Maastricht Treaty was ratified have not been challenged so far.[8]

---

[5]Cf. the seminal book by de Grauwe (2014), particularly at p. 23 et seq., and also Enderlein (2010).

[6]Article 125, paras. 1 and 2, TFEU, 2nd half sentence, respectively: "[...] without prejudice to mutual financial guarantees for the joint execution of a specific project.". Explanation in Smulders and Keppenne (2015), para 16.

[7]Ruffert (2013a).

[8]89 Entscheidungen des Bundesverfassungsgerichts 155 at 204 et seq. (Maastricht) [unofficial English translation available at http://www.judicialstudies.unr.edu/JS_Summer09/JSP_Week_1/German%20ConstCourt%20Maastricht.pdf]: "Even after transition to the third stage, development of the monetary union is subject to foreseeable standards and thus to parliamentary accountability. The Maastricht Treaty governs the monetary union as a community committed to long-term stability, in particular to monetary stability. It is true that it is not possible to foresee whether it will actually be possible, using as a basis the provisions contained within the Maastricht Treaty, to maintain long-term stability for the ECU currency. The fear that the efforts to achieve stability will fail, which could then result in further concessions in terms of monetary policy on the part of the Member States, is, however, too intangible a basis upon which to claim that the Maastricht Treaty is legally vague. The Maastricht Treaty sets long-term standards which establish the goal of stability as the yardstick by which the monetary union is to be measured, which endeavour, by institutional provisions, to ensure that these objectives are fulfilled, and which finally do not stand in the way of withdrawal from the Community as a last resort if it proves impossible to achieve the stability sought. Pursuant to Art. 105, para. 1 of the EC Treaty, the primary objective of the ESCB shall be to maintain price stability. Art. 107 of the EC Treaty provides the ESCB with independence to exercise the powers and carry out the tasks and duties conferred upon it. The sixth consideration in the Preamble to the Maastricht Treaty demonstrates the Member States' resolve to establish economic and monetary union on the basis of a stable currency. Art. 2 of the EC Treaty states that the promotion of non-inflationary growth and of a high degree of convergence of economic performance is part of the task of the European Community. Art. 3 a, para. 2 of the EC Treaty states that the definition and conduct of a single monetary policy and exchange rate policy for which the Treaty provides shall have the primary objective of maintaining price stability. Furthermore, the EC Treaty includes provisions to enable the Member States, in their economic policy, to support and promote the stability of the European currency. Art. 3 a, para. 3 of the EC Treaty specifies stable prices, sound public finances and monetary conditions, and a sustainable balance of payments as guiding principles for the activities of the Member States (see also Art. 102 a, sentence 2 of the EC Treaty). The economic policies of the Member States are declared to be a matter of common concern, and their broad guidelines are to be co-ordinated and regulated by means of a recommendation from the Council (Art. 103 of the EC Treaty). Art 104 of the EC Treaty prohibits national central banks from granting overdraft facilities or any other type of credit

It is therefore by no means astonishing that Article 125, para. 1, TFEU was at the heart of the debate when the State debt crisis broke out in early 2010.[9] Perhaps we will never learn why the German Federal Government yielded to the pressure to prepare a rescue parcel for Greece although it had resisted for quite some time arguing that the no bail out-clause would not allow for such rescue. The clause became even more important when the EFSF was created, and certainly, the words of the then French Minister of Finance will not be forgotten: "We violated all the rules because we wanted to close ranks and really rescue the euro-zone."[10] At that time, also a significant number of scholars considered the said measures to be in breach with Article 125, para. 1, TFEU whereas others tried to justify them pointing at the voluntary character of the support for Greece and the establishment of the EFSF, at the wording of the provision or at more complex interpretive constructions.[11]

The ECJ's judgment in *Pringle*[12] was therefore most welcome for clarification and for the manifestation of the EU's ability to clarify legal uncertainties within its institutional framework.[13] Nonetheless, the approach of the judgment towards the interpretation of Article 125, para. 1, TFEU is flawed in several respects, so that the fundamental nature of the provision is not decently reflected. This applies to the interpretation of the wording

> [. . .] shall not be liable for or assume the commitments of [. . .]

which is supposed not to prevent the Member States from providing financial support to each other; the fact that the Advocate General quotes a provision from the German civil code (BGB) rules on tenancy law (!) does not enhance the

---

facility to bodies governed by public law or public undertakings of Member States, and from purchasing debt instruments directly from them. Except where prudential considerations are concerned, bodies governed by public law or public undertakings of Member States shall not be entitled to privileged access to financial institutions (Art. 104 a of the EC Treaty). Art. 104 b of the EC Treaty excludes the Community and any Member State from liability for and from assumption of the commitments of bodies governed by public law or of public undertakings of another Member State, which means that it is not possible for a Member State to evade the consequences of questionable financial policy. [. . .] This concept of the monetary union as a community of stability is the basis and object of the German Act of Consent.".

[9]First touch of this author: Interview in *Frankfurter Allgemeine Zeitung* No. 19 of 23 January 2010, p. 19.

[10]Available at: http://www.reuters.com/article/2010/12/18/us-france-lagardeidUSTRE6BH0V020101218.

[11]Breach of Article 125 TFEU: Louis (2010), p. 977 et seq.; Kube and Reimer (2010), p. 1912 et seq.; Faßbender (2010); Palmstorfer (2012); Siekmann (2013), p. 141; Ruffert (2011a), p. 1785 et seq. No breach: Wieland (2011), p. 342; Smits (2011), p. 111; Herrmann (2010a), p. 415; Harden et al. (1997), p. 153. Cf. also the differentiated approach of Calliess (2012), p. 154 et seq., and above all Calliess (2011), p. 256 et seq., in particular p. 268 et seq. More literature provided by Häde (2016), paras. 5 et seqq.

[12]ECJ 27 November 2012, Case C-370/12, *Pringle*.

[13]Mr. Pringle's standing under Irish law, however, was at least as questionable as Gauweiler's standing under German constitutional law (see below Sect. 2.2).

argumentative persuasiveness of the judgment in this regard.[14] Besides, the relationship of rule to exception which exists between Articles 122, para. 2, and 125 TFEU does not appear to be correctly understood by the Court.[15] But above all, the relationship between grammatical and teleological interpretation is very insecure: if direct loans and guarantees are allowed between Member States following the ECJ's view of the wording of Article 125, para. 1, TFEU—why the necessity of a teleological reduction and—somehow incidentally—the incorporation of the conditions from the new Article 136, para. 3, 2nd sentence, TFEU into the interpretation of Article 125, para. 1, TFEU?[16] Apparently, the Court sought a reason to set aside the effect of the new provision mentioned and could formally find it in the divergence of the entering into force of the ESM Treaty (8 October 2012) and Article 136, para. 3, TFEU (2 May 2013 and not yet foreseen at the date of the judgment in *Pringle*). That divergence enabled the Court to assess the whole rescue policy of the past two and a half years although what was at stake was only Ireland's ratification of the ESM Treaty.

Nevertheless, the judgment provided legal certainty at a crucial stage in the development of the EMU. Following the judgment, it has become clear on the one hand, that a fund for the repayment of pre-crisis State debts or the establishment of the so called "Eurobonds" as common State bonds of economically stronger and weaker Euro-zone Member States would require a formal Treaty amendment.[17] On the other hand, the judgment helped setting aside, together with the amendment in Article 136, para. 3, TFEU, the talk on "permanent breach of the law" which was and still is popular in some parts of the general debate in Germany and elsewhere.[18] However, this does not mean that an insolvency mechanism for Greece, keeping the Country within the Euro, would not have been the better alternative in early 2010. At least it would have better mirrored the revenue-risk-balance of the private creditors.

Following the fresh outbreak of the Greek crisis in 2015 which was consequential upon the irresponsible politics of the Tsipras Government and of its criminal-style Minister of Finance, Article 125, para. 1, TFEU had a comeback in legal argumentation. The decisive negotiations were also influenced by the position that

[14]AG Juliane Kokott, Conclusions to ECJ 27 November 2012, Case C-370/12, *Pringle*, No. 120, footnote 21. More convincing (but against the opinion taken here) Ohler (2013), paras. 13 et seq.

[15]ECJ 27 November 2012, Case C-370/12, *Pringle*, para. 131.

[16]ECJ 27 November 2012, Case C-370/12, *Pringle*, paras. 129 et seq. See the critical remarks by Ruffert (2013b), p. 258, and the extensive criticism by Tuori and Tuori (2014), p. 126 et seq. A decisively more positive view on this point is taken by Herrmann (2015), p. 8.

[17]Allemand (2012); de Gregorio Merino (2012), p. 1631; Heun and Thiele (2012), p. 980 et seq.; Mayer and Heidfeld (2012a), p. 131 et seq.; Mayer and Heidfeld (2012b), p. 424 et seq. A divergent view is taken by Piecha (2012). On the fund-solution, Schorkopf (2012).

[18]The speech of former Commission Vice President Viviane Reding at the 69th Deutscher Juristentag in Munich (18 September 2012), which deals with this matter, caused a lot of debate. Cf. also Müller-Graff (2015), pp. 163 et seqq.

Article 125, para. 1, TFEU—in the light of *Pringle*—would operate against debt relief which would therefore require at least a temporary "Grexit".[19] This position, however, maybe challenged as debt modification and *restructuring* is still possible in the framework of the conditionality necessary following either the judgment or the wording of Article 136, para. 3, 2nd sentence, TFEU.[20] But this was not the situation of the negotiations with Greece in 2015: the Greek Government, supported by its extreme left-wing claque, tried to talk the EU into *unconditional* debt relief, and some Governments even made signs to yield into this. Insofar, other Governments have taken a convincing position. The plea for *unconditional* debt relief can also not be based on a passage in the *Gauweiler* judgment which explains that rescue measures can include the risk of losses and losses as such.[21] Some argue that if losses can even be faced under Article 123 TFEU which is, according to *Pringle*, stricter than Article 125 TFEU,[22] the latter article would not prevent Member States from incurring losses in unconditional debt relief.[23] This is, with respect, a confusion of both articles and an over-interpretation of the relevant passage from *Gauweiler*. There is a difference between the purchase of bonds in the limits described by the ECJ in the range of discretion accorded to the ECB on the one hand and the overt renouncement abandonment of funds that were initially provided upon strict conditionality.

2.2 Law as Power: Distortions in National Constitutional Law

Before switching to the second judgment of the ECJ in matters of EMU, the judgment of 16 June 2015 on *OMT*, it is useful to have a glimpse on how national constitutional law may have been modified during the crisis. Without any doubt, the German Federal Government used the possible negative outcome of proceedings in the *Bundesverfassungsgericht* as a bulwark against pleas for the provision of even higher rescue funds. It is useful to explain that it is by no means a matter of course that constitutional law plays a role in this field. As late as in mid-2009, just half a year before the Greek *de facto* insolvency, the Court had formulated limits for the transfer of budgetary powers to the EU for the first time; we could also say on limits

[19]This legal view of the German Federal Ministry of Finance was published in a non-paper and distributed by the Green MEP Sven Giegold (available at http://www.sven-giegold.de/wp-content/uploads/2015/07/grexit_bundesregierung_non_paper_10_juli_2015.pdf). The same view was taken by Claudia Buch, "*Expliziter Schuldenerlass für Griechenland verletzt das No-Bail-out-Prinzip*", Interview of 1 August 2015, available at http://www.bundesbank.de/Redaktion/DE/Interviews/2015_08_01_buch_boez.html.

[20]Some conclusion as above: Mayer (2015). Similarly, Steinbach (2015).

[21]ECJ 16 June 2015, Case C-62/14, *Gauweiler*, para. 126.

[22]ECJ 27 November 2012, Case C-370/12, *Pringle*, para. 132.

[23]Divergent opinion: Goldmann (2015).

of budgetary powers of Parliament in general. The theoretical construction achieving this is highly questionable and has been called into question by scholars[24]:

> The German *Bundestag* must decide, in an accountable manner *vis-à-vis* the people, on the total amount of the burdens placed on citizens. The same applies correspondingly to essential state expenditure.[25]

The core of this power cannot be transferred to the EU—even not by an amendment of the *Grundgesetz*—because the EU is considered to be structurally unable to provide the necessary level of democratic legitimacy. Any change of this situation would need a vote of the German people under Article 146.[26]

The *Bundesverfassungsgericht* soon applied this jurisprudence to the Greek rescue package and then to the ESM Treaty. Initially, it searched for reasons to limit the amount of budgetary involvement of the Federal Republic of Germany to find out when the *Bundestag* would lose its budgetary range of manoeuvre for the future.[27] This was given up, and the reasoning is now to achieve long term preservation of the democratic principle (a reasoning that could also be applied to budgetary management beyond EU matters):

> Article 79 (3) of the Basic Law does not guarantee the unchanged further existence of the law in force but those structures and procedures which keep the democratic process open and, in this context, safeguard parliament's overall budgetary responsibility.[28]

What is more important than this presentation of case law is the role of the *Bundesverfassungsgericht* in the political process of dealing with the crisis. It lead to the Federal Government being successful in implementing conditionality and the need for parliamentary approval within the rescue packages. A bold construction of constitutional law strongly influenced European politics. Is this the role of constitutional law which we desire?

The ground on which the *Bundesverfassungsgericht* controls EU activity whether they are *ultra vires* is comparatively firm, in particular since the Court clarified its relationship towards the ECJ and declared that a preliminary reference

---

[24]From the enormous bulk of legal writings on the judgment cf. only Jestaedt (2009).

[25]Bundesverfassungsgericht, Judgment of 30 June 2009, translation available at http://www.bundesverfassungsgericht.de/SharedDocs/Entscheidungen/EN/2009/06/es20090630_2bve000208en.html;jsessionid=57638495472D1C3F681DB1D1DEE5267F.2_cid370, para. 256.

[26]Bundesverfassungsgericht, *supra*, note 25, paras. 244 et seqq.

[27]Bundesverfassungsrecht, Judgment of 7 September 2011, translation available at http://www.bundesverfassungsgericht.de/SharedDocs/Entscheidungen/EN/2011/09/rs20110907_2bvr098710en.html, para. 131. The Bundesverfassungsgericht is not the only national Court to decide on the rescue measures: cf. the overview given by Fines (2015).

[28]Bundesverfassungsgericht, Judgment of 12 September 2012, available at http://www.bundesverfassungsgericht.de/SharedDocs/Entscheidungen/EN/2012/09/rs20120912_2bvr139012en.html, para. 222.

was a necessary precondition to the assessment of an act as *ultra vires*.[29] This was applied with respect to *OMT*, and it lead to an excellent analysis of the OMT programme in the preliminary ruling of 14 January 2014.[30] Of course, the political position can be taken again: without that preliminary ruling we would have no limitation to the purchase of assets in the principle of proportionality and the necessary temporal distance between emission and purchase on secondary markets.[31]

The real problem lies in the *Bundesverfassungsgericht*'s concept of standing. Standing to claim constitutional limits to the EU's competences is accorded to every citizen, based on the principles of democratic election of the *Bundestag* (Article 38 *Grundgesetz*) together with the inviolability of the principle of democracy (Articles 20 (1), 79 (3) and 146 *Grundgesetz*).[32] This shall even apply if the claimant is an MP (and it's always the same MP. . .).[33] The dissenting opinions to the preliminary ruling in *OMT* have impressively shown where this can lead to.[34] Even if the *Bundesverfassungsgericht* now found the ECB had acted outside its powers, the consequences would be rather vague and abstract.[35] There is an obvious discrepancy between the precise analyses on the merits on the one hand and the construction of standing which is near to absurd on the other hand. Some authors compare the approach to standing to what the ECJ did in *Van Gend en Loos* to bring forward the implementation of (then) EEC law.[36]

2.3 Learning Law: Institutional Shifts

European Law is not just used as a (powerful) tool for argumentation. It also undergoes modification and adaption—it can be said that it is learning. This is

---

[29]Bundesverfassungsgericht, Order of 6 July 2010, available at http://www.bundesverfassungsgericht.de/SharedDocs/Entscheidungen/EN/2010/07/rs20100706_2bvr266106en.html. Cf. Schwerdtfeger (2015), p. 301 et seq. Still critical, Ludwigs (2015).

[30]Bundesverfassungsgericht, Order of 14 January 2014, translation available at http://www.bundesverfassungsgericht.de/SharedDocs/Entscheidungen/EN/2014/01/rs20140114_2bvr272813en.html, paras. 84 et seqq.

[31]On these criteria see Sect. 2.3.

[32]Bundesverfassungsgericht, *supra*, note 25; cf. in particular para. 179: "Article 146 of the Basic Law creates a right of participation of the citizen entitled to vote. Article 146 of the Basic Law confirms the pre-constitutional right to give oneself a constitution from which constitutional authority emanates and by which it is bound.". See the criticism in Ruffert (2011b), pp. 842 et seqq.

[33]Bundesverfassungsgericht (*supra*, note 25), para. 199.

[34]Dissenting opinions of judges Gerhardt and Lübbe-Wolff to Order of 14 January 2014 (*supra*, note 30). See also Ohler (2015b), p. 1006.

[35]Cf. the strong criticism expressed by Mayer (2014), pp. 490 et seqq.

[36]Gärditz and Hillgruber (2009), pp. 872 et seqq.

true concerning the role of the ECB. The political interest of Governments in ECB action is obvious; and even more: at the global scale, the independence of the ECB and its orientation towards monetary stability is exceptional. The theoretical background in economics is the function of a stable currency in fixing market prices as reliable indicators of scarcity following the concept of ordo-liberalism.[37] This is of course disputed amongst economists, but at least two matters can plausibly be claimed: first, the relaxation of monetary policy has contributed significantly to the financial crisis in 2007/2008. Second, monetary policy runs into difficulties if its potential for boosting the economy seems exhausted. We can see this in the US and in Japan particularly. All in all, there are comprehensible reasons for the prohibition of direct State budget funding.

In the beginning of the crisis, the focus was less on ECB activity, certainly due to the sheer volume of the rescue packages beyond ECB action. It is submitted, however, the massive purchase of loans in summer 2011 following the SMP programme meant nothing but building a rescue package for Italy (then governed by PM Berlusconi)—and was in breach of Article 123, para. 1, TFEU.[38] We can make this assessment today following the rules the ECJ established in the judgment of 16 June 2015:

> [...] the ESCB's intervention could, in practice, have an effect equivalent to that of a direct purchase of government bonds from public authorities and bodies of the Member States if the potential purchasers of government bonds on the primary market knew for certain that the ESCB was going to purchase those bonds within a certain period and under conditions allowing those market operators to act, de facto, as intermediaries for the ESCB for the direct purchase of those bonds from the public authorities and bodies of the Member State concerned.[39]

This was exactly what had happened in summer 2011.

Therefore, it is not really astonishing that the announcement to do "whatever it takes" (albeit "within our mandate")[40] caused fears that the principle of attributed powers would not be sufficiently respected in a decisive point. It is most remarkable that the ECJ overcame several obstacles to deliver its judgment of 16 June 2015. It rejected certain weak arguments against the admissibility of the reference—mainly brought by Governments who are in need of ECB support.[41] More importantly, the

---

[37]Eucken (1940), pp. 136 et seqq.

[38]An impressive presentation of the (conditioned!) asset-purchase is provided by Beukers (2013), p. 1598 et seq., who, however, does not share the opinion in the text above. Ohler (2015a), § 4/44, at least admits that there was a deliberate purchase of bonds from single, crisis-stricken Member States, but he considers the purchase to be in conformity with EU law (Ohler 2015b, p. 1004). A similar view is adopted by Herrmann (2010b). An even more rigid position than here is taken by Schmidt (2016), § 5/75; Seidel (2010); Siekmann (2013), p. 147 et seq.

[39]ECJ 16 June 2015, Case C-62/14, *Gauweiler*, para. 104.

[40]ECB Press Release of 26 July 2012, available at http://www.ecb.int/press/key/date/2012/html/sp120726.en.html.

[41]ECJ 16 June 2015, Case C-62/14, *Gauweiler*, paras. 18 et seqq. As far as can be seen, this is not treated in the impressive Special Issue of the Maastricht Journal of European and Comparative

Court made clear that the control of the ECB, its independence notwithstanding, was in the range of its judicial review and that there were clear yardsticks for ECB action: the principle of proportionality and the prohibition to circumvent Article 123, para. 1, TFEU as explained.[42] As a consequence, it is unlikely that the *Bundesverfassungsgericht* will not be able to handle the ECJ's ruling.[43] There will be no war of the Courts.[44]

Since the beginning of 2015—for roughly one year now—the world is different anyway. The ECB is undertaking Quantitative Easing (QE) following the Fed's example and purchases State bonds of up to €60 bn per month.[45] As the ECB can undertake open market transactions following its Statute, as the bonds are bought in secondary markets and as bonds of all Member States are bought following the distribution key of the Eurozone, it is difficult to claim that this was direct monetary financing of the Member States budgets.[46] Further, the ECB has a margin of appreciation when fighting price instability which may be in danger through deflation as well as through inflation,[47] although there is some argument amongst economists whether we are really facing deflation when excluding energy prices from analysis—which are independent of European economic policies. It also goes without saying that QE has a relaxing effect on the economies in Countries like France and Italy and thus reduces the pressure for reforms.[48]

The picture for the law is quite astonishing—it turns our idea of legal control upside down. The strongest measure with severe economic effects meets the least legal concerns. The intervention of the SMP programme, punctually deep as well, was probably in breach of EU law, but this will never be found by any Court. The only programme that came under comprehensive judicial scrutiny on national and supranational level was never applied. Only because the ECJ had the institutional

---

Law, Vol. 23 (2016) on "*The European Court of Justice, the European Central Bank, and the Supremacy of EU Law*".

[42]ECJ 16 June 2015, Case C-62/14, *Gauweiler*, paras. 34 et seqq., 66 et seqq., 93 et seqq. On this, Ohler (2015b), p. 1004 et seq., as well as Sauer (2015), p. 981.

[43]Bundesverfassungsgericht, Order of 14 January 2014, *supra*, note 30, para. 100. Meanwhile, the *Bundesverfassungsgericht* decided this way: Judgment of 21 June 2016 - 2 BvR 2728/13, 2 BvR 2729/13, 2 BvR 2730/13, 2 BvR 2731/13, 2 BvE 13/13, available at www.bundesverfassungsgericht.de.

[44]See Ohler (2015b), p. 1005, on remaining divergences. Sometimes, authors exaggerate in saying that the Bundesverfassunsgericht was dictating its result to the ECJ; cf. e.g. Anagnostaras (2015), p. 757 et seq.

[45]ECB, Economic Bulletin No. 1/2015, pp. 15 et seqq.; Decision (EU) 2015/774 of the European Central Bank of 4 March 2015 on a secondary markets public sector asset purchase programme, OJEU L121, 14 May 2015, pp. 20 et seqq. Cf. van den End et al. (2015).

[46]Thiele (2015), pp. 304 et seqq.; Lammers (2015), pp. 215 et seqq. However, a constitutional complaint is pending against the programme: https://www.uni-marburg.de/fb01/lehrstuehle/oeffrecht/horn/horn_dateien/vfb.pdf.

[47]Ohler (2015a), § 3/12.

[48]Cf. Müller-Graff (2015), pp. 164 et seqq., also to other factual consequences.

strength to formulate limits for ECB action, we need not deny the effectiveness of EU law in this context.

2.4 *Limits to Governance by Law*

The guiding force of the law is not visible at any time and everywhere in the EMU. Following the surprising move of the Greek Government to sign a new agreement in summer 2015 after chaotic weeks, it is by no means clear whether the greatest rescue programme under the ESM Treaty[49] is in conformity with legal requirements, and this follows the judgments reported so far.

Support for a Member State is provided for in great detail in the articles of the ESM Treaty. The State in need of stability support addresses a respective request to the Chairperson of the ESM Board of Governors. According to Article 13, para. 1, 3rd sentence (b), of the ESM Treaty, the Chairperson

> shall entrust the European Commission, in liaison with the ECB, [...] to assess whether public debt is sustainable.[50]

The result of this assessment in the case of Greece is as follows[51]:

> The high debt to GDP and the gross financing needs resulting from this analysis point to serious concerns regarding the sustainability of Greece's public debt. The concerns could be addressed through a far reaching and credible reform programme, very strong ownership of the Greek authorities for such a programme and, after full restoration of the loans agreements, debt-mitigating measures that would be granted only once the commitments to reform from the Greek authorities has been demonstrated. A very substantial re-profiling, such as a long extension of maturities of existing and new loans, interest deferral, and financing at AAA rates would allow catering for these concerns from a gross financing requirements perspective, though they would still leave Greece with very high debt-to-GDP levels for an extended period.

In short, there are most serious doubts, but if the Greek Government advances its reform programme in a credible way, such doubts can be met by debt restructuring measures, although Greece will be highly in debt for a very long time.[52] The Board

[49]In 2012/13 €41,3 bn were spent for the Spanish banking sector; this measure is completed. The current aid for Cyprus is roughly €9 bn. Cf. http://www.esm.europa.eu/assistance/index.htm.

[50]Cf. Ohler (2015a), § 4/56.

[51]European Commission, Debt sustainability analysis, Bundestagsdrucksache 18/5780, Anlage 4 zum BMF-Beschlußantrag, p. 3, also available at http://ec.europa.eu/economy_finance/assistance_eu_ms/greek_loan_facility/pdf/debt_sustainability_analysis_en.pdf.

[52]Article 6 of Regulation (EU) No. 472/2013 of the European Parliament and of the Council of 21 May 2013 on the strengthening of economic and budgetary surveillance of Member States in the euro area experiencing or threatened with serious difficulties with respect to their financial stability (OJEU L 140, 27 May 2013, pp. 1 et seqq.), which belongs to the "Two Pack", also demands for reticence: "The assessment of the sustainability of the government debt shall be based

of Governors did not see itself prevented from making the respective decision under Article 13, para. 2, of the ESM Treaty[53]—of course not, because there was agreement on the third Greek package on the highest political level. Of course there will be no procedure before the ECJ under Article 37 of the ESM Treaty, as no Member State will trigger the control of the Board of Governor's decision.[54] The Eurozone Members even organised bridge financing from the EU budget via the EFSM, providing for simultaneous compensation for Member States outside the Eurozone for the case of default.[55] However, doubts with respect to the legality of the Commission's assessment persist.[56] The perspective of future debt sustainability is something different from actual sustainability, even if the acting institutions are all vested with a broad margin of appreciation.

In this respect, it is most revealing to consider the wording of the IMF's assessment of public debt sustainability in Greece[57]:

> Greece's public debt has become highly unsustainable. This is due to the easing of policies during the last year, with the recent deterioration in the domestic macroeconomic and financial environment because of the closure of the banking system adding significantly to the adverse dynamics.

This highlights the 2nd sentence on the provision about debt sustainability:

> Wherever appropriate and possible, such an assessment is expected to be conducted together with the IMF; [. . .].

It is neither inappropriate nor impossible to consider the IMF's assessment in this matter. Obviously the Eurozone Member States are giving priority to their policy aims before legality. Although there is no procedure to challenge this, it does not raise trust in the sustainability—of the ESM Treaty.

Another argument against the rescue package must however be rejected. Many claim that the strict requirements in the Memoranda of Understanding (MoUs)

---

on the most likely macroeconomic scenario or a more prudent scenario and budgetary forecasts using the most up-to-date information and taking proper account of the outcome of the reporting [. . .] as well as any supervisory task exercised in accordance with point (b) of Article 3(3). The Commission shall also assess the impact of macroeconomic and financial shocks and adverse developments on the sustainability of government debt.". On this see Ohler (2015a), § 4/56.

[53]ESM Press Release of 17 July 2015, available at http://esm.europa.eu/press/releases/esm-board-of-governors-approves-decision-to-grant,-in-principle,-stability-support-to-greece.htm.

[54]On this procedure, Häde (2014), § 17/20.

[55]Council Regulation (EU) No. 2015/1360 of 4 August 2015 amending Regulation (EU) No. 407/2010 establishing a European financial stabilisation mechanism, OJEU L 210, 7 August 2015, pp. 1 et seqq.; Council Implementing Decision (EU) 2015/1181 of 17 July 2015 on granting short-term Union financial assistance to Greece, OJEU L 192, 18 July 2015, pp. 15 et seqq.; Council Implementing Decision (EU) 2015/1182 of 17 July 2015 approving the adjustment programme of Greece, OJEU L 192, 18 July 2015, pp. 19 et seqq.

[56]There are few if any writings on this, polemical articles that are not very helpful (and not very scientific) set aside: Prieto (2015).

[57]International Monetary Fund, IMF Country Report No. 15/186 of 14 July 2015.

would erode democratic Government in the "receiving Countries" whereas democracy was disproportionately stressed in "paying Countries".[58] This argument confuses cause and effect. In the case of default of a State in its own currency (the Euro) in 2010 the consequences for Greece would have been at least as hard as they are now.[59] The assumption of responsibility by the EU in providing for rescue packages does not change the fact that Greece was (and probably still is) unable to refinance itself in the capital markets. The contribution of the Euro-system to the exorbitant level of debt which is sometimes seen in the incitement to Greece and other Countries lying in low interest rates is sufficiently outweighed by the enormous size of the rescue measures, to say the least.

3 Consequences for European Law Scholarship

3.1 Chances for Enhancing the Profile of European Law in the EMU

The mentioned characteristics of law in the crisis-related jurisprudence of the ECJ and to a certain extent of national Constitutional Courts show that we can ascribe a decisive, crucial role to European Union law in the State debt crisis—and even more so in the design of the future EMU, a point that had to be omitted here—be it the argumentative force of law, its potential quality as a tool of power, its ability to learn but also its limits and the knowledge about them. This must have repercussions on European Union legal scholarship. Indeed, legal writings in EU law addressed the relevant issues after some hesitation and detracted the debate from the very exclusive circle of experts on currency and budgetary law. The focus has long been on single questions: prohibition of bail out, powers of central banks, constitutional framework, democratic legitimacy—and rightly so, because these are the questions that require thorough treatment.

At the same time, the situation offers the chance to sharpen European legal scholarship in pointing at legal insecurities of the politico-legal debate, and at best in eliminating them. There is no necessity for scholarship to be overly lenient towards the obvious needs for political decision making, so treaty provisions with a clear sense of steering EU politics such as Article 125 TFEU must be construed in a way giving them their *effet utile*. The same strict approach should apply to the activity of national (Constitutional) Courts; distortions must be named as such and shall be academically discussed. In most jurisdictions, strong academic criticism is taken seriously on the long run. It is also important to consider the stability and reliance of a given institutional system; changes in the role and performance of institutions with respect to their constitutional mandate must at least be discovered,

[58] Elaborated by Tryantafyllou (2014). Similarly, Dawson and de Witte (2016), p. 220.

[59] On this and the following, Ruffert (2015).

if not called into question following the standards of institutional principles and rules developed in EU law over time. And finally, the limits of legality are to be named and transgressions of the political actors to be designated as such: if the third rescue package for Greece is not easily to be reconciled with the provisions of the ESM, scholars should better not conceal that. The tasks of scholarship must be elaborated clearly.

3.2 National Imprint of Legal Arguments

An uncertainty arises from the fact that legal argumentation may be influenced by national legal cultures and political orientation. Why, to give an obvious example, are legal arguments criticising the various rescue measures mainly brought forward by German scholars (and with particular impetus) whereas in other Countries, even in those with similar interests (Netherlands, Finland, Austria) such arguments and the commitment of national Courts are far less important? Why is it so rarely analysed that the Countries in crisis, Greece, Spain, Portugal, Ireland—and Italy and France?—are in considerably different situations? It may be helpful to have recourse to social-psychological findings, but this has not yet been scrutinised in depth, at least not to the knowledge of the larger legal scientific community.[60] Other interpretations may be added, and we should find out more about the interrelationship of different nationally coined perspectives. There is a strong challenge to EU legal scholarship to overcome national separations in academic discussion on the pertinent issues.

3.3 Political and Economic Orientations: The Diverging Mantras of the Euro-Adversaries or of "Austerity"

Beyond national influence, legal arguments tend to be pre-conditioned by basic political and economic orientations. A triangle of forces—politics, economics, law—is created, and politics and economics are having repercussions on the element providing the structural coupling, which is law. Scholarship must react upon this to achieve two things at the same time: (1) to avoid ascribing steering forces to legal rules which they do not have and (2) to preserve the methodological autonomy of legal scholarship.

What is first of all needed is transparency concerning the respective political or economic orientation; some already fail at that point. Further, if law scholars are integrating arguments from political science or economics, it is certainly difficult to give them a foundation that would completely match the standards of the

[60]Explained and analysed in terms of history by Huber (2014).

neighbouring science. When we write articles on legal issues as legal scholars, we should not pretend to be social scientists or economists at the same time.[61] However, trans-disciplinary work is indispensable in complex matters such as the analysis of the past and future of the EMU. The only way to achieve this in a sound manner is to prove at least the plausibility of the assumptions made beyond legal statements, be it empirically, in economic theory or by practical arguments. Unfortunately, the tendency to adopt positions lacking a sense of complexity, to say the least, is obvious in this debate, and this is certainly due to the desire to impress the general public. Lack of complexity is not the privilege of those who have been opting against the common currency since the early 1990s. There is another, somehow penetrant line of argument in scholarship which attributes all symptoms of the crisis to a policy of "austerity" which it considers misdirected.[62] This may lead so far as to disregard knowledge we have had for more than 200 years such as *David Ricardo's* theory on comparative cost advantage to mark a pretended point in the debate on European politics or even law: competition as a zero-sum game.[63] The plausibility of this assumption is flawed, at the very latest since the ECB has begun performing QE in early 2015.

It is crucial for European legal scholarship to be informed about the state-of-the-art in neighbouring disciplines, and to be transparent about any borrowing from them. Legal scholarship does not improve if it is reduced to imitating layman positions from economics.

3.4 European Law Scholarship and the Course of Integration

What is most difficult is a third task. EU law has always been meant to deepen and broaden the process of European integration, and it has given this sense to its scholarship for a long time. There are derisive caricatures of this image of the EU law scholar which may be exaggerated (*Berufseuropäer*), but they underline the necessity always to reflect the position of EU law scholarship with respect to its subject matter. This is less than being partisan to a certain course of integration with arguments drawn from legal policy, but more than just describing how integration advances from a legal perspective. It is decisive that EU law provides effective instruments to the EMU, that it explains the conditions of their effectiveness and that it contributes to their continuous improvement. European integration is in a

---

[61]This is the general approach of Fabbrini (2016), p. 10. However, he does not constantly follow this line (see Ruffert 2016).

[62]Cf. e.g. Adalid (2015); Nicol (2015); Wilkinson (2015); Dawson and de Witte (2016), pp. 213, 214 and 223 in particular—and many more authors.

[63]Müller (2015), p. 159: "not all countries can become 'more competitive' at the same time"—the contrary of this is *Ricardo's* central point.

most difficult situation. Its preservation is the main task of European legal scholarship today.

References

Adalid S (2015) L'intégration financière – Grandeur et decadence du fédéralisme de marché. In: de la Rosa S, Martucci F, Dubout E (eds) L'Union européenne et le fédéralisme économique. Bruylant, Bruxelles, pp 261 et seqq
Allemand F (2012) La faisabilité juridique des projets d'euro-obligations. Revue trimestrielle de droit européen 48:553 et seqq
Anagnostaras G (2015) In ECB we trust... the FCC we dare! The OMT preliminary ruling. Eur Law Rev 40:744 et seqq
Beukers T (2013) The new ECB and its relationship with the Eurozone Member States: between central bank independence and central bank intervention. Common Mark Law Rev 50:1579 et seqq
Calliess C (2011) Perspektiven des Euro zwischen Solidarität und Recht – Eine rechtliche Analyse der Griechenlandhilfe und des Rettungsschirms. Zeitschrift für Europarechtliche Studien, pp 213 et seqq
Calliess C (2012) Finanzkrisen als Herausforderung der internationalen, europäischen und nationalen Rechtsetzung. Veröffentlichungen der Vereinigung der deutschen Staatsrechtslehrer 71:113 et seqq
Dawson M, de Witte F (2016) From balance to conflict: a new constitution for the EU. Eur Law J 22:204 et seqq
de Grauwe P (2014) Economics of Monetary Union, 10th edn. OUP, Oxford
de Gregorio Merino A (2012) Legal developments in the Economic and Monetary Union during the debt crisis: the mechanisms of financial assistance. Common Mark Law Rev 49:1613 et seqq
Enderlein H (2010) Die Krise im Euro-Raum: Auslöser, Antworten, Ausblick. Aus Politik und Zeitgeschichte, pp 7 et seqq
Eucken W (1940) Die Grundlagen der Nationalökonomie. Gustav Fischer Verlag, Jena
Fabbrini F (2016) Economic governance in Europe. OUP, Oxford
Faßbender K (2010) Der europäische "Stabilisierungsmechanismus" im Lichte von Unionsrecht und deutschem Verfassungsrecht. Neue Zeitschrift für Verwaltungsrecht, pp 799 et seqq
Fines F (2015) À propos de quelques limites constitutionnelles au fédéralisme économique européen. In: de la Rosa S, Martucci F, Dubout E (eds) L'Union européenne et le fédéralisme économique. Bruylant, Bruxelles, pp 213 et seqq
Gärditz KF, Hillgruber C (2009) Volkssouveränität und Demokratie ernst genommen – Zum Lissabon-Urteil des BVerfG. Juristenzeitung, pp 872 et seqq
Goldmann M (2015) Eine Schuldenrestrukturierung setzt keinen Grexit voraus!, available at www.verfassungsblog.de
Häde U (2014) Der Europäische Stabilitätsmechanismus (ESM). In: Hatje A, Müller-Graff P-C (eds) Europäisches Organisations- und Verfahrensrecht (Enzyklopädie Europarecht, Band 1). Nomos, Baden-Baden, § 17
Häde U (2016) Artikel 125 AEUV. In: Calliess C, Ruffert M (eds) EUV/AEUV, 5th edn. Beck, Munich
Harden I, von Hagen J, Brookes R (1997) The European constitutional framework for Member States' public finances. In: Andenas M, Gormley L, Hadjiemmanuil C, Harden I (eds) European Economic and Monetary Union: the institutional framework. Kluwer, Leiden, pp 139 et seqq

Herrmann C (2010a) Griechische Tragödie – der währungsverfassungsrechtliche Rahmen für die Rettung, den Austritt oder den Ausschluss von überschuldeten Staaten aus der Eurozone. Europäische Zeitschrift für Wirtschaftsrecht, pp 413 et seqq
Herrmann C (2010b) EZB-Programm für die Kapitalmärkte verstößt nicht gegen die Verträge. Europäische Zeitschrift für Wirtschaftsrecht, pp 645 et seqq
Herrmann C (2015) Die Wirtschafts- und Währungsunion: konstitutionelle und institutionelle Aspekte der wirtschaftspolitischen Steuerung innerhalb der Europäischen Union. In: Müller-Graff P-C, Schwarze J (eds) XXVI. FIDE-Kongress vom 28. Mai bis 31. Mai 2014 in Kopenhagen. Europarecht Beiheft 3, pp 7 et seqq
Heun W, Thiele A (2012) Verfassungs- und europarechtliche Zulässigkeit von Eurobonds. Juristenzeitung, pp 973 et seqq
Höpner M (2015) Der integrationistische Fehlschluß. Leviathan, pp 29 et seqq
Huber PM (2014) Verfassungsstaat und Finanzkrise. Nomos, Baden-Baden
Jestaedt M (2009) Warum in die Ferne schweifen, wenn der Maßstab liegt so nah? Der Staat 48:497 et seqq
Kube H, Reimer E (2010) Grenzen des Europäischen Stabilisierungsmechanismus, Neue Juristische Wochenschrift, pp 1911 et seqq
Lammers L (2015) Die Politik der EZB an den Grenzen ihres Mandats? Europäische Zeitschrift für Wirtschaftsrecht, pp 212 et seqq
Louis J-V (2010) Guest editorial: the no bailout clause and rescue packages. Common Mark Law Rev 47:971 et seqq
Ludwigs M (2015) Der Ultra-vires-Vorbehalt des BVerfG – Judikative Kompetenzanmaßung oder legitimes Korrektiv? Neue Zeitschrift für Verwaltungsrecht, pp 537 et seqq
Mayer F (2014) Rebels without a cause? Zur OMT-Vorlage des Bundesverfassungsgerichts. Europarecht, pp 473 et seqq
Mayer F (2015) Umstrittener Schnitt. Die Zeit, No. 31, 30 July 2015
Mayer F, Heidfeld C (2012a) Eurobonds, Schuldentilgungsfonds und Projektbonds – Eine dunkle Bedrohung? Zeitschrift für Rechtspolitik, pp 129 et seqq
Mayer F, Heidfeld C (2012b) Verfassungs- und europarechtliche Aspekte der Einführung von Eurobonds. Neue Juristische Wochenschrift, pp 422 et seqq
Müller J-W (2015) Should the EU protect democracy and the rule of law inside Member States? Eur Law J 21:141 et seqq
Müller-Graff P-C (2015) Europa-Idee in der Krise? Europarecht-Beiheft 2, pp 149 et seqq
Nicol D (2015) Swabian housewives, suffering southerners: the contestability of justice as exemplified by the Eurozone crisis. In: Kochenov D, de Búrca G, Williams A (eds) Europe's Justice Deficit. Hart, Oxford, pp 165 et seqq
Ohler C (2013) Artikel 125 AEUV. In: Siekmann H (ed) EWU – Kommentar zur Europäischen Währungsunion. Mohr Siebeck, Tübingen
Ohler C (2015a) Bankenaufsicht und Geldpolitik in der Währungsunion. Verlag C.H. Beck, München
Ohler C (2015b) Rechtliche Maßstäbe der Geldpolitik nach dem Gauweiler-Urteil des EuGH. Neue Zeitschrift für Verwaltungsrecht, pp 1001 et seqq
Palmstorfer R (2012) To bail out or not to bail out? The current framework of financial assistance for Euro-Area Member States measured against the requirements of EU primary law. Eur Law Rev 37:771 et seqq
Piecha S (2012) Die Europäische Gemeinschaftsanleihe – Vorbild für EFSF, ESM und Euro-Bonds? Europäische Zeitschrift für Wirtschaftsrecht, pp 532 et seqq
Prieto C (2015) Le traitement de la crise grecque, entre desolation et espoir. Revue trimestrielle de droit européen, pp 491 et seqq
Reding V (2012) Europa, das Recht und die deutschen Juristen: ein luxemburgischer Zwischenruf (Dok. SPEECH/12/614)
Ruffert M (2011a) The European debt crisis and European Union law. Common Mark Law Rev 48:1777 et seqq

Ruffert M (2011b) Die europäische Schuldenkrise vor dem Bundesverfassungsgericht – Anmerkung zum Urteil vom 7. September 2011. Europarecht, pp 842 et seqq
Ruffert M (2013a) Mehr Europa – eine rechtswissenschaftliche Perspektive. Zeitschrift für Gesetzgebung, pp 1 et seqq
Ruffert M (2013b) Case Note. Juristenzeitung, pp 257 et seqq
Ruffert M (2015) Europäische Demokratie in der Krise? In: Baldus C, Kainer F, Stumpf C (eds) Festschrift für Peter-Christian Müller-Graff zum 70. Geburtstag. Nomos, Baden-Baden, pp 710 et seqq
Ruffert M (2016) Book review. Common Mark Law Rev 53 (2016), 1473 et seqq
Sauer H (2015) Doubtful it stood...: competence and power in European Monetary and constitutional law in the aftermath of the CJEU's OMT judgment. German Law J 16:971 et seqq
Schmidt R (2016) Wirtschafts- und Währungspolitik. In: Schmidt R, Wollenschläger F (eds) Kompendium Öffentliches Wirtschaftsrecht. Springer, Heidelberg, § 5
Schorkopf F (2012) Verfassungsrechtliche Grenzen und Möglichkeiten für eine Umsetzung des Schuldentilgungspaktes des Sachverständigenrates, Gutachten, available at http://www.sachverstaendigenrat-wirtschaft.de/fileadmin/dateiablage/download/publikationen/rechtsgutachten_schuldentilgungspakt.pdf
Schorkopf F (2015) Der Europäische Weg, 2nd edn. Mohr Siebeck, Tübingen
Schulz-Forberg H, Stråth B (2010) The political history of European integration: the hypocrisy of democracy-through-market. Routledge, London
Schwerdtfeger A (2015) Europäisches Unionsrecht in der Rechtsprechung des Bundesverfassungsgerichts – Grundrechts-, ultra-vires- und Identitätskontrolle im gewaltenteiligen Mehrebenensystem. Europarecht, pp 290 et seqq
Seidel M (2010) Der Ankauf nicht markt- und börsengängiger Staatsanleihen, namentlich Griechenlands, durch die Europäische Zentralbank und durch nationale Zentralbanken – rechtlich nur fragwürdig oder Rechtsverstoß? Europäische Zeitschrift für Wirtschaftsrecht, pp 521 et seqq
Seidel M (2015) Europas Finanz- und Staatsschuldenkrise – Auswirkungen auf die Rechtsstaatlichkeit und die Demokratie in der Europäischen Union. In: Baldus C, Kainer F, Stumpf C (eds) Festschrift für Peter-Christian Müller-Graff zum 70. Geburtstag. Nomos, Baden-Baden, pp 735 et seqq
Siekmann H (2013) Mißachtung rechtlicher Vorgaben des AEUV durch die Mitgliedstaaten und die EZB in der Schuldenkrise. In: Möllers TMJ, Zeitler F-C (eds) Europa als Rechtsgemeinschaft – Währungsunion und Schuldenkrise. Mohr Siebeck, Tübingen, pp 101 et seqq
Smits R (2011) Perspectives on the euro crisis. Leg Issues Eur Integr 38:107 et seqq
Smulders B, Keppenne J-P (2015) Artikel 125 AEUV. In: von der Groeben H, Schwarze J, Hatje A (eds) Europäisches Unionsrecht, 7th edn. Nomos, Baden-Baden
Steinbach A (2015) "Haircut" für Griechenland? (Un-)mögliche Frisuren eines Schuldenschnitts, 13 July 2015, available at unter www.verfassungsblog.de
Thiele A (2015) Die EZB vor Gericht. Zeitschrift für Bankrecht und Bankwirtschaft/J Bank Law Bank 295 et seqq
Tryantafyllou D (2014) Die asymmetrische Demokratie. Europarecht, pp 458 et seqq
Tuori K, Tuori K (2014) The eurozone crisis. CUP, Cambridge
van den End JW, de Haan J, Kearney I (2015) Quantitative easing (QE) in the Euro area: an exposition. Zeitschrift für Staats- und Europawissenschaften, pp 87 et seqq
Wieland J (2011) Der Rettungschirm für Irland. Neue Zeitschrift für Verwaltungsrecht, pp 340 et seqq
Wilkinson MA (2015) The euro is irreversible! ... Or is it?: On OMT, austerity and the threat of "Grexit". German Law J 16:1049 et seqq

The Role of the ECJ Beyond EU Law

Roberto Baratta

Abstract When intended to complement EU law or to enlarge its application to Third Parties, international treaties can empower the ECJ with additional tasks beyond the realm of EU law. This paper explores both the potential and legal constraints of the ECJ's extra powers, building upon some selected cases of practice. It argues that if one looks at this practice in depth through the prism of the purposes for which such special category of treaties were enacted and the reasons that led to them, the common denominator for involving the ECJ can be identified in the need to safeguard their consistency with the fundamental role the ECJ enjoys in the EU legal order under Article 19 TEU. The reference to the ECJ, both for solving disputes between themselves and for protecting individual rights as guaranteed by EU law (or by provisions which are identical in substance to it), is not just in line with the principle of institutional conferral. It is also a route the Contracting Parties are bound to take in order to respect the autonomy of EU law.

Contents

1 Introduction

International instruments may empower the ECJ with additional tasks beyond the realm of EU law, *i.e.* outside its usual scope. Intended to complement EU law or to enlarge its application to Third Parties, they are a special set of international treaties

R. Baratta (✉)
Department of Political Science, University of Macerata, Piazza Strambi, Macerata 62100, Italy
e-mail: rb2030@live.it

L. Daniele et al. (eds.), *Democracy in the EMU in the Aftermath of the Crisis*,
DOI 10.1007/978-3-319-53895-2_19

strictly *related to EU matters* in the sense that their functioning involves the interpretation and application of its *acquis*, even when their core topic transcends it.

Although the Treaty of Lisbon set aside the former Article 293 TEC, which mainly served as a legal basis to confer the ECJ extra competences in the field of private international law,[1] the current institutional architecture still allows Member States to draw up international agreements supplying the ECJ with additional powers. Recent practice has confirmed this trend. A first group of such treaties are those concluded by many, but not necessarily all, Member States alone. Being limited to Union Members, these can be described as *inter se* agreements stipulated in their sovereign external capacity. A second group of agreements granting powers to the ECJ may be found in treaties concluded between the EU and Third States, which submit themselves to the jurisdiction of the ECJ mainly for solving disputes on the interpretation and application of the relevant instrument.

Academic lawyers have devoted little attention to this topic. Thus this paper explores both the potential and legal constraints of the ECJ's extra powers, building upon some selected cases of practice. It focuses as a starting point on a survey of the recent practice (Sect. 2). It then addresses the EU legal constraints when entering into international agreements related to EU matters (Sect. 3). Finally, conclusions will be drawn (Sect. 4).

2 Empowering the ECJ via *inter se* Agreements or Through Treaties Concluded with Third States: A Survey of Recent Practice

By concluding *inter se* agreements Member States have different options to grant extra powers to the ECJ. These agreements can be founded on explicit provisions of the Treaties (1). Moreover, as practice shows, they may originate from Member States' own will, regardless of the existence of a primary law provision enabling this action (2). Finally, a third possibility regards international treaties entered into the EU and Third States. These instruments may grant exclusive jurisdiction to solve disputes concerning the interpretation and application of the relevant instrument or other litigations arising out of this kind of relations in the course of the treaty (3).

(1) A first option is explicitly provided for in Article 273 TFEU.[2] It covers the power to adjudicate laid down in a "special agreement" for disputes that fulfil two requirements. On the one hand, *ratione personarum* these disputes must involve

---

[1]I am essentially referring to Brussels Convention on the jurisdiction and the enforcement in civil and commercial matters, and to the Rome Convention on the law applicable to contractual obligations.

[2]It reads as follows: "The Court of Justice shall have jurisdiction in any dispute between Member States which relates to the subject matter of the Treaties if the dispute is submitted to it under a special agreement between the parties".

Member States only; on the other hand, the agreement should relate "to the subject matter of the Treaties". The latter substantive condition reveals the material connection of the agreement with EU law.

Accordingly, Member States are capable of further reference to the ECJ on the basis of a *compromis*, which is presumably meant to specify the terms of the disputes and the legal framework within which the Court is to operate. It is arguable that such possibility could also be founded upon a more comprehensive agreement between Member States containing a broad *compromissory* clause for sets of disputes. Given its "international" foundation, in the sense that the Treaties do not confer ECJ such a power outright, it is *prima facie* an optional choice that Member States (or some of them) may or may not exercise.[3] In that sense, it must be distinguished from the ECJ's exclusive jurisdiction stemming from Article 344 TFEU. However, a different and more compelling construction—as it will be suggested *infra*—appears possible.

As is known, the most renowned examples of that approach arose in the Euro economic area, *i.e.* the ESM Treaty, the so-called Fiscal Compact (or *Pacte budgetaire*, *Patto di bilancio*, *Fiskalvertrag*), as well as the Agreement on the transfer and mutualisation of contributions to the Single Resolution Fund, which was negotiated between 27 Member States to complete the third pillar of the Banking Union.[4]

Being part of a broader set of EU measures to tackle the Eurozone crisis,[5] which also include the Banking Union and the ECB monetary *activism*,[6] all these treaties are built together upon a sort of political and legal equation—more solidarity (the ESM Treaty) needs more discipline (the Fiscal Compact), while the *Banking Union* system enhances the financial stability of the Eurozone as a whole. They may be considered as comprehensive tools to strengthen the new regulatory framework of the EU economic governance, namely for Eurozone States.[7] In all of these *inter se*

---

[3] *E.g.* Mazzarini (2014), p. 2154 et seqq.

[4] See Council No. 8457/14 EF 121 ECOFIN 342, 14 May 2014. This Agreement set out the international legal obligation to transfer the contributions raised at national level towards the Single Resolution Fund. Indeed, some Eurozone States did not agree to found that obligation upon the law of the Union. As a result, such obligation is established by the Agreement, which lays down the conditions upon which the Contracting Parties, in accordance with their respective constitutional requirements, have agreed to transfer the contributions that they raise at national level to the Fund.

[5] For an in-depth analysis of the economic narrative of the Eurozone crisis, see Tuori and Tuori (2014), p. 61 et seqq.

[6] Cf. Tuori and Tuori (2014), p. 101 et seqq. as regards the ECB's contribution to combating the sovereign debt crisis; Baratta (2014a).

[7] However the ESM Treaty, by granting of financial assistance to Member States that are experiencing severe financing problems, is in legal terms more innovative than the Fiscal Compact. By imposing a strict fiscal discipline, the latter is meant to reduce the risk of public debt crises but reflects to a large extent the normative content of EU secondary law. Yet they are linked because it was agreed that the granting of financial assistance in the framework of the new programmes under the ESM, is conditional, as of 1 March 2013, in the ratification of the Fiscal Compact "by the ESM Member concerned" (recital 5 of the ESM Treaty). For a comprehensive overview of the developments in the EU economic governance, see Borges (2012), p. 1 et seqq.; Smets (2012), p. 41 et seqq.; Viterbo and Cisotta (2012), p. 323 et seqq.; Adam (2013), p. 5 et seqq.; Tuori and Tuori (2014), p. 85 et seqq.; Tosato (2016), p. 223 et seqq.; Condinanzi (2016), p. 240 et seqq.; Daniele (2016), p. 253 et seqq.

agreements, the Contracting Parties decided to confer the ECJ some powers to adjudicate. Yet the compliance with the conditions provided for in Article 273 TFEU was called into question.

As regards the *ratione personarum* requirement enshrined in Article 273 TFEU, the Agreement on the Single Resolution Fund—irrespective of its unusual construct—seems to be fulfilled.[8] By contrast, for the ESM Treaty the approach should be more nuanced. The *Pringle* ruling[9] held that it was satisfied by the ESM judicial settlement of disputes set out in Article 37 of the ESM Treaty.[10] It is rightly so for disputes *between ESM States* in connection with the interpretation and application of the Treaty, including any dispute about the compatibility of the decisions adopted by the ESM with the same Treaty.[11] However the Full Court adopted a broad approach as to the issue of whether it can be seized for disputes arising between an ESM State and the ESM itself, which is deemed to act as an international organisation. It is in fact described as an international financial institution[12]; indeed it was conceived as an "international organisation under public international law".[13]

[8]It is worth noticing that the dispute settlement between the Contracting Parties covers the interpretation of the Agreement's provisions, as well as the allegation by one Party that another Contracting Party has not complied with its obligations under the Agreement. The ECJ's competence includes any disputes concerning the reimbursement the Contracting Parties owed to the Member State that is not participating in the Single Supervisory Mechanism and in the Single Resolution Mechanism ("non-participating Member State") for the amount that that non-participating Member State has paid in own resources corresponding to the use of the general budget of the Union in cases of non-contractual liability and costs related thereto, in respect of the exercise of powers by the institutions of the Union under the SRM Regulation (see Articles 14 and 15 of the Agreement). Moreover, according to the preamble No. 18, the ECJ has been granted the power to verify the existence of any fundamental change of circumstances and the consequences deriving from it. The preamble considers it a dispute concerning the application of the Agreement for the purposes of Article 273 TFEU that can therefore be submitted to the Court of Justice by virtue of that provision.

[9]ECJ 27 November 2012, Case C-370/12, *Pringle*. See Thym and Wendel (2012), p. 733 et seqq.; Craig (2013), p. 3 et seqq.; de Witte and Beukers (2013), p. 805 et seqq.; Munari (2015), p. 723 et seqq.

[10]According to Article 37, para. 2, of the ESM Treaty, the Board of Governors is to decide "on any dispute arising between an ESM Member and the ESM, or between ESM Members, in connection with the interpretation and application of this Treaty, including any dispute about the compatibility of the decisions adopted by the ESM with this Treaty". Under Article 37, para. 3, the dispute is to be submitted to the Court of Justice, if an ESM Member contests the decision of the Board of Governors. As is clear from recital 16 of the ESM Treaty, the Parties to the ESM Treaty based this role for the ECJ on Article 273 TFEU.

[11]All Eurozone States are Members of the ESM Treaty. Even though it is open to non-Euro Member States, none of these has joined.

[12]Article 1 of the ESM Treaty.

[13]Conclusion of the European Council of 24–25 March 2011.

If one distinguishes the ESM's subjectivity from its membership, it would be a legal fiction to hold, as the ECJ did, that.

> a dispute in which the ESM is a party may be considered to be a dispute between Member States within the meaning of Article 273 TFEU.[14]

Either the ECJ has deliberately circumvented the problematic tie between the ESM and its Members, which reflects a still unsolved theoretical issue concerning the (international) personality of an organisation possessing its own will as a *subject* distinct from its Contracting Parties[15]; or that passage of *Pringle* may be considered as an implied evidence of the thesis according to which an international organisation is but a tool in the hand of its Members, its distinct will being ultimately a legal fiction.[16]

Even during the negotiation of the Fiscal Compact, respect for the *ratione personarum* condition proved hard to achieve. The need to maintain the dispute as a strictly intergovernmental matter clashed with the political desire to involve the Commission in assessing the correct implementation of the balanced (or in surplus) budget rule (Article 3, para. 1, a, in domestic law according to Article 3, para. 2),[17] which is the only dispute falling under the power of the ECJ pursuant to Article 8 of that agreement.[18] This explains the crucial, but limited role given to the Commission in issuing a report on whether a Party implements the balanced budget rule into domestic law properly; and the automaticity of the ECJ involvement, should the

[14]See *Pringle* ruling, cit., para. 175 and Tuori and Tuori (2014), p. 159, who agrees with the reasoning of the ECJ.

[15]It seems worth adding that as a matter of principle an organisation-hood stems from possessing an its own distinct will, namely when its decision-making is based on majority voting, which is actually the way in which the ESM organs operate. Once its subjectivity is confirmed by the fact that it externally and effectively acts as an international legal subject, it should be considered as an entity different from its Members.

[16]Klabbers (2009), p. 35 et seqq.

[17]Article 3, para. 2, stipulates that "the rules mentioned under paragraph 1 shall take effect in the national law of the Contracting Parties at the latest 1 year after the entry into force of this Treaty through provisions of binding force and permanent character, preferably constitutional, or otherwise guaranteed to be fully respected and adhered to throughout the national budgetary process".

[18]Needless to mention that the Commission's task was seen as a political necessity to counter the habit of mutual indulgence amongst the Eurozone Governments (Baratta 2013, p. 31 et seqq.). As is known, Member States are to a large extent unwilling to dispute amongst themselves, as the practice related to Article 259 infringements illustrates (see recently Kochenov 2015).

Commission report negatively against a party (in that situation "[. . .] the matter will be brought to the Court of Justice [...] by one or more Contracting Parties").[19]

All in all, a solution consistent with the subjective condition in question seems to be achieved if one considers that the Contracting Parties' commitment operates in the sphere of their discretionary powers. Indeed Member States agreed to reduce their international discretion to lodge a claim in order to shape an enforcement system that admittedly suits them best. Nothing in the exercise of their international sovereignty seems to prevent them from agreeing *ex ante* to rely on the Commission's assessment, and as a result to subordinate their choice to bring claims before the ECJ to an external (and above all, independent) evaluation. Thus, as long as the Commission formally is not a part of the proceedings, the requirements of primary law appear to be met. Moreover, it seems reasonable to assume that conferring new monitoring tasks to the Commission does not alter its institutional character of being, amongst other functions, a "guardian" of the system.

Coming to the substantive condition set forth in Article 273 TFEU,[20] clearly it is met by the dispute settlement set out in the ESM Treaty. As the Full Court pointed out in *Pringle*, a dispute on the interpretation or application of that Treaty,

[19]This is not to say that the Commission will be a party in the proceedings (de Streel and Etienne (2012), p. 182 et seqq.; Rossolillo (2012), p. 10 et seqq.; Ubertazzi (2013), pp. 83 and 85–86). Indeed, such an outcome would hardly be in compliance with the EU legal framework. Thus, only States collectively (Article 8, para. 1, second sentence) or unilaterally (Article 8, para. 1, third sentence)—and, in the latter case, regardless of the Commission's report—have the legitimacy to lodge a case against another State. The dispute remains strictly intergovernmental even in the case where a Party persists in not taking the necessary implementing measures after the first judgement of the ECJ. Yet, this second action is not automatic and unilateral in nature ("a Contracting Party [. . .] may bring the case before the Court of Justice [. . .]", Article 8, para. 2, first sentence). The problem is the overall coherence of the system as far as the six "Arrangements Agreed" are concerned. In fact, on 2 March 2012 all the Signatories agreed to annex to the Minutes of the Signing of the Treaty six "Arrangements Agreed" deemed to be applied in relation to Article 8, para. 1, second sentence, should the Commission conclude in a report to the Parties that one of them has failed to comply with Article 3, para. 2, of the Fiscal Compact. The aim of the Arrangements is to enhance the automaticity of the judicial control by construing the action as a collective and obligatory tool—within 3 months of the Commission's report, the "Trio of Presidencies" (as set out in Annex I to Council Decision 2009/908/EU of 1 December 2009) will lodge an application "in the interest of, and in close cooperation with, all the Contracting Parties". Minimising the politicisation of the dispute is the aim pursued by the Annex. In addition, the same Arrangements are to be used in relation to Article 8, para. 2, should the Commission assess that a Party has not taken the necessary measures to comply with the judgment of the ECJ provided for in Article 8, para. 1, of the Treaty. Stepped outside the documents to submit to ratification by national Parliaments, according to international customary law they are interpretative criteria of Article 8. They aim at enhancing the automaticity of the judicial control by construing the action as a collective and obligatory tool should the Commission conclude in a report that one of them has failed to properly implement the balanced budget rule into domestic law or, at a possible later stage, that a Party has not taken the necessary measures to comply with the judgement of the ECJ. Doubts however may be raised as to the consistency of the Arrangements with the nature (non automatic and unilateral) of the action laid down in Article 8, para. 2. See however Adam (2013), p. 39; Bartoloni (2013), p. 96.

[20]Tizzano (1967), p. 244 (focusing on the objective nature of the connection with the EU law).

> is likely also to concern the interpretation or application of provision of European Union law,[21]

given the strong *conditionality* which is attached to the granting of financial assistance to Member States that are experiencing severe financing problems.[22] Moreover, there is a strong *personal* tie between the Eurogroup and the ESM due to the fact that the composition of the ESM Board of Governors and its Presidency corresponds to those of the Eurogroup.[23] The same holds true for the Agreement on the Single Resolution Fund that is strictly intertwined with several EU secondary law acts.[24]

(2) Recent practice shows a second model for granting extra powers to the ECJ through intergovernmental agreements. Unlike the treaties aimed at enhancing the economic governance just mentioned, that is an international route that is unfounded on a specific legal basis of the EU Treaty. Quite illustrative in this regard is the "Agreement on a Unified Patent Court", signed in 2013 by 25 Member States, which empowers the ECJ with a set of tasks in the new patent litigation system. Instead of making use of a special Treaty rule for conferring extra powers to the ECJ in the area of European patents,[25] Member States decided to set up a

---

[21]See *Pringle* ruling, para. 174.

[22]Under the ESM Treaty, the agreement to be negotiated with the relevant State must be consistent with EU law and particularly with the measures taken by the EU in the area of coordination of economic policy. Consequently, the conditions to be attached to financial assistance are mostly determined by EU law (see *Pringle* ruling, paras. 173–174).

[23]It has been remarked that "in spite of institutional separateness, a personal union between the ESM and the Union (euro-area) framework has been created" (Tuori and Tuori 2014, p. 95).

[24]It is quite a weird and hybrid construction since the Agreement is tied, firstly, with the Single Supervisory Mechanism established by Council Regulation (EU) No. 1024/2013 (OJEU L 287, 29 October 2013, pp. 63 et seqq.). It confers specific tasks to the European Central Bank (ECB) with regard to policies relating to the prudential supervision of credit institutions, as well as, while acting jointly with the national competent authorities, some powers of supervision over the credit institutions established in the Member States whose currency is the Euro, and in the Member States whose currency is not the Euro which have established a close cooperation with the ECB for supervision purposes. Secondly, the Agreement is tied with the Directive (EU) 59/2014 of the European Parliament and of the Council establishing a framework for the recovery and resolution of credit institutions and investment firms, aimed at harmonising national laws and regulations on the resolution of credit institutions and certain investment firms, including the establishment of national resolution financing arrangements. The international Agreement on the Single Resolution Fund was considered as necessary on the (debatable) assumption that the participating Member States (that are charged with raising the contributions on the institutions located in their respective territories according to the BRR Directive and the SRM Regulation) remain nonetheless sovereign and competent to transfer those contributions towards the Fund. Thus, the obligation to transfer the contributions raised at national level towards the Fund derives from the international Agreement itself and not by EU law, though there is a clear substantial connection between these components.

[25]I refer to Article 262 TFEU that allows the Council to confer jurisdiction on the ECJ in disputes relating to the application of acts in the field of European intellectual property rights. However, even the ECJ in its Opinion 1/09 (8 March 2011, *Draft agreement on the creation of a unified patent litigation system*) was not enthusiastic with the plan to set up a specialised body, most likely to be attached to the General Court (see Baratta 2014a, p. 296 et seqq.; Adam 2011, p. 277 et seqq.; Alberti 2012, p. 367 et seqq.).

judicature "common" to the participating States outside the architecture of EU law. It contains a truly peculiar design of judiciary, perhaps not always perfect, but closely integrated, and formally founded on international law, which is not so far from a federal concept of justice.

Be that as it may, due to this unique feature, the Patent Court has been shaped to ensure the effectiveness of EU law and the respect for the founding principles of the EU judicial system. It suffices to recall, firstly, that the Patent Court foundation lies explicitly on the primacy of EU law in a manner that is so wide in scope that is unprecedented even within the EU legal system. Secondly, Member States may be sued for violations of EU law according to the usual infringements procedures pursuant to Articles 258–260 TFEU. Thirdly, Member States are liable for damages caused by the Patent Court according to the *Köbler* ruling. Fourthly, the Patent Court is placed under the supervisory judicial model stemming from the classic preliminary ruling procedure. Needless to say the ECJ's decisions are binding upon the Parties.[26]

(3) A third model for conferring extra powers to ECJ can be found in international treaties concluded by the EU with Third Countries.

In that regard, the monetary Agreements with the Principality of Monaco, the Republic of San Marino, the Vatican City State, as well as the Principality of Andorra are meaningful examples.[27] By virtue of these Agreements based on the procedural provisions of Article 219, para. 3, TFEU,[28] entities outside the EU are entitled to use the euro as their official currency in accordance with the relevant EU *acquis* and to produce limited quantities of Euro coins with their own design on the national side (though they are not allowed to issue Euro banknotes). Moreover, these small sized States have undertaken to implement a set of EU law, which is listed in the annexes to the same Agreements. These cover the field of Euro banknotes and coins, as well as the prevention of both money laundering and of fraud and counterfeiting of cash and non-cash means of payment, including EU banking and financial law and relevant ECB legal acts and rules on statistical reporting requirements.[29] A mechanism of Joint Committees is in charge of deciding the deadlines for the implementation by the three micro States of the new legal acts and rules in those fields.[30]

---

[26]As to the features of this unusual judicial construct and for further references, see Baratta (2014b), p. 101 et seqq.

[27]See for instance the Monetary Agreement between the European Union and the Vatican City State (2010/C 28/05), OJEU C 28, 4 February 2010, p. 13 et seqq.; Monetary Agreement between the European Union and the Republic of San Marino (2012/C 121/02), OJEU C 121, 26 April 2012, p. 5 et seqq. See Maresceau (2014), pp. 151 et seqq., 186 et seqq.

[28]Martucci (2016), p. 114 et seqq.

[29]See Articles 8 of the Monetary Agreements with the Vatican City State and the Republic of San Marino. Balboni (2014), p. 405 et seqq., at 423.

[30]See Articles 11 of the Monetary Agreements with the Vatican City State and the Republic of San Marino.

It is worth noting, on the one hand, that they have accepted that the ECJ will have the *exclusive* competence for settling any dispute which may arise from the application of the relevant Agreement between the Parties (provided that they have not been resolved within the Joint Committee); and on the other hand, that the judgment of the Court is binding on the Parties, which are in addition bound to take the necessary measures to comply with the judgment within a period to be set out by the Court in its decision. In the event that one of the Contracting Parties fails to take the necessary measures to comply with the judgment, the other Party can immediately terminate the Agreement.[31]

Quite similarly, the Agreement on civil aviation between the European Community and the Swiss Confederation,[32] while aiming to establish reciprocal freedom of establishment,[33] and liberalisation of air traffic rights between any point in Switzerland and any point in the EU for carriers registered in both Parties,[34] lays down the exclusive competence of the ECJ for

> all questions concerning the validity of decisions of the institutions of the Community taken on the basis of their competences under this Agreement.[35]

A similar approach is provided for in the multilateral agreement establishing a "European Common Aviation Area", which is completed by the ECJ competence for dispute settlement whose decision is "final and binding".[36]

It would be interesting to comprehend the reasons for the positive response of third States to an international treaty implying the acceptance, in some important, albeit limited, fields of their sovereignty, both of an *external* decision-making process (*i.e.* the EU legislative and normative institutions) and an *exclusive* judicial body (the ECJ) in which they have no representative. The answers cannot but be speculative. The first one seems quite obvious: the legitimacy acquired by the ECJ and the need to guarantee the uniformity of EU law even when it is applied beyond its initial territorial scope. The second layer could be the difficulty and the costs of creating an international judge as efficient and reliable as the ECJ. The final, and perhaps the most important, reason could be the pursuit of a partial integration process into the EU legal order, implying the unilateral application of EU law in Third States so as to accept its normative and related judicial constraints.

This construct, albeit peculiar, should not be conceived in exclusively unidirectional terms as if it were a form of EU legal imperialism.[37] Yet somehow it is. It is

---

[31] See Articles 10 of the Monetary Agreements with the Vatican City State and the Republic of San Marino.

[32] Agreement between the European Community and the Swiss Confederation on Air Transport, OJEU L 114, 30 April 2002, p. 73 et seqq.

[33] Article 4.

[34] Article 15.

[35] Article 20.

[36] See Decision of the Council and of the Representatives of the Member States of the EU meeting within the Council of June 2006 (2006/682/EC), and the Multilateral Agreement, OJEU L 285, 16 October 2006, p. 1 et seqq., Articles 15, para. 3, and 20, para. 3.

[37] Balboni (2014), pp. 407, 420 and 429–430.

arguable that Third States seek to be integrated in the EU legal order—*rectius*, in some specific internal market and monetary fields—with the ensuing beneficial economic effects. Some provisions laying down the possibility to invoke rights which devolve from these agreements before national Courts[38] or the principle of mutual cooperation in order to achieve the objectives of the same agreements[39] or even prohibiting any discrimination on grounds of nationality,[40] are illustrative in that regard.

The problem is that this goal has not been achieved by Switzerland if one takes into account ECJ case law.[41] Therefore, this model of integration in the internal market needs to be improved and, under this perspective, in the near future to become the basis for re-shaping the economic treaty relationships with some Western European Countries (the small sized Countries, in particular) in accordance with Aricle. 8 TEU and the related Declaration No. 3 attached to the Treaty of Lisbon.

3 Legal Constraints When Entering Into International Agreements Related to EU Matters

The above-mentioned instruments offer peculiar constructs within which, as is self-evident, the adjudicative powers of the ECJ stem from the consent of the Members States and, in some cases, from that of the Union institutions and Third Parties, a consent that is grounded in agreements governed by international law. Even assuming that the ESM Treaty, the Fiscal Compact and the UPC Agreement pertain to the competence of the Member States—to their sovereignties, so to speak—the States' autonomous capacity to act at an international level does encounter some constraints. That is all the more true when that capacity affects matters already governed by the EU legal framework.

All these international treaties raise issues of consistency with primary law. One may argue that insofar as primary law provides for an explicit legal basis to confer extra powers to the ECJ, the main concern is ensuring compliance with the conditions laid down in the same legal basis. As discussed, the ESM Treaty, the Fiscal Compact and the Agreement on the Single Resolution Fund are illustrative case studies of Article 273 TFEU. This is not to neglect the issue regarding the legality of these controversial (international) instruments, in particular that to ascertain that resorting to revision of primary or secondary EU law is politically unfeasible before having recourse to international law agreements in EU related

[38]Article 22 of the Agreement on the European Economic Aviation Area.

[39]Article 3 of the Agreement on the European Economic Aviation Area.

[40]Article 4 of the Agreement on the European Economic Aviation Area.

[41]ECJ 12 November 2009, Case C-351/08, *Grimme*; 15 July 2010, Case C-70/09, *Hengartner*; 11 February 2010, Case C-541/08, *FokusInvest*.

matter. Yet the issue under discussion here is different: may Member States and, where relevant, political institutions resort to the ECJ via international instruments outside a specific legal basis empowering them to do so, namely when a legal basis does exist?

In theory, this issue appears more problematic where a specific legal basis is provided for but there is no corresponding will to apply it. It is worth recalling that when Member States and institutions desired to establish a Patent Court, a EU law-based judiciary, making use of Article 262 TFEU was certainly an available option. As the ECJ held in Opinion 1/09, that provision can be used to confer

> on the Court some of the powers which it is proposed to grant to the Patent Court.[42]

However, the ECJ added that it

> is not the only conceivable way of creating a unified patent court.[43]

In its vision, Article 262 TFEU is just an *option* for it "does not establish a monopoly for the Court" as regards disputes in the field of intellectual property rights.[44] Arguably, an explicit legal basis for conferring extra powers to the ECJ can be circumvented by concluding an international agreement. This reading of Opinion 1/09 would entail that when resorting to a primary law legal basis, it does not suffice that a given matter falls under an area of EU action. What is further required, arguing from the ECJ's reasoning, is that Member States and the relevant institutions must have a specific will for Union action. In that case Opinion 1/09 *de facto* encouraged Member States (and the Commission behind the scene) to follow an international path outside EU legal framework.

Even *Pringle* did not pose substantial limits to Member States' capability to resort to *inter se* agreements in matters potentially falling within the scope of the EU legal framework.[45] In fact, the ECJ acknowledged that Eurozone States were entitled to conclude an agreement between themselves for the establishment of a stability mechanism. It highlighted, among other arguments, that having recourse to Article 352 TFEU is not binding for the Union institutions.[46]

Looking at the treaties in question through the prism of the purposes for which they were enacted and the reasons that led to them, the common denominator for involving the ECJ can be identified in the need to safeguard the consistency of the relevant agreement with the fundamental role the ECJ enjoys in the EU legal order under Article 19 TEU ("it shall ensure that in the interpretation and application of the Treaties the law is observed"). In other words, increasing the role of the jurisdiction of the ECJ by virtue of *inter se* agreements seems to be a means to

---

[42]Cit., para. 61.

[43]Cit., para. 61.

[44]Cit., para. 62. Baratta (2011), p. 297 et seq.

[45]Tuori and Tuori (2014), p. 193 et seq.

[46]*Pringle* ruling, cit., para. 67. See the critical remarks rightly addressed to this ruling by Munari (2015), p. 733 et seqq.

ensure the full effect of EU law, its autonomy and, ultimately, the particular nature of the law established by the Treaties, even when the EU law is deemed to apply beyond its original architecture.

This is not to say that, as a matter of policy, Member States are uninterested in involving the ECJ for disputes arising from these specific normative frameworks: quite the contrary, for several reasons. First, the ECJ has achieved prestige and legitimacy in more than six decades of activity.[47] The high profile composition of the Court, including senior jurists from all the Member States and the overall legal reasoning of its judgments, are well known in the capitals. Although one might have a critical approach with this or that decision, the ECJ jurisprudence has achieved a coherent shape to which the Member States have generally adhered throughout the decades. Thus, it is almost a matter of course for them to rely on the ECJ's role to uphold EU law, in particular for pursuing possible violations and making agreements as judicially effective as possible, instead of relying on the systemic deficiencies of international law under the principles of State responsibility, reciprocity, reactions to alleged violations, countermeasures and so forth.[48] In addition, when Member States are seriously determined to ensure strict observation of the engagements embedded in *inter se* agreements, the involvement of EU institutions, including the ECJ, can actually be instrumental for depoliticising disputes in a complex context.[49]

Secondly, given the variety of means to solve international disputes, it would be far more problematic in legal terms (and more expansive) to produce new judicial bodies for each normative framework located in the international sphere.

Thirdly, Member States cannot but recognise, as the practice shows, that an *inter se* agreement related to EU matters enhances the fulfilment of the general goals of the Union, as these have a substantial connection with the *acquis*. Arguably, it is reasonable to uphold a broad interpretation of the objective condition set out in Article 273 TFEU, as Advocate General Kokott suggested in the *Pringle*

[47]As it has been pointed out, it is "one of the most powerful high courts in the world" (Stone Sweet (2011), p. 121.

[48]In any adjudicatory system, decision on compliance amounts to an issue of legality and legitimacy, which is vital even under international law (Huneeus 2013, p. 437 et seqq., at 440; and Kolb 2013, p. 810 et seqq., focusing on "les faiblesses de la sanction en droit international").

[49]Quite illustrative in that regard is the involvement of the Commission, an independent political institution, in the system of dispute settlement of the Fiscal Compact. Since the balanced budget rule (Article 3) plays a pivotal role in the architecture of that Treaty, the Contracting Parties needed to ensure its proper implementation by having recourse to a *super partes* assessment. See however Prete (2015), p. 81 et seqq. and 88. This author casts doubt about the effectiveness of Article 8 procedure, given the complexity of some of its wording. It should be recalled however that Article 8 is a compromise text that was hard to achieve. Moreover, complexity is not a unique feature of that provision. Unfortunately, uncertainties of legal texts are quite common in the EU secondary law for a number of reasons that cannot be summarised here (see Robinson (2014), p. 239 et seqq.; and therewith the contributions of M. Guggeis, R. Bray, R. Baratta, M. Mousmouti, H. Hanthaki and V. Voermans). It does not follow that these provisions are necessarily ineffective.

conclusions.[50] A similar logic underlies the judicial enforcement of the correct implementation of the balanced budget rule at a national level as laid out in the Fiscal Compact.[51]

However, being (or being sometimes forced to remain) outside the realm of the EU architecture, Members States are expected to pay careful attention to ensure the consistency of the concerned instrument with the EU law *acquis* as a whole. In particular, since the jurisdiction of the ECJ is inherently contentious, *inter se* agreements may not alter the nature of its function as construed by the Treaties.[52] As a result, ECJ's decisions in *inter se* agreements are to be binding. To put it differently, Member States, as well the EU institutions when they enter into agreements with Third States with the aim of *integrating* them within some monetary and economic fields of EU law, would be prevented from allocating a mere consultative power to the ECJ.

This inherent feature of the EU judicature may also explain why its role beyond EU law should in principle be limited to solving classical legal disputes. It is worth noticing for instance that under the Fiscal Compact, the scope of ECJ jurisdiction regards only the correct implementation of the balanced budget rule in domestic law, and no more than that. This provision is not meant to make justiciable the event in which a national authority approves an imbalanced budget. It would simply not fall within the ECJ competence. This is hardly a surprise because the vast majority of the Member States realised the need to stay outside the EU legal framework for political reasons, yet they still had to preserve the judicial nature of the ECJ. Its crucial task is to state the law (Article 19 TEU), without touching upon political or economic evaluations.

In short, by virtue of the principles of institutional conferral and separation of powers on which the Union is founded, the EU judges are not the appropriate organs to interfere in economic and political affairs. Therefore, should the Member States decide to repatriate the balanced budget rule into the realm of EU law, without laying down any *justiciability* restriction in that respect, clearly the ECJ would not challenge this new empowerment—or *rectius* it would not have the possibility to do so according to the founding principles of the current Treaties. However, one may reasonably expect that the ECJ will adopt a self-restrained approach such as that

[50]In this case Advocate General pointed out that "Since the allocation of tasks under Article 273 TFEU is dependent on a special agreement between the parties, it is moreover sufficient if the subject matter of such an agreement is related to the subject matter of the European Union Treaties. It is not a requirement that every single dispute arising from the ESM Treaty must imperatively be shown to be related to the European Union Treaties", cit., para. 186.

[51]This judicial remedy is instrumental to the proper application of the Stability and Growth Pact and namely to the related primary and secondary law. In that sense the balanced budget rule indeed shows a complementing link to the economic union, as Article 1, para. 1, of the Fiscal Compact further demonstrates as regards it as a whole.

[52]See ECJ 14 December 1991, Opinion 1/91, *Draft agreement between the Community, on the one hand, and the countries of the European Free Trade Association, on the other, relating to the creation of the European Economic Area*, para. 61.

usually applied whenever an institution possesses a margin of appreciation for evaluating monetary, economic, political and social data. The judiciary experience in the field of competition law and state aids is illustrative[53]; the same holds true if one looks at the *Gauweiler* ruling as recognising the technical assessment the ECB enjoys as an independent institution charged with exclusive monetary policy tasks.[54] For the ECJ is usually, and understandably, unwilling to substitute its view for that of the political institution concerned.

More in general, Member States are prohibited from concluding an *inter se* agreement that might affect common rules or alter their scope pursuant to Article 3, para. 2, TFEU).[55] Accordingly, an implied condition is that such agreement must respect the EU *acquis* as a whole. This explains the reason why the Court's attributed powers under the Fiscal Compact concern the transposition of the balanced budget rule (as well as the related correction mechanism) into domestic law, but not the concrete compliance with that rule in a given national budget.[56] It is actually an obligation differing from those falling within the scope of the exclusion clause provided for in Article 126, para. 10, TFEU. In sum, the drafters were careful not to encroach on that originally limited role of the ECJ.[57]

Therefore, as long as the powers and roles conferred to the ECJ are neither altered, nor undermined, primary law does not prevent Member States and EU political institutions from providing additional tasks to the EU judiciary under an international treaty. Certainly, this possibility is to be grounded on the need to ensure the full effect of EU law when it is deemed to apply beyond its original scope. Yet it cannot be ruled out *a priori*.[58] After all, ECJ case law has apparently endorsed the possibility of acquiring new powers under international agreements insofar as some foundational requirements are respected. Opinion 1/91 admitted in principle such an option,[59] as did the *Pringle* ruling with respect to Article

[53]In these areas, leaving aside compliance with procedural rules, including the provisions of reasons, judicial control is essentially limited to assessing whether the Commission accurately stated the facts and whether manifest errors of evaluation or misuses of power occurred.

[54]ECJ 10 June 2015, Case C-62/14, *Gauweiler and others*, para. 68 et seqq.

[55]This prohibition also stems from Article 3, para. 2, TFEU, even though that provision, read with Article 216 TFEU, governs the competence of the EU for agreements with third countries or international organisations. In any case, this is the approach apparently adopted by the ECJ in the *Pringle* ruling, cit., para. 101.

[56]Baratta (2013), Martucci (2016), pp. 763–764.

[57]See however Ziller (2012), p. 115 et seqq., at 129–133; Ziller (2013), p. 609, who states that Article 8 circumvents Article 126, para. 10, TFEU; likewise, Adam (2013), p. 40. For a different perspective, de Streel and Etienne (2012), pp. 182–185, at 184; de Witte (2012a), pp. 14–17, at 17.

[58]This is not to say that a difference cannot be made between the ECJ and other political institutions as regards the possibility to borrow the EU institutions under an international agreement (as noted by de Witte (2012b), p. 139 et seqq., at 155).

[59]See Opinion 1/91 in which the Court noted that: "Admittedly, there is no provision of the EEC Treaty which prevents an international agreement from conferring on the Court of Justice jurisdiction to interpret the provisions of such an agreement for the purposes of its application in non-member countries. Neither can any objection on a point of principle be made to the freedom which the EFTA States are given to authorize or not to authorize their courts and tribunals to ask the Court of Justice questions or to the fact that there is no obligation on the part of certain of those courts and tribunals to make a reference to the Court of Justice" (paras. 59 and 60).

273 TFEU.[60] Further, ECJ's Opinion 1/09 essentially suggested the creation of a "common" Patent Court situated within the judicial system of the EU and, consequently, capable of ensuring the full effectiveness and respect for the foundations of EU law.[61]

4 Conclusions

When Member States enter into agreements *strictly related to the subject matter of EU law*, the reference to the ECJ, both for solving disputes between themselves and for protecting individual rights as guaranteed by EU law, is not just consistent with the principle of institutional conferral. It is also a route they are bound to take in order to comply with the ultimate rationale of the EU system. In other words, awarding additional jurisdiction to the ECJ cannot be seen as a mere option.[62] It rather appears as an obligation insofar as *inter se* agreements may affect the autonomy of EU law and its effectiveness. After all, it seems vital for the EU legal order that, in order to forestall future differences of interpretation, its *acquis* is given a uniform interpretation and application irrespective of the circumstances in which it is to be applied.[63]

This holds true also for international agreements whose purpose is to create economic areas with Third States based on EU rules (or on provisions which are identical in substance to it) and equal conditions of competition, as well as to provide for adequate means of enforcement at administrative and judicial level. By affirming the exclusive jurisdiction of the ECJ, the underlying *rationale* is to ensure the uniform application of EU law. It seems a functionally persuasive ground even from the perspective of a Third State seeking to partially integrate itself into the economic and internal market area of the EU.

All in all, they are a *special* category of international treaties strictly intertwined with *the subject matter of EU law as a whole* since they are, as discussed, intended either to complement EU law or to enlarge its application to Third Parties. In this scenario empowering the ECJ with additional tasks (beyond the realm of EU law) appears the only way to preserve the autonomy of EU law.

---

[60]See *Pringle* ruling, cit., para. 170 et seqq.

[61]See Opinion 1/09, cit., para. 82.

[62]One could argue that for instance in the area covered by Article 273 TFEU, the ECJ is entitled to adjudicate an international dispute, which is outside the exclusive jurisdiction of the Court on disputes concerning the interpretation and application of the Treaties pursuant to Article 344 TFEU. Consequently, Member States would be empowered to confer with the ECJ but not obliged to do so. However, this perspective does not consider the underlying rationale of the ECJ involvement in *inter se* agreements as suggested above in the text.

[63]See by analogy ECJ 18 October 1990, Joined Cases 297/88 and 197/89, *Dzodzi*, para. 37; 16 June 1998, Case C-53/96, *Hermès*, paras. 24–33; 14 december 2000, Joined Cases C-300/98 and 391/98, *Parfums Christian Dior*.

As submitted, under certain conditions, additional tasks can and should be attributed to ECJ outside the Union framework.[64] The implied assumption is that the ECJ, while acting beyond EU law in the event of *inter se* agreements, does not affect the rights of the EU Member States not participating in the relevant instrument. Quite to the contrary, the EU judiciary continues to work in the general interest in accordance with the EU legal order as a whole. It would not be convincing to argue that Article 13, para. 2, TEU precludes allocation of new tasks to the institutions outside the EU legal framework unless a unanimous will in favour is expressed. This conclusion would hardly be consistent with both the general principles and the recent practice of *inter se* agreements. Moreover it would go too far. After all, the principle of conferral cannot be derogated with the blessing of the national Governments. Therefore, a unanimous will is not required in order to attribute additional tasks to the ECJ, provided that its role and nature is not altered.[65]

That being said, it seems also arguable that as a matter of policy, international *inter se* instruments related to EU law should remain exceptional tools justified in emergency situations. The ESM Treaty and the Fiscal Compact were conceived just as provisional and urgent (though necessary) measures.[66] The juxtaposition of the EU legal framework and an international instrument ratified by a limited number of Member States should be accepted on a temporary basis only. For such a mixture may reinforce the fragmentation and uncertainty of the legal framework and also, as far as the ESM Treaty and the Fiscal Compact are concerned, the division between the Euro area and non-euro area States. They raise legal issues and concerns (some of them examined above) not always easy to fit in the legal framework of primary law.[67] Although *inter se* agreements remain at Member States' disposal, as the ECJ held in *Pringle*, they

> are prohibited from concluding an agreement between themselves which might affect common rules or alter their scope.[68]

---

[64]*Pringle* ruling, cit. para. 74.

[65]See, in general, ECJ 10 April 1992, Opinion 1/92, *Draft agreement between the Community, on the one hand, and the countries of the European Free Trade Association, on the other, relating to the creation of the European Economic Area*, paras. 32 and 41; and 18 April 2002, Opinion 1/00, *Proposed agreement between the European Community and non-Member States on the establishment of a European Common Aviation Area*, para. 20; see also Opinion 1/09, cit. paras. 74-76.

[66]Particularly in the case of Fiscal Compact, that approach was in principle considered viable, provided that any inconsistencies with the law and related principles of the EU (*contra legem* provisions) had to be avoided. The ECJ jurisprudence is clearly oriented in the sense that the effects of a multilateral mixed agreement on the bilateral relations between Member States cannot affect primary law, as well as the allocation of responsibilities defined in the treaties (see, in that regard, ECJ 30 May 2006, Case C-459/06, *MOX Plant*, para. 123; Opinion 1/91, cit., para. 35, and Opinion 1/00, cit., paras. 11 and 12.

[67]Craig (2012), p. 231 et seqq.; Finscher-Lescano (2013), p. 9 et seqq.

[68]*Pringle* ruling, cit., para. 101.

Further, the method of concluding an international agreement among a limited number of Member States raises a *repatriation problem*.[69] As for instance the *sunset clause* in Article 16 of the Fiscal Compact recognises, the great majority of Member States already considered the need to bring its regime back within the EU system since that exceptional instrument was conceived in the middle of the crisis. Some provisions of the Fiscal Compact, subsequent to its adoption, have already been implemented within the EU legal order through secondary law.[70] In fact, experience shows inevitable disharmonies between the *inter se* agreement and the EU normative framework.

References

Adam S (2011) Le mécanisme prejudicial, limite fonctionelle à la competence externe de l'Union. Note sur l'avis 1/09 de la Cour de Justice. Cahiers de droit europèen

Adam R (2013) La riforma del governo economico dell'Unione europea. In: Bartoloni ME, Caligiuri A, Ubertazzi B (eds) L'Unione europea e la riforma del governo economico della zona euro. Editoriale Scientifica, Napoli

Alberti J (2012) Il parere della corte di giustizia sul Tribunale dei brevetti europeo e comunitario. Il Diritto dell'Unione Europea

Balboni M (2014) I rapporti tra Unione europea e i micro-Stati: verso una nuova fase? Studi in onore di L. Costato, vol 2. Jovene, Napoli

Baratta R (2011) National Courts as "Guardians" and "Ordinary Courts" of EU Law: Opinion 1/09 of the ECJ. Legal Issues of Economic Integration

Baratta R (2013) Legal issues of the "Fiscal Compact". Searching for a mature democratic governance of the euro? In: de Witte B, Héritier A, Techsel A (eds) The euro crisis and the state of European democracy. European University Institute, RSCAS, EUDO, Florence

Baratta R (2014a) I vincoli imposti dal fiscal compact ai bilanci nazionali. Federalismi.it, No. 17

Baratta R (2014b) The Unified Patent Court–What is the "common" trait about? In: Honorati C (ed) The EU patent protection. Lights and shades of the new system. Giappichelli, Turin

Bartoloni ME (2013) Il ruolo della Corte di giustizia dell'UE in base al TSCG. In: Bartoloni ME, Caligiuri A, Ubertazzi B (eds) L'Unione europea e la riforma del governo economico della zona euro. Editoriale Scientifica, Napoli

Borges A (2012) The role of public financial institutions. In: Allen F, Carletti E, Simonelli S (eds) Governance for the eurozone: integration or disintegration? FIC Press, Philadelphia

Condinanzi M (2016) L'Unione economica e monetaria e politica sociale. In: Tizzano A (ed) Verso i 60 anni dai Trattati di Roma. Stato e prospettive dell'Unione europea. Giappichelli, Torino

Craig P (2012) The stability, coordination and governance treaty: principle, politics and pragmatism. Eur Law Rev 37:231

Craig P (2013) Pringle: legal reasoning, text, purpose and teleology. Maastricht J Eur Comp Law 20:3

Daniele L (2016) Misure anti-crisi, riforma della *governance* della zona euro e assetto istituzionale della UEM. In: Tizzano A (ed) Verso i 60 anni dai Trattati di Roma. Stato e prospettive dell'Unione europea. Giappichelli, Torino

de Streel A, Etienne J (2012) Le Traité sur la stabilité, la coordination et la gouvernance au sein de l'Union économique et monetaire. Journal de droit européen

[69]That seems necessary also as regards the ESM Treaty, as suggested by Munari (2015), p. 736.

[70]See Articles 5 and 6 of the Fiscal Compact.

de Witte B (2012a) European stability mechanism and treaty on stability, coordination and governance: role of the EU institution and consistency with EU legal order. In: Challenges of Multi-tier Governance in the EU–Workshop 4th October 2012
de Witte B (2012b) Treaty games–law as instrument and as constraint in the euro crisis policy. In: Allen F, Carletti E, Simonelli S (eds) Governance for the eurozone: integration or disintegration? FIC Press, Philadelphia
de Witte B, Beukers T (2013) The court of justice approves the creation of the European stability mechanism outside the EU legal order. Common Mark Law Rev 50:805–848
Finscher-Lescano O (2013) Fiskalvertrag und unionsrecht. Unionrechtliche Grenzen völkervertraglicher Fiskalregulierung und Organleihe. Neue Juristische Wochenschrift
Huneeus AV (2013) Compliance with International court judgments and decisions. In: Alter KJ, Romano C, Shany Y (eds) Oxford Handbook of International Adjudications, Oxford University Press
Klabbers J (2009) An introduction to international institutional law, 2d edn. CUP, Cambridge
Kochenov D (2015) Biting Intergovernmentalism: The Case for the Reinventation of Article 259 of TFEU to Make It a Viable Rule of Law Enforcement Tool. Jean Monnet Working Paper Series 11/15, The Jean Monnet Center International and Regional Economic Law and Justice, New York School of Law
Kolb R (2013) Théorie du droit international, 2e edn. Bruylant, Bruxelles
Maresceau M (2014) Les accords d'intégration dans les relations de proximité de l'Union européenne. In: Blumann C (ed) Les frontières de l'Unione européenne. Bruylant, Bruxelles
Martucci F (2016) L'ordre économique et monetaire de l'Union européenne. Bruylant, Bruxelles
Mazzarini L (2014) Articolo 274 TFUE. In: Tizzano A (ed) Trattati dell'Unione europea, 2a edn. Giuffré, Milano
Munari F (2015) Da *Pringle* a *Gauweiler*: i tormentati anni dell'unione monetaria e i loro effetti sull'ordinamento giuridico europeo. Il Diritto dell'Unione Europea
Prete L (2015) Some brief comments on the procedures of enforcement of the fiscal compact, one year after its entry into Force. European Law Reporter, No. 3
Robinson W (2014) Introduction: EU legislation – a shared responsibility. Theory Pract Legis 2 (3):239
Rossolillo G (2012) The fiscal compact, the euopean stability mechanism and a two-speed Europe: institutional proposals for a government of the eurozone. The Federalist
Smets F (2012) Imbalances in the euro area and the ECB's response. In: Allen F, Carletti E, Simonelli S (eds) Governance for the eurozone: integration or disintegration? FIC Press, Philadelphia
Stone Sweet A (2011) The European court of justice. In: Craig P, De Búrca G (eds) The evolution of EU law. OUP, Oxford
Thym D, Wendel M (2012) Préserver le respect du droit dans la crise: la Cour de Justice, le MES et le mythe du déclin de la Communauté de droit (Arret Pringle). Cahiers de droit européen
Tizzano A (1967) La corte di giustizia delle Comunità europee. Jovene, Napoli
Tosato GL (2016) L'Unione economica e monetaria: evoluzione e criticità legali. In: Tizzano A (ed) Verso i 60 anni dai Trattati di Roma. Stato e prospettive dell'Unione Europea. Giappichelli, Torino
Tuori K, Tuori K (2014) The eurozone crisis. A constitutional analysis. CUP, Cambridge
Ubertazzi B (2013) Il quadro politico istituzionale secondo il TSCG. In: Bartoloni ME, Caligiuri A, Ubertazzi B (eds) L'Unione europea e la riforma del governo economico della zona euro. Editoriale Scientifica, Napoli
Viterbo A, Cisotta R (2012) La crisi del debito sovrano egli interventi dell'U.E.: dai primi strumenti finanziari al Fiscal Compact. Il Diritto dell'Unione Europea
Ziller J (2012) The reform of the political and economical architecture of the eurozone governance. A legal perspective. In: Allen F, Carletti E, Simonelli S (eds) Governance for the eurozone: integration or disintegration? FIC Press, Philadelphia
Ziller J (2013) Diritto delle politiche e delle istituzioni dell'Unione europea. Il Mulino, Bologna

The *OMT* Case: Institution Building in the Union and a (Failed) Nullification Crisis in the Process of European Integration

Lorenzo Federico Pace

I am indebted to Professor Massimo Luciani (University of Rome "La Sapienza") and Dean William Treanor (Georgetown Law Center) for insights into the US Nullification Crisis. This article was written during a Fulbright Schuman research period in Washington D.C. The present article is dedicated to Professor Ugo Villani on his 70th birthday. This article represents the literature and case-law as of January 2016.

Abstract This article examines the birth and development of the OMT programme and its implications for the EU integration process. It then analyses the *OMT* case from two perspectives. First, as an example of "Institution building" in the European Union: developments that lasted 2 years (2010–2012) and allowed the EU to establish a "permanent" programme which was capable of ensuring the effective exercise of ECB monetary policy. The legality of the OMT was recently confirmed by the Court of Justice in the *Gauweiler* judgment. Second, the *OMT* case reveals evident Member State dissatisfaction with the working of the European Union. This is highlighted in the *sui generis* 2014 preliminary reference of the German Constitutional Court, regarding the methods and the conclusion reached, on the legality of the OMT. The BVerfG reference led to the 2015 *Gauweiler* judgment. This position (as well as, before it, the position of the *Bundesbank* on the same issue) shows, ultimately, a distrust in the ability of the Union to enact, in the general interest of the Member States, measures in areas where the legislative power is now transferred to the European level. This situation resembles *mutatis mutandis* the 1832 "nullification crisis" between the State of South Carolina and the Federal Government of the United States of America. By analysing this phase of American legal history, the article tries to identify a common pattern of behaviour in "two tier legal systems"—such as the US and the EU—in their respective integration processes. This historical comparison sheds light on the peculiarity of

L.F. Pace (✉)
Department of Economics, University of Molise, Campobasso, Italy
e-mail: lorenzo.pace@unimol.it

L. Daniele et al. (eds.), *Democracy in the EMU in the Aftermath of the Crisis*,
DOI 10.1007/978-3-319-53895-2_20

the European integration process *vis-à-vis* the US experience and highlights the risks that lie ahead in EU integration.

Contents

> [T]he power of the States to interpose in order to protect their rights [...] like all other reserved rights [...] is to be inferred from the simple fact that it is not delegated [to the Federal Government]—South Carolina Exposition and Protest, 1828

> Even the [German] legislature that decides on integration [...] may not transfer sovereign powers to the European Union whose exercise would affect [its] constitutional identity—German Constitutional Court, 2014

1 Introduction

This article will consider the birth and development of the OMT (Outright Monetary Transaction) programme. This programme was designed by the ECB in one of the most dramatic moments of the history of the European Union, when the financial crisis was leading to the "implosion" of the Eurozone. This event, had it occurred, would probably have resulted in the "collapse" of the single market and, with it, the "disintegration" of the European Union and the end of the process of European integration started in the mid twentieth century.[1]

The *OMT* case will be addressed here from two perspectives. Firstly, as an example of "Institution building" in the European Union: developments that lasted

[1]This is the reconstruction presented by the Economist in *The future of the European Union: The choice*, in *The Economist*, 26 May 2012.

2 years (2010–2012),[2] allowed the EU to establish a "permanent" programme which would ensure the effective exercise of ECB monetary policy. The Court of Justice recently confirmed its legality in the *Gauweiler* judgment.[3] Secondly, the *OMT* case reveals evident Member State discomfort with Union action. This is highlighted in the *sui generis* preliminary reference of the German Constitutional Court—for the methods and the conclusion reached—on the legality of the OMT. This reference led to the *Gauweiler* judgment. This position (as well as, before it, the position of the *Bundesbank*) shows, ultimately, distrust in the ability of the Union to enact, in the general interest, measures in areas where legislative power is now transferred at the European level. From this point of view, this situation resembles *mutatis mutandis* the 1832 "nullification crisis" between the State of South Carolina and the Federal Government of the United States of America (see *infra*, Sect. 6).

After examining the "Institution building" period that led to the birth of the OMT programme, the article will discuss the preliminary ruling of the BverfG of January 2014 and the Court of Justice's judgment of June 2015. After presenting the facts and the theoretical basis of "nullification" in the United States—and in particular of the "Nullification Crisis" of the *Tariff Act* of 1832—the article identifies some elements in common between the nullification crisis and the reference of the BVerfG. The article ends with some conclusions on the OMT programme and on the future of the European integration process.

2 Preliminary Notes: The General Situation in the European Union at the Beginning of the Crisis, the European Financial Crisis as a Regulatory Crisis, Issues Regarding the Difficulty in Defining the Legal Means to Resolve the Crisis and the Reasons for Its Dynamics

The OMT (Outright Monetary Transaction) is a so-called unconventional monetary measure decided by the ECB in August/September 2012[4] during the height of the financial crisis that began at the end of 2009.[5] The crisis is at times wrongfully

[2]For sake of space this article will not take into consideration the complex stages leading to the creation of the OMT programme and the related legal issues to be addressed. For a discussion of both, see Pace (2014b), p. 2162.

[3]ECJ 16 June 2015, Case C-62/14, *Peter Gauweiler* v. *Deutscher Bundestag*.

[4]See Wendel (2014), p. 265; Editorial (2015), p. 232; Simon (2015).

[5]On the reconstruction of the cause of the economic and political crisis, see Tremonti (2014), p. 36. For a view of the future of the Union after the crisis, see Fabbrini (2015c). For a comprehensive reconstruction of the crisis and the role of the ECB, see Micossi (2015). For an overview of the regulatory changes after the crisis, Tosato (2014), p. 5.

dubbed as the "Euro crisis"; wrongfully because the Euro as a currency—at least until the end of the financial crisis in 2013—was never "in crisis".[6] The financial crisis was—as will be subsequently explained—a "Euro system" crisis ("Eurozone crisis"). In other words, it was a crisis related to unsatisfactory "Eurozone governance". The birth of the OMT programme (or better, its presentation) combined with the measures enacted in the meantime by the European Union brought the crisis to an end. As such, the OMT constitutes an ECB crisis management tool that was not set out in the original legal framework and consequently did not exist when the Eurozone crisis started. It is an "open market operation", pursuant to Article 18 ESCB Statute as well as being a Eurozone bond buying programme. Its function is to safeguard the effective exercise of the ECB's monetary policy. As such, the OMT is a permanent programme of the ECB monetary policy governance, unlike the "temporary" SMP.[7] Given its aims and structure, although it does not transform the ECB into a lender of last resort (or rather, cannot configure the ECB as such for sake of its legality), the OMT also guarantees indirectly the "irreversibility" of the Euro. The programme indirectly provides that States under economic/financial stress, already subject to a financial assistance programme of the bail-out fund and that still have access to capital markets, will not default on their debt (see *infra*, Sect. 3). This in turn excludes a situation of "contagion" between Eurozone States under financial stress and, ultimately, ensures the "irreversibility" (at least from an economic point of view) of the Euro.

---

[6]See Schmidt (2013).

[7]The ECB issued on 14 May 2010 the Decision ECB/2010/5 on the Security Market Programme (SMP). The programme's goal was to protect the orderly transfer of monetary policy in the context of the single monetary policy—a goal already identified and pursued in previous programmes of the ECB before 2010 (see former President Trichet (2010), p. 11). The SMP, in particular, was qualified as a "temporary" programme. It consisted in buying on the secondary market public and private debt bonds of Eurozone States, interest rates of which showed an excessive spread compared to those of other States. Its aim was to reduce such a spread through the principle of supply and demand. The intervention was necessary on the assumption that spreads would "segment" the European market into different Countries and prevent a proper transfer of ECB monetary policy impulses in the context of a single monetary policy. Although the ECB had already issued before 2010 measures to combat the crisis in order to safeguard the proper transfer of monetary policy, such an innovative programme—and potentially divisive, as we will see later—had never been adopted by the Central Bank. The programme was "informally decided" by the Governing Council on Thursday 6 May 2010 and formally announced as the SMP programme on 10 May (Walker et al. 2010). The fact that date of the announcement did not coincide with that of the "informal decision" was because the ECB wanted to wait and evaluate what the Member States would decide on 9 May. The programme was an open market operation. Its legal basis was Article 12, para. 1, Article 13, para. 1, and, in particular, Article 18, para. 1, ESCB Statute, as set out in chapter IV (entitled *Monetary Functions and Operation of the ESCB*). Notably, the ESCB Statute is a Protocol (No. 4) to the Treaties and as such is EU primary law (Article 51 TEU). This is an important aspect that will be discussed later. The SMP programme was then executed—during the development and the extension of the financial crisis in its four temporal phases (see Pace (2014b), p. 2152)—for the purchase of Greek, Irish, Portuguese, Italian and Spanish bonds, although in different ways.

The birth of the OMT occurred in an historic moment of great activity by the world's major central banks (USA, UK, Japan, China), all of which acted to solve or at least mitigate—each for its part—the effects of the most serious global financial crisis since the 1929 Wall Street Crash.[8] Central banks used, often for the first time, so-called unconventional monetary policy measures in order to try to resolve the crisis; i.e., programme that differed from usual conventional monetary policy measures (setting of money interest rates; the quantity of money in circulation in the different monetary systems, etc.).

The ECB's intervention during the Eurozone crisis was characterised—unlike the US Federal Reserve's[9]—by the fact that at its onset the overall governance of the Euro area did not have a crisis management system.[10] This absence was justified in the following terms by the *ex* member of the ECB Executive Board, Jürgen Stark:

> There were no bailouts or rescue facilities because they weren't ever supposed to be necessary.[11]

In other words, prior to the crisis, owing to a problem of unsatisfactory regulation by the Member States (based nevertheless on a clear political choice), there were no institutional tools to counter systemic crises relating to Member States' public debt or to address the impact of a crisis on the ECB's monetary policy. To use a metaphor, the creation of the European Monetary Union—as envisaged by the Maastricht Treaty and the related rules of secondary legislation—was like a car driving along a highway at 300 km/h without the necessary safety systems in place. The setting up of such a crisis management system in 1992 would however have required—as seen in the development of the Eurozone crisis after 2009—the establishment of other Union Institutions and ensuing debate about the birth of a so-called European Political Union. Clearly in 1992 Member States were not ready to undertake this process. However, in the course of the crisis, in only 5 years—a still relatively short period, especially when compared with the history of other legal systems—the European Union equipped itself with just such a crisis management system (a permanent rescue fund; OMT, etc.), as well as more stringent regulations *vis-à-vis* Eurozone States in economic matters (the Six and Two Packs modifying the Stability and Growth Pact, Fiscal Compact), as well as other important Institutions for the stability of the Euro area (the European banking union, etc.).[12]

---

[8]On ECB unconventional measures during the crisis from an economic point of view, see Cour-Thimam and Winkler (2013). On the reconstruction of the American and European financial crisis, see Irvin (2014).

[9]For a thorough explanation of the reasons for the US financial crisis, its evolution and solution, see Messori (2009). See also Geithner (2014) and Bernanke (2015).

[10]On the lack of a EU *crisis management system*, see Editorial (2015), p. 231.

[11]Zhong (2012).

[12]On the characteristics and effects of the new legislation, see Rossi (2012), p. 293; Baratta (2014) and (2015), p. 493; Porchia (2015). On the relationship between market regulation and containment measures in a financial crisis, see Gelpern (2009), p. 493.

The creation of a crisis management system, and its related institutions, was complicated by the nature in EU law of the legal competence in matters of economic and monetary policy. In fact, normative competence in matters of economic policy is allocated at Member State level (Article 4, para. 2 and Article 120 TFEU) and is coordinated at the EU level (Article 2, para. 3, Article 5, para. 1, Article 119, para. 1, Article 120 TFEU). Monetary policy is, however, an exclusive competence of the Union (Article 3, para. 1, t, TFEU; Article 119, para. 2, and Article 127 TFEU). This situation is not a "birth defect"[13] but rather is the result of a political choice made by Member States in the Maastricht Treaty. This fact has characterised the dynamics of the European integration process. However, this issue raises potential difficulties in identifying which Institution is responsible for the enactment of regulatory measures on economic and/or monetary issues. In fact, monetary policy measures have a natural effect on economic policy, just as economic policy measures have an indirect effect on monetary policy. This "natural interference" can generate doubts, as shown in the judgments *Pringle*[14] and *Gauweiler*,[15] about which authority is competent—and with what scope—to enact the relative measures. This in turn raises doubts about the legality of the measures produced.

In order to understand the dynamics of the Eurozone crisis, it has to be remembered that funds to create the aforementioned crisis management system (ESM, etc.) were outside the "great political agreement" of the European budget. In other words, the agreement where directly Eurozone States had to make available their own funds in order to create such a system. This was due to German opposition to creating a fully fledged bailout pursuant to EU law on the grounds that, on one hand, prior to such a bailout, controls on Member States' budgets would have been required and, on the other, that the setting up of a bailout fund may have been illegal and that it could have been struck down by the BVerfG.

This element gave an "intergovernmental" trend to the solution of the crisis—that is, a solution outside the EU Institutional system—by entering into international Treaties (Fiscal Compact, ESM, Banking union resolution fund, etc.).

This aspect put the German Government—as the most important Eurozone State from an economic point of view—in a conflict between the protection of the Eurozone—via the allocation of its funds for this purpose—and the protection of German taxpayers (and their federal budget). This "tension" was exacerbated by the fact that Germany had already approved in 2003 important (and politically costly) reforms, among other things, to its welfare system with the aim of reaching a sustainable State budget. This resulted in a refusal by the German electorate of the idea of having to use its own funds in order to "save" States in financial crisis that had a "less attentive" management of their public debt and had a "much more generous" welfare system than Germany's after the 2003 reform. It has to be

---

[13]Sauer (2015), p. 973.

[14]ECJ 27 November 2012, Case C-370/12, *Thomas Pringle* v. *Ireland*.

[15]On this case law, see Munari (2015), p. 723.

underlined that the German Government in order to enact the reforms mentioned above had deliberately violated in 2003, together with the French Government, the Stability and Growth Pact,[16] thus creating the conditions for the emergence of the 2009 crisis, as now agreed by many[17] and recently acknowledged by the President of the *Bundesbank*, Jens Weidmann.[18]

3 The OMT Programme as a Tool to Protect the Effective Exercise of the ECB's Monetary Policy; Its Features, Its Aim and Its Institutional Checks and Balances; the OMT Does Not Legally Transform the ECB in a Lender of Last Resort

The OMT, like the SMP, has the purpose—in the ECB objectives—of allowing the proper transmission of monetary policy impulses in the singleness of its monetary policy that otherwise would be impeded by the excessive spread in interest rates between different Eurozone States bonds. The programme is realised by the purchase on the secondary market of Eurozone States' bonds, without an *ex ante* limitation, whose interest rates are deemed to be irrationally high. Unlike the SMP, the OMT provides among its conditions for implementation that the States whose bonds the ECB plans to buy have already requested and obtained a financial assistance programme by the ESM. They should also have continued access to the capital market and the ECB would accept to be considered at the same level as other creditors for the bonds purchased (*pari passu*). The financial assistance programme in turn requires the positive vote of all Eurozone States in the ESM Board of

[16]On the relationship between the violation of the Stability and Growth Pact and the 2003 structural reforms in Germany, see the article by the SPD President and Vice-Chancellor Sigmar Gabriel (2014), p. 1.

[17]The 2003 breach of the Stability and Growth Pact by France and Germany, with the help of Italy, is now widely seen as the trigger for the 2009 financial crisis; influential personalities on this position include: Helmut Kohl (2014), p. 45; Juergen Stark (in Zhong (2012)); Mario Monti (24 November 2011 during the joint press conference with Chancellor German Merkel and French President Sarkozy); Romano Prodi (Dernbach, Meier (2015)). See also Zingales (2016).

[18]Weidmann (2016), para. 3.2. The *de facto* suspension of the Stability and Growth Pact, along with the severe limitations of the European statistical system for the correctness of the budgetary data provided by the Member States—already denounced by the ECA in 2001—created the situation which then led to the start of the financial crisis in 2009. It was well known that Greece had always had, except in 2006, a deficit/GDP *ratio* higher than the binding 3% (just as it was known that France, Portugal and Spain entered the Eurozone with a *ratio* in 1998 higher than 3%). The *de facto* suspension of the Stability Pact in 2003 by France and Germany made it concretely inapplicable to Greece what France and Germany had willfully violated. The mismanagement of the Greek crisis with the Franco-German Deauville Pact of October 2010 created a contagion effect to Ireland. The crisis then evolved to Portugal, Spain and Italy. On this point see Pace (2014b), p. 2162. See also ECJ 13 July 2004, Case C-27/04, *Commission* v. *Council*.

Governors. This gives each and every Eurozone State a veto power (pursuant to the joint reading of Articles 4, para. 3, and 5, para. 6, f, of the ESM Treaty) in granting the financial assistance programme to the requesting State as well as, ultimately, the ability of the ECB to activate the OMT in favor of the said State.

Through such prior authorisation, Eurozone States whose bonds the ECB intends to buy are bound to the economic measures imposed by the ESM, even in the case of an improvement in the bonds interest rate brought about by the execution of the OMT. This would in turn avoid the risk of moral hazard and the consequent possible breach of Article 123 TFEU that the SMP programme potentially created.

This prior authorisation also allows for a clear distinction between measures relating to monetary policy, defined and imposed by the ESM through the financial assistance programmes, and those of a monetary nature, decided and executed by the ECB. This eliminates doubts raised regarding the lawfulness of the SMP programme *vis-à-vis* the ECB mandate. Moreover, the structure of OMT guarantees that the ECB's intervention is limited to resolving temporary financial crises of specific Eurozone States (as demonstrated by the "maturity" of the bond purchased, that is between 1 and 3 years). As a measure aimed to safeguard the effective exercise of the ECB's monetary policy—and not being an economic stimulus programme as Quantitative Easing[19]– the liquidity issued on the market through the OMT is "sterilised", i.e., reabsorbed by the ECB itself.

The OMT, like the SMP, did not expressly provide for the allocation of losses between the ECB and the National Central Banks in case of default of those States targeted by the bond buying programme. This is because it is directly the primary EU law provision of Article 33 ESCB Statute that governs the allocation of losses pursuant to the principle of "full risk sharing", unlike the "partial risk sharing" principle that governs the QE programme and that, as such, raises some doubts concerning its legality.[20]

The OMT features were defined in the press release of 6 September 2012 only and no formal decision—differently from the SMP—was published in the Official Journal. Furthermore, this press release does not clarify the legal basis for the programme. The fact that the OMT—as stated in the press release—is to replace the SMP programme leads to the conclusion that the two programmes share the same legal basis, namely Article 18 ESCB Statute. This was later expressly affirmed by the ECB before the BVerfG.[21]

---

[19]*Introductory statement to the press conference (with Q&A) Mario Draghi – President of the ECB*, Frankfurt am Main, 22 January 2015.

[20]The question concerns the legality of a measure of secondary law—as the Governing Council's, decision although not published in the Official Journal—that defines the principle of *partial risk sharing* thus derogating from the principle of *full risk sharing* governed by a rule of primary law, i.e. Article 33 ESCB Statute relating to the division of any loss incurred in a ECB programme. It is said that this feature was a *condicio sine qua non* requested my some Member States' Central Banks in order to approve the programme. See *Introductory statement to the press conference (with Q&A) Mario Draghi – President of the ECB*, Frankfurt am Main, 22 January 2015.

[21]BVerfG, para. 11.

The OMT programme also has the important incidental effect—but not the primary one—of avoiding the risk of default of Euro States and thus of ensuring the irreversibility of the Euro. In fact, the intervention of the rescue fund only (with a capacity of intervention limited to €500 billion) cannot guarantee a limitless liquidity intervention in the event of a financial crisis of a Eurozone State of the economic dimension, for example, of Italy or Spain. This aspect would raise doubts in the market of the irreversibility of the Euro if a State were under financial stress and the rescue fund did not have sufficient liquidity to bail it out. This would create, on another side, a possible "contagion" effect between different Eurozone States under financial stress.

By contrast, ECB intervention with the OMT ensures that if a Eurozone State is in a economic/financial crisis and while it still has capital market access—and with the further requirement of the prior consent by the ESM of a measure of financial assistance—the interest rates of its bonds will always be kept within sustainable limits for the budget of the said Member State. In other words, as Mario Draghi pointed out from an economic (but not legal) point of view, the OMT has the effect of eliminating

> unfounded fears about the future of the euro area [...] and the only way to do so was to establish a fully credible back stop against disaster scenarios.[22]

From a legal point of view, the OMT does not transform the ECB into a Lender of Last Resort (LLR)[23] (or may be more correctly, a Buyer of Last Resort)[24] as has been argued.[25] In fact, the goal that the ECB pursues with the OMT is not to guarantee financial stability. The goal of OMT—as the goal of the whole policy of the ECB since the 2008 American financial crisis—is to safeguard the effective exercise of its monetary policy. The ECB's intervention is justified from a legal point of view by the fact that excessive differences in spreads between Eurozone bonds[26] may determine market segmentation thereby preventing the ECB impulses of monetary policy having the same effect in all States of the Eurozone. This in turn would violate the singleness of this policy. This does not exclude the OMT indirect effects of financial stability—and only in the presence of rigid OMT requirements. The programme therefore avoids default by a Eurozone State on its debt.[27] Moreover it excludes contagion among Eurozone States and, ultimately and indirectly, guarantees financial stability.

---

[22]Blackstone and Boston (2015).

[23]Tropeano (2015), p. 296.

[24]See the presentation by Viral Acharya (2016).

[25]See Editorial (2015). On closer inspection the authors in the last page of the text claim that the WTO would only have an "indirect lender of last resort effect", p. 238.

[26]This is because the Eurozone—unlike the US—has one monetary policy but 19 different economic policies. Therefore the Eurozone presents 19 different issuers of public debt bonds. This peculiarity creates the possibility of excessive spreads between bonds of different Eurozone States.

[27]See De Grauwe (2013), p. 520.

Ideally, the moral hazard implications of such a programme should have been addressed by an "external independent supervisor" rather than by the ECB itself.[28] In the absence of an intervention by the competent parties (European Institutions, Member States), these aspects ultimately had to be defined by the ECB directly within the Governing Council through the modification of the SPM programme structure. Member States could have prevented the ECB's intervention with the OMT—at least for a period of time—by applying the decision of the European Council of 26 June 2012.[29] However, they preferred to leave that role to the ECB endangering its independence and legitimacy and turning the ECB into a "lightning rod" for criticism—as the BVerfG reference shows—of actions that should have been carried out by other entities.

4 The BVerfG and the Reference to the Court of Justice *vis-à-vis* the OMT (or the SMP?): The Peculiar Application of the Protection of the Constitutional Identity Principle, the Hypothetical Nature of the Legal Concerns Regarding Article 123 TFEU and the Breach of Fundamental Principles of EU Law

As the OMT "Institution building" period was concluded on 6 September 2012 already in the following October some appeals were presented before the BVerfG in order to declare the EU law programme illegal under German Constitutional Law. The content of the subsequent referral of the BVerfG to the Court of Justice of 2 February 2014 shows a clear *trait d'union* between the German *Bundesbank* and the German Constitutional Court in continuing the same objections on the legality of the OMT programme.[30] In fact, also the BVerfG—as a result of the appeals brought in front of it—considers that the OMT programme is in breach of the ECB mandate and that it violates the prohibition of Article 123 TFEU. In particular, the BVerfG concludes[31] in its *sui generis* preliminary reference to the ECJ that the OMT is a breach of both European Union and German Constitutional Law. In particular, the Court threatens the disapplication of the programme by all German agencies, Federal and State (para. 30), in the absence of a corrective interpretation of the Court of Justice (para. 99). This conclusion of the BVerfG has been labeled as an

[28]See De Grauwe (2013), p. 527.

[29]See Pace (2014b), p. 2170.

[30]*Ibid.*

[31]Similarly, see Wendel (2014), p. 265.

> (offensive) invitation to the ECJ to restrict the implication of the OMT programme by means of interpretation.[32]

Although the Court is clearly referring to the legality of the OMT one could think that the BVerfG is writing with the legal structure of the SMP programme in mind. In fact, the German Court raises points of illegality of the OMT (OMT and breach of the ECB mandate; breach of Article 123 TFEU) which, although problematic in relation to the SMP, had been expressly addressed in the OMT.[33]

The BVerfG divides its referral essentially into two parts: the first part, in which it defines the features of its so-called *ultra vires* review on EU law measures, and the second part concerning the assessment of the legality—under EU law—of the OMT programme.

Some of the contributions in the German legal literature claim that the applicants to the BVerfG had no legal interest under German law to present a plea regarding the OMT.[34] In spite of this, the German Court took the opportunity of such an action to formulate and clarify in its first reference to the Court of Justice both the scope of its legal review of Union law legal measures and the cases, the methods and effects of its reference to the Court of Justice.

In the first place, it is relevant to point out—for what will be said later—that the BVerfG, recalling a previous case law and even before defining the conditions of its review of EU law measures, underlines the key role of the "cautious and friendly" interpretation of EU law in the *ultra vires* review (the so-called *Europafreundlich* interpretation). The BVerfG argues that the

> powers of control which are constitutionally reserved for the Federal Constitutional Court are only exercised in a manner that is cautious and friendly towards European law (para. 24),

a principle that would seem to be violated in the later part of the BVerfG's position in the reference.

Referring to the two cases of the BVerfG's legal review *vis-à-vis* EU law measures, both are based on an *ultra vires* review (paras. 24 and 27). The first case is the case

> based on manifest transgressions of power (para. 22).

The second is the case where

> an act of an institution or other agency of the European Union has consequences which affect the constitutional identity protected by Art. 79 sec. 3 GG (para. 27).

In other words, in this second case, the BVerfG defines an "open clause" with reference to the general principle of constitutional identity pursuant to which the legitimacy of Union measures can be reviewed at any time. This is so because

---

[32] Wendel (2014), p. 277.

[33] See above, Sect. 3.

[34] See Sauer (2015), p. 993, who critically argues that "the assumption that the ECB's OMT announcement affects or infringes the petitioners' rights under Article 38, paragraph 1 (1) of the Basic Law is refuted even on the basis of the FCC's substantive understanding of this right".

> even the [German] legislature that decides on integration [. . .] may not transfer sovereign powers to the European Union whose exercise would affect [its] constitutional identity (para. 27).

This principle, as we will see later on, is not so distant from the one expressed in the 1828 *South Carolina Exposition and Protest*.[35] The BVerfG underlines that its review differs from the one performed by the Court of Justice under the Member States' identity protection clause (Article 4, para. 2, TEU, para. 29). It can therefore reach different conclusions (as regards both legality and illegality) *vis-à-vis* the Court of Justice. This setting seems to breach one of the elements identified as typical in the relationship between the Court of Justice and national Courts, namely that of

> relatively narrow conception of national constitutional autonomy.[36]

Again with reference to the constitutional identity review, the BVerfG maintains that this principle—with the scope defined in the reference—is present also in the case law of other European Constitutional Courts (para. 30), a fact some legal scholar doubt.[37] In this respect, the BVerfG makes reference to case law of other Constitutional Courts where EU acts are reviewed by clear, precise and exact violations of fundamental provisions or principles of the relative national Constitution (what it is called in the Italian legal system, *il principio dei controlimiti*). The BVerfG otherwise supports something that is clearly different from *controlimiti*: it supports the unconstitutionality of a complex programme by the ECB after a complete reinterpretation of: the primary and secondary EU law provisions relevant to the case; the aim of the programme; and even the legal nature of the measures on which the programme is built. In this respect, the approach of the BVerfG with reference to the protection of constitutional identity is "rather unique in Europe".[38]

It must be added that this kind of review—taking into account also its wide scope—also seems to breach fundamental principles of EU law such as the principle of autonomy of the EU legal system and the role of the Court of Justice as a centralised body of binding interpretation of EU Law. The BVerfG's claims of the possibility of declaring EU legal measures unconstitutional in the absence of any breach (also not manifest) of secondary Union law *de facto* entails the obliteration (and the delegitimation) of the key role that the Court has played in the development of the EU legal system. This "delegitimation" has an effect, in turn, on the

---

[35]See Sect. 6.a.

[36]Tridimas (2015), p. 412.

[37]It has been argued that the case law of other constitutional courts invoked by the BVerfG is inconsistent with what the Court claims. See Claes and Reestman (2015), p. 970.

[38]Wendel (2014), p. 304. See the deep (and critical) examination of the quoted case-law by the BverfG, Claes and Reestman (2015), pp. 946 and 957.

equally fundamental principle of autonomy of the EU legal system.[39] This is ensured through the independent interpretation of EU law by the Court of Justice both *vis-à-vis* Member States and *vis-à-vis* other International Law Entities, as recently emphasised in the opinion 2/13.[40]

An act that is illegal pursuant to an *ultra vires* review is

> from the outset, inapplicable in Germany (para. 27).

The BVerfG clarifies that in neither of the two cases of *ultra vires* review will the judgments of the Court of Justice issued in a preliminary ruling be binding on the German Constitutional Court.[41] This statement is all the more objectionable because it undermines the role of the reference to the Court, which is—as argued by the Court in opinion 2/13—to

> ensure its consistency, its full effect and its autonomy as well as, ultimately, the particular nature of the law established by the Treaties.[42]

It is no coincidence that the BVerfG's claim was then openly contested by the Court of Justice in its judgment, one of the few criticisms of the Court directed to the BVerfG's reference.[43]

The BVerfG's concern in the *OMT* case would appear to be different from that of the *Bundesbank*'s, though both share the idea of the OMT's unlawfulness. In fact, the real concern of the BVerfG, ultimately, is the inability of the *Bundestag* to exercise its powers of control over the federal budget as provided by the Federal Constitution, powers which, in the BVerfG's view, qualify the German constitutional identity (para. 28).

It is important to emphasise that, from a legal point of view, these BVerfG's concerns are irrelevant to the legality of the OMT programme pursuant to Union law, as confirmed by the judgment of the Court of Justice.[44] This point should already resolve the BVerfG's doubts.

---

[39]See, e.g., ECJ 5 February 1963, Case 26/62 *NV Algemene Transport- en Expeditie Onderneming van Gend en Loos* v. *Netherlands Inland Revenue Administration*; 15 July 1964, Case 6/64 *Flaminio Costa* v. *ENEL*; 9 March 1978, Case 106/77 *Amministrazione delle finanze dello Stato* v. *SpA Simmenthal*; 3 April 1968, Case 28/67 *Molkerei-Zentrale Westfalen/Lippe GmbH* v. *Hauptzollamt Paderborn*; 19 November 1991, Joined Cases C-6/90 and C-9/90 *Andrea Francovich and Danila Bonifaci* v. *Italy*. On the key importance of the principle of independence also in different branches of EU law see Pace (2014a), p. 141.

[40]ECJ 18 December 2014, opinion 2/13, *Accession of the European Union to the European Convention for the Protection of Human Rights and Fundamental Freedoms*, para. 176. In this sense, Sauer (2015), p. 1001.

[41]Para. 27.

[42]ECJ 18 December 2014, opinion 2/13, para. 176.

[43]Para. 16 of the judgment reads: "It must also be borne in mind that it is settled case-law of the Court that a judgment in which the latter gives a preliminary ruling is binding on the national court, as regards the interpretation or the validity of the acts of the EU institutions in question, for the purposes of the decision to be given in the main proceedings". As noted also by the Editorial (2015), p. 227, and also by Claes and Reestman (2015), p. 969.

[44]Court judgment, para. 123.

Apart from this, one could question whether the BVerfG's concerns are well founded. In particular, these concerns seem to be founded on the fact that the OMT programme, unlike other crisis management tools (first of all the ESM), does not define *ex ante* in an International Treaty the size of the financial assistance of each State. The fear of the BVerfG seems to be that

> the Eurosystem would in any case be available as a 'lender of last resort' for the government bonds in question (para. 94).

If this is the point and also the aim of the German Court, the erroneous (and unlawful) setting of the BverfG is evident. It aims at controlling and limiting the exercise of ECB monetary policy, that is, eliminating the key OMT feature of not having an *ex ante* "firepower" limit. This in turn means tampering with a key ECB aspect, which is its independence also from the Member States, independence that is governed entirely pursuant to EU primary law, i.e., by an International Treaty, as the BVerfG seems to ask. If this were the case, it would be contrary to the usual German stance of always protecting the ECB's independence[45] (Importantly, see the open criticisms of the German Finance Minister of April 2016 on the ECB policy and the response of the ECB President Mario Draghi defending the independence of the European Central Bank).[46] Furthermore, notwithstanding the erroneous classification by the BVerfG from a legal point of view of the ECB as a lender of last resort under the OMT programme,[47] the German Court's concerns have already been answered by the ECB during the action before the BVerfG and without the German Court contesting it (para. 12).[48] Moreover, such concerns (that is, the alleged inability of the *Bundestag* to exercise its powers of control over the federal budget as provided by the Federal Constitution) appear to be purely hypothetical[49] against the following facts: the ESCB Statute specifically provides for guarantees to cover losses of the action of the ECB in the form of reserves of the ECB and of the National Central Banks; as already underlined above, Union primary law expressly sets out—in Article 33 ESCB Statute—the allocation of loss arising from an ECB programme. Moreover, from one side the BVerfG imagines a (hypothetical and not actual) loss of the *Bundestag* control over the federal budget expenditure—a loss which, if existent, was introduced by the Maastricht Treaty, an International Treaty. On the other hand, in the BVerfG's consideration not enough weight is given to the (concrete and real) amounts of interest that the Eurosystem (and the Governments of the Eurozone States area through their national banks) have profited from. For instance, interest gained from

[45]Walker et al. (2010).

[46]Allen (2016).

[47]See Sect. 3.

[48]In particular, the ECB has argued that "there is no liability risk for the national budgets because the European System of Central Banks has ensured sufficient risk prevention, mostly through provisions and reserves. If losses occur nevertheless, they can be carried forward and balanced with revenues in the Following Years" (para. 12).

[49]In this sense, see also Sauer (2015), p. 992.

the execution of the SPM programme amounted to around €14 billion in 2012 alone. This interest could then cover for any future losses caused (in hypothesis) by the execution of the OMT on the financial buffers of the ECB and on the National Central Banks, as pointed out by the ECB before the BVerfG.[50]

The BVerfG from this (erroneous) assumption and with the aim of proving the illegality of OMT, construes—as will be seen later—EU primary law—and not only secondary law, as it claims[51]—to be in open violation of a *Europafreundlich* interpretation of Union law, an obligation that the German Court has imposed on itself (para. 24).[52]

Furthermore, the BVerfG interpretation in order to claim that the OMT is unlawful strays in some parts of the reference so far from the clear text of EU law primary law provisions that it complicates—through its interpretation—the same predictability of rights and obligations contained in the Treaty; predictability that the BVerfG underlines is decisive for evaluating the legality of Union law measures (para. 21).[53] Here reference in particular is made to the nature of monetary policy open market operations pursuant to Article 18 ESCB Statute and to the opposite conclusion of the BVerfG. It argues in fact that the OMT—measure *ex* Article 18 ESCB Statute—would be a measure of economic policy. In other words, as will be seen shortly, the BverfG's interpretation of primary and secondary Union law leads to a reconstruction of the OMT programme so far from the intention of the ECB and of EU law—as moreover demonstrated in the subsequent judgment of the Court of Justice—that one might wonder (maybe naively) what is the point for the German Court to assess this programme so oddly reconstructed as an *ultra vires* act.[54]

Coming to the substantive assessment, the BVerfG argues that the OMT is in violation of the mandate of the ECB because it views it as an economic measure. The BVerfG argues that this programme

> aims to neutralize spreads on government bonds of selected Member States of the euro currency area which have emerged in the markets and which adversely affect the refinancing of these Member States (para. 70).

---

[50]See Steen (2013).

[51]BVerfG judgment, para. 24.

[52]Goldmann (2015), p. 9, points out that in the reference the two elements of the BVerfG in its *ultra vires* review, that is the actual breach of EU law and the manifest breach of EU law, coincide in this way ultimately forcing the Court of Justice to either reach the BVerfG conclusion or to create a conflict with the position of the German Court. Equally critical, Claes and Reestman (2015), p. 969; Sauer (2015), p. 998.

[53]Para. 21.

[54]Sauer (2015), p. 997, argues that: "The FCC has deliberately confounded the doctrines of ultra vires review and of constitutional identity review, the review of EU measures and of domestic actions, the review of positive actions and of omissions, as well as of repressive and of preventive legal protection in order to disguise that it primarily addresses constitutional policy concerns".

It would thus be a

> functional equivalent to an assistance measure of the above-mentioned institutions – albeit without their parliamentary legitimation and monitoring (para. 78).

However, the Court, in order to reach this conclusion, fully overturns the structure of the OMT as defined by the ECB.[55] In fact, the ECB drafted the programme based on the following four pillars: 1. Identification of the reason for the financial stress of some Eurozone States (i.e., the fear of financial institutions of the possible collapse of the Eurozone); 2. The aim of the OMT (i.e., the protection of the successful transfer of ECB monetary policy impulses and its singleness); 3. Legal means used for this purpose (i.e., monetary policy measures consisting in open market operations pursuant to Article 18 ESCB Statute); and 4. The expected results of the OMT programme (i.e., the reduction of the interest spreads amongst Eurozone States' bonds).

The BVerfG's position regarding these four elements is as follows: 1. It decisively rejects the argument of the ECB—formulated in the exercise of its exclusive competence in the field of monetary policy—regarding the reasons for the financial stress of some Eurozone States. It accepts, however, the view provided by the German central bank (that is, "the convincing expertise of the *Bundesbank*", paras. 70–71)[56]; 2. It holds irrelevant in its judgment the ECB's goal of protecting the successful transfer of monetary policy and its singleness (para. 95). However it must be noted that this goal was already identified by the ECB well before the SMP programme of 2010[57]; 3. It configures ECB measures pursuant to Article 18 ESCB Statute as economic policy measures[58] without contesting the ECB differing claim. In fact the European Central Bank had argued during the plea before the BVerfG that open market operations are typical instruments of monetary policy,[59] as shown also by the experience of the US Federal Reserve[60]; 4. It does not take into consideration that the mere presentation of the OMT programme obtained the desired result without using cash from the budgets of the ECB, from National Central Banks' or even from those of the Member States'.

As mentioned previously, the way the BVerfG reconstructs the OMT programme seems to be contrary to the principle of *Europafreundlich* interpretation of Union law identified by the German Court itself. In addition, the assessment of the legality of the BVerfG is based on a wrong configuration of the OMT, at least from the point of view of EU law—with a further violation of the principle of *Europafreundlich* interpretation—also clarified by other elements: i.e. by the

---

[55]Para. 69.

[56]Paras. 70–71.

[57]See Pace (2014b), p. 2172.

[58]With particular reference to the legal nature of the OMT programme, as recalled, the BVerfG considered the OMT not as "an act of monetary policy, but mainly an act of economic policy" (para. 69).

[59]Similarly, see Wendel (2014), p. 294.

[60]On this point, see Zaring (2015).

criticism that the German Court held in relation to the so-called "By-passing" (para. 79)[61] and the so-called "Parallelism" between OMT and ESM. Finally the BVerfG comes to an unresolvable contradiction with reference to the purpose of the preliminary concession by the ESM of a programme of financial assistance to a Eurozone State under financial stress before the ECB can start an OMT programme.[62]

As regards the application of Article 123 TFEU—namely the review of the legality of the OMT effects—the BVerfG finds it difficult to interpret this prohibition in the absence of any case law by the Court of Justice. Such an absence should have persuaded the BVerfG to adopt a more cautious interpretation of this provision and not to reach a conclusion as definitive as the one contained in the referral; i.e., the breach of Article 123 TFEU by the OMT programme. This, also in view of the fact that it was questioned whether the legal doctrine quoted by BVerfG in the reference, supports what the German Court claims.[63]

The construction of the prohibition made by the BVerfG is questionable. The Court begins by defining a very wide prohibition (i.e. a "broader prohibition of monetary financing", para. 85). It then lists a series of indications of the OMT effects (some of which are merely potential and hypothetical, paras. 86–94).[64] The joint effect of the different indications would demonstrate—according to the German Court—the breach of Article 123 TFEU by the OMT.

A similar construction of the prohibition transforms the prohibition of Article 123 TFEU and cases of its violation, recalling Hegel, into a "night in which all cows are black".[65] In fact the breach of a prohibition—whose aim and scope is defined in a very wide way—is established on the basis of indications (potential and hypothetical) of the effects of the OMT (moreover, a programme never implemented).

---

[61]The BVerfG argues that, since the OMT is set up as an operation similar to those governed by Articles 12, para. 1, and 18 of the ESM Treaty for the Eurozone financial stability—i.e. buying bonds on the secondary market—, this is an instrument of ECB economic policy.

[62]The BVerfG comes to an unresolvable contradiction when, on the one hand, it claims the danger exists that the ECB—in the absence of any legal constraint—can act "every time the monetary policy transmission mechanism is disrupted" (para. 97). On the other hand, the BVerfG does not consider that the legal constraint of the ECB for the implementation of OMT—OMT operation subject to the authorisation by the ESM of a financial programme—has precisely the function of creating the "constraint" that the BVerfG requires in the action of the Central Bank. The BVerfG then maintains that this constraint violates the autonomy of the ECB. This was later denied by the Court of Justice because, as expressed in the characteristics of OMT, there is no automaticity between approval of a measure by the ESM and the execution of OMT.

[63]Wendel (2014), p. 298, writes: "Again it is astonishing to see how the Second Senate's majority tries to back up its argument with references to external sources which do not at all underpin its argument".

[64]The BVerfG goes so far as to identify evidence of breach of Article 123 TFEU in the fact that the ECB retains bonds until maturity (para. 90). However, this behaviour is not only not expressly prohibited by EU primary law (i.e. Article 18 ESCB Statute), but is part of the natural discretion of Central banks in this context. See, on the US experience Zaring (2015).

[65]On the "peculiarities" of the reading of Article 123 TFEU by the BVerfG, see Wendel (2014), p. 275; Sauer (2015), p. 982.

From this point of view the BVerfG construction is also in breach of the need of predictability of the Treaty rules—and those of prohibition in particular—that the BVerfG first calls as essential (para. 21).

5 The Court of Justice and the *Gauweiler* Judgment, in Other Words: The Legality of the Aim of the OMT Programme and of Its Checks and Balances

As recalled above, the Court of Justice in the *Gauweiler* judgments of June 2015 held the OMT programme to be legal. For the purposes of this article, this judgment is important first because it demonstrates the inaccuracy of the criticisms made towards the OMT by both the *Bundesbank* and the BVerfG. Second, the judgment is also of interest for the way in which the Court finds, from a legal standpoint, the legality of the OMT goals and for the way it finds that the check and balances defined in the OMT ensure the achievement of (only) these goals.[66] This also shows how the slow process of "Institution building" of the OMT programme (2010–2012) has led to the enactment of a legitimate programme under EU law. Applying the reasoning of the Court in *Gauweiler* to the SMP programme, this shows that that programme was probably unlawful pursuant to EU law.[67] Third, the judgment issued was rightly called a "model of restraint".[68] The Court in its judgment does not in fact seek confrontation with the BVerfG—confrontation that was already created with the previous *Mangold/Honeywell* judgment.[69] It tries to show the legality of the OMT "on the force of its substantive arguments".[70]

---

[66]For an interpretation in law and economics of the *OMT* case, see Lombardo (2015), p. 195.

[67]This should not be a surprise. The fact that the ECB has issued a measure that can be *ex post* considered unlawful—i.e. the SMP decision and not just individual purchases of specific Eurozone States Bond—is the consequence of the lack of a crisis management system at the time of the creation of EMU. Hence the need for the ECB to develop such a SMP programme during the crisis—in a "learning by doing" way—in order to protect its monetary policy. This is the result of the urgency with which the EU institutions have had to respond to the European financial crisis. Even in 2010 one of the bailout funds was issued on the basis of a deliberately erroneous legal basis. In fact the first rescue fund had been established with the Regulation (EU) No. 407/2010 having as legal basis Article 122, para. 2, TFEU. This was the only reference in the Treaty that would justify the creation of a solidarity fund. The funds established under this legal basis, however, are designed to help a Member State when it "is in difficulties or is seriously threatened with severe difficulties caused by natural disasters or exceptional occurrences beyond its control". This was clearly not the situation facing Greece in 2010. In spite of this, the Eurozone established such a fund, though making it clear in the conclusions of the 2012 European Council that this was to be the last time such a legal basis would be used for such purposes.

[68]See Editorial (2015), p. 227. Goldmann (2015), p. 13, approves the method of assessment of the Court, as it would allow "constitutional pluralism".

[69]See the critical words of Skouris (2009), p. 775 ss.; Tizzano (2011), p. 223.

[70]See Claes and Reestman (2015), p. 970; see also Editorial (2015), p. 231.

On the other hand, a confrontation between Courts would have been probably counterproductive especially taking into account the position of the Court. The Court of Justice in fact is legally speaking in a stronger position—also considering the legal nature of Union law (see *infra*, Sect. 6.b)—against the BVerfG because of the legal consequences of a judgment of the German Court in conflict with EU law. A judgment in violation of the EU obligations could lead, ultimately, to the imposition by the Court of Justice itself of a financial penalty on the State in default at the end of an infringement procedure (Articles 258–260 TFEU). Fourth, the conclusions of the judgment are also proof of the absence of a manifest breach of EU law in the OMT programme[71] as requested by the BVerfG in its *ultra vires* review of EU law measures. Moreover these conclusions also show how the interpretation of the BVerfG is far from being *Europafreundlich*, a prerequisite that, again, the German Court sets in its *ultra vires* review case-law. This fact is well highlighted in the completely different reasoning of the Court of Justice and that of the BVerfG with reference to the same legal issues of Union law raised by the German Court. Fifth, *Gauweiler* is important because it confirms the principle set out in *Pringle*[72] regarding the decision as to the competence (and the competent Institution) to issue a measure in economic or monetary matters. What is key in order to assess the legality of a similar measure is "the objectives sought by a programme" (para. 53) and not the "indirect effects" (para. 52) it may have on other policies. The possible "spillover effect" on other policies is irrelevant and is a product of the natural interference between the monetary and economic policy.

With reference to the first question regarding the legality of the OMT within the confines of the ECB mandate, the Court departs significantly from the BVerfG's line of reasoning. As already seen above, the German Court started its assessment by defining what in its view was the goal of the programme. It concludes that the OMT Programme was a measure of economic policy outside the mandate of the ECB and, as such, illegal.

The Court of Justice could have responded to what has been called an "attack" on the Court[73] by making reference only to the type of measures used for this programme, namely, open market operations governed by Article 18 ESCB Statute. While the Court, at the end of its reasoning, reaches this very conclusion, in order to respond to the BVerfG it uses a more complex and organic motivation following a typical reasoning of its case law in order to define the content (and limits) of a specific legislative competence attributed to the Treaty. Having ascertained that the OMT is a measure of monetary policy (para. 56), the Court then refutes the

[71]In this sense, see Sauer (2015), p. 971.

[72]ECJ 27 November 2012, Case C-370/12, *Pringle*, para. 56.

[73]Fabbrini (2015b). See Simon (2015), p. 1048, who argues in a surprising way that the postponement of the BVerfG "will go down as a masterpiece of truly cooperative constitutional pluralism in the history of European jurisprudence".

correctness of the issues raised by the BVerfG with reference to the issues of "selectivity",[74] "parallelism"[75] and "by-pass".[76] By doing so, it gives full prominence to the complex structure of the OMT programme and of its checks and balances.

Following its reasoning, the Court then assessed the proportionality of the OMT programme[77] after having defined the scope of judicial review by the Court of Justice in similar cases. That is, with measures where an Institution like the ECB is called

> to make choices of a technical nature and to undertake forecasts and complex assessments, it must be allowed, in that context, a broad discretion (para. 68).

Inside this evaluation, considering the suitability of the programme to achieve the objectives that the ECB established, the Court divides its review into two parts. In the first, the Court finds the ECB's "analysis of the economic situation of the euro", on the basis of which the OMT was then developed, is not "vitiated by a manifest error of assessment".[78] It then assesses the suitability of the OMT to concretely combat the causes of the crisis as devised by the ECB.[79] After assessing that the OMT reached its goal, the Court states that:

> the ECB's assertion [that this goal was achieved] has not been challenged in these proceedings (para. 79).

Having affirmed the suitability of the measure (para. 80), the Court assesses the proportionality test in the strict sense (para. 81). With this aim in mind, the Court emphasises once again the structure of the programme defined by the Governing Council of the ECB and its checks and balances. In particular, the Court lists a number of factors which show that the measure does not go beyond what is necessary to achieve its objective (paras. 82–90), among them the volume of purchases (para. 88) and the selectivity of the programme (para. 89). Interestingly, these are exactly the same elements identified by BVerfG, with the opposite reading, as indications of the programme's illegality.[80] Finally, the Court ends with reference to proportionality, claiming that the ESCB

> weighed up the various interests in play so as to actually prevent disadvantages from arising, when the programme in question is implemented, which are manifestly disproportionate to the programme's objectives (para. 91).

---

[74]Paras. 58–65.

[75]Paras. 59–62 and 64.

[76]Para. 65.

[77]This assessment of proportionality is required, according to the Court, pursuant to Articles 119, para. 2, TFEU, 127 TFEU, 5, paras. 1 and 4, TEU (paras. 66 and 67). On this, see Harbo (2015), p. 23.

[78]Paras. 73–75.

[79]Paras. 76–78.

[80]Paras. 88–89.

The task of the Court with respect to Article 123 TFEU is more complex than the first one. This is due primarily to the absence of case law on the point.[81] It also stems from the intrinsic difficulty of defining the content and scope of a prohibition that could have significant consequences in the future for EU Institutions in exercising their powers. The BVerfG's reading of the prohibition of Article 123 TFEU—with its wide scope and unclear content—is rejected by the Court. This was also due to the mere fact that such an interpretation—as noted correctly by the Court—would be in conflict with a provision of primary law, i.e., Article 18 ESCB Statute (paras. 95–96). The Court, given the special nature of the prohibition and the possibility that it can be "circumvented" (as indicated in BVerfG, para. 86), defines a complex evaluation scheme in order to ascertain the breach of Article 123 TFEU. This requires, first, identifying the content of the prohibition that the Court defines as a prohibition of "all financial assistance from the ESCB to a Member State" (para. 95). Following its evaluation scheme, the Court finds positively that: 1. The purchase of Government bonds on the secondary market is not as such in breach of Article 123 TFEU[82]; 2. Buying bonds on the secondary market pursuant to the OMT programme cannot have effects equivalent to the purchase in the primary market[83]; and 3. Buying bonds on the secondary market pursuant to the OMT programme cannot cause conduct by the Member States contrary to the objective of the prohibition. Its object is defined by reference to the *travaux préparatoires* of the Maastricht Treaty, that is:

> [to] encourage the Member States to follow a sound budgetary policy, not allowing monetary financing of public deficits or privileged access by public authorities to the financial markets to lead to excessively high levels of debt or excessive Member State deficits (para. 100).[84]

6 The 2014 Reference of the BVerfG to the Court of Justice and the Nullification Crisis of the Tariff Act of 1832: Differences and Similarities

From what we have so far observed, it would seem that the various objections raised against the OMT firstly by the *Bundesbank* from an economic point of view (risks of imbalances in the monetary system; uncontrolled increase in inflation, etc.) and then by the BVerfG from a legal point of view (OMT programme in breach of the ECB mandate; breach of Article 123 TFEU; negative consequences on the budgets of the Eurozone States; confusion between economic and monetary policy, etc.) are groundless. These facts raise a significant issue: namely, that of the existence a

[81] Bandilla (2011), p. 1; D'Acunto (2014), p. 1317; Salvadori (2014), p. 937.

[82] Para. 95.

[83] Paras. 100, 104 and 106–108.

[84] Paras. 109, 111–112, 114, 118–120 and 127.

non-veiled mistrust with regard to the ability of an EU Institution to issue—and this certainly applies to OMT—measures in order to protect the general interest of the EU (see *infra*, Sect. 6.b). In order to better understand the significance of the *OMT* case in the context of the European integration process, it seems useful to place it in a historical perspective. This will be done by recalling here—with all the obvious differences but also the similarities between the two events—the-so-called "Nullification Crisis" of 1832 between the Federal Government of the United States of America and the State of South Carolina. This event, so distant in many respects from the *OMT* case, could indicate, however, a similar pattern of behavior of Member States in "Two Tier legal systems", like the United States and the European Union, in specific moments of their development. This in turn could be useful to understand and predict, to some degree, the future development of the European integration process and the dangers it could face.

The nullification crisis arose some 40 years after the entry into force of the Federal Constitution (1787) and, in particular, with the enactment in 1828 of the federal *Tariff Act*.[85] The Act *inter alia* increased significantly import duties for goods in the Union. The law was designed to protect, according to some, the industrial economy of the northern States of the American federation with significant adverse effects on the economy of the southern States. In 1830, the Parliament of South Carolina, one of the States that claimed to be damaged by this legislation, debated the so-called "*South Carolina Exposition and Protest*". The document singled out the legal and economic grounds of the unconstitutionality of the *Tariff Act* with particular reference, among other things, to the absence of fiscal legal competence of the Federal Government in the Federal Constitution. The *Exposition* argued that the majority system provided by the Federal Constitution was becoming as tyrannical as the British monarch prior to American independence. The Member States, however, were prepared to oppose this situation. In particular, if the Federal Government exceeded its power by issuing unconstitutional law, such as—in their opinion—the *Tariff Act*, Member States had the right to protect their citizens by "nullifying" such regulations and "placing" their authority between their people and the Government of the United States.[86]

The theoretical basis of that power, which is said to go back to Thomas Jefferson and James Madison in the 1798 *Kentucky* and *Virginia Resolution* and developed in this case by John C. Calhoun,[87] was based on the nature of the Constitution. The theory was based on the idea that the Federal Constitution was created by the Peoples of the different individual sovereign States. States remained as such holders

[85]See McDonald (1985) and Jensen (1981).

[86]Woods Jr. (2010), p. 110.

[87]As well as the basic theory of *nullification,* the text was written by John C. Calhoun, then Vice President under John Quincy Adams, and then, in 1830, Vice President under Andrew Jackson. He resigned from that post in 1832 because of disagreements with Jackson himself. He then entered, during the so-called *Nullification crisis,* in the Federal Senate representing the State of South Carolina.

of "States' rights" in order to protect themselves from possible violations of the Federal "compact". This was justified by the fact that:

> [T]he power of the States to interpose in order to protect their rights [...] like all other reserved rights [...] is to be inferred from the simple fact that it is not delegated [to the Federal Government].[88]

In the event, the Federal Government issued unconstitutional pieces of legislation because *inter alia* it went beyond the powers transferred by the Member States, individual States—not so differently from what was claimed by the BVerfG in 2014—retained the power to nullify them and therefore they should not be applied on their territory even without prior judgment of the Supreme Court, as was required by the Federal Constitution.

Based on this, already in 1830 the Parliament of South Carolina had discussed whether to convene a Conference to "nullify" the federal law of 1828. Then, in 1832, when the rules of the *Tariff Act* were again modified by federal law allegedly favoring further the production and commercial interests of the northeast States, the Governor of South Carolina, James Hamilton, summoned the State Legislature in a special session that authorised the election of delegates to nullify that law. The conference adopted on 24 November 1832 an Order of nullification.[89] The Order declared the laws of 1828 and 1832 unconstitutional and void and prohibited the collection of the taxes foreseen by the laws. The Order—not unlike the claim of the BVerfG in the 2014 reference—clarified that the federal law was not applicable in the territory of South Carolina and that the contents of the order would be executed by all State officials. The Order also set forth that in the event of military force by the Federal Government used to collect the proceeds defined by the *Tariff Act*, such action would lead to the secession of the South Carolina from the Union.[90] Tensions rose following the intransigent response of the President of the Union, Andrew Jackson,[91] who threatened to send in the US Army after having pushed through the *Force Bill*. Congress, in order to defuse a potentially critical situation for the Union, issued on 1 March 1833 legislation which provided for a compromise that envisaged the gradual reduction of the controversial taxes. Congress also decided to approve the so-called *Force Bill*. The South Carolina Parliament, at the news of the proposed Act, quashed the order of nullification of the previous *Tariff Act* and accepted the compromise, however, issuing an ordinance of nullification of the *Force Bill*.[92]

The comparison between the "Nullification Crisis" and the *Tariff Act* of 1832 allows us to see the *OMT* case, recalling Spinoza, *sub specie aeternitatis*. Clearly, I do not want to argue here that the BVerfG reference and its content may have the

---

[88] 1930 *South Carolina Exposition and Protest*.

[89] Woods Jr. (2010), p. 112.

[90] Mason (1964), p. 108.

[91] See Jackson's Proclamation to the People of South Carolina, 10 December 1832, in Richardson (1911), p. 640 et seqq.

[92] Mason (1964), p. 56.

effects that the theories underlying the nullification crisis caused 30 years later in the US, i.e., the secession of the South American States and the ensuing civil war. Instead, I wish here to try to identify a pattern of behaviour of "Two Tier legal systems", such as the US and the EU, in order to underline current and future possible difficulties in the process of European integration.

Returning to the comparison between the two events, the State Legislation of South Carolina declared nullified a federal law—despite the absence of a previous judgment of the Supreme Court, as the Constitution set forth—as purportedly unlawful and therefore in breach of the Federal Constitution. In much the same manner the BVerfG had declared the OMT unconstitutional "subject to the interpretation by the Court of Justice of the European Union" (BVerfG, para. 55) because it considered that it was illegal under EU law.

Regarding the differences between the two events, the most obvious relates to the nature of the legal entities in question, that is, a State, in the case of the United States, and an International Organisation, although of "new genre in the field of international law",[93] in the case of the European Union. As a result of this, in the case of the *Tariff Act* and the following nullification, the Federal Government in order to bring South Carolina under Constitutional legality could only intervene with the US Army in order to enforce the law of the Federal *Tariff Act* (as evidenced by the enactment of the 1832 *Force Bill*). The subsequent secession of South Carolina in 1860 was the ultimate consequence of the exercise of power of nullification. In the European Union, the legal consequence of the potential nullification of the OMT (especially in the face of an assessment of the lawfulness of the OMT programme by the Court of Justice) would be—as already underlined above—the possible start of an infringement procedure under Article 258 TFEU against Germany for breach of its obligations under EU law. This would lead ultimately and in the manner provided for in the EU Treaty to the issue of financial sanctions decided by the Court of Justice in order to make the German Republic comply with its obligations under EU law (Articles 258–260 TFEU).

In this sense, however, both South Carolina, with its "*South Carolina Exposition and Protest*", and the German BverfG, with its preliminary ruling, argue—as clarified above—positions that are alien to the legality, respectively, of the United States and of the European Union.

A second difference is that, although in the case of the *Tariff Act* it was the "weak" States of the South that sought nullification, in the *OMT* case, it is the Institutions of an "economically strong" State of the North that seeks the nullification. Given these differences, and as a result of the different legal entities taken into account, the answer to the crisis of South Carolina was, ultimately, the secession from the American Federation in 1860. The response of Germany to the European situation is, as a State of "weight" in the EMU, the opposite. The response is not to disengage from the integration process—as in the case of South Carolina—but to gain more control in European affairs. It does not seem a coincidence—for

[93]ECJ 5 February 1963, Case 26/62, *Van Gend & Loos*.

instance—that people in the sphere of German influence have recently been appointed in key European economic policy entities.[94] This is of course a legitimate choice to the extent that this is not a violation of the representation of other Member States in the European Institutions.

Worryingly however, the nullification of the *Tariff Act* and the BVerfG's OMT reference have something closely in common. In fact, the theory behind nullification was based on a State's mistrust of the Federal Government (and Constitution) in defining measures (the *Tariff Act*) in the general interest of the United States. Similarly, the position of the BVerfG reveals mistrust of the EU institutions and their ability to define policies (legitimate under EU law) in the interest of the entire EU (or rather, towards Eurozone States).[95] In this case, the general European Union interest is in fact protected by a (lawful) ECB measure, the OMT programme. This has the goal of protecting the effective exercise by the Central Bank of its monetary competence (see *supra*, Sect. 3). On the other side, the BVerfG claims that the OMT programme is in breach of EU law and of the German constitutional identity. The specific criticisms raised by the BVerfG in its reference (*inter alia*, the peculiar application of the protection of the constitutional identity principle) put the German interests there underlined at odds with those of the (lawful) OMT programme up to the point of criticising the ECB's independence *inter alia* from Member States (see *supra*, Sect. 4). In this respect, the preference that the BVerfG gives to the "convincing expertise of the *Bundesbank*" (para. 71) rather than to the competent EU Institution dealing with monetary policy, the ECB, is telling.

Consequently, the idea of "geographic[ally] discriminated parts of the Union" defined by John J. Calhoun[96]—on the basis of which he developed the theory of nullification of federal laws—was functional to give back protection and weight to the interests of the Southern States of the Union, protection and weight that was "diluted" in the mechanisms of the Federal Government. Equally, in the *OMT* case, reference by the BVerfG to the principles of the protection of constitutional identity—especially in the excessively wide scope adopted by the German Court—is a legal technique aimed at bringing back to Member State level the control of policies (and its—lawful—measures as the OMT programme) already transferred to European level and governed by the laws of the Union. It is no coincidence that the ultimate consequences of the declaration of unconstitutionality

[94]This list of positions covered by German nationals as indicated by Fubini (2015): President of the European Parliament (Martin Schulz); the Chairman of ESM (Klaus Regling); President of the European Investment Bank (Werner Hoyer); Governor of the Development Bank of the Council of Europe (Rolf Welzel); President of the Bank for International Settlements (Jens Weidmann); the EIB Secretary-General (Klaus Troemmel). Germany in the person of the Minister of Finance would have endorsed the appointment of the Austrian Wilhelm Molterer as Managing Director of the European Fund for Strategic Investments (Juncker Fund), who was subsequently appointed to that position.

[95]Fairless and Blackstone (2012).

[96]See Calhoun (1851).

of the OMT by the BVerfG would be to decide (and impose) what the German representatives in the ECB Governing Council could not impose when defining the SMP (see the resignation of *Bundesbank* President Axel Weber[97] and of Jürgen Stark, member of the Executive Board[98] in 2011) and the OMT programme (see the only vote inside the Governing Council against the adoption of the OMT programme cast by the *Bundesbank* President Jens Weidman),[99] i.e. to impose their veto. It is in fact clear that if the BVerfG were to conclude that the OMT programme was illegal—with the resulting non-participation of German Institutions in the programme, primarily the *Bundesbank*—this would mean, regardless of the real effects of non-participation on OMT implementation,[100] concretely in the eyes of the financial markets (and not only theirs) the failure of the OMT programme. This would cast new doubts on the solidity and irreversibility of the Euro and, perhaps, the credibility of the European integration process itself.

7 Conclusions

One way to regard the *OMT* case might be simply as an important decision in which the Court of Justice recognised the legality of this programme. However, the *OMT* case is much more than that. It represents, in the first place, a typical example of the dynamics of the European integration process. That process requires major problems within the European area to occur before their causes are addressed and resolved.[101] In this case, the need to create the OMT programme stems from the absence of a crisis management system at the time of the creation of the Euro. It took the 2009 European financial crisis—the causes of which go back to the 2003 breach of the Stability and Growth Pact by France and Germany[102]—to push the Union to create such a crisis management tool. With reference to monetary policy, in particular, one had to wait until June 2012 and the risk of the Eurozone "breaking up"—and with it the risk of the European integration process coming unraveled—for the OMT

---

[97]See Walker and Galloni (2011).

[98]See The Wall Street Journal Europe, 28 June 2012.

[99]Fairless (2012).

[100]Sauer (2015), p. 988.

[101]Ultimately, the process of European integration, as started in the twentieth century, can be seen as a solution to the crisis of the European area after the tragic attempt of Nazi Germany to dominate Europe. This was in turn a consequence, from a legal-economic point of view, of the contradiction between the size reached at that time by the scope of the activities of firms and markets—a supranational dimension—and the purely national scope of European States power to regulate the economy. The solution of this "contradiction" in the European area was the creation of a common market among European States; an integrated market not too dissimilar from that of the United States of America. On this, see Pace (2007), p. 5.

[102]See above, Sect. 2.

programme to be created.[103] This delay had an obvious cost in terms of the trust and support of EU citizens in the European integration project.[104]

Secondly, the *OMT* case is an interesting case of Institution building. It provides a "privileged view" by which to understand the institutional dynamics in the EU. In this respect the *OMT* case shows how the ECB—also because of its independence—was able to define in 2 years (2010–2012) an effective and "permanent" protection programme for the exercise of its monetary policy.[105] The "long path" to the OMT—the result being essentially a compromise brokered in the General Council—has allowed the programme not only to be effective, as demonstrated in practice by the facts of 2012,[106] but also to be lawful under EU law, as concluded by the Court in its judgment of June 2015. According to the reasoning of the judgment, the previous SMP programme would probably have been as such illegal—and not only the 2011 Italian Bond purchase[107]—pursuant to EU law. The OMT programme, because of its features, has an important indirect effect of making the default of a Eurozone State unlikely and thus ensuring the irreversibility of the Euro without transforming the ECB—from a legal point of view—into a lender of last resort.[108]

The *OMT* case should also be considered as a *sui generis* referral to the ECJ by the BVerfG—that is, *sui generis* in terms of the way in which it was proposed and its conclusions—to the Court of Justice in 2014. The doubts expressed in it by the BVerfG *vis-à-vis* the OMT are on the one hand understandable in view of both the novelty of the ECB's so-called unconventional measures (e.g. the OMT) and the lack of Court of Justice case law on Article 123 TFEU. On the other hand, however, such legal concerns seem focused on issues (OMT and the ECB mandate; infringement of Article 123 TFEU), which, although legally problematic with reference to the SMP (2010), had been expressly contemplated and resolved with the OMT (2012).[109] All these facts make it difficult to understand the way in which the referral was proposed and difficult to understand its "conclusive" findings; that is, the illegality of OMT. The BVerfG's conclusion as expressed in the preliminary reference seems to have been due to different reasons. First, there is a certain "jealousy" of the German Court of its independence and an "ill-concealed" irritation at being legally obliged—for the first time—to request an interpretation of the law in order to issue its final decision. Secondly, this position appears to be due to the difficulty of individual Member States (especially those as economically important as Germany) and their Institutions (that is, the *Bundesbank*) to accept the loss of

[103]See above, Sect. 2.

[104]Schmidt (2015).

[105]See above, Sect. 3.

[106]See Pace (2014b), p. 2175.

[107]So seems to claim M. Ruffert in this volume, *The EMU in the ECJ – A New Dimension of Dispute Resolution in the Process of European Integration.*

[108]See above, Sect. 3.

[109]See above, Sect. 3.

"weight" and "steering capability" with reference to competences that have been transferred to the Union level, such as monetary policy, and the effects these EU policies have within individual Member States. This is shown, in fact, by a non-veiled mistrust on the part of the Member States (and the *Bundesbank* and the BVerfG in this case) of the ability of the Union Institutions to enact measures (see *supra*, Sect. 6.b)—albeit legitimate, such as the OMT—to protect the general interest of the Union. This conclusion is also reinforced by the fact that all objections raised against the OMT, from an economic point of view by the *Bundesbank* and from a legal standpoint by the BVerfG, proved to be unfounded.[110]

This observable mistrust in the Union is also manifested by the BVerfG through the definition and scope of the review of EU measures in order to protect the so-called "German Constitutional identity". This setting sows "seeds" of instability within the EU system. This approach would seem to violate fundamental principles of EU law that are strongly underlined by the Court of Justice in its recent opinion 2/13; namely that of the role of the Court of Justice as a centralised body of binding interpretation of EU law and, consequently, the principle of autonomy of the EU legal system.[111]

These "seeds" would create even greater instability if other Member States (or all the 28) were to start claiming the illegality of EU measures—with the dubious scope defined by the BVerfG—with a view to protecting their alleged constitutional identity, and then "nullifying" (or attempting to nullify) EU measures. A similar danger was underlined by the US President Andrew Jackson during the nullification crisis of 1832, an event that has some similarities with the BVerfG referral.[112] As Jackson said:

> Admit this doctrine [of State nullification], and you give to the States an uncontrolled right to decide, and every law may be annulled [by the States] under this pretext.[113]

In view of this, it is important to note that, in addition to criticism on this specific reference to the Court of Justice from the point of view of German law,[114] a strong criticism of the BVerfG case-law is also emerging from eminent German jurists.[115]

---

[110]See above, Sect. 3.

[111]See above, Sect. 4. See also Claes and Reestman (2015), p. 969. Fabbrini (2015a), p. 1003, argues that the nullification of the OMT by the BVerfG "would be clearly unlawful" and that it would endanger the primacy of EU law.

[112]See above, Sect. 6.a.

[113]Jackson's Proclamation to the People of South Carolina, 10 December 1832, cited above. Similarly, Wendel (2014), p. 286, notes that the interests linked to national identity must not necessarily prevail, "otherwise EU law would be subject to 28 potential identity caveats".

[114]In addition to the already quoted articles, see among others Denninger (2016); Wendel (2014), p. 273: "The Federal Court is adjudicating in an area for which it is not competent neither in a legal nor in a technical sense"; Sauer (2015), pp. 990 and 999: "Whatever solution the FCC is going to prefer, it should keep an eye on its mandate under the Basic Law".

[115]See the comment to the BVerfG *Lissabon Urteil* by Mestmäcker (2010), p. 35.

Some of them have not hesitated to criticise the case-law of the BVerfG discussed above, with one scholar declaring that the German Constitutional Court case-law

> is full of big words but in the end contains only small judgments.[116]

Against the generalised criticism of the preliminary reference of the BVerfG,[117] and also of the convincing *Gauweiler* judgment, the German Court is unlikely to confirm the final judgment in its assessment of the unconstitutionality of the OMT, leaving it then space only for the formulation of general disapproving criticism.[118]

What is most worrying is that the reference of the BVerfG seems to recreate the "'struggle' between the [European] periphery and the [German] center" whose elimination was indicated in 2011 by a great German and European, Helmut Schmidt, as the "original reason for European integration".[119] The removal of this "struggle", which for example programmes such as the OMT have the objective of eliminating, is all the more important because it is "an indispensable condition for the solution of the very precarious European crisis" in which we live.[120] A few years later, in 2016, Romano Prodi, former President of the EU Commission, reflecting on this "very precarious European crisis", defined it as a key transition moment for the future of the EU. Using some strong figurative words, he said the EU

> is in mid-stream. The problem is that we have to go on to the other side, we have to [have] more Europe, if not, [the EU will] disappear from the face of the earth.[121]

Again, the analogy to the US in the mid-1830s presents itself. The US was then likewise in a mid-stream and succeeded "in going on to the other side of the river", eventually becoming, in the twentieth century, a world leader. But only after resolving some not unimportant issues at the level of both its central Government and its Member States.

PS This article was concluded in January 2016. On 21 June 2016 the BVerfG gave its final judgments in the *OMT* case following the 2015 Court of Justice *Gauweiler* decision. As the title of the present article suggests, it was indeed a "(failed) nullification crisis". In fact, as anticipated in the present text, the German Court did not confirm the final judgment in its assessment of the unconstitutionality of the OMT. It holds in fact the OMT programme to be lawful. In the judgment reasoning, the BVerfG criticises some aspects of the *Gauweiler* judgments and sets

---

[116]Isensee (2013), p. 10.

[117]However, see the positive attitude *vis-à-vis* the BVerfG reference by the Kronberger Kreis (Feld et al. 2016).

[118]Goldmann (2015), p. 14, suggests ways for the BVerfG to avoid "the humiliation of recognizing the position taken in its referral as erroneous". See also Sauer (2015), p. 999.

[119]Schmidt (2011). This reading coincides with that, from an economic point of view, of De Cecco (2014), p. 31.

[120]Schmidt, *ibid.*

[121]Interview with Romano Prodi, "*Berlino ha sbagliato e ha aggravato la situazione*", Il Sole 24 Ore, 14 January 2016, p. 1.

out some additional implementing conditions to the OMT programme. These are not provided for by the *Gauweiler* judgment but are implicitly contained in the 2012 ECB decision. For my reading of the BVerfG judgment and of the "winners" and "losers" of the final showdown on the "*OMT* case", see my article: "*And indeed it was a (failed) nullification crisis: The OMT judgment of the German Federal Constitutional Court and the winners and losers of the final showdown in the OMT case*" in *SIDI Blog* (www.sidiblog.org), September 2016, at https://goo.gl/gNM5Hd.

References

Acharya V (2016) Presentation. Lender of Last Resort vs Buyer of Last Resort_–The Impact of the European Central Bank Actions on the Bank-Sovereign Nexus. First Annual Interdisciplinary Sovereign Debt Research and Management Conference, Georgetown University Law Center, 21 January 2016

Allen K (2016) Mario Draghi defends ECB independence after German criticisms. The Guardian. com, 21 April 2016

Bandilla W (2011) Art. 123. In: Grabitz E, Hilf M, Nettesheim M (eds) Das Recht der Europäischen Union: EUV/AEUV. Beck, München, p 1 et seqq

Baratta R (2014) I vincoli imposti dal fiscal compact ai bilanci nazionali. www.federalismi.it, No. 17

Baratta R (2015) Diritto e prassi evolutiva dell'Eurogruppo. Il Diritto dell'Unione Europea, p 493 et seqq

Bernanke B (2015) The courage to act: a memoir of a crisis and its aftermath. WW Norton & Company, New York

Blackstone B, Boston W (2015) Draghi Defends Bond Programme in Germany. The Wall Street Journal Europe, 11 March 2015

Calhoun JC (1851) A disquision on government. Press of Walker and James, Charleston, South Carolina

Claes M, Reestman JH (2015) The constitutional protection of national identity and the limits of European Integration at the occasion of the *Gauweiler homes*. German Law J, p 946 et seqq

Cour-Thimam P, Winkler B (2013) The ECB's monetary policy Non-Standard Measures. ECB Working Paper Series, No. 1528

D'Acunto S (2014) Art. 123 TFUE. In: Tizzano A (ed) Trattati dell'Unione europea, 2ª edn. Giuffré, Milano, p 1317 et seqq

De Cecco M (2014) The core country and the rest: how the Monetary Union (mal) functions and the future of the Euro. Review of Economic Conditions in Italy, p 31 et seqq

De Grauwe P (2013) The European Central Bank as lender of last resort in the government bond markets. CESifo Econ Stud 59(3):520 et seqq

Denninger E (2016) Die OMT-Klagen. DPCE, forthcoming

Dernbach A, Meier A (2015) Ex-Kommissionspräsident Prodi im Interview: "Griechenland wird seine Schulden niemals zurückzahlen". Der Tagesspiegel, 11 February 2015

Editorial (2015) On courts of last resort and lenders of last resort. Eur Constit Law Rev 232 et seqq

Fabbrini F (2015a) After the OMT case: the supremacy of EU law as the guarantee of the equality of the Member States. German Law J 1004 et seqq

Fabbrini S (2015b) Dall'integrazione alla disintegrazione. Il Sole 24 Ore, 13 December 2015

Fabbrini S (2015c) Which European Union? Europe After the Euro Crisis. Cambridge University Press, Cambridge

Fairless T (2012) Draghi vs. Weidmann Part. II: Top ECB Officials round on Bundesbank. The Wall Street Journal Europe, 3 August 2012

Fairless T, Blackstone B (2012) President Says ECB Bond Buying Serves Germany's Interest. The Wall Street Journal Europe, 25 September 2012

Feld LP, Fuest C, Haucap J, Schweitzer H, Wieland V, Wigger BU (2016) Dismantling the Boundaries of the ECB's Monetary Policy Mandate. Stiftung Marktwirtschaft, No. 61

Fubini F (2015) La Germania prende tutto nelle poltrone europee. Il Corriere della Sera, 1 October 2015

Gabriel S (2014) Perché perdere Londra sarebbe la fine del sogno europeo. Il Corriere della Sera, 30 June 30, 2014

Geithner TF (2014) Stress test: reflections on financial crises. Broadway Books, New York

Gelpern A (2009) Financial crisis containment. Connecticut Law Rev 493 et seqq

Goldmann M (2015) Constitutional pluralism as mutually assured discretion: the ECJ, the BVerfG, and the ECB. Maastricht J Eur Comp Law 9 et seqq

Harbo TI (2015) The function of proportionality analysis in European law. Brill, Leiden

Irvin N (2014) The Alchemists: three central bankers and a world on fire. Penguin Books, New York

Isensee J (2013) Große Worte, kleine Urteile. Handelsblatt, 13 June 2013, p 10 et seqq

Jensen M (1981) The new nation. A history of the United States during the confederation 1781–1789. Northeastern University Press, Boston

Kohl H (2014) Aus Sorge um Europe: Ein Appell. Droemer Knaur, München

Lombardo S (2015) The independence of the European Central Bank between Monetary Union and Fiscal Union: the OMT case as a conflict among non-majoritarian institutions. Law Econ Yearly Rev 195 et seqq

Mason AT (1964) The states rights debate. Antifederalism and the constitution. Prentice-Hall Inc., Upper Saddle River, New Jersey

McDonald F (1985) Novus Ordo Seclorum. The intellectual origins of the constitution. University Press of Kansas, Lawrence, Kansas

Messori M (2009) The financial crisis: understanding it to overcome it. Assogestioni

Mestmäcker EJ (2010) Im Schatten des Leviathan. Anmerkung zum Urteil des BVerfG vom 30.6.2009. Europarecht, p 35 et seqq

Micossi S (2015) The Monetary Policy of the European Central Bank (2002–2015). www.ceps.eu

Munari F (2015) Da Pringle a Gauweiler: i tormentati anni dell'unione monetaria e i loro effetti sull'ordinamento giuridico europeo. Il Diritto dell'Unione Europea, p 723 et seqq

Pace LF (2007) European antitrust law. Edward Elgar, Cheltenham

Pace LF (2014a) Dura lex sed lex: the parent-subsidiarity relationship in EU antitrust law and the AEG Telefunken presumption – independence of the EU legal system, effectiveness of competition law and protection of fundamental rights. In: Cisotta R, Marquis M (eds) Litigation and arbitration in EU competition law. Edward Elgar, Cheltenham, p 141 et seqq

Pace LF (2014b) La crisi del "sistema euro" (2009–2013): cause, fasi, players e soluzioni. In: Studi in onore di Giuseppe Tesauro. Editoriale Scientifica, Napoli, p 2162 et seqq

Porchia O (ed) (2015) *Governance* economica europea. Editoriale Scientifica, Napoli

Richardson JD (ed) (1911) A Compilation of the Messages and Papers of the Presidents. Vol. II. Bureau of National Literature and Art Inc., New York

Rossi LS (2012) "Fiscal Compact" e Trattato sul Meccanismo di Stabilità: aspetti istituzionali e conseguenze dell'integrazione differenziata nell'UE. Il Diritto dell'Unione Europea, p 293 et seqq

Salvadori M (2014) Art. 123 TFUE. In: Pocar F, Baruffi MC (eds) Commentario breve ai Trattati dell'Unione europea. 2ª edn. Cedam, Padova, p 937 et seqq

Sauer H (2015) Doubtful it Stood ... : Competence and Power in the European Monetary and Constitutional Law in the Aftermath of the CJEU's OMT Judgment. German Law J 973 et seqq

Schmidt H (2011) Rede "Deutschland und mit und für Europa" von Federal Chancellor Helmut Schmidt a.D. beim ordentlichen SPD-Bundesparteitag am 4. Dezember 2011 in Berlin. www.spd.de

Schmidt H (2013) Der Euro ist prima! Handelsblatt, 17 June 2013

Schmidt VA (2015) The Eurozone's Crisis of Democratic Legitimacy: Can the EU Rebuild Trust and Public Support for European Economic Integration? DG ECFIN Economic Discussion Paper No. 15 (Sept. 2015), http://ec.europa.eu/economy_finance/publications/eedp/dp015_en.htm

Simon S (2015) Direct cooperation has begun: some remarks on the judgment of the ECJ on the OMT decision of the ECB in response to the German Federal Constitutional Court's first request for a preliminary ruling. German Law J 1025 et seqq

Skouris V (2009) Les rapports entre la Cour de Justice européenne et les juridctions constitutionnelles nationales. Il Diritto dell'Unione Europea, p 775 et seqq

Steen M (2013) ECB unveils € 1.1 bn profit on bonds crisis. Financial Times, 21 February 2013

Tizzano A (2011) La Corte di giustizia dell'Unione europea e la Corte costituzionale italiana. In: Pace LF (ed) Nuove tendenze del diritto dell'Unione europea dopo il Trattato di Lisbona. Giuffrè, Milano, p 223 et seqq

Tosato GL (2014) La riforma costituzionale sull'equilibrio di bilancio alla luce della normativa dell'Unione: l'interazione fra i livelli europeo e interno. Rivista di diritto internazionale, p 5 et seqq

Tremonti G (2014) Bugie e Verità. Mondadori, Milano

Trichet J-C (2010) State of the Union: the financial crisis and the ECB's response between 2007 and 2009. J Common Mark Stud 11 et seqq

Tridimas T (2015) The ECJ and the national courts. In: Arnull A, Chalmers D (eds) European Union Law. Oxford University Press, Oxford, p 412 et seqq

Tropeano D (2015) Lender of last resort. In: Rochon LP, Rossi S (eds) The encyclopedia of central banking. Edward Elgar, Cheltenham, p 296 et seqq

Walker M, Galloni A (2011) Germany's Central Bank Chief Resigns. The Wall Street Journal Europe, 12 February 2011

Walker M, Forelle C, Blackstone B (2010) Currency Union Teetering, "Mr. Euro" Is Forced to Act. The Wall Street Journal, 27 December 2010

Weidmann J (2016) Solidität und Solidarität in der Europäischen Währungsunion. Rede bei der deutschen Botschaft in Rom, 26 April 2016, para. 3.2

Wendel M (2014) Exceeding judicial competence in the name of democracy: the German Federal Constitutional Court's OMT reference. Eur Constit Law Rev 265 et seqq

Woods TE Jr (2010) Nullification. How to resist Federal Tyranny in the 21st century. Regnery Publishing Inc., Washington

Zaring D (2015) Law and custom on the federal open market committee. Law Contemp Probl 78 (3)

Zhong R (2012) The Last Hawk in Europe. The Wall Street Journal Europe, 28 June 2012

Zingales L (2016) La strada mai battuta per evitare l'Eurogermania. Il Sole 24 Ore, 14 January 2016

Part V
Concluding Remarks

Economic and Monetary Policies as Essential Elements of the EU Constitutional Debate

Lucia Serena Rossi

Abstract Until not so many years ago, the EU economic and the monetary policies were quite snubbed fields of research by the majority of the legal doctrine, although with some excellent exceptions. The same two policies are today at the core of a wide constitutional debate, which involves essential issues such as democracy, fundamental rights, national sovereignty and institutional competences.

This debate concerns the aims, the tools and the methods of those two policies, that are formally separate, and submitted to different rules, but in practice strictly intertwined and reciprocally influencing. Opposite values are increasingly confronted: effectiveness vs. legitimacy, solidarity vs. responsibility, and loyal cooperation vs. vital national interests.

The debate is even more critical at political level. Since the Member States of the EU—and even more so the States of the Eurozone—seem not to share the same views about the aims and the means of those policies, the latters have become a cause of European division rather than of European integration. In such a confrontational situation the general interest should be promoted by the EU independent institutions. This raises the issue of the power of the European Commission and of the European Central Bank.

On the one hand, weakening the role and the independence of those institutions doesn't increase the democracy of the system and risks leaving the economic and the monetary policies in the sole hands of the most powerful State(s). The more those institutions are committed to the general interest and remain strongly independent from the national Governments, the better the principle of equality of Member States, provided for by Article 4 TEU can be ensured.

On the other hand, in order to strengthen the democracy and the legitimacy of policies that have become so important and so directly impinging on the daily life of the EU citizens, the accountability and the transparency of those institutions should be increased and the European Parliament should be more involved. The public

L.S. Rossi (✉)
Department of Legal Sciences, University of Bologna, Bologna, Italy
e-mail: lsrossi@cirdce.unibo.it

L. Daniele et al. (eds.), *Democracy in the EMU in the Aftermath of the Crisis*,
DOI 10.1007/978-3-319-53895-2_21

debate must also be encouraged, through national Parliaments and civil society, in order to highlight what the common aims and the appropriate tools are.

But what is the general interest? Of all the EU policies, these specific ones are the most influenced by economic theories, which claim to be "scientific" but, differently form what happens in the "hard sciences", are uncertain, multiple and provisional, more capable to explain the crises *ex post* than to forecast and prevent them *ex ante*. The coexistence of different theories is therefore able to support the most disparate policy views of the different Member States and a common vision about the real aims of the economic and monetary policy is more and more difficult to be shared.

The EU Treaties and legislation are mainly oriented to protect the monetary stability. Stability is essential and a framework of common rules is necessary for ensuring it. However a policy cannot be just a system of economic formulas or technical rules. Rules must be the instruments for implementing shared political aims in the general interest. They should be flexible to allow the system to adjust to changing contexts. And when they prove to be—or to have become—unapt to respond to the general needs they must be changed. In 2002 Romano Prodi labelled as "stupid" the Stability Pact for its excessive rigidity. In the following years it become clear that the respect of that Pact was almost impossible for some States of the Eurozone, starting from Germany and France. And when the world financial crisis burst, the response by the Member States Governments—and by the European institutions—has been to adding more rigidity and more stringent obligations, with the Fiscal Compact and the European Semester. The future will tell us whether all this added new cleverness or more stupidity to the European Monetary Union. But these measures were adopted as a reaction to the international market pressure, which was dictated more by ideological than "scientific" grounds. Therefore, a new open-minded review of those parameters should now be undertaken, asking whether or not they can be still considered as sound, sustainable and defensible at the light of the practice.

Moreover, probably the many problems raised today by the economic and monetary policies are dues not solely by the Stability Pact and the cleverness or stupidity of the existing fiscal rules, but also by the fact that, since the creation of the EMU, an imbalance of competences was established between the two policies fields in spite of their close relations.

The "original sin" was to give the EU a full exclusive competence in the monetary policy, but only a weak coordinating competence—mainly based on the open coordination method—in the economic matters, which remained with the competence of the Member States. The Treaty of Lisbon (Article 5 TFEU) affirms that the Member States shall coordinate their economic policies within the Union, while the Council can only adopt measures such as broad guidelines. Specific provisions however can apply to the Member States whose currency is the Euro.

But the two policies are strictly interconnected and they necessarily meet in the "fiscal" domain. If they pursue different interests a strong conflict may arise between the general EU and the national dimensions. The result is a system where the Eurozone States are forced in the same cage of common fiscal rules but compete on the ground of economic policies, which remain national, and keep quarrelling on how one should interpret the monetary and fiscal constraints, in order to promote their individual national economy.

The genetic weakness of the EU economic policy fully emerges in times of crisis. The response adopted so far by the EU institutions and by the Member States, mainly consisted in introducing new fiscal rules and constraints, while a modest support to the economic growth has only be pursued through a—quite bureaucratic—use of EU funds and programmes.

However any rule of European law ought to be interpreted in the light of the EU fundamental values: the principle of solidarity,[1] as well as the principles affirmed by Article 4 TEU, that is conferral, equality of the States before the law, respect for their constitutional identity, and sincere cooperation. The many tensions that the economic and monetary policies create in the EU ought to induce to reframe them in the light of those principles. Indeed the EU constitutional values must be respected by EU law even in the most "technical" fields and must inspire the EU policies.

The brief remarks above aim to emphasise that a wide reflection on the economic and monetary policies is more than ever necessary. This book is particularly valuable, because it offers so many and rich contributions which provide a critical and multi-faceted analysis of all the aspects of the EU economic and monetary policies, with a particular attention to their constitutional profiles.

The first part of this volume analyses the impact of the EMU on the principle of democracy and the role of the different European institutions. The tension between technocracy and democracy is typical in the monetary and economic policies also at national level. It becomes even more evident at EU level, where a "democratic *deficit*" is still perceived as a general problem, notwithstanding the fact that the powers of the European Parliament have been increasingly extended. If from one side it can't be denied that the management of those policies—in particular the monetary one—requires technical skills and knowledge that can be difficult to find outside dedicated institutions, on the other side it is suggested that the "democraticity" of these policies should be improved, under the existing Treaties or by modifying them. Notably it is necessary to make the technical institutions more accountable and transparent,[2] and to more involve democratic institutions such as the European Parliaments and the national Parliaments.[3]

The issue of the interinstitutional balance of powers also becomes particularly delicate in the EMU, where the ordinary institutions play new roles and new institutional frameworks are developed.[4] In what we could call the "fiscal galaxy" the international, intergovernmental and supranational dimensions combine in a

---

[1]On the application to the EMU of the principle of solidarity—affirmed by Articles 2 TEU, 122 TFEU and by many other provisions of the EU Treaties, see Mc Donnell (2014), pp. 57–92.

[2]See the suggestions advanced by Smits, p. 51 et seqq and Martines, p. 141 et seqq.

[3]See the contributions of Starita, p. 3 et seqq; Martucci, p. 27 et seqq; De la Parra, p. 101 et seqq.

[4]See Lionello, p. 179 et seqq; Fasone, Fromage, p. 161 et seqq; Simone, p. 195 et seqq.

fast development. The traditional conflict between community and intergovernmental methods can maybe seem today scarcely meaningful. As Angela Merkel held recently, the "Union method" may be regarded as a synthesis of the other two.[5] However the question remains whether the Member States would be prepared to transfer more sovereignty to supranational and independent institutions or would rather prefer not go any further than the present situation for fear of an excessive "centralisation" of powers in the Eurozone.[6]

The second part of this book is focused on the powers of the European Central Bank, the institutions that is at the head both of the Euro monetary policy and of the banking supervision. This institution is becoming more and more important as it probably saved the Euro, assuming the initiative in the first month of the crisis, when the other EU institutions proved to be unable to act.[7] The ECB is and must be a strongly independent institution, but cannot fill by itself the lack of leadership within the other institutions of the Eurozone, which are paralysed by the vetoes of the Member States.[8]

The third part deals with the great constitutional issues raised by the European Banking Union. New legal instruments have been adopted,[9] but the overall framework still shows incompleteness and contradictions.[10] In the Banking Union the general interest is confronted with individual rights and economic freedoms and the solidarity burden has been diverted from the public dimension to the private economic system.

Finally, the last part of this book reflects on the role of judges.[11] Whether or not the ECB interprets in a too creative way its own competence, to what extent the existing EU rules can be extensively interpreted or must be reviewed, and what are the limits to the national sovereignty that are necessary for ensuring—in the view of the general interest—the effectiveness and the coherence of the EU monetary and economic policies, all these issues are the playfield for a dialogue (or a conflict[12]) between the ECJ and the constitutional or supreme judges of the Member States.

We could conclude recognising that extraordinary times may call for extraordinary measures, and acknowledging that when times are fast changing also the law quickly develops. Since international treaties—by their nature—take a very long time to be negotiated and enter into force, it is inevitable that new legal rules develop beyond them, in the institutional practice and in the jurisprudence. The judges have a bridging role, interpreting the rules, filling the gaps of the latters and trying to give coherence to the system.

---

[5]See Allemand, p. 73 et seqq.

[6]See Fabbrini, p. 121 et seqq.

[7]See Cafaro, p. 217 et seqq; Peroni, p. 249 et seqq.

[8]See Bassan, p. 235 et seqq.

[9]See Viterbo, p. 267 et seqq; Cisotta, p. 283 et seqq.

[10]See Ortino, p. 299 et seqq; Ruccia, p. 319 et seqq.

[11]See Baratta, p. 353 et seqq; Pace, p. 371 et seqq.

[12]See Ruffert, p. 335 et seqq.

But the experience shows that when the EU legal system has evolved in order to keep the pace with the reality, then the EU Treaties—sooner or later—must be amended.

Reference

Mc Donnell A (2014) Solidarity, flexibility and the Euro crisis. In: Rossi LS, Casolari F (eds) The EU after Lisbon. Springer, Berlin, pp 57–92